MW01251869

PERSONAL PROPERTY
SECURITY LAW

Other books in the *Essentials of Canadian Law* Series

Statutory Interpretation

Intellectual Property Law

Income Tax Law

Immigration Law

International Trade Law

Family Law

Legal Ethics & Professional Responsibility

Copyright Law

Remedies: The Law of Damages

Individual Employment Law

The Law of Equitable Remedies

Administrative Law

Ethics and Canadian Criminal Law

Public International Law

Environmental Law 2/e

Securities Law

Constitutional Law 2/e

Youth Criminal Justice Law

Computer Law 2/e

The Law of Partnerships and Corporations 2/e

The Law of Torts 2/e

Media Law 2/e

Maritime Law

Criminal Law 3/e

Insurance Law

International Human Rights Law

Legal Research and Writing 2/e

The Law of Evidence 4/e

The Law of Trusts 2/e

Franchise Law

The Charter of Rights and Freedoms 3/e

ESSENTIALS OF
CANADIAN LAW

PERSONAL
PROPERTY
SECURITY
LAW

RONALD C.C. CUMING
University of Saskatchewan, College of Law

CATHERINE WALSH
McGill University, Faculty of Law

RODERICK J. WOOD
University of Alberta, Faculty of Law

IRWIN
LAW

Personal Property Security Law
© Irwin Law Inc., 2005

All rights reserved. No part of this publication may be reproduced, stored in a retrieval system, or transmitted, in any form or by any means, without the prior written permission of the publisher or, in the case of photocopying or other reprographic copying, a licence from Access Copyright (Canadian Copyright Licensing Agency), 1 Yonge Street, Suite 1900, Toronto, Ontario, M5E 1E5.

Published in 2005 by

Irwin Law
347 Bay Street
Suite 501
Toronto, Ontario
M5H 2R7

www.irwinlaw.com

ISBN: 1-55221-110-X

Library and Archives Canada Cataloguing in Publication

Cuming, Ronald C.C.
    Personal property security law / Ronald C.C. Cuming, Catherine Walsh, Roderick J. Wood.

(Essentials of Canadian law)
Includes bibliographical references and index.
ISBN 1-55221-110-X

    1. Security (Law)—Canada. 2. Personal property—Canada. I. Wood, Roderick J. II. Walsh, Catherine (Catherine A.) III. Title. IV. Series.

KE1042.C84 2005   346.7107'4   C2005-905865-X
KF1050.C84 2005

The publisher acknowledges the financial support of the Government of Canada through the Book Publishing Industry Development Program (BPIDP) for its publishing activities.

Printed and bound in Canada.

1 2 3 4 5   09 08 07 06 05

SUMMARY
TABLE OF CONTENTS

PREFACE   *xxv*

LIST OF CANADIAN PERSONAL PROPERTY SECURITY ACTS
AND ABBREVIATIONS   *xxix*

CHAPTER   1: Introduction and General Considerations   *1*

CHAPTER   2: The Concept of Security Interest and Scope of the *Personal Property Security Act*   *58*

CHAPTER: 3: Conflict of Laws   *118*

CHAPTER   4: Creation of a PPSA Security Interest   *161*

CHAPTER   5: Perfection   *200*

CHAPTER   6: The Registration System   *225*

CHAPTER   7: Buyers and Lessees of Collateral   *278*

CHAPTER   8: Competitions between Secured Parties   *308*

CHAPTER   9: Security Interests in Negotiable and Quasi-negotiable Collateral   *380*

CHAPTER 10: Competitions with Other Claimants   *395*

CHAPTER 11: The Effects of Bankruptcy and Insolvency Proceedings on Security Interests   *425*

CHAPTER 12: Following and Tracing into New Forms of Collateral   *452*

CHAPTER 13: Remedies   *511*

CHAPTER 14: National and International Security Interests   *584*

TABLE OF CASES   623

INDEX   659

ABOUT THE AUTHORS   671

DETAILED TABLE OF CONTENTS

PREFACE *xxv*

LIST OF CANADIAN PERSONAL PROPERTY SECURITY ACTS AND
ABBREVIATIONS *xxix*

CHAPTER 1:
INTRODUCTION AND GENERAL CONSIDERATIONS *1*

A. **Evolution of Personal Property Security Law** *1*

    1) The Idea of Secured Credit *1*
    2) Background *2*
    3) The *Personal Property Security Act* *3*

B. **Objectives of the PPSA** *4*

    1) Comprehensiveness *4*
    2) Flexibility *4*
    3) Fair and Efficient Enforcement *5*
    4) Protection of Information Needs of Third Parties *5*
    5) An Efficient Registration System *6*
    6) Certainty and Predictability in the Ordering of Priorities *7*
    7) Facilitation of Interprovincial and International Financing *8*

C. **Provincial and Territorial Variations** *8*

    1) Background *8*
    2) Variations between the Ontario PPSA and the Other Acts *10*
    3) Other Variations *10*

D. **Key Concepts** *12*

1) Security Interest   12
2) Debtor   13
3) Secured Party   16
4) Attachment   17
5) Perfection   18
6) Priority   18
7) Security Agreement versus Financing Statement   19

E. The Personal Property Classification System   19

1) Collateral   19
2) Sub-categories   20
3) Consumer Goods, Equipment, and Inventory   20
4) Land-related Goods   21
5) Land-related Intangibles   22

F. Interpretation   23

1) Conflict between Acts   23
2) Interpretation of Other Acts   24
3) Harmonization of Secured Transactions Law   24
4) Preservation of Complementary General Law   25
5) Inherent Interpretive Policies   26
6) Good Faith and Commercial Reasonableness   27

G. Knowledge and Notice   29

1) Meaning of "Knowledge"   29
2) Effective Notice   31

H. Federal Secured Transactions Law   33

I. The Proposed *Uniform Securities Transfer Act* (USTA)   35

1) Introduction   35
2) Objectives   36
3) Key Concepts   36
4) Scope of Proposed Amendments to the PPSA   38

J. Other Reform Initiatives   38

1) PPSA Reform   38
2) Abolition of *Bank Act* Security   39
3) The *Cape Town Convention on International Interests in Mobile Equipment*   39
4) The *Hague Convention on Investment Securities Held with an Intermediary*   41
5) The *UN Convention on the Assignment of Receivables in International Trade*   41

K. UCC Article 9   42

1) Historical Influence   42

2)   Comparison with the PPSA   43

L.   **Secured Transactions Law of Quebec**   47

1)   Introduction   47
2)   Forms of Security   48
3)   Assignments and Long-term Leases   50
4)   Priority Consequences of Failure to Publish (Perfect)   51
5)   Advance Registration and Multi-agreement Registration   51
6)   Purchase Money Super-priority   51
7)   Capacity of Consumers and Enterprises to Grant Security   52
8)   Scope of Buyer in the Ordinary Course of Business Rule   54
9)   Serial Number Identification   54
10) Enforcement   55

Further Readings   56

CHAPTER 2:

THE CONCEPT OF SECURITY INTEREST AND SCOPE OF THE *PERSONAL PROPERTY SECURITY ACT*   58

A.   **The Definition and Central Concept of Security Interest**   58

1)   A Unitary Concept   58
2)   Hypothecation   60
3)   Transactions outside the Hypothec Concept   61

B.   **The Non-traditional Transactions: Conditional Sales Contracts, Leases, Consignments, and Trusts**   64

1)   Introduction   64
2)   Security Leases   67
     a)   The Relevance of Characterization of Leases   67
     b)   The Nature of the Task   68
     c)   A "Substance" or "Function" Test   69
     d)   Factors Pointing to a Security Lease   70
          i)   Automatic Vesting of Ownership or Obligation to Purchase   71
          ii)   The Lease Term and the Commercially Useful Life of the Goods   71
          iii) Lessee's Payment Obligation   71
          iv)   The Price of an Option to Purchase or Renew (Accumulated Equity)   72
          v)   Open-end Leases   73
          vi)   The Role of the Parties   74
          vii) Contractual Remedies   75
3)   Security Consignments   75
     a)   The Relevance of Characterization of Consignments   75

b)   The Nature of the Task   76
c)   The Primary Factor Pointing to a Security Consignment   79
d)   Other Relevant Factors   79
4)   Security Trusts   80
a)   A Trust That Secures Payment or Performance of an
Obligation   80
b)   Trust or Security Agreement   81
c)   Trust and Security Agreement   82
d)   Side-by-side Trust and Security Agreement   84

C.   Transactions on the Line   85

1)   Introduction   85
2)   Some Examples   86
3)   The Special Case of Subordination Agreements   87

D.   The Deemed Security Agreements   90

1)   Introduction   90
2)   A Transfer of an Account   92
3)   A Transfer of Chattel Paper   92
4)   A Commercial Consignment   93
5)   A Lease for a Term of More than One Year   94
6)   Sale of Goods without Change of Possession   96

E.   Excluded Interests and Transactions   96

1)   Non-consensual Liens, Charges, and Deemed Trusts   96
2)   Security Interests Arising under Federal Law   98
3)   Interests in or Claim under a Contract of Annuity or Policy of
Insurance   99
4)   Pawn Transactions   101
5)   Interests in Land and Interests in Payments Connected with
Land   101
a)   The Ontario Approach   102
b)   The Alternative Approach   103
6)   Remuneration for Personal Services   105
7)   Other Exclusions   106
a)   Transfer Where Transferee Performs the Contract and a
Transfer for Collection   106
b)   Sale of Accounts or Chattel Paper in a Sale of a Business   106
c)   Tort Claims   107
d)   Sellers' Right of Disposal under the *Sale of Goods Act*   107

F.   The Effect of Restrictions on the Transfer of Assets   109

1)   What Is Property?   109
2)   Licences and Quotas   109
3)   Other Types of Unassignable Property or Property Subject to
Transfer Restrictions   112

4)   First Nations Property Situated on a Reserve   *114*

Further Readings   *116*

CHAPTER 3:
CONFLICT OF LAWS   *118*

A.   **Introduction and General Considerations**   *118*

1)   Scope of Chapter   *118*
2)   Importance of Choice of Law Rules   *119*
3)   Overview of PPSA Conflicts Regime   *119*
4)   Choice of Law and Territorial Scope of PPSA   *121*
5)   Importance of Inter-jurisdictional Uniformity in Choice of Law Rules   *122*
6)   Mandatory Nature of Choice of Law Rules on Validity and Perfection   *124*
7)   Exceptions to the General PPSA Rules   *125*

B.   **Preliminary Interpretive Issues**   *126*

1)   "Attachment"   *126*
2)   "Perfection"   *127*
3)   "Effects of Perfection or Non-perfection" and Priority   *128*

C.   **Applicability of Law of the Jurisdiction Where the Collateral Is Located**   *129*

1)   Ordinary Goods   *129*
2)   Relocation of Goods: Reperfection Requirement   *130*
3)   When Do Goods Change Location?   *131*
4)   Intervening Buyers and Lessees of Relocated Collateral   *132*
5)   Relocated Goods: Law Applicable to Priority   *133*
6)   Goods Intended for Export   *135*
7)   Goods in Transit   *136*
8)   Possessory Security Interests in Money and Documentary Collateral   *137*

D.   **Applicability of Law of the Jurisdiction Where the Debtor Is Located**   *137*

1)   Mobile Goods   *137*
2)   Non-possessory Security Interests in Money and Negotiable Documentary Collateral   *139*
3)   Pure Intangibles   *140*
4)   Determining the Location of the Debtor   *141*
5)   Impact on Perfection of a Post-attachment Change in the Location of the Debtor   *143*
6)   Transfer of the Collateral to a Transferee Located in Another Jurisdiction   *144*

7) Special Priority Rule Where Applicable Legal System Does Not Have a Public Registration System *145*
8) *Renvoi* *147*

E. **Law Applicable to Enforcement** *149*

1) Procedural Aspects *149*
2) Substantive Aspects *150*

F. **Transactional Scope of PPSA Conflicts Rules** *153*

1) Security Interests in Proceeds *153*
2) Characterization of "Security Interests" *155*
3) Application of PPSA Rules beyond Secured Transactions *156*

G. **Impact of Bankruptcy Proceedings on Choice of Law** *157*

H. **Pending Reforms: Investment Property** *158*

Further Readings *159*

CHAPTER 4:

CREATION OF A PPSA SECURITY INTEREST *161*

A. **Introduction** *161*

1) "Attachment" *161*
2) *Inter Partes* and Third-party Attachment *162*
3) Relationship among Attachment, Perfection, and Priority *162*

B. **"Value is given"** *163*

1) "Value" *163*
2) Antecedent Debt *164*

C. **"Debtor has rights in the collateral"** *164*

1) Rights versus Ownership *164*
2) Exceptions to *Nemo Dat* *165*
3) Impact of PPSA on Characterization of Debtor's Rights *166*
4) Deemed Security Interests *167*
5) "Debtor" *168*
6) After-acquired Collateral *169*
7) After-acquired Consumer Goods *171*
8) Future Property and Analogous Categories *172*
9) Repossessed or Returned Goods *174*
10) Attachment of a Floating Charge *174*
11) Postponement of Attachment *175*

D. **Written Security Agreement or Possession** *177*

1) Introduction *177*

2) Possession as a Substitute for a Signed Descriptive Security Agreement *178*

3) Relationship between Evidentiary Requirement and Priority *180*

E. **Mandatory Content of Written Security Agreement** *182*

F. **Charging Language** *183*

G. **Debtor Signature** *184*

H. **Collateral Description** *186*

1) Permissible Descriptions *186*
    a) Description by Item or Kind *186*
    b) All-inclusive Description *187*
    c) All-inclusive Collateral Description Subject to Specified Exclusions *188*

2) Identifiability *189*

3) Commercially Responsive Interpretation *189*

4) Location and Supplier Qualifiers *190*

5) Ambiguity and Extrinsic Evidence *192*

6) Proceeds *193*

I. **Effectiveness of the Terms of the Security Agreement** *194*

1) General Principle *194*

2) Statutory Constraints Imposed by the PPSA *194*

3) Statutory Constraints Imposed by Other Acts *195*

J. **The Secured Obligation** *196*

1) General Principle *196*

2) Future Advances, Interest, and Maintenance Charges *196*

3) All-obligations Clauses *198*

K. **Debtor's Right to A Copy of The Written Security Agreement** *199*

Further Readings *199*

CHAPTER 5:
PERFECTION *200*

A. **The Concept: Its Source and Meanings** *200*

B. **Loss and Continuity of Perfection** *202*

C. **Perfection Steps** *203*

D. **Perfection by Registration** *205*

1) Introduction *205*

2) Registration, Knowledge, and Constructive Knowledge *205*

3) Notice Registration *206*

4) Access to Details of a Security Agreement *207*

E. **Perfection by Possession** *211*

1) Introduction *211*
2) What Constitutes Possession *212*
3) Perfection by Seizure or Repossession *214*

F. **Perfection of a Security Interest in Goods in Possession of a Bailee** *217*

G. **Automatic Perfection** *218*

1) Introduction *218*
2) Automatic Perfection of Foreign Security Interest *218*
3) Automatic Perfection of Security Interests in Proceeds *220*
4) Other Instances of Automatic Perfection *221*
5) Automatic Perfection under Proposed Changes Associated with the Proposed *Uniform Securities Transfer Act* *223*

H. **Perfection by Control** *223*

CHAPTER 6:

THE REGISTRATION SYSTEM *225*

A. **Introduction and Background** *225*

1) Scope of Chapter *225*
2) Pre-PPSA Registration Systems *226*

B. **The PPSA Registration System: General Considerations** *227*

1) Nature of the Personal Property Registry *227*
2) Advance Registration *228*
3) One Registration for Multiple Security Agreements *229*
4) Distinction between PPSA Registry and a Title Registry *231*
5) Access to Off-record Information *231*
6) Mandatory Discharge or Amendment of Registration *233*
7) Registration and Search Criteria *238*
8) Client Access to the Registry for Registration and Searching *239*
9) Effective Time of Registration *240*
10) Liability for Errors or Omissions *242*
11) Registration Not Constructive Notice *245*
12) Transactional Scope of Registry: Non-PPSA Transactions *246*

C. **Required Registration Data** *247*

1) Debtor Name and Address *247*
2) Individual versus Enterprise Debtors *248*
3) Name Rules for Individual Debtors *249*
4) Birth Date of Individual Debtors *251*
5) Enterprise Debtors *251*
6) Name and Address of Secured Party *254*
7) Description of General Collateral *254*

8) Description of Serial Numbered Goods   255
9) Description of Proceeds   259
10) Duration of Registration   259

D. **Subsequent Changes**   260

1) Introduction   260
2) Transfer of a Security Interest   261
3) Subordination of Priority   262
4) Change in Debtor Name or Transfer of Collateral   262
5) Addition of Collateral   266
6) Renewal   267
7) Correction of Erroneous Lapse or Discharge   267

E. **Effect of Errors or Omissions on Validity of Registration**   269

1) The Verification Statement   269
2) Objective Test for Invalidity   269
3) Error in Debtor Name   270
4) Error in Serial Number   273
5) Error in Debtor Name Where Serial Number Correct   273
6) Error in General Collateral Description   274
7) Entry of Serial Number Description in General Collateral Field   275

Further Readings   277

CHAPTER 7:

BUYERS AND LESSEES OF COLLATERAL   278

A. **The Context**   278

B. **Priority of Buyers' and Lessees' Interests Over Unperfected Security Interests**   279

C. **Priority of Buyers' and Lessees' Interests Over Perfected Security Interests**   284

1) Implied Power of Sale or Lease Given to a Debtor   284
2) Buyers or Lessees of Goods in the Ordinary Course of Business   286
    a) The Concept   286
    b) What Is a Sale in the Ordinary Course of [the Seller's] Business?   288
        i)   The Consideration   288
        ii) Passage of Property to the Buyer   289
        iii) What Is Ordinary Course?   291
        iv) Ordinary Course of Business "of the Seller"   292
        v)   Security Interests Given by a Prior Seller   294
3) Buyers of Serial Numbered Goods   295
4) Buyers of Low-value Goods   297

5) The Effectiveness of Automatically Perfected Security Interests against Buyers *298*

6) Interface with *Sale of Goods Act* and *Factors Act* Buyer-protection Provisions *302*

CHAPTER 8:

COMPETITIONS BETWEEN SECURED PARTIES *308*

A. **The Structure of the PPSA Priority Rules** *308*

B. **The Residual Priority Rule** *309*

1) The First-in-time Rule *309*
2) The Relevance of Knowledge *312*
3) Change in the Method of Perfection *313*
4) Priorities and Multiple Security Agreements *314*
5) Future Advances and All Obligations Clauses *316*
6) "Assignment" of the Financing Statement *321*
7) Motor Vehicles and Serial Numbered Goods *323*
8) The Double-debtor Problem *324*
9) Amalgamations *328*

C. **Purchase Money Security Interests** *329*

1) Justification for Superpriority *330*
2) Definition of Purchase Money Security Interests *331*
    a) Security Interests Taken by Sellers *332*
    b) Enabling Loans *332*
    c) Deemed Security Interests *335*
3) Procedural Requirements *336*
    a) Purchase Money Security Interests in Non-Inventory *336*
    b) Purchase Money Security Interests in Inventory *337*
    c) Determining the Date of Possession *340*
4) The Double-debtor Scenario *341*
5) Maintaining Purchase Money Security Interest Status *341*
    a) The Effect of Cross-collateralization *341*
    b) Consolidation of Debts and Refinancing *345*
    c) Paying Out Purchase Money Security Interests Held by Third Parties *350*
6) Purchase Money Security Interests in Accounts or Chattel Paper as Proceeds of Inventory *353*
7) Competing Purchase Money Security Interests *354*

D. **Production Money Security Interests in Crops and Animals** *356*

E. **Priorities under the Proposed Changes Associated with the *Uniform Securities Transfers Act*** *359*

F. **Date of Resolution of Priority Competitions** *362*

G. Reperfection of a Security Interest   *363*

H. Subordination Agreements   *368*

1) The Nature and Varieties of Subordination Agreements   *368*
2) Subordination and Priorities   *371*
3) Subordination Clauses Distinguished from Other Contractual Provisions   *373*

I. Other Principles Affecting Priorities   *374*

1) Bad Faith   *374*
2) Estoppel   *377*
3) Subrogation   *378*

Further Readings   *379*

CHAPTER 9:

SECURITY INTERESTS IN NEGOTIABLE AND QUASI-NEGOTIABLE COLLATERAL   *380*

A. Introduction   *380*

B. Traditional Negotiable Property   *381*

1) Money   *381*
2) Instruments and Negotiable Documents of Title   *382*
3) Securities   *386*

C. Chattel Paper   *389*

1) Chattel Paper: A *Sui Generis* Type of Collateral   *389*
2) Competing Security Interests in Chattel Paper   *391*
3) Breakdown of the Chattel Paper Concept   *394*

CHAPTER 10:

COMPETITIONS WITH OTHER CLAIMANTS   *395*

A. Competing Interests under Money Judgment Enforcement Law   *395*

1) Introduction   *395*
2) The Traditional Approach   *396*
    a) Binding Effect of a Writ of Execution   *396*
    b) Prior Security Interests and Subsequent Writs of Execution   *398*
3) The Judgment Creditor as Chargeholder   *402*
    a) The New Judgment Enforcement Systems   *402*
    b) The Saskatchewan and Northwest Territories Approaches   *404*
4) Future Advances and the Position of Unsecured Creditors   *405*

B. Priority Competitions with Non-consensual Security Interests   *406*

1) Taxonomy of Non-consensual Security Interests   *408*

a)   Liens *408*
b)   Rights of Distress *409*
c)   Statutory Security Interests and Charges *409*
d)   Statutory Deemed Trusts *409*
e)   Statutory Rights of Attachment of Debts *410*
f)   Procedural Devices *410*
2)   The Resolution of Priority Competitions *411*
a)   Determining the Legal Parameters of the Non-consensual Security Interest *411*
b)   Priority Rules Contained in the PPSA *411*
i)   Commercial Liens on Goods *412*
ii)   Effect of Non-perfection of the Security Interest *413*
c)   Other Legislative and Common Law Priority Rules *414*
d)   Order of Attachment *415*
3)   The Effect of Bankruptcy on Priorities *416*
a)   Crown Claims *416*
b)   Deemed Statutory Trusts *418*
c)   Preferred Claims *419*
d)   The Use of Bankruptcy to Invert Priorities *420*

C.   **Priority Competitions over Trust Property** *421*

1)   Trust Property Acquired before the Creation of a Security Interest *422*
2)   Trust Property Acquired after the Creation of a Security Interest *423*

Further Readings *424*

CHAPTER 11:
THE EFFECTS OF BANKRUPTCY AND INSOLVENCY
PROCEEDINGS ON SECURITY INTERESTS *425*

A.   **Introduction** *425*

B.   **The Effect of Bankruptcy Law on the Rights of Secured Creditors** *426*

1)   The Definition of Secured Creditor under the BIA *426*
2)   The Traditional Approach *427*
3)   The Effect of Bankruptcy Law on the Priority Rights of Secured Creditors *428*
4)   The Effect of Bankruptcy and Insolvency Law on Enforcement Rights of Secured Creditors *429*

C.   **The Efficacy of After-acquired Property Clauses in Bankruptcy** *430*

D.   **The Effect of Discharge of the Bankrupt Debtor on a Security Interest** *438*

E.   **The Status of a Trustee under the PPSA**   *441*

   1)   The Interface between the PPSA and the BIA   *441*
   2)   Reperfection and the Status of the Trustee   *443*
   3)   The Special Status of the Trustee under the PPSA   *444*
   4)   The Exemptions Issue   *447*

Further Readings   *451*

CHAPTER 12:
FOLLOWING AND TRACING INTO NEW FORMS OF COLLATERAL   *452*

A.   **Overview**   *452*

   1)   Following and Tracing   *452*
   2)   Following Collateral into New Products   *453*
   3)   Tracing Value into New Assets   *454*
   4)   Tracing and Identifying Proceeds   *455*

B.   **Proceeds**   *456*

   1)   Extension of the Security Interest to Proceeds   *456*
     a)   The Statutory Right to Proceeds   *456*
     b)   Advantages of a Proceeds Claim   *459*
     c)   Enforcement against Both the Original Collateral and the Proceeds   *460*
   2)   The Definition of Proceeds   *462*
     a)   Application to Later Generation Proceeds   *462*
     b)   The Debtor's Interest Requirement   *462*
     c)   The Requirement of a Dealing   *464*
     d)   The "Identifiable or Traceable" Requirement   *465*
   3)   The Tracing Rules   *466*
     a)   Are PPSA Tracing Rules Different from Conventional Tracing Rules?   *466*
     b)   The Lowest Intermediate Balance Rule   *468*
     c)   Tracing and Multiple Claimants   *470*
     d)   The Relevance of Wrongdoing   *472*
     e)   Tracing through Payment of a Debt   *475*
     f)   The Functional Equivalence Rule   *476*
   4)   Perfection and Priorities   *478*
     a)   The Ontario and Manitoba Perfection Provisions   *478*
     b)   The Perfection Provisions of the Other Jurisdictions   *479*
     c)   Priority of Security Interests in Proceeds   *482*

C.   **Returned or Repossessed Goods**   *482*

   1)   Reattachment of the Inventory Financer's Security Interest   *483*
   2)   The Chattel Paper Financer's Interest   *484*

3)   The Account Financer's Interest   486
4)   The Resolution of Priority Competitions   486
    a)   The Situation outside of Ontario and the Yukon   486
    b)   The Ontario Provision   487
    c)   The Yukon Provision   489

D. Fixtures and Crops   489

1)   The Definition of Fixtures   490
2)   The Priority of a Security Interest in Fixtures   492
3)   The Role of Real Property Priority Rules   494
4)   Enforcing Security Interests in Fixtures   496
5)   Security Interests in Crops   497

E. Accessions   498

1)   The Definition of Accessions   499
2)   The Priority of a Security Interest in Accessions   500
3)   Enforcing Security Interests in Accessions   502

F. Manufactured and Commingled Goods   503

1)   Continuation of the Security Interest in the Product or Mass   503
2)   Perfection of the Security Interest in the Product   505
3)   Competing Security Interests in the Separate Components   506
4)   Competing Security Interests in a Component and a Product   508
5)   Valuation Limits on Continued Security Interests   509

Further Readings   510

CHAPTER 13:
REMEDIES   511

A. Introduction   511

1)   Personal Claims and Proprietary Claims   511
2)   Secured and Unsecured Creditors' Remedies   512

B. The Nature and Scope of Part 5   514

1)   Transactions Not Caught by Part 5   515
2)   Contractual Modifications to Part 5   516
3)   Disposition of Real and Personal Property   518
4)   Enforcement against Third Parties   519
5)   Who Is the Debtor?   520

C. Default   521

1)   Defining the Events of Default   522
2)   Acceleration Clauses and Insecurity Provisions   523
3)   The Reasonable Notice Doctrine   523
4)   The Statutory Notice of Intention to Enforce a Security   526

5)   Other Provincial Pre-seizure Notice Requirements   527

D.   Seizure   528
1)   The Right to Seize the Collateral   529
  a)   Peaceable Recaption   529
  b)   Restrictions on Self-help Remedies   530
  c)   Constructive Seizure   531
  d)   Seizure by Judicial Action   532
2)   Property Exempt from Seizure   533
3)   Custodial Duties of the Secured Party   534

E.   Redemption and Reinstatement   535
1)   The Right to Redeem   536
  a)   What Must Be Tendered?   536
  b)   Application of Equitable Principles   538
2)   Reinstatement   538

F.   Sale of the Collateral   539
1)   Method of Sale   540
2)   Notice of Disposition   542
3)   The Standard of Commercial Reasonableness   544
4)   Assessment of the Price: Wholesale or Retail?   546
5)   Recourse and Repurchase Agreements   547
6)   The Purchaser's Title   549
7)   Surplus and Deficiency   549
  a)   Disposition of a Surplus   550
  b)   Limitations on Deficiency Actions   551

G.   Retention of the Collateral in Satisfaction of the Obligation   552
1)   Statutory Foreclosure   553
2)   The Legal Consequences of Foreclosure   554
3)   Constructive Foreclosure   555
4)   Contractual Foreclosure   556

H.   Enforcement against Intangibles and Chattel Paper   558
1)   Direct Collection Rights of Secured Parties   558
2)   Rights of Third-party Account Debtors   560
  a)   Defences and Set-off   560
  b)   The Account Debtor's Obligation to Pay on Notification   561
  c)   Post-assignment Contractual Modifications   562
3)   Set-off and the Right to Proceeds   562

I.   Receiverships   564
1)   Regulation of Receiverships   564
2)   The Status and Legal Effect of a Receivership   566
3)   Deemed Agency Clauses   568

J.   Enforcement by Subordinate Secured Parties   *569*

1) Pre-emption by the Senior Secured Party   *569*
2) Marshalling of Securities   *571*
3) Obligations of the Junior Secured Party   *572*

K.   Supervisory Power of the Court   *574*

L.   Remedies against a Secured Party for Non-compliance with the PPSA   *576*

1) The Statutory Right of Action   *577*
2) Effect on Deficiency Claims   *578*

M.   Personal Claims Available to a Secured Party   *578*

1) Conversion and Detinue   *579*
2) Restitutionary Claims   *581*
3) Actions for Recovery of Money   *582*

Further Readings   *583*

CHAPTER 14:
NATIONAL AND INTERNATIONAL SECURITY
INTERESTS   *584*

A.   *Bank Act* Security   *585*

1) Availability of the Security   *585*
2) The Security Agreement   *586*
3) The Rights Obtained by the Bank   *587*
4) Registration   *588*
5) Fixtures   *589*
6) Fishing Vessels   *589*
7) Resolution of Priority Competitions with PPSA Security Interests   *589*
    a) The *Bank Act* Priority Provisions   *590*
    b) Application of the PPSA Priority Rules   *592*
    c) Double Documentation and Election   *594*
    d) *Bank Act* Security and Proceeds   *595*
8) Other Priority Competitions   *596*
9) Enforcement   *597*
10) Reform of the *Bank Act* Security Provisions?   *599*

B.   Security Interests in Ships   *600*

1) *Canada Shipping Act* Ship Mortgages   *600*
2) The Relevance of Canadian Maritime Law   *601*
3) Priority Competitions with Provincial Security Interests   *602*
4) Enforcement of the Ship Mortgage   *603*

C. Security Interests in Intellectual Property   *604*

D. Security Interests in Railway Assets and Rolling Stock   *607*

E. The *Convention on International Interests in Mobile Equipment*, 2001   *607*

    1) Introduction   *607*
    2) Types of Transactions to Which the Convention Applies   *609*
        a) Approach to Characterization of Transactions: Security Agreements, Leases, and Conditional Sales Contracts   *609*
        b) Non-consensual Rights or Interests   *610*
        c) Assignments   *611*
        d) Sales of Aircraft Objects   *611*
    3) The International Element   *611*
    4) The Priority Structure   *612*
    5) Post-default Rights and Remedies   *613*
    6) Insolvency   *613*
    7) Features of the International Registry   *614*
        a) A Single International Registry   *614*
        b) Guarantee of Reliability   *615*
        c) Notice Registration   *615*
        d) Pre-agreement Registration   *615*
        e) Compulsory Discharge   *616*
    8) Interface between the Convention and the PPSA   *616*
        a) Side-by-side Secured Financing Systems   *616*
        b) Matters Implicitly Left to Domestic Law   *616*
            i) Limited Application of the Convention: Size and Use of Aircraft   *616*
            ii) Proceeds   *617*
            iii) Accessions   *618*
            iv) Transition   *620*
            v) Sales of Aircraft Objects   *621*

Further Readings   *622*

TABLE OF CASES   *623*

INDEX   *659*

ABOUT THE AUTHORS   *671*

PREFACE

Secured transactions under the *Personal Property Security Act* (PPSA) are at the forefront of commercial law in both law faculty curricula and legal practice in common law jurisdictions of Canada. This book responds to what the authors believe to be a long-standing need for a comprehensive treatise on secured financing under the Act. Other publications in the field, including our own, have tended to focus on the PPSA of a particular province or adopted an annotative or section-by-section commentary style. Although these approaches are valuable, we felt that a Canada-wide treatise style treatment would convey more effectively the interrelationship among the various parts of the Act as well as the essentially unitary character of secured lending law in all PPSA jurisdictions. While we offer detailed analysis of the substantive differences among the various Acts, our initial instinct that a comprehensive presentation was feasible for most issues worked out remarkably well in the writing of this book. One of our goals in adopting this approach was to contribute to the continued harmonization of the law in this area by encouraging a vision of PPSA law, including judicial precedent, as generally borderless in character.

This book is essentially a doctrinal work. We have identified the policy rationales for particular provisions where relevant to their interpretation and we have included the occasional call for reform of particular areas. Nonetheless, the book does not analyze, let alone challenge, the broader underlying economic or social theory of secured lending. Our goal was to present what we hope to be an accurate and complete account of the current state of the law of secured transactions under the PPSA. We trust it will prove to be very valuable to law students and law professors for the purposes of both introductory and advanced courses in secured transactions. However, our intended readership goes beyond legal education. The book has been designed to be of assistance to anybody seeking general or specialized guidance, but especially to judges, lawyers, secured creditors and their debtors, and trustees in bankruptcy and other insolvency law practitioners.

Our concept of the PPSA as a single statute, despite some provincial and territorial variations, is reflected in the method of citation we adopted. As a general rule, we refer to the PPSA in the text of the book in the singular ("the PPSA" or "the Act"). In citing particular provisions of the Act in the footnotes, we give the relevant section numbers for each PPSA jurisdiction (referred to in abbreviated form) in order of their relative commonality in section numbering from highest to lowest. We have used the following abbreviations.

A:	Alberta	BC:	British Columbia
M:	Manitoba	NB:	New Brunswick
NL:	Newfoundland and Labrador	NWT:	Northwest Territories
NS:	Nova Scotia	Nu:	Nunavut
O:	Ontario	PEI:	Prince Edward Island
S:	Saskatchewan	Y:	Yukon

The following is a typical example:

PPSA (M, NWT, Nu, S) s. 65; (NB, PEI) s. 66; (NL, NS) s. 67; A s. 67; BC s. 69; Y s. 62.

In structure, the book follows, in part, the structure of the PPSA itself, with successive chapters devoted to the PPSA concept of a security interest and the scope of the Act, conflict of laws, the creation of a security interest, perfection, priorities, and default remedies. In the area of priorities, we decided that a more refined approach would better convey the different policies at stake depending on the category of competing claimant. The result is discrete chapters on priority competitions involving buyers and lessees, other secured parties, and other competing interests, notably judgment creditors, bankruptcy trustees, and non-consensual security interests.

The negotiable or quasi-negotiable character of certain categories of collateral raises special considerations at the level of both perfection and priorities. We therefore decided to devote a separate chapter to the special perfection and priority rules governing security interests in money, negotiable instruments and documents of title, securities, and chattel paper. The transformation of the original collateral into new forms also requires specialized legal treatment at the level not just of perfection and priority but also with respect to default remedies. Consequently, we included a discrete chapter on following and tracing the original collateral, covering security interests in replacement proceeds, accessions, commingled or processed goods, fixtures, and crops.

Although the PPSA provides the principal legal framework for secured transactions, it intersects with federal law at various points. This book deals extensively with these points of intersection. The impact of federal bankruptcy and insolvency proceedings on PPSA security interests is the subject of a separate chapter as are the specialized federal security regimes governing security in personal property taken by banks under the *Bank Act* and in ships under Canadian maritime law. The special limitations created by federal law on reserve-based personal property are also addressed.

Increasingly, the law of secured lending is influenced by international developments and we have also addressed the potential impact of recent international texts, notably the *Aircraft Protocol* to the *Cape Town Convention on International Interests in Mobile Equipment*, the *Hague Convention on the Law Applicable to Certain Rights in Respect of Securities Held with an Intermediary*, and the *United Nations Convention on the Assignment of Receivables in International Trade*.

Pending reforms at the domestic level include the proposed *Uniform Securities Transfer Act* and the complementary amendments that will be made to the PPSA on its adoption. In view of the importance of this form of collateral, and the current inadequacy of the PPSA treatment of security interests in securities held with an intermediary, we decided to include a relatively detailed treatment of the USTA reforms where relevant throughout the book.

This book is restricted to the Canadian law of personal property security as reflected in the PPSA. It does not, in other words, cover the regime for security in movable property found in the Quebec *Civil Code*. However, in view of the national character of many secured lending transactions, we decided to include a brief synopsis of the most salient points of commonality and difference between the PPSA and the *Civil Code* in the introductory chapter. We also included a comparative analysis of the PPSA choice of law rules for security interests with those found in the *Civil Code* in the conflict of laws chapter. Both chapters also incorporate some comparative reference to Article 9 of the *Uniform Commercial Code* in the United States.

This book is a collaborative effort. Although the various chapters had principal authors, they are unsigned and, because of the approach used, they reflect our combined efforts and ideas. As a result, the book as a whole represents more than what each of us might have produced on our own. As we progressed in the writing of the book, our individual viewpoints proved to be compatible or complementary on most points. However, a number of issues inevitably emerged on which we discovered that, at least initially, we held widely differing opinions. We found the process of working through our respective viewpoints to be stimulating and educative and we are grateful to each other for the patience and good humour which made it possible to produce a synthesis of our individual ideas. In the few instances where we were not able to reach agreement, we decided to simply present the different possible approaches in a neutral fashion leaving it to the wisdom of the reader to come to her own conclusions.

No doubt some differences in writing style remain between the various chapters. However, we have tried to minimize these by adopting common style guidelines. For example, we all agreed to include, where useful, concrete factual scenarios to illustrate the operation of the various rules and to minimize substantive discussion in the footnotes. We also settled on the use of "it" as the appropriate pronoun in referring to the secured party and on the random use of feminine and masculine pronouns ("she," "he") in referring to the debtor (this decision was based simply on the practical reality that most secured parties are legal entities whereas debtors may be either legal entities or natural persons and either men or women).

This book does not purport to be a digest or provide an analysis or critique of all Canadian cases dealing with the PPSA. Our approach was to cite leading, highly controversial, or conflicting decisions that are relevant to an exploration of the conceptual structure and functioning of the Act. Similarly, while we included lists of "additional readings" at the end of most chapters, no attempt was made to cite all of the legal literature on the PPSA.

Two of us, Catherine Walsh and Ronald Cuming, are indebted to the third, Rod Wood, for being willing to take on the additional onerous tasks of acting as repository of the various iterations of the chapters, preparing the index and acting on our behalf in communications with the publisher.

We would like to thank Irwin Law Inc., and particularly Mr. Jeffrey Miller, for their encouragement and patience over the long gestation period of this book.

September 2005   Ronald C.C. Cuming
                                                            Catherine Walsh
                                                            Roderick J. Wood

LIST OF CANADIAN PERSONAL PROPERTY SECURITY ACTS AND ABBREVIATIONS

APPSA   Alberta, *Personal Property Security Act*, R.S.A. 2000, c. P-7

BCPPSA   British Columbia, *Personal Property Security Act*, R.S.B.C 1996, c. 359

MPPSA   Manitoba, *Personal Property Security Act*, C.C.S.M. c. P35

NBPPSA   New Brunswick, *Personal Property Security Act*, S.N.B. 1993, c. P-7.1

NLPPSA   Newfoundland and Labrador, *Personal Property Security Act*, S.N.L. 1998, c. P-7.1

NWTPPSA Northwest Territories, *Personal Property Security Act*, S.N.W.T. 1994, c. 8

NSPPSA   Nova Scotia, *Personal Property Security Act*, S.N.S. 1995-96, c. 13

NuPPSA   Nunavut, *Personal Property Security Act*, S.N.W.T. 1994, c. 8

OPPSA   Ontario, *Personal Property Security Act*, R.S.O. 1990, c. P.10

PEIPPSA   *Prince Edward Island, Personal Property Security Act*, R.S.P.E.I. 1988, c. P-3.1

SPPSA   Saskatchewan, *Personal Property Security Act, 1993*, S.S. 1993, c. P-6.2

YPPSA   Yukon, *Personal Property Security Act*, R.S.Y. 2002, c. 169

CHAPTER 1

INTRODUCTION AND GENERAL CONSIDERATIONS

A. EVOLUTION OF PERSONAL PROPERTY SECURITY LAW

1) The Idea of Secured Credit

The idea of secured credit has been around as long as the concepts of private property and freedom of contract. The basic premise is straightforward. A debtor gives her creditor a proprietary interest in one or more of her assets on the understanding that if she defaults the creditor can look to the value of those assets to satisfy the debt.

The proprietary character of a security interest typically confers three basic rights on the secured party, namely: (1) the right to enforce the security interest against the collateral in the event of default; (2) the right to preference in payment, to the extent of the value of the collateral, over unsecured creditors upon an insolvency of the debtor; and (3) the right to follow the collateral and to assert the security interest against a third party to whom it has been transferred.

This book examines the legal framework for secured credit set out in the *Personal Property Security Act* (PPSA). First proclaimed by Ontario in 1976, the PPSA is in force today in all nine common law provinces and the three federal territories.[1]

---

1   In order of implementation, see: Ontario, 1976 (S.O. 1967, c. 73, in force 1 April 1976, replaced by S.O. 1989, c. 16, in force 10 October 1989); Manitoba, 1978 (S.M.

2) Background[2]

The oldest and most widely recognized consensual security device is the classic pledge or pawn, constituted by the debtor's transfer of possession of the collateral to the secured party on the understanding that the secured party is entitled to sell the collateral if the debtor defaults on her loan obligation. In some legal systems (an ever decreasing number), the pledge is still the only device available to secure personal property. However, Canadian (and English) common law long ago rejected the presumption of fraud historically associated with the grant of a security interest without a transfer of possession of the collateral to the secured party. This paved the way for the recognition of two additional forms of security, both of which enabled the debtor to remain in possession of the collateral. The first was the chattel mortgage, constituted by the transfer of title to the collateral to the secured party on condition that title would be transferred back to the debtor upon satisfaction of the secured obligation. The second was the equitable charge. Unlike the mortgage, the charge did not depend on the formal transfer of title to the collateral. It was purely hypothecary in character. The secured party's proprietary interest was created simply by the agreement of the debtor that the secured party could appropriate the value of the collateral to satisfy the secured obligation in the event of the debtor's default.

The widespread availability of non-possessory security devices supported the early development and steady growth of secured financing in the common law colonies that were to become Canada. By 1849, non-possessory security had become sufficiently commonplace to cause the Legislative Assembly of the Province of Canada to enact legislation requiring the public filing of chattel mortgages. By the turn of

---

1973, c. 5, in force 1 September 1978, see now R.S.M. 1987, c. P35); Saskatchewan, 1981 (S.S. 1979–80, c. P-6.1, in force 1 May 1981, replaced by S.S. 1993, c. P-6.2, in force 1 April 1995); Yukon Territory (O.Y.T. 1980, c. 20, 2d Sess, in force 1 June 1982, see now R.S.Y. 1986, c. 130); Alberta (S.A. 1988, c. P-4.05, in force 1 October 1990); British Columbia (S.B.C. 1989, c. 36, in force 1 October 1990); New Brunswick, 1995 (S.N.B. 1993, c. P-7.1, in force 18 April 1995); Nova Scotia, 1997 (S.N.S. 1995-96, c. 13, in force 3 November 1997); Prince Edward Island, 1998 (S.P.E.I. 1997, c. 33, in force 27 April 1998); Newfoundland, 1999 (S.N. 1998, c. P-7.1, in force 13 December 1999); Northwest Territories (S.N.W.T. 1994, c. 8, in force 7 May 2001); Nunavut (Nunavut Consolidated Acts, in force 7 May 2001).

2   On the pre-PPSA legal framework for personal property security, see, for example, Jacob S. Ziegel, "Canadian Chattel Security Law: Past Experience and Current Developments" in J.G. Sauveplanne, ed., *Security over Corporeal Movables* (Leiden: A.W. Sitjhoff, 1974).

the twentieth century, chattel mortgage legislation had come into force in all the common law provinces and the Northwest Territories.

By this point in history, the English floating charge had come into common use in the corporate financing sector in both England and Canada. The distinctive feature of the floating charge was that it enabled a non-specific charge to be taken over all of the undertaking of a corporation or over generic categories of circulating assets such as inventory and accounts receivable. Ultimately, separate registry systems were established for charges and mortgages — fixed or floating — granted by corporations to secure bonds or debentures.

The statutory recognition of assignments, beginning with Ontario in 1872, gave added legal efficacy to the assignment by a business of its accounts receivable by way of sale or security. By 1913, Saskatchewan had enacted legislation requiring the registration of security and non-security assignments of book debts by merchants and traders (other than those already subject to the registration regime for secured bonds and debentures granted by corporations). Assignment of Book Debts Acts were ultimately brought into force throughout common law Canada and in the territories.

Historical Canadian secured financing patterns were not merely a copy of English common law practices. The best example of this is the conditional sales contract. Like the mortgage, the efficacy of the conditional sales contract depended on the secured party holding title to the collateral. Unlike the mortgage, it was based on the retention of title by the secured party rather than the transfer of title by the debtor.[3] Of only recent vintage in England, the conditional sales contract had come into widespread use in Canada and the United States as early as the 1860s and 1870s to finance the acquisition of both consumer and business assets. Beginning in 1882, the common law provinces and the territories adopted legislation to provide for the public registration of both conditional sales contracts and hire purchase leases.

3) The *Personal Property Security Act*

The ad hoc evolution of personal property financing in Canada eventually led to a highly fragmented legal framework. There was no single law of personal property security. Each security device was instead governed by its own peculiar mix of statutory, common law, and equitable

---

3   On the pre-PPSA differences between the retention and grant of title for security purposes, see Michael G. Bridge *et al.*, "Formalism, Functionalism and Understanding the Law of Secured Transactions (1999) 44 McGill L.J. 567 at 597–98.

principles. The priority complexities created by the fragmentation in the substantive law were exacerbated by the co-existence of disparate and sometimes overlapping registration systems and policies.

The growing unhappiness of the business and legal communities with this state of affairs ultimately led to the adoption of the *Personal Property Security Act*. Inspired by Article 9 of the U.S. *Uniform Commercial Code* (UCC), the PPSA was enacted to modernize, rationalize, and consolidate personal property security law. Ontario was the first jurisdiction to adopt a PPSA. Initially enacted in 1967, the development of a computerized electronic registry to complement the Act took considerably longer than expected, with the result that the Act was not proclaimed in force for almost another decade. Following Ontario's lead in 1976, the PPSA was proclaimed in force by Manitoba in 1978, Saskatchewan in 1981, the Yukon Territory in 1982, Alberta and British Columbia in 1990, New Brunswick in 1995, Nova Scotia in 1997, Prince Edward Island in 1998, Newfoundland in 1999, and the Northwest Territories and Nunavut in 2001.

B. OBJECTIVES OF THE PPSA

1) Comprehensiveness

Although it preserves and protects the conventional rights of a secured party, the PPSA introduced a significant number of innovative features. Most important is the establishment of a comprehensive statutory framework to govern the creation, perfection, priority, and enforcement of security interests in all types of personal property. The key to the success of this objective is the adoption of a functional concept of security. "Security interest" is defined by the Act in generic terms to mean an interest in personal property that secures payment or performance of an obligation, without regard to the form of the transaction and without regard to the location of title to the collateral as between the secured party and the debtor.

2) Flexibility

Although the "security interest" concept adopted by the PPSA captures the traditional security devices, the Act detaches the legal incidents associated with taking security from the parties' choice of a security instrument. Distinctions between security interests are instead drawn along functional lines designed to accommodate both existing commercial practices and new financing techniques.

3) Fair and Efficient Enforcement

In principle, a secured party's proprietary rights in the collateral are limited by the function of taking security. Ownership remains in the debtor and the secured party's proprietary interest is limited to the value of the secured obligation. The PPSA recognizes the limited nature of the secured party's rights and the concomitant need to protect the debtor and interested third parties against a self-interested or improvident realization of the collateral. Although the parties are free to define the events of default that will trigger the secured party's rights of enforcement, the enforcement process itself is subject to mandatory procedural standards.

Sale of the collateral is the principal remedy, with the secured party obliged to account for any surplus proceeds, and the debtor subject to a personal liability to pay any shortfall. Exercise of the remedy is subject to minimum advance notice requirements, and the debtor is entitled to arrest the process at any point prior to final disposition by paying the secured obligation and the accrued costs of enforcement, and remedying any other act of default.

Where the collateral takes the form of an account owing by a third party to the debtor, the Act entitles the secured party to collect payment directly from the account debtor according to the same legal framework that applies to collections under a sale of receivables. This is subject to the important distinction that the secured party is obliged to hand over any surplus proceeds once the secured obligation is satisfied.

As an alternative to sale or collection, the PPSA permits a secured party simply to take the collateral in full satisfaction of the secured obligation. However, the secured party's right to take the collateral in payment is regulated in a manner designed to respect the hypothecary character of its proprietary interest. Exercise of the remedy depends on the post-default voluntary consent of the debtor and third parties with an interest in the collateral including subordinate secured parties. If any objection is raised — as it invariably will be where the anticipated market value of the collateral exceeds the secured obligation — the secured party must revert to the ordinary remedy of sale with the concomitant obligation to account for any surplus value.

4) Protection of Information Needs of Third Parties

Protection of a secured party's proprietary rights must be balanced against the need to ensure that third parties are not prejudiced by the existence of undisclosed "secret liens" in assets in a debtor's possession. The PPSA reconciles these objectives through two mechanisms. First, the security agreement must satisfy certain evidentiary requirements before it can be enforced against third parties: the secured party must take possession of the collateral or the debtor must sign a security agreement that describes the collateral. Second, the security interest must be perfected. Subject to the exceptional recognition of temporary automatic perfection, the Act recognizes only two perfecting steps: taking possession of the collateral or registration of the security interest in the Personal Property Registry established by the Act.

5) An Efficient Registration System

While registration requirements for non-possessory security devices have long been a feature of Canadian law, they developed incrementally. As noted earlier, chattel mortgages, assignments of book debts, corporate securities, and conditional sale and hire purchase agreements each had their own registration regime. The PPSA replaced the old systems with a single consolidated Personal Property Registry.

The PPSA registration regime is vastly more efficient than its predecessors. The pre-PPSA registries were document-filing systems of the kind still used in some jurisdictions for registering title to land. Registrants were required to file the actual security documentation. The PPSA instead adopts notice registration. All that has to be registered is a simple notice (called a financing statement) containing the basic information necessary to alert a searcher to the potential existence of a security interest — the names and addresses of the parties, a description of the collateral, and the duration of the registration. There is no need to file the underlying security documentation, or even tender it for scrutiny.

Notice registration removed any obstacle to advance registration and the PPSA confirms that a financing statement may be registered before or after a security agreement is made or a security interest attaches. Notice registration also eliminated the necessity for a one-to-one relationship between each registration and each security agreement, and the Act confirms that a single registration is effective to perfect a security interest arising under multiple agreements between the same parties.

The advent of computer technology represents the single most important contribution to the efficiency of the PPSA registration system. The records under the pre-PPSA registration statutes were maintained in paper form. Registrations had to be entered manually by the registry staff and searches had to be performed on-site. In a number of provinces, the records were maintained on a county-by-county basis, requiring complex internal rules to deal with the impact of relocation of the debtor or collateral to a different county. In contrast, registrations in the Personal Property Registry are stored in digital form in a single centralized database. Computerization has all but eliminated the archival burden on the registration system. It has also facilitated direct client access to the registry. Indeed, today, the vast majority of registrations and searches are conducted by the clients themselves — often using Internet access.

6) Certainty and Predictability in the Ordering of Priorities

Security is useful because it can reduce the priority risk attached to credit. However, risk reduction is dependent upon the certainty and predictability of the legal rules governing a secured party's priority status against competing claimants. Under pre-PPSA law, certainty and predictability were severely compromised.

First, priority between security interests was not necessarily determined by the order of registration. Actual knowledge of a prior unregistered security interest defeated a registered security interest. Secured parties could not therefore rely on registration to protect their priority ranking. If they had any inkling that the debtor might have had dealings with another secured party, their priority was vulnerable to challenge.

Second, even if the legislature had been inclined to eliminate the actual knowledge qualification, they could not have done so. So long as security interests covering the same asset were required to be registered in different regimes depending on the nature of the security device or the status of the debtor, adoption of a strict first-to-register rule was unworkable.

Third, registration under prior law did not displace the mix of common law and equitable rules that determined the priority status of a security interest against subsequent interests. It merely preserved whatever rights the secured party had under those rules. The operation of a number of those rules depended on whether or not the third party had taken with notice of the prior registered security interest. Although the issue attracted considerable litigation, there was considerable uncertainty as to whether registration constituted constructive knowledge for this purpose. This led to the rather bizarre result that a third party was sometimes better off for not having taken the precaution of searching.

By establishing a single comprehensive registration system, the PPSA greatly enhanced certainty and predictability for secured parties. Under the Act, priority among registered security interests is determined by the order of registration without regard to actual knowledge, and a registered or otherwise perfected security interest is normally guaranteed priority against other classes of subsequent claimants. The Act recognizes certain exceptions to both these principles for reasons of commercial practice or commercial convenience. However, these exceptions are expressed by the PPSA in explicit unambiguous language. Judicially developed theories of constructive notice or equitable subordination have no role to play. Indeed, the Act expressly disclaims the role of registration as constituting constructive knowledge for the purposes of those PPSA rules where actual knowledge still plays a role.

7) Facilitation of Interprovincial and International Financing

Secured transactions frequently involve connections to more than one province or country. The drafters of the PPSA recognized the importance of providing certainty and predictability on the applicable law. The Act contains statutory choice of law rules for four issues: (1) the validity of a security interest; (2) the requirements for registering or otherwise perfecting a security interest so as to ensure its effectiveness against third parties; (3) the priority effects of perfection or non-perfection; and (4) the enforcement rights of the secured party against the collateral.

The statutory choice of law rules are significant even in cases where all of jurisdictions to which a particular transaction is connected have enacted a PPSA. Although a common portal for electronic access to the registry databases of multiple PPSA jurisdictions is becoming available, each jurisdiction's registry remains legally distinct and perfection by registration in one does not constitute perfection by registration in all. Thus, guidance remains necessary on which jurisdiction's PPSA applies to perfection in order for secured parties to select the correct provincial or territorial registration venue. Moreover, the PPSA is not identical among all jurisdictions in which it has been enacted. Choice of law guidance is therefore also critical on the issues of the priority effects of perfection or non-perfection and enforcement.

C. PROVINCIAL AND TERRITORIAL VARIATIONS

1) Background

The incremental nature of the PPSA reform process has led to some variation in the different versions of the Act.

The 1976 Ontario Act was the product of a Committee of the Commercial Law Section of the Ontario Branch of the Canadian Bar Association. A committee of the Commercial Law Section of the Canadian Bar Association produced a *Model Uniform Personal Property Security Act* in 1970, subsequently revised and adopted by the Uniform Law Conference of Canada as the *Uniform Personal Property Security Act, 1982*. Neither version was ever implemented (although the 1970 Model influenced the 1973 iteration of the Manitoba Act).

National harmonization efforts having failed, the four Western provinces and the (then) two territories formed the Western Canada Personal Property Security Act Committee in 1986 to promote uniformity of PPSA legislation in the member jurisdictions.[4] By 1990, the annual meetings of the committee had attracted participants from Ontario, the Atlantic Provinces, and the federal government, prompting it to "nationalize" its status and goals. A new constitution was proclaimed at the 1991 meeting, reconstituting the committee as the Canadian Conference on Personal Property Security Law (CCPPSL) with a mandate "to encourage and facilitate the harmonization and compatibility of provincial, territorial and federal personal property security law." Quebec is now an annual participant, and the Conference has adopted a bilingual name.[5]

The conference's harmonization goals have been remarkably successful. The PPSA is broadly uniform in all provinces and territories, with one minor and one major exception. The minor exception is the Yukon PPSA. Because the Yukon PPSA parallels the 1981 version of the Saskatchewan PPSA, which in turn informed the work of the CCPPSL, the extent of variation is minor. The major exception is the Ontario PPSA. Although the original Act of 1976 was substantially revised and re-enacted in 1989, the Ontario law- makers did not take harmonization into account in the revision process. A 1993 report of a committee of the Ontario Branch of the Canadian Bar Association which would have led to greater harmonization was never implemented.[6]

---

4   The driving spirit behind the committee (now the conference) was and remains one of the co-authors of this text, Ronald Cuming.

5   Canadian Conference on Personal Property Security Law/Conférence Canadienne sur les Sûretés Réelles Mobilières.

6   Canadian Bar Association, Ontario, Submission to the Minister of Consumer and Commercial Relations concerning the *Personal Property Security Act* and the *Repair and Storage Liens Act* (Toronto: June 1993).

2) Variations between the Ontario PPSA and the Other Acts

The differences between the Ontario Act and its counterparts are the subject of issue-by-issue analysis throughout the book. For immediate purposes, it is enough to emphasize that the differences go beyond details to include some fairly fundamental points.

For example, unlike the other Acts, the Ontario PPSA does not apply to "deemed security interests" in the form of commercial consignments and true leases for a term of more than one year. The Ontario Act also places less significance on the information disclosure function of registration. This is reflected in differences in the provisions dealing with reinstatement of an inadvertently lapsed or discharged registration and the collateral description requirements for financing statements.

Differences also exist in the important area of priorities. For example, the Ontario Act does not provide detailed guidance on the priority status of creditors and transferees of negotiable collateral who deal with the debtor in the ordinary courses of the debtor's business. As the book explains, a practical consequence of this difference is that the Ontario courts have had to place more emphasis on theories derived from general law, for example, implied waiver, in resolving these conflicts.

The Ontario Act is rather more favourable to the interests of the secured party as against the debtor, compared to the other Acts. An important symbolic example is the absence in the Ontario version of provision for an overarching obligation of good faith and commercial reasonableness.

The same philosophical difference is seen in the provisions dealing with the rights of a secured party as against third parties. For example, the Ontario Act allows a post-default seizure of the collateral by a secured party to compensate for failure to perfect a non-possessory security interest by registration. The Ontario Act also gives broader protection to secured parties as against buyers and lessees of collateral.

3) Other Variations

For the most part, the other differences among the Acts are relatively insignificant. For example, the Acts in force in the four Atlantic provinces extend the concept of a deemed security interest to capture a sale of goods outside the ordinary course of business where the seller remains in possession beyond a reasonable period. They also adopt the Ontario policy on the scope of the exclusion of wage assignments.

Some differences are more significant. Four stand out in particular.

The first concerns the effectiveness of a security interest against the debtor's judgment creditors. An increasing number of PPSA jurisdictions provide for the registration of a notice of judgment or writ of execution in the Personal Property Registry with priority then determined by the order of registration. The wisdom of including judgment creditors within the PPSA registration and priority system is generally conceded. The failure of all jurisdictions to implement that approach is more a reflection of reform inertia and insufficient reform resources than any real policy divide.

The second point of difference may reflect a deeper policy division. Traditionally, common law legal systems have not imposed on secured parties the same exemptions from seizure that restrict the enforcement rights of a judgment creditor. A number of PPSA jurisdictions now qualify the right of a secured party to enforce a non-purchase money security interest against certain basic necessaries. They also provide a judicial discretion to stay enforcement against consumer goods in cases of serious hardship or where enforcement is not economically justified. Other provinces, including Ontario, have not been inclined to take this step.

A third important source of variation is in the design and operation of the registration system. To some extent this is simply a product of the incremental nature of PPSA reform; each jurisdiction quite naturally took advantage of technological advances that had occurred by the time of implementation of its own system. Other variations stem from differences in policy views on such issues as registry access, whether the system should build in some level of forgiveness for error in the entry of registration data, and the extent of the information disclosure function of the registry. These variations are not mere background technicalities: they can have a significant impact on the legal question of whether a security interest has been properly registered so as to be legally perfected against third parties.

Another difference is in the rules governing priority in accounts as between the holder of a purchase money security interest in inventory claiming the accounts as proceeds of the inventory and the holder of a prior registered security interest in the accounts as original collateral. The western provinces and the three territories have one rule, the Ontario Act has another, and the Acts in the four Atlantic provinces reflect yet a third approach. In practice, these differences have generated remarkably little controversy or litigation, suggesting that the priority issue is being dealt with effectively through intercreditor priority agreements.

D. KEY CONCEPTS

1) Security Interest

The PPSA is concerned solely with security interests that arise by virtue of an agreement between the parties. Although there are a variety of security interests that are created by law, these are not discussed in this book except to the extent that a priority competition arises between a consensual security interest and a non-consensual security interest.

The concept of consensual security interest adopted by the Act is intended to be exhaustive. A transaction will give rise to a security interest within the meaning of the Act if the following four requirements are satisfied:

1. The transaction creates or evidences a proprietary interest in an asset in favour of a creditor.
2. The asset is personal property.
3. The creditor's proprietary interest functions to secure payment or performance of an obligation.
4. The interest arises out of an agreement between the parties.

The PPSA concept of security goes beyond conventional common law ideas to include financing arrangements generated by the creditor's retention of title — for example, conditional sales and financing leases. By conceptualizing these transactions as secured in character, the Act effectively treats the buyer/lessee as the owner of the collateral with the seller/lessor having merely a security interest.

The impact of the functional concept of security adopted by the PPSA on conventional property concepts has been recognized beyond disputes directly governed by the Act. To cite the most prominent examples, it has informed decisions of the Supreme Court of Canada dealing with the effectiveness of security interests in bankruptcy and insolvency[7] and priority between a PPSA secured party and claimants holding a non-consensual interest in the collateral.[8]

The PPSA concept of security interest also captures certain deemed secured transactions; namely, an assignment of accounts or chattel paper, and, except for the Ontario Act, a commercial consignment and a true lease for a term of more than one year; the Atlantic Acts also extend to a sale of goods outside the ordinary course of business where the seller remains in possession after the sale. Although these transactions do not

---

7   *Re Giffen*, [1998] 1 S.C.R. 91.
8   *Royal Bank v. Sparrow Electric*, [1997] 1 S.C.R. 411.

give rise to a security interest, they raise the same policy concerns insofar as third parties would face difficulties in verifying the title of the person in possession or control of the "collateral" in the absence of a public registration requirement of the kind applicable to true security interests. These deemed secured transactions fall within the Act only for the purposes of perfection and priority. They are excluded from the enforcement regime for the obvious reason that the deemed debtor does not retain any interest in the "collateral" in need of protection.

2) Debtor

The PPSA defines "debtor" to mean a person who owes payment or performance of the obligation secured.[9] The definition is intended to complement the Act's generic concept of a security interest as an interest in personal property that secures payment or performance of an obligation. Thus, it does not matter what formal label is assigned to the debtor in the security documentation. Whether called a mortgagor, a chargor, a pledgor, a buyer, a lessee, or any other term, the important question is whether the person qualifies as the obligor on the obligation secured by the security interest.

The person who owes payment or performance of the obligation secured by a security interest may not be the same as the person who owns or has rights in the collateral. In the commercial context, for example, it is not uncommon for an obligation owing by a corporation to be secured by assets owned by a parent or subsidiary corporation, or by a principal shareholder in the case of a privately held corporation. In the consumer context, a family member or close personal friend may likewise allow his or her assets to stand as collateral for another's credit obligation.

The PPSA specifies that "debtor" means a person who owes payment or performance of the obligation secured, "whether or not [that] [the] person owns or has rights in the collateral." The concept thus includes both the grantor of the security interest and the person who is personally liable on the obligation secured by that security interest. However, it does not necessarily follow that every provision of the Act that refers to "debtor" includes both the owner and the obligor.

Except for the Ontario Act, the PPSA definition of debtor draws a distinction between provisions dealing with the collateral and provisions dealing with the obligation secured. Debtor means the grantor in the former instance and the obligor on the secured obligation in the

---

9   PPSA (A, BC, NWT, Nu, O, Y) s. 1 (1); (M, NB, PEI) s. 1; (NL, NS, S) s. 2.

latter instance. Nonetheless, the two categories are not always to be treated as mutually exclusive. The term "debtor" refers to both "if the context permits." Thus each section of the Act must be examined to determine whether its underlying objectives relate to the interests of both the owner of the collateral and the obligor, or only the owner, or only the obligor.

For example, in the context of the registration provisions of the Act, debtor generally means the owner as opposed to the obligor because the aim of registration is to provide a means for third parties dealing with the collateral to determine whether it may be subject to a security interest. Thus, a secured party need not name a debtor who does not own or have rights in the collateral on a registered financing statement. On the other hand, when it comes to the post-default enforcement rights and obligations of the debtor and the secured party, both the owner and the obligor have an equal claim to protection, the owner because the result of enforcement will be to appropriate the value of her property, and the obligor because the amount realized by the enforcement proceedings will determine the existence and extent of her personal liability for any deficiency.

The Ontario definition of debtor does not expressly clarify that the term may mean only the owner, or only the obligor, or both, depending on the nature and purpose of the relevant statutory provision. However, the authors are of the view that a contextual reading is supported by ordinary principles of interpretation.[10]

The need for a contextual approach to the term "debtor" is helpful in sorting out an issue on which there is controversy in the Ontario case law. This is the issue of whether the term includes a personal guarantor or other secondary obligor on the obligation secured. *Prima facie* they qualify under the Act's definition of debtor as meaning a person who owes payment or performance of an obligation,[11] notwithstanding that their liability is contingent on non-performance by the primary obligor. That this is the intent of the PPSA is confirmed by the express exclusion of "guarantors" and "indemnitors" from the statutory right to reinstate the security agreement.[12] By negative inference, the term "debtor" must include a secondary obligor where the context permits.

---

10 This is also the view taken by Jacob S. Ziegel and David L. Denomme in *The Ontario Personal Property Security Act Commentary and Analysis*, 2d ed. (Markham: Butterworths, 2000) at 12–13.

11 PPSA (A, BC, NWT, Nu, O, Y) s. 1(1); (M, NB, PEI) s. 1; (NL, NS) s. 2; S s. 2(1).

12 PPSA (BC, M, NB, Nu, NWT, S) s. 62(1); (A, NL) s. 63(1); NS s. 63(2); PEI s. 62(2); Y s. 60(1).

Unfortunately, the Ontario Act does not exclude guarantors from its reinstatement provisions,[13] and a number of lower court decisions support the view that guarantors are excluded from the concept of debtor, even for the purposes of the secured party's statutory obligation to give advance notice of an intended disposition of the collateral to the debtor.[14] In the view of the authors, these decisions are wrong. The same policies that demand protection of the primary obligor generally extend to the secondary obligor, with the exception of rights that are clearly limited to the primary obligor, for example, rights of reinstatement. This view is generally supported by the case law under Article 9. For example, most courts in the United States have held that a guarantor is to be considered a debtor for the purposes of receiving the pre-disposition notice.[15]

A related issue is whether a guarantor is permitted to contract out of the right to receive the pre-disposition notice or any other of the debtor protection measures set out in Part 5. The authors share the prevailing view in the United States that the statutory provision that prevents the waiver or variation of rights by the debtor extends to a guarantor as well.[16]

To complement the extension of the PPSA to certain deemed security interests, the definition of debtor includes an assignee, a consignee, a lessee, and a seller, as the case may be. A second situation where the term "debtor" must be read in an extended sense is where the debtor transfers the collateral in circumstances where the transferee takes subject to the security interest under the priority provisions of the Act. To accommodate this eventuality, debtor is defined to include a transferee of or a successor in interest to the debtor for the purposes of the provisions of the Act that deal with the following matters:

- the rights and obligations of the secured party and the debtor;
- perfection by possession;
- automatic temporary perfection where the collateral is returned temporarily to the debtor;

---

13   OPPSA s. 66(1).

14   See *Lewinsky v. Toronto-Dominion Bank* (1995), 9 P.P.S.A.C. (2d) 169 (Ont. Ct. Gen. Div.); *Travel 'N' Save Inc. v. Roynat Inc.* (1992), 13 C.B.R. (3d) 21 (Ont. Ct. Gen. Div.); *Moskun v. Toronto-Dominion Bank* (1985), 5 P.P.S.A.C. 221 (Ont. H.C.J.). But see, on the other hand, *Donnelly v. International Harvester Credit Corp. of Canada Ltd.* (1983), 2 P.P.S.A.C. 290 (Ont. Co. Ct.); *Canadian Imperial Bank of Commerce v. Moshi* (1989), 9 P.P.S.A.C. 275 (Ont. H.C.J.), rev'd on other grounds (1992), 3 P.P.S.A.C. (2d) 86 (Ont. C.A.).

15   See B. Clark, *The Law of Secured Transactions Under the Uniform Commercial Code*, revised edition (Arlington: A.S. Pratt & Sons, 2001) at ¶4.03[3][b][xiv].

16   *Moskun v. Toronto-Dominion Bank*, above note 14.

- the secured party's right to take possession of the collateral and to enforce the security agreement;
- the title acquired by the purchaser on an enforced disposition of the collateral by the secured party (the purchaser takes free of the interest of the debtor);
- the title acquired by a purchaser from the secured party who takes the collateral in satisfaction of the obligation secured (the purchaser takes free of the interest of the debtor); and
- liability for damages for non-compliance with the Act.

A transferee, in her capacity as an "owner" of the collateral, may also be entitled to the benefit of the enforcement protections available to the contractual debtor. The Act requires the secured party to give notice of an intended disposition of the collateral to any person who is known by the secured party to be an owner of the collateral. The persons entitled to receive a notice thereby acquire the right to redeem the collateral prior to disposition and to payment of any surplus remaining after a disposition. Similarly, where the secured party proposes to take the collateral in satisfaction of the secured obligation, a notice must be given to the transferee in his or her capacity as a person known by the secured party to be an owner of the collateral and the transferee thereby acquires the right to object to the proposal and force a disposition by sale.

The Ontario PPSA differs from the other Acts in its treatment of transferees as debtors. Although the statutory definition of debtor extends to a transferee from or a successor in interest to the original debtor, the Ontario Act does not specify the statutory provisions to which this extended interpretation is meant to apply. Nonetheless, "debtor" cannot be read as always including a transferee throughout the Act. Provisions premised on the existence of a direct contractual relationship between the secured party and the "debtor" cannot logically apply to a transferee. So, for example, while the Act states that "the debtor" is personally liable to pay any deficiency owing on the secured obligation after the proceeds derived from a disposition of the collateral have been applied in satisfaction of the secured obligation, this cannot be read as including a transferee in the absence of a direct undertaking to assume the personal obligations of the transferor.

3) Secured Party

The Act adopts the generic term "secured party" to designate the person who holds a security interest, whether for that person's benefit or for the benefit of another person (as in a syndicated secured loan arrangement), or as a trustee under a trust indenture (who holds the security interest as representative of all the debenture-holders).[17] The definition also extends to a receiver for the purposes of the provisions enumerated in the definition. This ensures that a receiver is subject to the obligations imposed by the PPSA enforcement regime even where the receiver is not appointed by the secured party (as in the case of a court appointment), and even where the security agreement under which the receiver is appointed purports to make the receiver an agent of the debtor rather than the secured party.

As with the definition of debtor, the term "secured party" is meant to be read in conjunction with the PPSA concept of a security interest as an interest in personal property that secures payment or performance of an obligation, regardless of the form of the transaction or the location of title as between the secured party and the debtor. Thus, it does not matter what formal label is assigned to the secured party in the security documentation. Whether called a mortgagee, a chargee, a pledgee, a seller, a lessor, or any other term, the important question is whether the person holds a security interest in the functional sense contemplated by the Act.

As noted earlier, the PPSA concept of security interest also captures certain deemed secured transactions that do not secure payment or performance of an obligation; namely, an assignment of accounts or chattel paper, and, except for the Ontario Act, a commercial consignment and a true lease for a term of more than one year; the Atlantic Acts also extend to a sale of goods outside the ordinary course of business where the seller remains in possession after the sale. Since the Act defines "secured party" as a person who has a security interest, it follows that the term includes both secured parties in the ordinary sense and those who hold a deemed security interest.

4) Attachment

The PPSA uses the term "attachment" to describe the creation of the security interest as distinct from the entry into of the security agreement. Until attachment occurs, no security interest exists and the secured party's rights against the debtor are purely personal and contractual. Conversely, once a security interest attaches, the secured party acquires proprietary rights in the collateral.

---

17   PPSA (A, BC, NWT, Nu, O, Y) s. 1(1); (M, NB, PEI) s. 1; (NL, NS) s. 2; S s. 2(1).

Under the Act, attachment requires the satisfaction of three conditions.[18] First, the secured party must give value. Second, the debtor must have rights in the collateral. Third, the parties' agreement must satisfy the evidentiary requirements imposed by the Act; that is, either possession of the collateral by the secured party or completion of a security agreement signed by the debtor that describes the collateral.[19] Satisfaction of the third requirement is necessary only for attachment as against third parties. As between the secured party and the debtor, satisfaction of the first two requirements is enough.

5) Perfection

To acquire the best rights possible against third parties, the security interest must also be perfected. Under the Act, a security interest is perfected only when it has attached *and* all steps necessary to perfect it have been performed.[20] Except for the limited situations in which perfection is automatic for a temporary period, the Act recognizes only two possible perfecting steps: registration of a financing statement[21] or taking possession of the collateral.[22]

6) Priority

Perfection, while distinct from priority, is nonetheless intertwined with priority. Until a security interest is perfected, it cannot be set up against the debtor's bankruptcy trustee or judgment creditors or against a buyer or lessee of the collateral who takes without knowledge.[23] In addition, a perfected security interest takes ahead of an unperfected security interest regardless of the time of attachment or knowledge, and ranking among competing perfected security interests is generally determined by the order of registration, taking possession, or automatic perfection, as the case may be.[24]

---

18   PPSA (A, BC, M, NB, PEI, Nu, NWT, S) s. 12(1); (NL, NS, Y) s. 13(1); O s. 11(2).
19   PPSA (A, BC, M, NB, PEI, S) ss. 12(1)(c), 10(1); (NL, NS) ss. 13(1)(c), 11(1); O ss. 11(2)(c), 11(1); Y ss. 13(1)(c), 8(1).
20   PPSA (A, BC, M, NB, NWT, Nu, O, PEI, S) s. 19; (NL, NS) s. 20; Y s. 18.
21   PPSA (A, BC, M, NB, NWT, Nu, PEI, S) s. 25; (N, NS) s. 26; (O, Y) s. 23.
22   PPSA (A, BC, M, NB, Nu, NWT, PEI, S) s. 24(1); (NL, NS) s. 25 (1); O s. 22; Y s. 22(1).
23   PPSA (A, BC, M, NB, Nu, NWT, O, PEI, S) s. 20; (NL, NS) s. 21; Y s. 19.
24   PPSA (A, BC, M, NB, Nu, NWT, PEI, S) s. 35(1); (NL, NS) s. 36(1); O s. 30(1); Y s. 34(1).

7) Security Agreement versus Financing Statement

As noted earlier, the PPSA adopts notice registration in place of the old document filing approach to perfection of non-possessory security interests. Instead of filing the security agreement itself, a separate notice called a financing statement is registered typically in electronic form.[25] In approaching the Act, it is critical to keep in mind the different legal functions performed by the statutory provisions governing the security agreement and the financing statement. Compliance with the evidentiary requirements imposed by the Act for security agreements is essential to the attachment of a non-possessory security interest,[26] while a validly registered financing statement is essential to its perfected status.[27]

E. THE PERSONAL PROPERTY CLASSIFICATION SYSTEM

1) Collateral

Collateral is the general term adopted by the Act to designate personal property that is subject to a security interest.[28] By virtue of the definition of security interest this includes assets subject to a deemed security interest. It also includes assets that fall within the definition of proceeds[29] derived from the original collateral to which an automatic security interest attaches under the Act.[30]

Many of the provisions of the Act apply generally to collateral regardless of the type of personal property involved. However, other sections regulate only certain types of personal property. It is therefore important to approach the PPSA with at least a preliminary understanding of its property classification scheme in mind.

---

25   PPSA (A, BC, M, NB, NWT, Nu, PEI, S) s. 25; (N, NS) s. 26; (O, Y) s. 23.
26   PPSA (A, BC, M, NB, PEI, S) s. 12(1); (NL, NS) s. 13(1); O s. 11(2); Y s. 13(1).
27   PPSA (A, BC, M, NB, NWT, Nu, PEI, S) s. 25; (N, NS) s. 26; (O, Y) s. 23.
28   PPSA (A, BC, NWT, Nu, O, Y) s. 1(1); (M, NB, PEI) s. 1; (NL, NS) s. 2; S s. 2(1).
29   PPSA (A, BC, NWT, Nu, O, Y) s. 1(1); (M, NB, PEI) s. 1; (NL, NS) s. 2; S s. 2(1).
30   PPSA (A, BC, M, NB, NWT, Nu, PEI, S) s. 28(1); (NL, NS) s. 29(1); O s. 25(1); Y s. 26(1).

2) Sub-categories

The PPSA definition of personal property contemplates seven categories, each of which is independently defined: goods, a document of title, chattel paper, a security, an instrument, money, or an intangible.[31] Collectively, these categories cover every conceivable kind of personal property. This is accomplished by defining the term "intangible" as a residual category, thereby ensuring the inclusion of assets that do not fit within the other six categories.

3) Consumer Goods, Equipment, and Inventory

For some purposes, the PPSA sub-classifies goods, according to the debtor's use, into consumer goods, equipment, and inventory. Consumer goods are defined as goods that are used or acquired for use primarily for personal, household, or family persons. Inventory is defined to include stock held by a person for sale or lease, goods furnished under a contract of service, raw materials or work-in-progress, and materials used or consumed in a business. The reference to goods "used or consumed in a business" does not include goods that are simply utilized in a business (such as a truck that is used to make deliveries). The term "used" means used up or depleted, as in the case of fuel that is used in a manufacturing plant or paint that is used in an automotive body shop. Equipment is a residual category, encompassing all goods held by a debtor other than as inventory or consumer goods.

The definition of consumer goods differs from the concept of a consumer product often used in consumer protection legislation. Under, for example, the New Brunswick *Consumer Product Warranty and Liability Act*, the characterization of a product as a consumer product depends on whether the goods are of a kind that are commonly used for personal, household, or family purposes in the abstract.[32] In contrast, the characterization of consumer goods for the purposes of the PPSA turns on the actual use to which they are put by the debtor. If the goods are put to both a business and a personal use by the debtor, it is clear from the wording of the definition that it is the primary use that is determinative. The characterization of goods as equipment or inventory likewise depends on the actual use to which the goods are put by the debtor as opposed to the use to which such goods might commonly be put in the abstract.

---

31   PPSA (A, BC, NWT, Nu, O, Y) s. 1(1); (M, NB, PEI) s. 1; (NL, NS) s. 2; S s. 2(1).
32   S.N.B. 1978, c. C-18.1, s. 1(1) ("consumer product").

Since the debtor's use may change over time, the PPSA (except for the Ontario and Yukon Acts) provides guidance on when the characterization is to be made. In the absence of a rule to the contrary, the determination is made as of the time the security interest attaches, regardless of any subsequent change in the use to which they are put by the debtor.[33]

4) Land-related Goods

In addition to tangible personal property in the pure sense, the PPSA definition of goods also encompasses land-related personal property in the form of fixtures, growing crops, and minerals.[34] Fixtures are considered to constitute goods to which a PPSA security interest can attach, whether attachment occurs before or after the goods are affixed to land. Growing crops constitute personal property capable of being subjected to a PPSA security interest as soon as the crops become growing corps. Because of their hybrid character (they normally pass with a transfer of the land), the Act provides special perfection, priority, and enforcement rules to resolve competitions between a PPSA security interest and an interest in the land to which the fixtures or growing crops are attached. There is no need for an equivalent set of rules in the case of minerals[35] and trees[36] (timber, in the parlance of the OPPSA) because they do not become personal property for the purposes of attachment of a PPSA security interest until the minerals are extracted or the trees are severed.[37] This is compatible with the PPSA definitions of goods and minerals as excluding minerals until they are extracted and trees until they are severed.[38] This compatibility is absent in the Ontario Act, which defines goods as including minerals and hydrocarbons to be extracted and timber to be severed.[39] This inconsistency was apparently

---

33 PPSA (BC, NWT, Nu, S) s. 1(4); (M, NB) s. 2(2); (NL, NS) s. 3(2); A s. 1(5). For an example of an express rule to the contrary, see PPSA (A, BC, M, NB, PEI, S) s. 10(4); (NL, NS) s. 11(4); (O, Y) no equivalent provision.
34 PPSA (A, BC, NWT, Nu, O, Y) s. 1(1); (M, NB, PEI) s. 1; (NL, NS) s. 2; S s. 2(1). Crops, fixtures and minerals are themselves separately defined.
35 Minerals are defined to include oil, gas, and hydrocarbons.
36 Except for nursery trees and the like which are included in the definition of crops.
37 PPSA (A, BC, M, NWT, Nu, S) s. 12(3); (NB, PEI) s. 12(4); (NL, NS) s. 13(4); (O, Y) s. 11(3).
38 PPSA (A, BC, NWT, Nu, O, Y) s. 1(1); (M, NB, PEI) s. 1; (NL, NS) s. 2; S s. 2(1).
39 OPPSA s. 1(1).

not intentional but resulted from an oversight by the drafters of the 1989 version of the OPPSA.[40]

5) Land-related Intangibles

Except for the Ontario Act, the PPSA excludes land-related intangibles in the form of accounts from its scope.[41] The only exception is where the account is evidenced by a security or an instrument that provides for a mortgage or a charge on land that is not specifically identified in the security or instrument.[42] In contrast, the Ontario PPSA applies to the assignment by a mortgagee, lessor, or chargor of rights to payment owing under a mortgage, charge, or lease, so long as the assignment does not purport to also transfer an interest in the land to which the debt relates.[43]

The general PPSA approach is designed to ensure that competing interests in land-related rights to payment are regulated exclusively by land law.[44] Under the Ontario approach, both land and personal property law end up having a role to play, similar to the role played by each in relation to a security interest in a fixture or growing crops. The Ontario Act permits a secured party with a PPSA interest in a right to payment under a lease, mortgage, or charge of real property to register a notice of the interest in the personal property registry and in the land registry for the district in which the relevant parcel of land is located.[45] If the competing interests are all PPSA interests, the PPSA governs priority and it is irrelevant whether the interest is or is not also registered in the land registry. However, if the competition is between the holder of an interest in the land who also thereby acquires a right in the land-related payments, and a transferee of the right to payment *simpliciter,* priority depends on who registers first against the land.[46]

The difference between the two approaches is based on perceived commercial practice. The general PPSA approach assumes that registrants and searchers expect to rely on the land registry system when-

---

40 Ziegel and Denomme, above note 10 at 131.
41 PPSA (A, BC, M, NB, NWT, Nu, PEI, S, Y) s. 4; (NL, NS) s. 5.
42 See the definitions of instrument and security in PPSA (A, BC, NWT, Nu, Y) s. 1(1); (M, NB, PEI) s. 1; (NL, NS) s. 2; S s. 2(1).
43 OPPSA s. 4(e).
44 For background reading, see Law Reform Commission of British Columbia, *Report on Land-Related Interests and the Personal Property Security Act* (Victoria: Attorney-General, May 1995).
45 OPPSA s. 54(1)(b).
46 OPPSA s. 36.

ever a transaction involves land-related debt whether or not assigned separately from the land.[47] Ironically, this policy was influenced by a decision under the 1976 Ontario PPSA in which the Ontario Court of Appeal ruled that a mortgage debt is not to be separated from the land to which it is connected in determining priorities between competing assignees of the same account.[48]

F. INTERPRETATION

1) Conflict between Acts

In the interests of certainty and predictability, the drafters of the PPSA sought to create a comprehensive statutory regime governing all significant legal aspects of secured transactions. They therefore included a provision specifying that the PPSA, as a general rule, prevails in the event of a conflict with other legislation of the enacting province or territory.[49]

At first impression, the primacy of the PPSA over other statutes is contradicted by the express preservation, elsewhere in the Act, of constraints imposed by "any other Act" on the effectiveness of a security agreement.[50] However, it is possible (and necessary) to read the two provisions in harmony. If the PPSA in general prevails over other enactments, the potential constraints imposed by other Acts must be restricted to situations where the issue addressed by the other Act is not addressed by the PPSA with the result that there is no conflict between the two enactments. The most important example of this involves the priority of a security interest governed by the PPSA as against statutory security interests or privileges whose status is governed by other law.

Consumer protection legislation constitutes an exception to the general rule that the PPSA prevails over other Acts.[51] The extent of the exception varies. The Ontario Act, for example, refers only to the *Con-*

---

47   To avoid gaps and overlaps, the land registration statutes of the relevant PPSA jurisdictions expressly confirm that they apply to the creation or transfer of land-related rights to payment except for the instruments and securities exceptions recognized by the PPSA.

48   *Re Urman* (1983), 44 O.R. (2d) 248 (C.A.), rev'g (1981), 1 P.P.S.A.C. 340 (Ont. H.C.J.).

49   PPSA (M, NWT, Nu) s. 69; (NB, PEI) s. 70; (NL, NS, Y) s. 71; A s. 74; BC s. 73.

50   PPSA (A, BC, M, NB, Nu, NWT, O, PEI, S) s. 9; (NL, NS) s. 10; Y no equivalent provision.

51   PPSA (M, NWT, Nu, S) s. 69; A s. 74; (NB, PEI) s. 70; (NL, NS, Y) s. 71; BC s. 73; O s. 73.

sumer Protection Act of that province.[52] No mention is made of other potentially applicable consumer legislation, such as the *Business Practices Act*[53] and the *Pawnbrokers Act*.[54] Some commentators see these omissions as inadvertent and have expressed the hope that the Ontario courts might read the reference to the *Consumer Protection Act* in a generic sense.[55] The other Acts avoid the risk of an inadvertent omission by using a catch-all reference to any provision in any Act for the protection of consumers.[56] Certain of the Acts also preserve other special legislation, notably the *Agricultural Implements Act* and the *Saskatchewan Farm Security Act* in the case of the Saskatchewan PPSA,[57] and the *Land Titles Act* in the case of the British Columbia PPSA.[58]

2) Interpretation of Other Acts

PPSA jurisdictions generally combined enactment of the PPSA with complementary and consequential amendments to other legislation to bring it into line with the Act's concepts and terminology. For additional certainty, the PPSA itself specifies that a reference in other Acts to any of the pre-PPSA security devices, for example, a chattel mortgage or a conditional sale, is deemed to be a reference to the corresponding kind of security agreement under the PPSA.[59] The Ontario Act lacks this provision, which leads to uncertainty as to the meaning of the outdated references in other Ontario statutes, such as the reference to a "mortgage" of "goods or chattels" in the *Commercial Tenancies Act*.[60]

3) Harmonization of Secured Transactions Law

The Acts in effect in the Atlantic provinces include an interpretation principle, derived from the U.S. *Uniform Commercial Code*,[61] directing

---

52 OPPSA s. 73, preserving the *Consumer Protection Act*, R.S.O 1990, c. C.31.
53 R.S.O. 1990, c. B.18.
54 R.S.O. 1990, c P.6.
55 Ziegel and Denomme, above note 10 at 576.
56 PPSA (M, NWT, Nu, S) s. 69; (NB, PEI) s. 70; (NL, NS, Y) s. 71; A s. 74; BC s. 73.
57 SPPSA s. 69(1).
58 BCPPSA s. 74(1).
59 PPSA (M, NWT, Nu, S) s. 70; (NB, PEI) s. 72; (NL, NS) s. 73; A s. 73; BC s. 75; Y s. 70.
60 R.S.O. 1990, c. L.7, s. 31(2); see further Ziegel and Denomme, above note 10 at 80.
61 § 1-102 of the UCC directs that it is to be liberally construed and applied to promote its underlying purposes and policies, one of which is to "make uniform the law among the various jurisdictions."

that the Act is to be interpreted and applied, insofar as the context permits, in a manner that promotes the interjurisdictional harmony of personal property security law in Canada.[62] Even in the absence of an explicit directive of this kind, the courts have taken the desirability of interprovincial harmonization into account in determining the substantive effect to be given to variations among the Acts.[63]

Indeed, the courts have been prepared to adopt a comparative approach to interpretation beyond the PPSA world, drawing on the case law under Article 9, where the same concept or principle underlies both regimes.[64] In principle, the same openness should be extended to the jurisprudence under the *Civil Code of Québec*, again to the extent of any commonality in concepts or policies.

4) Preservation of Complementary General Law

Although it seeks to codify the full range of specialized rules applicable to secured transactions in personal property, the PPSA necessarily operates against the backdrop of the general private law of the enacting jurisdiction. To this end, the Act expressly preserves the supplementary application of "the principles of the common law, equity and the law merchant" except where inconsistent with the PPSA.[65]

Most issues relating to the formation and contractual validity of security agreements continue to be governed by general contract and agency doctrine, subject to such exceptions as the special evidentiary requirements imposed by the PPSA. Other more specialized doctrines that have been identified as relevant supplementary sources include:

- the principle of sheltering under which a transferee from a transferor who took free of a security interest is entitled to shelter under the transferor's indefeasible title as against the secured party;[66]

---

62 PPSA (NB, PEI) s. 2(5); (NL, NS) s. 3(5).

63 See, for example, *Toronto Dominion Bank v. RNG Group Inc.* (2002), 61 O.R. (3d) 567, 38 C.B.R. (4th) 110, 4 P.P.S.A.C. (3d) 182 (S.C.J.); *GMAC Commercial Credit Corp. Canada v. TCT Logistics Inc.*, 2004 CarswellOnt 1283 (Ont. C.A. Apr 02, 2004), aff'g (2002), 36 C.B.R. (4th) 37, 4 P.P.S.A.C. (3d) 107 (Ont. S.C.J.).

64 *Gimli Auto Ltd. v. BDO Dunwoody Ltd.* (1998), 219 A.R. 166 (C.A.) at paras. 15–16; *Re Stelco Inc.*, 2005 CarswellOnt 1537 (Ont. C.A. Apr 26, 2005) at paras. 18–19.

65 PPSA (M, NWT, Nu, S) s. 65(2); A s. 66(3); BC s. 68(1); (NB, PEI) s. 65(1); (NL, NS) s. 66(1); O s. 72; Y s. 63(1).

66 See, for example, *Willi v. Don Shearer Ltd.* (1993), 107 D.L.R. (4th) 121 (B.C.C.A.).

- the common law right of a secured party to bring an action in conversion against a transferee from the debtor in the event of an unauthorized disposition of collateral;
- the common law right to bring an action in tort for wrongful seizure of collateral;
- the common law right to sue for slander of title; [67]
- the equitable doctrine of marshalling under which a prior-ranking secured party can be required to enforce its security interest against collateral not subject to a subordinate interest before resorting to the collateral in which there is a common interest.

5) Inherent Interpretive Policies

The PPSA is founded on certain legislative policies that generally inform its interpretation.

The first and most obvious of these is the advancement of commercial certainty and predictability. This is a primary value in commercial law generally. Its principal application in the PPSA context takes the form of an appropriate reluctance to countenance judicial glosses on the statutory rules, especially those dealing with priority. For example, in *GE Capital Canada Acquisitions Ltd. v. Dix Performance*,[68] the court observed:

> [W]hen interpreting commercial legislation of this nature and where it is consistent with the wording of the statute, the Court should try to achieve the objectives of simplicity and certainty. The Court ought to strive for interpretations that, where possible, recognize the importance to the business and financial community of being able to achieve compliance with regulatory requirements in as simple and in as certain a manner as is consistent with the intention of the Legislature as expressed in the language of the statute. In striving for simplicity, judicial interpretation should minimize to the extent possible the cost of regulatory compliance; achieving the equally important goal of certainty will similarly minimize the generation of post filing litigation challenging such compliance.

Further authority can be found in *Re West Bay Sales Ltd. and Hitachi Sales Corp. of Canada Ltd.*[69] in which the court stated:

---

67   See, for example, *Osman Auction v. Murray* (1994), 6 P.P.S.A.C. (2d) 211 (Alta. Q.B.).
68   (1994), 8 P.P.S.A.C. (2d) 197 (B.C.S.C.).
69   (1978), 20 O.R. (2d) 752 (H.C.J.).

It would be redundant, uninformative and costly to require inventory financing and deliveries to be the subject of multiple registrations and the resulting searches, tracing and legal proceedings to ascertain whether particular items of inventory among a multitude have become the subject of a security agreement. The business community have simplified the process, and it is not the intent of the Legislature to complicate it by unnecessary formality."

A second important policy is the preservation of internal coherence within the PPSA. This policy requires that individual provisions of the Act be interpreted not in isolation but in light of the implications of a particular reading on the logic or workability of other provisions. In *Agricultural Credit Corporation of Saskatchewan v. Royal Bank of Canada*,[70] the court stated: "The applicable canons of interpretation dictate that the section be interpreted contextually and be read in relation to the whole Act. Using this approach one quickly recognizes that the underlying concept of PPSA is a rejection of the system of 'transaction filing' and the adoption of the system of 'notice filing.'"

Third, the drafters were concerned to advance party autonomy and flexibility in the relationship between the secured party and the debtor. It follows that constraints on freedom of contract should not be readily implied in the absence of clear legislative direction.

Finally, and related to these, the PPSA is designed to increase efficiency for all actors involved in, or affected by, a secured transaction so as to promote greater access to secured credit at lower cost. An important example is the rejection of the role of knowledge in ordering priority among competing secured parties. This policy has particular significance in the context of the PPSA registration system and the rules dealing with the adequacy of a registration, because it is in this context that the need to balance the interests of the secured party and the public becomes most prominent.

6) Good Faith and Commercial Reasonableness

The PPSA imposes an overarching obligation on all parties to act in good faith and in a commercially reasonable manner in the exercise of their rights, duties, and obligations under the security agreement, the Act, and any other applicable legislation.[71] The pervasive nature of this duty means that it must be kept in mind in interpreting every provision of the Act

---

70   [1994] 7 W.W.R. 305 (Sask. C.A.).
71   PPSA (M, NWT, Nu, S) s. 65(3); (NB, PEI) s. 65(2); (NL, NS) s. 66(2); A s. 66(1); BC s. 68(2); Y s. 62(1).

that deals with the rights and obligations of any person. The Yukon and Ontario Acts do not have an equivalent provision. However, the Ontario Act obligates a secured party to exercise its collection and disposition rights on enforcement in a commercially reasonable manner.[72]

The PPSA also uses the standard of good faith and commercial reasonableness as part of the criteria for determining when a modification of a contract between a debtor/assignor and an account debtor is binding on a secured party/assignee. The absence of good faith also constitutes the standard of liability for loss or damage caused by advice tendered by a registry employee or agent.

Comparative guidance on the meaning of the good faith aspect of the standard may be sought in UCC Article 9, which defines good faith to mean "honesty in fact."[73] In other words, the question is whether the particular person acted with a subjective honest intent in the particular circumstances. This accords with the test adopted in other commercial law statutes, notably the *Bills of Exchange Act* which provides "a thing is deemed to be done in good faith, within the meaning of this Act, where it is in fact done honestly, whether it is done negligently or not."[74]

Assuming bad faith can be shown, what are the consequences? The Act recognizes a general right of action in favour of the victim of a breach of any obligation imposed by the PPSA for loss or damage caused by the breach.[75] In addition, bad faith may be grounds for disqualifying a person from relying on her statutory rights. For example, while good faith was historically equated with taking without actual knowledge of an anterior security interest, knowledge is relevant under the PPSA only if the particular rule specifically makes the absence of knowledge a condition of priority. To reinforce this point, the Act expressly confirms that a person does not act in bad faith *merely* because the person acts with knowledge of the interest of some other person.[76] Nonetheless, actual knowledge combined with other factors — for example, knowledge plus abuse of a non–arm's length relationship, or knowledge plus positive misleading or fraudulent conduct — may deny a person the right to rely on an otherwise applicable PPSA priority rule.[77]

---

72   OPPSA ss. 61(2) and 63(2).
73   § 9-102(a)(43).
74   *Bills of Exchange Act*, R.S.C. 1985, c. B-4, s. 3.
75   PPSA (M, NWT, Nu, S) s. 65; (NB, PEI) s. 66; (NL, NS) s. 67; A s. 67; BC s. 69; Y s. 62.
76   PPSA (M, NWT, Nu, S) s. 65(4); (NB, PEI) s. 65(3); (NL, NS) s. 66(3); A s. 66(2); BC s. 68(3); (O, Y) no equivalent provision.
77   See, for example, *Canadian Imperial Bank of Commerce v. A.K. Construction (1988) Ltd.* (1995), 9 P.P.S.A.C. (2d) 257 (Alta. Q.B.); *Carson Restaurants Inter-*

The commercial reasonableness aspect of the standard finds its principal practical significance in the context of the PPSA enforcement regime. The Act gives the secured party enormous flexibility in determining the method, manner, time, venue, and other terms relating to a disposition of collateral. The commercial reasonableness standard provides an important corrective against any abuse of this flexibility. The commercial reasonableness standard, unlike good faith, is dependent on an understanding of what is considered reasonable by those involved in the particular industry or practice under scrutiny, as opposed to the subjective understanding of the particular person whose conduct is in issue. This does not necessarily mean that expert evidence has to be led in every instance. For example, a court should feel perfectly competent in ruling that a disposition of high-value, industry-specific collateral through advertisement in the classified section of a general newspaper is not commercially reasonable without needing to hear from experts in the industry.

However, for matters going beyond obvious commercial common sense, an allegation of commercially unreasonable conduct will need to be buttressed by evidence of what is considered reasonable conduct among participants in the relevant activity or sector. For comparative confirmation of this point, reference may be made to UCC Article 9, which declares a disposition of collateral to be commercially reasonable if made "(1) in the usual manner in any recognized market; (2) at the price current in any recognized market at the time of the disposition; or (3) otherwise in conformity with reasonable commercial practices among dealers in the type of property that was the subject of the disposition."[78]

G. KNOWLEDGE AND NOTICE

1) Meaning of "Knowledge"

With limited exceptions involving negotiable collateral, knowledge of a competing security interest is irrelevant in determining priority among competing security interests under the PPSA. Where the competing interest is that of a buyer or lessee, however, taking with knowledge

---

national Ltd. v. A-1 United Restaurant Supply Ltd. (1988), [1989] 1 W.W.R. 266 (Sask. Q.B.); Fotti v. 777 Management Inc. (1981), 2 P.P.S.A.C. 32 (Man. Q.B.). For an illustrative U.S. decision to a similar effect, see Thompson v. United States, 408 F.2d 1075 (8th Cir. 1969).

78   § 9-627(b).

can still play a role. For example, a buyer of collateral takes subject to an unperfected security interest where the buyer acquired the collateral with actual knowledge of that security interest. Knowledge may also be relevant to priority in other contexts. For example, a secured party is subordinated for advances made after acquiring knowledge of the competing claim of a judgment creditor. Another example is the obligation of a secured party to amend a registration on acquiring knowledge that the debtor has transferred the collateral or changed its name.

The Act provides guidance on when knowledge is acquired where the issue is relevant. The test is an objective one. The issue is not whether the person subjectively or consciously knew the fact in question, but whether the information was acquired in circumstances where a reasonable person would take cognizance of it.[79]

Where the "person" is a corporation or other enterprise, questions may arise as to whose attention the information must come in order for the knowledge of that person to be attributed to the corporation or enterprise as a whole. The PPSA supplies specific guidance on this issue. In all cases, including the government, knowledge acquired by a senior employee having responsibility for the matters to which the knowledge relates is sufficient.[80] For bodies corporate, partnerships, and the membership of unincorporated associations, the Act gives additional alternatives. For bodies corporate, the acquisition of knowledge by a managing director or officer suffices, as does receipt by the body corporate's registered office or its attorney for service of a written notice setting out the relevant information. In the case of a partnership, knowledge acquired by any one of the general partners or by a person having control or management of the partnership business suffices. In the case of the membership of an unincorporated association, knowledge acquired by all the members or by a managing director or officer suffices.

The rules do not purport to determine what kind or degree of information communicates "knowledge" of a security interest or other relevant fact. Is actual knowledge required or is it sufficient that a person

79 PPSA (A, BC, NWT, Nu, S) s. 1(2); (NB, PEI) s. 2(1); (NL, NS) s. 3(1); M s. 2; O s. 69; Y no equivalent provision.
80 On the meaning of "senior employee" in the context of these rules, see *Re Wendrick's Furniture Warehouse Ltd.* (1994), Ontario Court (Gen. Div.) unreported (court file no. 31-282881), as cited by Ziegel and Denomme, above note 10 at 562. Unlike the other Acts, s. 69 of the Ont. PPSA does not provide explicit guidance on the meaning of knowledge in the context of the government and the membership of unincorporated associations. However the reference to a senior employee in the rules for bodies corporate and partnerships may be extended by analogy.

has knowledge of facts from which the relevant fact might be inferred on further investigation? The point has been litigated in the context of whether a secured party who receives notice that bankruptcy proceedings have been commenced against the debtor in a different jurisdiction thereby acquires knowledge of a change in the location of the collateral or debtor to that province for the purposes of the PPSA conflicts regime. In *Re Searcy*, the court concluded that the secured party was not required to speculate as to the implications of knowledge of other facts and that actual knowledge that the collateral was physically in that other jurisdiction was required.[81]

The *Re Searcy* approach has generally been followed,[82] including in cases dealing with the question of whether a buyer of an automobile takes without knowledge of an extraprovincial security interest that has not yet been re-perfected following relocation of the goods to the enacting jurisdiction. The sale transaction normally includes a transfer of registration with the local provincial motor vehicle registry. If the date of initial registration is recent, does knowledge of this fact impose an obligation of positive inquiry on the purchaser to investigate the possibility that the motor vehicle only recently entered the province? In the view of the authors, the answer is no. Buyers and lessees should not be under an obligation to investigate every Personal Property Registry in Canada on the chance that, because the registration was recent, the vehicle may have been located in another province where it was made the object of a security interest. This view is supported by a Saskatchewan decision.[83] More generally, anything less than actual knowledge of the relevant fact should not be sufficient to constitute knowledge unless the information in question unambiguously supports that inference.[84]

2) Effective Notice

The PPSA contemplates the sending of a notice or demand for a wide variety of purposes. In the interests of certainty, the Act supplies gen-

---

81   *Re Searcy* (1991), 2 P.P.S.A.C. (2d) 219, 8 C.B.R. (3d) 11 (B.C.S.C.).

82   See, for example, *Associates Commercial Corp. v. Scotia Leasing Ltd.* (1995), 24 B.L.R. (2d) 310 (Ont. Ct. Gen. Div.). For pre-PPSA decisions to the same effect, see *Re Country Kitchen Donuts Ltd.* (1980), 34 C.B.R. (N.S.) 252 (Ont. H.C.J.). See also *Re Simi Ltd.* (1987), 59 O.R. (2d) 139 (H.C.J.), aff'd (1988), 9 P.P.S.A.C. 46 (C.A.).

83   *Bauer Enterprises Ltd. v. Chrysler Credit Canada Ltd.* (1999), 181 Sask. R. 278 (Q.B.); but see *General Motors Acceptance Corp. of Canada v. Midway Chrysler Plymouth Ltd.* (1987), 7 P.P.S.A.C. 156 (Man. Q.B.), aff'd (1987), 8 P.P.S.A.C. 13 (Man. C.A.).

84   This was the situation in *HSBC Bank Canada v. Expressway Concrete Supply Ltd.* (1999), 1 B.L.R. (3d) 147, 14 C.B.R. (4th) 1 (Ont. S.C.J.).

eral guidelines on acceptable methods of service.[85] Table 1 summarizes
these rules (subject to minor variations in the Ontario Act).

Table 1   *Permissible Methods for Serving PPSA Notices*

Status of Recipient	Permissible Manner of Service
An individual	• personal service; • registered mail addressed to the individual by name at the individual's residence; or • if the individual is the sole proprietor of a business, registered mail addressed to the individual by name at the address of the business.
A partnership	• personal service to one or more of the general partners or to any person having control or management of the partnership business; • registered mail addressed to one or more of the general partners, or to any person having control of management of the partnership business, at the address of the partnership business.
A body corporate	• personal service to an officer or director of the body corporate or to the person in charge of any office or place of business of the body corporate or to the registered or head office of the body corporate; • registered mail addressed to the body corporate at its registered or head office.
A municipality	• personal service to the mayor, deputy-mayor, clerk of any solicitor of the municipality; • registered mail addressed to the municipality, or to the mayor, deputy mayor, clerk or any solicitor of the municipality, at the principal office of the municipality.
An unincorporated association	• direct personal service to an officer of the association or to a person in charge of any office or premises occupied by the association; • registered mail addressed to an officer of the association at the address of the officer.
The Crown in Right of the Enacting Province	• in accordance with the *Proceedings against the Crown Act* of the enacting jurisdiction.

The Act also lays down a default rule governing the time of receipt
of a notice or demand where registered mail is used. This will be the

---

85   PPSA (M, NWT, Nu, O, S) s. 68(1); (A, BC) s. 72(1); (NB, PEI) s. 69(1); (NL, NS)
s. 70(1); Y s. 65(1).

time of receipt, or the expiry of ten days after the date of registration, whichever is earliest.[86] Except for the Ontario Act, there is an explicit exception in the event of an interruption in postal services. In that event, the time of actual receipt controls. The above rules are purely facilitative. Other generally accepted modes of delivery, including electronic modes, may also be used.[87]

In situations where delivery must be made on a secured party named in a registration, the Act provides an alternative rule. Delivery by personal service or registered mail to the most recent address of the secured party as it appears in the records of the Personal Property Registry is sufficient.[88] This creates a significant incentive for secured parties to maintain the currency of their address particulars in the registry record.

H. FEDERAL SECURED TRANSACTIONS LAW

Although secured transactions law is primarily provincial, the federal Parliament has a limited power to legislate in the area of credit and security ancillary to several specific heads of federal constitutional jurisdiction.

The most important example is the *Bank Act*[89] regime for security granted in favour of federally regulated banks by business debtors and primary producers (including farmers, fishers, and aquaculturalists), enacted pursuant to federal jurisdiction over "banks and banking."

There is also the regime for ship's mortgages and maritime liens arising under Canadian maritime law enacted as an aspect of federal jurisdiction over "navigation and shipping" and other maritime subjects. The ship's mortgage regime is statutory.[90] The regime for maritime liens is derived from English maritime law referentially incorporated

---

86   PPSA (M, NWT, Nu, S) s. 68(2); (A, BC) s. 72(2); (NB, PEI) s. 69(2); (NL, NS) s. 70(2); O s. 68(4); Y s. 65(2).

87   *Electronic Documents and Information Act*, S.S. c. E-7.22; *Electronic Commerce and Information Act*, S.M. 2000, c. 32, C.C.S.M. c. E55; *Electronic Commerce Act 2000*, S.O. 2000, c. 17; *The Electronic Commerce Act*, S.N.S. 2000, c. 26; *Electronic Transactions Act*, S.B.C. 2001, c. 10; *Electronic Transactions Act*, S.A. 2001, c. E-5.5; *Electronic Transactions Act*, S.N.B. 2001, c. E-5.5; *Electronic Commerce Act*, S.P.E.I. 2001, c. 31, R.S.P.E.I., c. E-4.1; *Electronic Commerce Act*, S.N.L. 2001, c.E-5.2.

88   OPPSA s. 68(1). In the other Acts, the rule is separately stated in each of the provisions dealing with service on a secured party named in a financing statement.

89   S.C. 1991, c. 46 (s. 427, am. 1992, c. 27, s. 90).

90   *Canada Shipping Act, 2001*, S.C. 2001, c. 26, ss. 65–72.

into Canadian law by the *Federal Courts Act*.[91] That Act also vests *in rem* rights of action against maritime property in favour of certain maritime creditors.[92] Creditors, including ship mortgagees, tend to prefer the Federal Court *in rem* process because it is best equipped to ensure an effective collective execution of all real rights, whether arising under Canadian law or foreign law, in a vessel or other maritime object.

Federal law in other areas pre-empts the application of the provincial and territorial regimes only to a limited extent.

The *Canada Transportation Act*[93] provides a federal registration venue, as an alternative to PPSA registration, for security interests in railway assets and rolling stock, but does not otherwise address the legal implications of security interests in these types of assets.

The six federal intellectual property statutes[94] — enacted pursuant to the federal jurisdiction over "intellectual property" and "trade and commerce" — do not expressly address the grant of security in the forms of intellectual property within their scope. They apply only to the extent that the provisions regulating the assignment of intellectual property rights, the federal registration of such assignments, and the priority effect of federal registration can be interpreted as including assignments made for security purposes.[95]

Federal authority over "Indians and Lands Reserved for Indians" has resulted in the insulation of the reserve-based movable and immovable property of "Indian" and "band" debtors from the reach of security interests and from seizure by unsecured creditors.[96]

Finally, federal authority over "bankruptcy and insolvency" means that upon the debtor's insolvency, the status, ranking, and enforceabil-

---

91   R.S.C 1985, c. F-7, ss. 2(1) (definition of "Canadian maritime law"), 22(1), 42. And see *International Terminal Operators Ltd. v. Miida Electronics Inc.*, [1986] 1 S.C.R. 752.

92   Ss. 43(2)–(3).

93   S.C. 1996, c.10, ss. 104–5.

94   *Patent Act*, R.S.C. 1985, c. P-4; *Copyright Act*, R.S.C. 1985, c. C-42; *Trade-marks Act*, R.S.C. 1985, c. T-13; *Industrial Design Act*, R.S.C. 1985, c. I-9; *Plant Breeders' Rights Act*, S.C. 1990, c. 20; *Integrated Circuit Topography Act*, S.C. 1990, c. 37.

95   In order to reduce the prevailing uncertainty on this question, the Law Commission of Canada has made recommendations for reform of the law that would, among other things, create a federal registry system in respect of security interests in intellectual property: Law Commission of Canada, *Leveraging Knowledge Assets — Reducing Uncertainty for Security Interests in Intellectual Property* (2004) (posted at www.lcc.gc.ca — Research Projects — Federal Security Interests). For background reading, see H. Knopf, ed., *Security Interests in Intellectual Property* (Toronto: Carswell, 2002).

96   *Indian Act*, R.S.C. 1985, c. I-5, ss. 29, 37(1), 89.

ity of security interests otherwise regulated by one or another of the provincial regimes may be affected by federal law. The principal statute is the *Bankruptcy and Insolvency Act* (BIA).[97] Until 1992, the BIA was oriented almost entirely toward liquidation proceedings, its reorganization provisions rendered all but dormant by the high level of deference exhibited to the rights of secured parties. The void was filled by the federal *Companies' Creditors Arrangement Act* (CCAA).[98] Originally conceived to facilitate the reorganization of major public companies during the economic depression of the 1930s, the CCAA establishes a skeletal framework for arrangements with creditors. In 1992, the BIA was amended to add a detailed reorganization proposal process which extends to both secured and unsecured creditors. By that point, arrangements under the CCAA had proved enormously popular, at least for reorganizations demanding the kind of flexibility and discretion available under its judicially established process. Consequently, the decision was made to leave both statutory options in place. In addition to the BIA and the CCAA, there is also the federal *Winding-up and Restructuring Act*,[99] the exclusive liquidation mechanism for banks and insurance and trust companies.

Federal legislation in the areas outlined above can have a significant impact on the operation of the PPSA in relation to particular issues. While this book is not intended to be a treatise on federal law as it relates to secured transactions, issues of common concern or overlap with the PPSA are addressed in detail.

I. THE PROPOSED *UNIFORM SECURITIES TRANSFER ACT* (USTA)

1) Introduction

The proposed *Uniform Securities Transfer Act* (USTA)[100] will have a significant impact on the conceptual structure and substantive operation

---

97 *Bankruptcy and Insolvency Act*, R.S.C. 1985, c. B-3, as amended (most importantly by S.C. 1992, c. 27 and S.C. 1997, c. 12).
98 R.S.C. 1985, c. C-36.
99 R.S.C. 1985, c. W-11.
100 The ULCC-approved version of the USTA, together with previous consultative drafts, and related material (including comments received) are posted at www.osc.gov.on.ca under "Hot Topics." See also Eric T. Spink and Maxime A. Paré, "The *Uniform Securities Transfer Act*: Globalized Commercial Law for Canada" (2003) 19 B.F.L.R. 322.

of the PPSA. The USTA is designed to regulate the transfer and holding of securities and interests in securities. In tandem with the proposed complementary amendments to the PPSA, it also governs the grant of security interests in this type of collateral.

The project was developed by Canadian Securities Administrators at the request of the Uniform Law Conference of Canada. A consultation process with interested stakeholders has been ongoing since June 2002 and both the Act and the consequential amendments to the PPSA are now at a mature stage.

2) Objectives

Securities were traditionally held and transferred in a direct holding system in which the owner had a direct relationship with the issuer. The owner either held physical possession of a negotiable security certificate or would be recorded as owner on the issuer's register. Although the traditional direct holding system still operates, the great majority of publicly traded securities are today held and traded through a multi-tiered pyramid of intermediaries. The basic aim of the USTA is to provide a legal framework that accommodates the reality of this indirect holding system.

The USTA is modelled almost precisely on Article 8 of the U.S. *Uniform Commercial Code.* The complementary amendments to the PPSA also adhere very closely to the corresponding provisions in Article 9. This reflects a second objective of the legislation: to make Canadian securities transfer as uniform and harmonious as possible with that of the United States. This has been justified in turn by the perceived need to maintain the competitiveness of Canadian capital markets in view of the already existing close integration between the Canadian and U.S. markets.

3) Key Concepts

In the indirect holding system, an investor's interests in securities are held and transferred through entries in the books of the investor's broker or other intermediary. The investor's intermediary in turn has its interests recorded on the books of another intermediary often located in a different jurisdiction. At the top of what may be a lengthy chain of intermediaries, most securities are held by central securities depositories or settled through clearing systems such as the Canadian Depository for Securities Limited (CDS) in Canada, the Depository Trust and Clearing Corporation (DTCC) in the United States, and Euroclear and Clearstream in Europe.

The book-entry system facilitates the rapid and efficient trading of vast quantities of securities at a global scale. However, the enormity of the volume and scale also increases the systemic risk to the liquidity of financial markets. Systemic risk refers to the risk that the inability of one market actor to meet its obligations will cause other actors in the chain to be unable to meet their obligations. To contain that risk, the USTA follows Article 8 in adopting a conceptual framework in which interests in securities held through the indirect system are represented by financial accounts. The financial accounts concept in effect treats each account between each set of parties in the tier of intermediaries as a separate and distinct asset with the rights of each account-holder limited to the obligations owed to them by their own intermediary. Since an account-holder has no rights against the issuer or any other upper-tier intermediary, the systemic risk posed by the failure of any intermediary in the chain is contained.

The emergence of the financial accounts concept is reflected in the adoption of a new general category of collateral called "investment property." The proposed amendments to the PPSA define investment property as including "a security, whether certificated or uncertificated, security entitlement, [and a] securities account." Each of these terms is then separately defined.

Although the definition of security includes uncertificated securities as well as certificated negotiable securities, it tracks the conventional concept of a security as the bundle of intangible rights held by an investor against the issuer. In contrast, the definitions of security entitlement and securities account reflect the different conceptual nature of account-based interests in securities.

Security entitlement is defined to mean the bundle of rights described in Part 6 of the USTA held by a person who holds a financial asset through an intermediary as against that intermediary. The definition of a "financial asset" is very broad and includes not just securities and security entitlements but also bills of exchange and a variety of other investment products. However, in order for a security entitlement to exist, the financial asset must be held by a securities intermediary in a securities account. Securities account is defined in turn as an account to which a financial asset may be credited in accordance with an agreement under which the person maintaining the account undertakes to treat the account-holder as entitled to exercise the rights that constitute the financial asset. Thus, the financial asset concept is relevant only if the financial asset is credited to a securities account. In other words, the USTA and the PPSA govern the transfer or grant of security in financial assets only to the extent that they are held in a securities account. Even then, the collateral is not the financial asset itself but the security entitlement — the rights accorded the account holder by the USTA against the intermediary.

4) Scope of Proposed Amendments to the PPSA

The new conceptual structure for investment property is designed to support the addition of new substantive rules governing the creation, perfection, priority, and enforcement of security interests in investment property. The impact of the proposed amendments is reviewed in the individual chapters of this book that deal with these issues.

Reform of the substantive law would not reduce systemic risk without some assurance that the USTA or some equivalent legal framework applied to the validity, perfection, and priority of security interests in investment property. Accordingly, the proposed amendments to the USTA and PPSA include new choice of law rules designed to give the parties to a securities account agreement control over the law applicable to the validity and proprietary effects of their relationship.

J. OTHER REFORM INITIATIVES

1) PPSA Reform

The Commercial Law Strategy of the Uniform Law Conference of Canada (ULCC) includes a component aimed at the reform of Canadian secured transactions law.[101] The work produced to date includes a discussion paper that identifies possible areas for PPSA reform.[102] In addition, in 2003, the Conference approved recommendations aimed at the harmonization and clarification of the PPSA provisions governing choice of law and anti-assignment clauses affecting receivables and chattel paper.[103] Although the recommendations were preceded and

---

101 A description of the strategy is posted at www.ulcc.ca under Commercial Law Strategy.

102 R.C.C. Cuming & Catherine Walsh, *A Discussion Paper On Potential Changes to the Model Personal Property Security Act of the Canadian Conference on Personal Property Security Law Part 1 (covering sections 1 to 41)* (posted at www.ulcc.ca under Proceedings of Annual Meetings — 2000 Victoria BC — Commercial Law Documents).

103 *Reform of the Law of Secured Transactions — Report of the Working Group 2002-2003* (posted at www.ulcc.ca under Proceedings of Annual Meetings — 2003 Fredericton NB — Commercial Law Documents).

supported by a consultative process, no jurisdiction has taken any active steps towards implementation to date.

2) Abolition of *Bank Act* Security

The ULCC and the Law Commission of Canada recently undertook a joint project to examine the possibilities for reform of the increasingly controversial bank security device established by section 427 of the federal *Bank Act*. At its 2003 meeting, the ULCC adopted a resolution recommending its outright abolition.[104] This was followed in 2004 by a report to Parliament issued by the Law Commission of Canada recommending abolition.[105] The commission's report focused on the redundancy of the federal system in light of the modern reforms to the provincial and territorial regimes for security in personal property, the loss of certainty and predictability created by dual provincial and federal systems, and the perceived inequity of a specialized security regime for only one class of credit supplier.

3) The *Cape Town Convention on International Interests in Mobile Equipment*

Adopted in 2001, the *Cape Town Convention on International Interests in Mobile Equipment*[106] seeks to establish an internationally uniform legal regime to govern financing transactions involving high-value equipment of the kind that is commonly moved across borders, such as aircraft and rolling stock, or that lacks a territorial *situs* altogether, such as space assets. The convention applies to "international interests" defined in broad terms to include not only the creation of a charge but also the retention of title under a conditional sales contract, as well as leasing transactions. The substantive scope of the convention is equally broad. The convention contemplates the establishment of international registries for the public disclosure and ordering of priorities among international interests and between an international interest and third

---

104 The resolution is posted at www.ulcc.ca under Proceedings of Annual Meetings — 2003 Fredericton NB — Civil Section Minutes and Resolutions. The background report is posted at the same site under Proceedings of Annual Meetings — 2003 Fredericton NB — Commercial Law Documents.

105 Law Commission of Canada, *Modernizing Canada's Secured Transactions Law: The Bank Act Security Provisions* (2004). (The report is posted at www.lcc.gc.ca under Research Projects — Federal Security Interests.).

106 The Convention is posted at www.unidroit.org under Adopted Texts — Convention on International Interests in Mobile Equipment (Cape Town, 2001).

parties including third-party buyers, judgment creditors, and a trustee in bankruptcy. The convention also includes substantive provisions on the requirements for creation of an international interest and its enforcement, although room has been left for the continued application of national law at the enforcement level.

The convention is designed to be implemented incrementally through the use of asset-specific protocols that adapt the general provisions of the convention to the financing practices applicable to the particular type of asset. Thus far, a protocol has been adopted for only aircraft equipment,[107] but draft protocols are in preparation for railway rolling stock[108] and space assets.[109]

Canadian representatives were instrumental in persuading Unidroit to take on the convention project, and Canadian representatives were actively involved in the development of the regulations for the registry contemplated by the convention and in the development of new protocols. Implementation of the convention and the aircraft protocol into Canadian law can be expected. Model implementing legislation has already been developed by a working group composed of representatives from the federal government and the provinces and territories under the auspices of the federal Department of Justice and the ULCC. Ontario and Nova Scotia have already passed implementing legislation[110] though it is not yet in force.

Upon the implementation of the convention, security interests in aircraft collateral will need to be registered in the international registry established under the convention and aircraft protocol to preserve their effectiveness and priority status against competing registered interests. The convention regime does not however supplant the PPSA. The Act will continue to be relevant for matters not addressed in the convention.

---

107 The aircraft Protocol is posted at www.unidroit.org under Adopted Texts — Protocol to the Convention on International Interests in Mobile Equipment on Matters Specific to Aircraft Equipment (Cape Town, 2001).

108 The draft rolling stock protocol is posted at www.unidroit under Works in Progress — Work Programme — International Interests in Mobile Equipment — Study LXXII — Preliminary Draft Protocol on Matters Specific to Railway Rolling Stock.

109 The draft space property protocol is posted at www.unidroit under Works in Progress — Work Programme — International Interests in Mobile Equipment — Study LXXII — Preliminary Draft Protocol on Matters Specific to Space Assets.

110 *International Interests in Mobile Equipment Act (Aircraft Equipment), 2002,* S.O. 2002, c. 18; *International Interests in Mobile Aircraft Equipment Act,* S.N.S. 2004, c. 5.

4) The *Hague Convention on Investment Securities Held with an Intermediary*

Adopted in 2001, the *Hague Convention on the Law Applicable to Certain Rights in Respect of Securities Held with an Intermediary*[111] establishes a uniform choice of law regime to govern the validity, third-party effectiveness, and priority of ownership and security interests in interests in securities held with an intermediary in the indirect holding system. Canada's active support of the convention supports the likelihood of its eventual implementation. In the meantime, the choice of law regime contemplated by the proposed USTA and the complementary PPSA amendments, although not perfectly identical to the Hague solution, is sufficiently similar to be compatible with its broad policy objectives.

Following the completion of the Hague securities convention, Unidroit commenced work on a project aimed at the international harmonization of the substantive rules regarding securities held with an intermediary. Initiated in 2001, the work is being pursued on a "fast-track" basis and a preliminary draft convention was produced in December 2004.[112] Although compatible at the broad policy level with the USTA, the drafting style and conceptual structure of the draft convention, unlike the USTA, is not tied precisely to the UCC Article 8 model.

5) The *UN Convention on the Assignment of Receivables in International Trade*

Another recent international development of note is the adoption in 2000 of the *United Nations Convention on the Assignment of Receivables in International Trade*.[113] The convention establishes substantive and choice of law rules to govern the assignment of and grant of security in monetary receivables. Implementation in Canada would add a helpful level of clarification on a variety of issues, particularly those relating to the relationship between the account debtor and an assignee or secured party on which the existing Canadian provincial and territorial law is

---

111 The convention is posted at www.hcch.net under International Commercial and Finance Law — Securities held with intermediaries.

112 The preliminary draft convention is posted at www.unidroit.org under Work Programme — Transactions on transnational and connected capital Markets — Study LXXVII — Study 78: Securities held with an intermediary.

113 The convention is posted at www.uncitral.org under General Assembly Resolutions — 56th Session 2001 — A/RES/56/81 United Nations Convention on the Assignment of Receivables in International Trade.

underdeveloped at both the substantive and choice of law levels. Other issues addressed by the convention are reflected only in the non-Ontario versions of the PPSA with the result that implementation would indirectly bring about greater national uniformity. Canada was an active participant in the Working Group that produced the convention and a background report recommending implementation — commissioned jointly by the ULCC and the federal Department of Justice and forming the basis for a resolution adopted by the ULCC at its annual meeting in St. John's in August 2005 to establish a federal-provincial Working Group to draft implementing legislation and complementary reforms.[114]

K. UCC ARTICLE 9

1) Historical Influence

The deficiencies in the old law that led to the passage of the PPSA were not unique to Canada. In all common law legal systems, a century and more of *ad hoc* response to commercial demands for an ever-expanding cushion of assets to secure loan and purchase credit had produced deep fragmentation in the legal doctrine and theory.

Article 9 of the *Uniform Commercial Code* (UCC) represented the first attempt at a comprehensive rationalization of personal property security law. The idea of a uniform commercial code was endorsed by the National Conference of Commissioners on Uniform State Law in 1940 and shortly afterwards attracted the co-sponsorship of the American Law Institute (of *Restatement* fame). In 1944, the Uniform Commercial Code Project was formally launched under the direction of the realist scholar and commercial lawyer, Professor Karl Llewellyn, as Chief Reporter, with Soia Mentschikoff as Associate Editor. The first version of the UCC, published as the "1952 Official Text" was completed in 1951. The result still stands as the most widely influential work that either co-sponsor has produced. Beginning with Pennsylvania in 1953, the UCC has been adopted by all fifty of the American states (including the civil law state of Louisiana), as well as the District of Columbia and the Virgin Islands. Of all the UCC articles, Article 9 easily qualifies as the most innovative and successful.

With fifty separate jurisdictions, the commercial pressures for harmonization in the United States were immense. Moreover, the need

<hr>

114 The text of the pre-implementation report will be posted at www.ulcc.ca under Proceedings of Annual Meetings — St. John's (NL) — Commercial Law Documents.

for reform was particularly pressing. The U.S. courts showed a level of hostility to open-ended secured financing not seen in other common law systems, exemplified most dramatically by the refusal to endorse the all-inclusive floating charge on a business's assets. [115]

The most significant intellectual achievement of Article 9, and the feature that explains its attractiveness as a model for the PPSA, is the unifying concept of a single generic security interest. Working independently of each other, Professor Grant Gilmore of Harvard Law School and Professor Allison Dunham of the University of Chicago (initially the Chief Reporter for Article 9), arrived at the conclusion that the old system of discrete security devices for specific categories of personal property was no longer needed. Gilmore was invited to join Dunham as a co-reporter for Article 9. Together, they transformed their common insight into a statutory framework for financing transactions in which distinctions among creditors and security interests are based overtly on functional rather than formalistic distinctions.

2) Comparison with the PPSA

Although it owes a significant intellectual debt to Article 9, the PPSA is not simply a restatement of that model recast in the Canadian common law drafting style.[116] The PPSA came of age after the computer revolution, and Canada has been a global pioneer in the design and operation of electronic secured transactions systems. In contrast, the states enacting Article 9 initially adopted manual filing systems, frequently on a county-by-county basis. Centralized electronic filing is a fairly recent phenomenon in the United States, and its full implications are only now being worked out.

The differences extend beyond infrastructure to substantive policy. For example, the PPSA reflects the historically more liberal Anglo-Canadian attitude to secured transactions. The best illustration of this is the difference in the approach to the sufficiency of an "all present and after-acquired property" clause to describe the collateral in a security agreement. Under the PPSA, this is a valid description, whereas Article 9 continues to disallow the use of supergeneric descriptions in security

---

115 The story of the evolution of American personal property security law, including the transformation achieved by Article 9, is explained comprehensively by Grant Gilmore in his unparalleled two-volume work: G. Gilmore, *Security Interests in Personal Property* (Boston: Little, Brown, 1965).

116 See generally Ronald C.C. Cuming and Catherine Walsh, "Revised Article 9 of the *Uniform Commercial Code*: Implications for the Canadian PPSAs" (2001) 16 B.F.L.R. 339.

agreements.[117] It is not that Article 9 prohibits a debtor from giving an all-assets security interest. What is prohibited is to say so. Instead, the various genres or items of collateral must be listed. Collectively, they can add up to the debtor's entire asset base, but if this is stated explicitly, the security agreement is defective. It seems the drafters felt it should not be "too easy" for a debtor to bind all personal property in favour of a particular creditor.[118]

Article 9 was substantially revised and reissued in 2001. In some respects, the 2001 version has brought the two models into closer harmony. This is not due, as may have been the case in the past, to the conscious emulation of certain features of Article 9 in the PPSA. The harmonization traffic is in the opposite direction. Current Article 9 adopts a number of features which, while novel in the Article 9 context, had already been adopted by the PPSA. For example, a series of significant transactions brought within Article 9 for the first time already fall within the reach of the PPSA (with the exception of Ontario in some instances), including security agreements covering deposit accounts as original collateral, outright sales of all monetary intangibles, true commercial consignments, and consensual security agreements entered into by government debtors.

Post-default enforcement is another area where the recent amendments to Article 9 were already approximated in the PPSA. For example, in line with the PPSA, Article 9 now adopts a rebuttable presumption rule for determining deficiency rights where a creditor has failed to comply with its statutory enforcement obligations.[119] Other examples include clarification that a creditor who elects the remedy of "consensual strict foreclosure" obtains the collateral free of subordinate interests,[120] and the introduction of a requirement for notice of an intended

---

117 § 9-108(c), § 9-203(b)(3)(A). However, a supergeneric description is permitted in the financing statement perfecting the security agreement: § 9-504(2).

118 William J. Woodward, "The Realist and Secured Credit: Grant Gilmore, Common Law Courts, and the Article 9 Reform Process" (1997) 82 Cornell L. Rev. 1511 at 1527–28 and note 85.

119 § 9-626(4) creates a rebuttable presumption that a complying sale would have generated proceeds equal to the secured debt. It is then up to the creditor to lead evidence to show that a disposition conducted in accordance with Article 9 would have yielded less that the debt. The PPSA (except for the OPPSA) also relies on a shift in the burden of proof to determine a non-complying creditor's entitlement to a deficiency, with the secured party carrying a somewhat broader burden in consumer goods cases.

120 § 9-622.

disposition of collateral to be sent to secured parties who have filed financing statements.[121]

The following is a non-exhaustive list of other revisions introduced into Article 9 for the first time in 2001 for which analogous provision already existed in the PPSA (with the exception of the Ontario Act in some cases):

- the addition of instruments to the types of collateral capable of perfection by registration;[122]
- a special priority rule for contests between supplier and lender purchase money security interests in the same collateral;[123]
- explicit confirmation of the acceptability of all-inclusive collateral descriptions in financing statements (for example, "all assets" or "all personal property");[124]
- rules requiring secured parties to discharge ("terminate") a registration on satisfaction of the secured obligation;[125]
- the extension of the existing overarching requirement of "good faith" beyond honesty in fact to include the observance of reasonable commercial standards of fair dealing;[126]

---

121 § 9-611(c) requires that notice be sent to the debtor and any secondary obligors. In non-consumer cases, notice must also be sent to any secured party with a filed and indexed financing statement, any secured party who has perfected under specified statutes (e.g., under a state motor vehicle title certificate statute), and any person who has given actual notice of an interest in the collateral. Under the PPSA, the same notice obligation applies in consumer and non-consumer cases without distinction. In PPSA jurisdictions that provide for registration of judgments in the Personal Property Registry, notice must also be sent to all subordinate registered judgment creditors. § 9-611(c)(3)(B) requires notice to be sent to all secured parties of record, not just subordinate interests.

122 § 9-312(a). Old § 9-304 required possession. The PPSA permits registration as a perfection step for all types of collateral including instruments and money. Unlike the PPSA, § 9-312 does not permit a security interest in money to be perfected by registration; it can only be perfected by possession under § 9-313.

123 § 9-324(g) awards first priority to the supplier over the lender. This is in line with the PPSA approach.

124 § 9-504.

125 Under § 9-513, a termination must be filed within twenty days of debtor demand if the secured obligation has been satisfied and there is no commitment for further advances. In consumer cases, the creditor must file within one month even without debtor demand. § 9-625(e)(4) imposes penalties for failure to file. The PPSA contains broadly analogous provisions.

126 § 9-102. A similar overarching obligation of good faith and commercial reasonableness is found in the PPSA, except for the Ontario Act.

- imposition of a statutory liability on secured parties to pay deemed damages for non-compliance with certain mandatory Article 9 obligations;[127]
- model rules for production-money security interests;[128]
- confirmation that the term "inventory" includes goods leased by the debtor to others as well as goods held for lease;[129] and
- confirmation that the lapse of a financing statement does not retroactively subordinate the associated security interest to the interest of a pre-lapse lien creditor including a bankruptcy trustee (who is a deemed lien creditor under article 9).[130]

In other respects, however, the 2001 iteration of Article 9 has reduced the commonality historically enjoyed with the PPSA. To some extent, this is a function of its increased complexity. The new Article 9 is a far more detailed statute than its predecessors. A numerical comparison illustrates the change. The old Article 9 contained 55 substantive sections. The 2001 version has been expanded to 126 substantive sections (excluding transitional provisions and conforming amendments) including 36 new sections for which no previous counterparts existed.

In part this may be because the 2001 version of Article 9 emerged from a lengthy consultation process in which the drafters were sometimes persuaded to sacrifice the simplicity of general rules in order to satisfy the demands of diverse constituencies. An illustration is the substantially more complex conceptual structure adopted for monetary intangibles so as to enable the application of special rules — more accurately exemptions from Article 9's general policy of public registra-

---

127 § 9-625(e) ($500).

128 Appendix II to the 2001 version of Article 9 contains model definitions and special priority rules for production money security interests held by secured parties who extend new value used in the production of crops. Because no consensus emerged among the drafters on this issue, the model provisions were included as an optional appendix rather than as part of the uniform statutory text of Article 9 itself. The PPSA (except for the OPPSA) provides for special production money priority for security interests taken to finance inputs in crops, farm animals, and fish.

129 § 9-102.

130 § 9-515(c). The PPSA achieves the same result indirectly: the wording of the provisions subordinating unperfected security interests to unsecured creditors and the bankruptcy trustee make it clear that the secured party prevails so long as the security interest is perfected when the interest of the creditor or bankruptcy trustee arises. The wording in the OPPSA on this point is more ambiguous than in the other Acts and may raise problems equivalent to those which inspired the need for clarification in Article 9: OPPSA ss. 20(1) (a)(ii)–(iii), (b).

tion — to satisfy the demands of large financial institutions. Another example is the result of a compromise decision between groups representing financers and consumers to remove consumer transactions from Article 9's enforcement regime, leaving most significant issues to be resolved judicially or through state-by-state regulation.

From a Canadian perspective, the most important area of difference is the conflict of laws. Whereas the PPSA draws a basic distinction between tangible and intangible collateral for the purposes of determining the law governing perfection, the latest revision introduced a unitary choice of law rule into Article 9. Perfection of non-possessory security interests in all forms of collateral is now governed by the law of the location of the debtor subject to very limited exceptions.[131] The new rule was motivated by a desire to reduce transaction costs and priority risk in interstate transactions involving tangible collateral — notably inventory and equipment — located in multiple states. Registration in a single state now suffices to perfect a security interest in the debtor's assets wherever located, and whether tangible or intangible. However, the effects of perfection or non-perfection and other priority issues continue to be governed for tangible collateral, as a general rule, by the law of the location of the collateral.[132]

L. SECURED TRANSACTIONS LAW OF QUEBEC

1) Introduction

The legal regime for conventional hypothecs (consensual security interests) on movables established by the *Civil Code of Québec*[133] shares a basic philosophical commonality with the PPSA. Security can be granted in any kind of movable property, present or after-acquired,[134] to secure any kind of obligation, past, current, or future, determinate or indeterminate.[135] Non-possessory hypothecs must be published by registration in a centralized electronic registry to take effect against

---

131 § 9-301(1).

132 § 9-301(3)(C).

133 S.Q. 1991, c. 64, in force 1 January 1994 [*Civil Code*].

134 Art. 2666.

135 Arts. 2687, 2688. Where the obligation secured by a hypothec is indeterminate, the secured party cannot exercise its enforcement rights upon the debtor's default until the claim is made "liquid and exigible": art. 2748 (para. 2). Although the PPSA does not say this expressly, the same limitation flows from the very

third parties,[136] with priority among registered hypothecs determined, as a general rule, by the order of registration[137] regardless of actual knowledge.[138] The hypothecary creditor's enforcement rights on default are roughly the same as though available to secured parties under the PPSA. In addition to their personal rights of action, they may sell the collateral,[139] take the collateral in full satisfaction of their claims,[140] take possession of the collateral for the purposes of administering it,[141] and, where the collateral takes the form of accounts owing to the debtor, directly collect the accounts from the account debtors.[142] As is the case under the PPSA, exercise of these default rights is subject to procedural rules designed to protect the interests of the debtor and third parties in any surplus value in the collateral.

There are important differences as well. We deal with the differences at the level of choice of law in some detail in chapter 3. Otherwise, this book does not address the secured transactions law of Quebec. Nonetheless, in view of the national context of many PPSA financing transactions, we thought it important to include a comparative synopsis of the most significant aspects of the *Civil Code* regime in this chapter.

2) Forms of Security

The *Civil Code* adopts a unitary security institution — the hypothec — for all security interests, consensual or non-consensual, possessory or non-possessory, in all forms of property, movable or immovable, corporeal or non-corporeal.[143] However, the hypothec is treated as conceptually distinct from security generated by the retention or transfer of title[144]

---

nature of a security interest as being a limited proprietary interest measured by reference to the value of the secured obligation.

136 Art. 2663. And see the *Regulation respecting the Register of personal and movable real rights*, R.Q. c. C.c.Q., r.5.

137 Arts. 2941, 2945.

138 Art. 2693.

139 Arts. 2748 (para. 2), 2784–90 (sale by the secured creditor), 2791–94 (sale by judicial authority).

140 Arts. 2784 (para. 2), 2778–83.

141 Arts. 2748 (para. 2), 2773–77.

142 Arts. 2743–47.

143 Art. 2660.

144 Art. 1745 ff (instalment sales under which seller reserves ownership until full payment of the sale price); art. 1750*ff* (sales with a right of redemption constituted by a transfer of ownership subject to the reservation of a right to redeem it); art. 1842 ff (leasing or *crédit-bail*); 1851 (lease or *appelé bail*). The *Civil Code* also preserves certain non-consensual real remedies in favour of unpaid sellers

or by a trust.[145] Even when used to secure a loan or the acquisition price of a movable, such devices continue to be governed by the articles of the *Civil Code* that apply to the particular institution rather than by the regime for hypothecs. The Supreme Court had this to say about the conceptual division in its recent decision in *Lefebvre (Trustee of); Tremblay (Trustee of)*:[146]

> This distinction between security and rights of ownership remains a fundamental element of the classification of real rights in property law in the *Civil Code of Québec*. The right of ownership, which is the fundamental real right that theoretically confers full legal control over property, can be distinguished from a security such as a hypothec, which is an incidental real right. One author characterizes incidental real rights as "real rights of security" (droits réels de garantie) that relate to the monetary value of a thing rather than to the thing itself and are designed to complement another right by securing it or guaranteeing the payment of a claim.

At the level of publication (perfection), the practical impact of this conceptual division is minimal since the *Civil Code* extends the same rules that apply to hypothecs to these other juridical institutions where they are employed as security.[147] In *Ouellet (Trustee of)*[148] — the companion decision to *Lefebvre* — the Supreme Court ruled that the debtor's trustee in bankruptcy is not a third party for the purposes of the *Civil Code* requirement that instalment sales must be published by registration to be effective against third parties. The Court acknowledged, however, that its ruling for the purposes of future cases had been overtaken by intervening amendments made to the *Bankruptcy and Insolvency Act's* definition of "secured creditor" by the *Federal Law — Civil Law Harmonization Act No. 1*.[149] These amendments equate a reservation of ownership in an instalment sale to secure the purchase price with hypothecary security for the purposes of bankruptcy proceedings involving the instalment buyer. It follows that in future cases

---

of movables: see art. 1740 (unpaid seller's pre-delivery legal right of resolution); art. 1741 (unpaid seller's thirty-day post-delivery legal right of revendication).

145 Art. 1263 (acknowledging that the purpose of a trust may be to secure the performance of an obligation).

146 *Lefebvre (Trustee of); Tremblay (Trustee of)*, [2004] 3 S.C.R. 326 at para. 21 [*Lefebvre*].

147 Arts. 1745 (para. 2), 1749 (paras. 2–3) (instalment sale); art. 1750 (para. 2) (sale with a right of redemption); art. 1263 (trust); art. 1847 (leasing); art. 1852 (lease).

148 [2004] 3 S.C.R. 348.

149 S.C. 2001, c. 4, ss. 25–28.

the rights of an instalment seller who has retained ownership to secure the purchase price is of no effect against the trustee if it is not published.

The amendments also cover security in the form of a sale of property by the debtor to a creditor subject to a right of redemption, and a trust of property constituted by the debtor in favour of the creditor as trustee, where these transactions operate to secure an obligation. On the other hand, the amendments do not convert lessors — even where the lease functions economically to secure the purchase price — into secured creditors for bankruptcy purposes. Accordingly, the Court's ruling in its companion decision in *Lefebvre* that the trustee is not a third party for the purposes of the *Civil Code* requirement for publication of long term leases of movables means that an unpublished lease of movables is nonetheless effective against the trustee in the event of the lessee's bankruptcy.

The *Civil Code*'s parallel treatment of hypothecs and title-based security devices also extends to the enforcement context. Creditors who employ non-hypothecary security are bound by the enforcement obligations that apply to hypothecary creditors.[150] Again, there is one significant exception. Lessors under leasing or lease arrangements are not bound by the hypothecary enforcement regime even where the arrangements operates as the functional equivalent of an instalment sale.

3) Assignments and Long-term Leases

Like the PPSA, the *Civil Code* extends the publication (perfection) requirements that apply to movable hypothecs to assignments of claims (intangible obligations owing to the debtor),[151] and to leases of movables for a period of more than one year, even where these transactions do not function as security.[152] There are two significant differences. Only assignments of universalities of claims need be publicized by registration; specific assignments are exempt. Second, as noted earlier, the Supreme Court of Canada recently ruled that an unpublished long-term lease remains effective against the lessee's trustee in bankruptcy on the theory that the trustee is not a "third party" within the meaning of the *Civil Code* provisions requiring publication of a lease for a term of more than one year.[153]

---

150 Art. 1749 (para. 1) (instalment sale); art. 1756 (sale with a right of redemption); art. 1263 (para. 2).
151 Art. 1642.
152 Art. 1852.
153 *Lefebvre*, above note 146.

4) Priority Consequences of Failure to Publish (Perfect)

Under the *Civil Code*, a hypothec may be set up against third parties only when it is published by registration or debtor dispossession.[154] The PPSA begins from the converse presumption of *nemo dat quod non habet* (no one can give that which she has not). Security interests are presumed to take effect as soon as they are constituted. It follows that third parties are protected from an unperfected security only if they can point to an explicit source of protection. However, the PPSA subordinates an unperfected security interest against most significant categories of third-party interests, thereby minimizing any real differences between the regimes. An unperfected security interest taken under the PPSA is nonetheless capable of binding at least some categories of third-party claimants against whom an unpublished *Civil Code* hypothec would be ineffective. For instance, the PPSA does not explicitly protect transferees of collateral who do not give value, transferees who take with knowledge of an unperfected security interest, or creditors who hold security under the federal *Bank Act* or by virtue of a non-consensual security interest arising under some other statute. It follows that a PPSA secured party will be entitled to follow its security into the hands of third parties in these categories, notwithstanding failure to register, unless in the case of non-PPSA secured creditors, the statute governing their rights confers independent protection.

5) Advance Registration and Multi-agreement Registration

A PPSA secured party is permitted to register in advance of the actual execution of the security agreement, with priority then dating back to the time of registration and a single registration is effective to publicize security taken under successive security agreements. In contrast, registration is possible under the *Civil Code* only after the hypothec has come into existence and it is assumed that each registration relates to a separate hypothec.

6) Purchase Money Super-priority

The PPSA awards super-priority to a secured party who finances the debtor's acquisition of the very assets in which security is taken. A so-called purchase money security interest takes priority over a prior security interest covering after-acquired assets of the relevant kind.

---

154 Arts. 2663, 2703, 2934.

The *Civil Code* also awards super-priority to hypothecary creditors who provide purchase money financing as against the holder of a prior hypothec on the debtor's after-acquired property. However, this is restricted to sales credit extended by vendors.[155] A hypothec to secure loan credit does not qualify, even if the purpose of the loan is to finance the acquisition of assets.

Instead of relying on a vendor's hypothec, a purchase money financer has the option of achieving super-priority through financing arrangement designed to prevent the assets from entering the debtor's patrimony: for example, an instalment sale pending payment of the price, or a leasing or lease contract. Whichever form of security is chosen, the conditions for achieving or preserving super-priority are the same: the financer must register within fifteen days of the transaction.[156]

Under the *Civil Code*, reservations of ownership under instalment sales can also be used to finance the debtor's ongoing acquisition of inventory and a single registration is effective to publicize the financer's rights of ownership in a universality of inventory.[157] As under the PPSA, there is no grace period for effecting registration. However, unlike the PPSA, the *Civil Code* does not require the inventory financer to also give notice to prior registered creditors holding hypothecary security in assets of the same kind.

7) Capacity of Consumers and Enterprises to Grant Security

There are no limitations on who may take consensual security under the *Civil Code*. The position with respect to who may grant consensual security is more complicated. There are no *a priori* limitations, assuming the grantor has legal capacity, for "movable hypothecs with delivery," that is, the classic possessory pledge.[158] However, with the exception of a hypothec on a road vehicle or other movable property determined by regulation,[159] a non-possessory hypothec on movables can

---

155 Art. 2954.
156 Art. 2954 (vendor's hypothec); art. 1745 (para. 2) (instalment sale); art. 1847 (leasing); art. 1852 (lease).
157 Art. 2961.1. And see art. 52.2 of the *Regulation respecting the Register of personal and movable real rights*, above note 136.
158 Arts. 2665 (para. 2), 2681.
159 The following additional types of movable property have been designated by regulation as property on which a natural person who does not operate an enterprise may grant a movable hypothec without delivery: a caravan or a fifth-wheel; a mobile home; a boat; a personal watercraft; an aircraft. See the *Regula-*

be granted by a natural person only where he operates an enterprise and the hypothec may only charge the property of the enterprise.[160] While a leasing transaction similarly may be entered into for business purposes only,[161] no equivalent restriction applies to leases or to security generated through the transfer or retention of title or through a security trust. Moreover, where the transaction takes the form of an instalment sale, a sale with right of redemption or rights under a lease of more than one year, publication is required only where the transaction pertains to a road vehicle or the other categories of movable property designated by regulation as property in which a non-enterprise debtor can grant a non-possessory hypothec.[162]

With the exception of a security trust, these non-hypothecary security devices by their nature do not readily permit non-possessory security to be granted over a debtor's intangible assets. In contrast, except for the prohibition on the grant of security in after acquired consumer goods, the PPSA does not restrict the ability of consumers to charge the full range of their tangible and intangible assets. On the other hand, the *Civil Code* recognizes the effectiveness of a possessory hypothec over a wider range of intangible movables than the PPSA. The intangible need not be represented by a negotiable document to be effectively pledged by delivery. An ordinary monetary claim, for example, a deposit account, can be published (perfected) by delivery.[163] The Supreme Court of Canada has ruled that publication by delivery occurs once the debtor has transferred effective control of the claim to the hypothecary creditor by giving the creditor the right to collect directly in the event of

---

tion respecting the Register of personal and movable real rights, above note 136, art. 15.02.

160 Arts. 2683–86; and see s. 27 of the *Special Corporate Powers Act*, as amended by s. 643 of the *Act respecting the implementation of the Civil Code*. Carrying on an enterprise is seen as producing, administering or alienating property. There is no requirement for the enterprise to make a profit or that it be for business purposes. Thus manufacturing operations, farming, forestry, and fishing operations, social and athletic clubs, and so on are all carrying on an enterprise.

161 Art. 1842 (para. 3).

162 Art. 1745 (para. 2); (instalment sale); art.1750 (para. 2) (sale with a right of redemption); art. 1263 (trust); art. 1847 (leasing); art. 1852 (lease). Pursuant to art. 15.01 of the *Regulation respecting the Register of personal and movable real rights*, above note 136.

163 Art. 2710 (providing that: "A movable hypothec on a claim held by the grantor against a third person or on a universality of claims may be granted with or without delivery.").

default, and the necessary steps have been taken so that the hypothec may be set up against the account debtor of the claim.[164]

8) Scope of Buyer in the Ordinary Course of Business Rule

Under the *Civil Code*, a buyer who acquires assets under a sale effected in the ordinary course of the transferor's business takes free of any hypothec granted in those assets, whether or not the hypothec is registered and whether or not the buyer has actual knowledge.[165] The ordinary course of business exception applies even where the hypothec was granted by a predecessor in title to the immediate seller. Under the PPSA, on the other hand, protection is limited to security interests granted by the immediate seller

In a similar vein, where the sold property was financed through a instalment sale, the creditor's right under the *Civil Code* to have the sale annulled and to revendicate the property from the third-party buyer is conditional on reimbursement of the purchase price if the property was sold in the ordinary course of business of an enterprise.

9) Serial Number Identification

The PPSA requires specific serial number identification to achieve effective registration or priority where the collateral is a relatively high-value tangible asset for which a unique serial number or other identifier is available. This includes motor vehicles and (with the exception of Ontario), aircraft, trailers, mobile homes, and boats not subject to the federal ship's registry. The *Civil Code* likewise requires registration of a serial number description for road vehicles, broadly defined.[166]

---

164 *Re Blouin (sub nom. Caisse Populaire Desjardins de Val-Brillant v. Blouin)*, [2003] 1 S.C.R. 666. As the Court observed, for a hypothec on a claim to be set up against the account debtor, all that is required is that the account debtor either acquiesce in the hypothec or receive a copy or pertinent extract or other evidence of the hypothec: arts. 2710 (para. 2), 1641.

165 The rule is not stated expressly in the *Civil Code*; it arises by necessary inference from art. 2700 (para. 1).

166 See arts. 15, 20 of the *Regulation respecting the Register of personal and movable real rights*, above note 136.

10) Enforcement

While the basic philosophy is much the same, the *Civil Code* enforcement regime for hypothecs differs from that found in the PPSA on a number of quite fundamental points.

First, while both regimes require the secured party to give advance notice to the debtor and interested third parties of the exercise of an enforcement remedy, this obligation is cast on the secured party directly by the PPSA. Although the debtor must also receive direct notice under the *Civil Code*, the hypothecary creditor is additionally required to file the notice in the secured transactions registry, and it is then up to the registrar to notify third parties holding registered rights in the same collateral.[167]

Second, the PPSA releases the secured party from the obligation to give advance notice where the collateral is perishable, or apt to decline speedily in value, or where its value is set by objective market factors outside the control of the secured party. The range of circumstances where this is possible is far more circumscribed under the *Civil Code*, and creditors will normally have to seek explicit judicial permission if they wish to act before the expiry of the minimum-notice period.[168]

Third, the PPSA empowers a secured party to take unilateral possession of the collateral on default so long as this can be done without provoking a breach of the peace. Under the *Civil Code*, the hypothecary creditor must obtain a court order for forced surrender unless the person against whom enforcement is exercised consents in writing to turn the collateral over to the creditor at the agreed time or abandons it for the purposes of enabling the creditor to take possession.[169]

Fourth, the PPSA gives secured parties near-absolute flexibility and discretion in the timing, mode, method, and general conduct of the sale process. Although secured parties (and debtors) are subject to an overriding obligation to act in good faith and in a commercially reasonable manner, there is no *a priori* supervisory structure built into the enforcement process — a complainant must apply to the courts for relief.

In contrast, the *Civil Code* prescribes two modes of sale: sale by the creditor and sale under judicial authority.[170] Although sale by the creditor is, in principle, just as flexible as under the PPSA, the regime

---

167 Arts. 2757–58, 3017.
168 Arts. 2759 and 2767.
169 Arts. 2763–65.
170 Arts. 2784–90 (sale by the creditor); arts. 2791–94 (sale by judicial authority).

is structured such that creditors elect sale by judicial authority in most cases. Sale by judicial authority has an equivalent effect to a sale under the execution process contained in the *Code of Civil Procedure of Québec*: it purges the relevant assets of virtually all encumbrances, whether prior or subordinate to that of the enforcement creditor.[171] In a sale by a creditor, on the other hand, the sale releases the hypothec of the enforcing creditor and any prior-ranking claims; the purchaser takes subject to claims subordinate to that of the enforcing creditor.[172] It follows that an hypothecary creditor, in order to ensure that the proceeds will be applied in satisfaction of its hypothec, will almost invariably elect sale by judicial authority. The rule under the PPSA, and in common law generally, is the precise opposite: the purchaser acquires the asset free of the enforcing creditor's security, and any subordinate ranking claims.

Finally, in PPSA jurisdictions, the institution of the receivership, and the receiver-manager, enables a secured party to appoint a receiver — either by agreement between the debtor and creditor or by application to the court — to take over the management of the encumbered assets on the debtor's default with a view to their ultimate disposition. The remedy is particularly valuable where a secured party holds a general security interest in all the assets of an enterprise because it permits continued operation of the business as a going concern, with a view to its ultimate disposition as such, rather than on a piecemeal basis. Although the *Civil Code* envisages a similar remedy — the appointment of an administrator of the property of another — the regime regulating the powers and duties of the creditor/administrator is somewhat more onerous.[173]

FURTHER READINGS

BOODMAN, M., "The Nature and Diversity of Personal Property Security Systems in Canada" (1992) 23 R.G.D. 109

BRIDGE, M.G., "How Far is Article 9 Exportable?: The English Experience" (1996) 27 Can. Bus. L.J. 196

BRIDGE, M.G. *et al.*, "Formalism, Functionalism, and Understanding the Law of Secured Transactions" (1999) 44 McGill L.J. 567

---

171 Art. 2794.
172 Art. 2790.
173 Arts. 2773–27, 1306*ff.*

CUMING, R.C.C., "Judicial Development of Personal Property Security Law: The Contribution of the Saskatchewan Court of Appeal" (1999) Sask. L. Rev. 19

CUMING, R.C.C. & C. WALSH, "Revised Article 9 of the Uniform Commercial Code: Implications for the Canadian Personal Property Security Acts" (2001) 16 B.F.L.R. 339

GRENON, A., "Major Differences Between PPSA Legislation and Security over Movables in Quebec under the New Civil Code" (1996) 26 Can. Bus. L.J. 391

LAW REFORM COMMISSION OF SASKATCHEWAN, *Tentative proposals for a new Personal Property Security Act* (Saskatoon, Sask.: The Commission, 1990)

MACDONALD, R.A., "Modernization of Personal Property Security Law: A Quebec Perspective" (1985) 10 Can. Bus. L.J. 182

WALSH, C., "New Brunswick's New Personal Property Security Regime: A 1990s Version of a '1960s Model of a 1930s Idea'?" (1994) 9 B.F.L.R. 261

ZIEGEL, J.S., "The New Ontario Personal Property Security Act: Ambiguities, Unresolved Issues and Challenges" (1989–90) 5 B.F.L.R. 31

ZIEGEL, J.S., "The New Provincial Chattel Security Law Regimes" (1991) 70 Can. Bar Rev. 681

ZIEGEL, J.S., "Amendments to the Ontario Personal Property Security Act: Submission of the CBAO [Canadian Bar Association — Ontario] Personal Property Security Committee" (2000) 15 B.F.L.R. 279

THE CONCEPT OF SECURITY INTEREST AND SCOPE OF THE *PERSONAL PROPERTY SECURITY ACT*

A. THE DEFINITION AND CENTRAL CONCEPT OF SECURITY INTEREST

1) A Unitary Concept

The concept of security interest is at the core of the PPSA.[1] The Act applies only to transactions that create or provide for security interests or that are deemed to create security interests.[2] In the context of the PPSA itself, there is no need to determine the nature of a security interest other than to recognize that it is an interest that gives to the secured party the rights against specified kinds of competing claimants and

---

1   Issues relating to the creation of a security interest, including questions of rights in the collateral and attachment, are dealt with in chapter 3.

2   It is clear that a security agreement is a necessary but not sufficient condition for the creation of a security interest. All of the statutory prerequisites for its creation must be met: an agreement through which it is recognized that the secured party has or is to have a "security interest," the giving of value by the secured party, and the holding or acquisition of rights in the collateral by the debtor. A security interest is created by a security agreement only in the sense that a security agreement is a *sine qua non* of the existence of a security interest. The making of a security agreement by the parties provides the legally relevant evidence of their intentions that one party is to have a security interest in property of the other. Once the existence of this evidence coincides with the existence of the other prerequisites, the security interest attaches.

against the debtor that are set out in the Act. However, it is relevant in other contexts to identify the central concept of the PPSA.[3] Most pre-PPSA forms of security agreements used in Canada involved transfers of legal or equitable title.[4] The PPSA makes it clear that this is not required or even relevant.[5] Many security interests are created under transactions that provide for nothing more than the recognition that the secured party has a security interest in identified personal property of the debtor. However, when the rights of a secured party or debtor come into conflict with those of a third-party claimant in a context not regulated by the PPSA, it may be necessary to determine the nature of a security interest in order to determine the outcome of the conflict.

Not all security interests falling within the scope of the Act are conceptually the same. This is a product of several factors examined later in this chapter. The term "security interest" is defined in the Act as "an interest in personal property that secures payment or performance of an obligation."[6] This definition must be read in the context of the scope section of the Act that provides that the Act applies "to every transaction that in substance creates a security interest ..." and that provides a non-exclusive list of transactions that are to be treated as creating or providing for security interests.[7]

---

3   The authors do not agree that the approach described by Professor Grant Gilmore, one of the architects of Article 9, applies to the PPSA. Professor Gilmore concluded that the definition of "security interest" in UCC § 1-201(37) is "essentially a declaration of faith.... What is important to remember is that, ultimately, the Article 9 security interest floats, unmoored, in a void. Whether any particular transaction creates 'an interest ... which secures ... an obligation' is a question for judicial determination." See G. Gilmore, *Security Interests in Personal Property*, vol. 1 (Boston: Little, Brown, 1965) at 334–35.

4   There are circumstances in which it remains important to use traditional forms of charging clauses in agreements. Of particular importance in this respect are title retention clauses in secured sales agreements. See, for example, s. 89(1) of the *Indian Act*, R.S.C. 1985, c. I-5 (re-en. 1988, c. 23, s. 12) which provides different rights depending upon whether the security agreement is a conditional sales contract or another type of security agreement. See also chapter 14, A.7.a "The *Bank Act* Priority Provisions."

5   PPSA (A, M, NB, PEI, S) s. 3(1); (BC, NWT, Nu) s. 2(1); (NL, NS) s. 4(1); O s. 2(a); Y s. 2.

6   PPSA (A, BC, NWT, Nu, O, Y) s. 1(1); (M, NB, PEI) s. 1; (NL, NS) s. 2; S s. 2(1).

7   Above note 5. The definition and the scope section are tied together in the definition of security agreement — "an agreement that creates or provides for a security interest." PPSA (A, BC, NWT, Nu, O, Y) s. 1(1); (M, NB, PEI) s. 1; (NL, NS) s. 2; S s. 2(1).

2) Hypothecation

Standing alone, the definition of security interest is both too broad and too narrow to define accurately the concept in the Act. It is too narrow in that it does not describe common law interests arising under transactions such as conditional sales contracts and security leases that are within the scope of the Act. It is too broad in that it can be read as applying to non-consensual security interests that are not within the scope of the Act.[8] However, it does describe the central concept that characterizes the great bulk of interests to which the Act applies.

This central concept has the following features.[9] It assumes that the debtor has or will acquire a property interest in personal property. By agreement between the debtor and the creditor,[10] that interest is charged or is to be charged with or encumbered by an interest granted in favour of the creditor[11] for the purposes of securing performance of an obligation of a debtor.[12] This concept is not new — it was a feature of Roman law (hypothec)[13] and was recognized in Equity (equitable

---

8   The Act applies only to interests arising under a consensual arrangement (contract) and those that are given by the PPSA itself. Except to the extent that it provides a priority rule for repairers' liens, it does not apply to interest that arise by operation of law. See *Canadian Imperial Bank of Commerce v. 64576 Manitoba Ltd.* (1990), 79 C.B.R. (N.S.) 308 (Man. Q.B.), aff'd (1991), 2 C.B.R. (3d) 4 (C.A.). The Ontario PPSA is an exception to this generalization. See s. 20(1)(a)(i).

9   The conceptualization of a security interest under the Act applies only to transactions that function as secured financing arrangements (above note 5), not to those that do not but are deemed to be security agreements in order to bring them within the publication and priority regimes of the Act (see PPSA (A, M, NB, PEI, S) s. 3(2); (NL, NS) s. 4(2); (NWT, Nu) s. 2(2); (O, Y) s. 2(b); BC s. 3). The common law characteristics of these transactions remain undisturbed except to the very limited extent it is necessary to deem them to have characteristics of security agreements for clearly limited purposes.

10   The term "creditor" is used although the obligation secured need not be a debt. A security interest can secure payment or performance of any obligation.

11   The interest can be one that is recognized in law or equity. Consequently, a contractual equitable assignment (i.e., an agreement to assign or transfer a future chose-in-action) is a security agreement that gives rise to a security interest as soon as the debtor acquires a property interest in the property described in the agreement. See *356447 British Columbia Ltd. v. Canadian Imperial Bank of Commerce*, [1998] 9 W.W.R. 59 (B.C.C.A.).

12   The transaction may involve two "debtors": a principal debtor and a guarantor. See the definition of debtor: PPSA (A, BC, NWT, Nu, O, Y) s. 1(1); (M, NB, PEI) s. 1; (NL, NS) s. 2; S s. 2(1).

13   See P. Van Warmelo, *An Introduction to the Principles of Roman Civil Law* (Cape Town: Juta, 1976) at 116–19.

charge).[14] In traditional legal terms, a PPSA security interest has most of the characteristic of an interest arising under a hypothecation agreement.[15] A security interest does not involve any dealing with the title to or ownership of the collateral.[16] The rights of the secured party are not those of an owner or title-holder; their only role is to provide an alternative source of compensation should the debtor fail to perform her obligations to the secured party. Under the common law, when the debt secured by a mortgage is discharged, the ownership of the mortgagee has to be re-transferred to the debtor. Where a hypothecation is involved, the charge (security interest) on the debtor's property, being accessory only, simply disappears; there is nothing to re-transfer to the debtor.[17]

The conceptualization of a security interest as being in the nature of a hypothec, while useful in the context of situations where an interest not governed by the PPSA is in competition with a security interest, is not important where the competing interests are all governed by the PPSA priority rules. This is so since the PPSA, unlike prior law, does not adopt the principle of *nemo dat quod non habet* (no one can give that which he does not have) as the basis for its priority structure. This being the case, it is not necessary or relevant to quantify the debtor's interest in the collateral; although it is relevant, for the purpose of attachment that the debtor have some property rights in the collateral.

3) Transactions outside the Hypothec Concept

Despite conceptualization of the security interest as a hypothec, the Act contains a list of transactions that must be treated as creating security interests without regard to their form.[18] Included in the list are

---

14   See generally E.I. Sykes and S. Walker, *The Law of Securities*, 5th ed. (Sydney: The Law Book Company Limited, 1993) at 193–99.

15   However, the enforcement rights of a secured party under the PPSA do not parallel those of a creditor under a Roman Law hypothec or an equitable charge.

16   The Act states that no regards is to be paid to the person who has title when determining whether a transaction creates a security interest. PPSA (A, M, NB, PEI, S) s. 3(1); (BC, NWT, Nu) s. 2(1); (NL, NS) s. 4(1); (O) s. 2(a); (Y) s. 2.

17   While the conceptualization of a security interest as an interest arising out of hypothecation is useful in some contexts, that usefulness is limited. Whatever analogies can be drawn with financing devices of non-PPSA law, ultimately it is necessary to recognize that the features of a security interest must be gleaned from the various incidents given it by the provisions of the PPSA.

18   See, PPSA (A, M, NB, PEI, S) s. 3(1); (BC, NWT, Nu) s. 2(1); (NL, NS) s. 4(1); O s. 2(a); Y s. 2.

chattel mortgages, floating charges,[19] pledges, trust indentures and trust receipts,[20] assignments, consignments, leases, trusts, or transfers of chattel paper.[21] However, this section does not have a role in defining the essential nature of a security interest. Its purpose is to bring within the regime of the Act traditional types of secured financing devices[22] and other devices that function as security devices. This is made clear by the opening words of the section: "without limiting the generality of clause (a)." The policy basis for this aspect of the Act is examined below.

The conceptualization set out above raises the question as to whether a transfer of possession of the collateral by the debtor to the secured party results in a qualitatively different type of security interest than one that does not arise in this way. To put the issue in more direct terms: does a pledge remain a separately identifiable type of security agreement under the PPSA? There is nothing in the Act to suggest that a security interest arising under a transaction that, under prior law, would be a pledge is any different than a security interest arising under any other type of security agreement. Indeed, it is possible to go one step further in the analysis and to conclude that, along with the conditional sales, chattel mortgages, and other types of traditional financing devices, the concept of pledge as a *sui generis* type of secured transactions has disappeared under the Act. What has taken its place is a security agreement that explicitly or implicitly provides for perfection of the security interest through transfer of possession of the collateral to

---

19 The floating charge is essentially hypothecatory in nature. However, because of the limitations of the equitable charge, a floating charge agreement generally gives to the chargee powers that are consistent with those of a mortgagee.

20 At common law, a trust receipt is an arrangement associated with a pledge. A pledgee who releases goods to the pledgor for a special purpose such as sale or processing can take a trust receipt from the pledgor under which the latter acknowledges that the goods and the proceeds are held in trust for the pledgee. In this way the pledge is maintained. See *Re David Allester Ltd.*, [1922] 2 Ch. 211.

21 The OPPSA s. 2(a) includes "equipment trust" and "debenture" in the list. The reference to "equipment trust " was likely copied from the United States *Uniform Commercial Code* because the equipment trust was not a type of transaction in common use in Canada prior to enactment of the Ontario Act. The reference to "debenture" must be read in context since, technically, the term refers to a corporate debt obligation. There is no requirement the obligation be secured. However, it can be assumed that, in this context, the term refers to a corporate obligations secured by some form of security agreement in personal property.

22 The OPPSA s. 2(a) does not include a security trust in the list of transactions deemed to create a security interest. However, this is not significant since the list is not exhaustive.

the secured party.[23] Essentially, the transaction is nothing more than a generic security agreement; the possession by the secured party merely provides one of the two methods of proof of the existence of the security interest where a competition with third party interests is involved and is one of the various methods of perfection available to the secured party.[24] The secured party can release the collateral to the debtor without in any way affecting the nature of its interest. Its failure to obtain a written security agreement from the debtor and register a financing statement relating to the security interest affects only the enforceability and priority of the security interest against third parties without in any way affecting the nature of its interest. Further, if the secured party initially chooses perfection by possession but changes its mind and later perfects by registration before releasing possession of the collateral to the debtor, the security interest is treated as having been continuously perfected. By contrast, at common law the change from a pledge to a chattel mortgage resulted in the creation of an entirely different kind of security interest.[25]

---

23   In *Re M.C. United Masonry Limited* (1983), 2 P.P.S.A.C. 237 (Ont. C.A.) the court concluded that a security interest in shares came into existence as soon as a security agreement was executed and the agreement and the shares were delivered to the secured party. However, it is clear that the court viewed the delivery of the shares (along with the agreement) to the secured party as evidence of the intention of the parties that a security interest would be created rather than as a prerequisite to the creation of a security interest in the form of a pledge. The Court treated possession as a method of perfection and not the central factor in the creation of the security interest.

24   In *Tureck v. Hanston Investments Ltd.* (1987), 30 D.L.R. (4th) 690 (Ont. H.C.J.) the secured party sought "foreclosure" of his security interest in shares and perpetuation of the debt secured. His claim for relief was grounded on the argument that he held an equitable mortgage on the shares. It was argued in reply, and accepted by the court, that the security agreement provided for a pledge of the shares, and that foreclosure was not available as a remedy in such circumstances. The conclusion of the court with respect to the characterization of the transaction as a pledge was superfluous to the judgment since it correctly ruled that the transaction was governed by the Ontario Act which provides for non-judicial foreclosure.

25   All Acts permit perfection of security interests in all types of collateral by registration. The change from possession to registration may in some situations affect the "quality" of perfection that the security interest has. PPSA (A, BC, M, NB, PEI, NWT, Nu, S) s. 31; (NL, NS) s. 32(1); Y s. 30(1). See also O s. 28(6)–(8). However, this has nothing to do with the nature of the security interest, but is a product of the public policy decision to facilitate the free transferability of certain types of property interests.

B. THE NON-TRADITIONAL TRANSACTIONS: CONDITIONAL SALES CONTRACTS, LEASES, CONSIGNMENTS, AND TRUSTS

1) Introduction

The Act[26] applies to a conditional sale, a security lease, a security consignment,[27] and a security trust.[28] It is in the context of these transactions that the hypothec characterization described becomes inapposite. It is not possible, as it is for example in the context of a chattel mortgage, to simply re-characterize the transfer of a title to the secured party as the recognition of a statutory charge. At common law a conditional buyer, lessee, or consignee cannot be treated as charging her interest in the property being purchased or the goods being leased or consigned. No such interest exists other than the limited property interest incidental to possession of tangible property.

The drafters of the Act apparently proceeded on the assumption that a conditional sales contract is a transaction that conceptually approximates a traditional security agreement. This assumption was very likely induced by a strong line of authority in pre-PPSA Canadian cases supporting the position that an equitable interest (or implied statutory interest of some kind) commensurate with the value of the payments made by a conditional buyer passes to the buyer. However, these cases involved application of provincial Conditional Sales Acts that gave a "redemption" right to the conditional buyers.[29] This approach cannot be used to bring conditional sales contracts into the hypothecation concept of security interest set out above. A security interest comes into existence (that is, attaches) as soon as the debtor "has rights in

---

26   PPSA (A, M, NB, PEI, S) s. 3(1); (BC, NWT, Nu) s. 2(1); (NL, NS) s. 4(1); O s. 2(a); Y s. 2.

27   The terms "security lease" and "security consignment" are not used in the Act. They are used in this book to identify leases and consignments that are functionally security agreements. These should not be confused with "leases for a term of more than one year" and "commercial consignments" that are deemed security agreements for limited purposes by all Acts other than the OPPSA.

28   The term "security trust" is not used in the Act. It is used in this book to label trusts that are functionally security agreements. The OPPSA s. 2(a) refers to an equipment trust, a trust indenture and a trust receipt, but not a simple trust. The interface between the PPSA and trust law is addressed later this chapter.

29   See, for example, *C.C. Motor Sales Ltd. v. Chan*, [1926] S.C.R. 485 at 491, Newcombe J.; *Commercial Credit Corp. v. Niagara Finance Corp.*, [1940] S.C.R. 420.

the collateral."[30] However, it would be bootstrapping in the extreme to conclude that a buyer gets rights in the collateral because he is given a right of redemption under Part 5 of the PPSA. Under the PPSA, a security interest comes into existence as soon as the conditional sales contract for specific goods is executed. At that date, the buyer may have paid nothing and, consequently, would have nothing to redeem. In any event, even though a conditional buyer is seen as acquiring a property right in the goods commensurate with the amount paid, it is not this interest that is charged by the seller's interest.

A traditional conditional sales agreement provides that the seller "reserves" title and ownership under the conditions of the contract have been performed by the buyer. However, there is no basis for the conclusion that, under the PPSA, the nature or quantum of the security interest involved is any different from that which the seller would have if he had "taken" a security interest in the property sold after transferring title to the buyer.[31] Nor is there warrant for the conclusion that the conceptual mechanics for the creation of an interest by reservation are any different from those involved where the security interest is granted in property owned by the buyer. In other words, reservation does not involve the retention of a security interest and the transfer of the "balance" of the proprietary interest in the collateral to the debtor. If, as is noted above, a security interest is in the nature of a hypothec on the ownership rights of the debtor in the collateral, there is nothing for the secured party to "reserve" or retain; the security interest in the debtor's interest in the collateral attaches once the prerequisites to its existence have been fulfilled. Under the hypothecation characterization of a security agreement, the buyer acquires rights in the collateral as soon as the contract of sale is entered into.[32]

---

30   See PPSA (A, BC, M, NB, NWT, Nu, PEI, S) s. 12; (NL, NS) s. 13; (O, Y) s. 11.
31   See *National Trailer Convoy of Canada Ltd. v. Bank of Montreal* (1980), 1 P.P.S.A.C. 87 (Ont. H.C.J.); *Joseph Group of Companies Inc. v. Pickles Tents and Awnings Ltd.* (1981), 2 P.P.S.A.C. 1 (Man. C.A.); *Banque Nationale de Paris (Canada) v. Pine Tree Mercury Sales Ltd.* (1983), 42 O.R. (2d) 303 (Co. Ct.); *Haibeck v. No. 40 Taurus Ventures Ltd.* (1991), 2 P.P.S.A.C. (2d) 171 (B.C.S.C.).
        The differences between a security agreement that provides for the retention of title to the collateral and one in which the security interest is created by a transfer of title remain important where the security interest is in competition with an interest arising outside the Act. See chapter 14, A.7.a, "A Single International Registry."
32   This was recognized by the drafters of the *Uniform Commercial Code*. They provided for statutory recharacterization of conditional sales contracts and security leases. See UCC 1-203 which provides that "The retention or reservation of title by a seller or goods notwithstanding shipment or delivery to the buyer (§ 1-201(35)) is limited in effect to a reservation of a 'security interest.'"

Even if it were possible to shoehorn conditional sales contracts into the hypothecation concept of security interest through identification of some type of property interest in the buyer recognized at common law or equity, this would not be enough. No similar approach is possible in the context of security leases or security consignments since there is no basis in non-PPSA law for the conclusion that a lessee or consignee acquires any interest in leased or consigned personal property other than possession.

It is the view of the authors that the explanation for the inclusion of conditional sales contracts,[33] security leases, security consignments, and security trusts within the scope of the PPSA cannot be found in a conceptualization of these transactions as being in the nature of a hypothecation. A brief examination of the history of the pre-2000 versions of Article 9 of the *Uniform Commercial Code*, the conceptual and structural model for the PPSA, reveals why this is so. The goal of the drafter of Article 9 was to merge separate streams of personal property security law into a single system. In this respect, the goal was principally a pragmatic one; conceptualization, at least in traditional terms, was not important — indeed, it was to be avoided. Conceptualization of these transactions under prior law was the basis for determining priority rules and enforcement rights. Since Article 9 and the PPSA contain their own integrated priority and enforcement rules, it was important to avoid importation of prior law into the new system.

What was common to the forms of transactions that were the focus of the attention of the drafter was that they all had essentially the same function: to provide or recognize through contract that a person to whom an obligation was owed has an interest in personal property that would permit that person to look to the property as a source of compensation should the obligation not be performed. The effect of the transaction, not its form or the way in which the interest arose, was to be determinative.[34] This approach was carried over to the PPSA. Conditional sales contracts, security leases and security consignments and security trusts are included within the PPSA because functionally they are security agreements.[35]

---

33   A battle between characterization based on function and characterization based on legal doctrine occurred in the British courts in the context of title retention sales contracts. See *Armour v. Thyssen Edelstahlwerk AG,* [1991] 2 A.C. 339. For a good analysis of the recent cases, see I. Davies, *Textbook on Commercial Law* (London: Blackstone Press, 1992) at 259–70.

34   See, W.L. Tabac, "The Unbearable Lightness of Title under the *Uniform Commercial Code*" (1991) 50 Md. L. Rev. 408 at 409.

35   For a robust academic criticism of this approach, see M.G. Bridge, R.A. Macdonald, R.L. Simmons, and C. Walsh, "Formalism, Functionalism and Understanding the Law of Secured Transactions" (1999), 44 McGill L.J. 567.

These transactions are treated for the purposes of the PPSA as creating security interests even though they may not be so conceptualized under non-PPSA law.[36]

2) Security Leases

a) The Relevance of Characterization of Leases

The issue of characterization of leases arises under all Acts.[37] Under the Ontario Act, characterization of a lease as a bailment (true lease) or a security agreement (security lease) is required in order to determine whether the Act applies to it. If a transaction is found to be a security lease, it is subject to all provisions of the Ontario Act, including those dealing with perfection and priority,[38] in the same way as any other security agreement. However, if the transaction is characterized as a bailment, it is not within the scope of the Act. The relationship between the parties and the priority rights of the lessor are determined under the principles of the common law.[39] In all other PPSA jurisdictions, characterization of leases is relevant principally in the context of the *inter partes* rights of lessors and lessees.[40] The reason for this is that

---

36   As to the influence of PPSA conceptualization of these transactions outside the PPSA, see the discussion in chapter 10, B.2.c, "Other Legislative and Common Law Priority Rules."

37   Generally, Canadian courts have accepted the principle that characterization of a transaction is a matter for the *lex fori*. See *Gimli Auto Ltd. v. BDO Dunwoody Ltd.* (1998), 160 D.L.R. (4th) 373 (Alta. C.A.); *Juckes (Trustee of) v. Holiday Chevrolet Oldsmobile (1988) Ltd.* (1990), 82 Sask. R. 303 (Q.B.). However, in *GMAC Commercial Credit Corp. Canada v. TCT Logistics Inc.* (2004), 238 D.L.R. (4th) 487, 6 P.P.S.A.C. (3d) 163, 45 B.L.R. (3d) 68, 70 O.R. (3d) 321 the Ontario Court of Appeal refused to characterize a transaction (lease) under the Ontario PPSA when it was applying s. 7 of that Act that specifies the applicable law. The Court concluded that the transaction should be characterized under the law made applicable by s. 7 of the Ontario Act. The conclusion in *Re Intex Moulding Ltd.* (1987), 38 D.L.R. (4th) 111 (Ont. H.C.J.) that characterization of a lease as a security agreement or bailment is a matter for the proper law of the contract should not be followed.

38   The great bulk of cases coming before the Ontario courts involving characterization of leases deal with the issue as to whether a registration relating to the transaction is required under the Act.

39   This "all or nothing" approach applies in some other jurisdictions to legislation, other than the PPSA, that contains provisions affecting "security agreements" or "security interests." See, for example, *The Exemptions Act*, R.S.S. 1978, c. E-14, ss. 1.1 and 5(2); *The Executions Act*, R.S.S. 1978, c. E-12, ss. 2 and 2.2. See also *Law of Property Act*, R.S.A. 2000, ss. 51–53.

40   See, for example, *R. Clancy Heavy Equipment Sales Ltd. v. Joe Gourley Construction Ltd.*, [2001] 1 W.W.R. 681 (Alta. Q.B.).

all features of these Acts, other than post-default enforcement (Part 5), apply to true leases having a term of more than one year.[41] For all practical purposes,[42] it is only when a lessee or a third-party claims rights under Part 5 that the issue arises. If the transaction is a security lease, the lessor is a secured party who is required to comply with the regulatory scheme applicable to enforcement of security interests. If it is a true lease, the lessor is in law the owner of the leased property and the lessee has only the common law rights of a defaulting lessee.

b) The Nature of the Task

There are no explicit rules or guidelines in the PPSA that can be applied when determining whether a particular transaction is a true lease or a security lease. While the courts have developed a substantial body of case law that identifies the range of factors involved, there are no formulae that can be used in the characterization process. It is often the case that in a single transaction, some of the factors point to a security lease while others point to a true lease. The task was accurately described through mixed metaphors by Justice Farley of the Ontario Supreme Court:

> Unfortunately there are no tags or labels which may be read with ease and "certainty" ("certainty" in the same way that a laboratory is able to conduct a DNA test and give probabilities or odds). Rather the task involves a weighing of the various material matters involved. It is not a simple analysis of determining between black and white but rather the shade of grey where all factors are weighed in the balance as to whether the scales tip towards a true lease relationship — or alternatively against being a true lease relationship."[43]

The difficulties involved are amplified when the court fails to understand the operational concepts and policies of the PPSA or overlooks the express wording of the Act.[44]

---

41 PPSA (A, M, NB, PEI, S) s. 3(2); (NL, NS) s. 4(2); (NWT, Nu) s. 2(2); (O, Y) s. 2(b); BC s. 3.

42 It is theoretically possible, but practically very rare, to encounter a lease for a term of one year or less that is a security lease.

43 *Re Philip Services Corp.* (1999), 15 C.B.R. (4th) 107 at 109. The case did not involve characterization for the purposes of the PPSA. The issue before the court was whether a transaction in the form of a lease was lease within the meaning of s. 11.3(a) of the *Companies' Creditors Arrangement Act*. The court applies the same approach as is used in the decisions involving scope of the PPSA.

44 See, for example, *Centennial Plymouth Chrysler (1973) Ltd. v. Conlin* (2000), 15 P.P.S.A.C. (2d) 206 (Ont. S.C.J.) in which the court mistakenly concluded that

c)   A "Substance" or "Function" Test

The PPSA prescribes a "substance test" for determining whether a particular transaction is a security agreement.[45] This is also referred to as a "function test." Both call for an answer to the question: what was the imputed goal or intention of the parties[46] to the transaction as determined by the circumstances surrounding its creation and the effect its terms could reasonably be expected to produce? By answering this question, the function or substance of the transaction is identified.

One approach to characterization of a lease as security lease or true lease is to inquire as to whether the transaction has the characteristics more consistent with a sale than a bailment. In other words, the inquiry focuses on whether the lessor has the rights of a bailor or all or most of the rights of a seller or sales financer and the lessee has the rights and obligations of bailee or those of a buyer of the property. These rights and obligations, however, are not necessarily the ones that the common law ascribes to these types of transactions. The PPSA[47] precludes characterization of transactions on the basis of the form of the transaction or the locus of title to the collateral — the factors that would be primary indicia under the common law. It is generally accepted by the courts that the focus is on the economic rights and obligations of the parties to the transaction.[48]

In *Adelaide Corp. v. Integrated Transportation Finance Inc.*,[49] Blair J. of the Ontario Supreme Court employed a different approach. He concluded that the central issue is not whether the transaction is a true lease, on the one hand, or a conditional sales contract or, for that matter, a security lease on the other; it is whether or not the lease, as a lease, has as well the characteristics of a transaction securing payment or performance of an obligation. This approach does not involve a search for characteristics that point to a seller-buyer or sales financer-buyer rela-

---

the policy basis for expanded scope of the Ontario PPSA was consumer protection. Several courts have relied on retention of title by the lessor as evidence of a true lease. See, for example, *Kodak Canada Ltd. v. Jesi Estates Inc.* (1990), 1 P.P.S.A.C. (2d) 154 (Ont. Ct. Gen. Div.). This ignores the clear statement in the Act that title is not relevant to the determination.

45   Above note 5.

46   While some of the case law refers to the "intention of the parties" as a factor, it is clear that this is the objective or imputed intention of the parties.

47   Above note 5.

48   See generally R.C.C. Cuming, "True Leases and Security Leases under Canadian *Personal Property Security Acts*" (1982–83) 7 Can. Bus. L.J. 251. This approach is reflected in professional accounting rules, (see *Handbook of the Canadian Institute of Chartered Accountants*, § 3065). See also Tax Interpretation Bulletin IT-233R, Lease-option agreements; Sale-leaseback agreements dated 11 February 1983.

49   (1994), 111 D.L.R. (4th) 493 (Ont. Gen. Div.).

tionship; it involves a search for the principal function of the lease. If its function is to secure payment or performance of an obligation, it may be a lease, but it is also a transaction to which the PPSA applies.

However, in the recent decision of the Ontario Court of Appeal in *GMAC Commercial Credit Corp. Canada v. TCT Logistics Inc.*[50] the court rejected the suggestion that the approach taken in the *Adelaide* case results in the creation of a separate category of transaction — a true lease that secures payment or performance of an obligation. It concluded that a lease has as well the characteristic of securing payment or performance of an obligation is a "financing lease," that is, a security agreement within the scope of the Ontario Act.

It is the view of the authors that it is both useful and realistic to employ an analogy to secured sales transactions when determining whether a lease is a security agreement falling with the PPSA. It is useful in that the sales analogy provides guidance as to what factors (other than transfer of ownership) point to the existence of a security agreement. It is realistic since transactions labelled as leases are very often used as sales financing devices.[51]

d) Factors Pointing to a Security Lease

It would be naive to assert that a totally consistent approach has been employed by courts when applying the substance test of the PPSA to the characterization of leases. With very few exceptions,[52] courts have generally been reluctant to give broad scope to the substance test in this context.[53] However, it is possible to identify a range of factors that have been accepted as indicia of security leases. As noted above, these factors are ones that are significant from an economic perspective and not a traditional legal perspective. They focus principally on the economic interests of the parties to the transaction rather than on the locus of title or the label the parties use. If the effect of the transaction

---

50   Above note 37.

51   The reason for using this form of agreement may not be to avoid regulation under the PPSA. For example, a transaction in the form of a lease may be used in order to attract taxation outcomes more favourable to one or both of the parties than would prevail if the transaction were in the form of a secured sales agreement. See, for example, *Gatx Corporate Leasing Ltd. v. William Day Construction Ltd.* (1986), 60 C.B.R. (N.S.) 319 (Ont. H.C.J.).

52   See *Adelaide Corp. v. Integrated Transportation Finance Inc.*, above note 49.

53   However, this is not so in the context of application of the substance test to determine whether a lease is a true lease under s. 11.3(a) of the *Companies' Creditors Arrangement Act.* See *Re Smith Brothers Contracting Ltd.* (1998), 13 P.P.S.A.C. (2d) 316 (B.C.S.C.); *Re Philip Services Corp.*, above note 43.

is to give to the lessee economic rights substantially equivalent to those of a buyer or owner of the property, a security lease is indicated.

The following factors are indicative of transactions that in substance are security agreements. Not every aspect of the substance test described in the following paragraphs has been applied or recognized in existing case law. However, it is the view of the authors that those factors for which authority cannot be cited can be safely extrapolated from the test. The authors have not listed all the cases dealing with this issue. Prominent decisions and examples of decisions that reflect accurate application of the substance test have been cited.

i)   Automatic Vesting of Ownership or Obligation to Purchase
If the lease provides that ownership of the leased property automatically vests in the lessee upon expiry of the term or upon payment of a specified amount, or the lessee is contractually obligated to buy the property, the transaction is a security lease. This is the case under both the PPSA and the common law.[54] If the lessee is obligated to purchase the leased property at the end of the term, the transaction is treated from its inception as a secured sale.[55]

ii)   The Lease Term and the Commercially Useful Life of the Goods
In economic terms, an owner of goods has the right of use and possession of the leased property for all of its commercially useful life. Accordingly, a lease term (or terms[56]) for substantially all of the commercially useful life[57] of the leased property points to the existence of a security lease.[58]

iii)   Lessee's Payment Obligation
If the lessee is obligated to pay an amount that is equivalent to or greater than the capital cost of the leased property and an amount equivalent to the cost of the money invested in the property, there is evidence that the lessee has acquired the economic equivalent of ownership of

---

54   See *Lee v. Butler* (1893), 2 Q.B. 318 (C.A.); *Helby v. Mathews*, [1895] A.C. 471 (H.L.).

55   See *Federal Business Development Bank v. Bramalea Ltd.* (1983), 144 D.L.R. (3d) 410 (Ont. H.C.J.), aff'd 150 D.L.R. (3d) 768 (Ont. C.A.).

56   If the lease is automatically renewed or the lessee is obligated to renew the lease, the result is the same.

57   In this context, commercially useful life means the period during which the goods have market value other than as scrap or as parts.

58   This right is almost always accompanied by an obligation to pay at least the equivalent of the lessor's capital investment and an amount attributable to the cost of use of the funds invested.

the leased goods.[59] However, this factor alone should not be conclusive. If it is accompanied by the right to possession of the goods for all or substantially all of their useful life, it is conclusive. The only thing the lessee does not get under the transaction is legal title, something that is irrelevant under the substance test of the PPSA.

Some leases provide that the rental payments will be "credited against" the amount payable by the lessee to exercise a purchase option in the contract. This feature alone is not indicative of a security lease. What is important is the relation of the "new money" the lessee must pay to exercise the option to the value of the goods at the time the option is exercised. If the amount of the new money is equivalent to the approximate market value of the goods, the credit amount is of no significance.[60]

If the payments to be made by the lessee apply as well to other obligations without clear delineation as to the amount that is to be allocated to rights acquired in the leased goods, there is evidence that the lessee is acquiring the goods, not just leasing them at a specified lease rate.[61]

iv) *The Price of an Option to Purchase or Renew (Accumulated Equity)*
Where the lease has a term of less than the full useful life of the property and contains a provision giving the lessee an option to purchase the leased property, or to renew the term of the lease for the balance of its useful life, the amount that must be paid to exercise the option is a strong indicator of the nature of the transaction. By itself, the fact that an option exists is of no significance. Furthermore, if the amount payable under the option appears to have been arbitrarily chosen, it should not be considered as a relevant factor.[62] What is important is whether the option price indicates that the lessee has acquired an "equity" in the goods through the lease payments that have been made prior to the date the option can be exercised.

---

59   See, for example, *Standard Finance Corp. v. Coopers & Lybrand Ltd.*, [1984] 4
     W.W.R. 543 (Man. Q.B.); *Re Econo Transport Inc.* (1982), 43 C.B.R. (N.S.) 230
     (Ont. S.C. Master); *Leaseway Autos Ltd. v. Sinco Sportswear Ltd.* (1986), 45 Sask.
     R. 254 (Q.B); *Canadian Western Bank v. Baker* (1999), 15 P.P.S.A.C. (2d) 247
     (Sask. Q.B.), aff'd 2000 SKCA 108; *Case Credit Ltd. v. Poirer* (1999), 186 Sask. R.
     153 (Q.B.).
60   See, for example, *Continental Bank v. Sheridan Equipment Ltd.* (1986), 60 C.B.R.
     (N.S.) 14 (Ont. H.C.J.).
61   See *Re Philip Services Corp.*, above note 43 (characterization for the purposes of
     the *Companies' Creditors Arrangement Act*, R.S.C. 1985, c. C-36, s. 11.3(a)).
62   See, for example, *Standard Finance Corp. v. Coopers & Lybrand Ltd.*, above note 59.

If the option provides for payment of an amount that is significantly below the market sale price of the property,[63] or, in the case of renewal, significantly below market rental rate for the property, it is most likely that the lessor has recovered the difference between the option price and the market price through payments made prior to the date the option can be exercised. Consequently, the lessee has acquired an equity in the goods to the extent of this difference. Under these circumstances, it is predictable at the date when the agreement is executed that the lessee will exercise the option because the lessee can acquire ownership of the goods or extended right to possession of the goods under the lease renewal at less than their market value.[64] In order to avoid distortions resulting from unexpected depreciation or appreciation in the value of the goods, the market value, for the purpose of this test, is the value estimated at the date the contract was entered into.

If no specific option price is set out in the agreement but is left to be determined on the basis of objective factors at the date the option is exercised, the transaction is not likely to be viewed as a security agreement unless it is an open-end lease (discussed later in this chapter).

The fact that the option price equals the fair market value of the goods does not necessarily point to a true lease. If the option is exercisable only after the expiry of a term that approximates the useful life of the goods, or if, in any event, the lessee is obligated to pay the equivalent of the capital cost of the equipment and a credit charge, the amount required to exercise the option is not relevant.[65]

v) Open-end Leases
An open-end lease is one having a term considerably less than the useful life of the leased property. The lessee does not have an exclusive

---

63   In the earlier cases, this was misleadingly referred to as a "nominal amount." See, for example, *Re Ontario Equipment (1976) Ltd.* (1981), 125 D.L.R. (3d) 321 (Ont. H.C.J.), aff'd (1983), 141 D.L.R. (3d) 766n (Ont. C.A.).

64   A small accumulation of equity through lease payments is not determinative unless there are other factors that point to the existence of a security lease. See *Continental Bank of Canada v. Sheridan Equipment Ltd.*, above note 60; *R. Clancy Heavy Equipment Sales Ltd. v. Joe Gourley Construction Ltd.*, above note 40. However, see *Finchside International Ltd. v. Roy Foss Motors Ltd.* (1994), 29 C.B.R. (3d) 108 (Ont. Ct. Gen. Div.) in which the court first concluded that the option price was well below the estimated market value but then concluded that a true lease was involved.

65   See *Canadian Western Bank v. Baker*, above note 59; *Re Bronson* (1996), 39 C.B.R. (3d) 33 (B.C.S.C.); *Re Smith Brothers Contracting Ltd.*, above note 53 (characterization for the purposes of the *Companies' Creditors Arrangement Act*, above note 61, s. 11.3(a)).

option to purchase the goods, but may have a right of first refusal to purchase them at fair market value at the end of the lease term. What distinguishes this type of lease are the following features: (1) at the end of the term, the goods must be offered for sale in the market by the lessor (although the lessee may be given the right to buy them at their appraised value); (2) the lessee is obligated to pay to the lessor the difference between the amount recovered from the sale and a pre-determined amount set out in the lease contract; and (3) if the amount recovered by the lessor on resale exceeds this amount, the surplus is paid to the lessee.

While this type of transaction does not have the usual indicia of a security lease, an economic analysis of its effect reveals that it is a financing transaction and not a true lease.[66] An incident of ownership of property is gain from appreciation or loss from depreciation in the value of the goods. An open-end lease has the effect of guaranteeing the lessor recovery of its capital investment and a credit charge. Any unusual depreciation (or appreciation) of the goods accrues to the lessee.

vi) The Role of the Parties

The role of the lessor may be an indicator of the nature of the transaction. For example, where a financial lease is involved, the lessor's role is generally not that of a typical lessor holding an inventory of goods for lease to the public. In a tri-partite financial leasing arrangement, the leased equipment and its supplier are chosen by the lessee. The lessor steps into the picture by buying the property from the supplier and "leasing" it to the lessee. Since the role of the lessor is essentially that of a financer, it will usually ensure through the terms of the lease full recovery of the costs of the property and a charge for use of its capital. If the lessee is obligated to pay these amounts, a security lease is involved.[67] However, not all financial leasing transactions are in this

---

66   See *Crop & Soil Service Inc. v. Oxford Leaseway Ltd.* (2000), 186 D.L.R. (4th) 85 (Ont. C.A.); *Re Cronin Fire Equipment Ltd.* (1993), 21 C.B.R. (3d) 127 (Ont. Ct. Gen. Div.); *HOJ Franchise Systems Inc. v. Municipal Savings & Loan Corp.* (1994), 6 P.P.S.A.C. (2d) 302 (Ont. Ct. Gen. Div.). Compare *MTC Leasing Inc. v. National Bank*, [1997] 9 W.W.R. 228 (Man. Q.B.), aff'd [1999] 6 W.W.R. 587 (Man. C.A.). It is the view of the authors that the Manitoba courts failed to apply an economic analysis in this case with the result that the decision should not be viewed as authoritative or persuasive outside Manitoba.

67   See, for example, *Standard Finance Corp. v. Coopers & Lybrand Ltd.*, above note 59; *Adelaide Capital Corp. v. Integrated Transportation Finance,* above note 49. Compare *MTC Leasing Inc. v. National Bank, ibid.* For the authors' assessment of the decision in this case, see above note 66.

form. In some cases, the lessor is prepared to take the risk of recovering the balance of its investment through a sale of the leased property after it has been returned at the end of a term that is less than the full useful life of the property.

Provisions in a lease requiring the lessee to insure the goods, bear the risk of loss or damage, and keep them in good repair are of little value in the characterization process. These provisions are often found in both true leases and security leases.[68]

vii) Contractual Remedies

Lease provisions that give the lessor default remedies characteristic of a financing transaction and inconsistent with a lease point to the existence of a security lease. An instalment financing transaction will almost always provide for acceleration of the total amount payable under the transaction in the event of default by debtor. This reflects the existence of an obligation of the debtor to pay a defined amount of principal and interest to the financer. Under common law rules of contract a lessor is entitled to damages for breach of contract that may vary depending upon the circumstances of the breach.[69]

3) Security Consignments

a) The Relevance of Characterization of Consignments

The issue of characterization of consignment agreements arises under all Acts. Under the Ontario Act, characterization of a transaction labelled a consignment as a security agreement (security consignment) or some other type of agreement is required in order to determine whether or not the Act applies to it.[70] If a transaction is found to be a security consignment, it is subject to all of the provisions of the Act, including those dealing with perfection and priority, in the same way as any other security agreement. However, if the transaction is found not to have the characteristics of a security agreement, it is not within the scope of the Act. The relationship between the parties and the priority rights of the lessor are determined under the principles of the common law. In all other PPSA jurisdictions, it is necessary to recognize three types of consignments. As is the case under the Ontario Act, a security consign-

---

68 See, for example, *Continental Bank of Canada v. Sheridan Equipment Ltd.*, above note 60.

69 See *Re Philip Services Corp.* above note 43; *Re Bronson,* above note 65; *Standard Finance Corp. v. Coopers & Lybrand Ltd.*, above note 59.

70 OPPSA s. 2(ii).

ment is a security agreement and, as such, is subject to all of the provisions of the Act. Where a "commercial consignment"[71] is involved, all features of the Act, other than post-default enforcement (Part 5), apply. If the consignment is neither a security consignment nor a commercial consignment, no aspect of the transaction is governed by the PPSA.

In the following paragraphs, the approach used by the courts for determining whether a transaction labelled a consignment is a security consignment is discussed. The scope and relevance of "commercial consignments" under the Act other than the Ontario Act are examined later in this chapter.

b) The Nature of the Task

Prior to the enactment of the PPSA, Canadian courts generally were vigilant in identifying attempts to use the façade of consignments to protect sellers against the claims of creditors of their buyers. An aspect of this approach is the rule that in cases where a supplier claims goods in the hands of a trustee in bankruptcy on the basis that the goods were consigned to the debtor prior to the bankruptcy, the onus of proving that the supply contract was a true consignment and not a secured contract of sale rests with the supplier.[72] This rule of evidence was confirmed by the Ontario Court of Appeal in the context of a case involving the Ontario Act.[73]

The PPSA does not provide a test for distinguishing consignments that are security agreements from non-security or true consignments. Consequently, the principles of the common law to the extent that they focus on the substance of the transaction in question are to be applied

---

71 PPSA (A, BC, NWT, Nu, Y) s. 1(1); (MB, NB, PEI) s. 1; (NL, NS) s. 2; S s. 2(1).
72 See, for example, *Re Askin* (1960), 1 C.B.R. (N.S.) 153 (Ont. H.C.J.); *Re Granite Jewellery Ltd.* (1965), 7 C.B.R. (N.S.) 215 (Ont. H.C.J.); *Bank of Montreal v. Colossal Carpets Ltd.* (1977), 2 B.L.R. 196 (B.C.S.C).
73 *Seven Limers Coal & Fertilizer Co. Ltd. v. Hewitt* (1985), 52 O.R. (2d) 1 (Ont. C.A.) and *Access Cash International, Inc. v. Elliot Lake and North Shore Corporation for Business Development* (2000), 1 P.P.S.A.C. (3d) 209 (Ont. S.C.J.). No similar approach appears to have been taken where it is alleged that a "lease" is a disguised security agreement. There is nothing in the wording of the applicable scope provisions of the PPSA that would appear to justify having one approach to the onus of proof where consignments are involved and a different approach where leases are involved. However, the difference in approach might be justified on the basis that consignments generally involve inventory while leases generally involve equipment. The assumption on which the special rule for consignments was historically based was that it is objectionable for suppliers of inventory to use consignment arrangements as disguised, unregistered security agreements to protect inventory collateral from the creditors of their customers.

in the determination.[74] The term "consignment" is widely used in business dealings to denote a range of different types of transactions. The difference between a true consignment and a security agreement are easily stated in general terms. In *Access Cash International, Inc. v. Elliot Lake and North Shore Corporation for Business Development*[75] the court listed the features of a true consignment as follows: The merchant is the agent of the supplier. Title in the goods remains in the supplier. Title passes directly from the supplier to the ultimate retail purchaser and does not pass through the merchant. The merchant has no obligation to pay for the goods until they are sold to a third party. The supplier has the right to demand the return of the goods at any time. The merchant has the right to return unsold goods to the supplier. The merchant is required to segregate the supplier's goods from his own. The merchant is required to maintain separate books and records in respect of the supplier's goods. The merchant is required to hold sale proceeds in trust for the supplier. The supplier has the right to stipulate a fixed price or a price floor for the goods. The merchant has the right to inspect the goods and the premises in which they are stored. The goods are shown as an asset in the books and records of the supplier and are not shown as an asset in the books and records of the merchant. The shipping documents refer to the goods as consigned. The supplier maintains insurance on the goods after they are delivered to the merchant. It is apparent from the merchant's dealings with others that the goods belong to the supplier rather than the merchant.

Essentially, a consignment involves the relationship of principal and agent[76] between the transferor and the transferee of

---

74   See generally B. Colburn, "Consignment Sales and the *Personal Property Security Act*" (1981-82) 6 Can. Bus. L.J. 40; P.G. Bevans, "Consignment Transactions and the Personal Property Security Act" in R. Miner, ed., *Current Issues in Canadian Business Law* (Toronto: Carswell, 1986) at 289–316; J. MacFarlane, "Sale of Goods on Consignment" (1936–37) 22 Proceedings of Canadian Bar Association 175.

75   Above note 73.

76   In *Re Toyerama* (1980), 34 C.B.R. (N.S.) 153 (Ont. H.C.J.), Saunders J. stated at 157: "[t]he absence of an agency relationship does not necessarily mean that the agreement is not one of consignment. A consignment contract has been described as one of bailment and where, as here, there is a fixed return to the supplier, the agency relationship is not essential to render it a consignment agreement."

This conclusion may well have been induced by the imprecise way in which the term "consignment" is used in the business community. The term is sometimes used to refer to a sale on approval, sale or return or other types of bailment arrangements under which the bailee may become owner of the bailed goods upon the exercise of an option or the fulfillment of some other condition precedent. Indeed, the facts of the *Toyerama* case can be viewed as supporting the

goods.[77] Under a true consignment, the owner of property delivers possession of goods to another person whose role it is to sell the goods as agent for the owner.[78] While the consignee-agent will have obligations to the consignor-principal under this arrangement, and may well be a trustee of property of the consignor-principal, these obligations are not secured either by the ownership of the consignor-principal in the consigned property or by the beneficial interest he acquires under the trust. Under a security agreement, the debtor is not an agent; he buys and sells on his own account. His implicit obligations are not those of a fiduciary of the transferor, they are those of a buyer of goods. The secured party remains "owner" under a security agreement since in this way he is seeking to secure himself against non-performance of the transferee-debtor's obligations. A consignor remains owner until sale of the consigned goods. The goods are in the hands of the agent with the objective of having them sold by the agent on behalf of the consignor to a third party or, in some cases, to the consignee, as buyer.

Often transactions labelled consignments have some features that indicate a principal-agent relationship and others that point to a secured sales transaction.[79] The role of the court is to determine which group of features predominates. A factor that in some cases further complicates the determination is that the performance of a contract does not match that contemplated by its terms, with the result that the nature of the transaction cannot be determined by reference to the terms of the written contract.[80] To determine the substance of the agreement, the court will look both to the terms of the contract itself and the conduct of the parties in relation to that contract.[81] In case of a conflict between the two, conduct appears to be the more important indicator.

---

conclusion that a bailment for sale transaction was involved. However, the more accurate use of the term is confined to principal-agent arrangements under which the agent is authorized to sell the goods on behalf of his principal.

77   Bailment with an option to purchase the goods, such as a contract for sale or return or delivery on approval, is not a consignment. Nor, without more, is it a security agreement. The bailor is not an agent and the retained ownership of the bailor does not secure an obligation of the bailee.

78   *Langley v. Kahnert* (1905), 36 S.C.R. 397 at 401–2; *Re Stephanian's Persian Carpets Ltd.* (1980), 34 C.B.R. (N.S.) 35 (Ont. H.C.J.).

79   See, for example, *Convoy Supply Canada Ltd. v. Northern Credit Union Ltd.*, (2001) 2 P.P.S.A.C. (3d) 231 (Ont. S.C.J.).

80   See, for example, *Farwest Systems (Receiver of) v. Omron Business Systems Corp.* (1988), 69 C.B.R. (N.S.) 82 (B.C.S.C.).

81   See, for example, *Convoy Supply Canada Ltd. v. Northern Credit Union Ltd.*, above note 79; *Glengarry A.E.T. Inc. (Trustee of) v. Manhattan Electric Cable*

c) The Primary Factor Pointing to a Security Consignment

While there are several indicia of a consignment, there is one that is determinative. A principal-agent relationship does not entail an obligation on the part of the agent to purchase the goods delivered on consignment. The role of the agent-consignee is to sell the goods to a third person on behalf of the principal-consignor. Generally, property in the goods passes from the consignor to the buyer from the consignee. The consignor is a facilitator. Consequently, even though a contract contains other features characteristic of a true consignment, it is a security consignment within the scope of the PPSA if the consignee is under obligation to purchase the goods delivered to her under the contract[82] or to account for a predetermined amount whether or not the goods are sold.[83] The absence of such an obligation precludes characterization of the relationship as that of secured party and debtor.[84] While the presence of a legal obligation to buy the goods excludes the possibility of the transaction being characterized as a consignment, the absence of a contractual provision requiring the payment of a price for the goods does not necessarily establish the existence of a consignment. Such an obligation may be implicit in the arrangement where, for example, the consignee loses the right to return goods after the expiry of a specified period of time.[85]

d) Other Relevant Factors

A consignee has the legal right to return to the consignor any of the consigned goods without obligation.[86] This is a corollary of the lack of an obligation to buy the goods.[87] However, a right to return goods for

---

Corp. (1986), 6 P.P.S.A.C. 112 (Ont. H.C.J.); *Re Rivabo Truck Bodies Ltd.* (1975), 20 C.B.R.(N.S.) 252 (Ont. S.C. Reg.); *In Re Richardson* (1931), 13 C.B.R. 38 (Ont. S.C.).

82 See *Re Bristol Yacht Sales Inc.* (1984), 51 C.B.R. (N.S.) 279 (B.C.S.C.); *Langley v. Kahnert* (1905), above note 78. However, see, *Re Toyerama*, above note 76, in which the court concluded that the transaction was a "consignment" even though the bailee did not have a right to return the bailed goods.

83 *Convoy Supply Canada Ltd. v. Northern Credit Union Ltd.*, above note 79.

84 In *Glengarry A.E.T. Inc. v. Manhattan Electric Cable Corp.*, above note 81, the court concluded that the transaction was a consignment even though a term of the agreement described it as a security agreement.

85 *Re Dupuis Frères Limitée* (1979), 28 C.B.R. (N.S.) 313 (Que. S.C.). In such a case, it may be necessary to make the determination as to whether the transaction was a sale from the beginning or became a sale only when the period of time for return of the goods expired.

86 See *Re Stephanian's Persian Carpets Ltd.*, above note 78.

87 In *Re Toyerama*, above note 76, the court found that there was doubt as to whether or not the bailee had a right to return the goods to the bailor. It concluded, however, that there was no obligation on the part of the bailee to pay for

credit against an obligation to pay for the goods does not provide evidence of a consignment.

As agent, a consignee is obligated to recognize the consignor's right to the proceeds of the disposition of the goods or a specified portion of those proceeds.[88] However, since "trust proceeds" clauses are a common feature of security agreements under which inventory is collateral, such a clause by itself has neutral significance. It will have significance as a characterization factor only when found along with other indicia of a consignment.

There are several factors that, by themselves, are outside a pure principal-agent relationship but which do not necessary preclude the finding of a consignment arrangement if they are accompanied by other factors that indicate a consignment. For example, a consignment may provide that the consignee is free to set the sale price of the goods at any level above that set by the consignor and is entitled to retain as remuneration the difference between the sale price and the set price.[89] A true consignment may provide that the consignee is obligated to bear the risk of loss of or damage to the consigned goods,[90] or has the right to elect to buy the consigned goods and then sell them on his own account.[91]

4) Security Trusts

a) A Trust That Secures Payment or Performance of an Obligation
The PPSA includes in the illustrative list of security agreements a "trust … that secures payment or performance of an obligation."[92] This is in

---

items not sold to others or not taken to the bailee's retail store. In the absence of an obligation to purchase the items remaining in the bailee's warehouse, the lack of a right to return the items would lead to the conclusion that the consignee held the goods under some type of compulsory bailment arrangement. There was, however, no evidence to support this conclusion.

88 See *Bank of Montreal v. Colossal Carpets Ltd.* (1977), 2 B.L.R. 196 (B.C.S.C.); In *Re Richardson*, above note 81.

89 See *Re Stephanian's Persian Carpets Ltd.*, above note 78; *Langley v. Kahnert*, above note 78; *Re Alcock, Ingram & Co.*, [1924] 1 D.L.R. 388 (Ont. S.C.A.D.).

90 See *Re Stephanian's Persian Carpets Ltd.*, ibid.

91 *Ibid.*; *Langley v. Kahnert*, above note 78.

92 PPSA (A, M, NB, PEI, S) s. 3(1); (BC, NWT, Nu) s. 2(1); (NL, NS) s. 4(1); O s. 2(a); Y s. 2. OPPSA s. 2(a) does not include a trust in the list of transactions falling deemed to create a security interest. However, it refers to an equipment trust, a trust indenture and a trust receipt. Since the list of included transactions does not exhaust the types of transactions to which the Act applies, this difference between the OPPSA and the PPSA is not significant. The analysis in this part of the book applies equally to all Acts.

addition to the traditional types of financing transactions mentioned in the list, such as trust indentures,[93] that contain trust elements. While under pre-PPSA law trusts were not considered to be security devices unless they were part of a trust indenture, courts were quite prepared to recognize that they could have this effect.[94] Consequently, even without an express mention of trust in the PPSA, the general substance test of the section would bring within the scope of the Act a trust that secure payment or performance of an obligation.

When determining in a particular situation whether or not a trust falls within the scope of the PPSA, it is necessary to distinguish three different patterns: (1) where the transaction is a trust but not a security agreement; (2) where the arrangement is both a trust and a security agreement; and (3) where a trust and a security agreement are used separately as part of the same transaction.

b) Trust or Security Agreement

Even though a trust gives rise to an obligation on the part of the trustee to pay money or other value to a beneficiary, it is not necessarily a trust within the scope of the PPSA (that is, a security agreement). For a trust to be a security trust, its function must be to secure an obligation, not just embody the obligation as an inherent aspect of the trust relationship.

One test that has been applied by the courts to determine whether a transaction is a trust or security agreement is whether the relationship between the parties is that of creditor and debtor or trustee and beneficiary. Only when a creditor-debtor relationship exists can a security agreement be involved.[95] If, for example, the relationship is one of principal and agent,[96] the obligation owing by the trustee to honour the express or implied terms of the trust is endemic to the relationship[97] and not one

---

93 See D.W.M. Waters, *The Law of Trusts in Canada*, 2d ed. (Toronto: Carswell, 1984) at 449–51.

94 See *Flintoft v. Royal Bank of Canada*, [1964] S.C.R. 631; *Ford Tractor Equipment Sales Co. of Canada Ltd. v. Otto Grundman Implements Ltd. (Trustee of)* (1969), 72 W.W.R. 1 (Man. C.A.). See Donovan W.M. Waters, "Trusts in the Settling of Business, Commerce and Bankruptcy" (1983) 21 Alta. L. Rev. 395 at 418–20.

95 See, for example, *Re Skybridge Holidays Inc.* (1998), 13 P.P.S.A.C. (2d) 387 (B.C.S.C.), aff'd (1999), 11 C.B.R. (4th) 130 (B.C.C.A.); *Gervais (Guardian ad litem of) v. Yewdale* (1993), 6 P.P.S.A.C. (2d) 62 (B.C.S.C.).

96 *Graff v. Bitz (Trustee of)* (1991), 2 P.P.S.A.C. (2d) 262 (Sask. Q.B.).

97 See, for example, *Canadian Pacific Airlines Ltd. v. Canadian Imperial Bank of Commerce* (1987), 42 D.L.R. (4th) 375 (Ont. H.C.J.); *Air Canada v. M. & L. Travel Ltd.* (1993), 108 D.L.R. (4th) 592 (S.C.C.).

created by agreement between the parties.[98] Of course, an agency relationship does not preclude the creation of a security agreement between the parties where an interest is taken in property of the agent to secure a separate obligation owing by the agent to the principal.[99]

While this test can be helpful in some situations, its usefulness is limited. Unless the contract between the parties falls within a recognized category, such as agency, that does not involve a creditor and debtor relationship, this approach may not lead to a relevant conclusion; it may just beg the question. The existence of an equitable debt owing by a trustee to a beneficiary does not lead to the conclusion that a security agreement is involved.

c) Trust and Security Agreement

It is clear from the wording of the PPSA[100] that the drafter contemplated situations in which a trust arrangement created by contract is also a security agreement. The result is that two legal regimes apply to a trust that secures payment or performance of an obligation: equity and the PPSA. Since a trustee and beneficiary can be in a debtor-creditor relationship, the issue to be determined in this context is whether the trust is being used as the vehicle to secure the obligation that is the basis of this relationship or is merely the source of the obligation. Under a security trust either the secured party or the debtor can be the trustee or the beneficiary.

A trust and a security agreement co-exist in the following situations:

Pursuant to an agreement with B, A transfers property to C to be held on the trust condition that, in the event of non-performance of an obligation owing by A to B, the property will be transferred to B or disposed of and the proceeds applied to discharge the obligation owing by A to B. The beneficial interest of B under the trust is a security interest.

Pursuant to an agreement with B, A transfers property to B to be held on the trust condition that, in the event of non-performance of an obligation owing by A to B, B will be entitled to retain the property or may sell it and apply the proceeds to the obligation owing by A to B. B's title as trustee and

---

98 Where the relationship between the principal and agent arises out of a commercial consignment, the beneficial interest of the consignor-principal is a security interest under the PPSA since a commercial consignment is deemed to be a security interest under all Acts other than the OPPSA. See PPSA (A, M, NB, PEI, S) s. 3(2); (NL, NS) s. 4(2); (NWT, Nu) s. 2(2); BC s. 3; Y s. 2(b).

99 *Re Sims Battle Brewster & Associates Inc.* (1999), 13 C.B.R. (4th) 269 (Alta. Q.B.).

100 PPSA (A, M, NB, PEI, S) s. 3(1); (BC, NWT, Nu) s. 2(1); (NL, NS) s. 4(1); O s. 2(a); Y s. 2.

B's potential beneficial interest in the property that is the object of the trust constitute a security interest.

Pursuant to an agreement with B, A settles property on himself on the trust condition that it will be transferred to B or be sold and the proceeds applied to an obligation owing by A to B if A fails to discharge an obligation owing to B.[101] A is both settlor and trustee and the beneficial interest that B acquires under trust law is a security interest that secures the separate obligation of A.[102]

However, a trust does not involve a security agreement where the beneficial interest of the beneficiary is not related to an obligation of the trustee other than the obligation to fulfill the terms of the trust.

No security interest is involved where A transfers property to B or B receives property to which A is entitled on the expressed or implied trust condition that B will hold it for the benefit of A or for some other specified purpose. B, the trustee, has an obligation that is a condition of the trust; however, the performance of that obligation is not secured by an interest held by A,[103] it is the purpose of the trust.

No security interest is involved where A transfers money to B on the condition that the money will be used to purchase an airline ticket for A using the money. A trust of the money may arise; however, the beneficial interest in the money held by A as a result of this trust does not secure the obligation of B to carry out the terms of the trust, i.e., to purchase the ticket.[104]

No security interest is involved in an arrangement under which A loans money to B for the expressed purpose of paying specified creditors of B. The money is held by B as trustee under an express or resulting trust for A, with a power to pay that money to the specified creditors.[105] If the money is not paid to the creditors, it must be returned to A. B's trust obligations to pay the creditors or return the money to A are not obligations secured by A's beneficial interest under the trust.[106]

---

101 See *Flintoft v. Royal Bank of Canada*, above note 94; *Ford Tractor Equipment Sales Co. of Canada Ltd. v. Otto Grundman Implements Ltd. (Trustee of)*, above note 94.

102 See Waters, above note 93 at 84–85.

103 *Ogden v. Award Realty Inc.* (1999), 14 P.P.S.A.C. (2d) 99 (B.C.S.C.).

104 *Skybridge Holidays Inc.*, above note 95.

105 *Twinsectra Ltd. v. Yardley*, [2002] 2 A.C.164 (H.L.).

106 See *Gignac, Sutts v. National Bank of Canada* (1987), 5 C.B.R. (4th) 44 (Ont. H.C.J.). See also *Barclays Bank Ltd. v. Quistclose Investments Ltd.*, [1970] A.C. 567 (H.L.). This case has been the focus of considerable academic analysis. See, for example, D.R. Klinck, "The Quistclose Trust in Canada" (1994) 23 Can. Bus.

d) Side-by-side Trust and Security Agreement

The decision of the Ontario Court of Appeal in *Re Berman*[107] involved, but did not adequately address, an important public policy issue that arises where a trust arrangement and a security agreement are related transactions. Berman obtained a loan from a trust company that was invested with the company in a retirement savings plan. Under the *Income Tax Act*, the trust company was trustee of the plan. To secure the loan Berman executed a letter of direction that authorized the trust company to apply the proceeds of any redemption of the plan against the loan indebtedness. Berman's trustee in bankruptcy sought to defeat the trust company's claim to the investment on the grounds that the letter created a security interest in the invested money in favour of the company. This security interest was not perfected. The Court concluded that, while a security interest was created, the trust company did not have to rely on it. The company could repay itself from the investment proceeds as an incidence of its rights as a trustee to be paid out of trust property.

An implication of the decision is that where both PPSA and trust law apply to a relationship, a secured party can choose the source of law most advantageous to it. The issue could arise in other contexts. Many inventory financing agreements contain "trust proceeds clauses" under which the debtor agrees to hold proceeds from the disposition of collateral "in trust" for the secured party. If the *Berman* approach were applied, the failure on the part of the secured party to perfect its security interest in the proceeds would not affect its priority in relation to the debtor's trustee in bankruptcy. Further, the consequences of non-compliance with the perfection rules of the PPSA would depend upon whether the secured party happened also to be a trustee.[108]

It is the view of the authors that the *Re Berman* decision should not be followed in other Canadian jurisdictions to the extent that it is viewed as giving to a secured party the power to rely on rights arising under a trust as an alternative to reliance on its security interest. As a matter of public policy and commercial predictability, it is important that the PPSA be seen as the primary source of law dealing with legal issues addressed at the same time in the legislation and in trust law.

L.J. 45; M.G. Bridge *et al.*, above note 35 at 616; W. Swadling, ed., *The Quistclose Trust: Critical Essays* (Oxford: Hart Publishing, 2004).

107 (1979), 105 D.L.R. (3d) 380 [*Re Berman*].

108 See *McArthur (Trustee of) v. Canadian Imperial Bank of Commerce* (1986), 5 P.P.S.A.C. 187 (Ont. H.C.J.).

In *Re Whaling*,[109] the Ontario Court of Appeal stated that the decision in *Re Berman* stands for the proposition that where a beneficiary of an RRSP and the depository of that RRSP agree that the depository may access the funds in the RRSP to satisfy a debt, the depository may, upon the bankruptcy of the beneficiary, set off the funds in the RRSP against the debt owed to the depository by the beneficiary. The issue before the Court in *Re Whaling* was whether or not it is possible to have a security interest in an RRSP created under subsection 146(1) of the *Income Tax Act*. It concluded that it is and that such an interest (referred to as a "charge") was created as a result of an acknowledgment very similar to the one in *Re Berman*. The Court did not confirm the ruling in *Re Berman* that a trustee has a right to set off debts owing by a beneficiary to the trustee in his personal capacity.[110] Nor did it address the basic issue in *Re Berman* as to whether a secured party can rely on trust law to escape the consequences of the priority rules of the PPSA.

C. TRANSACTIONS ON THE LINE

1) Introduction

The elimination of form as a determinant of the existence of a security agreement necessitates a close look at some types of transactions that, on the surface, appear to fall outside the scope of a PPSA but that may provide for interests that fall on one side of the line or the other, depending upon the presence or absence of a feature. In each case, it is necessary to determine whether the essential characteristics of a security agreement are present. This involves answering the question: does the transaction involve the contractual recognition or creation of an interest in the personal property of one person that secures an obligation owing to another person?[111] A lien or charge, such as a repairer's lien or charge arising under a taxation statute, does not qualify because this type of interest arises by operation of law. It is not a consensual interest. The "interest" involved must be a real right in personal property in the sense that it is exercisable against not only the obligor but

---

109 (1998), 6 C.B.R. (4th) 1.
110 In *McMahon v. Canada Permanent Trust Co.*, [1980] 2 W.W.R. 438, the British Columbia Court of Appeal concluded that there is no such right. The Court expressed its disagreement in this respect with the decision in *Re Berman*.
111 See, for example, *Farm Credit Corp. v. Valley Beef Producers Co-operative Ltd.* (2002) 36 C.B.R. (4th) 121 (Sask. C.A.); *Toronto Dominion Bank v. East Central Feeder Co-operative Ltd.*, (2001), 2 P.P.S.A.C. (3d) 283 (Ont. S.C.J.).

also against third parties with subsequent interests in the property. A contractual licence to take property in satisfaction of an obligation does not qualify. Often, whether or not a security interest has been created will depend upon the wording of a contract between the parties.

2) Some Examples

The following are examples of transactions that fall on one side or other of the line between security agreement and an agreement that falls outside the scope of the Act.

- A guarantee does not create a security interest[112] unless the guarantor also gives as security an interest in his property to secure performance of the guarantee contract.[113]
- An agreement in an underwriting arrangement to recognize "equitable remedies" does not create a security interest.[114]
- A "negative pledge" clause or negative covenant in a loan agreement under which the borrower covenants not to encumber or dispose of some or all of her personal property until the loan is repaid does not create a security interest since, standing alone, the covenant does not create an interest in the property of the borrower.[115] A negative pledge clause in a security agreement cannot prevent the covenantor from giving another effective security interest in the collateral.[116]
- A contractual right of distress under which a lessor is given the right to seize and sell personal property of a tenant in the event of nonpayment of rent is not, without more, a security agreement since it does not give to the lessor an interest in the tenant's property.[117] However, a contractual "lien" or "charge" given to a carrier or storer should be treated as a security interest since the wording evidences the grant of a proprietary interest in the relevant goods in favour of the storer or carrier.
- A surety who has discharged a debtor's obligation to a creditor is automatically subrogated to any rights, including a security inter-

---

112 *Toronto Dominion Bank v. Gottdank* (2000), 1 P.P.S.A.C. (3d)67 (Ont. S.C.J.).

113 *Toronto Dominion Bank v. McCowan* (1995), 20 B.L.R. (2d) 138 (Ont. C.A.).

114 *Magellan Aerospace Ltd. v. First Energy Capital Corp.* (2000), 1 P.P.S.A.C. (3d) 297 (Alta. Q.B.), aff'd [2001] 8 W.W.R. 448 (Alta. C.A.).

115 *Frado v. Bank of Montreal* (1984), 34 Alta. L.R. (2d) 293 (Q.B.); *Swiss Bank Corp. v. Lloyds Bank Ltd.*, [1981] 2 All. E.R. 449 (H.L.).

116 PPSA (A, BC, M, NB, NWT, Nu, PEI, S) s. 33(2); (NL, NS) s. 34(2); O s. 39; Y s. 32.

117 See *First National Bank v. Cudmore* (1917), 10 Sask. L. R. 201 (C.A.).

est, held by the creditor to secure the obligation.[118] While the surety ends up as a secured creditor in relation to the debtor, the right to be recognized as such is not a security interest.[119] That right arises by operation of law.

- Set-off, whether contractual or procedural, does not involve a security interest because neither party to the set-off acquires a property interest.
- A sale on COD terms does not create a security interest unless there are provisions in the agreement or a related agreement indicating that the seller is retaining title until payment or otherwise has a security interest in the goods after delivery.[120]

3) The Special Case of Subordination Agreements

A subordination agreement generally entails an agreement of a creditor, often referred to as a subordinating or "junior" creditor, to postpone or subordinate his rights against a debtor until the obligation owning by a common debtor to another creditor or specified group of creditors,[121] often referred to as the benefiting or "senior" creditor(s), has been discharged. The subordination agreement may be made between the subordinating creditor and a specified benefiting creditor or may be contained in the agreement between the subordinating creditor and the common debtor, in which case it benefits a specified class or group of creditors of the debtor. The subordination may result in a security interest held by the subordinating creditor being postponed to a security interest held by the benefiting creditor.[122] This type of subordina-

---

118 See *Re Windham Sales Ltd.* (1979), 31 C.B.R. (N.S.) 130 (Ont. H.C.J.); *Mercantile Law Amendment Act* (1856), 19 & 20 Vict. c. 97, s. 5. In some provinces, this provision was "received" as common law. In others, it has been copied into provincial statutes. See, for example, *Mercantile Law Amendment Act*, R.S.O. 1990, c. M.10, s. 2.
119 *Re Windham Sales Ltd.*, *ibid.*
120 *Joseph Group of Companies Inc. v. Pickles Tents & Awnings Ltd.*, above note 31; *Banque National de Paris (Canada) v. Pine Tree Mercury Sales Limited* (1983), 47 C.B.R. (N.S.) 300 (Ont. Co. Ct.); *Atlas Industries Ltd. v. Federal Business Development Bank* (1983), 50 C.B.R. (N.S.) 14, 3 P.P.S.A.C. 39 (Sask. Q.B.).
121 *Chiips Inc. v. Skyview Hotels Ltd.*, 21 Alta. L.R. (3d) 225, [1994] 9 W.W.R. 727, 27 C.B.R. (3d) 161, 7 P.P.S.A.C. (2d) 23, 155 A.R. 281, 73 W.A.C. 281, 116 D.L.R. (4th) 385 (C.A.).
122 See, for example, *Engel Canada Inc. v. TCE Capital* (2002), 34 C.B.R. (4th) 169 (Ont. S.C.J.); *Euroclean Canada Inc. v. Forest Glade Investments Ltd.* (1985), 54 C.B.R. (N.S.) 65 (Ont. C.A.).

tion is addressed in the PPSA.[123] However, a subordination agreement need not involve two security interests. It may be nothing more than an agreement that the benefiting creditor has the right to have the common debtor's obligation discharged in priority to an obligation owing to the subordinating creditor. Furthermore, a subordination agreement can entail a unilateral undertaking by the subordinating creditor to postpone priority to specific further creditors or specified categories of creditors.

A subordination agreement *simpliciter* does not involve creation of a new interest.[124] It is simply an agreement to postpone enforcement of the rights of the subordinating creditor to the rights of the benefiting creditor. However, there are circumstances in which a new interest in the form of a security interest may be created. If the relationship between the subordinating creditor and the benefiting creditor is one in which the latter is given an interest in the former's rights against the common debtor, a security agreement would result. The security interest arises out of the agreement to give to the benefiting creditor an interest in the common debtor's obligation owing to the subordinating creditor and the subordinating creditor's security interest relating to that obligation. The effect of the agreement is that, in the event of default by the common debtor in discharging his interest to the benefiting creditor, the benefiting creditor can gain recovery through reliance on her right to the money payable by the common debtor to the subordinating creditor or, in the event of non-payment, to enforcement of the subordinating creditor's security interest. In this context, the benefiting creditor is a secured party, the subordinating creditor is the debtor and the collateral is the obligation of the common debtor to the subordinating creditor and the security interest relating to that obligation. This obligation is an account (assuming it is a monetary obligation) and, as such, qualifies as collateral. The essential difference between a subordination agreement that creates a security interest and one that does not is that, under the former, the benefiting party gets a new interest that is not created under the latter.

A subordination *simpliciter* involves an agreement between SP1 and SP2 that SP1 will forebear enforcing its security interest against the common collateral until SP2 has enforced its security interest. The result is that, in the event of D's default, SP2 would seize and sell col-

---

123 For a more complete discussion of subordination agreements in the context of these sections, see chapter 8, H.2, "Subordination and Priorities."

124 A few Acts contain a provision stating a presumption that a subordination agreement does not create a security interest. See PPSA (BC, NWT, Nu, S) s. 40(2).

lateral up to the value of the subordination free from interference by SP1. In the event of SP1's bankruptcy and the refusal of SP1's trustee to honour the agreement, SP2 would have only an unsecured claim against SP1's estate.

A subordination agreement that creates a security interest is one in which SP1 agrees with SP2 that, in the event of non-payment of the debt owing by D to SP2, SP2 would be entitled to collect payments owing to SP1 by D or to assert SP1's security interest in the collateral securing D's obligation to SP1. In effect, SP2 has a security interest in SP1's security interest to secure D's obligation to SP2.

A subordination agreement that provides for a security interest is used when the parties want to give to the benefiting creditor the subordinating creditor's priority position. For example, where the subordinating creditor (SP1) has first priority and the benefiting creditor (SP3) has a third-priority position behind another creditor (SP2), the only effective way for SP1 to give his priority status to SP3 is to transfer his interest to SP3. In law, this will entail an assignment of SP1's right to payment from the common debtor. This would be an assignment of an account that falls within the PPSA.

There are important consequences associated with the use of a subordination agreement to create a security interest. Since the benefiting creditor acquires an interest in the account of the common debtor, it has priority over anyone else who thereafter acquires an interest in the account and over the subordinating creditor's judgment creditors and trustee in bankruptcy if the security interest is perfected. If no interest is created under the subordination agreement, the benefiting creditor's contract rights under the agreement cannot be asserted against a subsequent assignee of the account. Furthermore, if the subordinating creditor becomes bankrupt, those contract rights cannot be asserted against the trustee other than as the basis for an unsecured claim against the bankruptcy estate.

In order for a security interest to be created by a subordination agreement, there must be indication in the agreement that a property interest has been given to the benefiting creditor. Some Acts include a provision that, in effect, creates a presumption that a subordination agreement does not create a security interest.[125]

---

125 *Ibid.*

D. THE DEEMED SECURITY AGREEMENTS

1) Introduction

The creation, perfection, priority, registration, and conflict of laws provisions of all Acts except the Ontario Act apply to four types of transactions that are not functionally or conceptually security agreements: assignments (sales) of an accounts; assignments (sales) of chattel paper; leases for a term of more than one year; and commercial consignments.[126] The Ontario Act applies only to the first two.[127] The Acts in effect in Atlantic Canada provide a fifth type of deemed security interest, a sale of goods without a change of possession. The legislative technique used to bring these transactions within the relevant provisions of the Act is to deem them to create security interests.[128] However, the deeming effect does not extend to enforcement since these transactions do not involve the types of relationship that are characteristic of secured financing arrangements.[129]

The policy reason for including these transactions in the PPSA is clear. Endemic to each type of transaction is the potential for third-party deception and the consequent commercial disruptions that this entails. In the case of a lease and a consignment, there is a separation of ownership and possession, thus placing the lessee or consignee in a position to mislead third parties as to the extent of his interest in the goods in his possession. In the case of a transfer of an account, the transferor retains apparent control of the account even though she no longer owns or has an interest in it. By bringing these transactions within the scope of the registration and priority rules of the PPSA, third parties are placed in the position of being able to discover the existence of these interests before dealing with a lessee, consignee, or assignor. The policy basis for

---

126 PPSA (A, M, NB, PEI, S) s. 3(2); (NL, NS) s. 4(2); (NWT, Nu) s. 2(2); BC s. 3.

127 OPPSA s. 2(b).

128 PPSA (A, BC, NWT, Nu, O, Y) s. 1(1); (M, NB, PEI) s. 1; (NL, NS) s. 2; S s. 2(1).

129 The question arises as to whether OPPSA s. 61(2) applies to a non-security transfer account or chattel paper under an agreement that gives the transferee a right of recourse against the transferee. The Act does not specifically state that Part V does not apply to these transactions. However, by inference, the Part does not apply unless there is a debtor-creditor relationship and the credit has an interest in property that secures the debtor's obligation. There is no such relationship in a recourse assignment. Nevertheless, section 61(2) expressly applies to such an assignment. This confusion does not exist in the other Acts all of which make it clear that Part V does not apply to non-security transactions governed by other features of the Act. PPSA (A, M, NB, NWT, Nu, PEI) s. 55(1); (BC, S) s. 55(2); (NL, NS) s. 56(2); Y s. 53(2).

including transfers of chattel paper is somewhat different. Prior to the implementation of the Acts, the law applicable to the various interests involved in chattel paper was unclear. One of the innovative features of the PPSA was to establish an entirely new regime for security interests in this unique type of property. Since this regime could be applied equally well to competing claims by successive transferees of chattel paper as to competing security interests in chattel paper, the decision was made to include absolute transfers within its scope.

A conceptual issue arises in the context of the extension of the Act to consignments, leases, and transfers of accounts. In order to bring these transactions within the operation of the Act, it is necessary to deem them to create security interests and to treat the consignor, lessor or accounts transferee as a secured party and a consignee, the lessee or accounts transferor as a debtor. In order for a security interest to attach, it is necessary that the debtor have rights in the collateral.[130] However, under non-PPSA law the debtors in these transactions have no rights in the collateral other than possessory rights in the case of leases and consignments. All Acts other than that of Ontario address the matter in the context of leases and consignments by providing that, for the purposes of the attachment requirement, a lessee under a lease for a term of more than one year and a consignee under a commercial consignment has rights in the goods when the consignee obtains possession of them pursuant to the lease or consignment.[131] However, these Acts do not address the position of the transferor of an account or chattel paper.

It is the view of the authors that this omission in the PPSAs does not warrant a different approach to transfers of accounts of chattel paper. As noted above, the legislative intention behind extending the scope of the Act to absolute transfers of accounts is to avoid third-party deception. The mechanism through which this is accomplished is to deem the transfer to be a security agreement providing for a deemed security interest. It follows that the account transferor is deemed to have rights in the account after transfer to the extent this is necessary to support the conclusion that an attached security interest exists.[132] Similar rea-

---

130 PPSA (A, BC, M, NB, NWT, Nu, PEI, S) s. 12(1); (NL, NS) s. 13(1); O s. 11(2); Y s. 11(1).

131 PPSA (A, BC, M, NWT, Nu, S) s. 12(2); (NB, PEI) s. 12(3); (NL, NS) s. 13(3); Y s. 11(2).

132 This approach was inferentially taken in *Agent's Equity Inc. v. Hope* (1996), 40 C.B.R. (3d) 310 (Ont. Ct. Gen. Div.); and *TCE Capital Corp. v. Kolenc* (1999), 172 D.L.R. (4th) 186 (Ont. Div. Ct.), aff'g (1998), 3 C.B.R. (4th) 98 (Ont. Ct. Gen. Div.). In these cases, the courts concluded that there is no requirement that the transferor of an account have a property interest after the transfer in order for

soning applies to sales of chattel paper. This issue is revisited in more detail in chapter 4.

2) A Transfer of an Account

All Acts include within their scope[133] absolute transfers of accounts other than types of transfers expressly excluded.[134] The transfer may be of a single account to a factor[135] or a block of accounts. The law of equity provides that an agreement to assign a future account gives rise to an automatic transfer of the account or charge on the account as soon as it comes into existence. Since the principles of equity are imported into the PPSA,[136] an agreement to transfer or assign a future account should be treated as giving rise to a deemed security interest as soon as the account comes into existence.[137] A trust arrangement under which a creditor agrees to hold her interest in an account in trust for another person would also fall within this aspect of the PPSA. Conceptually, there is a notional transfer of the equitable interest from the creditor as creditor to the creditor as trustee.

It is clear that the assignment step in a securitization transaction involving accounts falls within the PPSA. The sale of a block of loans (accounts), which is the first step in a securitization of the accounts, is a deemed security interest under the PPSA, with the result that the registration and priority provisions of the Act apply.

3) A Transfer of Chattel Paper

Chattel paper is the label given to a type of property that was not recognized as such under prior law. The term refers to a writing that evidences both a monetary obligation and a security interest in or lease of

---

the trustee in bankruptcy to defeat the transferee's interest under section 20(1) of the OPPSA.

133 In the balance of this part, a reference to scope of a PPSA should be read as not including Part 5(V) enforcement provisions of the Act.

134 PPSA (A, BC, M, NB, PEI, S) s. 4; (NWT, Nu, Y) s. 3; (NL, NS) s. 5; O s. 4(1).

135 *TCE Capital Corp. v. Kolenc*, above note 132 (Ont. Div. Ct.).

136 PPSA (M, NWT, Nu, S) s. 65(2); (NB, PEI) s. 65(1); (NL, NS) s. 66(1); A s. 66(3); BC s. 68(1); O s. 72.

137 See *356447 British Columbia Ltd. v. Canadian Imperial Bank of Commerce*, [1998] 9 W.W.R. 59 (B.C.C.A.). For an examination of this issue in the context of bankruptcy of the debtor, see chapter 11, C, "The Efficacy of After-acquired Property Clauses in Bankruptcy."

goods.[138] Chattel paper is treated as a unique type of collateral in order to ensure that the law reflects commercial practices under which these interests are transferred through the transfer of the documents providing for them.[139]

The most common situation in which chattel paper arises is where goods are sold under a secured instalment sales contract or leased under a long-term lease. The contracts used in these transactions are chattel paper under the Acts. The seller or lessor then sells or gives a security interest in the chattel paper to a financing institution. Under the PPSA, the seller is the debtor, the financial institution is the secured party and the chattel paper is the collateral.

Although chattel paper is sometimes taken as collateral, in the great bulk of cases it is sold to a financing organization. However, methods of dealing with this type of property and the priority issues that arise when it is dealt with, for the most part, are the same whether the interest of the transferee is that of a secured party or a buyer. For this reason, sales of chattel paper are included in all Acts with the result that the regime applicable to security interests in chattel paper applies with equal effectiveness to sales of chattel paper.[140]

4) A Commercial Consignment

All Acts, other than that of Ontario, provide that true (that is, non-security) "commercial consignments" fall within their scope. While the separation of possession and ownership is endemic to consignment arrangements, not all consignments fall within the scope of the PPSA. As a result of the definition of commercial consignment,[141] the Act applies only to consignments under which both the consignor and the consignee are in the business of dealing in goods of the description consigned.[142] Consequently, the consignment by a consumer of her property to a commercial consignee would not be caught by the Act. Consignments to auctioneers and to consignees who are generally known to their creditors to be selling or leasing goods for others are outside the scope of the Act.[143] There is no need to subject these types

---

138 PPSA (A, BC, NWT, Nu, O, Y) s. 1(1); (M, NB, PEI) s. 1; (NL, NS) s. 2; S s. 2(1).

139 See generally PPSA (A, BC, NB, NWT, Nu, PEI) s. 31(6); (M, S) s. 31(7); (NL, NS) s. 32(6); O s. 28(3); Y s. 30(5).

140 As to whether sales of chattel paper under a recourse agreement falls within Part V of the OPPSA, see above note 129.

141 PPSA (A, BC, NWT, Nu, Y) s. 1(1); (M, NB, PEI) s. 1; (NL, NS) s. 2; S s. 2(1).

142 See *National Bank of Canada v. Makin Metals Ltd.*, [1994] 4 W.W.R. 707 (Sask. C.A.).

143 See above note 141 for a definition of commercial consignment.

of consignments to the public disclosure requirement of the Act since the potential for deception of third parties resulting from the separation of possession and ownership is small.

The exclusion of consignments to consignees "generally known" by their creditors to be selling or leasing goods of others contains a test that is not always easy to apply. The knowledge that is relevant is not the knowledge of a particular creditor[144] or knowledge relating to a particular consignment. What is required is a generalized knowledge among creditors of the consignee. Saskatchewan courts have concluded that this is established through objective evidence, including signage at the consignee's premises or proof of a general understanding of this in the community in which the consignee carries on business.[145] Whether this approach applies where all or most of the creditors do not have a presence in the local community of the consignee is doubtful.

5) A Lease for a Term of More than One Year

The PPSA, except that of Ontario, deems true leases (that is, non-security leases) of goods having a term of more than one year to be security agreements. Leases for less than one year fall outside the Act.

Much of the uncertainty as to what constitutes a lease for a term of more than one year has been removed by the elaborate definition of the term contained in the Act.[146] In effect, the Act will apply in any case in which the lessee remains in possession of the leased property for a period of time in excess of one year.

A lease for an indefinite term, although determinable at the option of one of the parties, falls within the Act.[147] A lease for a term of less than one year that is automatically renewable for one or more terms, the total of which exceeds one year, is deemed to be a lease for a term of more than one year. In neither case is it relevant that at the time the issue arises the lessee has been in possession of the leased property for more than one year. What is important is that this potential exists under the terms of the lease.

---

144 See *Canadian Imperial Bank of Commerce v. Westfield Industries Ltd.* (1990), 86 Sask. R. 1 (Q.B.).

145 See *Royal Bank v. Autotran Manufacturing Ltd.*, [1991] 6 W.W.R. 238 (Sask. Q.B.), aff'd [1992] 3 W.W.R. 455 (Sask. C.A.). This decision was based on the definition of commercial consignment that referred to general knowledge in the area in which consignee carries on business. The definition now refers only to the knowledge of creditors of the consignee.

146 PPSA (A, BC, NWT, Nu, Y) s. 1(1); (M, NB, PEI) s. 1; (NL, NS) s. 2; S s. 2(1).

147 *Gelowitz v. Garcon Enterprises Ltd.* (1995), 132 Sask. R. 273 (Q.B.).

The definition addresses the case of an overholding lessee. Where the lease has an initial term of one year or less and the lessee remains in possession or substantially uninterrupted possession of the leased property after the expiry of the term with the consent of the lessor, the lease is deemed to be a lease for a term of more than one year as soon as, but not before, the duration of the lessee's possession exceeds one year. Accordingly, a lease for a term of one year or less that does not fall within one of the other two categories set out in the definition remains outside the scope of the Act until the lessee has been in possession or substantially uninterrupted possession for more than one year. During the initial one-year term of the lease, non-PPSA law governs all priority issues associated with conflicting claims relating to the lease property. However, once the lessee's possession extends beyond the one-year period, the Act applies. The lease is thereafter treated as creating a security interest with the result that priority issues involving interests or claims arising after (but not before) this point are addressed by the relevant provisions of the PPSA.

Not all leases for a term of more than one year are deemed to create security interests. A lease of household furnishings or appliances as part of a lease of land where the goods are incidental to the use and enjoyment of the land and leases of prescribed goods are outside the Act.[148] In addition, the deeming effect does not apply to a lease where the lessor is not regularly engaged in the business of leasing goods. What constitutes regular engagement in the business of leasing has been addressed by courts. Under the approach taken in these decisions, the frequency with which the lessor engaged in leasing prior to entering into the lease in question was not the determining factor. So long as leasing is part of the regular business of a person, the volume of leasing business undertaken is not significant.[149] The word "regularly" modifies "business" rather than "engaged."

---

148 Above note 146. No jurisdiction has added to the exemption through regulation.
149 *Paccar Financial Services v. Sinco Trucking Ltd.* (1987), 7 P.P.S.A.C. 176 (Sask. Q.B.), rev'd on other grounds (1989), 57 D.L.R. (4th) 438 (Sask. C.A.); *Planwest Consultants Ltd. v. Milltimber Holdings Ltd.* (1995), 32 Alta. L.R. (3d) 397 (Q.B.); *David Morris Fine Cars Ltd. v. North Sky Trading Inc.*, [1994] 9 W.W.R. 680 (Alta. Q.B.), aff'd (1996), 38 Alta. L.R. (3d) 428 (C.A.); *East Central Development Corp. v. Freightliner Truck Sales (Regina) Ltd.* (1997), 12 P.P.S.A.C. (2d) 328 (Sask. Q.B.).

6) Sale of Goods without Change of Possession

The Acts in effect in the four Atlantic Canada provinces include in their scope "sales without a change of possession."[150] The purpose for doing so is to provide public disclosure of the ownership rights of a buyer who leaves goods in the possession of the seller after property in the goods has passed to him under a sale not in the ordinary course of business of the seller. For a full discussion of the operation of this feature and a comparison with parallel provisions contained in the legislation of other jurisdictions, see chapter 7.

E. EXCLUDED INTERESTS AND TRANSACTIONS

1) Non-consensual Liens, Charges, and Deemed Trusts

The concept of security interest, while generally broad enough to encompass all forms of interests in personal property that secure obligations, does not have this scope in the context of the PPSA. A security interest under the PPSA must be one that has been created by or provided for in a transaction in the form of a security agreement[151] or one that arises pursuant to a provision of the PPSA.[152] Consequently, a lien or charge that arises by operation of law is not a security interest under the Act.[153] While a repairer's lien results from an agreement to have the personal property repaired or improved, its source is not the agreement. It arises without regard to whether or not it is mentioned in the agreement. Most non-possessory liens arise under statutory regimes that provide for their creation, priority, and enforcement.[154]

Out of an abundance of caution, the drafter of the PPSA decided to remove any doubt in the matter by including a provision excluding from

---

150 NB ss. 1 and 3(2)(d); (NL, NS) ss. 2 and 4(2)(d); PEI ss.1 and 3(2)(d).

151 PPSA (A, M, NB, PEI, S) s. 3(1); (BC, NWT, Nu) s. 2(1); (NL, NS) s. 4(1); O s. 2(a); Y. s. 2.

152 A security interest in proceeds arises automatically without the need for a reference to it in a security agreement. PPSA (A, BC, M, NB, NWT, Nu, PEI, S) s. 28(1); (NL, NS) s. 29(1); O. s. 25(1); Y s. 26(1).

153 Legislation under which some liens arise provide for the registration of the claim of lien in the Personal Property Registry. See, for example, *Repair and Storage Lien Act*, R.S.O. 1990, c. R.25; *The Commercial Liens Act*, Stat. Sask. 2001, c. C-15.1. However, this does not bring the liens within the scope of the PPSA.

154 *Ibid.*

the scope of the Act "a lien, charge or other interest given by statute or rule of law."[155] This decision proved to be fortunate since the limitation of the scope of the Act to consensual relationships appears not to have been obvious.[156] While the PPSA does not treat a repairer's lien as a security interest, it does peripherally address rights that arise under such a lien.[157] Otherwise, the general rule is that, unless the statute creating the lien or charge in competition with a security interest specifically so provides,[158] priority is based on the principle of first-in-time, first-in-right. This is qualified in Ontario by a provision of the Ontario Act that subordinates an unperfected security interest to "a person who has a lien given under any other Act or by a rule of law."[159]

---

155 Section 4(1)(a) of the OPPSA refers only to "a lien given by statute or rule of law." However, it is the view of the authors that the term "lien" is used in its broadest sense in this provision to include any encumbrance, whether described as a "lien" or a "charge" in the statutory provision under which it arises. Section 4(1)(b) of the OPPSA excluded from the scope of the Act "a deemed trust arising under any Act, except as provided in section 30(7)." Section 30(7) provides that a security interest, other than a purchase money security interest, in an account or inventory and its proceeds is subordinate to the interest of a beneficiary of a trust arising under the *Employment Standards Act* or the *Pension Benefits Act*.

156 See *Commercial Credit Corporation v. Harry D. Shields Ltd.* (1980), 112 D.L.R. (3d) 153 (Ont. H.C.J.), aff'd 122 D.L.R. (3d) 736 (Ont. C.A.); *Dubé v. Bank of Montreal* (1986), 5 P.P.S.A.C. 269 (Sask. C.A.) (the lien created when a landlord exercises a right of distress is excluded from the Act); *International Harvester Credit Corporation of Canada Limited v. Frontier Peterbilt Sales Ltd.*, [1983] 6 W.W.R. 328 (Sask. Q.B.) (repairer's statutory lien); *Canadian Imperial Bank of Commerce v. Maidstone Farming Ltd.* (1984), 46 O.R. (2d) 699 (Co. Ct.) (warehouse operator's lien); *Canadian Imperial Bank of Commerce v. 64576 Manitoba Ltd.* (1991), 77 D.L.R. (4th) 190 (Man. C.A.) (lien given to utility supplier).

157 PPSA (A, BC, M, NB, NWT, Nu, PEI, S) s. 32; (NL, NS) s. 33; (Y, O) s. 31. This section gives first priority over security interests to a repairer's lien arising as a result of the provision, in the ordinary course of business, of services or materials in connection with the collateral.

158 *Leavere v. Corporation of The City of Port Colborne* (1995), 122 D.L.R. (4th) 200 (Ont. C.A.). For an examination of the priorities between liens and security interests, see R. Wood and M. Wylie, "Non-Consensual Security Interests in Personal Property" (1992), 30 Alta. L. Rev. 1055.

159 O s. 20(1)(a). The effect of this provision is addressed in chapter 10, B.2.b.ii "Effect of Non-perfection of the Security Interest."

2) Security Interests Arising under Federal Law[160]

The courts have been required to address a feature of the PPSA that was not likely given much consideration by the drafters of the original Ontario Act. The PPSA expressly applies to every transaction that in substance creates a security interest. The concept of security interest is described in the PPSA in generic terms.[161] Clearly, a transaction that gives rise to a section 427 *Bank Act*[162] security creates a security interest. However, this security interest arises under and is governed by a conceptually different regime established through federal legislation.

The potential for confusion resulting from the overlap of the PPSA and the *Bank Act* has been eliminated in all Acts other than the Ontario Act and the Yukon Act.[163] They expressly exclude from their scope security agreements governed by an Act of Parliament that deals with the rights of parties to the agreement or the rights of third parties affected by a security interest created by the agreement, including an agreement governed by sections 425 to 436 of the *Bank Act*.[164]

There is no uncertainty as to the effect of the final part of this provision. A *Bank Act* security agreement does not create a PPSA security interest. However, the scope of the remaining part of this provision is not as clear. To be excluded from the PPSA, the security agreement must be "governed" by federal legislation. It is not clear what constitutes being governed in this context. On one reading of the provision, all that is required is that federal legislation "deals either with rights of parties to the security agreement or the rights of third parties affected by a security interest arising under the agreement." Under this approach, so long as federal legislation either addresses the rights of the parties to the agreement or the rights of third parties, the PPSA does not apply. It is the view of the authors that this interpretation is not warranted. Simply because federal legislation addresses in some way the rights of the parties to the agreement is not a basis for concluding that the agreement is excluded from the PPSA. It is our view that the term "governed" suggests a federal regime that replicates or substan-

---

160 For a more extensive examination of security interest arising under federal law, see chapter 14.

161 O s. 2.

162 S.C. 1991. c. 4.

163 PPSA (A, BC, MB, NB, PEI, S) s. 4; (NL, NS) s. 5; (NWT, Nu) s. 3.

164 These provisions do not deal with situations in which a bank acquires under separate agreements a s. 427 security and a PPSA security interest in the same collateral to secured the same obligation. The issues that arise in this context are addressed later in this book. See chapter 14, A "*Bank Act* Security."

tially replicates the PPSA regime. An example of such a regime is the *Canada Shipping Act, 2001*[165] that provides for the creation, registration, priority, and enforcement of ship mortgages.[166]

While some federal intellectual property statutes provide expressly for assignments of rights and specify consequences for non-compliance with statutory registration requirements,[167] it is the author's view that this legislation should not be viewed as "governing" security interests in this type of property. This legislation applies only incidentally or inferentially (if at all) to security interests in intellectual property rights.[168] The pre-emption of the PPSA by federal law should be limited to issues that the federal regime expressly addresses. Beyond this, the PPSA provides the default regime.

3) Interests in or Claim under a Contract of Annuity or Policy of Insurance

An important category of interests excluded from the scope of the PPSA is security interests in or claims in or under annuity contracts or insurance contracts.[169] The exclusion does not extend to a right to pay-

---

165 S.C. 2001, c. 26, ss. 65–72. While there is no judicial authority on the question as to whether the PPSA applies to a registerable but unregistered ship, the lack of registration does preclude the Federal Court from having power to issue an order under s. 44 of the *Canada Shipping Act* dealing with possession of a ship sought by a conditional seller who has registered its "ownership" interest as a security interest under the PPSA. See *General Motors Acceptance Corporation v. Furjanic* (1994), 7 P.P.S.A.C. (2d) 52 (F.C.T.D.) In *Re Doucet* (1983), 150 D.L.R. (3d) 53 (Ont. H.C.J.) the court concluded that the rights of a mortgagee to enforce a chattel mortgage against a vessel that is not required to be but has been registered under the *Canada Shipping Act* is preserved by the Act. However, presumably registration of a ship mortgage on the vessel under the *Canada Shipping Act* would displace the priority structure of the PPSA that might otherwise be applicable to conflicting interests in the vessel. See chapter 14 for further discussion of security interests governed by the *Canada Shipping Act*.

166 However, not all vessels are subject to this regime. Security interests in small craft that are licensed under the *Small Vessels Regulations* of the *Canada Shipping Act* are within the scope of the PPSA.

167 See, for example, *Copyright Act*, R.S.C. 1985, c. C-42, s. 57(3). See chapter 14 for a discussion of security interests created under federal intellectual property law.

168 See R. Wood, "Security Interests in Intellectual Property: Rationalizing the Registries" in Howard P. Knopf, ed., *Security Interests in Intellectual Property*, (Scarborough, Ont.: Thomson Carswell, 2002) 669 at 670–89.

169 Above note 163. While there is no legislative record of the policy basis for this exclusion, a plausible explanation is that the drafters concluded that assignments of insurance interests were adequately addressed under insurance law.

ment under a policy of insurance for loss or damage to collateral.[170] The term "contract of annuity" is not confined to contracts with insurance companies. What is excluded from the Act is a contract under which a stated sum of money is payable at regular intervals[171] from a fund or source in which the annuitant has no further property beyond the right to claim payment.[172]

An insurance policy, other than one covering loss or damage to collateral, that provides for insurance payments to a third party is not within the scope of the Act.[173] Competing interests in rights under contracts of insurance are governed by the *Insurance Act*,[174] which contains a modified statutory version of the traditional principle in *Dearle v. Hall*.[175] Priority is given to the first assignee to notify the issuer. In *Re Stelco Inc.*,[176] the Ontario Court of Appeal concluded that an insured's assignment to an insurance premium financer of unearned insurance premiums payable by an insurance company was not a security agreement governed by the Ontario Act. The Court, following American jurisprudence, reasoned that the premium financing company's right to a refund under the assignment was a right under the insurance contract in the sense that the premium financing agreement identified the insurance contract giving rise to the insured's right to a refund. It follows from this reasoning that the assignment of any money the payment of which arises out of or is associated with an insurance contract to which the assignor is a party is not an assignment within the scope of the PPSA. This raises the question as to whether the exclusion applies to the

---

For a judicial discussion of the background to this exclusion, see *Re Stelco Inc.* (2004), 6 P.P.S.A.C. (3d) 268 (Ont. S.C.J.), rev'd 2005 CarswellOnt 1537 (C.A.). However, it is the authors' view that this exclusion is hard to justify given the frequency of use of insurance interests as collateral to secure loans. It is anomalous that security interest in this type of collateral should be subject to a regime different from that applicable to other types of intangible collateral.

170 Above note 163.

171 An obligation to make unequal payments is an insurance interest, but not an annuity. See *The Insurance Act*, R.S.S. 1978, c. S-26, s. 2(kk); *Insurance Act*, R.S.O. 1990, c. I.8, s. 1 (for a definition of life insurance).

172 See *Re Rektor* (1983), 47 C.B.R. (N.S.) 267 (Ont. H.C.J.).

173 It is the authors' view that the decision of the Ontario Supreme Court in *Re Paul* (1986), 5 P.P.S.A.C. 86 is incorrect to the extent that the court ruled that a provision of an insurance contract requiring payment for loss compensation to a secured party was outside the exclusion in that it did not amount to a "transfer of an interest in a policy of insurance."

174 *The Insurance Act*, R.S.S. 1978, c. S-26, s. 162; *Insurance Act*, R.S.O. 1990, c. I.8, s. 200.

175 (1823), 3 Russ. 1, [1824-34] All E.R. Rep. 28.

176 Above note 169.

following situation. A, an insured, assigns to B money payable under an insurance policy. B gives C a security interest in his rights under the A-B assignment. Clearly the exclusion would apply to the A-B assignment. However, would it would apply to the security interest given by B to C? In *Re Rapid Auto Collision Ltd.*[177] the Ontario Supreme Court concluded that the exclusion did not apply to an assignment by an auto repair business of money owing by its customers, to be paid to the repairer by insurance companies which had insured the customers against damage to their vehicles. In this case, the assignor was not legally entitled to payment from the insurance companies. Payment was made by the companies as a matter of convenience for the insured customers. What was assigned was the customer accounts and not the customers' rights to payment under their insurance policies. However, if the repairer had acquired the legal right to obtain payment directly from the insurance companies, the interest it assigned would have been an interest in an insurance policy under the approach taken in *Re Stelco*.

4) Pawn Transactions

The Ontario Act excludes from its scope "a transaction under the *Pawnbrokers Act*."[178] No similar exclusion is found in the other Acts which exclude only from the enforcement part of legislation "a transaction between a pledgor and a pawnbroker."[179] The difference between the Ontario Act and other Acts is fundamental. While all Acts leave to other law the regulation of the rights of pledgors and pawnbrokers *inter se*, the Acts of jurisdictions other than Ontario apply to security interests created by pawns all aspects other than enforcement. Given that property pawned could very easily be subject to a prior PPSA security interest, it is difficult to see the justification for the broad scope of the Ontario exclusion.

5) Interests in Land and Interests in Payments Connected with Land

The problem of separating interests in personal property from interests in land in order to confine the application of the PPSA to security interests in the former has been addressed differently by the Ontario Act, on the one hand, and the Acts of other jurisdictions, on the other.

---

177 See *In Re Rapid Auto Collision Ltd.* (1983), 3 P.P.S.A.C. 187 (Ont. S.C.).

178 OPPSA s. 4(d). See *Pawnbrokers Act*, R.S.O. 1990, c. P.6

179 PPSA (A, M, NB, NWT, Nu, PEI) s. 55(1); (BC, S) s. 55(2); (NL, NS) s. 56(2); Y s. 53(2).

a)   The Ontario Approach

Section 4(1)(e) of the Ontario Act excludes from its scope the creation or transfer of an interest in real property, including a mortgage, charge, or lease of real property. However, the exclusion does not apply to an assignment of a right to payment under a lease charge or mortgage where the assignment does not convey or transfer the assignor's interest in the real property. Two important issues are associated with this feature of the Act. The first is whether it is conceptually possible to transfer lease, charge, or mortgage payments, or payments under an agreement for sale of land without at the same time transferring the leased land, the charge, the mortgage, or the seller's interest. Assuming this is possible, the second issue is the source of priority rules when an assignment of lease, charge, or mortgage payments transferred apart from the leased land, charge, or mortgage is in competition with a subsequent interest acquired in the land.

The second issue is answered by the Ontario Act. Under section 36, a security interest in lease, charge, or mortgage payments is subordinate to the interest of a person who acquires for value the lessor's interest in the leased land, the chargee's interest in the charge or the mortgagee's interest in the mortgage, as the case may be, if the security interest is not registered in the appropriate land registry office before the interest of such person is registered in the land registry office.[180]

The first issue is not directly addressed in the Act. However, the mention of the transferability of rights to payments under leases, charges, or mortgages in section 4(1)(e) is a clear expression of the decision of the Ontario Legislature to recognize this form of transfer of interests in land as being within the scope of the Act. Although the opening words of section 4(1)(e) appear to recognize that an interest in land is involved, clause (ii) refers to a form of agreement that, on its term, does not transfer the assignor's interest in the land. However, this clause need not be viewed as a statutory reversal of the common law principle that a lease, charge, or mortgage payment cannot be transferred without transferring an interest in the leased land, charge, or mortgage. Its effect is to apply the PPSA priority regime to the interests in land that are implicitly transferred under such agreements. This approach is confirmed by section 36, which provides priority rules where a prior assignee of lease, charge, or mortgage payments is in competition with a transferee of the lessor's interest in the leased property or the "real

---

180   Section 54(1)(b) of the Ontario Act permits and regulates registration in a land registry office.

property thereby demised"[181] or a transferee of the charge or mortgage, as the case may be.

Section 4(1)(e) does not directly address assignments of payments owing under agreements for sale of land. In *Canadian Imperial Bank of Commerce v. Yorkshire & Canadian Trust Ltd.*[182] a majority of the Supreme Court concluded that such an assignment necessarily carries with it the seller's equitable obligation to transfer an interest in the land when the final payment has been made. The decision of the Ontario Court of Appeal in *Irving A. Burton Ltd. v. Canadian Imperial Bank of Commerce*[183] may be viewed as a contradictory ruling although the issue appears not to have been argued before the Court.

b) The Alternative Approach

The approach to the problem of separating real from personal property interests contained in the PPSAs, other than that of British Columbia and Manitoba, is uniform and more direct.[184] These Acts exclude from their scope any transaction that creates or transfers an interest in land, including a lease[185] or that provides for the creation or transfer of a right to payment that arises in connection with an interest in land,[186] other than a right to payment that is evidenced by a security or instrument. While these payments are treated at law as being personal

---

181 These words were apparently designed to give priority to a mortgagee who, under the terms of the mortgage, is entitled to go into possession and collect lease payments of tenants of the mortgagee. See Ontario, Minister's Advisory Committee on the Personal Property Security Act, *Report of the Minister's Advisory Committee on the Personal Property Security Act* (Toronto: Ministry of Consumer and Commercial Relations, 1984) at 57–58. However, until the mortgagee goes into possession, the right to the rental payments remains with the secured party who has acquired an interest in them under a contract referred to in s. 4(1)(e)(ii).

182 [1939] 1 D.L.R. 401 (S.C.C.).

183 (1982), 134 D.L.R. (3d) 369 (Ont. C.A.). See also *Iverson Heating Ltd. v. Canadian Imperial Bank of Commerce* (1983), 43 A.R. 142 (Alta. Q.B.) in which the court concluded that an assignment of payments by itself under an agreement for sale could not support a caveat under the Alberta *Land Titles Act*.

184 PPSA (A, M, NB, PEI, S) s. 4; (NWT, Nu, Y) s. 3; (NL, NS) s. 5.

185 The BCPPSA specifically excludes licences issued under s. 10 of the *Forest Act*, petroleum and natural gas leases under *the Petroleum and Natural Gas Act*, leases issued under the *Coal Act* that confer the right to produce the coal, a mineral claim or placer claim under the *Mineral Tenure Act*, and "any similar interest that is prescribed for the purposes of this section." No additional categories have been prescribed.

186 The MPPSA includes within its scope a transfer of rental payments under a lease of land. See s. 4(f).

property in some contexts,[187] the potential for conflict between security interests in the payments and associated real property rights was apparently enough to convince legislators that no attempt should be made to craft a workable set of PPSA priority rules to accommodate these features of two systems.[188]

The PPSA contains an exception to the exclusion of transactions that provide for the creation or transfer of an interest in a right to payment that arises in connection with land. Negotiable debt instruments[189] that are dealt with in the market may well be secured by an interest in real property. For example, in order to raise capital a mortgage company may issue transferable debt obligations secured in part by its mortgage holdings. If one of these debt obligations (that is, instruments) is purchased by an investor who then gives a security interest in it, the background mortgage security does not exclude the security agreement from the operation of the PPSA. Consequently, if the investor gave two security interests in the instrument, the priority regime of the PPSA would apply. This would not be the case, however, if the document embodying the debt obligation specifically provided for or created a mortgage on identified land. Such a document falls out-

---

187 This approach does not eliminate all problems. For example, whether an overriding royalty or net profit interest created under an oil-and-gas lease is an interest in land or merely a personal interest is apparently a matter of the intention of the parties to the agreement creating the interest and not any *a priori* characterization of this type of interest. See *Bank of Montreal v. Dynex Petroleum Ltd.*, [2000] 2 W.W.R. 693 (Alta. C.A.), aff'd [2002] 1 S.C.R. 146.

188 In several provinces land law specifically addresses assignments of mortgage and lease payments. These provisions do not specifically refer to assignments of payments under agreements for sale of land. However, such an assignment likely creates a registerable interest in land since the debt and the assignor's interest in the land cannot be separated. See *Canadian Imperial Bank of Commerce v. Yorkshire & Canadian Trust Ltd.*, above note 182. See discussion of this issue above. The Alberta *Law of Property Act*, R.S.A. 2000, c. L-7, s. 63 deems an assignment of rental payments under a lease of land to be an equitable interest in land. As such it can be registered by caveat and is subject to the priority rules of the *Land Titles Act*. A similar approach is contained in the Saskatchewan *Land Titles Act, 2000*, S.S. 2000, c. L-5.1, ss. 17 and 144.

     All the Atlantic Canada provinces have brought land-related rights to payment within the scope of land registry or land titles Act. See, for example, *Registry Act*, R.S.N.B. 1973, c. R-6, s. 1.1 and the *Land Titles Act* S.N.B. 1981, c. L1.1., s. 2.1.

189 The text addresses the matter in the context of an instrument. However, the same explanation applies to a security. Both instrument and security are defined terms. PPSA (A, BC, NWT, Nu, Y) s. 1(1); (M, NB, PEI) s. 1; (NL, NS) s. 2; S s. 2(1).

side the definition of "instrument" and, as a result, is not caught by the exception to the exclusion of rights of payment arising in connection with an interest in land.

A somewhat different approach is contained in the BC Act. The definition of "instrument"[190] excludes negotiable debt obligations secured by a mortgage on land, "unless the interest being mortgaged is, itself, a mortgage on land." Consequently, a negotiable debt obligation that is technically a mortgage of a mortgage interest can qualify as an "instrument." Section 2(2) extends the scope of the Act to such an instrument unless it is registered under the *Land Title Act* or an application to register it under that Act has been made.

6) Remuneration for Personal Services

The PPSAs, other than the Ontario and Atlantic provinces Acts,[191] exclude from their scope the creation or transfer of an interest in present or future wages, salary, pay, commission, or other compensation for labour or personal services other than fees for professional services.[192] In several jurisdictions, the exclusion of wage assignments is of little significance since most such assignments are prohibited or very severely restricted.[193] The exclusion is much more significant in the context of assignments of non-wage income.

The courts have consistently held that real estate agents' and brokers' commissions are not "fees for professional services" and, as a result, assignment of them is not within the scope of the Act.[194] In *Re Lloyd*,[195] the Alberta Queen's Bench Court concluded that the juxtaposition of the words "commission" and "fees" in the section indicates that the former is not subsumed in the latter. In addition, the court concluded that the word "professional" refers to an occupation requiring special training in the liberal arts or science.

---

190 BCPPSA s. 2. See also the definition of security.

191 For example, section 4(d) of the NB Act excludes "the creation or transfer of an interest in present or future wages, salary, pay commission or any other compensation for work or services, the assignment or transfer of which is prohibited by any statute or rule of law."

192 PPSA (A, BC, M, NB, PEI, S) s. 4; (NWT, Nu, Y) s. 3; (NL, NS) s. 5.

193 See, for example, *Fair Trading Act*, R.S.A. 2000, c. F-2, s. 52; *The Assignment of Wages Act*, R.S.S. 1978, c. A-32, s. 2; *Employment Standards Act*, R.S.B.C. 1997, c. 113, ss. 21–22.

194 *F.W.C. Land Co. (Receiver-Manager of) v. Turnbull* (1997), 49 C.B.R. (3d) 82 (B.C.S.C.); *Ogden v. Award Realty Inc.*, above note 103.

195 (1995), 9 P.P.S.A.C. (2d) 107.

The effect of the approach taken in Ontario and in Atlantic provinces is to leave to non-PPSA law[196] the determination as to the validity of assignments of remuneration for personal services. However, to the extent such assignments are valid, the PPSA applies.

7) Other Exclusions

a) Transfer Where Transferee Performs the Contract and a Transfer for Collection

All Acts exclude an assignment or transfer of an unearned right to payment under a contract to a transferee who is to perform the transferor's obligations under the contract.[197] This exclusion addresses situations where there is little or no chance of third-party deception because the transferee steps into the shoes of the transferor who no longer is in a position to deceive third parties into thinking that he is entitled to payment under the contract.

The exclusion of transfers of accounts solely to facilitate their collection for the transferor found in all of the Acts[198] is warranted. Since the transferee remains the agent of the transferor, she is not an independent transferee so as to be capable of asserting priority over another transferee.

b) Sale of Accounts or Chattel Paper in a Sale of a Business

All Acts, other than that of Ontario, exclude a sale of accounts or chattel paper as part of a sale of a business out of which the accounts or chattel paper arose unless the seller remains in control of the business after the sale.[199] A very similar result prevails under the Ontario Act that excludes a sale of accounts or chattel paper as part of a transaction to which the *Bulk Sales Act*[200] applies.

The exclusion of sales of accounts and chattel paper incidental to the sale of a business is justifiable because, in this context, the potential that the assignor will be able to mislead other buyers of the accounts or chattel paper is very limited unless the substitution of the new owner for the former owner is not obvious as a result of the former owner remaining in control of the business.

---

196 See *Wages Act*, R.S.O. 1990, c. W.1, s. 7; and *Re Beaton* (1979), 30 C.B.R. (N.S.)
      225 (Ont. C.A.); *Employment Standards Act*, S.N.B. 1982, c. E-7.2, s. 38.
197 PPSA (A, BC, M, NB, PEI, S) s. 4; (NWT, Nu, Y) s. 3; (NL, NS) s. 5; O s. 4(1).
198 *Ibid.*
199 *Ibid.*
200 R.S.O. 1990, c. B.14.

c) Tort Claims

All Acts, other than that of Ontario, exclude the creation or transfer of an interest in a right to damages in tort.[201] The scope of this exclusion is unclear. A narrow interpretation of the provision would limit it to the assignment or transfer by a plaintiff in a tort action of prospective damages in the action or damages awarded but not paid. A permissibly broader interpretation is that it applies to an amount payable under a settlement agreement that terminates or precludes the recovery of damages in a court action. In *Alberta Opportunity Co. v. Dobko*,[202] the Alberta Queen's Bench Court concluded that the exclusion applied to an assignment of insurance proceeds payable to a plaintiff and held in a trust account of the plaintiff's lawyer. The court followed an earlier Alberta decision in which the court took the position that the exclusion should be given a broad interpretation,[203] and found that the solicitor was the agent for the assignor and, as such, merely held the money on her behalf. This finding leaves open the question as to whether the exclusion would apply in a case of an assignment of an account owing by a deposit-taking institution that represents proceeds of a successful tort action. Unlike the plaintiff's solicitor in the *Alberta Opportunity* case, the institution would not be the agent of the assignor and the account would not be owing by the defendant or the defendant's insurer. What would be assigned would not be "a right to damages in tort."

d) Sellers' Right of Disposal under the *Sale of Goods Act*

Under section 20(2) of the Ontario *Sale of Goods Act*[204] (and identical provisions contained in Sale of Goods Acts of all other PPSA jurisdictions), where goods are shipped and by the bill of lading are deliverable to the order of the seller or the seller's agent, the seller in the absence of evidence to the contrary is deemed to reserve the right of disposal. Generally, this right is relied upon to ensure payment of the price of the goods shipped under the bill of lading. Consequently, the use of an order bill of lading, when this form of shipping contract is a matter of agreement between the seller and the buyer, may be seen as a method of creating a security interest in the goods in order to secure payment of the price. For obvious reasons, legislators did not intend this result. It is long-established commercial practice for seller to use order bills of

---

201 PPSA (A, BC, M, NB, PEI, S) s. 4; (NWT, NU, Y) s. 3; (NL, NS) s. 5.

202 (1995), 9 P.P.S.A.C. (2d) 72.

203 *Gauthier Estate v. Capital City Savings & Credit Union Ltd.* (1992), 3 P.P.S.A.C. (2d) 176 (Alta. Q.B.).

204 R.S.O. 1990, c. S.1.

lading in this way without intending that, in the event of non-payment, a secured party-debtor relationship exists and that, in the context of the PPSA, Part 5 would have to be complied with.[205] It is for this reason that the definition of security interest contained in all Acts, other than the Ontario Act, provides that the term does not include the interest of a seller who has shipped goods to a buyer under a negotiable bill of lading or its equivalent to the order of the seller or its agent, unless the parties have otherwise evidenced an intention to create or provide for a security interest in the goods.[206]

The issue is addressed differently in the Ontario Act. Subsection 4(2) of the Ontario Act has been interpreted as having a broader effect than its counterparts in the other Acts. The subsection provides that the "rights of buyers and sellers under section 20(2) ... of the *Sale of Goods Act* are not affected by" the Act. The "right" of the seller under section 20(2) is the right to the *prima facie* presumption that the seller who ships under an order bill of landing reserves "the right of disposal."[207] The effect of preserving a right of disposal until conditions are fulfilled is described in section 20(1) of that Act. Despite the delivery of the goods to the buyer, the property in the goods does not pass to the buyer until those conditions have been fulfilled. Consequently, even though the goods have been delivered to the buyer, a reservation of a right of disposal through the use of an order bill of lading gives to the seller the functional equivalent of a perfected purchase money security interest without the need to comply with the PPSA so long as there is no evidence that the seller has surrendered its right of disposition.[208]

The approach contained in the other Acts has a much narrower effect. Since their only effect is to exclude from the definition of "security interest" the implication of reservation of title associated with the use of an order bill of lading, a contractual right of disposition (that is, retained ownership) that continues after delivery of the goods might very well be viewed as a security interest subject to the PPSA.

---

205 In *Barclays Business Credit, Inc. v. Fletcher Challenge Canada Ltd.* (1993), 13 O.R. (3d) 118 (Gen. Div.) the court concluded that an additional reason for section 4(2) of the OPPSA is to relieve the seller from the need to be concerned about competing security interests that might have priority.

206 PPSA (A, BC, NWT, Nu, O, Y) s. 1(1); (M, NB, PEI) s. 1; (NL, NS) s. 2; S s. 2(1).

207 Presumably, this is treated as an implied term in the contract with the buyer that can be overridden by provisions in the contract or conduct of the seller that indicates otherwise.

208 *Barclays Business Credit, Inc. v. Fletcher Challenge Canada Ltd.*, above note 205.

F. THE EFFECT OF RESTRICTIONS ON THE TRANSFER OF ASSETS

1) What Is Property?

By definition, a security interest is an interest in personal property.[209] Consequently, it is not possible to have a security interest in something that is not property. The failure of the common law to give precision to the concept of personal property creates peripheral uncertainty with respect to the application of the Act. Modern commercial law has accepted an increasing number of interests that are treated as property including interests that originally were treated as *in personam* rights. The most common interest of this kind is a simple debt. The creditor entitled to payment has only a personal right against the debtor to receive payment. However, the creditor can give to a third party a right in that right to payment. In the event of the bankruptcy of the creditor, the transferee of the right has priority to it over the creditor's trustee. In this sense, the personal right is property.

2) Licences and Quotas

The need to define what is meant by "property" under the PPSA has arisen in the context of attempts to take security interests in licences or agricultural quotas.

The term "licence" is used to refer to a range of different rights. A licence can be contractual or statutory, transferable or non-transferable. Generally, the term is used to refer to a grant of permission or authority given to a person to do some lawful act that that person otherwise could be precluded from doing.[210] Whether or not the right is "property" will depend upon a number of factors involving principally the extent to which the holder of the right can transfer it[211] and can

---

209 PPSA (A, BC, NWT, Nu, O, Y) s. 1(1); (M, NB, PEI) s. 1; (NL, NS) s. 2; S s. 2(1).

210 An agreement under which the owner of personal property is permitted to install and operate equipment on the land and premises of another person is a licence that does not entail a property interest. See *Wal-Mac Amusements Ltd. v. Jimmy's Dining and Sports Lounge*, [1997] 7 W.W.R. 358 (Alta. C.A.).

211 "It is submitted that the true test (of the existence of a property interest in a right) is as to whether the right, that is the *res* itself, can be dealt with and assigned.... The mere fact that it can be computed in terms of monetary value is not conclusive." E.I. Sykes and S. Walker, above note 14 at 9.

prevent its summary revocation or termination.[212] A licence coupled with a grant is proprietary.[213] While an *indicium* of a property interest is free transferability, it is not the only operative factor in the determination as to whether a licence is property. As a practical matter, however, the secured party may not be able enforce the security interest in the event of default by the debtor by compelling its transfer. However, in this case, the secured party may look to the proceeds as its security so long as the perfection requirements with respect to the proceeds have been met.[214]

The answer to the question as to whether it is possible to take a security interest in an agricultural production licence or quota has been influenced by controversial decisions in the Ontario Court of Appeal.[215] The Court concluded that tobacco production and milk production quotas (as distinct from money derived from the quotas) are not personal property under Ontario law. However, these decisions have been distinguished on the grounds that the legislation under which the quotas were granted gave to the granting agency unfettered discretion as to the granting and withdrawal of the quotas. Where this does not

---

212 See *Re Foster* (1992), 89 D.L.R. (4th) 555 (Ont. Ct. Gen. Div.) (taxi licence); *Sugarman v. Duca Community Credit Union Ltd.* (1998), 38 O.R. (3d) 429 (Gen. Div.), aff'd (1999), 44 O.R. (3d) 257 (C.A.) (nursing home licence). In *Re T. Eaton Co.* (1999), 14 C.B.R. (4th) 288 (S.C.J.), Farley J. of the Ontario Superior Court observed that these decisions can be explained on the basis of a very expanded view of personal property under the PPSA.

213 The issue as to whether a property interest can be created in a licence is important in cases when the licencee's trustee in bankruptcy uses the licence to generate income. The general rule is that, in the absence of a security interest in the licence, the creditor has no claim to the proceeds generated from the disposition of the licence. See *Irving B. Burton v. CIBC* (1982), 36 O.R. (2d) 703 (C.A.); *Kent Steel Products Ltd. v. Arlington Management Consultants Ltd.* (1967), 62 D.L.R. (2d) 502 (Man. C.A.). As to whether a pre-bankruptcy assignment of the proceeds can be enforced against the trustee see *Holy Rosary Parish (Thorold) Credit Union Limited v. Premier Trust*, [1965] S.C.R. 503 and chapter 11.

214 See, for example, *Agricultural Credit Corp. of Saskatchewan v. Featherstone (Trustee of)*, [1996] 8 W.W.R. 281 (Sask. Q.B.).

215 *National Trust Co. v. Bouckhuyt* (1987), 39 D.L.R. (4th) 60 (Ont. H.C.J.), rev'd 43 D.L.R. (4th) 543 (Ont. C.A.); *Canadian Imperial Bank of Commerce v. Hallahan* (1990), 69 D.L.R. (4th) 449 (Ont. C.A.), leave to appeal to S.C.C. refused (1991), 74 D.L.R. (4th) viii (S.C.C.); *Bank of Montreal v. Bale* (1991), 5 O.R. (3d) 155 (Gen. Div.), aff'd (1992), 4 P.P.S.A.C. (2d) 114 (Ont. C.A.). See also *Ontario Dairy Cow Leasing Ltd. v. Ontario Milk Marketing Board* (1990), 1 P.P.S.A.C. (2d) 149 (Ont. Ct. Gen. Div.), rev'd on other grounds (1993), 38 A.C.W.S. (3d) 807 (Ont. C.A.) and *Sanders v. British Columbia (Milk Board)* (1991), 77 D.L.R. (4th) 603 (B.C.C.A.) (milk production quota not property for which compensation must be paid).

exist, the right involved is more likely to be viewed as property.[216] The approach of the Ontario Court of Appeal was not followed in *Saskatoon Auction Mart Ltd. v. Finesse Holsteins*[217] in which the court concluded that a milk quota was property of the grantee subject to a security interest even though, under the regulations of the milk marketing board, it was declared to be property of the board.[218] The court also noted that while the board had control over the transfer of the quota, permission was frequently given with the result that the quota was viewed as having significant marketable value.[219]

The Saskatchewan Act explicitly confirms that "licences" constitute property that can be made the object of security so long as the licence is transferable, even if transfer is subject to restrictions or requires the consent of the licensing authority.[220] However, the secured creditor's power to realize its security by sale must be exercised in conformity with the terms and conditions governing the transfer of the licence.[221]

The Saskatchewan provisions codify the results reached in the *Saskatoon Auction Mart Ltd.* case. In the view of the authors, this jurisprudence should be treated as persuasive authority in the other provinces

---

216 It has been argued that the test as to whether a quota or licence should be collateral is subjective to the parties involved. "We are bound to reiterate that regulatory controls should play no role in determining what may be the subject of a security interest. If the transaction is not illegal it should be left to the secured party to determine whether the licence makes suitable security and to run the risk of the transfer not being approved if the secured party seeks to enforce the security interest." J.S. Ziegel and D. Denomme, *The Ontario Personal Property Security Act Commentary and Analysis* (Aurora, Ont.: Canada Law Book, 1994) at 36–37. The authors do not repeat this assertion in their second edition. This approach is difficult to accept. The Ontario Court of Appeal is technically correct in its conclusion that a security interest under the PPSA is an interest in personal property. A contractual agreement that a right is property does not make it property.

217 [1993] 1 W.W.R. 265 (Q.B.).

218 The SPPSA now includes "licence" in the definition of "intangible" and defines "licence" as "a right, whether or not exclusive, to manufacture, produce, sell, transport or otherwise deal with personal property or to provide services that is transferable by the grantee with our without restriction or consent of the grantor." See ss. 2(1)(w) and 2(1)(z).

219 However, these factors were not considered significant to the determination in the *National Trust Co. v. Bouckhuyt* decision of the Ontario Court of Appeal, above note 215.

220 The Saskatchewan Act includes "licence" in the definition of "intangible" and defines "licence" as "a right, whether or not exclusive, to manufacture, produce, sell, transport or otherwise deal with personal property or to provide services that is transferable by the grantee with our without restriction or consent of the grantor." See ss. 2(1)(w) and 2(1)(z).

221 SPPSA ss. 57(3), 59(18).

and territories. In other words, the authors do not endorse the more restrictive position adopted by the Ontario courts holding that security taken in rights of this kind falls outside the scope of the Ontario PPSA on the questionable theory that non-transferable licences do not constitute property within the meaning of the PPSA.

3) Other Types of Unassignable Property or Property Subject to Transfer Restrictions

Legal restrictions on the debtor's right to transfer collateral[222] do not preclude attachment of a security interest, whatever impact it may have on the secured creditor's direct enforcement rights. A security interest granted in confidential information attaches according to the ordinary PPSA rules, notwithstanding that the secured party's enforcement rights must be exercised in a manner that respects the debtor's duty of confidentiality.[223] However, an attempt to create a security interest in claims owing by the government fails if the debts owing by the Crown are prohibited by statute.[224]

A debate has arisen in the context of attempts to take security interests in registered retirements savings plans (RRSP) that fall within section 146(2)(c.3) of the *Income Tax Act*.[225] This section sets out conditions

---

222 *Ibid.*

223 In *Re Axelrod* (1994), 20 O.R. (3d) 133, 8 P.P.S.A.C. (2d) 1 (Ont. C.A.), aff'g (1994), 16 O.R. (3d) 649 (Ont. Ct. Gen. Div.), it was held that a security interest was capable of attaching to a dentist's patient records notwithstanding the dentist's overriding fiduciary duty and duty of confidentiality towards his patients. As explained by Arbour J.A. (as she then was) at 139:

> I see no difference between a dentist's entitlement to sell his or her practice, and a dentist's entitlement to pledge records. Both can be accomplished in a manner compatible with a dentist's professional responsibilities, as long as the dentist acts with the utmost good faith and loyalty in protecting the patient's confidence. The doctor may use the records to pursue his or her self-interest, so long as it does not conflict with the duty to act in the patient's best interests.

See also *Josephine V. Wilson Family Trust v. Swartz* (1993), 6 P.P.S.A.C. (2d) 76 (Ont. Ct. Gen. Div.). See also *Re Gauntlet Energy Corp.* (2003), 36 B.L.R. (3d) 250 (Alta. Q.B.) (the fact that confidential seismic information was not property for purposes of criminal law did not preclude finding that data was personal property in the nature of an intangible for the purposes of the PPSA).

224 *Marzetti v. Marzetti*, [1994] 2 S.C.R. 765. The decisions of Saskatchewan courts to the contrary are in error. *Orr & Co. v. Saskatchewan Economic Development Corp.* (1994), 24 C.B.R. (3d) 196, 6 P.P.S.A.C. (2d) 350, 119 Sask. R. 121 (Q.B.), aff'd (1994), 125 Sask. R. 80 (C.A.).

225 R.S.C. 1985, c. 1 (5th Supp.).

that must be met for a "depositary" RRSP. These conditions include: (1) the depositary has no right of offset as regards the property held under the plan in connection with any debt or obligation owing to the depositary, and (2) the property held under the plan cannot be pledged, assigned, or in any way alienated as security for a loan or for any purpose other than that of providing for the annuitant, commencing at maturity, a retirement income. In *Bank of Nova Scotia v. Phenix (Trustee of)*[226] the Saskatchewan Court of Appeal concluded that section 146 precluded the use of an RRSP as collateral under a security agreement. However, in *Re Whaling*[227] the Ontario Court of Appeal rejected this conclusion. The Court ruled that the creation of a security interest in (or contractual right of set-off relating to) a deposit resulted in its deregistration as an RRSP;[228] it did not invalidate the security interest or set-off right. It is the view of the authors that the approach of the Ontario Court of Appeal in this matter is the correct one. The conditions of section 146(2)(c.3) of the *Income Tax Act* do not go to the existence or validity of a security interest. They relate to the existence of a depositary RRSP.

The PPSA, with the exception of the Ontario Act, expressly permits the grant of security in (and the assignment of) accounts owed by a third party — the "account debtor" — to the assignor/debtor, notwithstanding a prohibition in the contract between the account debtor and the assignor/debtor under which the account arises.[229] Although the account debtor remains free to claim damages from the assignor/debtor for any actual loss or damage caused by breach of the "anti-assignment" clause, the security interest is effective and enforceable as between the assignor (debtor) and the assignee/secured party, and as between the assignee/secured party and the account debtor.

The common law rule applies in Ontario (as well as in the other PPSA jurisdictions with respect to accounts falling outside the scope of the Act). At common law, an anti-assignment clause does not nullify the grant of a security interest as between the debtor and the secured party, but the account debtor is entitled to plead the clause as a defence to a demand

---

226 (1989), 9 P.P.S.A.C. 95 (Sask. C.A.). See also *Re Baitinger*, [2002] 8 W.W.R. 686 (Sask. Q.B.).

227 Above note 109. The Court expressly rejected the conclusion of the British Columbia Court of Appeal in *Re Leavitt*, [1998] 3 W.W.R. 140 (B.C.C.A.). See also *Caisse Populaire Desjardins de Val-Brilliant v. Blouin* (2003), 225 D.L.R. (4th) 577 (S.C.C.).

228 This does not apply to a non-depository RRSP. See *Corscadden v. Crown Life Insurance Co.* (1994), 129 Sask. R. 244 (Q.B.).

229 PPSA (BC, M, NWT, Nu, S) s. 41(9); (NB, PEI) s. 41(10); NL s. 42(1); NS s. 42(10); Y s. 39(5); O no equivalent provision.

for payment by the assignee/secured party.[230] The practical effect of this is that while the assignee/secured party must enforce its rights through the assignor/debtor and cannot proceed directly against the account debtor, the security interest will nonetheless be effective against competing third-party creditors and the assignor/debtor's bankruptcy trustee.

4) First Nations Property Situated on a Reserve

The *Indian Act*[231] provides as follows:

> **88.** Subject to the terms of any treaty and any other Act of Parliament, all laws of general application from time to time in force in any province are applicable to and in respect of Indians in the province, except to the extent that those laws are inconsistent with this Act or any order, rule, regulation or by-law made thereunder, and except to the extent that those laws make provision for any matter for which provision is made by or under this Act.

> **89.** (1) Subject to this Act, the real and personal property of an Indian or a band situated on a reserve is not subject to charge, pledge, mortgage, attachment, levy, seizure, distress or execution in favour or at the instance of any person other than an Indian or a band.

> (2) A person who sells to a band or a member of a band a chattel under an agreement whereby the right of property or right of possession thereto remains wholly or in part in the seller may exercise his rights under the agreement notwithstanding that the chattel is situated on a reserve.

These provisions have a direct effect on the application of the PPSA to property of "an Indian or band."[232] The case law has provided considerable guidance as to their effect.

---

230 See *Rodaro v. Royal Bank of Canada*, [2000] O.J. 272 (S.C.J.), approving *Yablonski v. Cawood (c.o.b. Cawood Walker)* (1997), 143 D.L.R. (4th) 65 at 76 (Sask. C.A.) (which held that even if a contract contains a prohibition on assignment, the assignment would still be effective as between assignor and assignee; such a prohibition merely prevents the assignee from having direct recourse against the non-consenting party to the assigned contract).

231 R.S.C, 1985, c. I-5, s. 89; R.S., 1985, c. 17 (4th Supp.). It is not clear whether a band can waive the application of section 89. In a New Brunswick case, it was assumed (without argument on the point) that this was possible. See *Kingsclear Indian Band v. J.E. Brooks & Associates* (1991), 118 N.B.R. (2d) 290 (C.A.).

232 *Kostyshyn (Johnson) v. West Region Tribal Council Inc.* (1992), [1994] 1 C.N.L.R. 94 (F.C.T.D.) See also *Afton Band of Indians v. Attorney General of Nova Scotia* (1978), 3 R.P.R. 298 (N.S.T.D.).

Section 89 of the *Indian Act* does not apply to a security agreement with an Inuit, Metis, and non-status Indians since such persons do not fall within the definition of "Indian" in the *Indian Act*. Similarly, a corporation is not an Indian band within meaning of the *Indian Act* even if it has its registered office on a reserve and even if its shareholders are registered Indians.[233] The result is that that a First Nations debtor corporation does not receive the benefits of or disadvantages resulting from section 89. Furthermore, the corporation as creditor is subject to the section 89 prohibition on taking security interests in and seizure of property on an reserve.

A security interest taken on collateral that is clearly located on a reserve is invalid unless it falls within the exception of section 89(2). If the collateral is clearly located off the reserve, the prohibition does not apply.[234] Where the collateral is mobile goods, the relevant test is whether the paramount location of the goods is on or off the reserve as determined by the overall pattern of safeguarding and use.[235] Generally, in cases involving intangible assets such as a receivable (for example, income or a bank account), the situs is determined using an approach that is very similar to that contained in conflict of law principles. The principal factor in the determination is the location of the account debtor. Consequently, where the account debtor is not located on the reserve, the account does not fall within the protection of the subsection 89(1).[236]

A debtor cannot deliberately relocate what are evidently off-reserve assets to an on-reserve location so as to take advantage of the subsection 89(1).[237] Property belonging to a First Nations person that is invol-

---

233 *First Nations Farm Credit (Manitoba) Corp. v. McKay* (2000), 149 Man. R. (2d) 311 (Q.B.).

234 *Maracle v. Ontario (Minister of National Revenue)*, [1993] O.J. 1173 (Gen. Div.).

235 *Wahpeton Dakota First Nation v. Lajeunesse* (2002), 223 Sask. R. 77 (C.A.), leave to appeal to S.C.C. refused 232 Sask. R. 160n (S.C.C.).

236 The most recent decision on this matter is that of the Manitoba Court of Appeal. In *McDiarmid Lumber Ltd. v. God's Lake First Nation*, 2005 CarswellMan 33 (leave to appeal to S.C.C. granted, August 2005), the court analyzed prior decisions of the Supreme Court of Canada in which a more expansive "connecting factors test" was employed and came to the conclusion that the Supreme Court never intended that this test be applied to the determination under s. 89 as to where an intangible is located. It concluded that the common law test continues to apply. See also *Canadian Imperial Bank of Commerce v. E & S.L. Liquidators*, [1995] 1 C.N.L.R. 23 (B.C.S.C.) and *Fisher v. Seton Lake Indian Band*, [1995] B.C.J. 2512 (S.C.).

237 *Nathanson, Schachter & Thompson v. Sarcee Indian Band*, [1994] 6 W.W.R. 203 (B.C.C.A.).

untarily removed from a reserve by virtue of an illegal police seizure does not thereby lose the protection from seizure afforded by section 89.[238]

The prohibition on taking and enforcing security in section 89 does not apply to a seller who takes or reserves an interest in property sold on credit as security for part or all the unpaid purchase price. The term "person who sells" in section 89 presumably includes an assignee of a such person. Consequently, a lender could gain the advantage of the exception by entering into a tripartite arrangement with the seller and buyer in which the lender provides the seller with the upfront purchase monies in exchange for an assignment of the seller's reservation of title rights against the buyer under its conditional sales agreement with the buyer. This aspect of section 89 reflects the failure on the part of Parliament to bring this feature of the *Indian Act* in line with developments in provincial personal property security law resulting from the enactment of the PPSA which abandons the formal distinction between security by grant and by reservation of title.

FURTHER READINGS

BRIDGE, M., R. MACDONALD, R. SIMMONDS, & C. WALSH, "Formalism, Functionalism, and Understanding the Law of Secured Transactions" (1999) 44 McGill L.J. 567

CUMING, R.C.C., "True Leases and Security Leases Under Canadian Personal Property Security Acts" (1982–83) 7 Can. Bar Rev. 251

KLINCK, D.R., "The Quistclose Trust in Canada" (1994) 23 Can. Bus. L.J. 45

LAW COMMISSION OF CANADA, *Final Report, Leveraging Knowledge Assets, Reducing Uncertainty for Security Interests in Intellectual Property* (Ottawa: Law Commission of Canada, 2004)

LAW COMMISSION OF CANADA, *Final Report, Modernizing Canada's Secured Transactions Law: The Bank Act Security Provisions* (Ottawa: Law Commission of Canada, 2004)

WATERS, D.W.M., "Trusts in the Settling of Business, Commerce and Bankruptcy" (1983) 21 Alta. L. Rev. 395

---

238 *Vincent c. Quebec*, [1995] 3 C.N.L.R. 204 (Que. C.A).

WOOD, R.J. & M. WYLIE, "Non-Consensual Security Interests in Personal Property" (1992) 30 Alta. L. Rev. 1055

WOOD, R.J., "Security Interests in Intellectual Property: Rationalizing the Registries" in H.P. Knopf, ed., *Security Interests in Intellectual Property* (Scarborough: Carswell, 2002) at 669

CHAPTER 3

CONFLICT OF LAWS

A. INTRODUCTION AND GENERAL CONSIDERATIONS

1) Scope of Chapter

This chapter is concerned primarily with the statutory choice of law rules for security interests contained in the PPSA although occasional comparative reference will be made to the counterpart rules of the *Civil Code of Québec* (*Civil Code*) and Article 9 of the *Uniform Commercial Code* (UCC). Reference is sometimes also made to other relevant rules of Canadian private international law.

The PPSA rules apply to security interests in personal property, not proprietary interests in movables generally. Yet, if the law applicable to security interests differs from that applicable to ownership and other types of non-security interests, there is a risk of conflicting priority determinations under the different applicable laws in relation to the same item of collateral. Consequently, this chapter also addresses the desirability of drawing by analogy on the PPSA rules in the judicial development of choice of law rules for movables generally, particularly in relation to the critical issues of perfection and priority.

The insolvency of the debtor is the crucible in which the power of a security interest is tested. Consequently, this chapter also covers the impact of bankruptcy or insolvency proceedings on the law applicable to security interests.

118

The PPSA conflicts regime is not necessarily suitable for all categories of collateral. Chapter 1 of the book examined pending reforms with respect to two categories of collateral: investment property and mobile equipment commonly used across borders. When implemented, these reforms will have an impact on the conflicts rules outlined in this chapter. Chapter 1 also discussed the *United Nations Convention on the Assignment of Receivables in International Trade*. Although implementation plans are only at a very preliminary stage, the convention offers persuasive authority on a number of issues on which the private international law rules in Canadian common law jurisdictions are underdeveloped, including the law applicable to the rights of a secured party against the account debtor where the collateral takes the form of an account.

2) Importance of Choice of Law Rules

The various versions of the PPSA sometimes differ on significant issues. The PPSA varies even more substantially from the security regimes contained in the *Civil Code* and UCC Article 9.[1] Beyond Canada and the United States, the differences can be dramatic with many legal systems not sharing the same level of commitment to the concept of a public registration system for non-possessory security interests.

In view of these differences, it is critical for the parties to a security agreement — and third parties potentially affected by their transaction — to determine which jurisdiction's laws apply to a given issue. The drafters of the PPSA recognized the importance of certainty and predictability at the choice of law level. Explicit guidance is provided on the law applicable to four issues: the validity of a security interest, perfection, the effects of perfection or non-perfection (priority), and enforcement.

3) Overview of PPSA Conflicts Regime

Property rights in immovables have always been governed by the law of their location (*lex rei sitae*). However, rights in movables were historically subject to the law of the domicile of their owner (*lex domicili*). This idea is captured in the old maxims, *mobilia personam sequuntur* (movables follow the person) and *mobilia ossibus inherent* (movables inhere in the bone). These maxims were justified by the exigencies of global trade and the stateless and impermanent quality of movable property:

---

1   For a comparative overview of some of the principal differences, see chapter 1.

In a country a great part of whose commercial capital is employed abroad, it is particularly proper that such capital over which the trader has disposing power although situated out of the Kingdom, should be considered as referable to the *domicilium* of the owner.[2]

It was not until the nineteenth century that the *lex domicili* was replaced by the *lex rei sitae* for private commercial transactions.[3] Although partly influenced by emerging territorial theories of choice of law, the *lex rei sitae* rule was primarily justified on pragmatic grounds: the convenience of having a single choice of law rule for movables and immovables, the realities of practical enforcement, and the reasonable expectations of the parties.

Today, the *lex rei sitae* rule is still widely accepted, but only as a starting point. For intangible assets, more specialized connecting factors are emerging,[4] including a variation of the old *lex domicili* of the owner rule for accounts.[5] The PPSA reflects — indeed it was at the forefront of — these trends.

In identifying the law applicable to the validity, perfection, and effects of perfection or non-perfection of a security interest, the PPSA employs two basic connecting factors: the location of the collateral and the location of the debtor. For goods generally, the law of the jurisdiction where the collateral is located applies,[6] subject to a special destination rule for goods intended for export.[7] For intangibles and for goods that are inherently mobile, the law of the jurisdiction in which the debtor is located applies.[8] For money and reified intangibles (securities, chattel paper, and documents of title), the rule varies depending on whether

---

2   *Phillips v. Hunter* (1795), 2 H. B.I. 409, as quoted by Martin Wolff, *Private International Law*, 2d ed. (Oxford: Clarendon, 1950) at 502–76.

3   *Winans v. Attorney-General*, [1910] A.C. 27 at 32. The law of the domicile retains currency in the context of choice of law for succession to movables on death, and for matrimonial property.

4   See, for example, the *Hague Convention on the Law Applicable to Certain Rights in respect of Securities held with an Intermediary, 2001*. The convention is posted at www.hcch.net under International Commercial and Finance Law — Securities held with intermediaries.

5   See, for example, art. 22 of the *United Nations Convention on the Assignment of Receivables in International Trade*, 2001. The convention is posted at www.uncitral.org under General Assembly Resolutions — 56th Session 2001 — A/RES/56/81 United Nations Convention on the Assignment of Receivables in International Trade.

6   PPSA (A, BC, M, NB, NWT, Nu, O, PEI, S) s. 5(1); (NL, NS) s. 6(1); Y s. 4(1).

7   PPSA (A, BC, M, NB, NWT, Nu, O, PEI, S) s. 6(1); (NL, NS) s. 7(1); Y s. 5(1).

8   PPSA (A, BC, M, NB, NWT, Nu, O, PEI, S) s. 7(2); (NL, NS) s. 8(2); Y s. 6(1).

the security interest is possessory (law of the location of the collateral)[9] or non-possessory (law of the location of the debtor).[10]

When it comes to enforcement, the basic dividing line is between issues relating to the procedural and the substantive aspects of enforcement. For procedural aspects, the *lex rei sitae* applies for tangible collateral and the *lex fori* (law of the forum) applies for intangibles. The proper law of the security agreement applies to the substantive aspects.[11]

In addition to these general rules, the PPSA adopts special perfection rules where the collateral or the debtor, as the case may be, changes location to the enacting jurisdiction. The secured creditor is given a grace period to reperfect its security interest in accordance with the perfection requirements of the enacting jurisdiction.[12] These rules, strictly speaking, are not choice of law rules. Rather, reperfection within the stipulated grace period operates to preserve the perfected status of the security interest from the time of its initial perfection in the jurisdiction where the collateral or debtor was located at the time the security interest attached. The distinction here is a subtle but important one and its implications are revisited later in the chapter.

4) Choice of Law and Territorial Scope of PPSA

In *Holland v. Chrysler Credit Canada Ltd.*,[13] the territorial scope of application of the Alberta PPSA was analyzed according to the traditional proximity test of the level of factual connection between the transaction and Alberta. Where the issue is one to which the PPSA supplies a choice of law rule, this kind of analysis is inappropriate. Through the enactment of choice of law rules, each PPSA legislature has already expressed its intention on the question of the territorial scope not just of other laws but also its own PPSA. Thus, the substantive provisions of the Alberta Act governing the validity and perfection of a security interest apply to litigation taking place in Alberta only to the extent that the choice of law rules in the Alberta PPSA lead to the application of Alberta law. If the Alberta choice of law rules point to the application of some other province's law, for example that of Quebec or Ontario, then

9 PPSA (A, BC, M, NB, NWT, Nu, O, PEI, S) s. 5(1); (NL, NS) s. 6(1); Y s. 4(1).
10 PPSA (A, BC, M, NB, NWT, Nu, O, PEI, S) s. 7(2); (NL, NS) s. 8(2); Y s. 6(1).
11 PPSA (A, BC, M, NB, NWT, Nu, O, PEI, S) s. 8(1); (NL, NS) s. 9(1); Y s. 7(4).
12 PPSA (A, BC, M, NB, NWT, Nu, O, PEI, S) s. 5(3), 7(3); (NL, NS) s. 6(3), 7(3); Y s. 4(2), 6(3).
13 (1992), 5 Alta. L.R. (3d) 258, 134 A.R. 130, P.P.S.A.C. (2d) 250 (Q.B.).

the issue will be governed by the substantive provisions of the *Civil Code of Québec* or the Ontario PPSA, and not the Alberta PPSA.

At the most practical level, the choice of law provisions of the PPSA determine where registration must be made to ensure perfected status. As already noted, these provisions employ different connecting factors for different categories of collateral. It follows that multiple registrations may be required for a single secured transaction. Consider, for example, a debtor with a head office in British Columbia and inventory at locations in Alberta and Saskatchewan with accounts owing to it from customers across Canada. For the accounts, registration will be required in British Columbia, as the jurisdiction in which the debtor is located. However, for the inventory, registration will also be required in Alberta and Saskatchewan as the out-of-province situs of the inventory.

5) Importance of Inter-jurisdictional Uniformity in Choice of Law Rules

The PPSA does not address the jurisdiction of the courts over secured transactions disputes that have an extraprovincial connection. Nor does it cover issues relating to the recognition of extraprovincial judgments involving security interests. These matters are left to be determined by the general rules of private international law of each province and territory.

The common law (and constitutional) rules governing jurisdiction and the effects of foreign judgments have undergone fundamental change as a result of a series of Supreme Court of Canada decisions beginning in 1990.[14] An analysis of the rather complicated state of the current law is not within the scope of this book.[15] For present purposes, it is sufficient to recognize that the courts of more than one province or state may have authority to adjudicate a dispute where a secured transaction has factual connections to multiple places. For example,

---

14   See in particular: *Morguard Investments Ltd. v. De Savoye*, [1990] 3 S.C.R. 1077; *Hunt v. T & N plc*, [1993] 4 S.C.R. 289; *Beals v. Saldanha*, [2003] 3 S.C.R. 416.

15   See Nicholas Rafferty, gen. ed., *Private International Law in Common Law Canada: Cases, Text and Materials*, 2d ed. (Toronto: Emond-Montgomery, 2003) cc. 6-8; Janet Walker & Jean-Gabriel Castel, *Canadian Conflict of Laws*, 6th ed. looseleaf (Markham: Butterworths, 2005), cc. 11, 13-14. The ULCC has adopted three uniform acts aimed at codification of the current law: (1) *Court Jurisdiction and Proceedings Transfer Act* (1994); (2) *Enforcement of Canadian Judgments (and Decrees) Act* (1997); and (3) *Enforcement of Foreign Judgments Act* (2003). The text of these acts, and their enactment status, is posted at www.ulcc.ca under Uniform Statutes (note that the term enacted does not necessarily mean that the statute has been proclaimed in force in the designated jurisdictions).

if the defendant is resident in Ontario, and the collateral is goods located in Quebec and New York, a claimant will usually have a choice of bringing action in Ontario on the basis of the defendant's residence or in Quebec and New York on the basis of the location of the collateral. Where multiple litigation sites are possible, a defendant in an action brought in one venue may be entitled to invoke the doctrine of *forum non conveniens* to have the case heard in a more appropriate venue.[16] However, that doctrine does not necessarily ensure that all disputes in relation to the same collateral will be heard before the courts of a single province or state.

If there are multiple litigation sites, each court will apply the choice of law rules in force in its own jurisdiction to determine the applicable law. If the dispute comes before the Ontario courts, the Ontario courts will apply Ontario choice of law rules to determine the law applicable to a security interest in collateral located in Quebec and New York. If the same security interest is the subject of proceedings in Quebec, the applicable law will be determined by reference to the choice of law rules in the *Civil Code*. If New York is the forum, then choice of law will be decided by the conflicts regime contained in the New York version of Article 9.

If all the provinces or states to which a transaction is connected have identical choice of law rules, then the outcome of any dispute will, in principle, be identical regardless of where the litigation takes place. In the absence of uniformity, however, forum shopping is encouraged, and, where third parties are involved, there is a risk of conflicting priority determinations.

The courts have paid close attention to the importance of inter-jurisdictional uniformity at the choice of law level in interpreting the conflicts provisions of the PPSA. They have refused, for example, to allow minor variations in drafting between different versions of the PPSA,[17] or between the PPSA and Article 9,[18] to lead to a different interpretation where the basic policy underlying the relevant provision is the same. In an even more significant expression of comity, the Ontario Court of Appeal cited the importance of nationally-standardized choice of law rules in applying

16   On the *forum non conveniens* doctrine generally, see *Amchem Products Inc. v. British Columbia Worker's Compensation Board*, [1993] 1 S.C.R. 897; *Spar Aerospace Ltd. v. American Mobile Satellite Corp.*, [2002] 4 S.C.R. 205. On the application of the doctrine in the context of secured transactions cases, see *Mithras Management Ltd. v. New Visions Entertainment Corp.* (1992), 90 D.L.R. (4th) 726 (Ont. Ct. Gen. Div.); *Toronto Dominion Bank v. Hudye Soil Services Inc.*, [2000] 9 W.W.R. 272 (Man. Q.B.).

17   *Toronto Dominion Bank v. RNG Group Inc.* (2002), 61 O.R. (3d) 567 at para. 43 (S.C.J.).

18   *Gimli Auto Ltd. v. BDO Dunwoody Ltd.* (1998), 219 A.R. 166 (C.A.) at para 16.

the Ontario conflicts rule on mobile goods to a true lease even though it did not give rise to a security interest under the substantive provisions of the Ontario Act.[19] Although the lessor was from Ontario, the transaction bore strong connections to Alberta, and the Alberta PPSA (in company with the other Acts except that of Ontario) deems a true lease for a term of more than one year to be a security interest. In concluding that the term security interest for the purposes of the conflicts rules of the Ontario Act should be expanded to accommodate the Alberta concept, the Court cited the need "to avoid the inconsistencies, and the potential forum shopping, that might result from [instead] applying the law of the place where the dispute is adjudicated (the lex fori)."[20]

Harmonization at the interpretation level is possible only if all regimes share the same basic underlying policies. In fact, there are differences on a number of conflicts issues between the PPSA, the *Civil Code*, and Article 9. Because secured transactions frequently involve factual connections between a PPSA jurisdiction and Quebec or the United States, comparative reference will be made throughout this chapter to these other regimes.

6) Mandatory Nature of Choice of Law Rules on Validity and Perfection

To what extent are the secured party and the debtor free to choose a different governing law than the law designated as applicable by the PPSA? Clearly, a contractual choice of law clause cannot bind third parties. It follows that the parties cannot avoid the legal system to which the PPSA refers issues of perfection and the effects of perfection or nonperfection by selecting a different governing law.[21] The proposition is a long-standing one, codified rather than introduced by the PPSA.[22]

When it comes to the issue of the law applicable to the validity of a security interest, a distinction is normally drawn between the substantive requirements for attachment of a security interest as a property right and the validity of the security agreement as a matter of general contract law (for example, contractual capacity, effects of misrepresentation). Only the proprietary aspects are subject to the PPSA choice of law rule for validity. The law applicable to the contractual aspects is determined by the general choice of law rules for contract.

---

19   *GMAC Commercial Credit Corp. Canada v. TCT Logistics Inc.* (2004), 6 P.P.S.A.C. (3d) 163 (Ont. C.A.).
20   *Ibid.* at para. 27.
21   *Gimli Auto Ltd. v. BDO Dunwoody Ltd.*, above note 18.
22   See, for example, *Harrison v. Sterry* (1809), 5 Cranch 289 at 298.

Should a further distinction be drawn between the validity of the security interest as between the parties and as against third parties? In the view of the authors, this distinction is unworkable. For example, whereas the PPSA requires a security interest to be in writing only for the purposes of effectiveness against third parties, Article 9 of the UCC[23] and the *Civil Code*[24] both require writing as a precondition to the effectiveness of the security interest even between the parties. If the parties to a transaction otherwise governed by the *Civil Code* or Article 9 were able to choose the law of a PPSA jurisdiction to determine validity, this would defeat the intention of the legislatures in these jurisdictions to promote writing as an essential condition of the validity of the security interest, that is, as a precondition to the secured party being able to assert any rights against the collateral.

7) Exceptions to the General PPSA Rules

Certain of the Acts qualify the rules covered in this chapter by establishing exceptional rules for specific types of collateral.

First, except for the Ontario Act, the PPSA establishes an exception to the general debtor-location rule for the validity and perfected status of security interests in intangibles where they take the form of accounts resulting from the sale of minerals at the minehead or hydrocarbons at the wellhead. If the security interest in the accounts is provided for in a security agreement executed before the minerals or hydrocarbons are extracted and attaches upon their sale, issues relating to the validity, perfection, and effects of perfection of the security interest are governed by the law of the jurisdiction in which the minehead or wellhead is located.[25] The same rule applies to a security interest in extracted minerals or hydrocarbons provided for in a security agreement executed prior to extraction that is intended to attach upon extraction.[26] Derived from Article 9,[27] the assumption underlying these provisions is that issues of validity, perfection, and the effects of perfection will and should be governed by the real property mortgage law of the jurisdiction in which the land from which the minerals or hydrocarbons are to be extracted is located.

Second, the Acts in effect in British Columbia, Nunavut, and the Northwest Territories also state a special choice of law rule for security

---

23   § 9-203(b).
24   Art. 2696.
25   PPSA (A, M, NB, PEI, S) s. 7(6); (BC, NU, NWT) s. 7(7); (NL, NS) s. 8(6); Y s. 6(6); O no equivalent provision.
26   *Ibid.*
27   § 9-301(4).

interests in foreign registered ships, referring issues of validity, perfection, and the effects of perfection to the law of the jurisdiction where the ship is registered at the time that the security interest attaches.[28] Even in the absence of an equivalent provision, it is the view of the authors that the same rule applies in other PPSA jurisdictions as a result of federal jurisdiction over Canadian maritime law, a body of law that includes the choice of law aspects of matters falling within the purview of maritime law. This is subject to one qualification. While the conflicts rules of Canadian maritime law refer issues relating to the validity and perfection of ship's mortgages to the law of the jurisdiction under which the mortgage arises — effectively, the law of its state of registration — it is for the substantive rules for Canadian maritime law as the law of the forum, once it recognizes the right, to set the priorities to be accorded to that security interest as against other maritime competing claimants.[29]

B. PRELIMINARY INTERPRETIVE ISSUES

1) "Attachment"

The PPSA refers the validity and perfection of a security interest to the law of the jurisdiction where the collateral or debtor is located, as the case may be, at the time of "attachment."[30] Attachment is a term of art in the PPSA (and UCC Article 9) contexts. Even when used in other legal systems, it may have a different meaning (for example, attachment of an English floating charge). For the purposes of choice of law, a more functional concept is needed. The PPSA attachment rules establish the requirements for the creation of a security interest. It follows that the time of attachment for the purposes of the PPSA choice of law rules is the time at which the requirements for the creation of a security interest under the applicable law have been met.

If the dispute before the court involves the issue of non-compliance with the creation rules of the applicable law, this leads to something of a logical conundrum. How can the court apply the law of the jurisdiction where the collateral or the debtor is located at the time of attachment,

---

28   PPSA (BC, NU, NWT) s. 7(6).

29   *Todd Shipyards Corp. v. Altema Compania Maritima S.A.* (1972), [1974] S.C.R. 1248, 32 D.L.R. (3d) 571, [1974] 1 Lloyd's Rep. 174; *Marlex Petroleum Inc. v. The "Har Ra,"* [1987] 1 S.C.R. 57, aff'g [1984] 2 F.C. 345 (C.A.).

30   Location of collateral: PPSA (A, BC, M, NB, NWT, Nu, O, PEI, S) s. 5(1); (NL, NS) s. 6(1); Y s. 4(1). Location of debtor: PPSA (A, BC, M, NB, NWT, Nu, O, PEI, S) s. 7(2); (NL, NS) s. 8(2); Y s. 6(1).

if it is argued that no security interest ever attached? The same problem arises in the context of choice of law for contract. The "putative proper law" solution that has been adopted in that context applies, in the view of the authors, to the secured transactions context. Applying this approach, the applicable law is that of the jurisdiction whose rules would have applied to the issue of the validity of the security interest but for the failure of the secured creditor to comply with that law. For example, suppose a security interest in the form of a hypothec is granted in goods located in Quebec but the parties have not reduced their agreement to writing at the time the dispute arises. The substantive effect of this failure under the law of Quebec is to nullify the hypothec.[31] Under the PPSA choice of law rules, the law of Quebec — as the law of the location of the collateral — would have applied had the security interest been validly created. In the view of the authors, Quebec law therefore applies to the issue of nullity as the putative applicable law.

The putative proper law approach is reflected in article 8(1) of the *Rome Convention*:[32] "The existence and validity of a contract, or any term of a contract, shall be determined by the law which would govern it under this Convention of the contract or term were valid."

Article 8(2) of the convention contains a special rule designed to protect an individual from being taken to consent when, under that person's home law, there would be no consent: "Nevertheless, a party may rely upon the law of a country in which he has his habitual residence to establish that he did not consent if it appears from the circumstances that it would not be reasonable to determine the effect of his conduct in accordance with the law specified in [paragraph 8(1)]."

Of course, the *Rome Convention* binds only the European parties to it. However, it carries significant persuasive weight as a modern restatement of the general multilateral consensus on the appropriate choice of law response to this issue.[33]

2) "Perfection"

At the substantive level, the PPSA draws a distinction between the attachment of a security interest and its perfection. Although attachment

---

31   Art. 2696.

32   *Convention on the Law Applicable to Contractual Obligations (Rome Convention)*, opened for signature in Rome on 19 June 1980 (80/934/EEC). The text of the *Rome Convention* is posted at www.rome-convention.org.

33   Art. 12 of the *Inter-American Convention on the Law Applicable to International Contracts* sets out a very similar rule. The text of this convention is posted at oas.org under Treaties.

or creation is an element of perfection, a security interest is not perfected until it is registered or otherwise perfected. In other legal systems, the distinction between creation and third-party effectiveness may
be non-existent. Instead, a security interest, for at least some types of
transactions, may be treated as taking effect against third parties immediately upon completion of the transaction. For example, under the
Civil Code, an instalment sale in which the seller retains title to secure
the price must be published by registration only in the case of a sale of a
road vehicle, boat, aircraft, or similar high-value asset.[34] Otherwise, the
retention of title is effective against third parties *per se*. The same point
applies to true leases and true consignments in Ontario and the Yukon.
The Ontario and Yukon Acts do not deem these transactions to be "security interests" within the scope of the PPSA: the seller's or the lessor's
title may be set up against third parties without registration.

Except for the Yukon Act, the PPSA provides a functional equivalence test for determining when a security interest is perfected for conflict of law purposes. A security interest is perfected so long as it has a
status against third parties under the applicable law equivalent to that of
a security interest perfected under the PPSA.[35] If the applicable law does
not require a secured party to take any further step to protect or preserve its security interest, it will be regarded as perfected from the time
the agreement is concluded. Although the Yukon Act lacks an equivalent
provision, the same approach would be taken since the provision codifies
the findings in decisions under earlier versions of the PPSA.[36]

3) "Effects of Perfection or Non-perfection" and Priority

The PPSA choice of law rules for validity and perfection also apply to "the
effects of perfection or non-perfection."[37] A plain reading of the reference
to effects of perfection or non-perfection encompasses issues of priority
only to the extent that perfected or non-perfected status is a precondition
to the third-party effectiveness of the security interest (for example, pri-

---

34   Art. 1745 (para. 2); and see art. 15.01 of the *Regulation respecting the Register of
     personal and movable real rights*, R.Q. c. C.c.Q., r. 5.
35   PPSA (A, BC, M, NB, NWT, Nu, O, PEI, S) s. 8(2); (NL, NS) s. 9(2); Y no equivalent provision.
36   See *Re Bedard* (1983), 46 C.B.R. (N.S.) 172 (Ont. H.C.J.); *Juckes (Trustee of)* v.
     Holiday Chevrolet Oldsmobile (1983) Ltd. (1990), 79 C.B.R. (N.S.) 143, (*sub nom.*
     Juckes, Re) 68 D.L.R. (4th) 142, 1 P.P.S.A.C. (2d) 24 (Sask.Q.B.).
37   Location of collateral: PPSA (A, BC, M, NB, NWT, Nu, O, PEI, S) s. 5(1); (NL,
     NS) s. 6(1); Y s. 4(1). Location of debtor: PPSA (A, BC, M, NB, NWT, Nu, O, PEI,
     S) s. 7(2); (NL, NS) s. 8(2); Y s. 6(1).

ority as against a subsequent buyer or trustee in bankruptcy). The words do not necessarily include ranking rules even where the ranking rule is predicated on the order of perfection, for example, the first-to-register rule for competing security interests perfected by registration. Even if read to include ranking rules of this kind, not all priority issues are predicated on the order of perfection. Although a buyer or secured party normally takes subject to a prior perfected security interest, the PPSA recognizes numerous exceptions to this general rule (for example, the special protection given to ordinary course buyers of goods, ordinary course purchasers of negotiable collateral, and purchase money financers).

In practice, the courts have invariably assumed that the PPSA choice of law rules for perfection apply to all priority issues even where the issue does not directly relate to the effects of perfection or non-perfection.[38] In the view of the authors, this is the correct approach.[39] Certainty and predictability would be severely undermined if perfection and priority were to be governed by different laws.

C. APPLICABILITY OF LAW OF THE JURISDICTION WHERE THE COLLATERAL IS LOCATED

1) Ordinary Goods

As a general rule, the validity, perfection, and effects of perfection or non-perfection of a security interest in goods is determined by the law of the jurisdiction where the goods are located.[40] This is effectively a codification of the *lex rei sitae* rule, and the *Civil Code* adopts the same basic rule.[41]

The position under Article 9 is somewhat different. The law of the jurisdiction where the debtor is located governs perfection in all forms of collateral, whether tangible or intangible, subject to only limited exceptions.[42] However, the law of the jurisdiction where goods are located

---

38   See, for example: *Northwest Equipment Inc. v. Daewoo Heavy Industries America Corp.*, [2002] 6 W.W.R. 444 (Alta. CA); *Associates Commercial Corp. v. Scotia Leasing Ltd.* (1995), 10 P.P.S.A.C. (2d) 195 (Ont. Ct. Gen. Div.).

39   Article 9 now refers expressly to priority in addition to the effects of perfection or non-perfection: § 9-301–§ 9-306.

40   PPSA (A, BC, M, NB, NWT, Nu, O, PEI, S) s. 5(1); (NL, NS) s. 6(1); Y s. 4(1).

41   Art. 3102.

42   § 9-301(1). The principal exceptions are security interests in goods covered by a certificate of title (§ 9-303), deposit accounts (§ 9-304), investment property (§ 9-305) and letter-of-credit rights (§ 9-306). Also excepted are all possessory

continues to govern the effects of perfection or non-perfection, and priority.[43] Where a U.S. debtor is involved, or where the collateral includes goods located in the U.S., a prudent secured creditor may therefore wish to also perfect its security interest in the jurisdiction where the debtor is located while also verifying that it has the desired priority ranking under the law of the jurisdiction where the goods are located.

2) Relocation of Goods: Reperfection Requirement

The inherent mobility of goods makes it important to link their location with a specific temporal event for the purposes of applying the *lex rei sitae* rule. Under the PPSA, that event is the time of attachment, the point at which the security interest is created or attempted to be created.[44]

A post-attachment change in the location of the goods poses a risk for third persons who deal with the goods at their new location and who therefore would expect any security interest granted in the goods to be registered or otherwise perfected locally. The Acts address this risk by requiring local reperfection where goods subject to a security interest that attached abroad are brought into the enacting jurisdiction. To preserve continuity of perfection, the secured party is given a grace period for reperfection. The security interest "continues perfected" in the enacting province if it is registered or otherwise perfected in accordance with the enacting province's PPSA before the expiry of the earliest of the following periods:

- sixty days after the goods are brought into the province;
- fifteen days after the secured party has knowledge that the goods have been brought into the Province;[45] or
- before perfection lapses under the original *lex rei sitae*.[46]

If the extraprovincial security interest is perfected in time, it is regarded as having been continuously perfected from the time of initial perfection under the original *lex rei sitae*. If perfection is delayed or does not

---

security interests (§ 9-301(2)) as well as security interests in fixtures (where perfected by a so-called fixture filing), timber to be cut, and minerals to be extracted and related accounts (§ 9-301(3)–(4)).

43   § 9-301(3)(c).

44   PPSA (A, BC, M, NB, NWT, Nu, O, PEI, S) s. 5(1); (NL, NS) s. 6(1); Y s. 4(1).

45   On the question of how knowledge is acquired where the relevant person is a body corporate or the government or operates as a partnership or unincorporated association, see the analysis in chapter 1.

46   PPSA (BC, M, NB, NWT, Nu, PEI, S) s. 5(3); (A, O) s. 5(2); (NL, NS) s. 6(3); Y s. 4(2).

take place at all, the security interest is regarded as unperfected.[47] In other words, continuity of perfection is conditional on perfection before the expiry of the grace period. A secured party can perfect thereafter. However, perfection takes effect only from that point forward. The secured party loses any priority benefits that depend on continuous perfection, for example, priority over an intervening secured creditor.

The wording of the original Ontario PPSA implied that the secured party enjoyed the benefits of perfected status during the grace period whether or not the security interest was ever perfected in Ontario or was perfected in Ontario only after the expiry of the grace period. If this were the rule, third parties who dealt with the collateral during the grace period would have been subordinated to the security interest and would not have been entitled to take advantage of the subsequent lapse in perfected status. While there was some American jurisprudence supporting this result, it was rejected in the Ontario jurisprudence.[48] The current (1989) Ontario PPSA now conforms to that interpretation.[49]

In cases involving the relocation of goods to Quebec, the *Civil Code* establishes a similar reperfection requirement. Published (perfected) status is preserved only if the security is published in Quebec before the earliest of the cessation of publication (perfection) under the original *lex rei sitae*, the expiry of thirty days (as opposed to the sixty days afforded by the PPSA) after the goods enter Quebec, or fifteen days after the secured party finds out about the relocation.[50]

3) When Do Goods Change Location?

The PPSA does not define what constitutes "bringing" goods into the enacting jurisdiction so as to trigger the reperfection requirement. The case law, while sparse, supports a purposive interpretation.[51] Has the primary location of the goods shifted to a new jurisdiction so as to cause third parties there to reasonably believe that they can rely on local perfection rules when dealing with the goods?

Applying this approach, a change in the primary physical location of the goods will normally be sufficient for consumer goods, that

---

47   *Royal Bank v. Anderson (Trustee of)* (1986), 62 C.B.R. (N.S.) 1 (Sask. Q.B.); *Associates Commercial Corp v. Scotia Leasing Ltd.,* above note 38 at 318; *Re Kampman,* [2000] A.J. No. 1211 (Q.B.).

48   *Bachand v. Trans Canada Credit Corp.* (1980), 30 O.R. (2d) 405 (C.A.); *Re Adair* (1985), 15 D.L.R. (4th) 596 (Ont. C.A.).

49   OPPSA s. 5(1).

50   Art. 3104.

51   *Re Steed,* [2001] A.J. No. 262 (Q.B.) at para 6.

is, goods intended for personal family or household purposes. Thus, where a debtor ships household furnishings and other personal use goods to a new province, a finding that the goods have been "brought into the province" as of the date of their arrival will usually be possible without having to worry about whether the principal residence of the debtor changed at the same time.

For mobile goods, such as cars, the interpretation problems may be more acute. Where mobile goods constitute equipment, or inventory held for lease or leased by the debtor, the PPSA substitutes the law of the debtor's location for the *lex rei sitae* in order to avoid the difficulties of determining a stable location.[52] However, determination of the primary location remains necessary for consumer goods and inventory. Bringing a car into a province for the purposes of a road trip does not qualify, even though the car has been "brought into" the province as a physical fact.[53] On the other hand, if the debtor brings a car into the province in the course of establishing a residence there, the car will be considered to have been "brought into" the province, notwithstanding periodic trips back to the old province of residence,[54] and notwithstanding that the car remains registered at the old location after its physical relocation.[55]

A change in the debtor's intended residence is not always necessary. Something less may be enough, for example, bringing a vehicle into a province for use at a seasonal residence located there. In other words, the emphasis should be on the change in the apparent primary location of the goods as opposed to the debtor.

4) Intervening Buyers and Lessees of Relocated Collateral

A security interest in relocated collateral that is reperfected within the grace period will usually enjoy continuity of perfection. As a practical matter, this means that it can still be enforced against competing claimants. The PPSA establishes an important exception to that general rule. Buyers and lessees who acquire the collateral after its relocation but before reperfection take free of the security interest in the absence of actual knowledge.[56] For buyers, this means that they acquire full ownership of the collateral, free

---

52   PPSA (A, BC, M, NB, NWT, Nu, O, PEI, S) s. 7(2); (NL, NS) s. 8(2); Y s. 6(1). The special rule for mobile goods is discussed later in this chapter.

53   *Re Steed,* above note 51 at para 7.

54   *Ibid.*

55   *Re Arseneau* (2005), 7 P.P.S.A.C. (3d) 165 (N.S.S.C.).

56   PPSA (BC, M, NB, NWT, Nu, PEI, S) s. 5(3); (A, O) s. 5(2); (NL, NS) s. 6(3); Y s. 4(2). On the question of what constitutes knowledge for this purpose, and the extent to which knowledge may be inferred from other facts, see the analysis in chapter 1.

and clear of the proprietary rights of the secured party. For lessees, this means that they are entitled to enjoy possession of the collateral during the term of the lease without interference by the secured party except as authorized by the terms of the lease.

This special protection is restricted to buyers and lessees. The security interest will be considered perfected against a competing secured party who takes a security interest after the collateral is relocated as long as reperfection is effected before the grace period expires. The difference in treatment is justified on the theory that, unlike secured parties who are repeat players and can redistribute their losses, a purchase or lease typically represents a one-time transaction for the buyer or lessee.

The Ontario Act offers a more restrained measure of protection. Intervening buyers and lessees are protected only if the collateral acquired from the debtor qualifies as consumer goods.[57] Restricting the protection to consumer buyers is defended on the theory that commercial buyers are sufficiently sophisticated to know that they should investigate the anterior location of the collateral even if a search of the local registry does not disclose any registrations.

At the other extreme is the *Civil Code*. So long as the secured party complies within the applicable grace period, the publicized status of the security right is opposable against all third parties including intervening buyers and lessees.[58]

5) Relocated Goods: Law Applicable to Priority

Under the *Civil Code*, the validity of a security interest is governed by the law of the jurisdiction where the collateral is situated when the security interest is created,[59] whereas publication (perfection) and its effects are governed by the law of the jurisdiction where the collateral is *currently*

---

57 OPPSA s. 5(2). And see *General Motors Acceptance Corp. of Canada Ltd. v. Town & County Chrysler Ltd.*, 2005 CarswellOnt 1393 (Ont. S.C.J.). While the purchase contract must be with "the debtor," debtor is defined to include a transferee of the debtor or a successor to the debtor's interest in the collateral. Consequently, even if the initial sale by the debtor is made to someone who buys the goods as equipment or inventory, any sale by that person to a buyer who intends to use the goods as consumer goods would fall within the protection of s. 5(2).

58 This follows by negative inference from the fact that the only category of buyers protected by art. 3104 (para. 2) of the *Civil Code* are buyers who acquire the collateral in the ordinary course of business.

59 Art. 3102 (para. 1): "The validity of a movable security is governed by the law of the country in which the property charged with it is situated at the time of creation of the security."

situated.[60] Under this formulation, a change in the location of the collateral does not affect the law applicable to validity — thus avoiding the risk of retroactive invalidation — but it does bring about a change in the law applicable to perfection and the effects of perfection or non-perfection.

The PPSA does not make this distinction. Validity, perfection, and the effects of perfection or non-perfection are all governed by the law of the jurisdiction where the collateral is situated at the time of attachment of the security interest. This formulation apparently negates any role for the new *lex rei sitae* following relocation of the collateral except to the extent, as noted above, local reperfection is necessary in order to maintain continuity of perfection.

However, consider a priority conflict between the original secured party and the holder of a security interest granted in the goods following their relocation. If the effects of perfection of the first security interest are governed by the original *lex rei sitae*, and the effects of perfection of the second security interest are governed by the new *lex rei sitate*, which *lex rei sitae* governs a priority dispute between them?

As noted earlier, a plain reading of the reference to the law applicable to the "effects of perfection or non-perfection" does not encompass issues of priority except to the extent that perfected or non-perfected status is a precondition to the third-party effectiveness of a security interest. This opens the door to the continued application of the common law choice of law approach. At common law, the original *lex rei sitae* continues to apply *unless* it is displaced by a new right validly acquired in accordance with the new *lex rei sitae* as a result of events that occur there.[61] Under this approach, the priority rules of the original *lex rei sitae* would apply to contests involving third parties who acquired an interest in the collateral prior to relocation whereas the priority rules of the new *lex rei sitae* would govern contests between the original se-

---

60   Art. 3102 (para. 2): "Publication and its effects are governed by the law of the country in which the property charged with that security is currently situated." Article 9 adopts a similar formulation: § 9-301.

61   *Cammell v. Sewell* (1860), 5 H & N 728, 157 E.R. 1371 (Exch. Ct.) is usually cited as the foundational Anglo-Canadian authority. The leading English and Canadian cases applying the rule include: *Winkworth v. Christie Manson and Woods Ltd.*, [1980] 1 Ch. 496; *Century Credit Corporation v. Richard* (1962), 34 D.L.R. (2d) 291 (Ont. C.A.); *Maden v. Long*, [1983] 1 W.W.R. 649 (B.C.S.C.). Generally, see P.A. Lalive, *The Transfer of Chattels in the Conflict of Laws* (Oxford: Clarendon Press, 1955), especially at 175–84, and J.H.C. Morris, "The Transfer of Chattels in the Conflict of Laws" (1945) Brit. Y.B. Int'l L. 232, especially at 240–41. See also Schilling, "Some European Decisions on Non-Possessory Security Rights in Private International Law" (1985) 34 Int'l & Comp L.Q.

cured party and third party interests — including competing security interests — taken in the collateral after its relocation.

The courts have not addressed the issue of whether the common law approach continues to apply. In practice, where the contest has involved a post-relocation third-party interest, the courts have tended to assume that the priority rules of the new *lex rei sitae* govern.[62] On the other hand, in a case involving a priority contest between security interests that had both attached prior to relocation, the court ruled that the priority regime of the original *lex rei sitae* applied.[63] So the results in practice have tended to conform to the common law approach. On the other hand, in a recent Ontario decision involving a car sold in Quebec on instalment sales terms, the Ontario court applied Quebec law to determine priority as between the Quebec seller and a buyer who had purchased the car in Ontario after its removal into that province but before the Quebec seller had re-registered in the Ontario registry.[64] The instalment seller had re-registered in Ontario before the expiry of the sixty-day grace period required by the Ontario Act, and the court ruled that this had the effect of continuing and preserving the ownership rights of the conditional seller as against the buyer pursuant to the *Civil Code*. As in the other cases, however, the result would have been the same even if the Ontario priority regime had been applied.[65]

6) Goods Intended for Export

Particularly in purchase money financing transactions, the debtor may grant a security interest in goods that are intended to be removed immediately to the debtor's primary residence or place of business in another jurisdiction. In this situation, the law applicable to validity, perfection and the effects of perfection is the law of the jurisdiction to which the goods are to be exported provided two conditions are satisfied.[66] First, the parties must understand that the goods are to be kept in another jurisdiction when the security interest attaches. Second, the

---

62 See, for example, *Re Adair*, above note 48; *Holy Spirit Credit Union* v. *McMullan (Trustee of)*, [1994] M.J. No. 105 (Q.B.).

63 *Advance Diamond Drilling Ltd. (Receiver of)* v. *National Bank Leasing Inc.* (1992), 67 B.C.L.R. (2d) 173 (S.C.).

64 *General Motors Acceptance Corp. of Canada Ltd.* v. *Town & County Chrysler Ltd.*, above note 57.

65 The buyer did not qualify for protection under the special buyer protection rule in s. 5(2) of the Ontario Act because the buyer was a dealer who had purchased the car for resale, and the Ontario Act, as noted earlier, protects intervening buyers only where the goods are acquired by the buyer as consumer goods.

66 PPSA (A, BC, M, NB, NWT, Nu, O, PEI, S) s. 6(1); (NL, NS) s. 7(1); Y s. 5(1).

goods must in fact be removed to that other jurisdiction within thirty days after the security interest attaches. The aim of this exception is to relieve the secured party from the cost and expense of having to comply with the perfection rules of both jurisdictions. The thirty-day restriction on its availability limits the risk of third party dealings with the collateral before it is removed to its intended home.

The goods may subsequently be brought back into the enacting jurisdiction.[67] In that event, the security interest is subject to the same requirements for reperfection that apply where goods subject to a security interest that initially attached outside the enacting jurisdiction are brought into the jurisdiction for the first time.[68]

The thirty-day rule works well in the Canadian cross-border context, particularly since the *Civil Code* adopts a very similar rule.[69] Where the collateral is goods to be exported to or from the United States, however, the thirty-day rule may not provide adequate protection. Article 9 refers perfection (as distinct from the effects of perfection and priority) to the law of the location of the debtor regardless of whether the collateral is tangible or intangible.[70] To be sure that the perfected status of the security interest will be recognized in any litigation that may occur in the United States, a secured party will also need to perfect under that law.

7) Goods in Transit

The *Civil Code* adopts a special choice of law rule for goods in transit directing application of the law of the place of destination.[71] Under this

---

67   PPSA (A, BC, M, NB, NWT, Nu, O, PEI, S) s. 6(1); (NL, NS) s. 7(1); Y s. 5(1).

68   PPSA (A, BC, M, NB, NWT, Nu, O, PEI, S) s. 6(2); (NL, NS) s. 7(2); Y s. 5(2).

69   Art. 3103: "Any movable that is not intended to remain in the country in which it is situated may be charged with a security according to the law of the country for which it is destined; the security may be published according to the law of that country, but publication has effect only if the property actually reaches the country within thirty days of the creation of the security." Under the *Civil Code*, the term "country" refers to a territorial unit in the case of a country that comprises several territorial units each having law making authority; for example, within Canada, each province and territory is a "country" for the purposes of the *Civil Code*: art. 3077.

70   § 9-301(1). The traditional *lex rei sitae* rule continues to apply to security interests in goods covered by a certificate of title (§ 9-303), deposit accounts (§ 9-304), investment property (§ 9-305) and letter-of-credit rights (§ 9-306). Also excepted are all possessory security interests (§ 9-301(2)) as well as security interests in fixtures (where perfected by a so-called fixture filing), timber to be cut, and minerals to be extracted and related accounts (§ 9-301(3)–(4)).

71   See, for example, art. 2093 (para. 2) of the *Civil Code*: "real rights on property in transit are governed by the law of the country of their place of destination."

approach, perfection is governed by the secured transactions law of the place of destination. The PPSA does not address goods in transit. Subject to the thirty-day rule discussed in the preceding paragraph, a secured party may therefore have to perfect in accordance with both the law of the situs at the time of attachment and the law of the intended destination. Indeed, it may be prudent to perfect under the law of any jurisdiction in which the goods may come to rest during the course of transit.

8) Possessory Security Interests in Money and Documentary Collateral

The PPSA extends the *lex rei sitae* rule for the validity and perfected status of a security interest in ordinary goods to a security interest in money or documentary collateral that is in the possession of the secured party.[72] Unlike the case with goods, the various Acts do not provide a grace period for continuation of perfected status should the collateral be relocated to the enacting jurisdiction. The possessory character of the security interest means that the secured party has control over the movement of the collateral and can take whatever steps are needed to preserve its perfected or priority status in advance of the relocation.

D. APPLICABILITY OF LAW OF THE JURISDICTION WHERE THE DEBTOR IS LOCATED

1) Mobile Goods

Application of the *lex rei sitae* rule to perfection and priority is problematic in the case of inherently mobile goods, that is, goods that by virtue of their normal function are used in more than one state. A more stable connecting factor is needed to meet the demands of certainty and predictability. The PPSA substitutes the law of the jurisdiction where the debtor is located[73] on the theory that this is the law which commercially reasonable third parties would expect to apply in view of the mobile nature of the collateral.

The debtor location rule for mobile goods is not an optional alternative to the *lex rei sitae* rule.[74] Failure to perfect will be fatal to per-

---

72 PPSA (A, BC, M, NB, NWT, Nu, O, PEI, S) s. 5(1); (NL, NS) s. 6(1); Y s. 4(1).

73 PPSA (A, BC, M, NB, NWT, Nu, O, PEI, S) s. 7(2); (NL, NS) s. 8(2); Y s. 6(1).

74 For judicial confirmation, see, for example, *Trailmobile Canada Ltd. v. Kindersley Transport Ltd.* (1986), 7 P.P.S.A.C. 75, 54 Sask. R. 1 (Q.B.).

fected status even if the goods never physically enter the jurisdiction where the debtor is located and even if the security interest is perfected according to the *lex rei sitae*.[75] In other words, the test for whether collateral qualifies as mobile goods is not whether the particular debtor in fact uses the goods interprovincially or internationally. The question is whether the goods are of a type that in the abstract are normally used across borders.[76] This objective test dispenses with difficult issues of proof and with the need to ascertain whether or not the particular debtor has commenced to use or lease the goods across borders.

Goods used for the carriage or transport of persons or property across borders clearly qualify — for example, motor vehicles,[77] trailers, rolling stock, shipping containers, and airplanes. The concept also extends to assets that are relatively immobile when in use if they are normally moved from one location to another as the work demands, for example, road building, construction, and commercial harvesting machinery.[78]

The debtor location rule is limited to mobile goods held by the debtor as equipment, or as inventory leased or held for lease by the debtor to others.[79] The two categories are separate. In other words, equipment need not be equipment held for lease. Such an interpretation would be inconsistent with the very concept of equipment as defined in the PPSA and is illogical from the point of view of the policy behind the special choice of law rule for mobile goods.[80]

Mobile goods held by the debtor as consumer goods or as inventory for sale[81] fall within the general *lex rei sitae* rule. It follows that the type of seller makes a significant difference in determining where a prospective buyer or other third party must search for outstanding security interests. For example, for a motor vehicle used as equipment, the registration venue is the jurisdiction of the debtor's location, whereas if the same motor vehicle is used by the debtor as consumer goods, one looks to the jurisdiction where the vehicle itself is located.

---

75   *Gimli Auto Ltd. v. BDO Dunwoody Ltd.*, above note 18.

76   For judicial confirmation, see *ibid.*; *Toronto Dominion Bank v. RNG Group Inc.*, above note 17; *Westman Equipment Corp. v. Royal Bank*, [1982] 5 W.W.R. 475 (Man. Co. Ct.); *Trailmobile Can. Ltd. v. Kindersley Transport Ltd.*, above note 74.

77   *Gimli Auto Ltd. v. BDO Dunwoody Ltd.*, *ibid.*; *Ens Toyota Ltd. v. Megill Stephenson Co.* (1989), 9 P.P.S.A.C. 169 (Sask. Q.B.).

78   *Northwest Equipment Inc. v. Daewoo Heavy Industries America Corp.*, above note 38 (excavator).

79   PPSA (A, BC, M, NB, NWT, Nu, O, PEI, S) s. 7(2); (NL, NS) s. 8(2); Y s. 6(1).

80   *Toronto Dominion Bank v. RNG Group Inc.*, above note 17; *Gimli Auto Ltd. v. BDO Dunwoody Ltd.*, above note 18; *Holland v. Chrysler Credit Canada Ltd.*, above note 13..

81   On the PPSA classification of goods into "consumer goods," "equipment," and "inventory" for this and other purposes, see the analysis in chapter 1.

On this point the *Civil Code* differs from the PPSA. The *Civil Code* applies the law of the grantor's location to all goods ordinarily used in more than one jurisdiction, even where the debtor holds the goods as consumer goods or as inventory for sale.[82] In the case of consumer goods, this difference should not create great difficulties in practice. Since the location of the goods and the location of the grantor of the security will generally be identical, the different tests should lead to the same result. However, where the mobile goods are inventory held for sale in a number of jurisdictions, the differences between the Quebec rule and the PPSA rule become more significant. Where the financing transaction involves a connection to Quebec, a prudent secured party would therefore register in all jurisdictions where the inventory is located as well as in the jurisdiction where the debtor is located.

2) Non-possessory Security Interests in Money and Negotiable Documentary Collateral

The approach to choice of law for security interests in collateral in the form of money and documentary intangibles depends on whether the security interest is possessory or non-possessory. As already noted, for possessory security, the *lex rei sitae* rule applies.[83] For non-possessory security, the law of the location of the debtor governs.[84] This bifurcated approach creates difficulties in situations where a non-possessory security interest comes into a priority conflict with the interest of a buyer or secured party who has taken possession of the collateral. If the priority rules of the two jurisdictions are not the same, which should prevail?

The PPSA does not provide any explicit guidance in this scenario. The authors take the view that the law of the location of the collateral at the time the competing claimant took possession should apply. This is based on the theory that a person taking possession of money and documentary collateral, particularly negotiable or quasi-negotiable collateral, would reasonably expect local law to govern her rights against competing claimants.

The *Civil Code* is consistent with the PPSA in applying the law of the jurisdiction where the collateral is located to possessory security interests in money and documentary collateral.[85] However, the rule does not extend to chattel paper which is an unknown concept outside

---

82   Art. 3105 (para. 1).
83   PPSA (A, BC, M, NB, NWT, Nu, O, PEI, S) s. 5(1); (NL, NS) s. 6(1); Y s. 4(1).
84   PPSA (A, BC, M, NB, NWT, Nu, O, PEI, S) s. 7(2); (NL, NS) s. 8(2); Y s. 6(1).
85   Art. 3102; and see art. 3105 (para. 3).

the PPSA and Article 9. Instead the choice of law rule for pure incorporeal movables (intangibles) would apply, leading to application of the law of the debtor's location.[86]

3) Pure Intangibles

Application of the *lex rei sitae* rule to pure intangibles, such as accounts, is problematic because of the absence of any physical situs. There is a general consensus that the law governing the relationship between the assignor/debtor and the account debtor should govern the rights and obligations of a secured party or assignee against the account debtor. This is the rule found in the *United Nations Convention on the Assignment of Receivables in International Trade*,[87] the *Rome Convention*,[88] and the *Civil Code*.[89]

Application of that same law to rights against competing claimants would have the advantage of producing a single governing law for all third-party aspects of security in accounts. However, in the receivables financing context, this solution would impose unacceptable costs and inefficiencies. Where the security agreement covered accounts owing to the debtor by account debtors located in a number of provinces and states, the secured party would be forced to ascertain, and then perfect its security interest in accordance with, the law applicable to each debtor-account debtor relationship. The law applicable to priority might vary for different categories of accounts, increasing the costs of dispute resolution and insolvency administration. If the security agreement covered future accounts potentially owing by unidentified debtors, the secured party would not even be able to predict what law might apply.

Accordingly, the PPSA instead applies the law of the location of the debtor to the validity and perfection of security interests in intangibles including accounts.[90] This solution enables a security interest in a debtor's portfolio of present and future accounts to be taken and perfected in accordance with a single governing law, regardless of where the ac-

---

86 Art. 3105 (paras. 1–2).
87 Above note 5, art. 29.
88 Above note 32, art. 12(2).
89 Art. 3120: "The assignability of a claim and relations between the assignee and the assigned debtor [account debtor] are governed by the law governing relations between the assigned debtor [account debtor] and the assignor." Unfortunately, the *Civil Code* does not specifically state that this is also the choice of law rule for relations between a secured party and an account debtor where the transaction involves the grant of security in a claim as opposed to its outright assignment.
90 PPSA (A, BC, M, NB, NWT, Nu, O, PEI, S) s. 7(2); (NL, NS) 8(2); Y s. 6(1).

count debtors may be located or what law governs the debtor-account debtor relationship.

The debtor location rule has been adopted at the international level by the *United Nations Convention on the Assignment of Receivables in International Trade*.[91] It is also reflected in the *Civil Code* with one qualification. The law of the debtor's location applies only to the grant of security in pure intangibles.[92] A non-security assignment is governed by the general *lex rei sitae* rule,[93] which has traditionally been construed to mean the law governing relations between the debtor or assignee and the account debtor. If the traditional approach is applied, it follows that a priority contest between a secured party and an assignee would be governed by different and potentially conflicting laws.

Under the PPSA, a security interest is deemed to include a transfer of accounts. It follows that that the choice of law rule for a security interest in intangibles also applies to an outright assignment of accounts. However, for other categories of intangibles, for instance, non-monetary obligations, the potential for a conflict in the choice of law rules for security interests and transfers is also a risk. The point is revisited in more detail later in the chapter in the discussion on the need to take account of the PPSA rules in developing the choice of law principles governing movables generally.

4) Determining the Location of the Debtor

Where the *lex rei sitae* is the applicable law, determination of the location of the collateral at the relevant time is a purely factual inquiry. But if the applicable law is the law of the jurisdiction in which the debtor is located, a factual test is insufficient. Legal guidance is needed to avoid arbitrariness — for example, where the debtor happens to be at a secondary residence when the security interest attaches — and to provide certainty in ambiguous cases — for example, where the debtor has a business presence in more than one jurisdiction.

The drafters of the PPSA recognized the need to provide clear guidelines for determining the location of a debtor.[94] Under the Act, a debtor is deemed to be located at the debtor's place of business. A debtor who has no place of business is deemed to be located at his or her principal resi-

---

91   Above note 5, arts. 22, 30.
92   Art. 3105.
93   Art. 3097: "Real rights and their publication are governed by the law of the place where the property concerned is situated."
94   PPSA (A, BC, M, NB, NWT, Nu, PEI, S) s. 7(1); (NL, NS) s. 8(1); O s. 7(4); Y s. 6(2).

dence. Business debtors are deemed to be located at their place of business or chief executive office if there is more than one place of business. Thus a national or multinational debtor corporation is not necessarily located in its jurisdiction of incorporation but rather in the place where the management of the company is centred if that is in a different place.

Like the PPSA, the *Civil Code* refers to the law of the debtor's location for validity, publication and the effects of publication of a security interest granted in intangible property and "mobile goods."[95] However, the place where the grantor is located is not determined in the same manner. The *Civil Code* uses the concept of domicile. In the case of an individual, domicile equates with habitual residence.[96] In most situations, application of the law of habitual residence will not produce different results than under the PPSA. However, for legal persons, the *Civil Code* defines domicile by reference to the place in which the legal person maintains its head office.[97] In practice, this is often referred to as the registered office test, in view of the fact that corporations are generally required to designate a head office in their publicly filed constitutive documents.

Where a financing transaction includes a connection to Quebec, the secured party may need to take account of the difference between the *Civil Code* and the PPSA location rules. For example, if the debtor maintains its registered office in Quebec and its chief executive office in Ontario (or vice versa), a prudent secured creditor will need to register, and interested third parties will need to conduct searches, in the registries of both provinces. Moreover, since the priority effect of registration (or non-registration) may be different under the PPSA and the *Civil Code*, the secured party should also recognize that any priority dispute arising out of the transaction may be decided differently depending on whether it is adjudicated before the Ontario or the Quebec courts.

The ULCC has adopted recommendations calling for reform of the PPSA and the *Civil Code* to bring about national uniformity in the debtor location rules.[98] Under the proposed reform the location of a Canadian debtor with a business presence in more than one province or territory would be determined by a registered office test in line with the current *Civil Code* location rule, while a non-Canadian debtor would be considered located at its chief executive office in line with the current PPSA rule.

---

95   Art. 3105 (para. 1).
96   Art. 75.
97   Art. 307.
98   *Reform of the Law of Secured Transactions — Report of the Working Group 2002–2003* (posted at www.ulcc.ca under Proceedings of Annual Meetings — 2003 Fredericton NB — Commercial Law Documents).

5) Impact on Perfection of a Post-attachment Change in the Location of the Debtor

As a practical matter, the risk of a post-attachment change of location is much lower for the debtor than the collateral. The PPSA nonetheless addresses the possibility. The secured party is given a grace period to preserve continuity of perfected status in the event of a post-attachment change in the location of the debtor.[99] The period is the same as that which applies to a change in the location of collateral governed by the *lex rei sitae* rule. Reperfection must be effected before expiration of the earliest of the following time periods:

- sixty days after the debtor relocates to the other jurisdiction;
- fifteen days after the secured party has knowledge that the debtor has relocated; or
- before perfection ceases under the law of the jurisdiction where the debtor was located when the security interest attached.

There is a subtle but significant difference between the triggering of the grace period in the two situations. In respect of goods governed by the *lex rei sitae* rule, the grace period for reperfection applies only where the goods are relocated to the enacting jurisdiction.[100] In contrast, a security interest covered by the debtor location rule must be reperfected within the time periods prescribed by the enacting province's PPSA, even if the debtor relocates to some other jurisdiction and even if that other jurisdiction is not a PPSA jurisdiction.

The Ontario Act is different on this point. Reperfection in accordance with the time periods prescribed by the Ontario PPSA is required only if the debtor relocates to Ontario.[101] If the debtor relocates elsewhere, it is for the law of that other jurisdiction to determine what is needed to maintain continuity of perfection, including the availability and length of any grace periods.

Where the debtor relocates to another PPSA jurisdiction, the difference is inconsequential since the grace periods will be identical under both the law of the forum and the law of the new location. However, the debtor may relocate to a province or country where the grace periods for preserving perfected status are different. Consider the following scenario:

SP grants a security interest in mobile goods and intangibles while located in Saskatchewan. D later relocates to the state of New York. Three months

99 PPSA (A, BC, M, NB, NWT, Nu, PEI, S) s. 7(3); (NL, NS) s. 8(3); O s. 7(2); Y s. 6(3).
100 PPSA (A, BC, M, NB, NWT, Nu, PEI, S) s. 5(3); (NL, NS) s. 6(3); O s. 5(2); Y s. 4(3).
101 OPPSA s. 6(2).

later, SP finds out about the relocation and perfects its security interest in accordance with the New York version of UCC Article 9.

Article 9 of the UCC gives the secured party a grace period of four months to reperfect upon a change in the location of the debtor.[102] Consequently, continuity of perfection is preserved in the above scenario as a matter of New York law. However, in litigation in Saskatchewan, the Saskatchewan court will apply the shorter time periods prescribed by the Saskatchewan PPSA with the result that the security interest loses continuity of perfection.

The converse situation can also arise. Suppose that instead of changing location to New York, the debtor moves to Quebec and the secured party reperfects in Quebec within forty-five days of the relocation. So far as Quebec law is concerned, perfected status is lost since the *Civil Code* provides a maximum grace period of only thirty days for reperfection where a debtor relocates to that province.[103] However, in litigation in Saskatchewan, perfected status would be preserved by virtue of the lengthier sixty-day grace period recognized by the Saskatchewan PPSA.

6) Transfer of the Collateral to a Transferee Located in Another Jurisdiction

The location of the debtor can change indirectly as a result of a transfer of the collateral to a transferee at a different location. The following scenario illustrates this possibility:

D, located in Province X, grants a security interest in mobile goods and intangibles to SP1 who registers in Province's X registry. In breach of the security agreement between D and SP1, D transfers an interest in the assets to T, located in Province Y. T then grants a security interest in the same assets to SP2 who registers in Province Y's registry because this is where T is located.

---

102 § 9-316(a).

103 Art. 3106 of the *Civil Code* provides that a security interest governed by the law of the original location of the debtor is deemed to be published in Quebec, where the debtor subsequently relocates to Quebec, from the time of initial perfection so long as it is perfected before the any of the following events, whichever occurs first: (1) the cessation of the effectiveness of perfection under the law of the jurisdiction where the debtor was previously domiciled; (2) the expiry of thirty days from the time the debtor establishes his new domicile in Quebec; (3) the expiry of fifteen days from the time the secured party was advised of the new domicile of the debtor in Quebec.

In this scenario, the PPSA, except for the Ontario Act,[104] obliges SP1 to reperfect in accordance with the law of the jurisdiction where T is located (Province Y) naming T as a new debtor in order to preserve the perfected status of its security interest under D's home law (province X). The applicable grace periods are the same ones that apply in the case of a change in the location of the debtor.[105] If the security interest is perfected in the new jurisdiction within these time lines, it is deemed to be continuously perfected. If it is not, the security interest becomes unperfected.

The reperfection rule is intended to protect persons in the position of SP 2 in the above scenario who would reasonably presume that a search of the registry in the jurisdiction where T is located would disclose any security interests granted by T in the collateral. It is *not* intended for the benefit of T who ought to have verified the status of D's ownership by searching the registry in Province X in advance of her purchase. Consequently, failure to reperfect within the relevant time periods does not cause the security interest to become unperfected as against T but only as against a party taking from T such as SP2 in this scenario.[106]

A *transfer* of ownership or title is necessary to trigger the reperfection obligation. It has been held that delivery of possession of mobile goods to a consignee in another jurisdiction under a consignment for sale does not prejudice the perfected status of the security interest.[107]

7) Special Priority Rule Where Applicable Legal System Does Not Have a Public Registration System

Although perfection and priority are generally governed by the law of the jurisdiction where the debtor is located, the PPSA, except for the Ontario Act, creates an important exception where that jurisdiction does not have a registration system in place for publicly recording security interests.[108] In that event, the security interest must comply with the perfection requirements imposed by the PPSA of the enacting jurisdiction. Failure to comply does not affect perfected status. However, the security interest is subordinated to any third-party interest acquired in the collateral provided that the collateral (for example, mobile goods or

---

104 The *Civil Code* likewise does not require reperfection in the event of a transfer of collateral to a transferee located outside Quebec.

105 PPSA (A, BC, M, NB, NWT, Nu, PEI, S) s. 7(3); (NL, NS) s. 8(3); O s. 7(2); Y s. 6(3).

106 *Northwest Equipment Inc. v. Daewoo Heavy Industries America Corp.*, above note 38.

107 *Canadian Imperial Bank of Commerce v. A.K. Construction (1988) Ltd.* (1996), 186 A.R. 1 at 6 (Q.B.), aff'd (1998), 223 A.R. 115 (C.A.).

108 PPSA (A, BC, M, NB, NWT, Nu, PEI, S) s. 7(4); (NL, NS) s. 8(4); O no equivalent provision; Y s. 6(4).

a documentary intangible) was situated in the enacting province at the time of the dealing or, in the case of an account, the account was payable in the enacting province at the relevant time.

Neither the Ontario Act nor the Quebec *Civil Code* contains an equivalent rule. Even where the debtor is located in either jurisdiction, this difference is unlikely to create difficulties since both regimes establish a public registry for security interests and therefore fall outside the exception. The same is true where the debtor is located in the United States since Article 9 also establishes a public registry.[109] However, Article 9 does not require (and in some cases does not even permit) registration of a security interest in some forms of collateral. For example, a security interest in an account that takes the form of a deposit account with a financial or other deposit-taking institution can only be perfected by control, a concept that does not provide public disclosure of the existence of the security interest.[110] It is an open question whether the requirement for local perfection is triggered where the other jurisdiction does not provide for registration of security interests granted in the particular category of collateral, even though a general public registration system exists for other categories of collateral. Taking into account the objectives of the exception — to ensure third parties who deal with locally situated collateral are able to rely on a public record to determine if any security interests have been granted in the collateral — it would seem that the presence of a general registration system is not enough unless that system requires registration of the category of collateral in issue.

Where the debtor is located outside of Canada or the United States, there is a greater likelihood that the law of debtor's location may not provide for public registration. However, the exception is triggered only if the collateral is physically located in the enacting PPSA jurisdiction, or bears a strong connection to that jurisdiction as where collateral in the form of an account is payable there. These qualifications reflect the objective of the section: to protect local parties who would otherwise have no means of easily verifying whether collateral having a local connection is subject to a security interest under the law of the debtor's location.

In practice, it may not always be wise for third parties to rely wholly on the exception. There is a risk that the rights of competing claimants may end up being adjudicated elsewhere, for example where insolvency proceedings are commenced in the debtor's home jurisdiction, or where

---

109 § 9-501.
110 § 9-312(b)(1), § 9-314, § 9-104, § 9-342.

the location of the collateral (in the case of mobile goods and documentary intangibles) or of the account debtor (in the case of collateral in the form of accounts) changes after initial attachment of the security interest. If the choice of law rule of the court in which the issue is litigated refers to the law of the debtor's location, the special priority given to local interests by the PPSA will not be available.

8) *Renvoi*

Under the *renvoi* doctrine, a choice of law rule referring to the law of X jurisdiction does not refer only to the internal rules that the courts in X jurisdiction apply in domestic cases.[111] The forum court also takes account of the choice of law rule that the courts in jurisdiction X apply to cases having the same connections to other jurisdictions that are presented by the fact pattern in question. If the choice of law rule of X jurisdiction points to the application of a law other than X law, the forum court applies that other law. Technically speaking, the term "*renvoi*" (reference back) applies only where the choice of law rule of X jurisdiction refers back to the law of the forum. However, the term has come to include the situation where the choice of law rule refers the issue to a third law.[112]

The *renvoi* doctrine has attracted criticism as introducing an unacceptable level of uncertainty and unpredictability in the choice of law exercise. The applicable law ultimately depends not on the forum's own choice of law rules but on those of a foreign jurisdiction. From a policy perspective, this amounts to an abdication by the forum of the policy reasons underpinning its own choice of law rule. Moreover, if the forum court employs total *renvoi*– which is the only logically defensible approach — the analysis does not yield an applicable internal law if the other legal system also employs total *renvoi*.[113]

Renvoi is generally rejected in modern private international law regimes. The *Civil Code* expressly confirms that the choice of law rules set out in the *Civil Code* are to be read as referring only to the internal rules of the applicable law, that is, the rules that would be applied by that other legal system in a wholly domestic case.[114] The conflict of laws

---

111 For a good recent summary of the *renvoi* doctrine, see N. Rafferty, above note 15 at 487–90.

112 *Ibid.* at 487–88.

113 *Ibid.* at 489.

114 Art. 3080: "Where under the provisions of this Book [Book 10 — Private International Law], the law of a foreign country applies, the law in question is the internal law of that country, but not the rules governing conflict of laws."

regime in Article 9 also adopts the internal law approach[115] as does the *United Nations Convention on the Assignment of Receivables in International Trade.*[116] So far as Canadian common law is concerned, the few cases suggesting that *renvoi* might apply are dated, and "uncompelling in their reasoning."[117] Certainly, there seems to be general agreement that the doctrine should have no place in areas of the law where certainty and predictability are paramount values.

The PPSA, with the exception of the Ontario Act, contains an exception to the modern trend. In cases where the law of the jurisdiction in which the debtor is located applies, the Act states expressly that this includes the choice of law rules of that jurisdiction.[118] The reason goes back to the early days of PPSA reform in Canada. In its inception, the PPSA debtor location rule for mobile goods and accounts was somewhat novel, and there was a perceived need to respect the fact that other jurisdictions might continue to apply some variation of an artificial *lex rei sitae* approach.

The ULCC has adopted recommendations calling for the abolition of the vestiges of the *renvoi* doctrine in the non-Ontario Acts.[119] Pending implementation of that reform, the current wording creates difficulty only where there is a difference between the choice of law rules in the PPSA and the choice of law rules of the jurisdiction whose law is designated as applicable by those rules. The likelihood of a difference is rapidly diminishing. As a general rule, Article 9 and the *Civil Code* apply the law of the debtor's location to the same classes of collateral as the PPSA. Internationally, this is also increasingly the case at least where the collateral takes the form of accounts.[120]

However, there are situations where the *renvoi* doctrine must be kept in mind. Suppose that the debtor has offices throughout eastern Canada but maintains its chief executive office in Montreal and its registered office in Moncton. In this scenario, it will not be sufficient for the secured party to perfect its security interest under the internal law of Quebec even though the New Brunswick PPSA provides that perfection and the effects of or non-perfection are governed by the law of the

---

115 All of the choice of law rules in Article 9 refer to "the local law" of the designated jurisdiction: § 9-301–§ 9-306.

116 Above note 5, art. 5(i).

117 Rafferty, above note 15 at 490.

118 PPSA (A, BC, M, NB, NWT, Nu, O, PEI, S) s. 7(2); (NL, NS) s. 8(2); Y s. 6(1).

119 *Reform of the Law of Secured Transactions — Report of the Working Group 2002–2003*, above note 98.

120 This is the rule adopted in arts. 22 and 30 of the *United Nations Convention on the Assignment of Receivables in International Trade*, above note 5.

jurisdiction where the debtor maintains its chief executive office. Like the other Acts except the Ontario Act, the choice of law rule in the NB-PPSA refers not just to the internal rules of the law of the debtor's location but also to its choice of law rules. This produces a reference back to New Brunswick law since the Quebec choice of law rule defines the location of the debtor by reference to its registered office rather than its chief executive office. Furthermore, since Quebec law rejects the doctrine of *renvoi*, the New Brunswick court must accept the reference back to New Brunswick law as a reference to the substantive rules of the PPSA, not its choice of law rules. Accordingly the security interest will be considered perfected, even in proceedings before the New Brunswick courts, only if the security interest is registered or otherwise perfected under the NBPPSA.

Of course, even in the absence of *renvoi*, a prudent secured party would be well advised to take account of any differences in the choice of law rules of all jurisdictions to which the transaction is potentially connected. In the above scenario, even if the *renvoi* provision in the New Brunswick Act were repealed, the substantive rules of the New Brunswick Act would still end up being applied if the dispute were adjudicated before the courts of Quebec as opposed to New Brunswick. In proceedings in Quebec, the Quebec courts will apply their own choice of law rule, not the choice of law rule of the New Brunswick Act. In other words, elimination of the complications produced by *renvoi* cannot wholly eliminate complications posed by differences in the choice of law formulae. However, it would at least eliminate an additional source of complications.

E. LAW APPLICABLE TO ENFORCEMENT

1) Procedural Aspects

Procedural issues are governed, as a general rule, by the law of the forum, that is to say, by the law of the court that is seized of the matter.[121] The PPSA formulation departs somewhat from the general rule.[122] The law of the forum governs enforcement procedure only in the case of an intangible. Otherwise, the procedural law of the jurisdiction where the collateral is located at the time of enforcement applies.

---

121 The most recent Supreme Court analysis of the rule is found in *Tolofson v. Jensen*, [1994] 3 S.C.R. 1022.
122 PPSA (A, BC, M, NB, Nu, O, PEI) s. 8(1); (NL, NS) s. 9(1); Y, s. 7(4).

The PPSA formulation presumably reflects the inherent differences between enforcement against tangible and intangible collateral. For tangible collateral, enforcement typically requires physical seizure and sale of the collateral. The procedure by which this can be done necessarily depends on the local administrative and regulatory framework and is bound up with local concerns about preserving public order.[123] The PPSA reference to the procedural rules where enforcement rights are exercised thus makes sense in practical and policy terms.

For intangible collateral, enforcement usually takes the form of a demand by the secured party on the account debtor who owes payment or performance of an obligation to the debtor to instead render performance to the secured party. If the account debtor refuses, the secured party's recourse is to pursue an action in the courts against the account debtor (as reflected in the traditional common law term "*chose in action*" to describe intangible property). Since the method of enforcement may ultimately involve a court action against the account debtor, the drafters may have assumed that the applicable procedural rules should be those of the jurisdiction in which the court seized of the action is sitting.

2) Substantive Aspects

Substantive issues involved in the enforcement of the rights of a secured party against collateral are governed, according to the PPSA, by the proper law of the contract between the secured party and the debtor.[124] The Act does not attempt to define the "proper law of the contract," leaving that to general conflicts law.

Contracting parties are generally free to choose the proper law of their contract, even if they choose a legal regime to which their transaction bears no relationship.[125] The proximity principle enters into play

---

123 These same considerations likewise explain why the law governing execution of a judgment is that of the jurisdiction where the execution proceedings are carried out: see, for example, *Royal Trust Co. v. Kritzwiser*, [1924] 3 D.L.R. 596 (Sask. C.A.).

124 PPSA (A, BC, M, NB, NWT, Nu, O, PEI, S) s. 8(1); (NL, NS) s. 9(1); Y s. 7(4).

125 The leading Anglo-Canadian authority on the party autonomy principle in choice of law for contract is still *Vita Food Products Inc. v. Unus Shipping Co.*, [1939] A.C. 277 (P.C.) (on appeal from N.S.C.A.). For a modern codification of the principle, see art. 3111 (para. 1) of the *Civil Code*: "A juridical act, whether or not it contains any foreign element, is governed by the law expressly designated in the act or the designation of which may inferred with certainty from the terms of the act."

only if there is no agreement on the applicable law. In that event, the proper law is that of the legal system that bears the closest and most real connection to the transaction.[126]

The party autonomy principle is not unqualified. The parties to an otherwise domestic transaction cannot evade the mandatory principles of domestic law by a choosing a different governing law.[127] Under the PPSA, a secured party is obligated to give advance notice of enforcement action, to hand over any surplus after a forced disposition, to recognize the debtor's right to cure the default before disposition, and generally to act in good faith and in a commercially reasonable manner. In pursuing enforcement, the secured party remains subject to these obligations, even where a choice of law clause refers to a less restrictive regime.[128] Otherwise, the choice of law clause would provide an indirect means of escape from the PPSA prohibition against contracting out of the basic enforcement framework of the Act.[129]

Preservation of the mandatory enforcement rules of otherwise applicable domestic law is particularly significant in the consumer context. A number of PPSA jurisdictions have enacted special legislation limiting the exercise by a secured party of enforcement rights.[130] For example, the Ontario *Consumer Protection Act* requires a court order before a secured supplier of goods can repossess the goods if two-thirds or more of the price has been paid.[131]

In cases where the secured transaction contains an extraprovincial element, the issue becomes more complicated. Suppose that collateral

---

126 Unfortunately, the only serious Supreme Court authority on the point is somewhat dated: *Imperial Life Assurance Co. of Canada v. Colmenares*, [1967] S.C.R. 443. For a modern codification of the principle, see art. 3112 of the *Civil Code*: "If no law is designated in [the parties' juridical] act, or if the law designated invalidates the juridical act, the courts apply the law of the country with which the act is most closely connected, in view of its nature and the attendant circumstances."

127 See, for example, art. 3111 of the *Civil Code*: "A juridical act containing no foreign element remains, nonetheless, subject to the law of the country which would apply if [no law were] designated."

128 *Cardel Leasing Ltd. v. Maxmenko* (1991), 2 P.P.S.A.C. (2d) 302 (Ont. Ct. Gen. Div.).

129 PPSA (A, BC, M, NB, PEI) s. 56(3); (NL, Nu, NWT, NS) s. 57(3); O s. 59(5); Y s. 53.

130 Although the PPSA generally takes precedence in the event of a conflict with any other act, consumer protection legislation prevails over the PPSA: (M, NWT, Nu, S) s. 69; (NL, NS, Y) s. 71; (NB, PEI) s. 70; A s. 74, BC s. 73; O s. 73. See also chapter 1.

131 R.S.O. 1990, c. 31, s. 23.

is located in Quebec and the debtor is located in Ontario. Are the parties free to choose between the Quebec and Ontario enforcement law or even the law of some third jurisdiction? Or are they bound by the mandatory elements of the enforcement laws of both provinces?

There is little or no authority on the issue.[132] The point arose in *Alves Worms Ltd. v. Ford Credit Canada Ltd.*,[133] an Ontario case involving a seizure of collateral located in Quebec. The plaintiff argued that the secured party had failed to comply with the law of Quebec, which required a court order for repossession if 50 percent of the purchase price secured by the security interest had been paid. In the end it was unnecessary to decide whether the Quebec rule applied since the court found that the circumstances of the seizure were wrongful even as a matter of Ontario law.

One solution would be to apply the mandatory enforcement rules of the law governing the validity, perfection, and priority of a security interest. Under this approach, the mandatory enforcement rules of the debtor's location would govern in the case of security granted in mobile goods and intangibles, whereas the mandatory rules in force in the jurisdiction where the collateral is located would be determinative for security interests in ordinary goods and possessory security interests in documentary collateral. Two considerations can be advanced to support this solution. First, the law governing the validity of a security interest would seem to have the strongest economic and social interest in issues relating to the protection of the debtor's interest in the collateral. Second, restrictions on a secured party's enforcement rights are also aimed at the protection of third-party interests in the collateral and are therefore bound up indirectly with the law applicable to priority.

The suggested solution does not necessarily represent the best approach in all circumstances. Suppose the collateral takes the form of goods located in province X, the law of which imposes a "seize or sue"

---

132 In the context of personal security, the Alberta courts have ruled that non-compliance with the otherwise mandatory formality rules of the Alberta *Guarantees Acknowledgement Act* did not avoid a guarantee executed in Alberta by an Alberta guarantor where the contract of guarantee contained a choice of law clause in favour of Ontario law which did not impose any equivalent restrictions, notwithstanding that the only connection with Ontario was that it was the location of the head office of the counterparty: *Greenshields Inc. v. Johnston* (1981), 119 D.L.R. (3d) 714 (Alta. Q.B.), aff'd (1981), 131 D.L.R. (3d) 234 (Alta. C.A.). For a critique, see Vaughan Black, "The Strange Case of Alberta's Guarantees Acknowledgment Act: A Study in Choice-of-Law Method" (1987) 11 Dalhousie L.J. 208.

133 (1995), 10 P.P.S.A.C. (2d) 25 (Ont. Ct. Gen. Div.).

limitation on enforcement, but the debtor is located in province Y, the law of which empowers the secured party to seize and sell the collateral *and* to claim any resulting deficiency. In this scenario, it is not at all clear that the secured party's rights should be confined by X law. Rather, the question of the debtor's *personal* liability for any deficiency following the sale would seem to be of paramount concern to Province Y as the debtor's home jurisdiction. In the view of the authors, the court in this scenario should look carefully at the mandatory rules vying for application to determine whether their policy extends to the circumstances of the case, and, even if it does in the abstract, whether the benefit of applying the rule is outweighed by the loss of certainty and predictability it would produce in an interprovincial or international financing context. Application of the law of province Y in the above scenario is indirectly supported by the cases which characterize "seize or sue" and similar limitations as substantive rather than procedural in character so as to preclude their application where the only connection to the enacting jurisdiction is the fact that the collateral is located there at the time of seizure of the collateral.[134]

F. TRANSACTIONAL SCOPE OF PPSA CONFLICTS RULES

1) Security Interests in Proceeds

In principle, the same choice of law rules that apply to the original collateral also apply to a security interest in proceeds. It follows that where the proceeds take a different form than the original collateral, it may be necessary to perfect the security interest in more than one jurisdiction. Consider the following scenario:

Debtor's chief executive office is located in Saskatchewan. Debtor grants a security interest in its inventory located in Ontario to SP1 who perfects by registration in the Ontario Personal Property Registry. Debtor later grants a security interest in its accounts to SP2 who perfects by registration in the Saskatchewan Personal Property Registry. SP1 claims a security interest in the accounts as proceeds of its original collateral in priority to SP2.

---

134 See *243930 Alberta Ltd. v. Wickham* (1990), 75 O.R. (2d) 289 (C.A.), *Traders Finance Corp. v. Casselman*, [1960] S.C.R. 242, *Canadian Acceptance Corporation Limited v. Matte* (1957), 9 D.L.R. (2d) 304 (Sask. C.A.), *Livesley v. E. Clemens Horst Co.*, [1924] S.C.R. 605.

SP2 will prevail over SP1 in this scenario. Although registration in the Ontario Registry is sufficient to perfect SP1's security interest in the inventory, perfection of a security interest in intangibles is governed by the law of the location of the debtor. To ensure priority over SP2 as against the accounts, SP1 should have registered its security interest under the Saskatchewan PPSA.

Attention must also be paid to the law applicable to priority in the accounts. For example, under the Ontario PPSA, the holder of a purchase money security interest in inventory is entitled to superpriority in any accounts generated by the sale of the inventory as against a prior secured creditor claiming the accounts as original collateral.[135] While the Acts in the Atlantic provinces adopt a similar policy,[136] the rule in other PPSA jurisdictions is the opposite,[137] and purchase money superpriority in inventory is also restricted under Article 9.[138] It follows that the holder of a security interest in inventory located in Ontario cannot assume that its superpriority under the Ontario PPSA will carry over to any accounts generated by the sale of the inventory. While Ontario law governs the perfected and priority status of the security interest in the inventory, the law of the jurisdiction in which the debtor is located governs the priority status of a security interest in intangibles including accounts. If the debtor happens to be located in a jurisdiction that does not recognize an equivalent superpriority, the secured party will be subordinated to a prior security interest in the accounts taken and perfected under the law of that other jurisdiction.

Finally, in the inter-jurisdictional financing context, a secured party should not assume that its security interest will automatically continue into the proceeds of the original collateral. Although this is the rule under the PPSA, it is not necessarily the rule in other legal systems whose law may apply under the PPSA choice of law rules. For example, the scope of a proceeds security interest under the *Civil Code* is far more restrictive than under the PPSA.[139] Where there is a risk that an automatic right to proceeds will not be recognized under the law applicable to the validity of a security interest in collateral in the form of the particular proceeds, the secured party should ensure that

---

135 OPPSA s. 33(1).

136 PPSA (NB, PEI) s. 34; (NL, NS) s. 35.

137 PPSA (A, BC, M, NWT, Nu) s. 34; Y s. 33.

138 Under § 9-324(b), purchase money superpriority in inventory collateral carries over only to identifiable cash proceeds (defined in § 9-102) received on or before delivery of the inventory to a buyer.

139 Art. 2674.

the security agreement and registration covers all conceivable forms of proceeds as original collateral.

2) Characterization of "Security Interests"

As noted earlier, the PPSA requires reperfection where the debtor or the collateral, depending on the applicable choice of law rule, relocates to the enacting province.[140] The reperfection requirement is aimed at the protection of third parties who would reasonably expect the security interest to be registered or otherwise perfected in accordance with the requirements of the PPSA in effect in the jurisdiction where the debtor or collateral is currently located. If that goal is to be achieved, the enacting jurisdiction's understanding of what constitutes a security interest should be determinative, regardless of the characterization adopted by the initially applicable law. For example, if goods subject to a conditional sales agreement (instalment sale) entered into in Quebec are subsequently removed to a PPSA jurisdiction, the reperfection requirement is triggered even though the *Civil Code* does not include such a transaction within its concept of hypothecary security or may not require registration of conditional sale contracts covering the particular type of goods.[141]

The characterization issue is an important one even as between PPSA jurisdictions. The PPSA perfection and priority rules extend to certain "deemed" secured transactions even though they do not secure payment or performance of an obligation.[142] However, the scope of the deemed security concept differs among different jurisdictions. The Ontario PPSA does not extend to commercial consignments and true leases for a term of more than one year whereas, the Acts in the Atlantic provinces extend the deemed security interest concept beyond lease and consignments to include the interest of a buyer under a sale of goods without a change of possession outside the ordinary course of business.

If goods subject to a true lease initially governed by the Ontario PPSA are moved to any other PPSA jurisdiction, the lease must be perfected in accordance with the PPSA in effect at the new location,

---

140 PPSA (A, BC, M, NB, NWT, Nu, PEI, S) s. 5(3); (NL, NS) s. 6(3); O s. 5(2); Y s. 4(3).
141 On the differences between security in the form of a hypothec and security constituted by the retention or transfer of title under the *Civil Code*, including the publication (perfection) requirements applicable to each, see chapter 1.
142 For a detailed discussion of the PPSA concept of security interest, including deemed security interests, see chapter 2.

even though the lessor was not required to register to preserve its title against third parties while the goods were located in Ontario. Conversely, a lessor of goods initially subject to the New Brunswick PPSA need not worry about reperfection if the goods are moved to Ontario. This is the approach that has generally been applied by the courts[143] except in a few highly criticized Ontario cases.[144]

However, the forum court's own concept of security interest should not be determinative of the scope of application of its choice of law rules in all situations. As noted earlier, in *GMAC Commercial Credit Corp. Canada v. TCT Logistics Inc.*,[145] the Ontario courts were confronted with the issue of applicable law in the context of a true lease transaction involving mobile goods leased by an Ontario debtor but garaged in Alberta. Although the lease did not give rise to a deemed security interest under the substantive provisions of the Ontario Act, the Court of Appeal ruled that the term security interest for the purposes of the conflicts rules of the Ontario Act should be expanded to accommodate deemed security interests recognized by other PPSA jurisdictions to which the transaction bore a connection.

3) Application of PPSA Rules beyond Secured Transactions

In its ruling in *GMAC Commercial Credit Corp. Canada v. TCT Logistics Inc*,[146] the Ontario Court of Appeal emphasised the need "to avoid the inconsistencies, and the potential forum shopping" that might result from limiting the concept of security interest in financing transactions having connections to multiple jurisdictions by the forum's own definition.[147] In the view of the authors, these same considerations support the application of the PPSA choice of law rules by analogy to any trans-

---

143 *Re Tunney* (2000), 18 C.B.R. (4th) 311 (B.C.S.C.); *Juckes (Trustee of) v. Holiday Chevrolet Oldsmobile (1983) Ltd.*, above note 36; *McLean (Trustee of) v. General Motors Acceptance Corp.*, [1992] 3 W.W.R. 524 (Sask. Q.B.). For pre-PPSA authority to the same effect, see *Re Delisle* (1988), 69 C.B.R. (N.S.) 89 (B.C.S.C.); *Canron Inc. v. Ferrofab Ltée.* (1986), 7 B.C.L.R. (2d) 291 (B.C. Co. Ct.).

144 *Re Intex Moulding Ltd.* (1987), 7 P.P.S.A.C. 91 (Ont. H.C.J.); *Bank of Nova Scotia v. Gaudreau* (1984), 27 B.L.R. 101, (Ont. H.C.J.). The decision is generally regarded as mistaken: see, for example, J.S. Ziegel and David L. Denomme, *The Ontario Personal Property Security Act: Commentary and Analysis*, 2d ed. (Markham: Butterworths, 2000) at 84.

145 *GMAC Commercial Credit Corp. Canada v. TCT Logistics Inc.*, above note 19.

146 *Ibid.*

147 *Ibid.* at para. 27.

action that involve the creation or transfer of an interest in personal property. This approach eliminates the risk of conflicting rulings where a transaction is deemed to be a security interest in one jurisdiction but not in the forum. More generally, it ensures that the validity and priority of the interest of a transferee of personal property is governed by the same law that applies to the validity and priority of a security interest in the same item of property. In the case of accounts and chattel paper, this is already the rule. Since the PPSA deems a sale of accounts to be a security interest, the choice of law rule applicable to the validity and perfection of a security interest in accounts also applies to a sale of the same accounts. If different choice of law rules were instead applied, the rights of the transferee and the secured party might end up being governed by conflicting priority rules.

G. IMPACT OF BANKRUPTCY PROCEEDINGS ON CHOICE OF LAW

If bankruptcy proceedings are commenced against the debtor, the validity of a security interest, and its perfected and priority status, continues to be governed by the law applicable to it under the choice of law rules in effect in the bankruptcy forum.[148] So in an insolvency proceeding commenced in Alberta, the choice of law rules of the Alberta PPSA apply whereas in Ontario one looks to the Ontario PPSA.

The law of the jurisdiction where the insolvency proceedings are commenced (*lex concursus*) may restrict the rights of a secured creditor acquired prior to commencement under the applicable law. Under the *Bankruptcy and Insolvency Act*, there are three main sources of limitation.[149] First, the enforcement remedies of a secured creditor are normally stayed in the context of reorganization proceedings. Second, the secured creditor's rights in the collateral are diminished in favour of other creditors in a few very limited circumstances. Finally, the security interest may be refused recognition altogether under the avoidance provisions of the Act. The important point is that in the absence of explicit provisions of this kind, the validity, perfection and priority of the security interest continues to be governed by the law designated

---

148 Generally, see Catherine Walsh "The Operation of Security Interests in International Insolvencies," *Contemporary Law 1998: Canadian Reports to the 1998 International Congress of Comparative Law* (Cowansville: Yvon Blais, 1999) c. 5.

149 For a detailed analysis, see chapters 11 and 13.

as applicable under the general choice of law rules that would apply outside of insolvency.

H. PENDING REFORMS: INVESTMENT PROPERTY

When implemented, the proposed *Uniform Securities Transfer Act* (USTA), in tandem with the complementary amendments proposed for the PPSA,[150] will have a significant impact on the choice of law rules governing the transfer of and the grant of security in investment property. Under the current rules, as explained earlier, possessory security interests in collateral in the form of securities are governed by the law of the location of the collateral, whereas non-possessory security interests are governed by the law of the location of the debtor. Possessory security interests in securities are possible in practice, as a general rule, only where the security is held in certificated form so as to be capable of physical delivery.[151] Yet today an investor's interests in publicly-traded securities are typically held and transferred through entries in the books of the investor's broker or other intermediary. Since a security interest granted in securities held in the indirect system will

---

150 The proposed USTA and PPSA complementary amendments, together with previous consultative drafts, and related material (including comments received) are posted at www.osc.gov.on.ca under "Hot Topics." See also Eric T. Spink and Maxime A. Paré, "The *Uniform Securities Transfer Act*: Globalized Commercial Law for Canada" (2003) 19 B.F.L.R. 322.

151 Note, however, that for securities with a clearing agency, the non-Ontario Acts deem possession to have been taken when the appropriate entries have been made in the records of the clearing agency: see further chapter 9. Applied to the choice of law context, the deemed possession rule presumably means a secured party would be regarded as having taken a possessory security interest in securities recorded in the name of the debtor in the records of the Canadian Depository for Securities Limited (CDS) in Toronto, thereby triggering the *lex rei sitae* choice of law rule. But what is the location of the collateral in the context of securities held with a clearing agency? Is it where the records are kept? If so, and if the records are kept in Toronto, then the Ontario PPSA presumably applies. This creates conceptual difficulties since the Ontario Act does not contain a deemed possession rule for securities with a clearing agency with the result that the security interest might be characterized as non-possessory by Ontario law, leading to the application, under the doctrine of *renvoi* preserved by the non-Ontario Acts, to the law of the debtor's location. The foregoing scenario, and the enormous complications and uncertainties it presents, is only one example of why comprehensive reform of the PPSA choice of law rules for investment property is overdue.

necessarily be non-possessory in nature, it follows that the applicable law under the current rules will be the law of the debtor's location. There is a concern that this creates systemic risk in the indirect holding system since it leads to the potential application of different and possibly conflicting laws to each of the various investor accounts that make up an intermediary's portfolio.

To contain this risk, the USTA and related PPSA amendments proposes a new choice of law rule, derived from Articles 8 and 9 of the UCC, under which the law of the intermediary's jurisdiction, as a general rule, would govern issues relating to the validity, perfection and priority of security interests in security entitlements and security accounts, with the law of the intermediary's jurisdiction defined in the first instance by reference to the law specified in the agreement between the investor and the intermediary.[152] The proposed reforms would also address the law applicable to security interests in securities in the strict sense, that is, those held in the traditional direct holding system in which the owner had a direct relationship with the issuer. For certificated securities, the traditional *lex rei sitae* rule would apply: the law of the jurisdiction in which the certificate is located would govern. For uncertificated securities, the law of the issuer's jurisdiction would govern. These rules are also copied from UCC articles 8 and 9.[153]

FURTHER READINGS

Babe, J., "Canadian PPSA Conflict of Laws Rules" (1996) 13 Nat'l. Insolv. Rev. 3

Deschamps, M., "Les Conflits de lois en droit des sûretés au Canada et aux États-Unis: comparaison entre le Code civil du Québec, les PPSAs et le UCC" in *Développements récents en droit bancaire* (Cowansville, Qué.: Éditions Yvon Blais, 2003) at 123

Mendelsohn, M., "Security on Movables and Private International Law under the Quebec Civil Code" in *Cross-Border Transactions*, McGill University, Faculty of Law, Meredith Memorial Lectures, 1993 (Cowansville, Qué.: Éditions Yvon Blais, 1994) at 259

---

152 See UCC § 9-305, § 8-110.
153 *Ibid.*

TALPIS, J.A. & C. TROULIS, "Conflict of Laws Rules under the Civil Code of Quebec Relating to Security" in *Développements récents sur l'hypothèque* (Cowansville, Qué.: Éditions Yvon Blais, 1997) at 187

WALSH, C., "The Operation of Security Interests in International Insolvencies" in *Contemporary Law: Canadian Reports to the 1998 International Congress of Comparative Law, Bristol, U.K., 1998* (Cowansville, Qué.: Éditions Yvon Blais, 1999) at 193

ZIEGEL, J., "Ontario PPSA Choice of Law Rules and Ambulatory Definition of Security Interest" (Case Comm.) (2004) 40 Can. Bus. L.J. 412

CREATION OF A PPSA SECURITY INTEREST

A. INTRODUCTION

1) "Attachment"

For a security interest to come into existence, the parties must first conclude a security agreement. The formation of an effective security agreement depends on such essential elements as the existence and legal capacity of the debtor, the authority to act of the debtor's representatives, and the absence of any vitiating factors such as duress, *non est factum*, illegality, uncertainty, or fraud. All these matters are governed by the general law of contract, the supplementary application of which is expressly preserved by the PPSA.[1]

The formation of the security agreement as a matter of contract law is distinct from the creation of the security interest contemplated by that agreement. The PPSA uses the term "attachment" to denote the creation of the security interest itself.

Attachment requires the satisfaction of three conditions.[2] First, the secured party must give value. Second, the debtor must have rights in the collateral. Third, the parties' agreement must satisfy the eviden-

---

1   PPSA (M, NWT, Nu, S) s. 65(2); (NB, PEI) s. 65(1); (NL, NS) s. 66(1); A s. 66(3); BC s. 68(1); O s. 72; Y s. 63(1).
2   PPSA (A, BC, M, NB, PEI, Nu, NWT, S) s. 12(1); (NL, NS) s. 13(1); O s. 11(2); Y (s. 11(1).

tiary requirements imposed by the Act: that is, either possession of the collateral by the secured party or completion of a security agreement signed by the debtor that describes the collateral. The elements of attachment are the focus of this chapter.

2) *Inter Partes* and Third-party Attachment

Except for the Ontario Act, the PPSA distinguishes between the conditions for attachment as between the parties and as against third parties. For attachment between the secured party and the debtor, it is sufficient if value is given, and the debtor has rights in the collateral. Satisfaction of the evidentiary requirement is necessary only for third-party enforceability of the security interest.

The concept of a security interest attaching to property only as between the parties may seem anomalous. The principal value of a security interest, like any other property interest, lies in its *prima facie* opposability to third parties (in contrast to "mere" contractual obligations that bind third parties only with their consent). However, until the evidentiary requirement is satisfied, the security interest attaches only in the limited sense that the PPSA rules governing the parties' rights and obligations in relation to the collateral apply. This is most significant at the enforcement stage where the Act seeks to balance the need for an efficient liquidation process against the need to protect the debtor against a purely self-interested enforcement by the secured party.

The formulation of the attachment concept in the Ontario PPSA does not distinguish between *inter partes* and third-party attachment. That Act instead states simply that a security interest is not enforceable against third parties unless all three components of attachment have been satisfied.[3] However, it is well accepted that once value is given and the debtor has rights in the collateral, the security agreement becomes enforceable between the parties and the enforcement regime in Part 5 of the Ontario Act applies. In other words, the difference in formulation does not affect the result.

3) Relationship among Attachment, Perfection, and Priority

To acquire the best rights possible against third parties, the security interest must also be perfected. Perfection is the subject of chapter 5. This

---

3   OPPSA s. 11(1).

chapter is concerned with perfection only insofar as the attachment of a valid security interest is an essential component.[4]

Except for the fact that attachment is a precondition to the perfected status of a security interest, attachment, and priority are also separate concepts under the PPSA. However, the time of attachment may be determinative of priority in the following situations: (1) a contest between two unperfected security interests;[5] (2) a contest between the holder of a registered security interest that has not yet attached and a buyer of the collateral;[6] and (3) a contest between the holder of a PPSA security interest in goods that are subsequently affixed to real property and a person with an interest in the real property.[7]

B. "VALUE IS GIVEN"

1) "Value"

The secured party must have given value in order for a PPSA security interest to attach.[8] The value must be real value. A cheque that is dishonoured on presentation does not qualify.[9] On the other hand, the secured party is not required to actually advance loan funds or purchase money credit for attachment to occur. The Act defines "value" to mean "any consideration sufficient to support a simple contract."[10] Thus, value is given as soon as the secured party makes a binding commitment to extend credit to the debtor.[11] Similarly, a security interest continues to exist under a line of credit arrangement even if there is no indebtedness outstanding at a given time so long as the secured party

---

4   PPSA (A, BC, M, NB, NWT, Nu, O, PEI, S) s. 19, (NL, NS) s. 20; Y s. 18.

5   See chapter 8.

6   See chapter 7.

7   See chapter 12. And see *Business Development Bank of Canada v. S & S Mobile Refrigeration* (1996), 12 P.P.S.A.C. (2d) 298, 28 O.T.C. 48 (Ont. Ct. Gen. Div.); *Cormier v. Federal Business Development Bank* (1984), 25 B.L.R. 194, 3 P.P.S.A.C. 161 (Ont. Co. Ct.).

8   PPSA (A, BC, M, NB, PEI, Nu, NWT, S) s. 12(1)(a); (NL, NS, Y) s. 13(1)(a); O s. 11(2)(b).

9   *Dale Tingley Chrysler Plymouth Ltd. v. Chris & Don Enterprises Ltd.* (1994), 8 P.P.S.A.C. (2d) 191 (Sask. Q.B.), rev'd on other grounds (1995), 10 P.P.S.A.C. (2d) 112 (Sask. C.A.).

10   PPSA (S) s. 2(1); (A, BC, NWT, Nu, O, Y) s. 1(1); (M, NB, PEI) s. 1; (NL, NS) s. 2.

11   For judicial confirmation, see *Agricultural Credit Corp. of Saskatchewan v. Pettyjohn* (1991), 1 P.P.S.A.C. (2d) 273 at 282 ff (Sask. C.A.).

is obligated to continue extending credit.[12] Indeed, it has been held that a security interest granted under seal satisfies the requirement of value on the theory that a seal substitutes for consideration under general contract doctrine.[13] Of course, if there is no actual obligation outstanding at a given time, the existence of an attached security interest is of theoretical importance only. Without a determinate obligation, there is nothing for which enforcement against the collateral can be pursued.

2) Antecedent Debt

The definition of value extends to an antecedent debt or liability,[14] enabling past unsecured debt to be converted into secured debt. The same rule applied in pre-PPSA law on the theory that an unsecured creditor's willingness to forbear action on the outstanding debt constitutes sufficient new value to support the security agreement.[15] The statutory inclusion of past debt does away with the need to allege and prove forbearance. However, an arrangement to convert a debt from unsecured to secured status still remains subject to the provincial law on fraudulent conveyances and unjust preferences and to federal bankruptcy and insolvency avoidance law.[16]

C. "DEBTOR HAS RIGHTS IN THE COLLATERAL"

1) Rights versus Ownership

A security interest is a proprietary interest. As such, it requires a subject matter. If the asset does not yet exist or if the debtor has not yet acquired an interest in it, there is nothing to which the security right can attach.

---

12   *Central Guaranty Trust Co. v. Bruncor Leasing Inc.* (1992), 4 P.P.S.A.C. (2d) 229 at 234 ff (Ont. Ct. Gen. Div.).
13   *Heidelberg Canada Graphic Equipment Ltd. v. Arthur Andersen Inc.* (1993), 7 B.L.R. (2d) 236, 4 P.P.S.A.C. (2d) 116 (Ont. Ct. Gen. Div.).
14   PPSA (S) s. 2 (1); (A, BC, NWT, Nu, O, Y) s. 1(1); (M, NB, PEI) s. 1; (NL, NS) s. 2.
15   *O'Brien v. Stebbins*, [1927] 3 D.L.R. 274 (Sask. C.A.); *Royal Bank v. Kiska* (1967), 63 D.L.R. (2d) 582 (Ont. C.A.). And see the discussion in *Heidelberg Canada Graphic Equipment Ltd. v. Arthur Andersen Inc.*, above note 13..
16   See, for example, *Asklepeion Restaurants Ltd. v. 791259 Ontario Ltd.* (1998), 13 P.P.S.A.C. (2d) 295 (Ont. C.A.).

This basic idea is reflected in the requirement that the debtor must have "rights in the collateral" before a security interest can attach.[17]

While the debtor's rights must be proprietary in character, they need not amount to full ownership. Any type of proprietary interest is sufficient. This includes a right to possession. The courts have sometimes been wary of that proposition, no doubt out of concern for the rights of the true owner. For example, in *Agar v. 762250 Ontario Ltd.*,[18] the debtor had breached the terms of a co-tenancy agreement by granting a security interest in shares. Reasoning that the debtor had insufficient rights to grant a security interest in the shares, the court ruled that the secured party had therefore acquired the shares subject to "the equities" between the debtor and the other parties to the co-tenancy agreement.

In the view of the authors, the same result in cases of this kind is more coherently achieved by accepting that a debtor in lawful possession of collateral has sufficient rights to support attachment of a security interest. However, just because a security interest has attached does not mean that the secured party will prevail. The PPSA preserves the supplementary application of the "principles of the common law, equity and the law merchant" to the extent not inconsistent with the Act.[19] These principles include *nemo dat quod non habet* (no one can give that which she has not). If the debtor had no proprietary interest beyond possession to convey, then the security interest can only attach to that possessory interest. A possessory title is good against the whole world *except* the true owner.[20] The true owner (or co-owners in the foregoing scenario) will therefore prevail over the secured party.[21]

2) Exceptions to *Nemo Dat*

Exceptionally, the law may empower a debtor with only limited rights in collateral to grant a greater interest to a secured party than he possesses. The operation of these exceptions is preserved by the PPSA ex-

---

17 PPSA (A, BC, M, NB, PEI, Nu, NWT, S) s. 12(1)(b); (NL, NS, Y) s. 13(1)(b); O s. 11(2)(c).

18 (1994), 6 P.P.S.A.C. (2d) 292 (Ont. Ct. Gen. Div.).

19 PPSA (M, NWT, Nu, S) s. 65(2); A s. 66(3); BC s. 68(1); (NB, PEI) s. 65(1); (NL, NS) s. 66(1); O s. 72; Y s. 63(1).

20 *Armory v. Delamirie* (1722), 1 Str. 505, 93 E.R. 664, as applied in *Bird v. Ft. Frances*, [1949] 2 D.L.R. 791 (Ont. H.C.); *Canada (Attorney General) v. Brock* (1991), 59 B.C.L.R. (2d) 261 at 268 (as cited in *Gray v. Royal Bank* (1997), 143 D.L.R. (4th) 179, 12 P.P.S.A.C. (2d) 126 (B.C.S.C.)).

21 *Gray v. Royal Bank, ibid.*

cept to the extent they are inconsistent with the priority regime of the Act.[22]

For example, if a trustee conveys or grants security in trust property in breach of trust, the buyer or secured party will prevail over the equitable title of the trust beneficiary in the absence of knowledge of the trust. In situations of this kind, it is sometimes said that the debtor's legal power to grant a superior title to third parties constitutes sufficient rights in the collateral for the purposes of attachment. This approach collapses the distinction between attachment and priority. Analytically, it may be more accurate to say that the debtor's legal title constitutes sufficient rights to support attachment. The priority status of that right then turns on the applicable priority rule, whether it is *nemo dat* or some exception to *nemo dat*.

3) Impact of PPSA on Characterization of Debtor's Rights

Under the terms of a conditional sales contract or security lease, the seller or lessor purports to retain title to the goods, with the buyer or lessee having merely a possessory right. The courts have sometimes relied on the buyer's or lessee's possessory rights as constituting sufficient rights to support attachment of a competing security interest.[23] This approach fails to take into account the impact of the conceptual structure of the PPSA. Under the Act, a conditional sale or security lease is characterized as giving rise to a security interest. A secured transaction is inherently a relationship in which the debtor owns the collateral and the secured party has only a charge on the debtor's title. The buyer's or lessee's implicit ownership means that a competing security interest will attach to the goods, not merely to the debtor's possessory rights in the goods. The rights of the seller or lessor as against the competing secured party then depend upon the PPSA rules governing priority between secured creditors.

---

22   See the discussion in chapter 7 on the interrelationship between the PPSA and the provisions of the *Sale of Goods Acts* in effect in PPSA jurisdictions which empower a "seller in possession" without title to nonetheless convey title to third parties in certain circumstances.

23   *Euroclean Canada Inc. v. Forest Glade Investments Ltd.* (1985), 49 O.R. (2d) 769, 4 P.P.S.A.C. 271, 54 C.B.R. (N.S.) 65, 16 D.L.R. (4th) 289, 8 O.A.C. 1 (C.A.), leave to appeal to S.C.C. refused (1985), 55 C.B.R. (N.S.) xxvii, 16 D.L.R. (4th) 289n (S.C.C.); *Haibeck v. No. 40 Taurus Ventures Ltd.* (1991), 59 B.C.L.R. (2d) 229, 2 P.P.S.A.C. (2d) 171 (S.C.).

4) Deemed Security Interests

Except for the Ontario Act, the PPSA deems a lease for a term of more than one year and a commercial consignment to be secured transactions.[24] The rights of the lessor or consignor as against the holder of a security interest granted by the lessee or consignee are intended to be governed, not by the *nemo dat* doctrine, but by the PPSA rules governing perfection and priority between competing security interests. To bring these rules into play, the lessee or consignee must have sufficient rights in the collateral to support attachment of the competing security interest.

In grappling with this issue, the Saskatchewan courts ruled that the debtor's possessory rights constituted sufficient rights for the purposes of attachment.[25] That position has since been codified. Except for the Ontario Act, the PPSA now provides that a debtor has rights in leased or consigned goods for the purposes of attachment when the debtor obtains possession of them.[26]

This provision should not be interpreted as meaning that the consignee or lessee has only possessory rights in the collateral. The Act characterizes the parties' relationship as a deemed secured transaction with the result that ownership is deemed to vest in the lessee or consignee.[27] As deemed owner, the lessee or consignee has sufficient rights to grant a competing security interest in the goods themselves, not merely in the right to possession of the goods.

The Ontario Act is silent on the issue and the Ontario courts have expressed doubt about whether a debtor's possessory rights under a true lease or consignment constitute sufficient rights to support attachment.[28] In the Ontario context, the issue has little practical significance.

---

24 For a detailed analysis of deemed security interests, see chapter 2.
25 *Ford Credit Canada Ltd. v. Percival Mercury Sales Ltd.* (1986), 6 P.P.S.A.C. 288 (Sask. C.A.), additional reasons at (1986), 50 Sask.R. 270, aff'g on other grounds (1984), 34 Sask. R. 134, 4 P.P.S.A.C. 92 (Sask. Q.B.); *Gelowitz v. Garcon Enterprises Ltd.* (1995), 9 P.P.S.A.C. (2d) 212 (Sask. Q.B.); *International Harvester Credit Corp. of Canada Ltd. v. Bell's Dairy Ltd.* (1986), 50 Sask. R. 268, 6 P.P.S.A.C. 138 (Sask. C.A.), additional reasons at (1986), 50 Sask. R. 270, rev'g (1984), 4 P.P.S.A.C. 149 (Sask. Q.B.); *Farm-Rite Equipment Ltd. (Receiver of) v. Robinson Alamo Sales Ltd.* (1986), 5 P.P.S.A.C. 286 (Sask. Q.B.).
26 PPSA (A, BC, M, Nu, NWT, S) s. 12(2); (NB, PEI) s. 12(3); (NL, NS, Y) s. 13(3); O no equivalent provision.
27 This feature of the Act was not fully appreciated by the Saskatchewan courts in: *Farm-Rite Equipment Ltd. (Receiver of) v. Robinson Alamo Sales Ltd.*, above note 25; *Ford Credit Canada Ltd. v. Percival Mercury Sales Ltd.*, above note 25.
28 *Guaranty Trust Co. of Canada v. Canadian Imperial Bank of Commerce* (1989), 2 P.P.S.A.C. (2d) 88 (Ont. H.C.J.), aff'd (1993), 6 P.P.S.A.C. (2d) 51 (Ont. C.A.);

The Ontario PPSA applies to leases and consignments only where they function as disguised purchase money secured transactions. True leases or consignments fall outside the scope of the Act. It follows that even if the lessee or consignee's possession constituted sufficient rights to support attachment of a competing security interest, the lessor's or consignor's superior title would prevail under the *nemo dat* doctrine.

Deemed security interests fall with the scope of the PPSA only for the purposes of the rules governing perfection and priority. The Act does not otherwise deem the lessee or consignee to be the owner. A competing secured creditor will prevail only if the lessor or consignor fails to register its deemed security interest, or fails to satisfy the conditions for purchase-money priority.[29] Even then, the lessor or consignor as owner is entitled to claim any residual value left in the collateral after the obligation secured by the competing security interest is satisfied.

The same analysis applies where the deemed secured transaction takes the form of a sale of accounts or chattel paper or, in the context of the Acts in effect in the Atlantic provinces, a sale of goods without a change of possession. By deeming the interest of a buyer to be a security interest, the PPSA implicitly deems the seller to retain ownership for the purposes of supporting attachment under a subsequent sale or grant of security.[30] However, the seller's implicit ownership operates only for the purposes of applying the PPSA perfection and priority rules. Otherwise, the buyer is the owner.

5) "Debtor"

Normally, the person who grants the security is also the debtor of the secured obligation. However, security is sometimes granted to secure the obligation of a third person. This is reflected in the PPSA definition

---

Canadian Imperial Bank of Commerce v. International Harvester Credit Corp. of Canada Ltd. (1986), 4 P.P.S.A.C. 329 (Ont. H.C.J.), rev'd on other grounds (1986), 6 P.P.S.A.C. 273 (Ont. C.A). Compare with *Harry D. Shields Ltd. v. Bank of Montreal* (1992), 3 P.P.S.A.C. (2d) 115 (Ont. Ct. Gen. Div.); *CIBC v. Otto Timm Enterprises* (1996), 26 O.R. (3d) 724 (C.A.).

29   For recent judicial confirmation, see *Re Western Express Air Lines Inc.* (2005), 7 P.P.S.A.C. (3d) 229 (B.C.S.C.) at paras 10–17.

30   See Tamara Buckwold and Ronald C.C. Cuming, "The *Personal Property Security Act* and the *Bankruptcy and Insolvency Act*: Two Solitudes or Complementary Systems?" (1997) 12 B.F.L.R. 467 at 487. Compare with Michael Bridge, Roderick Macdonald, Ralph Simmonds, and Catherine Walsh, "Formalism, Functionalism and Understanding the Law of Secured Transactions" (1999) 44 McGill L.J. 568 at 586, n. 59.

of debtor as including either the person who owes the secured obligation or the person who owns or has rights in the collateral, or both,
depending on the context.[31] For the purposes of the requirement that
the debtor have rights in the collateral, debtor clearly means the person
who owns or who has the rights in the collateral.

6) After-acquired Collateral

The common law traditionally refused to accept the possibility that a
person could transfer or grant security in property not yet owned by
that person. For the property interest to come into existence there had
to be some specific act of appropriation following the debtor's acquisition of the asset. But equity, operating on the maxim "equity regards as
done that which ought to be done," treated a contract to give a present
security interest in after-acquired property as effective to convey an
equitable interest immediately on the debtor's acquisition of the property.[32] However, equity also "follows the law" and a security interest in
after-acquired property was therefore subordinated to the interest of a
subsequent purchaser or mortgagee of the legal title without notice.[33]
Moreover, registration of a security agreement containing an after-acquired property clause was not considered to be constructive notice for
this purpose, leading to the curious situation where one was actually
better off for not having searched the registry in advance of a purchase
or mortgage.[34]

In *Acmetrack Ltd. v. Bank Canadian National*,[35] the Ontario Court
of Appeal reversed its traditional position and ruled that registration
under the Ontario *Corporation Securities Registration Act* (CSRA) constituted constructive notice to other secured parties. This decision was
rendered after the OPPSA went into effect and during the period when
the CSRA still operated in parallel with the PPSA. The Court was possibly influenced by a desire to make the non-PPSA and PPSA positions

---

31   PPSA (A, BC, NWT, Nu, O, Y) s. 1(1); (M, NB, PEI) s. 1; (NL, NS) s. 2; S s. 2(1).
32   *Holroyd v. Marshall* (1862), 11 E.R. 999, [1861–73] All E.R. Rep. 414 (H.L.);
     Tailby v. Official Receiver (1888), 13 App. Cas. 523 at 545–49 (H.L.); *Lloyd v. Eu-
     ropean and North American Railway* (1878), 18 N.B.R. 194 (C.A.); *Vassie v. Vassie*
     (1882), 22 N.B.R. 76 (C.A.); *Fraser v. Macpherson* (1898), 34 N.B.R. 417 (C.A.).
33   The classic authority on the vulnerability of equitable security interests in after-
     acquired property to subsequent legal interests under pre-PPSA law is *Joseph v.
     Lyons* (1884), 15 Q.B. 280 (C.A.).
34   See *Blower v. Hepburn* (1980), 112 D.L.R. (3d) 474 (Alta. Q.B.) for a survey of the
     Canadian case law.
35   (1984), 12 D.L.R. (4th) 428 (Ont. C.A.).

as compatible as possible. In any event, the PPSA makes it clear that constructive notice by registration has no role to play in a statutory priority regime.[36]

The vulnerability of security interests in future property under prior law was not unjustified in policy terms. To have recognized a security interest in future property as effective at law would have enabled a secured party with an all-inclusive security interest to acquire a situational monopoly over the debtor's financing needs. So long as the security interest was treated as effective only in equity, the legal interest in specific assets remained available to secure more specialized or economically attractive sources of financing. The rule also carved out an important area of protection for a *bona fide* purchaser for value who, given the fragmented and incomplete character of the old registration regimes, could not reasonably be expected to bear the risk of a failure to consult the registry in advance of a purchase.

Under the PPSA, a security interest under a security agreement that covers after-acquired property attaches to that property in accordance with the terms of the agreement subject only to satisfaction of the criteria for attachment.[37] In other words, the security attaches as soon as the debtor has rights in the collateral, value is given and the evidentiary requirements for security agreements are satisfied.

The PPSA expressly disclaims the need for a subsequent act of appropriation of the after-acquired collateral. The OPPSA does not include this disclaimer. However, the Ontario courts have been just as willing as their counterparts in other provinces to recognize that a single security agreement is capable of effectively charging the after-acquired property of a debtor subject only to compliance with the rules for attachment.

If classification were needed, the effect is to convert all security interests in after-acquired collateral taken under the Act into statutory "legal" interests on an equal par with security interests in present collateral. But classification is generally not needed because priority turns on the detailed regime established by Part 3 of the Act. The policy concerns that influenced the legal/equitable classification under prior law have been dealt with directly in the fashioning of those rules.

Since the "rights in the collateral" requirement for attachment must be satisfied before attachment can occur, a security interest covering af-

---

36   PPSA (A, BC, M, Nu, NWT, S) s. 12(2); (NB, PEI) s. 47; (NL, NS) s. 48; O s. 47(5)(a); Y s. 52(3).

37   PPSA (A, BC, M, NB, Nu, NWT, PEI, S) s. 13(1); (NL, N) s. 14(1); O s. 12(1); Y s. 11(3).

ter-acquired property will attach to each new asset acquired by the debtor only at the point of acquisition. It follows that two or more security interests covering after-acquired collateral will attach simultaneously on the acquisition of the collateral by the debtor. In general, this does not generate significant difficulties since priority between perfected security interests is determined by the order in which the perfecting steps for each were taken, and a perfected security interest has priority over an unperfected security interest. However, if both interests are unperfected, the Act states that the order of attachment governs.[38] Where attachment is simultaneous, the rule becomes unworkable and the courts have held, correctly in the view of the authors, that priority goes to the first secured creditor who obtains a written security agreement.[39]

7) After-acquired Consumer Goods

Enabling debtors to grant security in their future assets to a single creditor is not uncontroversial, in part because of concerns with the situational monopoly thereby acquired over the debtor's access to secured financing. The PPSA establishes various mechanisms to alleviate this concern, including a prohibition (now deleted from the Saskatchewan Act) on the grant of security in after-acquired consumer goods.[40]

The consumer goods exception is directed at so-called add-on plans under which a finance company takes a general security interest in all of the debtor's household goods as additional security under a purchase-money financing arrangement or a blanket security agreement under which a lender is given a security interest in all present and future assets of a consumer debtor. Accordingly, the prohibition on the grant of security in after-acquired consumer goods does not apply to purchase money security interests. Unlike add-on security, which is used primarily for its *in terrorem* effect on the debtor, the imposition of a prohibition on purchase money financing for consumer goods would cause more harm than good.

There is a significant difference in the formulation of this prohibition in the Ontario Act.[41] The Ontario version does not make an explicit exception for purchase money security interests. Instead, the Act

---

38   PPSA (A, BC, M, NB, Nu, NWT, PEI, S) s. 35(1); (NL, NS) s. 36(1); O s. 30(1); Y s. 30(2).

39   *National Bank of Canada v. Merit Energy* (2001), 27 C.B.R. (4th) 283, 294 A.R. 1 (Q.B.).

40   PPSA (A, BC, M, NB, Nu, NWT, O, PEI, S) s. 13(2) (b); (NL, NS) s. 14(2) (b); Y s. 12(2).

41   OPPSA s. 12(2).

172 PERSONAL PROPERTY SECURITY LAW

creates a ten-day window after the secured party gives value for attachment of a security interest in after-acquired consumer goods. As a
result, if a debtor gets a bank loan to buy a car but fails to buy the car
within ten days from the date the bank commits to the loan, the security interest of the bank cannot attach.

The consumer goods exception does not apply to an accession or
to goods subsequently obtained by the debtor to replace the original
collateral. The Ontario formulation of the provision does not expressly
address replacement goods. However, a security interest in consumer
goods owned or acquired by the debtor within the ten-day window will
continue in replacement goods if they represent proceeds of that collateral. The Ontario Act provides that no security interest arises under an
after-acquired property clause to after-acquired consumer goods, subject to the ten-day window. A proceeds interest arises by operation of
the PPSA rather than through an after-acquired clause in the security
agreement. Therefore, the right to proceeds in Ontario is not affected
by the ten-day limit on security in after-acquired consumer goods.

Except for the Ontario Act, the wording of the PPSA is unclear on
whether the restriction against the grant of security in after-acquired
consumer goods prevents a security interest from arising in respect of
proceeds of consumer goods owned by the debtor when the security
interest was granted. In the view of the authors, it should not. Proceeds
do not constitute after-acquired property in the sense of bringing new
value into the debtor's asset base so as to fall within the policy underlying the restriction. Rather, they constitute the exchange value of the
original collateral.

8) Future Property and Analogous Categories

A distinction is sometimes drawn between after-acquired and future
property, with future property referring to property not yet in existence, as opposed to property in existence but not yet owned by the
debtor. Where security is granted in a debtor's future property, the attachment issue is not so much when the debtor acquired rights in the
collateral but rather when the property itself comes into existence so
as to support attachment. The PPSA provides express guidance on this
in two potentially troublesome cases: crops and the unborn young of
animals. The Act deems the debtor to acquire rights in crops when they
become growing crops and in animals when they are conceived.[42]

---

42   PPSA (A, BC, M, NB, Nu, NWT, PEI, S) s. 12(3); (NL, NS) s. 13(3); (O, Y) s. 11(3).

An analogous problem arises with personal property that begins life as real property. The question here is when the transformation to personal property occurs. Under the Act, a debtor is considered to acquire sufficient rights to support attachment in minerals when they are extracted, and in trees, other than those that constitute crops (timber in the OPPSA) when they are severed.[43] Except for the Ontario Act, this is compatible with the PPSA definition of "goods" and "minerals" as excluding minerals until they are extracted and trees until they are severed.[44] In contrast, the Ontario Act defines goods as *including* minerals and hydrocarbons to be extracted and timber to be severed.[45]

Although attachment of a security interest to growing crops occurs as soon as they qualify as such, the PPSA (except for the Saskatchewan Act) imposes a temporal limitation on attachment. The security interest does not attach to crops grown more than one year after the security agreement has been executed.[46] The only exception is where the crops are given as security in conjunction with a lease, purchase, or mortgage of land. If the parties agree, the security interest can attach to crops grown during the term of the lease, purchase, or mortgage.

The provision was carried over to the PPSA from earlier versions of UCC Article 9. It was intended to protect farmers, who are vulnerable to sudden and severe economic setbacks, from encumbering all their future expectations. The provision never found its way into the *Civil Code of Québec* and has been removed from UCC Article 9. It does not seem to have generated significant case law outside Saskatchewan[47] (where it has since been deleted from the PPSA). Presumably this is not because the prohibition is popular; rather that it can be escaped by resorting to *Bank Act* security.

The Ontario Act provides guidance on a fifth category of collateral.[48] A security interest in fish does not attach until the fish are caught.

---

43   PPSA (A, BC, M, NB, Nu, NWT, PEI, S) s. 12(3); (NL, NS) s. 13(3); (O, Y) s. 11(3).
44   PPSA (A, BC, NWT, Nu, O, Y) s. 1(1); (M, NB, PEI) s. 1; (NL, NS) s. 2; S s. 2(1).
45   OPPSA s. 1(1). This inconsistency was apparently not intentional but resulted from oversight by the drafters of the 1989 Ontario Act: see Jacob S. Ziegel and David L. Denomme, *The Ontario Personal Property Security Act: Commentary and Analysis*, 2d ed. (Markham: Butterworths, 2000) at 131.
46   PPSA (A, BC, M, NB, Nu, NWT, PEI, S) s. 13(2)(a); (NL, NS) s. 14(2)(a); O s. 12(2)(a); Y s. 12(2).
47   *Feduk v. Bank of Montreal* (1992), 3 P.P.S.A.C. (2d) 310 (Sask. Q.B.); *Kozak v. Gruza* (1989), 9 P.P.S.A.C. 221 (Sask. C.A.); *Legaarden v. Abernethy Credit Union Ltd.* (1991), 3 P.P.S.A.C. (2d) 292 (Sask. Q.B.); *Stusick v. C & M Holdings Inc.* (1995), 10 P.P.S.A.C. (2d) 213 (Sask. Q.B.).
48   OPPSA s. 11(3)(b).

Here, the question is not future property in the strict sense — clearly, the fish exist before they are caught — but rather what quality of control is necessary for the fish to leave the public domain and become the private property of the debtor. Presumably, the provision is not intended to cover fish cultivated in aquaculture, which are more appropriately analogized to farm animals, including the rule that a security interest attaches to the unborn young on conception.

9) Repossessed or Returned Goods

A buyer or lessee of goods takes free of any security interest granted by the seller or lessor if the transaction was authorized or took place in the ordinary course of the seller's or the lessor's business.[49] In other words, the sale or lease terminates the attached status of the security interest. However, if the goods are returned to, seized, or repossessed by the seller or lessor, the PPSA provides for the automatic reattachment of the security interest.[50]

10) Attachment of a Floating Charge

An equitable security interest in the nature of a so-called floating charge is classically described as hovering over the collateral without attaching to any specific asset until the charge is crystallized.[51] The floating charge as a distinct legal concept is irrelevant under the PPSA.[52] However, floating-charge terminology is sometimes still used in security agreements. In the early days of PPSA reform in Canada, it was argued that because floating charges under pre-PPSA law did not become specific until crystallization, the use of floating-charge terminology demonstrated the parties' intention to postpone attachment. The courts were unsympathetic.[53] Ontario is the only jurisdiction where the

---

49   For a detailed analysis, see chapter 7.
50   For a detailed analysis, see chapter 12.
51   For a comprehensive analysis, see Roderick J. Wood, "The Floating Charge in
     Canada" (1989) 27 Alta. L. Rev. 191.
52   For a detailed analysis, see chapter 2.
53   *Royal Bank of Canada v. G.M. Homes Inc.* (1984), 4 P.P.S.A.C. 116 (Sask. C.A.);
     Affinity International Inc. v. Alliance International Inc. (1994), 8 P.P.S.A.C. (2d) 73
     (Man. Q.B.), additional reasons at (1994), 8 P.P.S.A.C. (2d) 73 at 82 (Man. Q.B.),
     aff'd (1995), 9 P.P.S.A.C. (2d) 174 (Man. C.A.); *Transamerica Commercial Finance
     Corp. Canada v. Karpes* (1994), 8 P.P.S.A.C. (2d) 86; *Orr & Co. v. Saskatchewan
     Economic Development Corp.* (1994), 24 C.B.R. (3d) 196, 6 P.P.S.A.C. (2d) 350
     (Sask. Q.B.), aff'd (1994), 8 P.P.S.A.C. (2d) 83 (Sask. C.A.); *Rehm v. DSG Com-*

argument met with any success initially.[54] These maverick cases were quickly condemned in the literature[55] and not followed in subsequent decisions.[56] The later versions of the PPSA confirm expressly that a security interest in the nature of a floating charge is subject to the same attachment rules as any other type of security interest.[57]

11) Postponement of Attachment

The parties retain the freedom to postpone attachment if this is desirable. But for attachment to occur later than the date of execution of the security agreement, this intention must be stated specifically in the security agreement.[58] Otherwise, the security interest attaches upon the entry into of the security agreement, assuming the other requirements of attachment are satisfied.[59] There is no room to imply a postponement simply because the security agreement describes the security interest as a floating charge or entitles the debtor to deal freely with the collateral pending crystallization.[60] If the parties wish to postpone attach-

---

munications Inc., [1995] 4 W.W.R. 750, 9 P.P.S.A.C. (2d) 114, 33 C.B.R. (3d) 65, 129 Sask. R. 297 (Q.B.); *Russelsteel Inc. v. Lux Services Ltd.* (1986), 6 P.P.S.A.C. 107 (Sask. Q.B.); *Roynat Inc. v. United Rescue Services Ltd.* (1982), 2 P.P.S.A.C. 49 (Man. C.A.); *Irving A. Burton Ltd. v. Canadian Imperial Bank of Commerce* (1982), 2 P.P.S.A.C. 22, 36 O.R. (2d) 703 (C.A.); *National Bank of Canada v. Grinnell Corp. of Canada* (1993), 5 P.P.S.A.C. (2d) 266 (Ont. Div. Ct.); *Re Huxley Catering Ltd.* (1982), 2 P.P.S.A.C. 22 (Ont. C.A.).

54   *Royal Bank v. Inmont Canada Ltd.* (1980), 1 P.P.S.A.C. 197 at 205–7 (Ont. Co. Ct.); *First City Capital Ltd. v. Arthur Andersen Inc.* (1984), 46 O.R. (2d) 168 at 171 (H.C.J.); *Access Advertising Management Inc. v. Servex Computers Inc.* (1993), 21 C.B.R. (3d) 304, 15 O.R. (3d) 635, 6 P.P.S.A.C. (2d) 113 (Gen. Div.).

55   See J.S. Ziegel, "Floating Charges and the OPPSA: A Basic Misunderstanding" (1994) 23 Can. Bus. L.J. 470; K.C. Morlock, "Floating Charges, Negative Pledges, the PPSA and Subordination: *Chiips Inc. v. Skyview Hotels Limited*" (1995) 10 B.F.L.R. 405.

56   *Credit Suisse Canada v. 1133 Yonge Street Holdings* (1996), 28 O.R. (3d) 670, 11 P.P.S.A.C. (2d) 375, 40 C.B.R. (3d) 214, 26 B.L.R. (2d) 282 (Gen. Div.); var'd on other grounds (1998), 41 O.R. (3d) 632 (C.A.). See also *Royal Bank v. Sparrow Electric Corp.*, [1997] 2 W.W.R. 457, 46 Alta. L.R. (3d) 87, 208 N.R. 161, 143 D.L.R. (4th) 385, 44 C.B.R. (3d) 1, [1997] 1 S.C.R. 411, (*sub nom. R. v. Royal Bank*) 97 D.T.C. 5089, 12 P.P.S.A.C. (2d) 68.

57   PPSA (A, BC, M, NB, PEI, Nu, NWT, S) s. 12(1); (NL, NS) s. 13(1); O s. 11(2); Y s. 11(1).

58   *Ibid.*

59   *Redi-Mix Ltd. v. Hub Dairy & Barn Systems Ltd.* (1987), 7 P.P.S.A.C. 165 (Sask. Q.B.).

60   *Royal Bank v. G.M. Homes Inc.*, above note 53.

ment, they must enter into a specific agreement to this effect.[61] The Ontario version of this provision does not include the word "specifically," but the Ontario Court of Appeal has affirmed that the PPSA attachment rules contemplate only a fixed security interest.[62] The point is reinforced by the majority and minority opinions of the Supreme Court of Canada in *Royal Bank of Canada v. Sparrow Electric Corp.* [63]

Attachment is conceptually distinct from another issue historically associated with the floating-charge jurisprudence. This is the extent of the debtor's ability to dispose of the collateral to third parties free of the security interest. To avoid paralysis of the debtor's business operations, the courts found that a floating charge covering circulating assets carried with it an implied licence to deal with the collateral in the ordinary course of business. The licence extended beyond sales of inventory to include the grant of security in specific assets to another secured party so as to effectively give priority to the latter.

In the context of the Ontario Act, it has been suggested that where a security agreement uses the language of floating charge and covers the entirety of the debtor's revolving assets, it may be possible to rely on the pre-PPSA floating-charge jurisprudence to imply an authority for the debtor to grant a higher-ranking security in specific collateral.[64] The authors caution against that mode of analysis. The PPSA expressly states that a transferee of collateral takes free of a security interest where the dealing was expressly or impliedly authorized by the secured party.[65] Even where authority has not been given, the PPSA replaces the priority ground previously occupied by the implied licence jurisprudence with explicit priority rules that protect the title acquired by a buyer or lessee of goods in the ordinary course of business[66] and by a holder of money and a purchaser of negotiable and quasi-negotiable collateral.[67] Interestingly, the scope of explicit protection offered by the Ontario Act in the latter situation is not nearly as comprehensive.[68] The

---

61   PPSA (A, BC, M, NB, PEI, Nu, NWT, S) s. 12(1); (NL, NS) s. 13(1); O s. 11(2); Y s. 11(1).
62   *Credit Suisse Canada v. 1133 Yonge Street Holdings,* above note 56.
63   Above note 56.
64   Ziegel and Denomme, above note 45 at 130.
65   PPSA (A, BC, M, NB, PEI, Nu, NWT, S) s. 28(1); (NL, NS) s. 29(1); O s. 25(1); Y s. 26(1).
66   PPSA (A, BC, M, NB, PEI, Nu, NWT, S) s. 30(2); (NL, NS) s. 31(2); O s. 28(1); Y s. 29(1).
67   PPSA (A, BC, M, NB, PEI, Nu, NWT, S) s. 31; (NL, NS) s. 32; O s. 28; Y s. 30.
68   Compare the limited scope of OPPSA s. 28 with PPSA (A, BC, M, NB, PEI, Nu, NWT, S) s. 31; (NL, NS) s. 32.

argument that it may be possible to rely on the implied licence theory of the floating charge to give priority to a subsequent secured party may represent an attempt to compensate for the absence of sufficiently explicit protection in the PPSA itself.

In the view of the authors, the use of floating-charge terminology should not be presumed to imply a grant of authority to the debtor to dispose of the collateral to third parties free of the security interest. In the context of the floating charge, the old implied licence theory, though based on notions of estoppel and agency, was essentially a priority stratagem. The drafters of the PPSA adopted a fixed concept of security because they were confident that the work done by the floating charge concept would be more efficiently accomplished by a clear set of statutory priority rules. Although agency and even estoppel can still play a role depending on the facts of each case, the mere use of floating-charge terminology does not carry with it priority consequences.

D. WRITTEN SECURITY AGREEMENT OR POSSESSION

1) Introduction

Under pre-PPSA law, a non-possessory security interest was not subject to any writing or other evidentiary requirements in order for the interest to become enforceable against the debtor. The rule was different when it came to enforceability against third parties. Under the pre-PPSA registration statutes, a non-possessory security interest was considered void, as against creditors of the debtor and subsequent purchasers and mortgagees of the collateral unless the security agreement was evidenced by a written agreement executed by the debtor and filed in the appropriate registry.

The PPSA adopts notice registration in place of the pre-PPSA document-filing approach to registration. Instead of filing the security agreement itself, a separate financing statement is registered.[69] This change eliminates the practical need to have a written security agreement in order to effect registration. The PPSA drafters took full advantage of the increased flexibility. The Act allows for advance registration of a financing statement before any security agreement is ever entered into.[70]

---

69   PPSA (A, BC, M, NB, PEI, Nu, NWT, S) s. 25; (NL, NS) s. 26; (O, Y) s. 23.
70   PPSA (A, BC, M, Nu, NWT, S) s. 43(4); (NB, PEI) s. 43(5); (NL, NS) s. 44(5); O s. 45(2)–(3) (advance registration not allowed if the collateral is consumer goods); Y s. 42(8).

Moreover, a single registration can perfect security interests arising under multiple security agreements between the same parties covering the collateral described in the registered financing statement.[71]

In the PPSA notice system, registration merely signals that a security interest may exist in property falling within the registered collateral description. Whether a security interest actually exists depends on off-record evidence of the parties' agreement. In contrast, under the pre-PPSA document-filing systems in which a copy of a written security agreement had to be filed, registration provided *prima facie* proof to other creditors of the existence of the security interest and the date of its execution.

As a result of the move to notice registration, the PPSA imposes an independent evidentiary requirement for non-possessory security interests. Between the parties, an oral security agreement continues to be enforceable, subject to the general constraints that govern all contracts. However, for the security interest created by the agreement to become enforceable against third parties, the debtor must sign a security agreement that contains a description of the collateral.[72]

The function of the requirement for a signed descriptive security agreement is the same as under pre-PPSA law. It is intended to provide third parties, particularly third-party creditors, with objective written evidence of the actual existence of a security interest and to reduce litigation on the scope of the collateral agreed to by the debtor. The difference is that the security agreement itself is no longer part of the public registration record. Access is instead ensured by entitling creditors and other interested third parties to obtain a copy of the security agreement directly from the secured party who is also obligated to verify the current outstanding indebtedness and scope of the collateral.[73]

2) Possession as a Substitute for a Signed Descriptive Security Agreement

A written security agreement is not necessary if collateral is tangible and the secured party takes possession of the collateral.[74] Possession

---

71   PPSA (A, BC, M, Nu, NWT, S) s. 43(5); (NB, PEI) s. 43(6); (NL, NS) s. 44(6); O s. 45(4) (multi-agreement registration not allowed if the collateral is consumer goods); Y no equivalent provision.

72   PPSA (A, BC, M, NB, PEI, Nu, NWT, S) ss. 12(1)(c), 10(1); (NL, NS) s. 13(1)(c), 11(1); O s. 11(2)(c), 11(1); Y s. 13(1)(c), 8(1).

73   PPSA (A, BC, M, NB, O, PEI, Nu, NWT, S) s. 18; (NL, NS) s. 19; Y s. 17.

74   PPSA (A, BC, M, NB, PEI, Nu, NWT, S) s. 10(1); (NL, NS) s. 11(1); O ss. 11(2)(c), 11(1); Y s. 8(1). For judicial confirmation, see, for example, *977380 Ontario Inc. v. Roy's Towing Co.* (1997), 13 P.P.S.A.C. (2d) 201 (Ont. Ct. Gen. Div.).

adequately evidences both the debtor's consent to the security interest and the scope of the collateral covered by that interest.

Under pre-PPSA law, only "an actual and continued" change of possession of the collateral excused a secured party from having to file its security documentation in the pre-PPSA registry.[75] The same policy has been carried over to the PPSA. Constructive possession by the secured party of collateral that remains in the actual or apparent possession or control of the debtor or the debtor's agent does not substitute for a signed descriptive security agreement.[76] There is no equivalent provision in the Ontario Act, but the same rule should apply because possession by the debtor or anybody closely associated with the debtor would not provide sufficient evidence to third parties that the debtor's title is potentially encumbered.

In addition to satisfying the evidentiary requirement, taking possession of the collateral also operates to perfect a security interest under the Act.[77] With the exceptions of the Ontario, Manitoba, and Yukon Acts, possession by the secured party for the purposes of seizure or repossession does not qualify as an act of perfection.[78] The same disqualification does not apply to possession for the purposes of satisfying the evidentiary requirement.[79] The following scenario illustrates the operation of this distinction:

On day one, SP acquires an oral non-possessory security interest in D's collateral. On day ninety, SP seizes the collateral following D's default. On day ninety-five, D sells the collateral to Buyer.

In this scenario, SP's act of seizing the collateral is sufficient to satisfy the evidentiary requirement. However, while SP may win the battle, there is a serious risk of losing the war. SP's interest remained unperfected at the time of the sale to Buyer since seizure does not qualify as a sufficient possession for perfection purposes. An unperfected security interest is

---

75   See, for example, s. 3 of the now-repealed New Brunswick *Bills of Sale Act*: "A sale or mortgage that is not accompanied by an immediate delivery and an actual and continued change of possession of the chattels sold or mortgaged is void [against third parties] unless [registered]"; and note s. 1: "change of possession means such change of possession as is open and reasonably sufficient to afford public notice thereof."
76   PPSA (A, BC, M, NB, PEI, Nu, NWT, S) s. 10(2); (NL, NS) s. 11(2); Y s. 22(2).
77   PPSA (A, BC, M, NB, PEI, Nu, NWT, S) s. 24(1); (NL, NS) s. 25(1); O s. 22; Y s. 22(1).
78   *Ibid.* Section 22 of the *Yukon Act* does not state a rule one way or the other.
79   PPSA (A, BC, M, NB, PEI, Nu, NWT, S) s. 10(1); (NL, NS) s. 11(1); O ss. 11(2)(c), 11(1); Y s. 8(1).

ineffective against a buyer who takes without actual knowledge of the existence of the security interest.[80] Since SP had already seized the collateral by the time of the purported sale to Buyer, it is unlikely that Buyer will be in a position to claim he took without knowledge of the security interest. Nonetheless, one can imagine scenarios where Buyer could credibly claim ignorance of SP's interest — for example, where the sale negotiations commenced before the seizure by SP and Buyer did not verify D's continued possession before concluding the sale. In that eventuality, Buyer will prevail, except under the Ontario Act.[81]

3) Relationship between Evidentiary Requirement and Priority

Until the evidentiary requirement is satisfied, a security interest is unenforceable against third parties.[82] It follows that a third party who acquires an intervening interest in the collateral will generally take free of the security interest. Thus an oral non-possessory security interest is ineffective against a trustee in bankruptcy even if a financing statement in relation to that interest is registered before the bankruptcy commences.[83] Similarly, a purchaser or lessee of collateral in the debtor's possession takes free of a prior security interest, regardless of knowledge, if a signed descriptive security agreement has not been executed prior to the sale or lease. With respect to unsecured judgment creditors, the critical point will be when the collateral becomes bound by the judgment.[84]

---

80 PPSA (NB, PEI, Nu, NWT, S) s. 20(3); A s. 20(b); (BC, M) s. 20(c); (NL, NS) s. 21(3); (NWT, Nu) s. 20(1); O 20(1); Y s. 19(1). For a full analysis of the priority repercussion of failure to perfect, see chapter 5.

81 In contract to the other Acts, OPPSA s. 20(1) requires that the buyer also obtain possession of the collateral in order to prevail over an unperfected sercurity interest.

82 PPSA (A, BC, M, NB, PEI, Nu, NWT, S) s. 10(1); (NL, NS) s. 11(1); O ss. 11(2)(c), 11(1); Y s. 8(1).

83 For judicial confirmation, see, for example, *Atlas Industries v. Federal Business Development Bank* (1983), 50 C.B.R. (N.S.) 14, 3 P.P.S.A.C. 39 (Sask. Q.B.); *Toronto Dominion Bank v. Flexi-Coil Ltd.* (1993), 4 P.P.S.A.C. (2d) 288 (Sask. Q.B.); *Simonot v. Burlingham Associates Inc.* (sub nom. *Collins (Bankrupt), Re),* (1998), 165 Sask. R. 209, [1998] 8 W.W.R. 365, 4 C.B.R. (4th) 115 (Q.B.).

84 *Kawartha Consumers Co-Operative Inc. v. Debenture Holders of Kawartha Consumers Co-Operative Inc.,* [1999] O.J. No. 4367, 14 C.B.R. (4th) 210 (S.C.J.). In some jurisdictions, collateral is bound by a judgment on its seizure pursuant to judgment execution proceedings. In others, registration of a notice of judgment or a writ of enforcement in the Personal Property Registry is the decisive point. See also chapter 10.

The position is more controversial where the competing third-party interest is another security interest. Consider the following scenario:

On day one, SP1 enters into an oral security agreement with Debtor and promptly registers a financing statement in the Personal Property Registry. On day two, Debtor grants a security interest in the same collateral to SP2 pursuant to a written security agreement and SP2 registers a financing statement in the Personal Property Registry. On day three, Debtor signs a written security agreement evidencing the security interest previously granted to SP1.

In the Ontario Act, the evidentiary requirement is presented as one of the prerequisites to the attachment of a security interest. Attachment in turn is presented as a prerequisite to the third-party effectiveness of a security interest. It follows that SP1 has priority, notwithstanding that SP2's interest attached before SP1's security interest was reduced to writing.[85]

However, the formulation in the other Acts is somewhat different. As with the Ontario Act, satisfaction of the evidentiary requirement is a prerequisite to the third-party attachment of a security interest created by a security agreement. However, unlike the Ontario Act, the other Acts state the evidentiary requirement as a standalone provision, which is then incorporated by cross-reference into the rules governing third-party attachment.[86]

There is some debate on the significance of this difference. Some see the evidentiary requirement qualifying the operation of the priority rules that govern competing perfected security interests. On this view, if SP1 does not satisfy the evidentiary requirement before SP2's interest attaches, SP2 acquires a vested priority against SP1, regardless of the order of registration. Others take the position that the evidentiary requirement qualifies the general rule of priority only insofar as compliance is a precondition to the effectiveness and attachment of SP1's interest against SP2. On this view, it does not matter whether SP1 complies with the evidentiary requirement before or after SP2's interest attaches.[87]

From a policy viewpoint, both interpretations have their shortcomings. Proponents of the first point out that the objective of the evidentiary requirement is undermined if it can be complied with after the fact so as to make an oral non-possessory security interest retroactively enforceable against an intervening security interest. Proponents of the

---

85   *Rogerson Lumber Co. v. Four Seasons Chalet Ltd.* (1980), 113 D.L.R. (3d) 671 (Ont. C.A.), Houlden J.A.

86   PPSA (A, BC, M, NB, PEI, Nu, NWT, S) ss. 12(1)(c), 10(1); (NL, NS) s. 13(1)(c), 11(1); O s. 11(2)(c), 11(1); Y s. 13(1)(c), 8(1).

87   This latter interpretation was adopted in *674921 B.C. Ltd. v. Advanced Wing Technologies Corp.*, [2005] B.C.J. No. 1704 (S.C.).

second worry about the impact of such a rule on certainty and pre-dictability in priority ordering. If compliance with the evidentiary requirement is necessary before SP2's interest is acquired, SP2 would presumably also have to show that it had complied before SP1 reduced its own agreement to writing.

E. MANDATORY CONTENT OF WRITTEN SECURITY AGREEMENT

A typical security agreement will include terms covering such matters as:

- the amount of the secured debt, including interest and finance char-ges, and the terms of repayment and maturity;
- a description of the collateral;
- the duties of the debtor respecting the care of the collateral includ-ing any requirements to keep it in a specified location and to main-tain insurance coverage;
- restrictions on the debtor's freedom to take on additional secured or unsecured debt and generally to dispose of the collateral to third parties;
- the obligation of the debtor to remit proceeds of an authorized deal-ing with the collateral to the secured creditor or to maintain pro-ceeds in a separate trust account;
- a list of the events of default sufficient to trigger the secured credit-or's enforcement powers, such as a default in payment, failure of the debtor to comply with other duties and obligations under the agreement, an unauthorized disposition of the collateral or an un-authorized removal of the collateral from the jurisdiction, bankrupt-cy, insolvency or winding up, failure to pay specified debts to third parties, and the suffering of unpaid judgments;
- the power of the secured party to accelerate payment on default and default remedies generally;
- the power of the secured party to appoint a receiver and manager, where broad-based business financing is involved, and the powers and duties of the receiver and manager.

For the purposes of satisfying the evidentiary requirement, how-ever, it is unnecessary for all the terms of the parties' agreement to be set out in a written security agreement or equivalent record.[88] Only

---

88 For judicial confirmation, see, for example, *Astral Communications Inc. v. 825536 Ontario Inc. (Trustee of)* (2000), 46 O.R. (3d) 477, 128 O.A.C. 362, 183 D.L.R.

three components are required. First, the agreement must contain language sufficient to qualify it as a security agreement within the meaning of the PPSA, that is, an agreement that creates or provides for or evidences a security interest. Second, it must carry the debtor's signature. Third, it must set out a description of the collateral.

These requirements need not all be satisfied by a single document or record. A series of writings may be relied on provided that they sufficiently incorporate each other by reference,[89] and provided that the debtor's signature appears on the same document that contains the provisions that create or evidence the security interest.[90]

F. CHARGING LANGUAGE

To satisfy the evidentiary requirement, the Act requires that the debtor sign a document or equivalent record that qualifies as a security agreement. "Security agreement" is defined as an agreement that provides for or evidences the creation of a security interest.[91] It follows that a document that merely describes the alleged collateral — for example, an ordinary bill of sale — is insufficient. The document must contain "charging language"; that is, the document must evidence the named debtor's intention to grant an interest in the relevant assets to secure an obligation owing to the named secured creditor.[92] No particular wording is required; if the words in substance reflect the necessary intent, they are sufficient.[93]

(4th) 455, 15 C.B.R. (4th) 1, 15 P.P.S.A.C. (2d) 256 (C.A.); *Universal Handling Equipment v. Redipac Recycling* (1992), 4 P.P.S.A.C. (2d) 15 (Ont. Ct. Gen. Div.).

89 Compare with *Alberta Treasury Branches v. Faja Bison Ranch Inc.* (1994), 152 A.R. 112, 6 P.P.S.A.C. (2d) 205 (Alta. Q.B.).

90 *Universal Handling Equipment v. Redipac Recycling,* above note 88; *Re Dempster's Custom Sheet Metal Ltd.* (1983), 2 P.P.S.A.C. 308 (Ont. C.A.).

91 For the definition of security agreement see PPSA S s. 2(1); (A, BC, NWT, Nu, Y) s. 1(1); (M, NB, PEI) s. 1; (NL, NS) s. 2.

92 See, for example, *J.J. Riverside Manufacturing Ltd. v. E.J.W. Development Co.* (1981), 1 P.P.S.A.C. 330 (Man. Co. Ct.); *Stafford v. Sumbler* (1989), 9 P.P.S.A.C. 47 at 54 (Ont. Dist. Ct.); *Osman Auction Inc. v. Murray* (1991), 2 P.P.S.A.C. (2d) 236 (Alta. Q.B.); *Capital City Savings & Credit Union Ltd. v. Alberta Motor Products Ltd.,* 2003 ABQB 129, 5 P.P.S.A.C. (3d) 171; *Capital Plymouth Chrysler Inc. v. Euro Sport Auto Sales Ltd.* (1998), 14 P.P.S.A.C. (2d) 30 (Alta. M.). To the same effect under prior law, see *Devoe v. Long,* [1951] 1 D.L.R. 203 (N.B.S.C.(A.D.)). Compare with the anomalous decision in *Guntel v. Kocian,* [1985] 6 W.W.R. 458, 5 P.P.S.A.C. 109 (Man. Q.B.).

93 See, for example, *356447 B.C. Ltd. v. Canadian Imperial Bank of Commerce* (1998), 157 D.L.R. (4th) 682 at paras. 6 and 7 (B.C.C.A.).

The Ontario Act contains an anomalous saving provision under which a "security agreement is not unenforceable against a third party by reason only of a defect, irregularity, omission or error therein or in the execution thereof unless the third party is actually misled."[94] The provision was apparently inserted in the original Ontario PPSA in error and a modified version of it was carried over to the 1989 Act against the advice of the Minister's Advisory Committee.[95] It is clear that the omission of charging language is a fundamental defect, and is not capable of being cured by the saving provision.[96]

G. DEBTOR SIGNATURE

The omission of the debtor's signature is fatal to the enforceability of a security agreement against third parties.[97] This is the rule even in Ontario, notwithstanding the anomalous saving provision in that Act.[98] To interpret the saving provision to cure the complete absence of a signature would completely undermine the requirement of a signature.[99]

The person signing must have the authority of the debtor to give security on its behalf.[100] As to what is a sufficient signature, under the *Sale of Goods Act*, a letterhead or other imprint on the evidentiary document bearing the name of the party to be charged on a contract of sale suffices to satisfy the writing requirement imposed by that Act for a sale of goods above a specified value.[101] It has been suggested that these precedents should serve as persuasive authority under the PPSA.[102] However, judicial generosity on what satisfies the signature requirements of the *Sale of*

---

94 OPPSA s. 9(2).

95 See Ziegel and Denomme, above note 45 at 117–18.

96 *MacEwen Agricentre Inc. v. Bériault* (2002), 61 O.R. (3d) 63 (S.C.J.), distinguishing *Garry v. Sternbauer Estate* (2000), 1 P.P.S.A.C. (3d) 51 (Ont. S.C.J.). See also *Astral Communications Inc. v. 825536 Ontario Inc. (Trustee of)*, above note 88.

97 See, for example, *J.I. Case Credit Corp. v. Canadian Imperial Bank of Commerce* (1985), 5 P.P.S.A.C. 181 (Sask. Q.B.).

98 *Astral Communications Inc. v. 825536 Ontario Inc. (Trustee of)*, above note 88. See also *Universal Handling Equipment v. Redipac Recycling*, above note 88; *State Bank of India (Canada) v. Trutzschler GmbH & Co. KG.* (1997), 44 C.B.R. (3d) 299 (Ont. C.A.).

99 *Astral Communications Inc. v. 825536 Ontario Inc. (Trustee of)*, ibid.

100 For judicial confirmation, see *Atlas Industries v. Federal Business Development Bank*, above note 83; *Joseph Group of Companies Inc. v. Pickles Tent & Awnings Ltd.* (1981), 2 P.P.S.A.C. 1 (Man. C.A.).

101 Ziegel and Denomme, above note 45 at 133.

102 *Ibid.*

Goods Act reflects a lack of judicial confidence in the efficacy of the writing requirement in that context,[103] and the well-established reluctance on the part of the courts to apply *Statute of Frauds* requirements.

The authors do not support the automatic transferability of the *Sale of Goods Act* jurisprudence to the PPSA context. The writing requirement in the PPSA is, in part at least, different from that of the *Statute of Frauds*. The latter has only *inter partes* evidentiary significance, whereas the PPSA requirement has only third-party significance.

On the other hand, the authors do not advocate a technical or literal interpretation of the term "signature." It should be read in functional terms to mean any mark or symbol that in ordinary commercial practice is accepted as identifying a contracting party and signifying his or her consent to be bound by the contract terms to which the mark or symbol relates. The fundamental issue is whether what is alleged to constitute the signature can be taken as reliable evidence of the debtor's voluntary consent to the creation of the security interest.

The current version of Article 9 no longer refers to signing; rather, the security agreement must be authenticated by the debtor;[104] authenticated is then defined to include electronic methods of encryption.[105] In Canada, the *Uniform Electronic Commerce Act* provides for the interpretation of statutory writing and signature requirements, including those found in the PPSA, to accommodate the advent of electronic modes of communication and authentication.[106] Adopted by the Uniform Law Conference of Canada in 1999, the Act or its equivalent is now in force in all PPSA jurisdictions except for the Northwest Territories and Nunavut.[107]

---

103 M.G. Bridge, *Sale of Goods* (Toronto: Butterworths, 1988) at 86.

104 § 9-203(b)(3)(A).

105 § 9-102(a)(7).

106 The text of the *Uniform Electronic Commerce Act* is posted at www.ulcc.ca. The Act is designed to implement the principles of the *United Nations Model Law on Electronic Commerce*, developed by UNCITRAL and adopted by the General Assembly of the United Nations in November, 1996: www.uncitral.org. Both the *Uniform Act* and the *U.N. Model Law* apply beyond the scope of "commerce" in the strict sense to almost any legal relationship that may require documentation.

107 *Electronic Documents and Information Act*, S.S., c. E-7.22; *Electronic Commerce and Information Act*, S.M. 2000, c. 32, C.C.S.M. c. E55; *Electronic Commerce Act 2000*, S.O. 2000, c. 17; *The Electronic Commerce Act*, S.N.S. 2000, c. 26; *Electronic Transactions Act*, S.B.C. 2001, c. 10; *Electronic Transactions Act*, S.A. 2001, c. E-5.5; *Electronic Transactions Act*, S.N.B. 2001, c. E-5.5; *Electronic Commerce Act*, S.P.E.I. 2001, c. 31, R.S.P.E.I. 1988, c. E-4.1; *Electronic Commerce Act*, S.N.L. 2001, c. E-5.2.

H. COLLATERAL DESCRIPTION

1) Permissible Descriptions

Pre-PPSA law required that the collateral be sufficiently described in the security agreement to enable it to be identified.[108] This requirement enabled third parties dealing with assets in a debtor's hands to determine which of those assets were encumbered. It also served to deter a secured party from subsequently claiming a security interest in a greater range of collateral than had been actually agreed to.

Except for the Ontario and Yukon Acts, the PPSA adopts a somewhat different formula. In place of a general "identifiability" test, the Act authorizes alternative modes of description depending on the breadth of the relevant collateral.[109] The collateral description formulae authorized for security agreements are the same as those prescribed by regulation for financing statements (with the exception of the special rules for serial numbered goods).[110] This approach facilitates the registration process insofar as the collateral description contained in the security agreement can be re-entered on the financing statement without the need for any redrafting.

The Ontario Act incorporates the pre-PPSA test: a security interest is not enforceable against a third party unless the security agreement contains a description of the collateral "sufficient to enable it to be identified."[111] The Yukon Act adopts a similar test.[112] The question of whether this approach produces a different result is discussed later in this chapter.

a) Description by Item or Kind

The collateral may be described by item or kind. Description by item is appropriate in cases where the collateral consists of a specific item distinct from other items within the same genre, for instance, the "account owing the debtor under a contract entered into with Acme Co. on 17 September, 1990." Description by kind is appropriate where the collateral consists of all property within the specified genre, for instance, "all present and after-acquired accounts." In deciding on the appropriate

---

108 *McCall v. Wolff* (1885), 13 S.C.R. 130; *Hovey v. Whiting* (1887), 14 S.C.R. 515.
109 PPSA (A, BC, M, NB, PEI, Nu, NWT, S) s. 10(1)(b); (NL, NS) s. 11(1)(b).
110 For a detailed discussion of the collateral description requirements applicable to financing statements, including the special rules for serial numbered goods, see chapters 5 and 6.
111 OPPSA s. 11(2).
112 YPPSA s. 8(1)(c).

wording for a description by kind, the PPSA confirms that the parties may use the statutorily defined generic categories of personal property: chattel paper, documents of title, goods, intangibles, instruments, money, or securities.

More limited genres may also be used if the collateral consists of a genre within a genre. This is subject to one exception. The PPSA (except for the Manitoba, Yukon, and Ontario versions) expressly proscribes the use of the terms "consumer goods" and "equipment" to describe goods unless there is a further reference to the kind of goods.[113] This is because the statutory definitions of these terms do not refer to a kind of goods but rather to the particular use to which goods are put by the particular debtor.[114] It follows that if "consumer goods" or "equipment" were permissible descriptive terms, a third party dealing with goods in the debtor's possession would be forced to investigate the debtor's subjective use to know whether the goods in question were covered by the security agreement.

"Inventory" is also a use description rather than a kind or item description.[115] However, it is usually obvious to a third party which goods in a debtor's possession are being held as inventory. Accordingly, the Act authorizes the use of the term "inventory" to describe collateral but only while the goods in question are held by the debtor as inventory.[116] Should the debtor convert an item of inventory to a personal or capital use, the secured creditor will run afoul of the proscription against describing collateral as "consumer goods" or "equipment." This is a conscious departure from the general rule that the determination of whether goods are consumer goods, inventory, or equipment is made as of the time the security interest attaches, regardless of any subsequent change in use.[117]

b) All-inclusive Description

Where the collateral involves all of the debtor's present and after-acquired personal property, it is infeasible and unnecessary to require the secured party to use an item or kind description. Since the security

---

113 PPSA (A, BC, NB, PEI, Nu, NWT, S) s. 10(3); (NL, NS) s. 11(3); (M, O, Y) no equivalent provision.
114 For an analysis of the definitions of consumer goods and equipment, and the time at which the debtor's use is to be determined, see chapter 1.
115 For an analysis of the definition of inventory, see chapter 1.
116 PPSA (A, BC, NB, PEI, Nu, NWT, S) s. 10(4); (NL, NS) s. 11(4); (M, O, Y) no equivalent provision.
117 PPSA (BC, NWT, Nu, S) s. 1(4); A s. 1(5); (M, NB) s. 2(2); (NL, NS) s. 3(2); (O, Y) no equivalent provision.

interest is meant to attach to all the personal property of the debtor at any given time, the words "all present and after-acquired personal property" are sufficient to describe the collateral, and the PPSA expressly confirms the adequacy of an all-inclusive description of this type.[118] Under the pre-PPSA case law, an "all present and after-acquired property" clause was likewise considered sufficient to identify the collateral.[119]

c) All-inclusive Collateral Description Subject to Specified Exclusions

The parties may sometimes wish to exclude specified assets from the reach of a general security interest that is otherwise meant to cover all property of the debtor. Rather than requiring the parties to revert to an item or kind description, the Act authorizes the use of a statement that a security interest is taken in all of the debtor's present and after-acquired property except for specified items or kinds.

Where the exclusion relates to generic kinds of goods, it is impermissible to use the proscribed terms "consumer goods" and "equipment." Since the use of these terms is not permitted, it follows that an exception is also not permissible. After all, if the problem with these terms is that they depend upon the debtor's use and do not provide an actual description of the collateral, then this also holds true when they are used by way of exception. Suppose that the collateral description refers to consumer goods. Clearly, this is invalid. But suppose that the description instead refers to "all present and after-acquired personal property except inventory and equipment" (that is, it only covers consumer goods). This difference in wording does not make the description valid. The use of the term would not completely invalidate the description: it would remain valid in respect of the non-goods collateral. But it has the potential to invalidate the description to the extent that it covers goods.

The Act does not deal explicitly with the situation where the carve-out is in respect of a more limited kind of assets, for example, "all present and after-acquired goods other than motor vehicles." There is no reason in principle why this should not be permitted as an item or kind description.

---

118 For judicial confirmation, see, for example, *Orr & Co. v. Saskatchewan Economic Development Corp.*, above note 53.

119 See, for example, *Tailby v. Official Receiver*, above note 32; *Hovey v. Whiting*, above note 108; *Ball v. Royal Bank* (1915), 52 S.C.R. 254.

2) Identifiability

Although the OPPSA permits — indeed, encourages — the use of overinclusive generic collateral descriptions on financing statements, the collateral description contained in the security agreement is subject to the pre-PPSA identifiability test.[120] In contrast to the approach described in the preceding section, the Ontario Act states simply that a security interest is not enforceable against a third party unless the security agreement contains a description of the collateral "sufficient to enable it to be identified."[121] The test under the Yukon Act is similar: the collateral must be sufficiently described to enable the intended collateral to be distinguished from that which is not collateral.[122]

The authors are of the view that the different approaches should not, in general, lead to any difference in substantive result. The Ontario courts have affirmed the adequacy of the same kinds of generic and all-inclusive descriptions that the PPSA explicitly endorses.[123] As for whether "consumer goods" and "equipment" are sufficient descriptors, the Ontario and Yukon Acts do not expressly disqualify their adequacy (neither does the Manitoba Act). However, the authors are of the view that such descriptors should not qualify because the collateral cannot be identified without recourse to additional extrinsic evidence of the debtor's subjective use. It is true that the Ontario Act contains a curative provision not found in the PPSA under which an error or omission in the security agreement is not fatal unless it is shown to have actually misled a third party.[124] However, the Ontario Court of Appeal has held that where there is a conflict between the curative provision and the evidentiary requirements for security agreements, the latter is to prevail.[125]

3) Commercially Responsive Interpretation

The PPSA endorses generic descriptions in order to facilitate after-acquired asset financing and to avoid the risk of inadvertent exclusion. In line with this policy, the descriptive words used by the parties in the security agreement should be interpreted in light of commercial

---

120 PPSA O s. 11(2)(a); Y s. 8(1)(b).
121 OPPSA s. 11(2)(a).
122 YPPSA s. 8(1)(b).
123 See, for example, *Access Advertising Management Inc. v. Servex Computers Inc.* (1993), 6 P.P.S.A.C. (2d) 113 (Ont. Ct. Gen. Div.).
124 OPPSA s. 9(2).
125 *Astral Communications Inc. v. 825536 Ontario Inc. (Trustee of)*, above note 88.

realities. For example, the definition of goods in the current version of Article 9 expressly includes a computer program embodied in or accompanying goods that is ordinarily considered an inherent part of the goods or that is an aspect of the functionality of the goods.[126] The PPSA definition lacks equivalent language. Nonetheless, the authors are of the view that the descriptor "goods" in a security agreement (and indeed in the PPSA generally) should be interpreted in a like fashion. To require imbedded software to be separately identified would defeat reasonable commercial expectations.

4) Location and Supplier Qualifiers

Collateral descriptions that describe the collateral by item or kind sometimes contain a qualification that then limits the ambit of the collateral. For example, a secured party may be financing all the appliances contained in an apartment building, which it is also financing. However, the debtor may own and operate other apartment buildings that are not being financed by that secured party, and may wish to give security interests in the appliances to another lender. This can be accomplished by incorporating a location qualifier in the collateral description (for example, "all appliances located at 4539 Arcadia Avenue"). Similarly, a supplier may wish to take a security interest in all of the inventory that it supplies to the debtor, but not on any of the inventory that is being financed by other suppliers. This can be accomplished by incorporating a supplier qualifier in the collateral description (for example, "all stereo equipment supplied by Acme Co.").

If a supplier qualifier is used, it may be necessary to examine the actual invoices in order to determine which goods in the debtor's possession were supplied to the debtor by the secured party and which may have been supplied from another source. In the view of the authors, this does not make the collateral description inadequate. The requirement to include a collateral description in the security agreement does not mean that a third party should be able to determine which assets are covered by the security interest and which are not simply by looking at

---

126 § 9-102(a)(44): "The term [goods] also includes a computer program embodied in goods and any supporting information provided in connection with a transaction relating to the program if (i) the program is associated with the goods in such a manner that it customarily is considered part of the goods, or (ii) by becoming an owner of the goods, a person acquires a right to use the program in connection with the goods. The term does not include a computer program embedded in goods that consist solely of the medium in which the program is embedded."

the security agreement and nothing else. In *GE Capital Canada Acquisitions Inc. v. Dix Performance (Trustee of)*[127] and *Re Hickman Equipment (1985) Ltd.*[128] the Court observed that the necessary additional information can be obtained from the secured party through the PPSA demand procedure.[129] Further support for this proposition can be found in *Clark Equipment of Canada Ltd. v. Bank of Montreal.*[130] The charging clause in the security agreement covered "all products." The security agreement described products as "all new equipment and machinery manufactured or offered for sale by CLARK, and used equipment and machinery of the same general type whether or not manufactured or offered for sale by CLARK." The Court upheld the adequacy of the collateral description. The same approach was taken in *New World Screen Printing Ltd. (c.o.b.) New World Print) v. Xerox Canada Ltd.,*[131] where the collateral was described as "all present and future office equipment and software supplied or financed from time to time by the secured party (whether by lease, conditional sale, or otherwise) whether or not manufactured by the secured party or any affiliate thereof."

The use of a location qualifier similarly does not undermine the adequacy of the collateral description. It is sufficient to enable the collateral to be identified — goods at a particular location — notwithstanding that it may be necessary to physically go to the location in question in order to ascertain the collateral covered by the description.

If a location qualifier is used, there is a risk that the goods may later be removed to a new location. The mere possibility of this risk materializing should not invalidate the collateral description. Greater difficulties arise if the goods are in fact moved to a new location. Relocation makes it impossible for third persons to identify the collateral by visiting the specified location since the assets are no longer at that site. On the other hand, as long as it can be demonstrated that the goods in question were moved there from the location specified in the security agreement, the description remains adequate to describe the collateral in the sense of enabling it to be identified. The situation is no different than if collateral described as a red widget in the security agreement is later painted green by the debtor. Although the description in the security agreement no longer accurately describes the collateral, it is

127 [1995] 2 W.W.R. 738 (B.C.S.C.).
128 (2003), 224 Nfld. & P.E.I.R. 73, 5 P.P.S.A.C. (3d) 93 (Nfld. S.C.T.D.).
129 PPSA (A, BC, M, O, NB, PEI, Nu, NWT, S) s. 18; (NL, NS) s. 19; Y s. 17.
130 (1984), 8 D.L.R. (4th) 424 (Man. C.A.).
131 [2003] B.C.J. No. 2559 at para. 6 (S.C.).

still possible to show that the green widget constitutes the collateral referred to in the security agreement.

5) Ambiguity and Extrinsic Evidence

In general, the courts have adopted a commercially sensitive approach to the interpretation of collateral descriptions in security agreements. Indeed, if they have erred, it is in the direction of excessive generosity. A recent Newfoundland case provides a case in point.[132] A secured party sought judicial determination of whether the collateral descriptor "vehicles" meant vehicles in the conventional sense of cars and trucks or covered the entire inventory of the debtor, which also included earth-moving and paving equipment and attachments or accessions to such equipment. After ruling that extrinsic evidence of the factual background to the security agreement was admissible to determine the true intent of the parties in using the word "vehicles," the court concluded that it was intended to capture the entire inventory.

In the view of the authors, this decision goes too far. The interpretive issue at stake is not the true intention of the parties. Rather, the purpose of requiring a written collateral description is to enable third parties to identify which assets of the debtor are encumbered by security. To allow extrinsic evidence of the parties' subjective intention to vary the ordinary meaning of the words of the agreement defeats the purpose of the requirement.

The Act provides creditors and other interested third parties with the means to confirm which particular items are in fact collateral under a security agreement. In addition to requiring the secured party to supply a copy of the security agreement, they are also entitled to demand that the secured party verify which items on an itemized list of possible collateral accompanying the demand are actually collateral as of the date of the demand.[133] The availability of this procedure is seen by some as intended "to set the threshold of identification of the [collateral] at a relatively low level."[134]

---

132 *Re Hickman Equipment (1985) Ltd.,* above note 128.
133 PPSA (A, BC, M, O, NB, PEI, Nu, NWT, S) s. 18; (NL, NS) s. 19; Y s. 17.
134 *G.E. Capital Canada Acquisitions Ltd. v. Dix Performance (Trustee of),* above note 127 (stated in the context of upholding the adequacy of the collateral descriptor "shelving" against a challenge by the trustee in bankruptcy of the debtor; the authors are not in disagreement with the actual ruling; although the term "shelving" may be somewhat imprecise, the courts ought not to be overly technical or demanding in assessing the adequacy of the descriptors used by the

While the authors agree that a technical or overly demanding reading of collateral descriptions is to be resisted, they do not regard the availability of the verification procedure as validating the use of ambiguous collateral descriptions that make ascertainment of the collateral impossible. If descriptions that depend on extrinsic evidence for interpretation were adequate, the security agreement would no longer perform its intended evidentiary function.

6) Proceeds

Under the PPSA a security interest automatically extends to the proceeds of an unauthorized dealing with the original collateral by the debtor, as well as to any insurance or other compensation payable for the loss or destruction of the collateral.[135] The Act makes it clear that a security agreement is not unenforceable against third parties by reason only that it does not include a description of proceeds.[136]

The Ontario Act does not have an equivalent clarifying provision. However, the authors take the view that that Act likewise does not require the security agreement to refer specifically to proceeds. A proceeds security interest is not created by the security agreement: it is created by law under the PPSA. It is designed to protect the secured creditor against a loss of the value of its collateral as a result of its unauthorized disposition or accidental destruction. If the secured creditor were still required to expressly provide for a proceeds security interest in the security agreement, the automatic statutory protection would be meaningless.

The possible existence of a proceeds security interest means that third parties cannot place full reliance on the collateral description in the security agreement. Assets falling outside that description will also be subject to the security interest where they qualify as proceeds of the described collateral. The Act seeks to limit the risk to third parties by requiring a timely amendment of the registered collateral description to include a description of the proceeds. The risks are much greater in Manitoba and Ontario, which do not impose any equivalent obligation (except for motor vehicles held as consumer goods).

---

parties; the term "shelving" is sufficient to permit a third party to identify the collateral save in very borderline cases).

135   On the right to proceeds under the PPSA, see chapter 12.

136   PPSA (A, BC, M, NB, PEI, Nu, NWT, S) s. 10(5); (NL, NS) s. 11(5); O no equivalent provision.

I. EFFECTIVENESS OF THE TERMS OF THE SECURITY AGREEMENT

1) General Principle

The Act establishes a baseline presumption of freedom of contract — "Except as provided by this or any other Act, a security agreement is effective according to its terms."[137] The Ontario formulation adds the words "between the parties and against third parties."[138] The additional words do not change anything. The Act defines a security agreement as an agreement that creates or provides for or evidences a security interest. Thus, it is only the proprietary effect of the security agreement — the security interest itself — that is presumptively effective against third parties. The impact on third parties of the contractual aspects of the agreement depends on the general law of contract.[139]

The distinction between the contractual and proprietary aspects of a security agreement is especially significant in the context of credit sales. The PPSA explicitly preserves the normal application of sale of goods law to the seller-buyer aspect of the parties' relationship.[140] In other word, the Act is intended to regulate only the security aspect of the relationship between the parties. The sales aspect, including the seller's performance obligations with respect to the quantity, quality, and condition of the goods sold, continues to be governed by general contract and sale of goods law.

2) Statutory Constraints Imposed by the PPSA

The presumptive effectiveness of security agreements under the PPSA is expressly made subject to any statutory constraints found in the PPSA or any other Act.

Turning first to the PPSA, the most comprehensive example is the overriding obligation cast on all parties to exercise their rights and obligations under the Act in good faith and in a commercially reason-

---

137 PPSA (A, BC, M, NB, Ont, PEI, Nu, NWT, S) s. 9; (NL, NS) s. 10; Y no equivalent provision.
138 OPPSA s. 9(1).
139 The Act preserves the supplementary application of general contract law: PPSA (M, NWT, Nu, S) s. 65(2); A s. 66(3); BC s. 68(1); (NB, PEI) s. 65(1); (NL, NS) s. 66(1); O s. 72; Y s. 63(1).
140 PPSA (A, BC, M, NB, O, PEI, Nu, NWT, S) s. 15; (NL, NS) s. 16; Y s. 14.

able manner.[141] More particular examples fall into three main categories.

First, for the security interest contemplated by the security agreement to acquire full proprietary effect, the PPSA rules governing its attachment must be satisfied. These rules were examined in preceding sections of this chapter.

Second, the PPSA contains a number of specialized rules regulating the parties' rights in the collateral. Some of these are merely suppletive, that is, they apply only if the parties have not expressed a contrary intention. A good example is the regime governing the rights and obligations of the parties where the secured party is in possession or control of the collateral.[142] Others are mandatory, that is, they are not subject to contractual waiver or exclusion. The most significant example is the enforcement regime established by Part 5 of the Act. Part 5 lays down a series of mandatory rules and procedures designed to balance the secured creditor's interest in efficient enforcement against the need to protect the debtor (and third parties) from an unfair expropriation of the surplus value of the collateral over and above the amount necessary to satisfy the secured obligation. These rules are the subject of detailed analysis in chapter 13.

Third, the extent of the effectiveness of the security interest against third parties is determined by the perfection and priority rules of the Act, both of which are also the subject of separate chapters.

3) Statutory Constraints Imposed by Other Acts

The impact of the express preservation of constraints imposed by other statutes is greatly reduced by the rule that where there is a conflict between the PPSA and any other Act (except for an Act relating to the protection of consumers[143]), the PPSA prevails.[144] In light of this, the potential constraints imposed by other Acts are restricted to two situa-

---

141 PPSA (M, NWT, Nu, S) s. 65(3); A s. 66(1); BC s. 68(2); (NB, PEI) s. 65(2); (NL, NS) s. 66(2); Y s. 62(1); O no equivalent provision (but note OPPSA ss. 61(2), 63(2), under which the secured party is obligated to exercise collection and disposal rights on enforcement in a commercially reasonable manner).

142 Although these rules apply even in the case of pre-default possession, they have their greatest significance in the enforcement context and are therefore addressed in chapter 13.

143 PPSA (M, NWT, Nu, S) s. 69; A s. 74; BC s. 73; (NB, PEI) s. 70; (NL, NS, Y) s. 71; O s. 73. The SPPSA also preserves the application of *The Agricultural Implements Act* and *The Saskatchewan Farm Security Act.*

144 PPSA (M, NWT, Nu) s. 69; A s. 74; BC s. 73; (NL, NS, Y) s. 71 ; (NB, PEI) s. 70.

tions. The first is where the situation addressed by the other Act is not resolved by the PPSA. The most important example here relates to the priority of a security interest governed by the PPSA as against non-consensual security interests, charges, or liens whose status is governed by other law. To the extent that other law reduces the priority status of the PPSA security interest, it will prevail. The second category of constraints arises where constitutionally applicable federal legislation alters the rules established by the PPSA. The most important examples here are the priority and enforcement rules governing secured creditors contained in federal bankruptcy and insolvency legislation. Both categories of constraints are addressed in detail in other chapters.

J. THE SECURED OBLIGATION

1) General Principle

The PPSA defines a security interest as an interest that secures payment or performance of an obligation. The use of the term "payment" confirms that the obligation may be the payment of money and this will be the usual case. However, the explicit addition of the term "performance" confirms that the obligation in question need not be monetary or need not be monetary in the sense of a predetermined sum. Indeterminate, conditional, and secondary obligations also qualify so long as the obligation has become liquid when the secured party seeks to enforce its security interest.

2) Future Advances, Interest, and Maintenance Charges

In some cases, the obligation secured is not only indeterminate; it is a future obligation, as in the case of a security interest granted against a promise to supply a line of credit or to extend future advances. So long as the security agreement obligates the creditor to extend the future credit or make the advance, the security is constituted.[145] Similarly, a security for a line of credit or future advances survives, even where no money is actually owed to the creditor at the particular time. Of course, before the security interest can be enforced, there must be an outstanding obligation then in existence.

---

145 PPSA (A, BC, M, NB, PEI, Nu, NWT, S) s. 14; (NL, NS) s. 15; (O, Y) s. 13. And
     see *Humboldt Credit Union Ltd. v. Empire Shoe Store Ltd.* (1986), 7 P.P.S.A.C. 63
     (Sask. C.A.).

In addition to the amount of all advances made to the debtor, the security interest also secures the interest payable, subject to the limitations imposed by the federal *Interest Act*[146] and section 347 of the *Criminal Code*.[147] The PPSA also adds to the concept of future advance all costs incurred by the secured creditor in the preservation and maintenance of the collateral.

The Act does not automatically entitle a secured party to "tack" any and all future indebtedness to its initial security. As was the case under pre-PPSA law,[148] the security agreement must expressly state that the security is to cover future advances. The right to tack future advances, in other words, is a matter of contract and not a rule of substantive law. On the other hand, if the original security agreement does not contain a future advance clause, the parties are free to agree to one at a later date, either by way of amendment of the original agreement or as a term of a new agreement covering the same collateral.

At common law, a secured party who contracted for security to cover future advances was likewise entitled to tack all subsequent advances to the original security. To this general rule, there was one exception. The security interest was subordinated to an intervening security interest to the extent of advances made after the first secured party had knowledge of the intervening interest.[149] The rule applied to successive security interests in intangibles as well as goods.[150] The prior-ranking secured party was defeated only if he or she had knowledge of the intervening interest; registration was not notice for this purpose.[151] The

---

146 R.S.C. 1985, c. I-15

147 R.S.C. 1985, c. C-46, s. 347 makes it an offence to enter into an agreement for, or to receive, interest at a rate exceeding 60 percent per annum. The purpose of s. 347 is to aid in the prosecution of loan sharks. However, it is cast in comprehensive language and potentially applies to a broad range of sophisticated commercial credit transactions. In *Transport North American Express Inc. v. New Solutions Financial Corp.*, [2004] 1 S.C.R. 249 at para 32, the Supreme Court observed that the traditional rule that declared an illegal contract void *ab initio* is therefore not necessarily applicable in cases involving a breach of s. 347. Severance lies along a spectrum of available remedies. Depending on the circumstances, the court may exercise its discretion to find the whole agreement unenforceable or sever only the provision(s) that put the effective interest rate over 60 percent. The court's remedial discretion takes into account the seriousness of the illegality involved in any given case, the identity and nature of the parties and the broader contractual context.

148 On pre-PPSA law, see, for example, *Amherst Boot & Shoe Co. v. Carter* (1922), 50 N.B.R. 315 (C.A.).

149 *Hopkinson v. Rolt* (1861), 9 H.L.C. 514; *West v. Williams*, [1899] 1 Ch. 132 (C.A.).

150 *W. H. Fraser v. Imperial Bank of Canada* (1912), 47 S.C.R. 313.

151 *Pierce v. Canada Permanent* (1894), 25 O.R. 671 at 676 (H.C.J. Ch. D.).

PPSA eliminates this exception. Under the Act, a secured party has the same priority against intervening secured parties for future advances as it has for prior advances.[152]

The position is different if the intervening third party is a judgment creditor who has completed the steps required by the Act to prevail against an unperfected security interest. The secured party is subordinated to the extent of advances made after acquiring knowledge of the completion of these steps.[153] It is for this reason that the PPSA releases a secured party from any obligation to the debtor to make future advances where the secured party has knowledge of the intervening claim of a judgment creditor.[154]

3) All-obligations Clauses

It is up to the parties to contractually specify the obligation that is to be secured by the security interest. In some cases, the security agreement may specifically set out the amount of the secured debt, including interest and finance charges, and the terms of repayment and maturity. In many cases, the repayment terms are not found in the security agreement, but are instead found in a credit agreement or loan agreement. The security agreement may simply contain an all-obligations clause that provides that all present and future obligations are secured by the security agreement.

All-obligations (or dragnet) clauses of this kind do not seem to have attracted significant judicial scrutiny in Canada. However, there are Australian and US cases dealing with their effectiveness.[155] Where contained in standard form printed terms incorporated into a security agreement, there is some support for the proposition that the clause is to be construed having regard to the context of the secured transaction and the commercial purposes of the transaction which the clause is designed to serve. In other words, the plain language may not be taken at face value. The identity of the borrower matters. Some courts say that if the mortgage is between commercial parties there is no need for the court to intervene because these parties are of equal bargaining power.

---

152 For a detailed analysis, see chapter 8.
153 For a detailed analysis, see chapter 10.
154 PPSA (A, BC, M, NB, PEI, Nu, NWT, S) s. 14; (NL, NS) s. 15; (O, Y) s. 13.
155 For a comprehensive recent review, see R. Wood, "Turning Lead into Gold: The Uncertain Alchemy of 'All Obligations' Clauses" (2004) 41 Alta. L. Rev. 801. For an annotated survey of the U.S. case law, see William B. Johnson, "Construction and Effect of 'Future Advances' Clauses under UCC Article 9" 90 A.L.R. 4th 859.

This means the court interprets the words in their ordinary meaning. The other interpretation is often used where the debtor is not a commercial entity. On this view the clause may be "read down" to cover only those sums that would ordinarily be in the mind of the mortgagor as part of the mortgage debt.

K. DEBTOR'S RIGHT TO A COPY OF THE WRITTEN SECURITY AGREEMENT

If the security agreement is in writing, the PPSA requires the secured party to deliver a copy to the debtor within ten days after the execution of the agreement.[156] However, non-compliance does not invalidate the security agreement.[157] In the rare case where the secured party fails to comply after a request, the debtor may apply to the Court for a delivery order. The Act also gives a cause of action for non-compliance to any person to whom an obligation is owed under the Act. Damages are recoverable if the non-compliance caused reasonably foreseeable loss[158] or the obligation is one for the breach of which the Act awards deemed damages.[159] However, a secured party's breach of the delivery obligation does not attract deemed damages and it is difficult to envisage how the breach could cause actual loss to the debtor.

FURTHER READINGS

WALSH, C., "The PPSA Writing Requirement and Priority among Competing Perfected Security Interests" (1994) 9 B.F.L.R. 217

---

156 PPSA (A, BC, M, NB, PEI, Nu, NWT, S) s. 11; (NL, NS) s. 12; O s. 10; Y s. 9.
157 A seller's or lessor's failure to comply with the equivalent obligation under the pre-PPSA Conditional Sales Acts did not invalidate the conditional sales or hire purchase agreement: *Canadian Imperial Bank of Commerce v. Bedard* (1985), 63 N.B.R. (2d) 223 (Q.B.T.D.).
158 PPSA (NB, PEI) s. 66(2); (NL, NS) s. 67(2); (NWT, Nu) s. 65(2); A s. 67(1); BC s. 69(3); M s. 65(2); O s. 67(2); S s. 65(5); Y s. 62(2).
159 PPSA (M, NWT, Nu, S) s. 65(6); (NB, PEI) s. 66(3); (NL, NS) s. 67(3); (NWT, Nu) s. 65(2); A s. 67(2); M s. 65(2); (BC, O, Y) no equivalent provision.

CHAPTER 5

PERFECTION

A. THE CONCEPT: ITS SOURCE AND MEANINGS

The concept of perfection plays a central role in the operation of the PPSA system. The drafters of the PPSA adopted, perhaps unfortunately, the terms "perfected" and "perfection" from Article 9 of the *Uniform Commercial Code*, which in turn copied them from § 60 of the *United States Bankruptcy Code*, as it existed at the time Article 9 was drafted.[1] In the context of United States bankruptcy law, the term "perfection" means that a security interest has a status giving it invulnerability to defeat by the debtor's trustee in bankruptcy or judgment creditors.[2] However, it is not particularly helpful in the context of the PPSA to seek the meaning of the term in its origins. The scope of the concept can be determined only by reference to its use in the PPSA itself.

The principal use of the term perfection in the PPSA is to describe a priority status acquired by a security interest. The Act[3] provides that a security interest is perfected when it has attached (that is, has come

---

1   Now see 11 USC § 547.
2   11 USC § 547(e)(1)(B) provides that a transfer of personal property or a fixture is perfected when a creditor on a simple contract cannot acquired a judicial lien that is superior to the interest of the transferee.
3   PPSA (A, BC, M, NB, NWT, Nu, O, PEI, S) s. 19; (NL, NS) s. 20; Y s. 18.

into existence)[4] and all steps required for perfection have been completed, regardless or the order of occurrence. In other words, an extant security interest acquires the status of being perfected when a prescribed
step has been taken or the status is conferred (temporarily or permanently) by the Act.[5]

The starting point in the analysis of the concept of perfection is
recognition that a security interest is a property interest in the collateral. Proprietary rights generally confer priority status in the sense
of being effective against third parties under common law principles.
Perfection is the status that must be achieved if the property rights acquired under the hypothecation are to be protected against competing
rights in or claims to the hypothecated collateral. The Act inferentially
defines perfection, not by stating what it is, but by specifying the interests that can defeat (subordinate or cut off) a security interest that
is not perfected.[6] These interests include judgment creditors (under
prescribed circumstances),[7] the debtor's trustee in bankruptcy,[8] other
secured creditors,[9] and buyers of the collateral.[10]

However, the priority status of a perfected security interest is not
exclusive. There can be several perfected security interests in the same
collateral. Furthermore, it is relative, not absolute. Perfection is not invulnerability. The priority status a perfected security interest has depends upon the nature and status of the interest or interests with which
it is in competition. The relativeness of the status of perfection results
from the various priority rules contained in the Act and in related legislation. A perfected security interest can be defeated by other interests in
the collateral, including those of unsecured judgment creditors, other
secured creditors, and transferees of the collateral. Consequently, the
only generalized description of the concept of perfection that is possible is that it is a status that normally must be attained in order for a

---

4   PPSA (A, BC, M, NB, NWT, Nu, PEI, S) s. 12; (NL, NS) s. 13; (O, Y) s. 11.
5   As noted below, perfection does not always require the taking of a "perfection
    step." There are circumstances in which the Act confers the status automatically.
6   Lack of perfection does not result in a security interest being "void." It is still
    enforceable against the debtor and a donee of the collateral.
7   PPSA (NB, NWT, Nu, O, S) s. 20(1); (BC, M) s. 20(a); A s. 20(b); NL s. 21(2);
    NS s. 21(1); PEI s. 20(2); Y s. 19(1).
8   PPSA (NWT, Nu, O, PEI) s. 20(1); (BC, M) s. 20(b); (NB, S) s. 20(2); A s. 20(a);
    NL s. 21(1); NS s. 21(2); Y s. 19(1).
9   PPSA (A, BC, M, NB, NWT, Nu; PEI, S) s. 35(1); (NL, NS) s. 36(1); O s. 30(1);
    Y s. 34(1).
10 PPSA (NWT, Nu, O) s. 20(1); (BC, M) s. 20(c); (NB, S) s. 20(3); A s. 20(b);
    NL s. 21(2); NS s. 21(3); PEI s. 20(2).

security interest to have priority over other proprietary interests in the collateral.

B. LOSS AND CONTINUITY OF PERFECTION

Generally, the status of perfection is lost when the requirements for its existence are no longer present. It is lost if not replaced by another permissible method of perfection: when registration of a security interest expires or is discharged; when the secured party ceases to have possession of the collateral or a bailee ceases to hold on behalf of the secured party; or when the circumstances that resulted in automatic perfection no longer prevail or when a period of automatic perfection expires. Under the Ontario Act,[11] perfection by registration can be lost where the secured party fails within a specified period of time to correct the registration information to reflect a change in the name of the debtor or the transfer of the collateral to a third party or to perfect by taking possession of the collateral. However, the loss of perfection in these contexts may have no significance as a result of the operation of section 30(6) of the Ontario Act.

A change from one perfection step to another is not treated as new perfection so long as the security interest was perfected at the time the alternative perfection step was taken. This is made clear by a provision in the Act[12] that gives continuous perfection to a security interest that was originally perfected in one way and again perfected in some other way without an intermediate period when it was unperfected. The same approach applies when the change is from automatic perfection to perfection using one of the perfection steps.

Section 30(6) of the Ontario Act addresses another context within which continuity of perfection is recognized. It provides that when a security interest that is perfected by registration becomes unperfected and is again perfected by registration, the security interest is treated as having been continuously perfected from the time of first registration except with respect to "rights" in the collateral of a person acquired during the period when the security interest was unperfected. The continuity of perfection does not occur, however, if the new perfection is by a method other than registration. The section gives rise to several priority issues to the extent that perfection is not deemed to be continuous with respect to "rights" of a person acquired during the period

---

11   OPPSA s. 48.
12   PPSA (A, BC, M, NB, NWT, Nu, PEI, S) s. 23(1); (NL, NS) 24(1); (O, Y) s. 21(1).

when the security interest was unperfected. These issues are addressed in chapter 8.[13]

The other Acts address a similar situation with a priority rule rather than a perfection rule. They provide that when the registration of a security interest lapses or is discharged but is registered again within a specified period of time, the priority position of the security interest is retained in relation any other security interest that had a subordinate position prior to the lapse or discharge.[14]

A special application of the concept of continuous perfection of a security interest is found in a provision of the Act that gives an automatic security interest in proceeds.[15] A proceeds security interest is treated as being temporarily or continuously perfected, depending upon the circumstances. In effect, the security interest in the original collateral and the perfected status of that interest is treated as carrying over to the proceeds of collateral. The perfection rules for proceeds are addressed later in this chapter. For a complete discussion of the concept of proceeds, see chapter 12.

C. PERFECTION STEPS

The PPSA refers to "steps required for perfection."[16] It would be a mistake to read these words as suggesting that the taking of one of the steps results in perfection of a security interest. The steps are measures that must be taken to gain the status associated with perfection, but, by themselves, they do not result in that status. This is made clear in the various sections of the Act that deal with methods of perfection that contain the prefatory phrase "subject to section 19" (or its equivalent in each Act). This phrase was designed to indicate that a perfection step or method alone does not result in perfection.[17] Perfection is acquired

---

13 See chapter 8, G, "Re-perfection of a Security Interest."
14 PPSA (BC, M, NB, NWT, Nu, S) s. 35(7); (NL, NS) s. 36(7); A s. 35(8); PEI s. 35(6); Y s. 34(5).
15 PPSA (A, BC, M, NB, PEI, NWT, Nu, S) s. 28; (NL, NS) s. 29; O s. 25; Y s. 26.
16 Above note 3. The steps referred to are registration, transfer of possession of the collateral to the secured party or agent of the secured party, the issuance of a document of title by a bailee of the collateral in the name of the secured party or holding of the goods by the bailee as agent of the secured party. In the case of a financial asset, taking delivery or acquisition of control by the secured party will also constitute perfection steps under proposed amendments to the PPSA accompanying the proposed *Uniform Securities Transfer Act*. See s. 24.1.
17 This approach was not used in the drafting of the amendments to OPPSA.

only when there is a coincidence of the perfection step or method and attachment. It is permissible to effect a registration before a security agreement is executed or a security interest has come into existence,[18] and although registration is a "step required for perfection," it does not result in perfection. The status of perfection can only be acquired for a security interest that has come into existence (that is, has attached).

The status of perfection can be automatically acquired when the interest arises if the appropriate step has been taken or statutory conditions exist prior to the time of attachment. A perfection step can precede attachment of a security interest.[19] This feature is very important in the context of the priority rules of the Act, some of which date priority not from the date of perfection but from the date a perfection step has been taken.[20]

However, this is not the case under the Ontario Act when a security interest is perfected by possession. Section 30(2) of the Act provides that a security interest perfected by registration has priority over another security interest perfected otherwise than by registration if the registration occurred before the perfection of the other interest. In order for a security interest to be perfected by possession, it must attach. The issue that arises in the context of section 30(2) is displayed in the following scenario:

SP1 and Debtor agree that SP1 will have a security interest in an automobile that D intends to purchase from its owner. Before acquiring the automobile, SP1 takes possession of it under an agreement with SP1, D, and the owner. Thereafter, D agrees to give a security interest in it to SP2 who immediately effects a registration. Debtor then acquired ownership of the vehicle. The issue arises as to whether SP1 can date its priority from the date he took possession of the vehicle. If not, SP2 has priority.

The other Acts employ a different approach. They give priority on the basis of the earliest of registration of a financing statement or "possession of the collateral … without regard to the date of attachment of the security interest."[21] A technical argument, which the authors have concluded does not serve the apparent intent of the drafter, can be made that the transfer of the automobile from the owner to SP1 was not a transfer

---

18   PPSA (A, BC, M, NWT, Nu, S) s. 43(4); (NB, PEI) s. 43(5); (NL, NS) s. 44(5); O ss. 45(2) and (3); Y s. 42(8).
19   Above note 4.
20   Above note 9.
21   Above note 9.

of possession of property that is "collateral." Until a security interest attaches in property, that property is not collateral.[22] Consequently, if a secured creditor acquires possession of property that only later becomes property in which the debtor has an interest, the perfection step can be taken only when the debtor acquires those rights. In effect, the perfection step and perfection must occur contemporaneously.

D. PERFECTION BY REGISTRATION

1) Introduction

The registry system is a central feature of the PPSA regime. It is the principal mechanism making it feasible for a creditor to take an interest in property of a debtor and at the same time allow the debtor to remain in possession or control of the property without substantial risk to third parties who otherwise may be deceived by the debtor's continued possession or control into believing that the debtor has unencumbered ownership of the property. The public disclosure of the creditor's interest allows third parties to take prophylactic measures to avoid this priority risk.

The Act permits registration as a step for perfection of a security interest in any type of collateral.[23] However, it is not always the "best" step in that perfection in this form results in a weaker priority status than possession where negotiable collateral such as money, a negotiable instrument, a security or chattel paper is involved.[24]

2) Registration, Knowledge, and Constructive Knowledge

While the priority system of the Act is based on the assumption that registration provides the mechanism through which subsequent potential acquirers of interests in the collateral can inform themselves of the risk involved in dealing with debtors, it is not an element of the priority structure of the Act that registration gives constructive notice of

---

22   The term "collateral" is defined in the PPSA as "personal property that is subject to a security interest." PPSA (BC, NWT, Nu, O, Y) s.1(1); (MB, NB) s. 1(g); (NFL, NS) s. 2(g); A s. 1(1)(g); S s. 2 (1)(g).
23   PPSA (A, BC, M, NB, PEI, NWT,Nu, S) s. 25; (NL, NS) s. 26; (O, Y) s. 23.
24   See, for example, PPSA (A, BC, NB, PEI, NWT, Nu) s. 31(4); (M, S) s. 31(5); (NL, NS) s. 32(4); O s. 28(4); Y s. 30(4).

the existence of the security interest to which the registration relates. The Act provides that registration of a financing statement is not constructive notice or knowledge of its existence or contents to any person.[25] The PPSA priority regime does not take into account the subjective or objective knowledge of registration or lack of it on the part of parties with competing interests.[26] The priority status of a security interest is determined on the basis of the fact of registration (or lack thereof) and not on a presumption that the holder of a competing interest knows or should know that the registration exists.

3) Notice Registration

A registration can be effected before a security agreement has been executed between the parties identified in it or before a security interest to which it refers has come into existence.[27] It may relate to security interests arising under one or more existing or prospective security agreements.[28] This very high degree of flexibility is possible because the role of registration is not to make available to interested persons all the details of an existing security agreement between persons identified as secured party and debtor in the registration. Its role is to provide a notice of the existence or potential existence of a relationship between the identified persons that provides or will provide for a security interest or security interests in items or kinds of property described in it. A separate mechanism, examined in the following part of this chapter, is provided through which a third party can gain access to the details of an extant security agreement between the parties.

---

25   PPSA (A, BC, MB, NB, NWT, Nu, PEI, S) s. 47; (NL, NS) s. 48; O s. 47 (5); Y s. 52(3).

26   However, a few priority rules require that the competing subsequent interest be acquired without notice of a priority security interest. See, for example, above note 10.

27   Above note 18. However, under s. 45(2) of the Ontario Act, an effective registration is not possible before a security agreement providing for a security interest in consumer goods has been signed by the debtor.

28   PPSA (A, BC, M, NWT, Nu, S) s. 43(5); (NB, PEI) s. 43(6); (NL, NS) s. 44(6); O s. 45(4) (applicable to collateral other than consumer goods); Y s. 42.

4) Access to Details of a Security Agreement

The Act[29] contains a feature that is an important aspect of the system designed to give third parties the facilities through which they can reduce the legal risk that an interest in property acquired from debtors will be subordinated to prior security interests.[30] Under the notice registry system of the Act, only very minimal information relating to a relationship between a secured creditor and a debtor is available from the registry. This does not include the terms of a security agreement. Except where the collateral must be described by serial number, the description in the registration may be generic. When a security interest is perfected by possession or automatically perfected, no information as to the contents of the security agreement or the relationship of the parties is available to the public.

The approach employed by the Act is to require a secured party to respond to a demand from specified persons for details of the security agreement or a copy of it. The demand may be made by the debtor, a creditor,[31] a sheriff, a person with an interest in personal property of the debtor, or an authorized representative of any of them. The Ontario Act is somewhat more restrictive in that only a debtor, a judgment creditor, a person who has an interest in the collateral, or an authorized representative of such person is entitled to make the demand.[32]

---

29   PPSA (A, BC, M, NB, NWT, Nu, O, PEI, S) s. 18; (NL, NS) s. 19; Y s. 17.

30   However, in order to accurately assess this risk, the person acquiring this information must appreciate the way in which the priority system of the Act operates. For example, if the description of the collateral in a registration is "construction equipment," but the response to a demand reveals that the collateral is "cement mixer," the person who made the demand cannot assume that a security interest he thereafter takes in any item of construction equipment other than a cement mixer will have priority. Under the priority rules of the Act, any security interest in collateral falling within the description "construction equipment" arising under a security agreement executed at any time during the life of the registration will have priority over any other security interest, other than a purchase money security interest, in construction equipment. Priority is given to the first secured party to effect a registration (or acquired perfection in some other way).

31   In *Spir-l-ok Industries v. Bank of Montreal* (1985), 41 Sask. R. 128 (Q.B.), the court held that a secured party making a demand under (the former) SPPSA s. 18 was entitled only to disclosure of security interests in property in which it held a security interest. The court apparently failed to take into account that the secured party was also a creditor. There is nothing in s. 18 that limits the scope of the demand of a creditor.

32   In *Henry Weiner Ltd. v. Royal Bank,* (1986), 61 C.B.R. (N.S.) 317 (Ont. H.C.J.), the court concluded that a creditor who had filed a petition seeking a receiv-

This approach limits access to private commercial information to categories of persons whose rights have been or could be affected by the priority regime of the Act. Unlike the former document registry systems displaced when the Act was implemented, all of the details of the security agreements are not accessible by any person willing to pay the required search fee.

One category of persons not entitled to make a direct demand for information from the secured party is potential creditor grantors. On the surface this would appear to be anomalous since it is only through disclosure of this information that persons in this category can assess the legal risk of dealing with debtors. The difficulty is that there is no way to ensure that a person demanding the information is doing so for reasons of risk assessment rather than for some other purpose. Competitors or persons with malicious intent toward the debtor or the secured party could claim to be potential credit grantors. Information not disclosed in a registration is obtained by granting to the debtor the right to demand it. A potential credit grantor can use the debtor as its vehicle for obtaining the information important to risk assessment. Under the Act, the debtor may require the secured party to provide the specified information to any person at an address specified by the debtor. Under the Ontario Act, the secured party is required to give the information only to the debtor.

The Act requires disclosure to "a person with an interest in personal property of the debtor." This could be seen as defeating the policy of precluding unjustifiable disclosure of information as to the relationship between parties. However, the Act limits the scope of inquiry that can be demanded by such person. The person can demand a copy of information only with respect to a security agreement providing a security interest in property in which that person has an interest.[33] In effect, such person must specify in the demand the property in which the person holds an interest. Only then can the secured party determine whether or not it has a security interest in that property. A similar approach is contained in the Ontario Act, which limits the right to demand information to "a person who has an interest in the collateral."[34] All Acts appear to require that the person making the demand prove

---

ing order in bankruptcy against the debtor was a person having an "interest in the collateral." The decision is questionable. A petition gives no interest to the petitioning creditor.

33   PPSA (BC, M, NWT, Nu, S) s. 18(3); (NB, PEI) s. 18(4); (NL, NS) s. 19(4); A s. 18(2); (O, Y) no equivalent provision.

34   OPPSA s. 18(1).

that she has an interest in the "collateral" that is subject to the security interest. This is the onus that must be discharged under the Ontario Act by the person demanding the information when the secured party applies to a court for an exemption from the obligation to provide the demanded information.[35]

One of the items of information that may be demanded is a statement of the amount of indebtedness and the terms of payment or a written approval or correction of the information as to the indebtedness and terms of payment. Another item that may be requested is a written approval or correction of an itemized list of property claimed as collateral.[36] However, under section 18(2) of the Ontario Act, a trustee under a trust indenture is not required to provide this information. The other Acts do not relieve trustees from the obligation to respond to a demand, but give them a longer period of time to respond to a demand.[37] Presumably the experience in provinces other than Ontario attests to the weakness of the contention of trustees that it would be too onerous to require them to provide this information.

When a secured party fails to respond as required by the Act to a demand for information, a court may order compliance.[38] In addition, the Acts, other than the Ontario Act, give the court power to order that a security interest to which the information relates be unperfected or extinguished and any registration relating to it be discharged if its order to respond to the demand is not followed.[39] However, the court can also exempt the secured party from compliance or extend the period during which the response may be provided.[40]

---

35 OPPSA s. 18(8). This is a very peculiar provision. It purports to allow a court to grant an exemption from compliance with a demand for information, but only when the person making the demand cannot prove that he is in a category of persons entitled to make the demand. This is not an exemption, it is simply a case where the person making the demand has not met the requirements of the statute. The equivalent provisions in the other Acts provide for a genuine exemption. The secured party can be relieved from compliance even though the person making the demand falls within a qualifying category. PPSA (M, NB, NWT, Nu, PEI, S) s. 18(13); (NL, NS) s. 19(13); A s. 18 (9); BC s. 18(14); Y s. 17(8).
36 PPSA (BC, M, NWT, Nu, S) s. 18(2); (A, O) s. 18(1); (NB, PEI) s. 18(3); (NL, NS) s. 19(3); Y s. 17(1).
37 PPSA (BC, M, NWT, Nu, S) s. 18(7); (NB, PEI) s. 18(7); (NL, NS) s. 19(7); A s. 18(5); Y no equivalent provision.
38 PPSA (M, NB, NWT, Nu, PEI, S) s. 18(8); (NL, NS) s. 19(8); A s. 18(6); BC s. 18(9); Y s. 17(3); O no equivalent provision.
39 PPSA (M, NB, NWT, Nu, PEI, S) s. 18(12); (NL, NS) s. 19(12); A s. 18(8); BC s. 18(13); Y s. 17(6).
40 Above note 35.

A person who suffers loss or damage as a result of an unjustified failure to respond as required to a demand may recover resulting loss or damage[41] along with deemed damages.[42] Under the Ontario Act, where the secured party provides incomplete or incorrect information, the person making the demand and any person who reasonably may be expected to rely on the answer may recover resulting loss or damage.[43] The other Acts approach such a case differently. They provide that when a secured party supplies inaccurate information or a document other than a copy of the security agreement, the secured party is estopped as against the person who made the demand, or any person who can reasonably be expected to rely on the reply, from denying the accuracy of the information in the reply or that the document supplied is a true copy of the security agreement.[44]

The PPSA addresses situations where the demand for information has been made to someone who was a secured creditor but who has assigned her interest to someone else.[45] The former secured party is obligated to disclose the name and address of her immediate successor in interest and, if known, the current holder of the interest.[46] A court can order compliance with this requirement or order exemption from it.[47] In addition, a successor in interest is estopped as against a person who has made a demand to the former secured party for information

---

41   PPSA (M, NWT, Nu, S) s. 65(5); (NB, PEI) s. 66(2); (NL, NS) s. 67(2); A s. 67(1); BC s. 69(3); O s. 18(5) and (10); Y s. 62(2). The APPSA damages are recoverable only if the non-compliance was without reasonable excuse. Under the OPPSA, liability is strict.

42   PPSA (M, S) ss. 65(8)–(9); (NB, PEI) s. 66(5)–(6); (NL, NS) s. 67(5)–(6); (NWT, Nu) s. 65(7)–(8); A s. 67(3)–(4); BC s. 69(7)–(8); (O, Y) no equivalent provision.

43   OPPSA s. 18(5)(b) and (10)(b).

44   PPSA (M, NB, NWT, Nu, PEI, S) s. 18(14); (NL, NS) s. 19(14); A s. 18(10); BC s. 18(15); Y no equivalent provision.

45   No similar provision is contained in the YPPSA.

46   PPSA (M, NB, NWT, Nu, PEI, S) s. 18(9); (NL, NS) s. 1(9); A s. 18(7); BC s. 18(10); Y s. 17(4). OPPSA s. 18(6) requires disclosure of only the "latest" successor in interest known to the former secured party. Consequently, it is only when the former secured party has knowledge as to who currently holds the interest is she required to provide any disclosure under this provision. There is no requirement to disclose the identity of the person to whom she assigned her interest unless that person still holds the interest. See also OPPSA s. 56(6).

47   PPSA (M, NB, NWT, Nu, PEI, S) s. 18(10); (NL, NS) s. 19(10); A s. 18(6); BC s. 18(11); Y s. 17(3). Under OPPSA s. 18(6), there is no power to order compliance unless it is read into the very general power given by s. 18(10) to "make such order as it considers just." However, the person demanding the information may recover loss or damages resulting form the failure to reply or as a result of an incorrect or incomplete reply.

or who can reasonably be expected to rely on the reply received in response to the demand from denying the accuracy of the information in that reply.[48] However, the estoppel does not arise if it is established that such person knows the identity of the successor or if, before the demand was made, the registration was amended to disclose the successor as the secured party.

The Act addresses the legitimate concern of secured parties that they may be liable for disclosure of information to unauthorized persons.[49] The secured party is empowered to respond to a demand for information made by a person who purports to be someone entitled to it unless the secured party knows that this is not the case. However, the obligation to act in a commercially reasonable manner requires the secured party to take appropriate care in determining whether a demand has come from someone entitled to it.

E. PERFECTION BY POSSESSION

1) Introduction

One of the "perfection steps" or methods through which an attached security interest can gain perfected status is transfer of possession of the collateral to the secured party or agent of the secured party.[50] Where the collateral is goods held by a bailee, a form of perfection by possession occurs when the bailee issues a document of title in the name of the secured party or agrees to hold the goods on behalf of the secured party.[51] In the latter case, the bailee is treated as an agent of the secured party for this purpose with the result that the goods are treated as being in the possession of the secured party.[52]

Perfection by possession does not create a common law pledge. At common law, a pledge is a type of security arrangement with its own special characteristics. Under the Act, possession is one of the available steps for perfection of a security interest. Although perfection by posses-

---

48   No similar provision in contained in the OPPSA.

49   PPSA (M, NWT, Nu, S) s. 18(18); (NB, PEI) s. 18(17); (NL, NS) s. 19(17); A s. 18(14); BC s. 18(19); (O, Y) no equivalent provision.

50   PPSA (A, BC, M, NB, NWT, Nu, PEI, S) s. 24; (NL, NS) s. 25; O s. 22; Y s. 22.

51   PPSA (A, BC, M, NB, NWT, Nu, PEI, S, Y) s. 27(1); (NL, NS) s. 28(1); O s. 26(2).

52   *Ibid.* The section, other than O s. 26(2), refers to the bailee "holding on behalf of the secured party pursuant to section 24 (or equivalent section)."

sion can give higher priority than perfection by registration,[53] the use of this method of perfection does not result in a different type of security interest.

The Act provides that a security interest in all categories of collateral other than intangibles, may be perfected by the secured party taking possession of the collateral.[54] Intangibles are excluded from the list because it is not physically possible to take possession of an intangible.[55] Consequently, a financial institution that enters into a term-deposit contract (that does not meet the requirements of an "instrument"[56]) and thereafter loans money to the depositor cannot perfect a security interest in its obligation under the term deposit contract by possession.[57] This obligation is an account[58] and, consequently, an intangible.

2) What Constitutes Possession

Perfection by possession requires actual physical possession by the secured party or an agent or bailee[59] of the secured party other than the debtor or debtor's agent. The Act provides that a secured party does not have possession of collateral that is in the actual or apparent possession

---

53   For example, PPSA (A, BC, NB, NWT, Nu, PEI) s. 31(4); (M, S) s. 31(5); (NL, NS) s. 32(4); O s. 28(4); Y s. 30(4).

54   Above note 50. The section includes a reference to "security." Under proposed amendments to the PPSA to accompany the proposed *Uniform Securities Transfer Act*, the equivalent of perfection by possession will be taking delivery of a certificated security pursuant to section 79 of the *Uniform Securities Transfer Act*. See proposed APPSA ss. 24(3)–(4); OPPSA ss. 22(3)–(4). A new perfection step relating to securities, "control," will be introduced by these amendments. See proposed s. 4.1.

55   The reference to "negotiable document of title" in the section that provides for perfection by possession of the collateral indicates an intention on the part of the drafters to exclude non-negotiable documents of title. A possessor of a non-negotiable document of title other than the person named in the document as the person entitled to take delivery of the goods, has no rights to possession of the goods. However, possession of a negotiable document of title perfects a security interest in the goods covered by it. See PPSA (A, BC, M, NB, NWT, Nu, PEI, S, Y) s. 27(1); (NL, NS) s. 28(1); O s. 26(1).

56   PPSA (A, BC, NWT, Nu, O, Y) s. 1(1); (M, NB, PEI) s. 1; (NL, NS) s. 2; S s. 2(1).

57   A security interest in a taxi-cab licence cannot be perfected by possession of the car to which the licence relates because the collateral is the licence and not the vehicle. See *Re Foster* (1992), 89 D.L.R. (4th) 555 (Ont. Ct. Gen. Div.).

58   Above note 50.

59   *Ibid.*

or control of the debtor or debtor's agent.[60] Consequently, the common law concept of constructive possession has not been imported into the Act since it permits a debtor to be in apparent possession or control of the collateral.[61]

Special rules apply to perfection by possession of security interests in "securities"[62] including certificated, uncertificated, and immobilized shares and negotiable debt obligations. Where certificated shares are collateral, the secured party can perfect by taking physical possession of the certificates.[63] This is often accompanied by transfer of the certificate into the secured party's name.[64] However, a different approach is required where uncertificated securities or immobilized securities held by clearing agencies are taken as collateral.

Since by definition an uncertificated security is not in hardcopy form,[65] it is not possible to perfect a security interest in it by taking physical possession of a certificate. Nevertheless, the Act provides that it is possible to perfect a security interest in an uncertificated "security" by taking possession of it but does not indicate what constitutes taking possession in this context. In the absence of specific direction on the matter, it is reasonable to assume that possession by the secured party is obtained when the issuer or agent of the issuer records the interest of the secured party in its records either as a security interest or as ownership. As a practical matter, the issue does not arise since most provincial Business Corporations Acts do not recognize uncertificated securities. However, the Ontario *Business Corporations Act*[66] provides that an uncertificated security is delivered to a purchaser when the security is recorded in the records of the issuer in the name of the pur-

60 PPSA (A, BC, M, NB, NWT, Nu, PEI, S) s. 24(2); (NL, NS) s. 25(2); Y s. 22(2); O no equivalent provision. However, see *Re Darzinskas* (1981), 132 D.L.R. (3d) 77 (Ont. H.C.J.).
61 *North Western Bank Ltd. v. Poynter,* [1895] A.C. 56 (H.L.); *Young v. Lambert* (1870), L.R. 3 P.C. 142.
62 Defined in PPSA (A, BC, NWT, Nu, O, Y) s. 1(1); (M, NB, PEI) s. 1; (NL, NS) s. 2; S s. 2(1).
63 When this occurs, the secured party qualifies for the special priority given to a purchaser of a security. PPSA (A, BC, NB, NWT, Nu, PEI) s. 31(3); (M, S) s. 31(4); (NL, NS) s. 32(3); O s. 28(6)–(8); Y s. 30(3).
64 Theoretically, transfer in the secured party's name by itself is not sufficient since it is not mentioned in the PPSA as a perfection method.
65 An uncertificated security is a security that is not evidenced by a security certificate and the issue and any transfer of which is registered or recorded in records maintained for that purpose by or on behalf of the issuer of the security.
66 R.S.O. 1990, c. B.16.

chaser. This would be accepted by a court as transfer of possession for the purpose of perfection by possession under the Ontario Act.

Several Acts deal more specifically with security interests in securities (certificated or uncertificated) held by a clearing agency. The Ontario *Business Corporation Act* provides that securities held by a clearing agency (or its custodian or nominee) may be transferred or "pledged" by the making of an appropriate entry in the records of the clearing agency.[67] When a pledge or creation of a security interest is involved, the making of the entry has the effect of the pledgee or secured party taking possession of the security for the purposes of the Act.[68] A participant[69] who is a transferee or pledgee of a security held by a clearing agency is deemed to have possession of the security for the purposes of the Ontario Act.

The Acts of several other jurisdictions provide that where the collateral is a security, the transfer of which may be effected by an entry in the records of a clearing agency as provided in the law relating to the transfer of securities, the transferee or secured party is deemed to have taken possession of the security when the appropriate entries have been made in the records of the clearing agency.[70]

3) Perfection by Seizure or Repossession

There is divergence between the Ontario and Manitoba Acts, on the one hand, and all other the Acts, on the other, with respect to the issue of whether a security interest is perfected by possession when the secured party seizes the collateral from the debtor for the purposes of enforcement. The approach contained in the Acts of nine jurisdictions is that a security interest is not perfected by possession when that possession results from seizure or repossession.[71]

---

67   *Ibid.*, s. 85(1).

68   *Ibid.*, s. 85(4).

69   This term is not defined in the Act. However, it refers to a broker, bank or other institution that is directly associated with the clearing agency with the result that securities held by the agency may be noted in the records of the agency as belonging to that person or institution.

70   PPSA (M, NB, PEI) s. 2(4); (NL, NS) s. 3(4); (NWT, Nu) s. 1(6); BC s. 24(3); S s. 2(5); (A, O, Y) no equivalent provision.

71   PPSA (A, BC, NB, NWT, Nu, PEI, S) s. 24; (NL, NS) s. 25; O s. 22; Y s. 22. In *Key West Ford Sales Ltd. v. Rounis* (1998), 13 P.P.S.A.C. (2d) 102 (B.C.S.C.), the court held that when a seller terminated a contract and repossessed a vehicle as a result of a misrepresentation on the part of the debtor, the security interest was perfected by possession. The court failed to address the question as to how the

The Ontario[72] and Manitoba Acts expressly provide that "possession or repossession (or seizure)[73] of collateral by the secured party or on the secured party's behalf ... perfects a security interest." The Manitoba Act qualifies this with the requirement that the "possession, repossession or seizure [be] pursuant to a right given by the security agreement or this Act."[74] This qualifier removes the suggestion implicit in the Ontario Act that *de facto* possession of the collateral is enough even though that possession may have been gained through seizure of the collateral in a manner that violates the Act or the rights of the debtor or another person with an interest in the collateral.

The Ontario and Manitoba approach appears to be based on the conclusion that the function of possession by the secured party or agent of the secured party is to ensure that third parties are informed of the existence of the security interest. Possession by the secured party serves this goal regardless of the motive for taking possession. The approach contained in the Acts of all other jurisdictions has both conceptual and functional bases. There is a fundamental conceptual difference between perfection by possession and repossession or seizure after default. The surrender of possession of the collateral by the debtor to the secured party or agent of the secured party is voluntary on the part of the debtor and involves recognition by both parties that the secured party's interest is to be protected in this way.[75] Seizure is the involuntary taking of the collateral from the debtor by the secured

---

seller could be treated as continuing to have a perfected security interest once it elected to terminate the security agreement.

72 OPPSA s. 22.
73 MPPSA s. 24(1).
74 The inclusion of the word "seizure" in the Manitoba Act formulation eliminates the problem endemic to the Ontario Act that seizure by a secured party who did not have possession in the first place does not qualify since this is not "repossession." Of course, after seizure, such a secured party would be in possession. If this is all that is required, what function is to be given to the word "repossession"?
75 While, as noted elsewhere in this book, perfection by possession does not create a common law pledge, the circumstances under which it occurs parallel those when a pledge is being created. The debtor agrees that the secured party's interest is to be protected against loss to third parties by having the secured creditor take possession of the collateral. Somewhat anomalously, some OPPSA commentators treat perfection of a security interest by possession as creating a pledge, but at the same time support the Ontario approach in treating seizure and repossession as perfection. See J.S. Ziegel and D. Denomme, *The Ontario Personal Property Security Act, Commentary and Analysis*, 2d ed. (Toronto: Butterworths, 2000) at 177 and 179–80.

party as a result of the debtor's default. It is a compulsory enforcement measure that is closely circumscribed by the Acts.

The recognition of seizure or repossession as an appropriate perfection step gives rise to potential legal and factual problems the solutions to which may frustrate a central policy of the Act: to provide an orderly, predictable system for taking and enforcing security interests. In the great bulk of cases this form of perfection will be relied upon by secured parties who, for some reason, have failed to make use of the very accessible and inexpensive facilities for registration of security interests available in all jurisdictions. It can be seen as encouraging precipitous action and potential breaches of the peace. In the context of a priority competition with the debtor's trustee in bankruptcy, it is very likely to involve difficult questions of proof as to exactly when the secured party took possession, requiring the courts to determine sequences of events that occurred a few hours apart. It also holds the potential for difficult legal determinations. It is likely to induce litigation on esoteric questions such as: can there be a form of constructive possession when the debtor, a subordinate secured party or other person hides the collateral or otherwise takes illegal measures to prevent seizure or repossessions;[76] is seizure or repossession sufficient when it occurs before the debtor is in default or, for some other reason, the secured party is not entitled to seize or repossess the collateral?[77]

An example of the type of legal issues that are endemic to the Manitoba-Ontario approach was addressed by the Ontario Court of Appeal in *Sperry Inc. v. Canadian Imperial Bank of Commerce*.[78] The issue before the Court was whether possession of collateral by a receiver-manager — who had taken possession of collateral upon the debtor's default — qualified as perfection by possession. The receiver-manager had been appointed by the secured party pursuant to a power in the security agreement. The security agreement contained a standard agency clause

---

76   In *Key State Bank v. Voz* (1989), 9 P.P.S.A.C. 47 (Ont. Dist. Ct.) the court held that when the secured party was deprived of actual possession by the police, he remained in constructive possession sufficient to meet the requirement of the Act for perfection by possession. However, in *C.I.B.C. v. Melnitzer* (1993), 23 C.B.R. (3d) 161 (Ont. Ct. Gen. Div.) the court concluded that when the secured party was deprives of possession of the collateral through the fraudulent conduct of the debtor, the security interest in the collateral became unperfected.

77   This problem would not arise under s. 24(2) of the MPPSA. In order for seizure or repossession to qualify as a perfection step, it must occur "pursuant to a right given by the security agreement or this Act."

78   (1985), 17 D.L.R. (4th) 236 (Ont. C.A.). See also *Bank of Nova Scotia v. Royal Bank of Canada* (1987), 68 C.B.R. (N.S.) 235 (Sask. C.A.).

under which the receiver-manager was deemed to be the agent of the debtor. [79] The Court ruled that it is only when realizing on the collateral that the receiver is acting as the secured party. She remains the agent of the debtor when exercising the power contained in the security agreement to carry on the business of the debtor. It is only when there is objective evidence of the intention of the receiver-manager to dispose of the collateral for the purposes of enforcing the security interest that the receiver-manager's possession qualifies as perfection by possession. An indicium of this intention would be notice to the debtor of an intention to sell the collateral.[80]

F. PERFECTION OF A SECURITY INTEREST IN GOODS IN POSSESSION OF A BAILEE

A form of perfection that can be treated as a variant of perfection by possession occurs when a bailee of the debtor issues a document of title in the name of the secured party.[81] In addition, if a commercial bailee issues a negotiable document of title to the goods in its possession, perfection of a security interest in the document of title is deemed to be perfection of a security interest in the goods covered by it.[82] This latter form of perfection carries with it a special priority rule. Any security interest in the goods perfected after issue of the negotiable document of title is subject a security interest in the negotiable document of title. The security interest in the negotiable document of title can be perfected by registration,[83] possession by the secured party or his agent[84] or temporarily.

---

79 The clause, commonly found in security agreements that provide for the appointment of a receiver-manager in the event of default by the debtor, provided that the receiver-manager is agent of the debtor. The principal reason for including such clauses is to exonerate the secured party from liability for illegal acts of the receiver-manager. However, now see PPSA (M, NB, NL, NWT, Nu, PEI) s. 64(7); (A, NL, NS) s. 65(7); BC s. 66(1); S s. 64(8); Y s. 54(2); O no equivalent provision. These provisions empower a court to order the secured party to "make good a default in connection with the receiver's custody, management or disposition of the collateral of the debtor."

80 The decision was made under the former OPPSA. However, it is the authors' view that there is nothing in the current OPPSA or the MPPSA that produces a different result.

81 PPSA (A, BC, M, NB, NWT, Nu, PEI, S, Y) s. 27(1); (NL, NS) s. 28(1); O s. 26(1).

82 *Ibid.*

83 PPSA (A, BC, M, NB, NWT, Nu, PEI, S) s. 25; (NL, NS) s. 26; (O, Y) s. 23.

84 PPSA (A, BC, M, NB, NWT, Nu, PEI, S) s. 24; (NL, NS) s. 25; O s. 22; Y s. 22.

G. AUTOMATIC PERFECTION

1) Introduction

There is no general "grace period" given to a secured party during which a security interest is treated as perfected without a perfection step having been taken. However, there are several specific circumstances in which the Act grants the status of perfection to a security interest without the need on the part of the secured party to effect a registration relating to it or to take possession of the collateral. However, in most cases, it is not as effective as perfection by registration or transfer of possession of the collateral to the secured party.

The circumstances in which automatic perfection is granted and the preconditions to its availability vary widely. In some cases, the perfection is temporary and conditional[85] in the sense that it is recognized for a specified period of time only if a perfection step has been taken (or another type of temporary situation arises) before the expiry of the period. In others, it is temporary and unconditional[86] in that it is recognized for a specified period of time whether or not an alternative perfection step is taken before or after the expiry of that period. In other cases, it is unconditional and permanent.[87]

Under specified circumstances a purchase-money security interest is given a special priority if it is perfected within a specified period.[88] While these are priority rules, they allow for delayed perfection when the purchase money security interest is in competition with other interests specified in the provisions.

2) Automatic Perfection of Foreign Security Interest

The Act contains an elaborate set of rules specifying the circumstances under which the validity, perfection, and priority of foreign[89] security

---

85 PPSA (BC, M, NB, NWT, Nu, PEI, S) s. 5(3); (NL, NS) s. 6(3); A s. 4(2); O s. 5(2); Y. s. 6(3).

86 PPSA (A, BC, M, NB, NWT, Nu, PEI, S) s. 28; (NL, NS) s. 29; O s. 25; Y s. 26.

87 Under the proposed amendments to the PPSA, ss. 19.1 and 19.2, accompanying *Uniform Securities Transfer Act* automatic perfection can be permanent.

88 PPSA (A, BC, M, NB, NWT, Nu, PEI, S) s. 22(1); (NL, NS) s. 23(1); O s. 20(3); Y s. 20 and PPSA (A, M, NWT, Nu, S) s. 34(2); (BC, NB, PEI) s. 34(1); (NL, NS) s. 35(1); O s. 33(2); Y s. 33(1).

89 That is, security interests created under the law of another jurisdiction, whether Canadian or non-Canadian.

interests are recognized. When a priority contest arises in a jurisdiction involving a foreign security interest, one of the issues that may be involved is whether that interest is recognized under the laws of the jurisdiction as being perfected. The Act provides a period of temporary, conditional automatic perfection of such interests. A security interest that is perfected under the law that generally governs perfection remains perfected in the jurisdiction for a specified period of time after the collateral is brought into the jurisdiction[90] or debtor changes his location to the jurisdiction[91] if it remains perfected under the otherwise applicable law and is perfected under the law of the jurisdiction within that period of time. Failure to obtain perfection within the specified period of time results in the security interests being treated as unperfected as soon as the collateral is brought into the jurisdiction or the debtor changes his location to the jurisdiction, as the case may be.

An effect of conditional automatic perfection is that a person who acquires an interest in the collateral during the period of automatic perfection can take effective protective measures such as witholding a loan or grant of credit pending the expiry of the period. The person can rely on taking free from any foreign security interest in the collateral not otherwise perfected during the period. This approach would not produce the same result if the period of automatic perfection were absolute.

The priority status associated with the perfection granted by these provisions of the Act is more limited than it would be if the security interest were perfected in the jurisdiction through a perfection step. Under the Act,[92] a temporarily perfected foreign security interest is subordinate to the interest of a buyer or lessee of goods who acquired the interest without knowledge of the security interest and before it is perfected in the jurisdiction either by registration or by the secured party taking possession of the goods.[93]

---

90   Above note 85.
91   PPSA (A, BC, M, NB, NWT, Nu, PEI, S) s. 7(3); (NL, NS) s. 8(3); O s. 7(2); Y s. 6(3). The differences in approach between the OPPSA and the other Acts are examined in chapter 3, C.2, "Relocation of Goods: Re-perfection Requirement" and D.5, "Impact on Perfection of a Post-attachment Change in the Location of the Debtor."
92   Above note 85. The OPPSA protects only to buyers or lessee of consumer goods.
93   This weakness in perfection status applies only where the law applicable to validity is that of the location of the collateral when the security interest attached. It does not apply where the applicable law is that of the location of the debtor when the security interest attached.

3) Automatic Perfection of Security Interests in Proceeds

The Act gives temporary, unconditional perfection of a security inter-est in proceeds.[94] The security interest and its perfected status in the original collateral continues in the proceeds. However, the temporary perfection terminated fifteen days after the security interest attaches to the proceeds, unless it is otherwise perfected by any of the methods applicable to original collateral of the same kind. Under the Ontario Act, separate perfection of a security interest in proceeds is required when the security interest in the original collateral was perfected by possession.[95] In this case, the period of temporary, absolute perfection is ten days.[96]

The unconditionality of the automatic perfection provided by the Acts can be an important consideration in determining priorities. If the priority of a competing interest in the proceeds is based on the date the interest was acquired, a security interest in proceeds that is temporar-ily perfected at that date may well have priority even though it is never perfected. For example, if the debtor becomes a bankrupt during the period of automatic perfection, a proceeds security interest has priority over the debtor's trustee in bankruptcy even though the security inter-est is not otherwise perfected before the end of the period of automatic perfection or thereafter.[97]

A specialized variant of a security interest continued in proceeds is contained in a different provision of the Act. It gives to a secured party holding a security interest in chattel paper a statutory security inter-est in the goods to which the chattel paper relates, when those goods are returned to or repossessed by the original seller (debtor) or by the secured party.[98] The Act provides that this statutory security interest in the goods is unconditionally perfected for a period of fifteen days (ten days in Ontario) from the date of the return or repossession.[99]

---

94   PPSA (A, BC, NWT, Nu, S) s. 28(3); (NB, PEI) 28(4); (NL, NS) s. 29(1); M s. 28(2); O s. 25(4); Y s. 26(2). See chapter 12 for a detailed examination of secu-rity interests in proceeds.
95   Where a motor vehicle that is consumer goods is proceeds, the serial number must be registered if the security interest is to have priority over a good faith buyer. See OPPSA s. 25(5).
96   OPPSA s. 25(4).
97   See *Central Refrigeration & Restaurant Services Inc. v. Canadian Imperial Bank of Commerce* (1986), 47 Sask. R. 124 (C.A.).
98   PPSA (A, BC, M, NB, PEI, NWT, Nu, S) s. 29; (NL, NS) s. 30; O s. 27(1); Y s. 28.
99   PPSA (A, BC, M, NB, PEI, NWT, Nu, S) s. 29(4); (NL, NS) s. 30(4); O s. 27(4); Y s. 28(6).

4) Other Instances of Automatic Perfection

The Ontario and Yukon Acts provide that a security interest in an instrument, security, or negotiable document of title is perfected for ten days after it attaches, to the extent that it arises for new value secured by a written security agreement.[100] No similar provision is contained in the other Acts. This feature resembles a traditional "grace period" of the kind contained in the pre-PPSA Conditional Sales Acts, which gave a grace period of deemed registration between the date the conditional sales agreement was executed and the date it was in fact registered. The provision harkens back to the time when registry systems were primitive and perfection by registration was cumbersome and time-consuming. It was thought necessary to give to a secured party who most likely intended to perfect by registration a short grace period after the date the debtor obtained possession of the collateral to effect registration. Since modern registry systems are efficient and easily accessed, there is no longer a need for this concession to secured creditors.

Subject to the Yukon and Ontario exceptions just described, the Act addresses situations where the need for automatic perfection is most likely to arise.[101] They provide a period of automatic perfection when a security interest in one of the specified types of goods has been perfected by possession and it is commercially necessary for the secured party to release the collateral to the debtor in order to allow him to deal with it one of the ways specified in the section. In most cases, the release of the collateral to the debtor will be on the condition that, where a disposition, collection, or other dealing with the collateral is involved, the debtor will account to the secured party for the proceeds. The provision addresses a gap in the Act that gives automatic perfection to a security interest in the proceeds.[102] In order for a security interest in proceeds to be continuously perfected for the fifteen- (ten-) day period, the security interest in the original collateral must have been perfected when the proceeds were generated. The Act provides this perfection without the need to effect a registration in relation to the collateral.

While disposition of the collateral by the debtor need not be the reason for release of the collateral in the form of goods or a document of title to goods, it is clear that, in the great bulk of cases, disposition will eventually be involved. The principal exception would be cases

---

100 OPPSA s. 24(1) and YPPSA s. 25(1).
101 PPSA (A, BC, M, NB, NWT, Nu, PEI, S) s. 26(1); NL s. 27(2); NS s. 27(1); O s. 24(2); Y s. 25(2).
102 Above note 94.

where the secured party intends to perfect by having a document of title issued in his name or intends to take possession of a negotiable document of title. In these cases, the period of automatic perfection facilitates the shift from perfection by possession to perfection through the use of a document of title without having to bridge the gap between the two by registration.

This provision of the Act addresses perfection of security interests, not the priority of those interests. A security interest given automatic perfection under the section is vulnerable to defeat by interests that are given priority over security interests perfected by registration.[103] In addition, the Act provides that a buyer or lessee of goods who gives value and acquires her interest without knowledge of the security interest takes free of a temporarily perfected security interest.[104] In order to be protected, the debtor who sold or leased the goods need not be selling in the ordinary course of business. All that is required is that the buyer or lessee gives value and have acquired her interest without knowledge of the security interest. There is no equivalent of this provision in the Ontario Act.

An issue of interpretation arises in the context of the Ontario Act that is addressed in the other Acts. The other Acts provide that the automatic perfection given by the section is not affected by the lack of a written security agreement or the continued possession by the secured party as otherwise required by the Act.[105] No similar provision is found in the Ontario Act. It provides that a security interest is not enforceable against a third party unless it has attached and that a security interest attaches when a written security agreement has been signed by the debtor or the collateral is in the possession of the secured party or agent of the secured party.[106] However, in the situation contemplated by the provision that gives temporary perfection for released collateral,[107] neither of these conditions has been met. The security interest remains perfected after release of the collateral to the debtor, but it is unenforceable against a third party.

The Yukon Act provides another type of automatic perfection. Under section 24, a purchase-money security interest in consumer

---

103 PPSA (A, BC, M, NB, NWT, Nu, PEI, S) s. 31; (NL, NS) s. 31(2); O s. 28(1); Y s. 29(1). See amendments to APPSA ss. 31(3)–(4) and OPPSA ss. 28(6)–(7) accompanying the proposed *Uniform Securities Transfer Act*.
104 PPSA (A, BC, M, NB, NWT, Nu, PEI, S) s. 30(5); (NL, NS) 31(5); Y s. 29(5); O no equivalent provision.
105 *Ibid.*
106 OPPSA s. 11
107 OPPSA s. 24.

goods other than "special consumer goods" (serial numbered goods or goods of a value in excess of an amount specified in regulations) is perfected automatically upon attachment.

5) Automatic Perfection under Proposed Changes Associated with the Proposed *Uniform Securities Transfer Act*

Proposed amendments to the Act associated with the proposed *Uniform Securities Transfer Act* will provide for automatic attachment and perfection of a security interest in a security or financial asset arising in the context of transactions between persons in the business of dealing with securities or financial assets that provide for delivery against payment.[108] This special form of attachment and perfection also applies to a security interest in investment property, a commodity account or commodity contract created by a broker, securities intermediary or commodity intermediary, respectively.[109] This type of automatic perfection differs from other types in that it is both unconditional and is not temporary.

H. PERFECTION BY CONTROL

Proposed amendments to the PPSA associated with the proposed *Uniform Securities Transfer Act*[110] will introduce a new type of perfection — perfection by control — applicable to security interests in "investment property."[111] Perfection by control occurs when the creditor has taken whatever steps are necessary to be in a position to sell the collateral without any further action by the debtor. Where the collateral is a certificated security in bearer form, delivery[112] of the certificate to the se-

---

108 Proposed APPSA ss. 12.1(3) and 19.2(1); OPPSA ss. 11.1(3) and 19.2(1).
109 Proposed APPSA ss. 19.2(2)–(3); OPPSA ss. 19.2(2)–(3).
110 Above note 16.
111 This term is defined in the amendments as "a security, whether certificated or uncertificated, security entitlement, securities account, commodity contract or commodity account." See proposed changes to APPSA s. 1(1)(x.1); OPPSA s. 1(1). Each of the types of property set out in the definition are, in turn, defined in the amendments.
112 "Delivery" can be more or less than transfer of possession of the certificate. See *Uniform Securities Transfer Act* s. 79.

cured party constitutes control.[113] Where the collateral is a certificated security in registered form, delivery of the certificate accompanied by appropriate endorsement or registration of the certificate in the secured party's name constitutes control.[114] A secured creditor obtains control of an uncertificated security when the issuer registers the secured party or someone acting on behalf of the secured party as owner, or the issuer agrees to comply with instructions that are originated by the secured party without further consent of the debtor. A secured creditor obtains control of a security entitlement[115] by agreement with the debtor's intermediary to act on the creditor's instructions, or by having the security entitlements transferred into the creditor's securities account.[116]

---

113   APPSA ss. 1(1.1) and 24.1; OPPSA ss. 1(1.1) and 22.1; *Uniform Securities Transfer Act* s. 30.

114   *Ibid.*

115   This is a new form of property in which a security interest can be taken. See APPSA s. 1(1)(ss.2); OPPSA s. 1(1); *Uniform Securities Transfer Act* ss. 1(1)(gg) and 106–18.

116   APPSA ss. 1(1.1) and 24.1; OPPSA ss. 1(1.1) and 22.1; *Uniform Securities Transfer Act* s. 30.

CHAPTER 6

THE REGISTRATION SYSTEM

A. INTRODUCTION AND BACKGROUND

1) Scope of Chapter

The requirement that security interests be perfected to take full effect against third parties is examined in chapter 5. The usual mode of perfection — and the only one universally available — is registration in the Personal Property Registry established by the PPSA.[1] This chapter addresses the nature and operation of the registry, the registration process, the requirements for a valid registration, and the circumstances in which errors or omissions may prove fatal to perfected status.

The question of *where* registration should be made is dealt with in chapter 3 on conflict of laws. Chapter 14 addresses the question of whether alternative or supplementary registration may be required under federal law — in particular, under the federal intellectual property statutes (where the collateral is federally regulated intellectual property rights), the *Canada Shipping Act* (where the collateral is a ship registered in the federal ship registry), or the *Bank Act* (where the security is granted by a commercial debtor to a federally regulated bank). The question of whether supplementary filings in the land registry are

---

1   PPSA (A, BC, M, NB, NWT, Nu, PEI, S) s. 25; (NL, NS) s. 26; (O, Y) s. 23. Provision for the registry is made in PPSA (A, BC, M, NB, NWT, Nu, PEI, S) s. 42(1); (NL, NS) s. 43(1); O s. 41; Y s. 40.

required for fixtures and crops (and rents in the case of Ontario) to preserve priority against those with an interest in the related land is dealt with in chapter 12.

2) Pre-PPSA Registration Systems

Canadian law reflects a long-standing commitment to the principle that some form of public registration should be a precondition to the effectiveness of a non-possessory security interest against third parties.[2] The first public registry for personal property security dates back to pre-Confederation with the passage by the legislature of the Province of Canada in 1849 of the *Bills of Sale (and Chattel Mortgages) Act.* By the end of the nineteenth century all the common law provinces had enacted equivalent legislation.

The *Bills of Sale Act* required a sale or mortgage of goods without a change of possession to be registered on pain of subordination to subsequent purchasers and mortgagees, as well as unsecured creditors and their representatives. After the conditional sale came into common commercial use in Canada (*circa* the 1860s), legislatures in the common law jurisdictions began to impose a similar registration requirement, beginning about 1882. This policy was eventually reflected in the adoption of the *Uniform Conditional Sales Act* by the ULCC in 1922.[3]

The registration requirements for intangible assets in the form of accounts evolved along a more circuitous path. The early English common law struck upon notification of the account debtor as the closest functional equivalent to a physical transfer of possession. Under the rule in *Dearle v. Hall,*[4] priority between successive assignments or charges of the same obligation was determined by the order of notification to the account debtor, provided that the first-notifying creditor did not have actual knowledge of a prior assignment or charge when it acquired its own interest. The rule did not apply to a competition between the holder of an assignment or charge and a garnishing creditor or trustee in bankruptcy. To remedy the absence of any publicity mechanism to protect unsecured creditors, the federal *Bankruptcy Act* of 1919 em-

---

2   Generally, see R.C.C. Cuming, "Harmonization of Business Law in Canada," in Royal Commission on the Economic Union and Development Prospects for Canada [The Macdonald Report], *Report of the Royal Commission on the Economic Union and Development Prospects for Canada* (Ottawa: Minister of Supply and Services Canada, 1985) book 56.

3   See J.S. Ziegel, "Uniformity of Legislation in Canada: The Conditional Sales Experience" (1961) 39 Can. Bar Rev. 165.

4   (1828), 3 Russ. 1, 38 All E.R. 475.

powered a trustee in bankruptcy to avoid any general assignment of book debts, whether absolute or by way of security, which had not been registered. The new federal rule forced the provincial legislatures to establish a public registry system for assignments of and security interests in monetary intangibles. The typical legislative vehicle was the *Assignment of Book Debts Act* under which an unregistered assignment (defined to also include an assignment by way of security) was void not just against the assignor/debtor's unsecured creditors, but also against subsequent assignees and charge-holders.[5]

The proliferation of registry regimes for different categories of collateral and different kinds of security devices created particular difficulties for corporations, which in practice tended to charge all their assets by way of a single security device, the equitable charge. Some provinces, following the example of the *English Companies Act* of 1900, incorporated a registration system into their companies' legislation. In 1931, the ULCC adopted a Uniform *Corporation Securities Registration Act*. Enacted (in varying forms) in a number of common law jurisdictions, the Act made it possible to register the grant of security in both tangible (goods) and intangible (book debts) assets through a single registration. However, the new Act did not replace the other registration statutes. Its scope was restricted to corporate debtors and corporate debt instruments. Even then, security was defined in conventional terms to exclude security created by retention of title, that is, conditional sales agreements and financing leases.

B. THE PPSA REGISTRATION SYSTEM: GENERAL CONSIDERATIONS

1) Nature of the Personal Property Registry

The Personal Property Registry is very different from its predecessors. The functional concept of a security interest adopted by the Act has made it possible to consolidate all registrations in a single registry, regardless

---

5   However, the courts generally ruled that registration was not constructive notice for the purposes of the rule in *Dearle v. Hall* with the result that the first-registered assignee could still be defeated if a subsequent assignee was the first to notify the account debtor. It was not until the 1990s that the Nova Scotia Court of Appeal finally reversed this position, just prior to the advent of PPSA reform in that province: see Catherine Walsh, "Registration, Constructive Notice and the Rule in *Dearle v. Hall*: Judicial Reform in Nova Scotia" (1996) 12 B.F.L.R. 131.

of the form of the security instrument, the status of the debtor, or the nature of the collateral.[6] Moreover, the PPSA registration process itself is vastly more efficient. The pre-PPSA registries were document-filing systems of the kind used for registering title to specific parcels of land or specific ships. Registrants were required to file the actual security documentation itself. The PPSA instead adopts notice registration,[7] a concept first pioneered in Canada for security granted under the *Bank Act*. Only minimal information need be registered: the names and addresses of the parties, a description of the collateral, and the duration of the registration.[8] There is no requirement to file the underlying security documentation, or even tender it for scrutiny.

2) Advance Registration

Notice registration removes any obstacle to advance registration and the PPSA confirms that a registration may be made before or after a security agreement is made or a security interest attaches.[9] The 1989 version of the Ontario PPSA eliminated the bar on advance registration found in the original Ontario Act with one exception. If the collateral is consumer goods, the security agreement must have been signed by the debtor before registration can be made.[10]

The consumer goods exception creates complications where the collateral includes other assets in addition to consumer goods. Secured parties must make separate registrations if they wish to have the advantage of advance registration for collateral that is not consumer goods.

Two reasons have been advanced in support of the exception. The first is "minimizing the number of [registered] encumbrances on a consumer's title to his or her property."[11] The second is the concern that if advance registration were permitted, a registration made by a potential secured party with whom a consumer debtor had initiated inquiries

6   See chapter 2 for a detailed analysis of the PPSA concept of security interest.
7   PPSA (A, BC, M, NB, NWT, Nu, PEI, S) s. 25; (NL, NS) s. 26; (O, Y) s. 23.
8   The content and format requirements for registrations are prescribed in detail in the regulation under the PPSA: Alta. Reg. 95/2001; B.C. Reg. 227/2002; Man. Reg. 80/2000; N.W.T. Reg. 066-2001; N.B. Reg. 95-57; N.L.R. 103/99; N.S. Reg. 129/97; R.R.O. 1990, Reg. 912; P.E.I. Reg. EC270/98; R.R.S. c. P-6.2 Reg.1; Y.O.I.C. 1982/092.
9   PPSA (A, BC, M, Nu, NWT, S) s. 43(4); (NB, PEI) s. 43(5); (NL, NS) s. 44(5); O s. 45(2)–(3); Y s. 42(8).
10 OPPSA s. 45(2).
11 Jacob S. Ziegel and David L. Denomme, *The Ontario Personal Property Security Act Commentary and Analysis*, 2d ed. (Markham: Butterworths, 2000) at 370.

would discourage other potential secured parties from offering a more competitive deal if the debtor went on to comparison shop.[12]

There is no evidence from other PPSA jurisdictions that did not adopt this feature that these concerns were justified. Financial institutions are unlikely to engage in the time and expense of speculative registrations and advance registration does not seem to have significantly increased the number of registered encumbrances against consumer goods in these other jurisdictions. In any event, the Act empowers any person named as a debtor in a registration to execute a written demand to discharge the registration if no security agreement has been entered into between the parties.[13] Failure to comply exposes the secured creditor to liability for statutory damages,[14] and entitles the debtor to unilaterally bring about the discharge.[15] Significantly, this latter right is absent from the Ontario Act; the debtor must apply to the court for an order directed to the registrar to effect the discharge.[16]

3) One Registration for Multiple Security Agreements

In a notice-registration system, the registered notice is independent from the security documentation. It follows that there is no reason why a single registration cannot operate to perfect security interests arising under successive agreements between the same parties. Accordingly, the PPSA confirms that a single registration is effective to perfect a security interest arising under multiple agreements,[17] regardless of

---

12 *Ibid.*

13 PPSA (A, BC, M, NB, NWT, Nu, PEI, S) s. 50(3); (NL, NS) s. 51(3); O s. 56(2); Y s. 50(4).

14 PPSA (M, NWT, Nu, S) s. 65(6); (NB, PEI) s. 66(3); (NL, NS) s. 67(3); (NWT, Nu) s. 65(2); A s. 67(2); M s. 65(2); (BC, O, Y) no equivalent provision. The PPSA also creates a general cause of action to recover any reasonably foreseeable actual damages suffered by a person as a result of the failure of the defendant, without reasonable excuse, to discharge any duty or perform any obligation imposed by the Act. PPSA (M, NWT, Nu, S) s. 65(5); (NB, PEI) s. 66(2); (NL, NS) s. 67(2); (NWT, Nu) s. 65(2); A s. 67(1); BC s. 69(3); Y s. 62(2). The scope of the counterpart provision in the Ontario Act is more limited and does not extend to failure to discharge: OPPSA s. 67(2).

15 PPSA (A, BC, M, NB, NWT, Nu, PEI, S) s. 50(3); (NL, NS) s. 51(3); O s. 56(2); Y s. 50(4).

16 OPPSA s. 56(5).

17 PPSA (A, BC, M, Nu, NWT, S) s. 43(5); (NB, PEI) s. 43(6); (NL, NS) s. 44(6); O s. 45(4); Y no equivalent provision.

whether the agreements are related to one another or represent separate and distinct transactions.[18]

Even in the absence of a similar provision in an earlier version of the Saskatchewan Act, the Saskatchewan Court of Appeal concluded that under the theory of a notice-registration system, one registration can perfect multiple security interests arising from subsequent, unrelated transactions between the same parties.[19] The wording of the original Ontario PPSA precluded that interpretation, although the courts were prepeared to approve the use of a single registration to perfect security interests arising under successive security agreements where they formed part of a single ongoing transaction.[20]

The 1989 version of the Ontario PPSA brought the Ontario Act into line with the other Acts on this point, providing that "one registration may perfect one or more security interests created or provided for in one or more security agreements between the parties."[21] In *Adelaide Capital Corp. v. Integrated Transportation Finance Inc.*,[22] the court continued to insist on a linkage between security agreements and also rejected the possibility that a registration made in contemplation of one security agreement could perfect a security interest provided for in an earlier security agreement. The authors share the view of other commentators that this decision was contrary to the express language of the 1989 Ontario Act and incorrect in principle.[23] To clarify the situation, the Act was amended in 2000 to confirm that a single financing statement may perfect multiple security interests in multiple security agreements "whether or not (a) the security interests or security agreements are part of the same transaction or related transactions; or (b) the security agreements are signed by the debtor before the financing statement is registered."[24]

The Ontario Act continues to differ on one point. Multi-agreement registration is not permitted if the collateral is consumer goods.[25] To avoid the risk that a subsequent refinancing or other change will be

---

18   For recent judicial confirmation, see *Re Sokoloski*, (2002), 4 P.P.S.A.C. (3d) 178 (Alta. Q.B.); *Re Hickman Equipment (1985) Ltd.* (2004), 7 P.P.S.A.C. (3d) 56 (Nfld. C.A.).
19   *Royal Bank v. Agricultural Credit Corp. of Saskatchewan* (1994), 7 P.P.S.A.C. (2d) 1 (Sask. C.A.), rev'g (1991), 2 P.P.S.A.C. (2d) 338 (Sask. Q.B.).
20   *Re Better* (1989), 9 P.P.S.A.C. 158 (Ont. S.C.).
21   OPPSA s. 45(4).
22   (1994), 6 P.P.S.A.C. (2d) 267 (Ont. Ct. Gen. Div.).
23   *Personal Property Security Opinion Report*, § 5.3, note 340 at 85.
24   S.O. 2000, c. 26, Sched. B, s. 16(6) amending OPPSA s. 45(4).
25   OPPSA s. 45(4).

treated as a new security interest, requiring a new registration, secured creditors may choose to specify in the original agreement that the security interest in the consumer goods secures both existing advances and any future advances that may be agreed to between the parties.[26]

4) Distinction between PPSA Registry and a Title Registry

It follows from the adoption of notice-registration, and the concomitant features of advance registration and multi-agreement registration, that the existence of a registered financing statement does not mean that a PPSA security interest necessarily exists; only that one may exist or may be acquired in the future. In adopting this approach, the drafters recognized the fundamental difference between a system for recording title to assets and one for recording security interests. A title registry functions as a conclusive source of positive information for third parties about the current state of title to specific assets. A false registration creates the potential for prejudicial reliance by third parties who purchase or take security in assets in the belief that the registered owner is the true owner. To maintain the integrity of the registry record, some evidentiary proof of the underlying transfer documentation is needed.

In the case of a pure secured transactions registry, however, registration of notice of a security interest where none in fact exists cannot generate prejudicial reliance by potential secured creditors or purchasers. Unlike the case with a title transfer registry, it is the *absence* of registrations in a secured transactions registry on which prospective purchasers and secured creditors rely in deciding to advance funds. Faced with the priority risk presented by a prior registration, they can protect themselves by refusing to go ahead with the transaction unless the registration is discharged or unless the registered secured party undertakes to postpone or subordinate its interest. Since advance registration is permitted, this course of action is necessary in any event for protection against the priority that would otherwise attach to a security interest arising under a subsequent agreement covered by the pre-existing registration.

5) Access to Off-record Information

The old document-filing approach was motivated in part by the perceived need to protect other creditors from the risk that an alleged security agreement in fact reflected a collusive arrangement between

---

26   Ziegel and Denomme, above note 11 at 378.

an insolvent debtor and a preferred unsecured creditor to remove the debtor's assets from the reach of the debtor's other execution creditors. Requiring the security document to be filed provided presumptive evidence of its existence and the date of its execution.

Adoption of a notice registration approach means that the secured transactions registry no longer provides *prima facie* proof of the security interest. Its existence and scope instead depends on the off-record security agreement which, in the absence of possession, must be evidenced by a signed security agreement that describes the collateral to take effect against third parties.[27] To ensure that third parties have access to that evidence, the Act empowers existing creditors and their representatives to require the secured creditor to supply a copy of the security agreement and to furnish up-to-date details on the current status of the financing.[28]

The Ontario Act is somewhat more restrictive. Only judgment creditors, as opposed to unsecured creditors generally, are entitled to demand further information.[29] This limitation may have been based on the assumption that since a judgment is typically a prerequisite to the right of an unsecured creditor to initiate execution against a debtor's assets, the existence of a security interest is irrelevant to an unsecured creditor who has not yet obtained judgment. However, this fails to take into account the fact that the value of any outstanding security interests is part of the information required by an unsecured creditor in determining whether or not it is worthwhile to invest the time and expense involved in obtaining a judgment so as to be in a position to pursue execution.

In addition to unsecured creditors, the Act empowers existing secured creditors and any other third parties with an interest in the assets described in a registration to demand further information from the party named as secured creditor on the registration.[30] As with unsecured creditors, the existence and extent of a prior registered security interest will generally reduce the value of their interests. Moreover, their priority status may be capable of determination only by access to

---

27   For a detailed analysis of the evidentiary and attachment requirements of the Act, see chapter 4.

28   PPSA (A, BC, M, NB, O, PEI, Nu, NWT, S) s. 18; (NL, NS) s. 19; Y s. 17.

29   OPPSA s. 18(1).

30   Under the non-Ontario Acts, secured creditors are eligible to demand further information in their capacity as "creditors": PPSA (A, BC, M, NB, PEI, Nu, NWT, S) s. 18; (NL, NS) s. 19; Y s. 17. Because s. 18 of the Ontario Act applies only to "judgment creditors", existing secured creditors must instead rely on their status as persons with "an interest in the collateral."

further factual details about the secured transaction to which a registration relates. For example, a buyer or lessee of the collateral will generally take free of a registered security interest if it has not yet attached at the time of the sale or lease, and a purchase money security interest generally takes ahead of a prior-registered security interest covering after acquired property.

The Act also empowers the debtor to require the person named as secured party in a registration to supply a copy of the security agreement and to respond to a request for current details about the security agreement including confirmation about whether specified assets are or are not collateral.[31] Instead of responding to the debtor, the debtor can require the secured party to send the response directly to a named third party, such as a prospective purchaser or secured party.[32] A prospective purchaser is safe in relying on the secured party's direct assurance that no security interest currently exists; the Act subordinates an unperfected security interest to the interest of a buyer or lessee and perfection requires attachment as well as registration.[33] However, a prospective secured party cannot assume that it will have a first priority simply because the person named as secured creditor in a registration confirms that no security agreement exists with the debtor or that no indebtedness is currently outstanding. As explained earlier, the Act permits advance registration and multi-agreement registration and priority among competing security interests generally dates from registration, regardless of the order of attachment.[34] It follows that if the debtor later grants security to the first registered secured party, that security interest will have priority, provided that the collateral falls within the collateral description in the registration. For this reason, a subordination agreement is needed.

6) Mandatory Discharge or Amendment of Registration

Registration can have a prejudicial impact on the ability of the person named as debtor in the statement to sell or grant security in the collateral

---

31 PPSA (A, BC, M, NB, O, PEI, Nu, NWT, S) s. 18; (NL, NS) s. 19; Y s. 17.

32 Section 18 of the OPPSA does not expressly contemplate a demand by the debtor to forward the response to a third party. However, the demand must contain an address for reply and the same result can be achieved if the debtor supplies the third party's address as the address for reply

33 For a detailed analysis of priority between a secured party and buyers and lessees of the collateral, see chapter 7.

34 For a detailed analysis of priority among competing PPSA security interests, see chapter 8.

described in the statement. The Act supplies a number of measures to protect the debtor against the risk that a registration does not represent (or no longer represents) an existing or contemplated security interest.

First, the person named as secured party on a registration is required to send a copy of the registration or a verification statement relating to an electronic registration to the person named as debtor within thirty days (twenty days under the British Columbia Act) after registration, unless this right has been waived in writing.[35] In the absence of a written waiver, failure to comply exposes the secured party to liability to pay statutory damages to the debtor.[36] The theory is that by executing a written waiver, the debtor must be taken to have received notice of the registration or impending registration.

Second, where the registration relates to consumer goods, the secured party is under a statutory duty to register a discharge within thirty days after the obligations under the security agreement to which the registration relates have been performed.[37] Once again, non-compliance exposes the secured party to liability for statutory damages.[38] Under the Ontario version, the duty is triggered if the debtor's obligations "have been performed *or forgiven*." The addition of the words "*or forgiven*" should not lead to a difference in substance from the other Acts. Forgiveness equates to performance since it amounts to an agreement to change the content of the original performance obligation.

If the registration does not relate to consumer goods, or does not relate exclusively to consumer goods, the Act does not impose a posi-

---

35   PPSA (M, NB, PEI, Nu, NWT, S) s. 43(12); (A, NB, PEI) s. 43(11); (NL, NS) s. 44(11); BC s. 43(15); O s. 46(6); Y no equivalent provision.

36   PPSA (M, NWT, Nu, S) s. 65(6); (NB, PEI) s. 66(3); (NL, NS) s. 67(3); A s. 67(2); (BC, O, Y) no equivalent provision. The PPSA also creates a general cause of action to recover any reasonably foreseeable actual damages suffered by a person as a result of the failure of the defendant, without reasonable excuse, to discharge any duty or perform any obligation imposed by the Act. PPSA (M, NWT, Nu, S) s. 65(5); A s. 67(1); BC s. 69(3); (NB, PEI) s. 66(2); (NL, NS) s. 67(2); Y s. 62(2). The counterpart provision in the Ontario Act does not extend to a failure to send a verification statement: OPPSA s. 67(2).

37   PPSA (A, BC, M, NB, PEI, Nu, NWT, S, Y) s. 50(2); (NL, NS) s. 51(2); O s. 57.

38   PPSA (M, NWT, Nu, S) s. 65(6); A s. 67(2); M s. 65(2); (NB, PEI) s. 66(3); (NL, NS) s. 67(3); (BC, O, Y) no equivalent provision. The PPSA also creates a general cause of action to recover any reasonably foreseeable actual damages suffered by a person as a result of the failure of the defendant, without reasonable excuse, to discharge any duty or perform any obligation imposed by the Act. PPSA (M, NWT, Nu, S) s. 65(5); A s. 67(1); BC s. 69(3); (NB, PEI) s. 66(2); (NL, NS) s. 67(2); Y s. 62(2). The counterpart provision of the Ontario Act does not extend to failure to perform this obligation. OPPSA s. 67(2).

tive discharge obligation on the secured party.[39] The word "exclusively" is absent from the relevant provision of the Ontario Act.[40] This creates ambiguity in cases where a single registration relates to a security agreement that cover both consumer goods and additional collateral or to multiple security agreements covering consumer goods and additional collateral. Is the secured party required to discharge the registration even though the obligations secured by the additional collateral have not been performed? In the view of the authors, the answer is no. The requirement is triggered only "where all the obligations under a security agreement that creates a security interest in consumer goods" have been performed. The reference to "all the obligations under the security agreement" indicates that the secured party is not required to discharge the registration until the obligation secured by both the consumer goods and the additional collateral has been performed. On this interpretation, the result is the same as if the word "exclusively" had been explicitly included.

There are sound practical reasons for not imposing a positive discharge obligation in the commercial context. Commercial financing is typically a medium- to long-term arrangement, often involving a fluctuating line of credit rather than a lump sum loan, and a series of security agreements rather than a one-off loan or credit transaction. It would be contrary to the interests and intentions of both parties to require the secured party to register a discharge every time there was a temporary pause in financing. Indeed, such a requirement would be contrary to the spirit underlying the provisions allowing advance registration and multiple-agreement registration.

Even commercial financing arrangements are intended to come to an end at some point. In addition, the collateral description contained in the registration may be overly broad, including items or kinds of collateral that are not intended to be the object of any actual or contemplated security agreement between the parties. To address these contingencies, the PPSA empowers the debtor (and any person with an interest in the collateral described in the registration) to send a written demand to the secured party to discharge or amend the registration to reflect the actual status of their relationship.[41] The right is triggered by any of the following circumstances:

---

39 PPSA (A, BC, M, NB, PEI, Nu, NWT, S) s. 50(3); (NL, NS) s. 51(3); O s. 56(1); Y s. 50(4).
40 OPPSA s. 56(1).
41 PPSA (A, BC, M, NB, PEI, Nu, NWT, S) s. 50(3); (NL, NS) s. 51(3); O s. 56(1); Y s. 50(4).

- all the obligations under the security agreement to which the registration relates have been performed;
- the secured party has agreed to release all or part of the collateral
  described in the registration;
- the registered collateral description includes an item or kind of collateral that is not collateral under a security agreement between the
  secured party and the debtor; or
- no security agreement exists between the parties.[42]

An issue of interpretation arises when the registration relates to
more than one security agreement and the obligations under one or
more, but not all the agreements, have been discharged. It is the view
of the authors that, in order to have the right to demand discharge of
the registrations, the obligations under *all* the security agreements to
which the registration relates must be discharged. In other words, the
words "the agreement" should be read to include the plural. The contrary rule would undermine the rule permitting a single registration to
perfect multiple security agreements.

Unless the secured party obtains a contrary court order, non-compliance within the prescribed time period (fifteen days generally — forty
days under the Alberta Act) entitles the person making the demand to
statutory damages.[43] Even more importantly, the person making the demand is empowered to require the registrar to register the discharge or
amendment on proof to the registrar that the demand was made and not
met and after notice to the secured party.[44] The Acts of the four Atlantic
provinces dispense with the latter condition. Once the fifteen days expire without compliance, the debtor is entitled to register the discharge
or amendment unilaterally without having to go through the registrar.[45]

---

42   See, for example, *Mearford Energy Services Inc. v. Class M Planet Corporation*
      (2002), 3 P.P.S.A.C. (3d) 290 (Alta. Q.B.).
43   PPSA (M, NWT, Nu, S) s. 65(6); A s. 67(2); BC s. 69(4); (NB, PEI) s. 66(3); (NL,
      NS) s. 67(3); O s. 56(4); Y no equivalent provision. The PPSA creates a general
      cause of action to recover reasonably foreseeable actual damages suffered by a
      person as a result of the failure of the defendant, without reasonable excuse,
      to discharge any duty or perform any obligation imposed by the Act. PPSA
      (M, NWT, Nu, S) s. 65(5); A s. 67(1); BC s. 69(3); (NB, PEI) s. 66(2); (NL, NS)
      s. 67(2); Y s. 62(2). The counterpart provision in the Ontario Act is does not
      extend to failure to perform this obligation: OPPSA s. 67(2).
44   PPSA (A, M, NB, PEI, Nu, NWT, S, Y) s. 50(5)–(7); BC s. 50(5)–(8); (NL, NS) s.
      51(5)–(7); O no equivalent provision.
45   PPSA (NB, PEI) s. 50(5)–(7), (NL, NS) s. 51(5)–(7). The debtor is liable for
      statutory damages if a discharge or amendment is registered outside the cir-
      cumstances contemplated by the provision: PPSA (NB, PEI) s. 66(4); (NL, NS) s.

A court order is needed only where the security agreement to which a registration relates is a trust indenture. The reason for this exception lies in the need to protect the secured parties of the issuer of the trust indenture against the risk of an inadvertent, negligent, or fraudulent discharge by the trustee.

Although the provisions of the Ontario Act are somewhat different, the right to demand a discharge or amendment arises in substantially the same circumstances.[46] However, there is an important distinction when it comes to the consequences of non-compliance. Although the person making the demand is entitled to statutory damages under the Ontario Act, there is no statutory right to unilaterally bring about the amendment or discharge or require the registrar to do so. A court order is needed in all cases.[47]

In imposing the burden of enforcing compliance on the debtor, the Ontario drafters were worried about the risk that a debtor might register a discharge or amendment in circumstances not authorized by the provision. However, the PPSA gives the secured party who receives a demand the opportunity to obtain a court order prohibiting discharge or amendment.[48] Although the time period for obtaining an order is short, the procedure is summary and the court can always grant a temporary order preserving the registration until the matter is sorted out. Moreover, the registry automatically sends a verification statement to the secured party where a registration is discharged. Indeed, in the Atlantic provinces, the registry sends a verification statement when *any* change is made in the registered particulars; it need not amount to a discharge. If the discharge or amendment was not authorized, the PPSA entitles the secured party on receipt of the statement to reinstitute the registration without any loss in perfected status except as against intervening interests.

67(4). While personal liability may be of little comfort if the debtor is insolvent, the penalty of statutory damages supplies some deterrent for solvent debtors.

46 The person entitled to make a demand under s. 56(1)–(2) of the Ontario Act is "a person with an interest in the collateral." The debtor is not mentioned explicitly. Since the debtor clearly qualifies as a person with an interest in the collateral, the missing words are not significant. In addition, the Ontario Act does not oblige the recipient of the demand to register the amendment or discharge, only to deliver a completed financing change statement or certificate of discharge to the person making the demand.

47 OPPSA s. 56(4)–(5).

48 PPSA (A, M, NB, Nu, NWT, PEI, S) s. 50(5)–(7), BC s. 50(5)–(8), (NS NL) s. 51(5)–(7), Y s. 50(5). There is no similar provision in the Ontario Act but a secured party would be entitled to make an application for relief under s. 67(1)(e) which empowers a court to make any order necessary to protect the interests of any person in the collateral.

7) Registration and Search Criteria

Entries in a registry must be indexed according to set criteria to permit their efficient retrieval. As a general rule, registrations in the Personal Property Registry are indexed and searched by reference to the name of the debtor.[49] Debtor-name indexing greatly liberates the process of taking and perfecting security. Secured parties can perfect a security interest in a debtor's present and after-acquired personal property, or in generic categories of it, through a single one-time registration.

Debtor-name indexing has one drawback. If the debtor transfers the collateral, third parties who deal with the collateral in the hands of the transferee cannot protect themselves by conducting a search of the registry using the name of the transferee. The search will not disclose a security interest registered against the name of the original debtor.

In response to this problem, the PPSA provides for asset-based searching in respect of "serial numbered goods."[50] Serial numbered goods are relatively high-value assets for which there is likely to be a re-sale market and to which reliable numerical identifiers can be assigned. They are defined by regulation to include: a motor vehicle, trailer, mo-bile home (a manufactured home in British Columbia), aircraft, boat, or an outboard motor for a boat.[51] The Ontario and Yukon systems take a less expansive approach: numerical searching is available only in re-spect of motor vehicles.[52]

The registration number assigned by the registry to a previous registration constitutes the third available search criterion.[53] Unlike the other two criteria, it will not normally be useful for third-party searchers because it requires actual knowledge of the existence and details of the registration.

---

49   PPSA (A, BC, M, NWT, Nu, S) s. 48(1), (NB, PEI) s. 48(2), (NL, NS) s. 49(2), O s. 43(1), Y s. 41(1).

50   *Ibid.* Remote parties are also protected by the requirement for a secured party to amend its registration to disclose any transferee from the debtor as a new debtor once the secured party finds out about the transfer.

51   See, for example, NB Reg. s. 1 ("serial numbered goods," "aircraft," "boat," "mo-bile home," "motor vehicle" (note the exclusion of a "tractor"), "trailer"). On the scope of the motor vehicle definition, see *Royal Bank v. Steinhubl's Masonry Ltd.*, 2003 SKQB 299 (forklift qualifies).

52   PPSA O s. 43(1), Y s. 41(1).

53   PPSA (A, BC, M, Nu, NWT, S) s. 48(1), (NB, PEI) s. 48(2), (NL, NS) s. 49(2), Y s. 41(1). Although s. 43(1) of the Ontario Act does not provide expressly for regis-tration number searching, a search according to debtor name or serial number (motor vehicle identification number in the Ontario parlance) is required to disclose the registration number assigned to the registration.

It is technically possible to search using the secured-party name. This is done where there are "global changes" to a secured-party name. However, this type of search is not contemplated by the Act and is done only by registry staff. The identity of the secured party as a search criterion is irrelevant to the legal objectives of the registration system. The quantity and content of registrations by a particular supplier of secured credit may have practical commercial value for other credit suppliers, for example, as a source of a competitor's customer list. However, to allow public access for this purpose would violate reasonable commercial privacy expectations and might damage public trust in the system.

8) Client Access to the Registry for Registration and Searching

The registration records under the pre-PPSA registration statutes were kept in manual form. Moreover, except for corporation securities, a number of provinces maintained their personal property security registries in their county or district land registry offices. The decentralized nature of the records vastly complicated the search process and required complex internal rules to deal with the impact of relocation of the debtor or collateral within a province.

Registrations in the Personal Property Registry are stored in digital form in a single, centralized computer database. This feature greatly reduce the archival burden on the system and eliminates the need to conduct multiple regional searches.

A computerized database also facilitates direct client access to the registry records and all the systems authorize the electronic submission of registrations, and the electronic submission and retrieval of search requests and search results.[54] Most also authorize direct electronic access for the purposes of amendment or discharge.

Geographical equality of access is assured through various combinations of modes of access, depending upon the jurisdiction. These include: direct electronic access from the business premises of clients who have entered into an electronic access arrangement with the registry; attendance at a regional branch administered by the government or private agencies; and fax submissions as well as telephone access in the case of search requests.

---

54 To accommodate direct electronic registration, the PPSA defines "financing statement" and "financing change statement" to include data authorized by the regulations to be electronically transmitted to the registry to effect a registration: S s. 2(1); (A, BC, NWT, Nu, O, Y) s. 1(1); (M, NB, PEI) s. 1; (NL, NS) s. 2.

In the four Atlantic Provinces, electronic access — either from a client's premises or from a branch office of the registry — is the *only* available mode of access for both registration and searching.[55] Although electronic access is by far the most prevalent mode in the other jurisdictions, used in practice for more than 90 percent of registrations, clients retain the option of using a paper registration or submitting a paper search request.

9) Effective Time of Registration

As a general rule, priority between competing security interests that have been perfected by registration depends on the order of registration. It follows that the time at which each registration became legally effective is vital in determining priority among competing registered security interests. The time at which a registration takes legal effect is also critical to the resolution of priorities between a secured party and a buyer or lessee of the collateral, as well as the debtor's unsecured creditors and bankruptcy trustee, against whom a perfected security interest is generally effective.

The PPSA provides that a registration takes effect from the time assigned to it by the registry.[56] Where the registration data is electronically transmitted, the system assigns a time of registration only when the registration data has successfully been entered into the registry database. This means that the effective time of registration is coterminous with the time at which the registration becomes searchable by third parties.

In the Atlantic provinces, electronic registration is the only available mode of registration.[57] However, the other PPSA jurisdictions retain the option of using paper forms for registrations. In Ontario, the time of registration is assigned as soon as the paper statement is physically received in the offices of the registry.[58] The resulting time lag

---

55   The definitions of financing statement and financing change statement in the Atlantic Acts do not contemplate the use of paper registration forms; rather, the definitions are confined to the data authorized by the regulations to effect, amend, or discharge a registration. See PPSA (NB, PEI) s. 1; (NL, NS) s. 2.

56   PPSA (A, BC, M, NWT, Nu) s. 43(2); (NB, PEI) s. 43(4); (NL, NS) s. 44(4); O s. 51(3).

57   Thus, the definitions of financing statement and financing change statement in the Atlantic Acts do not contemplate the use of paper registration forms; rather, they refer simply to the data authorized by the regulations to effect, amend, or discharge a registration. See PPSA (NB, PEI) s. 1; (NL, NS) s. 2.

58   On the Ontario approach and practice, see generally Ziegel and Denomme, above note 11 at 445–46.

between the effective time of registration and the time of searchability creates a priority risk for third parties who may find themselves bound by a registration that has not yet appeared on the public record.[59] In cases where a paper statement was registered at a branch office, the time lag can be up to one business day or more because the paper form has to be couriered to the central office in Toronto before it is scanned or manually keyed into the database.

To deal with this problem, search results in Ontario indicate a "file currency date" that is earlier than the real time of the search. The file currency date means that the search result is only guaranteed to disclose the state of registrations up to that date. Somewhat confusingly, the file currency date is not a cut-off date. Electronic registrations made after the file currency date may and usually will show up on the search result. Nonetheless, the search result is guaranteed only up to that date. It follows that a competing secured party who perfects by registration, and other interested third parties, will have to conduct a second subsearch before being confident in advancing funds or otherwise acting in reliance on the registry record.

In the other jurisdictions where paper financing statements are used, the initial practice was also to assign a time of registration on physical receipt of the paper statement as opposed to entry of the information set out on the paper form into the registry data base by registry personnel. This practice is reflected in the provision found in certain of the Acts that "if two or more financing statements are assigned the same time, the order of registration is determined by reference to the registration numbers assigned to the financing statements in the registry office."[60] This provision was necessitated by the practice of assigning the same time to all registrations that arrived by mail on the same day. Although this practice reduced arbitrariness, it increased the risk that two or more registrations might be assigned the same time. In any event, it seems that the practice today is increasingly to assign the time of registration only upon entry of the information set out on the paper

---

59   On the problems posed by the effective time of registration issue, see further R.C.C. Cuming, "Modernization of Personal Property Security Registries: Some Old Problems Solved and Some New Ones Created" (1983–84) 48 Sask. L. Rev. 189 at 192.

60   PPSA (A, BC, M, NWT, Nu) s. 43(2). In contrast, the Atlantic Acts contemplate that the time of registration will be the same as the time at which the registration number is assigned: see PPSA (NB, PEI) s. 43(4), (NL, NS) s. 44(4). Since electronic registration is the only available medium of registration under the Atlantic Acts, the time and the number are always assigned contemporaneously by the computer system on completion of the registration.

form into the registry system so as to make registration and search-ability coterminous.[61]

10) Liability for Errors or Omissions

The Personal Property Registry is a publicly administered system in the sense that, while the maintenance of the system may be contracted out to the private sector, the administrative responsibility is vested in a publicly appointed registrar and public servants under her supervision.[62] To what extent are these public servants or the government as their employer, responsible for errors or omissions in the operation of the system? In practice, errors or omissions could cause loss in three situations.

The first is where an employee or representative of the registry is alleged to have given incorrect or misleading verbal advice or information. Here, the PPSA excludes liability unless the victim can show bad faith.[63] The Ontario Act goes a little further insofar as it preserves a victim's right of action under general law in respect of a tort committed by a registry employee.[64] The Alberta Act goes in the opposite direction by excluding liability altogether in this situation.[65]

The second potential area of liability is for loss caused by an error or omission in the information entered into the data base of the registry. Here, a distinction is drawn between paper and electronic registrations.

Where the registration data is submitted electronically, the registrant is responsible for entering the data directly into the registry database and thus bears the risk of any errors or omissions. Even if the problem could conceivably have been caused by a malfunction in the

---

61   For example, in e-mail correspondence with the authors, the administrators of the Saskatchewan system confirmed that "prior to 1995, the Saskatchewan PPR placed a date and time stamp on financing statements physically received"; however, "this practice is no longer followed." Since 1995, the practice has become to assign a registration number only "after the data has been entered into the system."

62   PPSA (A, BC, M, NB, PEI, NWT, Nu, Y) s. 42; (NL, NS) s. 43; S s. 40, s. 42; O s. 41. The situation in Alberta is somewhat exceptional. Alberta registry agents are clearly not public officials — the service is wholly privatized though the government retains liability for errors and omissions: see Roderick Wood, "The Evolution of the Personal Property Registry: Centralization, Computerization, Privatization and Beyond" (1996) 35 Alta. L. Rev. 45 at 55.

63   PPSA (M, NB, PEI, S) s. 52(2); BC s. 52(1); (NL, NS) s. 53(2); (NWT, Nu) s. 52(1.1); (A, Y) no equivalent provision.

64   OPPSA s. 42(6).

65   APPSA s. 52(4). The same is true under s. 51 of the Yukon Act.

system itself, the Act excludes liability for the failure of the system to effect an electronic registration or to effect it correctly.[66] The absence of a paper version of the registered data makes an allegation of systemic malfunction impossible to prove.

If a paper registration form is used, the registrant is likewise responsible for the correctness of the information entered on the form. However, the Act gives a cause of action for loss or damage caused by a failure on the part of registry staff to enter the information contained on the paper form into the registry database or to enter it accurately.[67]

The third situation where loss might be caused is where the registry issues a search result that contains erroneous or incomplete information notwithstanding entry of the correct search data by the registry client. In this situation, the Act recognizes liability for loss caused by an error or omission in a printed search result produced by the registry.[68] Issues of proof preclude an action where the claimant alleges an error in a search result viewed electronically or printed at the client's own premises.

Where the alleged error or omission consists in the inaccurate transcription by registry staff of information contained on a paper registration form into the registry database, the person normally entitled to compensation will be any third-party searcher, including a competing secured party, who suffered loss as a result of reliance on the misleading information in the registration.

---

66 PPSA (M, NB, PEI, S) s. 52(2); BC s. 52(1); (NL, NS) s. 53(2); (NWT, Nu) s. 52(1.1). The Alberta Act does not expressly exclude liability in this situation but the same result is achieved via the general exclusionary rule in s. 52(4) combined with s. 52(1) which recognizes an exception only where a paper registration form is used. The same approach is taken in s. 51 of the Yukon Act.

67 PPSA (A, M, NWT, Nu, S) s. 52(1). The BC Act does not create a statutory cause of action for loss or damage caused by Registry error in a paper registration; s. 52(2) merely limits whatever cause of action the victim may have at common law. The section explicitly limits liability where telephone or other remote electronic communication is used to transmit registered data. By negative implication, the door is left open for a common law action for Registry error in the handling of a paper registration. The Atlantic Acts do not recognize liability for error in entering paper registrations since electronic registration is the exclusive medium in those provinces. For the position in Ontario, see further discussion below.

68 PPSA (A, M, NB, NWT, Nu, PEI), s. 52(1); (NL, NS) s. 53(1). The BC Act does not create a statutory cause of action for loss or damage caused by registry error in the production of a search result; however, s. 52 does not exclude or limit whatever liability might exist at common law in this situation.

The position is different if the error or omission consists in the failure of the registry staff to enter the data on a paper financing statement into the system altogether. As explained in the preceding section, except in Ontario, it seems that the practice is to assign the time of registration only upon entry of the registration data into the database. It follows that where a paper financing statement is never entered into the system so as to be assigned a time, it never becomes legally effective and the person potentially suffering the loss will be the secured party whose security interest was never legally perfected as opposed to a third party searcher. The situation is different in Ontario where, as noted in the preceding section, the effective time of registration is assigned on physical receipt of the paper statement in the registry offices with the result that it takes legal effect as of that time as against third party searchers even if never actually entered into the system.

To the limited extent that liability is recognized, the normal mode of recovery, except in Ontario, is through a civil action for damages in the courts. The victim's right of action is prescribed by a special limitation period[69] and there is a monetary limitation on the quantum of allowable recovery.[70]

In Ontario, claims are processed through an application to the registrar for payment of compensation out of the Personal Property Security Assurance Fund.[71] Claims to the fund are subject to limits on quantum[72] and are prescribed by one year from the time that the claimant becomes aware of the loss or damage.[73] Claims are limited to loss caused by an error or omission in the registration or searching system.[74] To be eligible for compensation, the victim must have suffered

---

69 PPSA (M, NB, NWT, Nu, PEI, S), 52(3); A s. 52(2); BC s. 54(3); (NL, NS) s. 53(3); O s. 44(6); Y s. 51(2).

70 PPSA (A, M, NB, NWT, Nu, PEI, S) s. 54(1); (NL, NS) s. 55(1); O s. 44(2); Y s. 51(6); BC no equivalent provision.

71 OPPSA s. 44.

72 The total amount payable cannot exceed $1,000 in relation to any one security agreement: OPPSA s. 44(2). Claims in excess of that amount are paid *pro rata* according to the loss suffered by each claimant: s. 44(21). The amount payable at any given time is further limited to the actual amount in the fund less any approved unpaid claims: s. 44(4).

73 OPPSA s. 44(6).

74 OPPSA s. 44(1). The fund applies only to loss or damage caused by an error on the part of the registration system. Loss caused by an error in the registration or search criteria supplied by a registrant or a searcher clearly does not qualify: *Federal Business Development Bank v. Ontario (Registrar of Personal Property Security)* (1984), 7 D L R (4th) 479 (Ont. Div. Ct.).

the loss as a result of reliance on a certified printed search result or a certified copy of a paper registration form.[75]

The existence of the assurance fund does not preclude a civil action in all circumstances. Although employees and agents of the Ontario registry are protected from personal liability for good faith errors or omissions, the Crown remains liable for any tort committed by them.[76] However, the victim must elect between the two remedies. An application to the compensation fund precludes a civil action against the Crown, and the converse also holds true.[77]

Alberta has also established an assurance fund carried over from pre-PPSA law.[78] However, the fund exists merely as the source of payment of any damages recovered in a civil action. To this there is one exception. The provincial treasurer may pay a claim from the fund, without an action being brought, when authorized by the minister to do so, on the report of the registrar concluding that the claim is justified.[79]

11) Registration Not Constructive Notice

The question of whether registration constituted constructive notice of a security interest was important in prior law because of the complex of common law, equitable and statutory rules that made priority turn on whether a subsequent interest was acquired with notice of a prior interest.[80] The doctrine of constructive notice is irrelevant to the operation of the priority regime established by the PPSA. In order to forestall arguments relying on the concept, the Act expressly provides that registration of a security interest does not constitute constructive notice or knowledge of its existence.[81]

---

75   OPPSA s. 44(4).
76   OPPSA s. 43(5)–(6).
77   OPPSA s. 44(18), (19).
78   APPSA s. 51.1(1) (continuing the Chattel Security Registries Assurance Fund).
79   APPSA s. 54(4).
80   See, for example, J.S. Ziegel, "Registration Statutes and the Doctrine of Constructive Notice" (1985) 63 Can. Bar Rev. 629.
81   PPSA (A, BC, M, NB, NWT, Nu, PEI, S) s. 47; (NL, NS) s. 48; O s. 46(5)(a); Y s. 52(3). Although the doctrine of constructive notice or knowledge based on registration has no legal relevance to priority under the PPSA, taking with actual knowledge of a prior security interest is relevant to the priority of buyers and lessees of collateral under certain of the priority rules of the Act.

12) Transactional Scope of Registry: Non-PPSA Transactions

The mandate of the Personal Property Registry extends beyond registrations under the PPSA to include registrations that are permitted or required under any other Act to be made in the registry.[82] For example, the registry is the designated registration venue in provinces that have enacted legislation to allow for non-possessory, non-consensual liens in favour of repairers, transporters, and storers.[83]

Perhaps the most important category of non-PPSA registrations brought within the system are notices of judgments or writs of execution obtained by unsecured creditors. While not all jurisdictions have reformed their law to allow for this, the experience in those that have is highly positive. In addition to simplifying the judgment enforcement procedure, registration supports a more efficient and equitable system of ordering priorities between a secured party and a judgment creditor.[84]

Other examples are more unique to particular provinces. For example, in several of the Western provinces, the Personal Property Registry is used as the venue for registering floating charges on land for the purposes of land titles legislation,[85] and, in British Columbia, it is the venue for registrations under that province's *Manufactured Homes Act*.[86]

As a result of amendments made in 1992, the federal *Bankruptcy and Insolvency Act* now provides that statutory charges and liens in favour of the federal or provincial governments take effect, as a general rule, only when registered in a public registry available to all creditors.[87] The

---

82   PPSA (A, BC, M, NB, NWT, Nu, PEI, S) s. 42(1); (NL, NS) s. 43(1); O s. 41(1); Y s. 40.

83   See, for example, *Repairers' Lien Act*, R.S.B.C. 1996, c. 404, as am. S.B.C. 1997, c. 45, s. 53; *Repair and Storage Liens Act*, R.S.O. 1990, c. R.25; *Commercial Liens Act*, S.S. 2001, c. 15.1.

84   For a detailed analysis, see chapter 10.

85   See, for example, s. 198.1 of the *Land Titles Act*, R.S.B.C. 1991, c. 250, as am. R.S.B.C. 1996, c. 250 (Supp.), s. 4; 1997, c. 25, ss. 31–42. Generally see R.J. Wood, "The Floating Charge on Land in the Western Provinces" (1991) 20 Can. Bus. L.J. 132.

86   *Manufactured Home Act*, R.S.B.C. 1996, c. 280, as am. R.S.B.C. 1996, c. 280 (Supp.) ss. 1–9.

87   *Bankruptcy and Insolvency Act*, R.S.C. 1985, c. B-3, as substantially re-enacted by S.C. 1992, c. 27, provides in ss. 86–87 that Crown claims secured by a statutory security interest are reduced to unsecured status unless the "security is registered pursuant to a prescribed system of registration" s. 87(1). Under the regulations, a prescribed system is "a system of registration of securities that is available to Her Majesty in right of Canada or a province and to any other creditor holding a security, and is open to the public for inspection or for the

Personal Property Registry clearly qualifies, and a number of PPSA jurisdictions have expressly amended their legislation to provide for registration of Crown security interests in that venue.[88] Some provinces have
not taken this step principally because registration does not necessarily produce the desired outcome. Even when registered, the Crown lien
takes subject to all prior-registered security interests, at least in collateral
existing at the date of registration of the Crown lien. Therefore, it loses
the superpriority typically extended to it by the provincial or federal
statute under which it arises. Moreover, a registered Crown lien is effective only for the outstanding monetary amount specified in the registration so that constant amendments are needed to maintain the value of
the security as the defaults in payment accumulate. Finally, Crown liens
usually arise late in the life of a financially troubled debtor, and by the
time the default is discovered there is often insufficient value left in the
debtor's assets for the registration to produce any real benefit.

The use of the registry for disclosure of encumbrances created or
regulated by other laws offers searchers the convenience and efficiency
of a single search venue. Priority as between a PPSA security interest
and statutory security interests arising under other law is addressed
in chapter 14. However, two points are worthy of re-emphasis here.
First, the statutes authorizing the registration of non-consensual liens
do not necessarily provide uniform or clear rules on the priority effect
of registration. Second, not all non-consensual, non-possessory security interests are required to be registered.

C. REQUIRED REGISTRATION DATA

1) Debtor Name and Address

The name of the debtor is the only universally available criterion for
searching the records of the Personal Property Registry.[89] As such,
entry of the name and address of the debtor (or debtors if there are mul-

---

making of searches" (SOR/98-240, s. 1, s. 111 of the Bankruptcy and Insolvency
General Rules).

88 For example, in British Columbia, see the *Miscellaneous Registrations Act*, R.S.B.C.
1996, c. 312. In Ontario see, for example, s. 19.1 of the *Gasoline Tax Act*, R.S.O.
1990, c. G.5, as am. On the impact of the BIA amendments, see generally R.J.
Wood and M.I. Wylie, "Non-Consensual Security Interests in Personal Property"
(1992) 30 Alta. Law Rev. 1055 at 1095–98. And see further chapter 14.

89 PPSA (A, BC, M, NWT, Nu, S) s. 48(1); (NB, PEI) s. 48(2); (NL, NS) s. 49(2); O
s. 43(1); Y s. 41(1).

tiple debtors) is an essential component of a valid registration. Indeed, where electronic registration is used, most systems are programmed to reject a registration if the field for entering the debtor's name and address is not completed.

The PPSA definition of debtor includes both the person who owns or has rights in the collateral in which that person grants a security interest, and the person who owes payment or performance of the obligation secured by that security interest.[90] Where these are not the same person, the definition confirms that the meaning of debtor depends on the legislative context in which the term is used. Since the object of registration is to disclose the possible existence of a security interest in the identified collateral, it is obvious that the debtor whose name must appear on the registration is the person who owns or has rights in the collateral. A debtor who is only liable on the secured obligation need not be named even if that person is a guarantor of the secured obligation. Although a guarantor of a secured debt is entitled to an assignment by way of real subrogation of the security interest upon payment to the secured creditor, the guarantor does not acquire proprietary rights in the collateral unless and until the assignment actually takes place.

2) Individual versus Enterprise Debtors

A registrant must indicate whether the debtor is an "individual" or a "natural person," on the one hand, or an "enterprise,"[91] a "business debtor,"[92] or an "artificial body,"[93] on the other hand. Although the terminology varies, the basic dividing line is the same in all jurisdictions. For the sake of brevity, this text uses the terms "individual" and "enterprise." Accurate designation is essential because the two categories of debtors are stored in separate searchable fields within the registry database. A search in the enterprise database will not disclose a security interest registered against an individual debtor, and the converse is also true.

---

90   See the statutory definition of debtor in PPSA: S s. 2(1); (A, M, NB, NWT, Nu, PEI, Y) s.1; (BC, O) s.1(1); (NL, NS) s. 2(1). And see also the analysis of the definition in chapter 1.

91   This is the term used in the regulation under the Acts in the Atlantic provinces, the Northwest Territories, and Nunavut. See, for example, NB Reg. s. 19, 1 ("enterprise").

92   This is the term used in the regulation under the Acts in the Western provinces. See, for example, BC Reg. ss. 9(5), 1 ("business debtor name" and "artificial body").

93   This is the term used in the Ontario system. See Ont. Reg. ss. 16, 1 ("artificial body").

3) Name Rules for Individual Debtors

In identifying an individual debtor, the PPSA regulation requires entry of the surname (last name), the first (first given) name, and the first middle name (in Ontario, the initial of the first middle name).[94] The Canadian Conference on Personal Property Security Law (CCPPSL)[95] has approved the rules shown in Table 6.1 for determining an individual's correct legal name.

Table 6.1 *Name Rules for Individual Debtors*

Status of Individual Debtor	Documentary Source of Name
Born in Canada with birth registered in Canada	Birth certificate
Born in Canada but birth not registered in Canada	1) Current Canadian passport 2) If the debtor does not have a current Canadian passport, current Canadian social insurance card 3) If the debtor does not have a current Canadian passport or SIN card, current foreign passport from jurisdiction of habitual residence
Naturalized Canadian citizen (i.e., not born in Canada but a Canadian citizen)	Canadian citizenship certificate
Not born in Canada and not a Canadian citizen	1) Current Canadian visa 2) If the debtor does not have a current Canadian visa, current foreign passport issued by jurisdiction where debtor habitually resides 3) If the debtor does not have a current visa or current foreign passport, governmental birth certificate issued at debtor's birth place

Under the CCPPSL rules, the name shown on the document must be used, even if the individual goes by a nickname or a shortened form of name. However, to give *de facto* notice and thereby avoid future disputes, the commonly used name may be recorded as a separate debtor name.

---

94 In some communities, it is customary to use an individual's surname as the first name followed by their given name or names. If a registrant is not certain about the correct order of the names, prudence requires entry of the possible variations on separate debtor lines or fields.

95 On the history of the Conference, see chapter 1.

If a debtor has changed his or her name by marriage or in accord-ance with change of name legislation, the CCPPSL rules stipulate that the name of the debtor is the name adopted after marriage (if recog-nized in the debtor's jurisdiction of habitual residence)[96] or the name stated in the debtor's change of name certificate, as the case may be. If a married debtor uses both antenuptial and postnuptial names (for example, different names in professional versus personal or social con-texts), both names must be recorded. In the rare event no other rule covers a case; the default rule requires entry of the name that appears on any two of the following government-issued documents: a current motor vehicle operator's licence, a current vehicle registration, or a cur-rent medical insurance card.

The CCPPSL rules have been adopted in the Atlantic provinces, Al-berta, Manitoba, the Northwest Territories, and Nunavut.[97] In the other jurisdictions, the regulations do not stipulate an authoritative source. The evolution of the applicable rules has been left to the courts with somewhat mixed results.

The Ontario courts have concluded that the name appearing on the debtor's birth certificate is the correct name,[98] a conclusion supported by the authors, and reflected in the regulation under the Ontario Act.[99] A birth certificate rule is consistent with the general understanding of what constitutes an individual's legal name under vital statistics and change of name legislation. Most importantly, it ensures certainty and predictability for both registrants and searchers, and avoids the need for litigation on what constitutes the correct version of the *de facto* name.

Prior to the adoption of the CCPPSL rules by Alberta, the Alberta Court of Appeal ruled that the debtor's name for the purposes of the

---

96   In *Re Grisenthwaite* (1987), 7 P.P.S.A.C. 71 (Ont. S.C. (Mast.)), the debtor's first husband died and she remarried. She commonly used her first husband's surname, but she also used her new husband's surname. The debtor's occasional use of her second husband's surname meant that it was her legal surname at common law and under the Ontario *Change of Name Act* as it then read (R.S.O. 1980, c. 62, s. 2(1); see now S.O. 1986, c. 7 (now R.S.O. 1990, c. C.7)). The regis-tration used the surname of the debtor's first husband's and was therefore held to be invalid.

97   PPSA Reg: A s. 20; M s. 14; NB s. 20; NL s. 20; NS s. 20; NWT s. 19; PEI s. 19.

98   *Re Haasen* (1992), 8 O.R. (3d) 489 (Gen. Div.). For Canadian citizens born out-side Canada, the name appearing on the individual's Canadian citizenship cer-tificate has been held to be "the most practical and rational" source for OPPSA registration purposes: *C.I.B.C. v. Melnitzer (Trustee of)* (1993), 6 P.P.S.A.C. (2d) 5 at 43 (Ont. Ct. Gen. Div.); *Re Takhatalian* (1982), 2 P.P.S.A.C. 90 (Ont. H.C.J.). Compare with *Re Kniaziew* (1994), 8 P.P.S.A.C. (2d) 13 (Ont. Ct. Gen. Div.).

99   O Reg. ss. 3(1)(c), 16(1).

PPSA does not necessarily mean the name on the debtor's birth certificate or other legal name document. A variation suffices if the evidence shows that it is commonly used by the debtor.[100] Although the Court acknowledged the strong legal and policy arguments in favour of the birth certificate rule, it was unwilling to impose such a requirement on registrants in the absence of an explicit legislative directive. The British Columbia courts have adopted the same position, at least at the lower court level.[101]

These decisions may have been influenced by the fact that the challenge to the validity of the registration was brought by a trustee in bankruptcy. Courts have sometimes been unsympathetic to the trustee because of the absence of any risk of direct detrimental reliance on the Registry. However, the legislation does not leave any room for a "flexible" interpretation depending on the source of the challenge. Moreover, this attitude threatens the efficacy of the registry system. The general body of unsecured creditors represented by the trustee *do* rely on the Registry as an efficient source of reliable information about their enforcement rights against assets in the hands of a debtor.

4) Birth Date of Individual Debtors

If more than one grantor shares the same name, the provision of the debtor's address will often resolve the identity issue for searchers. However, where the name is a very common one shared by many individuals in the same community, the address may be insufficient and further inquiry may be needed. To assist in resolving the issue, the Ontario system requires the registration of the birth date of a debtor who is a natural person.[102] In the other provinces, the entry of a birth date is optional.

5) Enterprise Debtors

The enterprise classification is not synonymous with either a legal person or a business entity. In addition to corporations, the concept extends to partnerships, unincorporated associations or organizations, syndicates

---

100 *Miller, McClelland Ltd. v. Barrhead Savings & Credit Union Ltd.* (1995), 9
P.P.S.A.C. (2d) 102 (Alta. C.A.), rev'g (1993), 5 P.P.S.A.C. (2d) 163 (Alta. Q.B.).
See also *Re Paquette* (1993), 5 P.P.S.A.C. (2d) 136 (Alta. Q.B.), aff'd (1994), 6
P.P.S.A.C. (2d) 190 (Alta. Q.B.), application for reconsideration refused (1994), 6
P.P.S.A.C. (2d) 401 (Alta. Q.B.).
101 *Re Fraser* (1994), 6 P.P.S.A.C. (2d) 235 (B.C.S.C.); *Re Logan* (1992), 73 B.C.L.R.
(2d) 377 (S.C.); *Re Lazarchuk* (1994), 7 P.P.S.A.C. (2d) 155 (B.C.S.C.).
102 O Reg. s. 3(1)(c).

or joint ventures, estates of deceased individuals, trade unions, trusts, estates of bankrupts, and other enterprises that grant security in the assets "belonging" to the enterprise. Although nowhere said explicitly, the distinction between the two classifications lies in whether the transaction is entered into on behalf of the entity and in relation to the assets attributed to the enterprise. Thus, the concept does not include an individual who carries on a sole proprietorship, even if the business is operated under a name and style other than the individual's name. The individual's own name must be entered in the field designated for individual debtors in accordance with the rules governing individual debtors. To assist searchers to identify the relevant debtor, a registrant may also enter the individual's business name and style as a separate enterprise debtor in the same registration. This additional information is entirely optional, however, and has no legal effect.

If the debtor is a body corporate, the formal legal name for registration purposes is determined by the general law governing the particular type of body corporate. However, the regulations address the case where the name of the body corporate takes separate English and French forms or a combined English-French form or all three. Except in Alberta, all linguistic forms of the name must be entered as separate debtor names within the single registration.[103] In Alberta, only the form used in business dealings in Alberta need be included.

The formal legal name of the corporation must be entered. Trade names are not sufficient. So a numbered company (for example, "366551 Alberta Inc.") that does business under a trade name (for example, "M.S.T. Trucking Co.") must register by its numbered name and not its trade name.[104]

The PPSA Regulation also covers the use of abbreviations such as "Ltd.," "Inc.," and "Co." to indicate corporate status. The system has been programmed to disregard such terms in conducting a search for an enterprise debtor. Consequently, precision is not essential on this point and the registrant may enter, with or without a period, either the abbreviation or the full word.[105]

---

103 *Armstrong, Thomson & Tubman Leasing Ltd. v. McGill Agency Inc. (Trustee of)* (1993), 5 P.P.S.A.C. (2d) 231 at 234–36 (Ont. Ct. Gen. Div.).
104 *Case Power & Equipment v. 366551 Alberta Inc. (Receiver of)* (1994), 23 Alta. L.R. (3d) 361, 8 P.P.S.A.C. (2d) 267, 118 D.L.R. (4th) 637, 157 A.R. 212, 77 W.A.C. 212 (C.A.); *K.J.M. Leasing Ltd. v. Grandstrand Bros. Inc. (Receiver Manager of)* (1994), 7 P.P.S.A.C. (2d) 197 (Alta. Q.B.).
105 See *GMAC Leaseco Ltd. v. Royal Bank* (1992), 4 P.P.S.A.C. (2d) 4 (B.C.S.C.). Compare *Universal Handling Equipment v. Redipac Recycling* (1992), 4 P.P.S.A.C. (2d) 15 (Ont. Ct. Gen. Div.).

The rules governing the entry of the names of unincorporated enterprise debtors are summarized in Table 6.2.

Table 6.2 *Rules for Enterprise Debtor Names*

Type of Enterprise	Name Requirements
Estate of Deceased Individual	Name of the deceased individual followed by the word "estate"
Trade Union	1) Name of the trade union; and 2) Name of each person representing the trade union in the transaction giving rise to the registration.
Trustee acting for Named Trust	Name of trust as indicated in the document creating the trust followed by the word "trust" unless the name already contains that word
Trustee acting for Unnamed Trust	Name of at least one of the trustees, entered in the order of first name, middle name if any, and last name, followed by the word "trustee"
Trustee acting for Estate of a Bankrupt Individual	Name of the trustee, entered in the order of first name, middle name if any, and last name, followed by the word "bankrupt"
Trustee acting for Estate of a Bankrupt Enterprise	Name of bankrupt enterprise followed by the word "bankrupt"
Registered Partnerships	Firm name of partnership as stated in the certificate or declaration filed under the applicable partnership legislation
Any other Partnership	1) Firm name of partnership, if any, and the name of at least one of the partners; or 2) If the partnership does not have a name, the names of all of the partners
Syndicate or Joint Venture	1) Name of the syndicate or joint venture as stated in its constituting document; and 2) The name of all participants
Other Enterprise	1) Name of the association, organization or other enterprise (as stated in its constituting charter or other document if there is one); and 2) Name of each person representing the association, organization or other enterprise in the transaction giving rise to the registration

As the table indicates, a registrant is sometimes required to enter the name of a representative of the enterprise in addition to the name of the enterprise *per se*. If the representative is an individual, the name must be entered in the manner provided for entering the name of an individual debtor; if the representative is a body corporate, then the rules governing the entry of the name of a body corporate apply. A representative for these purposes is a person who has power to bind the enterprise or its officers or members and who has exercised that power in the formation of the transaction giving rise to the registration.

6) Name and Address of Secured Party

The PPSA Regulation prescribes the same rules for registering the name and address of the secured creditor that apply to the debtor. However, since the secured party name is not a search criterion, strict accuracy is generally not essential.[106] Substantial accuracy is nonetheless important since searchers will rely, and are entitled to rely, on the Registry record for the purposes of contacting the secured party to obtain further information concerning the secured transaction underlying the registration.[107] Consequently, incorrect information may expose the secured creditor to liability in the event of detrimental reliance by a third party on incorrect data.

7) Description of General Collateral

In theory, in a notice registration system, there is no absolute necessity for the registration to identify the collateral. However, the absence of a description would limit the debtor's ability to sell or grant security in assets that remain unencumbered. Prospective buyers and secured creditors would require some form of protection — for example, a release from the secured creditor — before entering into transactions involving any of the debtor's assets. The absence of a description would also diminish the information value of the registry record for insolvency administrators and judgment enforcement creditors.

For these reasons, the PPSA regulation requires a description of the encumbered assets to be registered. Two separate sections or fields are available for the description of collateral. One is for serial number goods, discussed immediately below. The other section is for all other collateral ("general collateral").

---

106 Compare with *John Deere Credit Inc. v. Standard Oilfield Services Inc.* (2000), 79 Alta. L.R. (3d) 166 (Q.B.), where an incorrect secured party name rendered the financing statement seriously misleading.

107 PPSA (A, BC, M, NB, NWT, Nu, O, PEI, S) s. 18; (NL, NS) s. 19; Y s. 17.

Except in Ontario, the rules governing general collateral descriptions for the purposes of registration are the same as the rules governing collateral descriptions in security agreements:[108] the collateral may be described by item or kind or as "all present and after acquired personal property" or as "all present and after acquired personal property" subject to specified item or kind exclusions. As in the case of a security agreement, a description of the collateral as consumer goods or equipment without further reference to the kind of collateral is inadequate for the purposes of registration; a description of collateral as inventory is adequate only while the collateral is held as inventory. These qualifications exist because "consumer goods," "equipment," or "inventory" only describe how the collateral is used by the particular debtor and are not in themselves reliable identifiers from the perspective of third parties. For example, a cow could be equipment, consumer goods, or inventory depending upon whether the cow is held for dairy farming purposes, for household purposes, or for sale.

The Ontario approach is very different. The description requirements for general collateral are so minimal that they diminish the ability of searchers to rely on the registry record in determining whether or not a particular asset is charged with security. The registrant need only place a checkmark in a box next to the generic category into which the collateral falls: consumer goods, inventory, equipment, accounts, or other (to be used where the collateral does not fall within the preceding categories or includes a combination of these categories, or covers all present and after acquired personal property).[109] Although the form allows for a more detailed textual description, this is purely optional.[110]

8) Description of Serial Numbered Goods

The individual or business name of the debtor, as the case may be, is a universal search criterion. Yet it is not always an adequate one. Suppose the debtor sells collateral subject to a registered security interest outright to a third party who, in turn, proposes to sell or grant security in it to a fourth party. Assuming the fourth party is unaware that the third party acquired the collateral from the original debtor, he or she will search the registry using only the third party's name. That

108 PPSA (A, BC, M, NB, NWT, Nu, PEI, S) s. 10(1)(b); (NL, NS) s. 11(1)(b); Y s. 8(1). For a detailed analysis of the description requirements for security agreements, see chapter 4.
109 O Reg s. 3(1)(f).
110 O Reg s. 3(1)(11).

search obviously will not disclose the registered security interest. This is sometimes referred to as the A-B-C-D problem.

To alleviate the risk faced by remote transferees, the PPSA requires a more specific serial number description to be registered in the appropriate field where the collateral consists of specified "large ticket" manufactured goods for which unique, accurate, and permanently affixed identification numbers or marks are available: motor vehicles, trailers, mobile homes, aircraft, boats, and outboard motors for boats. The Ontario and Yukon systems take a more circumscribed approach: serial number (vehicle identification number — VIN) description is required only if the collateral is a motor vehicle, with motor vehicle defined to exclude boats, aircraft, farm tractors, and road-building equipment.[111]

Table 6.3 shows the rules that are used to determine the serial number of goods falling within the definition of serial numbered goods in jurisdictions other than Ontario and the Yukon.

Table 6.3 *Rules for Determining Serial Numbers*

Type of Serial Numbered Goods	Serial Number
Combine, tractor, mobile home, or trailer	Manufacturer's serial number marked on or attached to the chassis
Any other motor vehicle including an automobile, truck, motorcycle, or motorized bicycle	Vehicle Identification Number (VIN) located on body frame
Boat registered, recorded, or licensed under the *Canada Shipping Act*	Registration or recording or licence number of boat assigned pursuant to the Act
Any other boat	Manufacturer's serial number marked on or attached to the boat
Outboard Motor	Manufacturer's serial number marked on or attached to the motor
Aircraft that must be registered under the law of a foreign state that is a party to the *Convention on International Civil Aviation*, 1944 (Chicago)	Registration marks assigned to airframe (omitting any hyphen)
Aircraft — any aircraft not mentioned above	Manufacturer's serial number marked on or attached to the Airframe

---

111 OPPSA s. 43(1); YPPSA s. 41(1).

In addition to the serial number itself (or at least the last twenty-five characters), the regulation stipulates that the description must also indicate the type of the collateral (for example, motor vehicle, boat) and the make, model, and model year of the collateral.

Boats registered under the *Canada Shipping Act* would normally be charged as security by way of a ship's mortgage under Canadian maritime law and registered in the *Canada Shipping Act* registry rather than the Personal Property Registry.[112]

Upon the enactment into Canadian law of the *Convention on International Interests in Mobile Equipment* and the associated Aircraft Protocol, security interests in aircraft objects (air frames, engines, and helicopters of the size and capacity set out in the protocol) will instead be registered in an international registry and the priority effects of registration will generally be determined by the convention as opposed to the PPSA.[113]

In interpreting any ambiguity in the definitions of the various categories of goods that constitute serial numbered goods, regard should be had to the purpose of the designation. Under this approach, serial numbered goods are goods that, because of their capacity for self-propulsion or their inherent portability, are particularly susceptible to being transferred from the debtor to a buyer and from one buyer to another through "secondhand" and "private sale" markets. This is in contrast to goods that, because of their inherent limited mobility or their association with a specific activity or place, are less susceptible to multiple resales, and for which third parties, as a general rule, are therefore adequately protected by a general collateral description.

Royal Bank v. Steinhubl's Masonry Ltd.[114] provides judicial support for this approach. The court was called upon to interpret the definition of motor vehicle in the serial numbered goods context. The PPSA regulation defines motor vehicle as a mobile device that is propelled primarily by any power other than muscular power: (1) in, on, or by which person or thing may be transported or drawn, and that is designed for use on road or natural terrain; or (2) that is used in construction or maintenance of roads. The court construed the term "natural terrain" in the context of this definition to have a meaning similar to that of "road," with the result that the term "motor vehicle" for the purposes of the regulation was interpreted to include self-propelled mobile devices

---

112 See also R. Wood, "The Nature and Definition of Federal Security Interests" (2000) 34 Can. Bus. L.J. 65 at 94–96.

113 See further chapters 1 and 14.

114 Above note 51.

with high mobility designed for use in relatively unrestricted places or facilities in contrast to self-propelled vehicles designed with limited mobility primarily for use in confined contexts. Applying this test, the forklift at issue in the case was held to fall into the first category (motor vehicle). Motorized wheelchairs and motorized wheelbarrows were offered as examples of the latter category (not serial numbered goods). This approach was based on the theory that the greater mobility and geographical scope of usage of goods in the first category rendered them more susceptible to the A-B-C-D problem at which the serial numbered registration requirement was directed.

For serial number searching to work, there must be a commensurate obligation on secured parties to register the number in the appropriate space or field. Such a requirement limits the ability of a secured party to perfect a security interest in after-acquired serial numbered goods through a single registration; an amendment will be needed to add the serial number as each new item is acquired by the debtor. However, serial number identification is not mandatory for all serial numbered goods. It is a precondition to a valid registration only for serial numbered goods that constitute consumer goods in the hand of the debtor.[115]

Where serial numbered goods are held by the debtor as equipment, entry of the serial number is optional in the sense that the security interest will still be considered perfected provided the goods are included in the general description of the collateral.[116] However, without the serial number, the secured creditor is at risk of subordination to a buyer or lessee of the collateral and to a competing secured creditor who includes the serial number in its registration.[117] The position is somewhat different in Ontario and the Yukon. In those jurisdictions the security interest is only subordinated to a buyer and not to another secured party.[118]

In the case of serial numbered goods held by the debtor as inventory, a serial number description is not required and provides no legal advantage. A contrary rule would impose an unworkable registration burden on secured parties, thereby undermining an important goal of

---

115 See for example NB Reg. s. 23(1)(a);O Reg. s. 3(7). And see further chapters 7 and 8.
116 See for example NB Reg. s. 23(1)(c); O Reg. s. 3(8). And see further chapters 7 and 8.
117 For secured parties see: PPSA s. 35(4); (A, BC, M, NB, NWT, NU, PEI, S) s. 35(4); (NL, NS) s. 36(4); for buyers see: PPSA (A, BC, M, NB, NWT, N, PEI, S) s. 30(6)–(7); (NL, NS) s. 31(6)–(7).
118 OPPSA s. 28(5); Y s. 29.

the PPSA — the facilitation of inventory secured financing. Moreover, serial number identification of inventory is unnecessary to protect third parties. Buyers and lessees who take in the ordinary course of the debtor's business will take free of the security interest in any event and a generic description of inventory adequately identifies the collateral for the purposes of other creditors and the debtor's insolvency administrator.

9) Description of Proceeds

The same collateral description requirements that apply to registrations covering original collateral, including the requirements for serial number description, also apply to a registration that is intended to cover proceeds of the original collateral. So, for example, a registration covering "inventory" would not cover "accounts" arising from the sale of the goods; accounts would need to be listed as a separate category of collateral.[119] The exceptions are Ontario and Manitoba where a simple check mark next to a "proceeds" box suffices except in the case of a motor vehicle where the VIN must be specified. In the Yukon Territory a box must be ticked where a party claims proceeds and where a purchase money security interest is claimed.[120] The effect of an error in respect of these requirements is uncertain.

10) Duration of Registration

The duration of secured financing relationships can vary considerably. The PPSA accommodates the need for flexibility by allowing registrants to self-select the desired term of the registration: anywhere from one to twenty-five whole years or infinity.[121]

The Ontario PPSA imposes one qualification on variable registration. If the collateral is consumer goods, the registration life is deemed to be five years unless a shorter period is specified.[122] This exception is intended to protect consumer debtors against the risk of stale registrations remaining on the record, thereby hampering their access to credit. In the view of the authors, this risk is sufficiently contained by

---

119 However, depending on the form that the proceeds take, the secured party may be able to rely on automatic perfection of its proceeds security interest. For a detailed analysis, see chapter 12.
120 See OIC 1982/092 s. 5.
121 NB Reg. s. 17; O Reg. ss. 3(1)(b), 3(4) and 3(6).
122 PPSA s. 55(5).

the statutory obligation cast on secured parties to discharge a registration against consumer goods within thirty days after all obligations under the security agreement that created the security interest have been performed,[123] with statutory damages payable in the event of non-compliance.[124]

To further encourage timely discharge, no fee is charged for entry of a discharge. To discourage excessive registration terms, fees are based on an incremental tariff related to the length of the registration life selected (with the exception of Nova Scotia which charges a flat fee).

D. SUBSEQUENT CHANGES

1) Introduction

A secured party may wish to amend a registration for a wide variety of reasons: for example, to correct an error or omission; to record the effect of a court order or a change in the name or address of a party; or to add or release an item of collateral or a debtor. As a general rule, a financing change statement is used to register any changes to the initial registration. In registering an amendment, the registrant is generally required to identify the registration number assigned by the registry to the original registration. It is essential that the number be accurate since it serves to link the information on the financing change statement to the "family" of registrations to which it relates.

Failure to register a financing change statement in relation to some types of changes may result in subordination to subsequent interests or loss of perfected status. In other cases, registration is optional in the sense that failure to register has no impact on perfected or priority status. The various possibilities are canvassed below.

---

123 PPSA (A, BC, M, NB, NWT, Nu, PEI, S, Y) s. 50(2); (NL, NS) s. 51(2); O s. 57.
124 PPSA (M, NWT, Nu, S) s. 65(6); A s. 67(2); BC s. 69(4); (NB, PEI) s. 66(3); (NL, NS) s. 67(3); O s. 57(2); Y no equivalent provision. The PPSA also creates a general cause of action to recover any reasonably foreseeable actual damages suffered by a person as a result of the failure of the defendant, without reasonable excuse, to discharge any duty or perform any obligation imposed by the Act: (M, NWT, S) s. 65(5); A s. 67(1); (NB, PEI) s. 66(2); (NL, NS) s. 67(2); Y s. 62(2). The scope of the Ontario provision is more limited and does not extend to failure to perform this obligation: OPPSA s. 67(2).

2) Transfer of a Security Interest

The PPSA makes it clear that if a secured party transfers a security interest perfected by registration, it is unnecessary to update the registration to disclose the identity of the new secured party.[125] Failure to record a transfer of the security interest does not undermine its searchability since the principal search criterion is the name of the debtor. Where a transfer is registered, this is effected by amending the original registration to delete the name of the original secured party and to add the name of the new secured party. In the case of a partial transfer, the original secured party will remain on the record and the registrant must describe the collateral affected by the transfer.

The situation is different where the security interest which is transferred is not perfected by registration at the time of the transfer. Here, the transferee will need to register in order to perfect the security interest (unless the security interest is one that was perfected by possession and possession has also been transferred). The Act confirms that the registration may name the transferee as the secured party.[126] There is no need, in other words, to first register in the name of the original secured party.

Although it is optional, registration of a transfer of a security interest is prudent. If the record is unchanged, the original secured party remains vulnerable to demands for information on the current status of a registered security interest. Failure to record the assignment may also entail potential loss for the transferee of the security interest. Both the secured party of record and a successor in interest are estopped from denying the validity of information supplied by the original secured party unless the transfer was registered or the person making the demand knew the identity and address of the transferee.[127]

A change in the identity particulars of the secured party may come about not as a result of a transfer of the security interest but because of a change in the name or the address of the original secured party. The registry systems have been designed to efficiently accommodate this eventuality. On submission of a global financing statement, registry

---

125 PPSA (A, BC, M, NB, NWT, Nu, PEI, S) s. 45(1); (NL, NS) s. 46(1); O s. 47(1); Y s. 44(1). For judicial confirmation, see *Kevill v. Trans-Canada Credit Corp.* (1979), 23 O.R. (2d) 432 (Co. Ct.); *Re Orion Truck Centre Ltd.* (2003), 17 B.C.L.R. (4th) 337 (S.C.).

126 PPSA (A, BC, M, NB, NWT, Nu, PEI, S) s. 45(3); (NL, NS) s. 46(3); O s. 47(2); Y s. 44(4).

127 PPSA (A, BC, M, NB, NWT, Nu, PEI, O, S) s. 18; (NL, NS) s. 19; Y s. 17.

staff will change the relevant particulars for all registrations of that secured party.

3) Subordination of Priority

Where a secured party agrees to subordinate or postpone a registered security interest to the interest of somebody else, the Act authorizes registration of an amendment to disclose the subordination.[128] Disclosure is optional, since the subordination only affects the priority position of the parties bound by it.

4) Change in Debtor Name or Transfer of Collateral

The transfer by the debtor of her interest in the collateral undermines the publicity function of registration. So does a change in the debtor's name. The debtor's name is the principal search criterion and a search using the debtor's new name or the name of the debtor's transferee will not disclose an interest registered against the old name or the original debtor.

Where the secured party gives its prior consent to the transfer by the debtor, the PPSA requires the secured party to amend the registration to disclose the transferee as a new debtor or to take possession of the collateral before the expiration of fifteen days after the transfer.[129] It is the transfer itself that triggers the running of the grace period, notwithstanding that the prior consent of the secured party indicates advance knowledge of the pending transfer.[130] "Prior consent" in this context clearly means consent to the transfer, not consent to the transfer free of the security interest. Otherwise, the security interest would not continue in the collateral in the hands of the transferee[131] and the question of preserving perfected status would not arise.

If the transfer by the debtor was unauthorized, the secured party is unlikely to have advance knowledge. The same risk is present where the legal name of the original debtor changes. There is no question that these changes still present a risk to third parties who deal with

---

128 PPSA (A, BC, M, NB, NWT, Nu, PEI, S) s. 45(6); (NL, NS) s. 46(6); O s. 50; Y s. 47(1).

129 PPSA (A, BC, M, NB, NWT, Nu, PEI, S) s. 51(1); (NL, NS) s. 52(1); O s. 48(1); Y s. 45(1).

130 *Tisdale Credit Union Ltd v. Fritshaw Farms Meat Processing Ltd.* (1989), 79 Sask. R. 162 (Q.B.).

131 PPSA (A, BC, M, NB, NWT, Nu, PEI, S) s. 28(1); (NL, NS) s. 29(1); O s. 25(1), Y s. 26(1).

the debtor under the new name or with the transferee, as the case may be. However, it would be unfair to require a secured party to respond to a change in circumstances of which it is still ignorant. Accordingly, the PPSA does not oblige the secured party to act until it "has knowledge of information required to register a financing change statement disclosing the transferee as the new debtor ... or the name of the new debtor."[132] Once knowledge is acquired, the secured party has fifteen days to either take possession of the collateral or amend its registration to disclose the name of the transferee or the new name of the debtor, as the case may be.

In a case where there are successive transfers of the collateral, it is pointless to require the secured party to register the name of the intermediate transferees if it does not become aware of their existence until after the collateral has already passed into new hands. Accordingly, the secured party is deemed to have met its obligations if it registers the name of the most recent transferee within fifteen days (thirty days in Ontario) after acquiring the knowledge necessary to trigger the amendment obligation.[133]

Except in Ontario, a secured party who fails to amend the record or otherwise perfect the security interest is subordinated against third-party interests acquired in the collateral after the expiration of the fifteen-day period. In other words, the secured party retains whatever priority it enjoyed against prior interests. This approach reflects the purpose of requiring disclosure: to protect third-party searchers dealing with a transferee from the original debtor or with the original debtor under her new name. Nonetheless, there is judicial support for the proposition that a trustee in bankruptcy has a sufficient interest *qua* representative of the debtor's creditors to qualify for protection.[134]

---

132 PPSA (A, BC, M, NB, NWT, Nu, PEI, S) s. 51(2); (NL, NS) s. 52(2); O s. 48(2)–(3); Y s. 45(2)–(3).

133 PPSA (BC, NB, PEI, NWT, Nu, S) s. 51(4); A s. 51(5); (NL, NS) s. 52(4); O s. 48(4); Y no equivalent provision.

134 *Re Stevens* (1993), 23 C.B.R. (3d) 46, 17 Alta. L.R. (3d) 99, 6 P.P.S.A.C. (2d) 231, (Q.B.); *Re Orion Truck Centre Ltd.,* above note 125. See also, in relation to the Ontario Act, *In Re Media Corporation* (1984), 3 P.P.S.A.C. 253 (Ont. H.C.J.); *Re Alduco Mechanical Contractors* (1979), 1 P.P.S.A.C. 142 (Ont. H.C.J.). But see *Re Hewstan* (1996), 42 C.B.R. (3d) 186, 12 P.P.S.A.C. (2d) 36 (B.C.S.C.). And note *Re Hickman Equipment (1985) Ltd.* (2003), 40 C.B.R. (4th) 69, 223 Nfld. & P.E.I.R. 21 (Nfld. S.C.T.D.) (within fifteen days of obtaining actual knowledge of transfer of collateral, secured creditor registered financing change statement naming transferee as debtor; registration of financing change statement made during stay period established by order with respect to a transferee under the *Companies' Creditors Arrangement Act* and continued by subsequent receivership order;

The secured party also retains priority against third-party interests acquired in the collateral during the fifteen-day period even if the registration is not amended before the expiry of that period. In other words, the grace period gives absolute rather than conditional protection subject to two important qualifications. First, a buyer or lessee of the collateral for value without knowledge takes free of the security interest if the sale or lease occurs before the secured creditor amends the registration or otherwise perfects the security interest, even if the sale or lease occurs within the fifteen-day grace period.[135] Second, the secured party retains priority over a competing security interest that is registered or perfected during the grace period only if the amendment is registered before the fifteen days expire.

Conversely, as between two secured creditors who acquire and perfect their security prior to the change of name or transfer, the first-ranking creditor retains its priority status even if the subordinate secured party registers an amendment to record the change of name within the required time period and the first-ranking creditor does not. The point arose in *Bank of Nova Scotia v. Royal Bank*[136] in which a transferee of collateral from the original debtor granted a security interest to SP2 who registered naming the transferee as debtor. SP2 knew of the prior security interest acquired by SP1 from the original debtor before registering (because a serial number search had revealed the registration). SP1 found out about SP2's registered interest when it attempted to enforce the security against the original debtor. SP2 made a second registration after SP1 found out about the transfer but before SP1 registered an amendment naming the transferee as a new debtor. SP1's registration was made outside the fifteen-day compliance period and SP2 attempted to rely on its second registration as giving it priority as an intervening secured creditor over SP1. The British Columbia court before whom the point arose ruled that the second registration by SP2 did not improve its priority position; a secured party like SP2 who takes a security interest from a transferee before a secured party in the position of SP1 has knowledge of the transfer cannot claim priority and the registration of a second financing does not change anything. In any event, the court reasoned, SP2 was acting in bad faith in attempting to

---

held, post-bankruptcy registration of financing change statement by creditor to disclose transfer is effective if made within the fifteen-day time limit established by the Act).

135   PPSA (A, BC, M, NB, NWT, N, PEI, S) s. 30 (5); (NL, NS) s. 31(5); Y s. 29 (5); O no equivalent provision.

136   (1998), 14 P.P.S.A.C. (2d) 10 (B.C.S.C.).

invoke the protection of the Act given that it had actual knowledge of SP1's security interest before registering the first time and given that SP1 had delayed registration of the amendment naming the transferee as a debtor by reason of the initiation of settlement negotiations between the two parties.

The approach under the Ontario Act is quite different. The grace period for compliance is somewhat more generous: thirty as opposed to fifteen days. However, failure to amend or otherwise perfect before the expiry of that period causes the security interest to become wholly unperfected.[137] It follows that the security interest will be subordinated even as against third-party interests acquired prior to the transfer. Priority status against prior claimants can be regained if the secured party amends the registration or otherwise perfects even if this occurs outside the grace period. The security interest is then deemed to have been continuously perfected from the time of the original registration except as against a person who acquired rights in the collateral during the period when the interest was unperfected.[138]

The question of whether amalgamation brings about a name change or transfer of collateral so as to trigger these re-perfection requirements has attracted some controversy. As a matter of corporate law, amalgamating companies do not terminate their legal existence upon amalgamation, but continue in the amalgamated company. It has therefore been held that amalgamation does not bring about a transfer of the collateral from the amalgamating companies to the amalgamated company.[139]

---

137 OPPSA s. 48.
138 OPPSA s. 30(6). In *In Re Media Corporation*, above note 134, the secured party did not file its amendment correcting the debtor's name until one day after a petition in bankruptcy was filed and it therefore lost out to the trustee in bankruptcy. There was another secured party in the picture who retained priority against the trustee notwithstanding that it too had not registered an amendment. However, the other secured party had the good fortune not to know of the name change. See also *Re Alduco Mechanical Contractors*, above note 134. But see *Re PSINet Ltd.* (2002), 32 C.B.R. (4th) 102 (Ont. C.A.), aff'g (2002), 30 C.B.R. (4th) 226 (Ont. S.C.J.) (permitting secured creditor to re-register without loss of priority against pre-lapse interests even though revival of original registration made after the commencement of reorganization proceedings under the *Companies' Creditors Arrangement Act*, R.S.C. 1985, c. C-36, and even though other creditors involved in that proceeding had been operating on the assumption that the secured creditor held only unsecured status).
139 *Heidelberg Canada Graphic Equipment Ltd. v. Arthur Andersen Inc.* (1992), 7 B.L.R. (2d) 236, 4 P.P.S.A.C. (2d) 116 (Ont. Ct. Gen. Div.).

As for whether a change of name occurs, it has been held that if the name of the amalgamated company in which the amalgamated company continues is different, there is a name change within the meaning of the PPSA.[140] Conversely, if the name of the amalgamated and amalgamating companies is the same, no amendment or other perfecting step is needed. Since the amalgamating company retains sufficient legal existence for the security interest to continue and since the names are the same, the original registration is not materially misleading to a third-party searcher dealing with the amalgamated company. This conclusion is supported by the decision of the Ontario Court of Appeal in *Charter Financial Co. v. Royal Bank*.[141] The Court held that where the original debtor company amalgamated before the secured party registered, the subsequent registration against the original amalgamating company was not materially misleading so as to invalidate the registration in view of the continued legal existence of the amalgamating company; third-party searchers would not be misled since the names of the amalgamating and amalgamating companies were intended to be the same.

5) Addition of Collateral

Should the debtor's financing needs change after the entry into of the original security agreement, the debtor may agree to grant security in additional collateral. Such a change can made by a financing change statement. A fresh registration is not required. Of course, the amendment is effective only from the date the financing change statement is registered. The security interest in the new collateral is not retroactively perfected to the date of the original registration.

The situation is different when the financing change statement reflects new collateral in the form of proceeds of the original collateral. Provided the applicable grace period for re-perfection is respected, the priority status of a perfected security interest in proceeds is the date of perfection of the original collateral.[142]

If the description in the original registration covers after-acquired collateral, there is normally no need to amend the registration. How-

---

140   *Re Yustin Construction* (1986), 5 P.P.S.A.C. 154 (Ont. H.C.J.); and see *Pudwill v. Royal Bank of Canada*, [2002] O.J. No. 1547 (C.A.). But see *Re Orion Truck Centre Ltd.*, above note 125 (*obiter*).
141   (2002), 159 O.A.C. 201, 4 P.P.S.A.C. (3d) 4 (Ont. C.A.)
142   PPSA (A, BC, M, NB, NWT, Nu, S) s. 35(3); (NL, NS) s. 36(3); O s. 30(5); Y no equivalent provision. For a detailed analysis, see chapter 12.

ever, as explained earlier, in the case of after-acquired serial number goods, it will be necessary to add the serial numbers by use of a financing change statement in order to obtain priority over certain competing claimants.

6) Renewal

The availability of variable registration periods significantly reduces the incidence of lapse. Nonetheless, subsequent events may change what initially seemed to be a generous estimate of the financing life of a transaction. In that event, the secured party will have to renew its registration in order to maintain its perfected status. A registration may be renewed any number of times so long as the renewal is registered before the previous registration expires. Renewal extends the registration life for the time period specified by the registrant.

A renewal must be made by registering a renewal of the original registration. If a fresh registration is instead made, continuity of perfection is lost even if it is registered prior to the expiry of the original registration and relates to the same debtor and the same collateral.[143]

7) Correction of Erroneous Lapse or Discharge

If registration lapses, the security interest remains valid and enforceable against the debtor.[144] But as against third parties, perfected status is lost. Even if a new registration is made, the perfected status of the security interest will date from the time of re-registration without any relation back to the original registration.[145]

To this there is one important exception. Except for the Ontario Act, the PPSA gives a secured party a thirty-day window in which to revive the perfected status of a lapsed or discharged registration so as to regain its priority ranking against prior secured creditors.[146] The security interest is then deemed to have been continuously perfected from the time of the original registration, except as against secured parties

143 *Black Hills Credit Union v. C.I.B.C.* (1988), 8 P.P.S.A.C. 199 (Sask. C.A.); *Saskatchewan Credit Union v. Bank of Nova Scotia* (1985), 5 P.P.S.A.C. 123 (Sask. Q.B.); *Moose Jaw v. Pulsar Ventures* (1985), 5 P.P.S.A.C. 133 (Sask. Q.B.).
144 *Canadian Imperial Bank of Commerce v. Klunkovski* (1983), 3 P.P.S.A.C. 216 (Ont. H.C.J.); *Fotti v. 777 Management Incorporated* (1981), 2 P.P.S.A.C. 32 (Man. Q.B.).
145 *Royal Bank v. Demyen (Trustee of)* (1986), 6 P.P.S.A.C. 240 (Sask. Q.B.).
146 PPSA (A, BC, M, NB, NWT, Nu, PEI, S) s. 35(7); (NL, NS) s. 36(7); Y s. 34(5).

who register or perfect a security interest, or advance new funds in relation to a prior perfected security interest, during the period when the registration record indicated that the registration had been discharged or had lapsed. Protection is limited to priority contests with other secured parties. Perfected status is lost as against a trustee in bankruptcy, buyer, judgment creditor, or other third party who enters the picture after the lapse or discharge but before the registration is revived.[147]

The procedure for reviving a lapsed or discharged registration varies. In some systems, the computer program does not permit further registrations to be made against a lapsed or discharged registration. In these systems, the secured party must make a new registration that indicates it is a re-registration and discloses the registration number of the original registration. In *Re UF Media Inc.*[148] the registration was made during the lapse period and referred to the registration number of the original registration but did not repeat the collateral description. The original registration having lapsed, it was no longer searchable by registration number. The Court of Appeal nonetheless upheld the effectiveness of the re-registration on the questionable theory that the omission of the collateral description was not seriously misleading since a reasonable searcher could have obtained a copy of the original registration from the secured party directly. The Court did not go so far as to suggest that the omission of a collateral description in an original registration would be curable.

Other systems have been programmed so that lapsed and discharged registrations remain searchable for a thirty-day period. In these systems, a secured party is able to revive the registration without having to make a new registration. In the latter case, the continued searchability of lapsed or discharged registrations does not affect their legal status. Until the registration is positively revived, third parties are entitled to act on the assumption that the security interest is no longer in existence or has become unperfected by lapse, as the case may be.

The Ontario Act contains a similar saving provision with one important difference.[149] Priority status can be revived as against interests over whom the secured creditor had priority before the lapse or discharge at any time. There is no thirty-day limitation on the right.[150]

---

147 *Bigstone Band Enterprises Ltd. (Re)* (1999), 15 P.P.S.A.C. (2d) 240 (Alta. Q.B.).
148 2003 CarswellBC 1760 (C.A.).
149 OPPSA s. 30(6).
150 For an illustration, see *Asklepeion Restaurants Ltd. v. 791259 Ontario Ltd* (1996), 11 P.P.S.A.C. (2d) 320, 6 O.T.C. 326 (Gen. Div.). And see *Re PSINet Ltd.*, above note 138 (secured creditor permitted to revive original registration without loss of priority against pre-lapse interests even though revival of original registra-

This more liberal approach increases the likelihood of new security interests entering the picture, thereby increasing the risk of circular priority contests.

E. EFFECT OF ERRORS OR OMISSIONS ON VALIDITY OF REGISTRATION

1) The Verification Statement

The PPSA regulation makes provision for the registrar to forward a verification statement of a registration to the registrant or secured party identified in the registration. The verification statement shows the data that was entered into the registry database, thereby giving the secured creditor an early opportunity to correct any errors or omissions through the registration of a financing change statement or by notification to the registrar in the case of registry errors. However, there is no legal requirement to review the verification statement, and mistakes sometimes go unnoticed. With the widespread use of electronic financing, the risk of registry error on data entry has diminished. Most often the cause is error on the part of the registrant. Indeed, challenges to the validity of a registration as a result of registrant error constitute the biggest source of litigation under the PPSA.

2) Objective Test for Invalidity

Not every error or omission invalidates a registration. Under the Act, the validity of the registration is not affected unless the mistake is "seriously misleading."[151] The Ontario Act uses the slightly different formulation of "materially misleading," but in the authors' view there is no substantive difference in the tests. In determining what constitutes a seriously misleading error, it is not necessary to show that anyone was actually misled, or, indeed whether a search was ever conducted by the party challenging the validity of the registration. Rather, the test is an

---

tion made after the commencement of reorganization proceedings under the *Companies' Creditors Arrangement Act,* above note 138, and even though other creditors involved in that proceeding had been operating on the assumption that the secured creditor held only unsecured status).

151 PPSA (A, BC, M, NWT, Nu, S) s. 43(6); (NB, PEI) s. 43(7); (NL, NS) s. 44(7); O s. 46(4); Y s. 64(1).

objective one. Is the error seriously misleading from the viewpoint of a hypothetical searcher of the system?[152]

From the viewpoint of the secured party, it may seem unfair to invalidate a registration as against a third party who was not actually prejudiced by a registration error. However, an objective standard avoids case-by-case litigation on the question of actual prejudice and promotes the integrity and reliability of the registration system. In any event, the function of registration is not limited to protecting the reliance interest of third parties. Registration also operates as an efficient means of demarcating the point at which secured parties can assert priority over the debtor's judgment creditors and trustee in bankruptcy and promotes the efficient ordering of priorities among secured parties.

The Ontario PPSA initially adopted an actual prejudice standard for determining incurable error. The 1989 version of the Act substituted the objective test: whether "a reasonable person is likely to be materially misled by the error or omission."[153] Initially, some Ontario courts attempted, in effect, to resurrect the old standard by examining the effect of the error from the viewpoint of a reasonable person having the same knowledge about the security interest as the person actually challenging the registration, typically a trustee in bankruptcy.[154] The integrity of the legislature's intention to impose a truly objective standard has now been affirmed by the Ontario Court of Appeal.[155]

3) Error in Debtor Name

Sometimes an error in the registered name of the debtor results from a simple failure to follow the rules outlined earlier concerning what

---

152 For judicial confirmation, see *Kelln (Trustee of) v. Strasbourg Credit Union Ltd.*, [1992] 3 W.W.R. 310 (Sask. C.A.); *General Electric Capital Equipment Finance Inc. v. Inland Kenworth Inc.* (1993), 81 B.C.L.R. (2d) 384 at 390 (S.C.); *General Motors Acceptance Corporation v. Trans Canada Credit Corp.* (1994), 6 P.P.S.A.C. (2d) 216 (Alta. Q.B.). Compare with *Re Munr* (1992), 77 B.C.L.R. (2d) 98 (S.C.). Compare also with the anomalous decision in *Harder v. Alberta Treasury Branches* (2004), 6 P.P.S.A.C. (3d) 346 (Alta. Q.B.).

153 OPPSA s. 46(4).

154 See, for instance, *General Motors Acceptance Corporation of Canada v. Stetsko* (1992), 8 O.R. (3d) 537 (Gen. Div.); *Re Rose* (1993), 6 P.P.S.A.C. (2d) 53 (Ont. Ct. Gen. Div.).

155 *Re Lambert* (1991), 2 P.P.S.A.C. (2d) 160 (Ont. Ct. Gen. Div.), rev'd (1994), 7 P.P.S.A.C. (2d) 240 (Ont. C.A.), leave to appeal to S.C.C. refused (1995), 33 C.B.R. (3d) 291n (S.C.C.). For a more recent attempt to reinvigorate the relevance of subjective knowledge, see *Harder v. Alberta Treasury Branches*, above note 152.

constitutes the correct name of the debtor as where the trade name of a debtor is entered instead of the actual name.[156] More often, however, the challenge is based on an alleged mistake in the name as entered.

A mistake that invalidates a registration in one jurisdiction may not do so in another. This is because the question of whether such an error is seriously misleading can only be decided in the context of the information storage and retrieval capabilities of each particular registry system. The issue is not whether the mistake appears to be minor or trivial in the abstract but whether it caused the registration not to be disclosed on a search of the system using the correct name of the debtor.[157]

In Ontario, *any* error or omission in the debtor's name invalidates the registration.[158] This is because a specific-name search in the Ontario system discloses only those names that precisely match the information entered by the searcher. Searchers can elect to perform a non-specific-name search that matches all information in the database to the first name and surname, ignoring initials and birth dates. However, it has been held that a reasonable searcher should not be expected to know the difference between the two types of searches and it is therefore the results obtained on a specific-name search that matter.[159]

The other registry systems have been programmed to automatically disclose both exact and inexact matches of names on a search result.

---

156 *Re Ovens* (1979), 1 P.P.S.A.C. 131 (Ont. C.A.); *K.J.M. Leasing Ltd. v. Grandstrand Bros. Inc. (Receiver Manager of)*, above note 104; *Re Barous* (1983), 3 P.P.S.A.C. 61 (Sask. Q.B.); *Re Hickson* (1984), 3 P.P.S.A.C. 263 (Man. C.A.); *Re Bellini Manufacturing & Importing Ltd.* (1981), 1 P.P.S.A.C. 259 (Ont. C.A.).

157 *Case Power & Equipment v. 366551 Alberta Inc. (Receiver of)*, above note 109 (*per* Hetherington J., Conrad J. concurring). *P.E.I. Lending Agency v. Island Petroleum Products Ltd.*(1999), 185 Nfld. & P.E.I.R. 78, 15 P.P.S.A.C. (2d) 111 (P.E.I.S.C.T.D). And see *K.J.M. Leasing Ltd. v. Grandstrand Bros. Inc. (Receiver Manager of)*, *ibid.*: "What a search under the incorrect name discloses is not the right question. Obviously a search under the incorrect name will disclose the … security. But it defies logic to say that a search under the incorrect name discloses the disputed security so the error is not seriously misleading. That is a circular argument. What is relevant is what a search under the right name will disclose. What will a searcher armed with the right name discover?"

158 *Re Gibbons* (1984), 4 P.P.S.A.C. 53 (Ont. C.A.); *Re Wilson* (1984), 4 P.P.S.A.C. 69 (Ont. H.C.J.). The only exception is where the collateral is a motor vehicle that is required to be described by its VIN (vehicle identification number) and the VIN is entered correctly: *Re Lambert*, above note 155 (discussed separately in this chapter).

159 *Re Weber* (1990), 1 P.P.S.A.C. (2d) 36 (Ont. H.C.J.); *Re Woolf* (1992), 7 P.P.S.A.C. (2d) 268 (Ont. Ct. Gen. Div.), appeal allowed on other grounds without addressing this point, 7 P.P.S.A.C. (2d) 276 (Ont. C.A.).

This allows more latitude for non-fatal errors and omissions than in Ontario. Nonetheless, not all similar matches are flagged and if the registration is not disclosed on a search using the correct name, the error or omission is *ipso facto* misleading, however minor it may seem in the abstract. It is not open to the court, in other words, to conclude that the system should have been programmed to disclose the name or number as an inexact match; the question is whether it was.[160] So, referring to "Granstrand Bros. Inc." as "Grandstrand Bros. Inc." might not appear to be an egregious error in the abstract. However, if the effect of the error is to cause the registration not to be disclosed on a search using the correct name of the debtor, it is nonetheless seriously misleading so as to invalidate the registration.[161]

If the registration appears on a search result as an inexact match, this does not necessarily mean that the error is not seriously misleading. The further question must then be asked whether an objective searcher could reasonably conclude that the inexact match referred to the debtor or serial numbered goods in question or was so closely similar as to prompt further inquiry.[162] If the discrepancy is minor and the registration and search data match in other particulars, then the searcher cannot simply ignore the result and the error will likely be discounted.[163] However, if the list of similar matches is lengthy or the discrepancies are major, a court might well conclude that the error was seriously misleading on the theory that a reasonably diligent searcher should not have to go to the effort of investigating each and every similar match disclosed to determine whether or not it refers to the debtor or collateral in question.

160 *Case Power & Equipment v. 366551 Alberta Inc.*, above note 104.
161 *K.J.M. Leasing Ltd. v. Grandstrand Bros. Inc. (Receiver of)*, above note 104.
162 *General Motors Acceptance Corp. of Canada v. Trans Canada Credit Corp.*, above note 152.
163 *Alberta Treasury Branches v. Triathlon Vehicle Leasing* (1992), 4 P.P.S.A.C. (2d) 163 (Alta. Q.B.), aff'g (1992), 4 P.P.S.A.C. (2d) 147 (Alta. Q.B.); *Chrysler Credit Canada Ltd v. Webber* (1993), 6 P.P.S.A.C. (2d) 106 (Alta. Q.B.), rev'd on reconsideration, [1994] A.J. No. 292 (Q.B.); *Buchan v. Saskatchewan Government Insurance*, [1997] S.J. No. 726, 13 P.P.S.A.C. (2d) 61 (Q.B.); *General Motors Acceptance Corp. of Canada v. Trans Canada Credit Corp.*, ibid.; *P.E.I. Lending Agency v. Island Petroleum Products Ltd.*, above note 157.

4) Error in Serial Number

As explained earlier, if the collateral is serial numbered goods (or a motor vehicle in Ontario), the searcher has the option of searching the registry according to the serial number (or VIN in Ontario) rather than the name of the debtor. The distinction between the Ontario and other systems in respect of incorrect entry of the debtor name also holds true when it comes to challenges based on an error in the entry of the serial number. While the Ontario system is programmed to return only an exact match for the correct VIN of a motor vehicle, the other systems have built in some capability for returning similar matches in the case of serial number searches. Where the serial number shows up as a similar match, the error is unlikely to be treated as seriously misleading unless the quantity of similar matches is so great that a searcher would not be able to conclude that the similar match likely referred to the goods in issue.

5) Error in Debtor Name Where Serial Number Correct

The omission of a serial number, or a seriously misleading error in the entry of a serial number, is treated as substantially misleading even if the debtor name is entered correctly.[164] The Ontario Court of Appeal has rejected the converse proposition, holding that a correctly registered serial number cures an error in entering the name of the debtor.[165] Although adopted by the British Columbia Court of Appeal,[166] the Ontario position has been rejected by the Saskatchewan, Alberta, and New Brunswick Courts of Appeal,[167] and this position has since been con-

---

164 *Bank of Nova Scotia v. Royal Bank*, above note 136; *Re Alda Wholesale Ltd.* (2001), 3 P.P.S.A.C. (3d) 52 (B.C.S.C.); *Primus Automotive Financial Services Canada Ltd. v. Kirkby (Trustee of)* (1998), 14 P.P.S.A.C. (2d) 273 (Alta. Q.B.); *Toronto Dominion Bank v. Flexi-Coil Ltd.* (1993), 4 P.P.S.A.C. (2d) 288 (Sask. Q.B.); *Trans Canada Credit Corp. Ltd. v. Walko* (1991), 2 P.P.S.A.C. (2d) 334 (Sask. Q.B.); *Re Fleurke* (1992), 4 P.P.S.A.C. (2d) 59 (Alta. Q.B); *Re Paterson* (1994), 8 P.P.S.A.C. (2d) 126 (Ont. Ct. Gen. Div.). Compare with the anomalous decision in *Harder v. Alberta Treasury Branches*, above note 152.
165 *Re Lambert*, above note 155.
166 *Gold Key Pontiac Buick (1984) Ltd. v. 464750 B.C. Ltd. (Trustee of)* (2000), 2 P.P.S.A.C. (3d) 206 (B.C.C.A.), rev'g (1999), 15 P.P.S.A.C. (2d) 46 (B.C.S.C.).
167 *Re Kelln*, above note 152; *Case Power & Equipment v. 366551 Alberta Inc. (Receiver of)*, above note 104; *Re Moncton Motor Homes & Sales Inc.* 2003 NBCA 26; *Primus Automotive Financial Services Canada Ltd. v. Kirkby (Trustee of)*, above note 164; *Buchan v. Saskatchewan Government Insurance*, above note 163; *Re Paquette*, above note 100.

firmed by legislative amendments in the Maritime provinces,[168]In the view of the authors and of commentators,[169] this represents the correct approach. Serial number searching was intended to be a supplementary mode of searching, not an alternative to debtor-name searching. The ability of a third party to place full confidence in either a debtor name or a serial number search is essential to the integrity of the registry system. Not all searchers will necessarily have ready access to the serial number of particular vehicles of the debtor. Even if access is available, not all searchers are sophisticated enough to appreciate the necessity to search by serial number. Finally, there are situations where the imposition of serial number searching imposes excessive transaction costs on searchers, for example, where the debtor in question holds many pieces of equipment that qualify as serial numbered goods.

6) Error in General Collateral Description

Where the collateral is all present and after-acquired property, a description in these terms is by definition adequate. Litigation on the sufficiency of a general description has therefore tended to involve cases where the collateral constitutes an item or kind of collateral. It is clear that a significantly misleading error or omission in the description of an item or kind of collateral, or failing to describe it at all, means that the security interest will not be considered perfected with respect to that item or kind of collateral.[170] The fact that the Act requires a secured party to respond to a demand indicating the actual collateral covered by the security agreement does not excuse the error; to hold otherwise would rob the description requirement of any meaning.[171]

---

168 PPSA NS ss. 44(8A)–(8B); PEI ss. 43(8.1)–(8.2); NB s. 43(8)–(8.1).
169 R.J. Wood, "Registration Errors and Search Criteria: *Gold Key Pontiac Buick (1984) Ltd. v. 464750 B.C. Ltd.*" (2001) 35 Can. Bus. L.J. 146; R.J. Wood, "Registration Errors under the OPPSA: *Lambert (Re)*" (1994–95) 24 Can. Bus. L.J. 444; David Denomme, "Search Again? Names, Numbers and Reasonable Persons" (2002) 17 B.F.L.R. 1; R.C.C. Cuming "Judicial Treatment of the Saskatchewan Personal Property Security Act" (1986-87) 51 Sask. L. Rev. 129 at 140–44.
170 *Gates Fertilizers Ltd. v. Waddell* (1985), 5 P.P.S.A.C. 79 (Sask. Q.B.); *Re Alda Wholesale Ltd.* (2001), 26 C.B.R. (4th) 1 (B.C.S.C.); *Re Noriega*, [2003] 7 W.W.R. 566, 42 C.B.R. (4th) 274, 15 Alta. L.R. (4th) 79 (Q.B.); Compare with *Re UF Media Inc.*, above note 148.
171 *Re Noriega, ibid.* As Master Funduk observed, while there are several decisions in which a complete failure to provide any collateral description was excused (*Elmcrest Furniture Manufacturing Ltd. v. 216200 Alberta Ltd (Receiver Manager of)* (1985), 41 Sask. R. 125 (Q.B.); *Mutual Life Assurance Co. v. Toronto Dominion Bank* (1995), 10 P.P.S.A.C. (2d) 182 (Man. Q.B.)), these cases were premised

A registration containing an invalid registration is invalid only with respect to the erroneously described collateral. The PPSA confirms that the validity of the registration in relation to other collateral that is correctly described is not affected.[172] Although the Ontario Act does not have this provision, the position in that province is the same since it merely codifies the doctrine of severability adopted by the Ontario courts in ruling on the effect of partial error under pre-PPSA registration law. [173]

A minor error in a general collateral description does not invalidate the registration if the other descriptors are sufficient to lead a searcher to conclude that the description covers the relevant item or kind of collateral. Moreover, if the erroneously described collateral also falls within a broader collateral description set out in the same registration, the registration may be saved. For example, in *Saskatchewan Economic Development Corporation v. Pryor*,[174] the registration contained the following description: "Rubber Tire Loader, Serial No. 9668." The serial number was incorrect and the registration did not specify any make, model number, or year. However, the rubber-tire loader was not required to be registered as serial numbered goods under the PPSA regulation and the registration also included a general collateral description covering "all personal property of the debtor now or hereinafter acquired." This latter description was held to be sufficient to give the secured party a perfected security interest in the rubber-tire loader.

7) Entry of Serial Number Description in General Collateral Field

Except in Ontario, a financing statement contains an independent field for describing collateral that falls within the definition of serial numbered goods. The financing statement also contains a general collateral description field. As explained earlier, collateral can be described by item or kind or by an all-encompassing description in this field. One issue that has arisen is whether the recording of a serial number in the general collateral field should qualify as a valid serial number descrip-

---

on the assumption that an error may be cured so long as no actual person was misled by the error; since the test is now clearly objective, these decisions lack any authoritative value.

172 PPSA (A, BC, NWT, Nu, S) s. 43(9); (M, NB, PEI) s. 43(10); (NL, NS) s. 44(10); Y s. 64(2); O no equivalent provision.

173 *Hunt v. Long* (1916), 27 D.L.R. 337 (Ont. S.C.A.D.).

174 (1992), 3 P.P.S.A.C. (2d) 235 (Sask. Q.B.).

tion where a description by serial number is required for a valid registration or is relevant to priority.

In *Commcorp Financial Services Inc. v. R & R Investments Corp.*,[175] a secured party registered a financing statement which included the serial number of a motor vehicle in the general collateral field. The debtor later gave a competing security interest to another secured party, who registered a financing statement that recorded the serial number in the serial number field. Except for the Ontario and Yukon Acts, the PPSA provides that serial numbered goods held by the debtor as equipment must be described by serial number in order to be considered perfected as against competing buyers and competing secured parties (who themselves have registered by serial number).[176] Master Funduk held that entry of a serial number description in the general collateral field satisfied this requirement, and gave priority to the first secured party. This decision was subsequently followed by courts in Prince Edward Island[177] and Nova Scotia.[178]

The authors are of the opinion that these cases are wrongly decided. The whole purpose of requiring serial number registration is to permit searching parties to conduct a search of the registry using the serial number of the collateral. When a serial number search is conducted, it is only information that is contained in the serial number field that is matched against the search criterion. Therefore, a serial number search will not disclose registrations in which the serial number is recorded in the general collateral field. In order to eliminate the risk to searchers represented by these decisions, a number of jurisdictions have found it prudent to clarify their legislation.[179]

---

175 (1995), 10 P.P.S.A.C. (2d) 87 (Alta. Q.B.).

176 For a detailed analysis of the perfection and priority rules associated with serial number registration, see chapters 7 and 8.

177 *Business Development Bank of Canada v. ABN Amro Leasing*, [2002] P.E.I.J. No. 18 (P.E.I.S.C.T.D.), aff'd 5 P.P.S.A.C. (3d) 76 (P.E.I.S.C.A.D.).

178 *Valley Vista Golf Course Ltd. (Receiver of) v. Maximum Financial Services Inc.* (2003), 214 N.S.R. (2d) 91 (T.D.).

179 See NBPPSA s. 43(8.1); and see the new definition of "seriously misleading defect, irregularity, omission or error" in NSPPSA s. 2 and PEIPPSA s. 1.

FURTHER READINGS

DENOMME, D.L., "Search Again?: Names, Numbers and Reasonable Persons" (2001) 17 B.F.L.R. 1

DENOMME, D.L., "Name/Number Tie-breaker (For Now)" (Case Comm.) (2004) 19 B.F.L.R. 295

WOOD, R. J., "The Evolution of the Personal Property Registry: Centralization, Computerization, Privatization and Beyond" (1996) 35 Alta. L. Rev. 45

WOOD, R. J., "Registration Requirements and Registration Errors under the APPSA" (Case Comm.) (1996) 27 Can. Bus. L.J. 132

WOOD, R. J., "Registration Errors and Dual Search Criteria" (Case Comm.) (2001) 35 Can. Bus. L.J. 146

BUYERS AND LESSEES OF COLLATERAL

A. THE CONTEXT

A security interest is a property interest in collateral. As such, it is an encumbrance or limitation on the ownership rights of the debtor that, under the common law principle, *nemo dat quod non habet* (one cannot give what one does not have), is not affected by a sale of the debtor's interest in the collateral to a buyer.[1] This principle, qualified by the requirement of perfection,[2] underlies the PPSA rules applicable to competitions between secured parties and buyers of collateral. In the absence of a special priority rule providing otherwise, an interest in collateral bought after a perfected security interest attaches is subject to the security interest.

However, an unqualified application of the *nemo dat* principle in the context of competing claims of secured parties and buyers is commercially unacceptable. A balance is required. Since buyers acquire their interests in a variety of contexts, no single approach can produce this balance in all situations. Consequently, the Act contains a range of priority rules applicable to buyers.

---

1   This is made clear by PPSA (A, BC, M, NB, NWT, Nu, PEI, S) s. 28(1); (NL, NS) s. 29(1); O s. 25(10); Y s. 26(1). This section provides that, where collateral is dealt with, the security interest continues in the collateral unless the secured party expressly or impliedly authorizes the dealing.
2   See chapter 5.

Set out in this chapter is a description and analysis of the priority rules through which the drafters of the Act sought to achieve this balance. While, for the most part, the analysis focuses on buyers of collateral, the priority rules examined apply also to lessees. However, there is an important difference between the position of a buyer and a lessee. A priority rule may provide that both a buyer and a lessee "take free from" a security interest. In the context of a buyer, this means that the security interest is cut off with the result that the buyer acquires the debtor-seller's ownership rights in the collateral free from the security interest. However, in the context of a lease, this only means that the security interest cannot be asserted against the lessee. The security interest is not cut off; it remains effective with respect to the reversionary interest of the debtor-lessor.[3]

Special priority rules apply to buyers of accounts, chattel paper, securities, instruments, documents of title, and money. These rules are addressed elsewhere in this book.

B. PRIORITY OF BUYERS' AND LESSEES' INTERESTS OVER UNPERFECTED SECURITY INTERESTS

One of the mechanisms contained in the Act designed to protect buyers of collateral from the effects of the *nemo dat* principle is a priority rule that, under prescribed circumstances, subordinates an unperfected security interest to the interest of a buyer. The functional basis of this rule is that perfection, other than temporary perfection, gives to potential buyers of collateral a prophylactic measure to avoid taking the collateral subject to a prior security interest. Disclosure of the existence of the security interest through one of the perfection steps enhances the ability of a potential buyer to assess the legal risk involved in buying the collateral. If, as a result of a failure on the part of the secured party to perfect its security interest, the buyer is denied the opportunity to employ this measure, the security interest is cut off through the sale of the collateral by the debtor to the buyer.

---

3   This feature is explicitly recognized in OPPSA s. 28(2); it is implicit in the other Acts.

The Act[4] provides that a security interest in goods is subordinate to the interest of a transferee,[5] other than another secured party, who gives value and acquires the interest without knowledge[6] of the security interest and before it is perfected. While the words "subordinate to" are used in the section, the legal effect of the priority rule is that an unperfected security interest is cut off by the sale of the goods to the buyer. The result is that the buyer acquires the debtor's interest free from the security interest and can pass it on in a sale to another buyer.[7]

The term "transferee" is not defined in the Act. However, it is the opinion of the authors that it includes a lessee of the collateral. As noted above, in the case of a lease, the security interest is not cut off. The lessee takes free from it, but it remains effective with respect to the debtor-lessor's reversionary interest in the collateral.

The term "value" includes any consideration sufficient to support a simple contract,[8] including a promise to pay the purchase price,[9] a

---

4   PPSA (NWT, Nu, O) s. 20(1); (BC, M) s. 20(c); (NB, S) s. 20(3); A s. 20(b); NL s. 21(2); NS s. 21(3); PEI s. 20(2).

5   In *Carr v. Shamrock Credit Union* (1987), 7 P.P.S.A.C. 66, the Saskatchewan Queen's Bench Court concluded that a "transferee" under SPPSA s. 20(3) included a recipient of property transferred pursuant to a vesting order made under matrimonial property legislation. In the opinion of the authors, this was a misapplication of the provision. Clearly, the section contemplates a consensual transfer of the property from the debtor to a buyer.

6   As to what constitutes "knowledge," see PPSA (A, BC, NWT, N) s. 1(2); (M, NB, PEI) s. 2(1); (NL, NS) s. 3(1)(c); O s. 69; S s. 2(2); Y no equivalent provision. See also PPSA (A, BC, MB, NB, NWT, Nu, PEI, S) s. 47; (NL, NS) s. 48; O s. 47(5); Y s. 52(3). For an examination of the concept, see chapter 1.

7   For judicial confirmation of the application in the PPSA context of what is sometimes called the "sheltering principle," see *Willi v. Don Shearer Ltd.* (1992), 3 P.P.S.A.C. (2d) 188 (B.C.S.C.), aff'd [1994] 2 W.W.R. 312 (B.C.C.A.).

8   PPSA (BC, NWT, Nu, O, Y) s. 1(1); (M, NB, PEI) s. 1; (NL, NS) s. 2; A s. 1(1); S s. 2(1).

9   It is the view of the authors that the Ontario Country Court decision in *Royal Bank v. Dawson Motors (Guelph) Ltd.* (1981), 39 C.B.R. (N.S.) 304, in which the court concluded that a contractual undertaking to pay the price of the goods was not value in the context of the former Ontario Act, is no longer relevant and should not be followed in any jurisdiction. Section 20 of the former Ontario Act provided that an unperfected security interest was subordinate to the interest of a transferee "to the extent that he gives value." The decision can be supported on the basis that these words allowed the court to quantify the consideration. These words are not found in the current Ontario Act or any other Act. Given the clear wording of the Act, it is not open for a court to place this gloss on its wording.

forbearance to sue,[10] and a binding commitment to grant credit.[11] Since there is no requirement that the buyer give "new value,"[12] the consideration for the sale can be cancellation of an antecedent debt or liability as contemplated by the definition of "value."[13] The definition of value refers only to consideration; it does not include a reference to sealed contracts as a substitute for consideration.[14]

Whether the buyer has met the requirements under which he is given priority is to be determined at the date the transfer takes place.[15] Consequently, if the security interest is perfected or the buyer acquires knowledge of the security interest after he has bought the goods, he takes free from the security interest. The correlative issue arises as to whether a buyer can assert priority over an unperfected security interest that was perfected at the time of the sale but became unperfected thereafter. The same reasoning applies; priority is determined on the basis of the relevant factors as they existed at the date of the sale.[16]

There is a very significant difference between the Ontario Act and all other Acts with respect to the need for the buyer to take delivery of the collateral in order to defeat an unperfected security interest. Under the Ontario Act, a buyer is protected only if she "receives delivery"

---

10   *Toronto-Dominion Bank v. Nova Entertainment Inc.* (1992), 7 Alta. L.R. (3d) 132 (Q.B.).

11   *Agricultural Credit Corp. of Saskatchewan v. Pettyjohn* (1991), 1 P.P.S.A.C. (2d) 273 (Sask. C.A.).

12   "New value" is defined in PPSA (A, BC, M, NWT, N) s. 1(1); S s. 2(1); in the Atlantic provinces Acts, "new value" is defined within the definition of value: (NB, PEI) s. 1; (NL, NS) s. 2; (O, Y) no equivalent provision.

13   By comparison, PPSA (A, BC, NB, NWT, Nu, PEI, S) s. 30(8); (NL, NS) s. 31(8); M s. 30(7); Y s. 29(4), O no equivalent provision, precludes a buyer from claiming priority under any of the rules of s. 30 on the basis of consideration in the form of discharge of a money debt or past liability.

14   However, at least one Ontario court concluded that a corporate seal imports consideration for the purposes of the OPPSA. *Heidelberg Graphic Equipment Ltd. v. Arthur Anderson Inc.* (1993), 4 P.P.S.A.C. (2d) 116 (Ont. Ct. Gen. Div.).

15   Section 20(1)(c) of the Ontario Act provides that "until perfected," a security interest in goods is not effective against a transferee, other than a secured party, who gives value and receives delivery of the goods without knowledge of the security interest. This formulation can be read as giving priority to a security interest that is perfected after the sale of the goods to a buyer. The words "until perfected" suggest that the priority rule does not apply if the security interest is perfected at any time before or after the sale. However, clearly this was not the intention of the Ontario Legislature.

16   *Alberta (Attorney General) v. Findlay*, [1996] 3 W.W.R. 514 (Alta. Prov. Ct.).

of the collateral[17] before the security interest is perfected. There is no similar requirement in the other Acts. The practical significance of this difference is apparent in the context of a scenario in which a buyer of goods, who has relied on a search of the registry that has disclosed no security interest in the goods, leaves the goods temporarily in the possession of the debtor-seller for repair, short-term storage, or some other reason. If the security interest is perfected any time after the date of the sale and before the buyer receives delivery of the goods, the Ontario Act gives priority to the secured party over the buyer even though the buyer has acted in good faith and may have transferred the purchase price to the debtor under circumstances in which it cannot be recovered. The other Acts protect the legitimate expectation of the buyer induced by the lack of perfection of the security interest at the date of the transfer; the Ontario Act does not.

The Ontario Act rule gives rise to a problem of interpretation in a case where the buyer is in possession of the goods at the date of sale as a lessee or bailee. It is physically impossible in such a situation for her to "receive delivery" of the goods. At best there can be a "constructive delivery" of the goods from her as lessee or bailee to herself as buyer. This presumably would be deemed to occur at the moment the sales agreement is signed or otherwise comes into effect.

A problem of interpretation of this feature of the PPSA[18] arises under all of the Acts where the contract between the debtor and the buyer is in the form of an agreement to sell under which the debtor-seller has retained title for security purposes. The provision expressly applies only where the transfer is "pursuant to a transaction that is not a security agreement."[19] The conditional sales contract between the debtor-seller and the buyer is a security agreement. However, it is the opinion of the authors that the purpose of this feature of the provision was to address a situation in which the debtor-seller gives another security interest in the collateral to another secured party. Since other priority rules of the Act deal with priority conflicts among secured parties,[20] there is no justification for excluding the application of the provision where the

---

17 See OPPSA ss. 25(5). However, there is no delivery requirement where there has been a sale in the ordinary course of business or where a motor vehicle that is proceeds is bought as consumer goods. OPPSA ss. 28(1) and 28(5).

18 Above note 4.

19 The same problem arises under OPPSA s. 20(1)(c) that applies to "a transferee who takes under a transfer that does not secure payment or performance of an obligation."

20 See, for example, PPSA (A, BC, M, NB, NWT, Nu, PEI, S) s. 35(1); (NL, NS) s. 36(1); O s. 30(1); Y s. 34(1).

debtor-seller is also a conditional seller-secured party. The provision should be read as applying to transferees who are buyers under conditional sales contracts. This is necessary in order to avoid an absurd result under which good faith buyers who acquire their interests under one type of sales contract are protected while those who acquire their interests under another type of sales contract are not. There is no policy reason why this distinction should be recognized.

Another issue of interpretation arises in a situation where the first transferee from the debtor who does not qualify for the protection of the priority rule (for example, he has knowledge of the unperfected security interest in the goods), transfers his interest to a buyer who does qualify. It is the opinion of the authors that the wording of the provision and the policy that underlies this feature of the Act supports the conclusion that the second buyer (or any qualifying subsequent buyer[21]) is entitled to the protection of the section. This is particularly so in the context of security interests in serial numbered goods sold to remote buyers who rely on the serial number of goods as the search criterion. However, even when serial numbered goods are not involved, a remote buyer should still be protected since he may trace the chain of ownership back to the original debtor and use that name as the search criterion.

Where the security interest is perfected at the time of the first sale by the debtor but unperfected at the time of a later sale to a second or subsequent buyer who meets the requirements of the provision,[22] the subsequent buyer takes free of the security interest for the same reason that a buyer from the debtor who meets the requirements of the provision is protected.[23]

---

21   In *Denolf v. Brown* (1994), 17 Alta. L.R. (3d) 374 (Q.B.), the court concluded that an execution creditor of a subsequent buyer who caused the collateral to be seized had priority over an unperfected security interest in the collateral. The decision was not based on the derivative nature of the interest of the execution creditors, but on the wording of s. 20(1)(a) of the Alberta Act which, at the time, provided that an unperfected security interest in collateral is subordinate to a creditor who causes the collateral to be seized to enforce a judgment.

22   This occurred in *Bank of Montreal v. Kalatzis* (1984), 37 Sask. R. 300, but the bank did not claim the goods from the subsequent buyer.

23   *Alberta (Attorney General) v. Findlay*, above note 16.

C. PRIORITY OF BUYERS' OR LESSEES' INTERESTS OVER PERFECTED SECURITY INTERESTS

1) Implied Power of Sale or Lease Given to a Debtor

The PPSA[24] provides that where collateral is dealt with, the security interest continues in the collateral unless the secured party expressly or impliedly authorizes the dealing. This provision can be seen as having two functions. The first is to state an essential attribute of the proprietary nature of a security interest: a security interest is a property interest that, subject to other requirements and priority rules of the Act, is not affected by the debtor's transfer of the collateral.[25] The second function is to recognize that, when a secured party expressly or impliedly authorizes the debtor to deal with the collateral, the security interest is affected to the extent of that authority.[26] Depending upon the scope of that authority, disposition to a buyer will result in extinguishment or subordination of the security interest.

The authority to deal with the collateral may be severely restricted. For example, if the debtor is given authority to deal with the collateral only with the prior express consent of the secured party, any disposition without that consent will have no effect on the security interest

---

24 PPSA (A, BC, M, NB, PEI, NWT, Nu, S) s. 28; (NL, NS) s. 29; O s. 25; Y s. 26.

25 *Lanson v. Saskatchewan Valley Credit Union Ltd.* (1998), 172 Sask. R. 106 (Sask. C.A.); *Northwest Equipment Inc. v. Daewoo Heavy Industries America Corporation*, [2002] 6 W.W.R. 444 (Alta. C.A.). The equivalent provision in the OPPSA, s. 25(1), appears on the surface to have a more limited function. By its express wording, it operates only when "the collateral gives rise to proceeds." However, it is the view of the authors that the provision should be given a broader interpretation so as to recognize a secured party's right to follow the collateral into the hands of a third party, even in the absence of a dealing generating proceeds. This view is supported by s. 9(1) of the Ontario Act which makes a security agreement effective against third parties in the absence of any contrary provision.

26 OPPSA s. 25(1) addresses only authority to deal with the collateral free of the security interest. The words "free of the security interest" were added in 2000 (s. 16(3) of Bill 119) on the recommendation of the Canadian Bar Association of Ontario PPLA Committee. The intent was to clarify the provision, i.e., to confirm that the right to follow the collateral is lost only if the secured party expressly or impliedly authorized the debtor to deal with the collateral free of the security interest. In other words, there is no indication that the words were intended to give the section a more restricted scope that its counterparts in other jurisdictions.

unless a priority rule of the Act dictates otherwise[27] or unless the sale is ratified after the event. The consent of the secured party is a condition that must be met before the sale takes place. If the condition is that the proceeds of the sale must be remitted to the secured party, or some other condition to be met after the sale takes place, the security interest is extinguished.[28] However, where the buyer agrees to the condition that the price of the collateral will be paid by him to the secured party, title to the property does not pass to the buyer free from the security interest until the condition is met.[29]

The underlying issue is whether or not the secured party has authorized the debtor to sell the collateral free of the security interest with the result that an unencumbered title passes to the buyer. If this authority has been given, the buyer should be protected even though the debtor-seller's authority to sell may have been conditioned on performance of some post-sale act such as remission of the proceeds. The buyer's title should not be subject to retroactive invalidation by reason of risks outside the buyer's control and against which the secured party could have protected itself by making the debtor's authority to sell conditional on direct payment from the buyer of the proceeds or payment into a special account. If the debtor-seller has extracted a direct payment condition from the buyer, the buyer must be taken to know that the debtor's authority to sell free of the security interest is conditioned on discharge of the secured obligation. In this case, the debtor has not been authorized to pass title free of the security interest.

The authority to deal with the collateral may be implied from the circumstances of the parties[30] or the conduct of the secured party. This conduct may involve an implicit waiver of an express provision in the

27   See *Royal Bank v. Gatekeeper Leasing Ltd.* (1993), 6 P.P.S.A.C. (2d) 92 (B.C.S.C.).

28   *Lanson v. Saskatchewan Valley Credit Union Ltd.*, above note 25; *Bank of Montreal v. L.S. Walker Machine Tools Inc. and Whitman Engineering Limited* (2000), 15 P.P.S.A.C. (2d) 236 (Ont. S.C.J.). It is the view of the authors that the opposing position taken by the Manitoba Queen's Bench Court in *Paccar Financial Services v. Chubey*, [1992] 2 W.W.R. 751 should not be followed.

29   *Canadian Commercial Bank v. Tisdale Farm Equipment Ltd.*, [1984] 6 W.W.R. 122, aff'd [1987] 1 W.W.R. 574 (Sask. C.A.).

30   See *Lanson v. Saskatchewan Valley Credit Union Ltd.*, above note 25; *Toronto-Dominion Bank v. Howitt Enterprises Ltd.* (1998), 13 P.P.S.A.C. (2d) 368 (Ont. Ct. Gen. Div.); *Gencare Services Ltd. v. Tolpuddle Housing Cooperative Inc.* (1993), 6 P.P.S.A.C. (2d) 340 (Ont. Ct. Gen. Div.). This was recognized under the common law. See *Dedrick v. Ashdown* (1888), 15 S.C.R. 227; *Delaney v. Downey* (1912), 2 W.W.R. 599 (Sask. K.B.); *Nourse v. Canadian Canners Ltd.*, [1935] O.R. 361 (C.A.).

security agreement requiring the prior consent of the secured party as a condition of the power to deal with the collateral.[31]

It is very common for secured parties who finance business inventory to give an express power to a debtor to sell collateral in the ordinary course of the debtor's business. Conditions placed on this power or any attempt to define in the agreement in a restrictive way what constitutes ordinary course of business do not prejudice the position of a buyer or lessee who acquires her interest in the ordinary course of business. This protection is not dependent in any way on the scope of authority given to the debtor it is based on the explicit priority rules of the Act dealing with ordinary course of business sales and leases that are the subject of the next section of this chapter.[32] It is the view of the authors that statutory recognition of the authority of the debtor to deal with the collateral includes authority to collect accounts subject to a security interest and use the proceeds for the debtor's purposes without having to account to the secured party.

2) Buyers or Lessees of Goods in the Ordinary Course of Business

a)   The Concept

The Act contains a priority rule that substantially affects the status of a perfected security interest in collateral in the form of goods.[33] Any sale or lease of the collateral by the debtor in the ordinary course of business results in the security interest being cut off, in the case of a sale, and abridged to the extent of the lessee's interest in the case of a lease,[34] unless the buyer or lessee knows that the sale or lease violates the terms of the security agreement.

---

31 This would be based on the common law principle of estoppel. See *Canadian Imperial Bank of Commerce v. Lush* (2001), 2 P.P.S.A.C. (3d) 61 and (2001), 2 P.P.S.A.C. (3d) 65 (N.B.Q.B.). The operation of the estoppel principle is preserved by PPSA (M, NWT, Nu, S) s. 65(2); (NB, PEI) s. 65(1); (NL, NS) s. 66(1); A s. 66(3); BC s. 68(1); O s. 72; Y s. 63(1).

32 PPSA (A, BC, M, NB, NWT, Nu, PEI, S) s. 30(2); (NL, NS) s. 31(2); O s. 28(1); Y s. 29(1). *Credit Suisse Canada v. 1133 Yonge Street Holdings* (1998), 5 C.B.R. (4th) 174 (Ont. C.A.).

33 *Ibid.*

34 The provision protecting ordinary course buyers (PPSA (A, BC, M, NB, NWT, Nu, PEI, S) s. 30(2); (NL, NS) s. 31(2); O s. 28(1); Y s. 29(1)) provides that the buyer or lessee takes free from any perfected or unperfected security interest in the goods. This does not mean that the lessee acquires ownership of the leased property It means that the security interest cannot be asserted against the

The policy underlying the section is that persons who buy goods in the ordinary course of business should not be required to take measures to protect themselves against the risk that the goods they buy are subject to prior perfected or unperfected security interests given by sellers with whom they deal.[35] A secured party who takes a security interest in goods of a debtor who is in the business of selling goods of that kind can expect that its security interest will be defeated by transactions with customers of the debtor.[36] The Saskatchewan Court of Appeal has taken the position that courts should give "a generally liberal interpretation to the phrase 'buyer … of goods sold … in the ordinary course of business of the seller,' in order to carry out the purpose of the ordinary course buyer rule: to protect the buying public in cases where the secured party furnishes goods which are sold to the public by the debtor in the regular course of the debtor's business. This comports with the underlying philosophy of the provision to protect the security interest so long as it does not interfere with the normal flow of commerce."[37]

The priority rule protecting ordinary course buyers is a rule of law; its function does not depend on any implied right of sale given to the debtor in the security agreement or otherwise. It operates even in the face of express limitations on the debtor's power of sale that would be effective where the sale is out of the ordinary course of business. The language of the provision makes it clear that knowledge on the part of the buyer that the goods being purchased in the ordinary course of business are subject to a security interest given by the seller is not relevant unless the buyer also knows that the sale is in violation of the security agreement. A buyer does not have the requisite knowledge of breach of a security agreement simply because she is aware that the debtor is in financial difficulties.[38]

---

lessee so long as the lease is extant. OPPSA s. 28(2) is more precise. It provides that a lessee takes free from a security interest in leased property to the extent of the lessee's rights under the lease.

35 *Northwest Equipment Inc. v. Daewoo Heavy Industries America Corporation*, [2002] 6 W.W.R. 444 (Alta. C.A.). PPSA, above note 32, provides that the buyer or lessee takes free from any perfected or unperfected security interest. The reference to "unperfected" is necessary since the requirements for priority over an unperfected security interest are different. Consequently, when the security interest is unperfected, the buyer can rely on either priority rule.

36 *Camco Inc. v. Frances Olson Realty (1979) Ltd.*, [1986] 6 W.W.R. 258 (Sask. C.A.); *Fairline Boats Ltd. v. Leger* (1980), 1 P.P.S.A.C. 218 (Ont. H.C.J.).

37 *Camco Inc. v. Frances Olson Realty (1979) Ltd., ibid.* at 276.

38 *Estevan Credit Union Limited v. Dyer*, [1997] 8 W.W.R. 49, additional reasons given, [1997] 8 W.W.R. 458 (Sask. Q.B.).

b)   What Is a Sale in the Ordinary Course of [the Seller's] Business?

i)   The Consideration

The ordinary course buyer and lessee protection provision of the Act applies to a "sale" or "lease" of goods. These terms are not defined in the Act. However, the Act provides some guidance.[39] A sale is generally a transaction under which the debtor's interest in the goods is transferred to a buyer in return for the payment of money or the promise to pay money. There is no requirement that the buyer take delivery of the goods. The Act provides that a transaction involving a transfer as security for a debt does not qualify.[40] A sale under which the consideration paid by the buyer is cancellation of part or all of a debt does not qualify as a sale in the ordinary course of business.[41] This feature of the Act requires clarification and, depending upon how it is interpreted, could produce commercially unacceptable results. The provision expressly removes from the scope of the ordinary course buyer priority rule a "transfer ... in total or partial satisfaction of ... a past liability." This would appear to exclude a sale under which part of the consideration is the discharge of a liability that arose between the parties under a prior sales contract. If, for example, the debtor agreed to allow the buyer to set off against the purchase price of the goods an amount owing by the debtor to the buyer as a result of a prior contract between the parties, the sale would not be a sale in the ordinary course of business.

It is the view of the authors that the exclusion should not be read as removing the sale from the protection of the ordinary course buyer priority rule unless the total purchase price is paid through total or partial satisfaction of an obligation owing by the buyer to the debtor.[42] The policy basis for excluding cancellation of debt as acceptable consideration in the context of sales or leases to which the buyer or lessee protection provisions apply is to ensure that the seller receives some proceeds to which the security interest in the sold or leased goods can attach. If the total consideration paid by the buyer or lessee is cancella-

---

39   PPSA (A, BC, NB, NWT, Nu, S) s. 30(8); (NL, NS) s. 31(8); M s. 30(7); Y s. 29(4); O no equivalent provision. See *Chrysler Credit Canada Ltd. v. M.V.L. Leasing Ltd.* (1993), 5 P.P.S.A.C. (2d) 92 (Ont. Ct. Gen. Div.).

40   *Royal Bank v. 216200 Alberta Ltd.* (1986), [1987] 1 W.W.R. 545.

41   Above note 39.

42   This is the approach taken by some courts in the United States when interpreting the equivalent provision of Article 9. See *General Electric Credit Corp. v. R.A. Heintz Construction Co.* 302 F. Supp. 958 (D. Or. 1969); *Walter E. Heller Western Inc. v. Bohemia, Inc.*, 655 P.2d 1073 (Or. App. 1982); but see *Franklin National Bank of Morrill, Nebraska*, 20 UCC Rep. Serv. 2d 1409 (Wyo. 1993).

tion of a debt owing by the seller or lessor, no proceeds are generated. However, if only part of the price paid is cancellation of the debt, the other part of the consideration received by the seller or lessor will be proceeds which, to the extent of their value, replace the collateral that has been sold or leased.

ii) Passage of Property to the Buyer

The lack of a definition of the term "sale" in the PPSA has given rise to the question as to whether the ordinary course buyer priority given by the Act[43] protects a buyer where the secured party takes steps to enforce its security interest before transfer of the debtor's interest in the goods to the buyer. There are contrary high-level judicial rulings on this issue.

In *Royal Bank v. 216200 Alberta Ltd.*,[44] the Saskatchewan Court of Appeal concluded that, when an inventory financer seized goods from a retailer who had agreed to order and deliver goods of that description to a customer, the buyer was not protected by the ordinary course buyer rule of the Saskatchewan Act since, at the time of seizure, goods meeting the contract description had not been appropriated to the sale contract with the result that property in the goods seized had not passed to the buyer. This was held to be so even though the buyer had paid part or all the purchase price of the goods ordered. The Court concluded that the rule should be read as incorporating in this context the rules on passage of property contained in the *Sale of Goods Act*.[45] The Court rejected the argument that the rule operates as soon as the contract of sale is made and that no regard should be had to the date property in the goods passes to the buyer.

The position of the Saskatchewan Court of Appeal was expressly rejected by the Ontario Court of Appeal in *Spittlehouse v. Northshore Marine Inc.*[46] In this case, the sales contract provided for the retention of title by the debtor (seller) pending payment of the total purchase price of the good purchased, a very expensive yacht. After the buyer had paid 90 per cent of the purchase price of the yacht and before it was delivered to the buyer, a secured creditor of the seller seized it to enforce a security interest given by the seller. The Court concluded that, if it were to apply the reasoning of the Saskatchewan Court of Appeal,

---

43   PPSA (A, BC, M, NB, NWT, Nu, PEI, S) s. 30(2); (NL, NS) s. 31(2); Y s. 29(1).
44   Above note 40. See also *Re Anderson's Engineering Ltd.*, (2002), 33 C.B.R. (4th) 1 (B.C.S.C.).
45   R.S.S. 1978, s. S-1.
46   (1994), 18 O.R. (3d) 60 [*Spittlehouse*].

injustice would result. Accordingly, it ruled that the *Sale of Goods Act*[47] is not relevant or material to the application of the ordinary course buyer rule of the Ontario Act in this context.[48] The Court did not express a clear opinion as to whether the section requires anything more than a sale of goods agreement between the parties in order to bring the section into operation.

The injustice of the approach taken by the Saskatchewan Court of Appeal is obvious where a sale of specific goods[49] is involved and the buyer has paid some or all of the purchase price and, for some reason, the title to the goods has not passed to the buyer. Furthermore, on the surface, the approach appears to be inconsistent with the Court's position, set out in *Camco Inc. v. Frances Olson Realty (1979) Ltd*,[50] that the ordinary course buyer rule should be given a broad interpretation so as to give maximum protection to buyers.

However, it is the view of the authors that the approach of the Saskatchewan Court of Appeal is technically more correct than that of the Ontario Court of Appeal and the one that produces the most consistent results. This is demonstrated in the following scenario. Assume that, as will almost always be the case where a competition exists between an inventory financer and a buyer in the ordinary course of business, the seller-debtor is insolvent at the time the priority competition arises. If the debtor is also a bankrupt, the buyer in the ordinary course of business will be competing not only with the inventory financer but also the debtor's trustee. Even if the approach in *Spittlehouse* is applied in the financer-buyer context, it cannot be applied in the trustee-buyer context because the determination as to whether or not property has passed to the buyer from the seller is determined under sale of goods rules. The buyer will defeat the claim of the trustee to the goods only when property

---

47   See *Sale of Goods Act*, R.S.O. 1990, c. S.1.

48   It is the view of the authors that the Court could have ruled in favour of the buyer without rejecting the approach taken by the Saskatchewan Court of Appeal. Since the sales contract between the seller and the buyer was a security agreement, for the purposes of the PPSA, the seller was a secured party and the buyer was the owner of the yacht. Under the reconceptualization that the Act imposes on conditional sales contracts, property in the yacht passed to the buyer as soon as the yacht was appropriated to the contract. The facts support the conclusion that this appropriation occurred before seizure of the boat by the secured party. See Jacob Ziegal, Commentary, "To what types of sale does section 28(1) of the OPPSA apply?" (1994–95) 24 Can. Bus. L.J. 457.

49   A sale of "specific goods" under the *Sale of Goods Act* is a sale of good identified and agreed upon at the time the sales agreement is entered into. See the *Sale of Goods Act*, above note 45, s. 2(1)(m).

50   Above note 36.

in the goods claimed by the buyer passed to her prior to the invocation of bankruptcy proceedings or when the court is prepared to order specific performance of the contract.[51] Otherwise the goods will be treated as part of the bankrupt's estate[52] subject, however, to the prior perfected security interest of the inventory financer.[53] The result is that the *Spittlehouse* approach provides protection to buyers in the ordinary course of business only in cases where bankruptcy of the debtor is not involved. It is well established that it is not an abuse of process for a secured party to invoke bankruptcy for the sole purpose of avoiding a priority rule of provincial law.[54] Consequently, inventory suppliers are given an inducement to invoke bankruptcy proceedings against debtors in order to defeat the claims of customers of the dealers who would otherwise be given priority under the *Spittlehouse* approach.

Acceptance of the approach of the Saskatchewan Court of Appeal as legally the most sound and consistent one should not be viewed as an argument for the position that the law in its present form in Saskatchewan in this respect is satisfactory. It is the view of the authors that the *Sale of Goods Act* should be amended to provide protection for pre-paying buyers of unascertained goods or specific goods the title to which does not pass at the date of the sale.[55] The approach of the Ontario Court of Appeal in *Spittlehouse* is inadequate not because the court's policy instincts were wrong but because it provides limited and easily-circumvented protection.

iii) What Is Ordinary Course?

While, ultimately, it is a finding of fact in each particular case, the courts have provided guidance in general terms as to the meaning of

---

51 *Re Anderson's Engineering Ltd.*, above note 44; *Western Canada Pulpwood & Lumber Co.* (1929), 11 C.B.R. 125 (Man. C.A.).

52 Except where the reason for the property not passing is its retention by the debtor to secure the purchase price of the goods.

53 *Bankruptcy and Insolvency Act*, R.S.C. 1985, c. B-3, s. 136(1).

54 *Bank of Montreal v. Scott Road Enterprises Ltd.* (1989), 57 D.L.R. (4th) 623 (B.C.C.A.).

55 The British Columbia Legislature has provided leadership in this respect. See Part 9, *Sale of Goods Act*, R.S.B.C. 1996, c. 410 which gives to a pre-paying buyer a statutory lien for the amount paid on all goods that are in or come into the possession of the seller and are held by the seller for sale that correspond with the description of or with any sample of the goods under the agreement to sell the property in which has not passed to a different buyer under a different contract of sale, and on any account in a savings institution in which the seller usually deposits the proceeds of sales.

"sale in the ordinary course of business."[56] Generally, a sale in the ordinary course of business includes a sale to the public at large of the type normally made by the vendor in a particular business, where the basic business dealings between buyer and seller are carried out under normal terms and consistent with general commercial practice. Generally, it does not include private sales between individual buyers, nor does it include a sale by a dealer under unusual circumstances.[57] For example, where a retail car dealer sold to a friend thirteen vehicles, chosen by the dealer, which comprised one-half of the dealer's used-vehicle inventory, the sale was found not to be made in the ordinary course of business.[58]

A sale in the ordinary course of business need not involve a sale by a retail seller to a customer on retail business premises. For example, a sale in the ordinary course of business can occur where cattle is sold by a farmer to another farmer[59] or grain is sold by a farmer to a feedlot,[60] and where an automobile dealer sells vehicles to another dealer.[61]

iv) *Ordinary Course of Business "of the Seller"*
There is a possible difference between the Ontario Act and the other Acts with respect to the test to be applied in the context of sales in the ordinary course of business. The other Acts refer to "goods sold or leased in the ordinary course of business of the seller or lessor …"[62] The Ontario Act refers to the sale or lease of goods "in the ordinary course of business."[63] This difference was considered important by the Saskatchewan Court of Appeal in *Camco Inc. v. Frances Olson Realty* (1979)

56 In *Fairline Boats Ltd. v. Leger,* above note 36, the court set out the following factors that should be considered: (1) whether the agreement is made at the business premises of the seller; (2) whether the buyer is an ordinary, everyday consumer, or a dealer or financial institution; (3) the quantity of the goods sold —a small numbers of items or a substantial proportion of the stock of the seller; (4) the price charged for the goods — the usual market price or a low price.
57 *Royal Bank v. 216200 Alberta Ltd.,* above note 40; *Northwest Equipment Inc. v. Daewoo Heavy Industries America Corporation,* above note 35.
58 *Estevan Credit Union Limited v. Dyer,* above note 38. See also *Re 547592 Alberta Ltd.* (1995), 10 P.P.S.A.C. (2d) 62 (Alta. Q.B.).
59 *Saskatchewan Wheat Pool v. Smith* (1996), 142 Sask. R. 285 (Q.B.), aff'd (1997), 152 Sask.R. 79 (C.A.).
60 *Agricultural Commodity Corp. v. Schaus Feedlots Inc.* (2001), 2 P.P.S.A.C. (3d) 270 (Ont. S.C.J.), aff'd (2003), 4 P.P.S.A.C. (3d) 266 (Ont. C.A.).
61 *Ford Motor Credit Corp. v. Centre Motors of Brampton* (1982), 137 D.L.R. (3d) 634 (Ont. H.C.J.); *Chrysler Credit Canada Ltd. v. M.V.L. Leasing Ltd.,* above note 39.
62 PPSA (A, BC, M, NB, NWT, Nu, PEI, S) s. 30(2); (NL, NS) s. 31(2); Y s. 29(1).
63 OPPSA s. 28(2).

Ltd.[64] The court concluded that the ordinary course buyer provision of
the Saskatchewan Act focuses on the business of the particular seller
whereas the equivalent provision of the Ontario Act involves the more
limited inquiry as to practices in the trade or industry as a whole.[65]
Consequently, when determining whether a condominium seller was
acting in the ordinary course of business when it sold appliances subject to perfected security interests along with the condominiums, it
was not considered relevant that appliances are generally sold in retail
stores. The court concluded that the mere fact that the seller was engaged in the selling of appliances as an incident to its primary business
of selling condominium units did not preclude a finding that the sales
were in the ordinary course of business of the seller.

Although the general tests developed by the courts provide sufficient guidance as to the proper application of the ordinary course of
business priority rule, there is one highly fact-dependent situation in
which general tests are not very helpful. This is where goods subject to
a security interest originally held by a business debtor as equipment
are then sold.[66] While there is no easy way to determine when the sale
of equipment becomes a sale in the ordinary course of business of the
seller, there are two factors that must be brought into the determination. These are the frequency with which the sales take place and the
circumstances in which they occur. Simply because a debtor is engaged
in business activity, it does not follow that any sale by the debtor of
its equipment is in the ordinary course of its business. However, if as
a regular part of carrying on its business, the debtor sell goods that
to that point were being used as equipment under circumstances in
which goods of that kind are generally sold, the sales are in the ordinary course of its business. The focus is on what is ordinary business
activity. "Ordinary" reflects frequency of sale or usual practices of the
seller or other participants in the same or similar businesses; "business" reflects the circumstances of the sales. Accordingly, if the circumstances of the sale parallel those of sales of inventory, the fact that

---

64 Above note 36.

65 *Ibid.* at 276.

66 See *Alberta Pacific Leasing Inc. v. Petro Equipment Sales Ltd.* (1995), 10 P.P.S.A.C.
    (2d) 69 (Alta. Q.B.). Some guidance can be obtained from decisions interpreting
    the words "regularly engaged in the business of leasing" found in the definition
    of "lease for a term of more than one year" in PPSA S s. 2(1); (M, NB) s. 1; A s.
    1(1); (BC, NWT, Nu, Y) s. 1(1); NS s. 2; NL s. 2; PEI s. 1. See *David Morris Fine
    Cars Ltd. v. North Sky Trading Inc.* (1994), 27 C.B.R. (3d) 252 (Alta. Q.B.), aff'd
    (1996), 38 Alta. L.R. (3d) 428 (C.A.); *Re Sinco Trucking Ltd.* (1987), 7 P.P.S.A.C.
    176 (Sask. Q.B.).

only one such sale has taken place should not preclude the conclusion that there has been a sale in the ordinary course of business.

v)   Security Interests Given by a Prior Seller

The Act[67] provides that a qualifying buyer takes or holds the goods bought in the ordinary course of business "free from" any security interest in the goods "given by the seller." It is clear that the reference to "seller" is to the person who had contracted with the buyer[68] and not to a prior seller who sold the goods to the person with whom the protected purchaser has contracted.[69] This being the case, the Act does not always protect buyers who acquire goods in the ordinary course of business. The limitations of this feature of the Act are most apparent in the context of situations where a buyer acquires goods from a dealer in used property. The buyer in such situation must take additional steps to avoid loss resulting from having to surrender the goods to the holder of a perfected security interest in the goods given by a person who sold the goods to the dealer or by someone earlier in the chain of ownership. This is demonstrated in the following scenario.

SP takes a security interest in a motor vehicle owned by D. This security interest is perfected. D trades-in (sells) the vehicle to Used Car Dealer as part of an arrangement to purchase a newer vehicle. Used Car Dealer sells the original motor vehicle to Buyer in the ordinary course of its business. D defaults in his obligation to SP and SP seizes the motor vehicle from Buyer. There is no priority rule that puts Buyer in the position of taking free from SP's security interest. The buyer in ordinary course priority rule applies only to a security interest given by Used Car Dealer. It does not apply to the security interest given by D.

Alternative protective measures are available to buyers of used goods. If the goods are serial numbered goods, in most situations, the buyer will be able to discover an earlier security interest through a registry search using the serial number of the goods.[70] If the price of

---

67   PPSA (A, BC, M, NB, NWT, Nu, PEI, S) s. 30(2); (NL, NS) s. 31(2); Y s. 29(1).

68   The ordinary-course buyer provision applies where the person who contracts with the buyer is acting as agent of the seller-debtor. See *National Trust Co. v. Kirch* (1993), 12 O.R. (3d) 781 (Gen. Div.).

69   See *General Motors Acceptance Corporation of Canada Ltd. v. Owens* (1993), 11 Alta. L.R. (3d) 269 (Q.B.); *Ensign Pacific Leasing Ltd. v. Lumar Auto Sales,* (1998), 52 B.C.L.R. (3d) 218 (S.C.).

70   The circumstances under which this is possible are discussed in the next section, "Buyers of Serial Numbered Goods." However, a serial number search will not be effective where the goods were inventory when the initial security inter-

the goods is not greater than $1,000, the buyer is protected by a special priority rule in all jurisdictions other than Ontario. [71]

3) Buyers of Serial Numbered Goods

There is a deficiency endemic to any registry system based on debtor name as the registration-search criterion. This is shown in the following scenario.

SP takes and perfects a security interest in collateral of D. D sells the collateral to B1 and then sells it to B2. If all B2 has is D's name as the search criterion, he will not be able to discover SP's registration unless B1 discloses the identity of the person (D) from whom he acquired the goods. The remedy for this deficiency is to give to B2 a search criterion he can use to discover SP's security interest. The serial number or other unique collateral identifier serves this purpose. It is for this reason that the PPSA provides that in specified circumstances, serial numbered goods collateral must be identified in a registration in the manner prescribed by regulations.

Generally, serial number registration requirements are most effective in cases where the collateral is goods that are highly mobile. This recognizes the susceptibility of these types of goods to being passed from the debtor to a buyer and from one buyer to another, often in second hand, private sale markets. Goods with limited mobility are more likely to stay in the debtor's possession or to be associated with a specific activity or place. As a result they are less susceptible to multiple transactions occurring under circumstances in which debtors' names are ineffective search criteria.[72]

The types of goods that are categorized as "serial numbered goods"[73] are much less numerous under the Ontario Act than under the other Acts. Under the regulations to these Acts, a motor vehicle (broadly defined), a trailer, aircraft, a boat, and an outboard motor for a boat are

---

est was taken and were initially sold by the debtor other than in the ordinary course of business. See *Royal Bank v. Wheaton Pontiac Buick Cadillac GMAC Ltd.* (1990), 88 Sask. R. 151 (Q.B.).

71   PPSA (A, BC, M, NB, NWT, Nu, PEI, S) s. 30(3); (NL, NS) s. 31(3); Y 29(3); O no equivalent provision. The effect of these provisions is examined later in the chapter in "Buyers of Low-value Goods."

72   *Royal Bank of Canada v. Steinhubl's Masonry Ltd.*, [2004] 1 W.W.R. 267 (Sask. Q.B.).

73   The term "serial numbered goods" is not used in the Ontario regulations. What is required is the vehicle identification number, which may be a serial number of the goods, however.

serial numbered goods.[74] In contrast, the special priority rules of the Ontario Act based on vehicle identification number registration apply only to a "motor vehicle" (albeit, equally broadly defined).[75]

The PPSA requires as a condition of perfection of security interests in serial numbered goods held by the debtor as consumer goods that registrations contain the serial numbers or vehicle identification numbers of the collateral.[76] The Act, other than the Ontario Act, employs a bifurcated approach where the serial numbered goods are held by the debtor as "equipment."[77] A security interest in (serial numbered goods) equipment that is registered using the name of the debtor as the registration criterion is perfected. However, unless the registration also includes the serial number of the equipment, the security interest is cut off when the goods are bought by a buyer who gave value and bought the goods without knowledge of the security interest.[78]

Section 28(5) of the Ontario Act provides that a buyer of a motor vehicle "classified as equipment of the seller" takes free from a security interest in the vehicle "given by the seller" unless the registration relating to the security interest contains the vehicle identification number of the vehicle or unless the buyer knew that the "purchase constituted a breach of the security agreement."[79] This approach is more limited in its effect as a buyer protection measure. It applies only to security interests given by the seller. Consequently, it has no value where the

---

74   See, for example, R.R.S., c. P-6.2, Reg. 1, ss. 2(b), (d), (n), (o), (u), and (w); 12, 13.

75   R.R.O. Reg. 912, ss. 1, 3(6)–(10). See also OPPSA s. 25(5).

76   PPSA (A, BC, NWT, Nu, S) s. 43(7); (M, NB, PEI) s. 43(8); (NL, NS) s. 44(8); (O, Y) no equivalent provision. See also R.R.S., c. P-6.2, Reg. 1, ss. 12–13 and R.R.O. Reg. 912, ss.1, 3(6)–(10). As to whether serial number alone is sufficient without the name of the debtor in a form that is not seriously misleading, see chapters 6 and 8.

77   For the definition of equipment, see PPSA (A, BC, NWT, Nu, O, Y) s. 1(1); (M, NB, PEI) s. 1; (NL, NS) s. 2; S s. 2(1).

78   PPSA (A, BC, M, NB, NWT, Nu, PEI, S) s. 30(6)–(7); (NL, NS) s. 31(6)–(7); Y s. 29(2); O no equivalent provision. A similar approach is taken with respect to a competing perfected security interest in the equipment. If the serial number of the collateral is not included in the registration, the competing, perfected security interest is given priority provided that the competing secured party included a serial number description in its own registration: PPSA (A, BC, M, NB, NWT, Nu, PEI, S) s. 35(4); (NL, NS) s. 36(4); (O, Y) no equivalent provision.

79   In this respect, the provision adds another kind of test where buyers out of the ordinary course of business are involved. OPPSA s. 20(1)(c) requires that the buyer be "without knowledge" of the unperfected security interest and that she take possession of the collateral. OPPSA s. 25(5) requires the buyer to be acting "in good faith." There is no requirement that the buyer take possession of the goods,

security interest in the equipment has been given by a remote party. In this respect, it contains the same limitation found in the ordinary course of business priority rule of the PPSA[80] examined earlier in this chapter. No such limitation is contained in the other Acts which apply to any security interest in the goods perfected by registration.

4) Buyers of Low-value Goods

All Acts other than the Ontario Act,[81] embody the policy decision that buyers or lessees of small-value consumer goods[82] acquired other than in the ordinary course of business of the seller should not be subjected to the cost and inconvenience of having to search the registry for any outstanding security interests.[83] In addition, it provides protection in some situations where a search of the registry would not reveal the registration because the person who is selling the goods is not the debtor.[84]

The circumstances under which this protection is provided are different from those in which the ordinary course of business priority rule functions. The protection is broader in scope in that the seller need not be selling in the ordinary course of business. It extends to all prior security interests in the goods, whether given by the seller or a prior owner of the goods. Otherwise the protection is narrower in scope. The price of the goods bought (or the value of the goods leased) must not exceed $1,000 or an amount prescribed by regulation. The buyer must be without knowledge of the existence of the security interest in the goods. It is not sufficient that she is unaware that the sale is in violation of a security agreement providing for the security interest.[85]

An uncertainty associated with application of this priority rule arises when a buyer purchases under a single contract several items of goods where no single item has a market value of more than $1,000 but

---

80 See text accompanying above note 68.
81 PPSA (A, BC, M, NB, NWT, Nu, PEI, S) ss. 30(3)–(4); (NL, NS) ss. 31(3)–(4); Y s. 29 (3); O no equivalent provision. The Yukon provision applies to all consumer goods other than "special consumer goods."
82 The SPPSA ss. 30(3)–(4) apply also to sales of goods purchased for farming purposes.
83 The provisions are generally referred to as the "garage sale" priority rule because it is in the context of purchases at garage sales that they will be most frequently relevant.
84 This is the so-called A-B-C-D problem endemic to a registry system that is based on the debtor name as the registration-search criterion.
85 The YPPSA s. 29(3) requires the buyer to take possession of the goods.

298 PERSONAL PROPERTY SECURITY LAW

the total price of all the items bought exceeds $1,000. It is the view of the authors that the word "goods" in this provision[86] should be interpreted in the singular. Only if the actual or imputed price of any one of the items purchased exceeds $1,000 should the protection of the provision be inapplicable with respect to that item. This conclusion is based on the assumption that it is only when the goods having a market value greater than $1,000 are involved that a buyer should be expected to incur the cost and inconvenience of a registry search. From a practical point of view, a secured party is likely to be concerned about the loss of its security interest to a good faith buyer only when the item of goods involved is of substantial value.

5) The Effectiveness of Automatically Perfected Security Interests against Buyers

The PPSA provides that in several specific contexts a security interest is perfected without the secured party having to take a perfection step (that is, registration or taking possession of the collateral).[87] While generally automatic perfection is temporary, the potential exists for buyer deception if automatically perfected security interests are given priority over buyers.

The PPSA gives automatic perfected status to a security interest in goods that attached while the goods were located in one jurisdiction but which are later relocated to a new jurisdiction. So long as perfection has not lapsed under the law of the original jurisdiction, the security interest is treated as continuously perfected provided it is re-perfected in accordance with new jurisdiction's PPSA before the expiration of a specified time period.[88]

This is subject to an important exception in favour of a buyer or lessee who acquires the goods after they are relocated to the new jurisdiction without knowledge of the foreign security interest and before it is re-perfected in accordance with the new jurisdiction's PPSA.[89] Under the Act a temporarily perfected foreign security interest is subordinate to the interest of a buyer of goods, other than goods of a kind that are

---

86   Above note 81.
87   For an examination of automatic perfection, see chapter 5.
88   PPSA (BC, M, NB, NWT, Nu, PEI, S) s. 5(3); (NL, NS) s. 6(3); A s. 4(2); O s. 5(2); Y. s. 4(3). For a detailed discussion of the impact of a post-attachment change in the location of goods on the law applicable to perfection and priority, see chapter 3.
89   *Ibid.*; Y no equivalent provision.

normally used in more than one jurisdiction and held by the debtor as equipment or inventory leased or held for lease by the debtor to others,[90] who acquired the interest without knowledge of the security interest and before it is perfected in the jurisdiction either by registration or by the secured party taking possession of the goods.

The protection granted to buyers and lessees under the Ontario Act[91] in the equivalent situation is somewhat narrower. A foreign security interest that is not perfected in Ontario at the time of the sale or lease is subordinate to a buyer or lessee who acquired the goods from the debtor in Ontario as consumer goods in good faith and without knowledge of the security interest. In other words, the buyer must have acquired the goods for personal, family, or purposes. If the goods are bought for use as equipment or inventory, the buyer is not protected. On the other hand, while the purchase contract must be with "the debtor," this would appear to include not only the debtor under the security agreement creating the security interest but also a transferee of the debtor or successor in to the debtor's interest in the collateral.[92] Consequently, even if the initial sale by the debtor is made to someone who buys the goods as equipment or inventory, any sale by that person to a buyer who intends to use the goods as consumer goods would appear to fall within section 5(2).

Under all the Acts, a very different approach applies where the foreign security interest is in goods that are of a kind that are normally used in more than one jurisdiction and held by the debtor as equipment or inventory leased or held for lease by the debtor to others.[93] Where this type of collateral is involved, the buyer must rely on public disclosure under the law of the jurisdiction where the debtor is located at the time the security interest attaches,[94] unless (with the exception of the Ontario Act) there is no public registry for security interests in that

---

90   See PPSA (A, BC, M, NB, NWT, Nu, O, PEI, S) s. 7; (NL, NS) s. 8; Y s. 6.
91   OPPSA s. 5(2).
92   While the purchase contract must be with "the debtor," the term "debtor" is defined in OPPSA s. 1 to include "a transferee of or successor to a debtor's interest in the collateral." Consequently, even if the initial sale by the debtor is made to someone who buys the goods as equipment or inventory, any sale by that person to a buyer who intends to use the goods as consumer goods would fall within OPPSA s. 5(2).
93   For a detailed discussion of the impact of a post-attachment change in the location of the debtor on the law applicable to perfection and priority, see chapter 3.
94   Above note 90.

jurisdiction.[95] The Act provides for a period of automatic perfection when the debtor changes location to another jurisdiction or transfers an interest in the collateral to a person located in another jurisdiction.[96] However, the Act contains no protection for persons who buy the collateral in reliance on a registry search made in the new jurisdiction during the period of automatic perfection unless under there is no public registry for security interests in that jurisdiction.[97]

The Act[98] gives temporary, unconditional perfected status to a security interest in proceeds. The security interest and its perfected status in the original collateral automatically continues in the proceeds. However, perfection terminates upon the expiration of fifteen days after the security interest attaches to the proceeds, unless it is otherwise perfected by any of the methods applicable to original collateral of the same kind. Under the Ontario Act, separate perfection of a security interest in proceeds is required when the security interest in the original collateral was perfected otherwise than by registration.[99] In this case, the period of temporary, unconditional perfection is ten days.[100]

In addition, the Act provides a specialized variant of the principle that a security interest continues in proceeds. This feature[101] gives to a secured party holding a security interest in chattel paper, a statutory security interest in the goods to which the chattel paper relates, when those goods are returned to or repossessed by the original debtor-seller or by the secured party. This statutory security interest in the goods is unconditionally perfected for a period of fifteen days (ten days under the Ontario Act) from the date of return or repossession of the collateral.[102]

---

95 PPSA (A, BC, M, NB, NWT, Nu, PEI, S) s. 7(4); (NL, NS) s. 8(4); Y s. 6(4); O no equivalent provision.

96 PPSA (A, BC, M, NB, NWT, Nu, PEI, S) s. 7(3); (NL, NS) s. 8(3); O s. 7(2); Y s. 6(3); O s. 7(2) addresses only the case where the debtor relocates to Ontario.

97 Above note 90.

98 PPSA (A, BC, NWT, Nu, S) s. 28(3); (NB, PEI) s. 28(4); (NL, NS) s. 29(1); M s. 28(2); O s. 25(4); Y s. 26(2). These provisions are examined in greater detail in chapter 12.

99 Where a motor vehicle that is consumer goods is proceeds, the serial number must be registered if the security interest is to have priority over a good faith buyer. For further discussion, see "Buyers of Serial numbered Goods."

100 OPPSA s. 25(4).

101 PPSA (A, BC, M, NB, NWT, Nu, PEI, S) s. 29; (NL, NS) s. 30; O s. 27(1); Y s. 28.

102 PPSA (A, BC, M, NB, NWT, Nu, S) s. 29(3); (NL, NS) s. 30(3); O s. 27(3); Y s. 28(4).

The Act[103] provides that a buyer of goods takes free from a security interest temporarily perfected as proceeds or returned or repossessed goods if the buyer gave value and bought the goods without knowledge of the security interest. The Manitoba Act provides this protection only in cases where the goods purchased are returned or repossessed.[104] There is no protection where the collateral is proceeds. Under the Ontario Act, there is no protection for buyers of goods that are proceeds automatically perfected during the ten-day period following their acquisition by the debtor unless the proceeds are in the form of a motor vehicle bought as consumer goods.[105] Nor is there protection under the Ontario Act for a buyer of returned or repossessed goods who acquired her interest during the ten-day period of temporary perfection following their return or repossession.[106] The failure of the Manitoba and Ontario Acts to provide protection to buyers of proceeds is consistent with the general approach contained in these Acts under which security interests in proceeds are deemed perfected without the need to take any additional perfection measure relating to the proceeds so long as the security interests in the original collateral were perfected by registration.

The Act[107] provides a short period of automatic perfection when a security interest in goods or in a negotiable document of title to goods has been perfected by possession and it is commercially necessary for the secured party to release the collateral to the debtor in order to allow him to deal with it one of the ways specified in the section. However, the Act[108] provides that a buyer or lessee of goods who gives value and acquires her interest without knowledge of the security interest takes free of a security interest temporarily perfected under these circumstances. This protection is not dependent upon the debtor having sold or leased the goods in the ordinary course of business. All that is required is that the buyer or lessee gives value and has acquired her interest without knowledge of the security interest.

The Yukon Act grants automatic permanent perfection to a purchase-money security interest in consumer goods (other than serial numbered goods and goods of a value in excess of an amount specified

---

103 PPSA (A, BC, M, NB, NWT, Nu, PEI, S) s. 30(5); (NL, NS) s. 31(5); Y s. 29(5).
The YPPSA requires that the buyer also take delivery of the goods.
104 MPPSA s. 30(2).
105 OPPSA s. 25(5).
106 OPPSA s. 27(4).
107 PPSA (A, BC, M, NB, NWT, Nu, PEI, S) s. 26; (NL, NS) s. 27; O s. 24(3); Y s. 25.
108 Above note 102. There is no equivalent of this provision in the OPPSA.

in regulations).[109] However, it also provides that a buyer or lessee of such goods takes free from a perfected security interest in such goods acquired for value, without knowledge of the security interest if the buyer or lessee receives delivery of the goods.[110]

6) Interface with *Sale of Goods Act* and *Factors Act* Buyer-protection Provisions

Consideration of the buyer in possession and seller in possession provisions of the *Sale of Goods Act*[111] (and, in some provinces, the *Factors Act*[112]) is required in order to get a complete picture of the position of a buyer of goods subject a security interest. These provisions were modified with the advent of the PPSA. In the following discussion, the Saskatchewan *Sale of Goods Act* (SGA) is referred to in the footnotes. Unless otherwise indicated, the Saskatchewan provisions are representative of the other SGAs (although the section numbering may differ).

The SGA gives power to a non-owning buyer or mercantile agent of the buyer who has possession of goods or a document of title to the goods with the consent of the buyer the power to sell, pledge, or otherwise dispose of the goods to a person who receives them or the document of title to them in good faith and without notice of any right of the seller in the goods. The effect of the sale, pledge, or disposition is the same as if the buyer were a mercantile agent in possession of the goods or documents of title with the consent of the owner.[113] The scope of this provision has been dramatically reduced in all jurisdictions so that it now applies only where the contract between the seller and buyer is not a security agreement that creates a security interest under the PPSA.[114] Consequently, it has little significance in the context of the priority regime of the PPSA affecting buyers of goods.[115]

The SGA also provides that when a person has sold goods (with the result that title to the goods passes to the buyer) but continues in

---

109 YPPSA s. 24.
110 YPPSA s. 29(3).
111 For example, R.S.S. 1978, c. S-1, s. 26; R.S.A. 2000, c. S-2, s. 26; R.S.B.C. 1996, c. 410, s. 30; C.C.S.M. c. S10, s. 28; C S.N.B. 1997, c. S-1, s. 24; R.S.N.W.T. 1998, c. S-2. s. 27 (also Nunavut); R.S.O. 1990, c. S.1, s. 25; R.S.Y. 2002, c. 198, s. 24.
112 For example, R.S.S. 1978, c. F-1, ss. 9–10; R.S.P.E.I. 1998, c. F-1, s. 9.
113 This section is subject to a gloss that is not examined in this text. See M.B. Bridge, *Sale of Goods* (Toronto: Butterworths, 1988) at 654–62.
114 See, for example, *The Sale of Goods Act*, R.S.S. 1978, c. S-1, s. 26(4). See also above notes 111, 112: A, BC, M, NB, NWT, Nu, PEI, O, Y.
115 See *Bank of Nova Scotia v. Steffens* (2002), 645 A.P.R. 299 (N.S.S.C.).

possession of the goods or document of title to the goods, the delivery or transfer of the goods or document by the seller or a mercantile agent acting for him, under a "sale, pledge or other disposition," to a person receiving the goods or document in good faith and without notice of the previous sale has the same effect as if the seller making the delivery or transfer was expressly authorized by the owner of the goods to do so.[116]

The effect of this provision is to give power to the seller in possession to dispose of or create a security interest in goods without the consent of their owner, the buyer who acquired title in the initial sale.[117] However, to defeat the interest of the initial buyer, the section requires "delivery or transfer of the goods or document of title" to and receipt of the goods by the subsequent secured party or buyer. There is debate in the case law as to whether constructive delivery of the goods is sufficient for this purpose. The dominant view, which the authors support, is that actual delivery is required.[118] On this view, the only type of security interest that a seller in possession is empowered by the SGA to create in the goods is a classic pledge, or, in the parlance of the PPSA a possessory security interest, that is, a security interest that is capable of attachment and perfection against third parties through possession of the collateral by the secured party or agent of the secured party.[119]

With the exception of Ontario, PPSA jurisdictions enable a buyer who has left the seller in possession to protect her title by registration in the Personal Property Registry. This provision addresses the problem that is displayed in the following scenario.

Seller sells goods to A, who then gives a security interest in them to SP1 who perfects the security interest by registration. Seller, who retained possession of the goods, sells and delivers them to B. Since the effect of the seller in possession section is to cut off A's interest, it follows that SP1's derivative interest is also cut off.[120] Thus, a security interest given by B to SP2 would

---

116 Section 26(1).

117 This power gives to the seller in possession "rights in the collateral" under PPSA (A, BC, M, NB, NWT, Nu, PEI, S) s. 12; (NL, NS) s. 13; (O, Y) s. 11.

118 See Bridge, above note 113 at 645–47.

119 The pledge has not survived as a *sui generic* type of security interest under the PPSA. However, its functional spirit has been preserved insofar as the PPSA recognizes that possession of the collateral by the secured party can substitute for a written security agreement for the purposes of third party attachment of a security interest (see also chapter 4) and also constitutes an effective alternative method of perfection (see also chapter 5).

120 *National Trust Company v. Kirch*, above note 68.

have priority even though SP1's security interest was perfected at the time of the sale by the seller to B.

The *Sale of Goods Acts* of all PPSA jurisdictions except Ontario and the Yukon Territory were amended to address problems that arose after the repeal of the Bills of Sales Acts (that provided for registration of sales transactions under which possession of the goods remained with the seller) that accompanied enactment of the PPSA.[121] Two different approaches have been taken.

Under the first approach,[122] the SGA has been amended to enable the initial buyer to protect its title against a subsequent sale or grant of security in the goods by a seller in possession where the subsequent transaction takes place outside the ordinary course of the seller's business. As soon as the interest of the initial buyer is registered in the Personal Property Registry, the seller in possession loses the power otherwise given by the SGA to create security interests in or convey title to the goods to other persons.

Section 26(1.1) of the Saskatchewan SGA is representative of this approach. The Act provides that section 26(1) does not apply to a sale, pledge, or disposition of goods or documents that is out of the ordinary course of business of the seller where, prior to the sale, pledge or disposition, the interest of the owner is registered in the Personal Property Registry. The effect of this provision is to reinstate the common law *nemo dat* rule when the initial buyer timely registers his ownership in the Personal Property Registry. The result is that, once this registration is effected, the seller in possession loses the power given by section 26(1) to create security interests or transfer ownership rights in the goods to other persons. The operation of this provision is shown in the following scenario.

Seller sells goods to A but retains possession of them. Immediately after the sale, A registers her ownership in the goods in the Personal Property Registry. Thereafter the seller, acting out of the ordinary course of business, sells or gives a security interest in the goods to B. Since A registered before the subsequent sale or grant of security by the seller, A's ownership or any perfected security interest in the goods given by A is not affected by the subsequent sale or grant of a security interest in the goods.

---

121 See Ontario Law Reform Commission, *Report on Sale of Goods* (Toronto: Ministry of the Attorney General, 1979) at 302–5.

122 See, for example, *The Sale of Goods Act,* above note 114. s. 26(1.1) and above note 111: A, BC, NWT, Nu, PEI.

Registration of the initial buyer's interest does not affect the operation of the seller in possession provision if the sale, pledge or disposition occurs in "the ordinary course of business of the seller." Consequently, in the above-noted scenario, A's interest would be subject to defeat even though it is registered if the subsequent sale or security interest granted by the seller in possession occurred in the ordinary course of her business.

Since the concept of "sale in the ordinary course of business of the seller" is not otherwise addressed in the SGA, it is reasonable to assume that the drafters of the amendment to the seller in possession provision intended that the case law dealing with the concept of a sale in the ordinary course of business in the PPSA[123] would be applicable.

It is clear that the drafters of the SGA amendment intended that the grant of a possessory security interest by a seller in possession would also prevail over the title of the initial buyer provided that the transfer of possession takes place in the ordinary course of the seller's business. However, the PPSA provides no guidance on what constitutes an ordinary course pledge as opposed to an ordinary course sale. It is the view of the authors that the concept should be given a narrow scope in the context of security interests. The public policy considerations that warrant protecting ordinary course buyers and lessees are inapplicable where the seller grants a security interest in goods he does not own. A secured party contemplating taking a possessory security interest in goods in the debtor's possession can discover the existence of the initial buyer's ownership rights through a search of the registry. Unlike buyers who deal with sellers acting in the ordinary course of business, secured parties can be expected to obtain a registry search before granting credit to sellers and taking security interest in good in their possession.

Under the second approach to the post-PPSA operation of the seller in possession provision of the SGA,[124] a "sale of goods without a change of possession," is deemed to create a security interest under the PPSA.[125] A transaction that qualifies as a "sale of goods without a change of possession" is then excluded from the scope of the seller in possession provisions of the SGA of the jurisdictions that have adopted this approach.[126] However, a deemed security interest in the nature of

---

123 PPSA (A, BC, PEI, S, NWT, Nu) s. 30(2).
124 See above note 112. Prince Edward Island has adopted both approaches.
125 PPSA NB s. 3(2); NS s. 4(2); NL s. 4(2); PEI s. 3(2). It is not a security interest, however, within Part 5 (enforcement). See, for example, NBPPSA ss. 3(2) and 55.
126 See, for example, NB SGA, s. 24(4). This change was not adopted in Price Edward Island.

a "sale of goods without a change of possession," is defined to exclude a sale in the ordinary course of business of the seller.[127] Consequently, where the initial sale is in the ordinary course of business of the seller, the interest of the initial buyer is not a security interest but is subject to the seller in possession exception to the *nemo dat* rule of the *Sale of Goods Act*.

There are functional, as well as conceptual, differences between these two approaches. Under the first approach — represented by the Saskatchewan SGA — the failure on the part of the initial buyer to register his ownership exposes him to loss of that ownership to a subsequent buyer or secured party to whom the seller delivers possession of the goods in the ordinary course of the seller's business. Under the second approach the consequences of non-registration are more significant. The buyer's ownership can be lost or subordinated not only to another buyer, but also to a secured creditor of the seller who has perfected his security interest by any method and to the seller's unsecured creditors or trustee in bankruptcy. This policy underlying this second approach represents a continuation of the old *Bills of Sale Act* policy that protected subsequent buyers, subsequent mortgagees, and creditors generally against the risk that goods in the possession of X in fact belonged to Y — often a related company — pursuant to a non-ordinary course of business sale.

There is another functional difference between the two approaches. Under the second approach, an initial buyer who acquires goods through a sale in the ordinary course of business of the seller cannot protect her ownership from the operation of the seller in possession provision of the *Sale of Goods Act* by registration in the Personal Property Registry. The initial buyer's interest is deemed to be a security interest only if the goods were acquired in a sale that was not in the ordinary course of business of the seller. This is not the case under the first approach. Registration of the initial buyer's interest bars application of the seller in possession exception to *nemo dat* whether or not that sale was one occurring in the ordinary course of business of the seller. However, this distinction is only relevant when the subsequent sale, grant of a security interest, or other disposition occurs out of the ordinary course of business of the seller. Under the first approach, registration protects the initial buyer's interest only when the subsequent transaction is not in the ordinary course of business of the seller.

Assume a seller sells goods to A but retains possession of them. If this is a sale in the ordinary course of business of the seller, A's inter-

---

127   This is a defined term in the relevant PPSAs. See NB s. 1; (NL, NS) s. 2; PEI s. 1.

est is not a deemed security interest under the second approach and, therefore, cannot be protected by registration from the effects of the seller in possession rule of the *Sale of Goods Act*. In contrast, under the first approach, A's ownership interest can be registered in the Personal Property Registry.

If thereafter the seller, acting outside the ordinary course of business, sells or gives a security interest in the goods to B, under the second approach, A's ownership is lost or subordinated to a buyer or secured party who takes possession of the goods and thereby qualifies for protection under the seller in possession rule of the SGA. Under the first approach, A's ownership is protected by the registration. However, under this approach, A's ownership would be lost or subordinated to a qualifying buyer or secured party if the subsequent sale or security agreement occurred in the ordinary course of business of the seller.

CHAPTER 8

COMPETITIONS BETWEEN SECURED PARTIES

A. THE STRUCTURE OF THE PPSA PRIORITY RULES

It is conventional to divide the priority rules of the PPSA that govern competitions between or among competing secured parties into two categories: (1) the special priority rules; and (2) the residual or general priority rule. The special priority rules provide for particular types of situations, most notably competitions involving purchase money security interests. The residual priority rule applies where the Act provides no other method for determining priorities among security interests. The collective operation of these two types of priority rules does not resolve all possible varieties of priority competition. The residual priority rule only covers competitions between parties with competing PPSA security interests in the same collateral. It is of no use in resolving competitions where one of the competing interests is not a security interest that is within the scope of the PPSA, for example, in a dispute between a secured party who holds a PPSA security interest and a claimant who has a non-consensual security interest, such as a landlord's right of distress. Nor can it be invoked to resolve a dispute between a secured party and a bank that holds a *Bank Act* security, at least in those provinces that have excluded the *Bank Act* security from the scope of the

PPSA. In these cases, the PPSA does not provide an answer, and in the absence of any legislation or special common law rule, the dispute is resolved by applying general principles of property law.[1]

In some cases, the special priority rules contained in the PPSA relate exclusively to security interests. For example, the purchase money security interest priority is available only to a secured party who obtains that kind of security interest. No other class of claimant is able to claim this priority. In other cases, the special priority rule in the PPSA is not restricted to secured parties, but may include other classes of claimants. For example, the PPSA contains special priority rules relating to negotiable forms of property. A purchaser who obtains possession of the property without knowledge of a prior security interest will typically be entitled to priority. These provisions apply not only to absolute transfers of the property (where the debtor transfers it by way of sale), but also to transfers by way of security (where the debtor gives a secured party a possessory security interest in the collateral). This chapter examines the PPSA priority rules that apply strictly to competitions between secured parties. The priority rules that are of a more general application (such as the priority rules governing negotiable or quasi-negotiable collateral) are discussed elsewhere.

B. THE RESIDUAL PRIORITY RULE

1) The First-in-time Rule

The residual priority rule of the PPSA uses a first-in-time approach to resolve priorities among competing secured parties. However, this temporal rule does not, for the most part, look to the time when the security agreement is executed or the time when the security interest arises in determining priorities. There is a substantial difference in the structure and wording of the residual priority rule between the Ontario Act and the Acts of the other jurisdictions. On most issues, this does not produce any difference in outcome, but on one important matter the wording does produce a different result.

The residual priority rule in the Ontario PPSA sets out four different cases organized according to the method of perfection of the

---

1 See chapter 10, B "Priority Competitions with Non-consensual Security Interests" and chapter 14, A "*Bank Act* Security."

competing security interests.[2] The first involves a competition between two security interests, both of which have been perfected by registration. In this case, priority is awarded to the first to register, regardless of the order of perfection. The second case involves a competition between a security interest that is perfected by registration and another security interest that is perfected otherwise than by registration. Here, priority is given to the registered security interest if registration occurred before the perfection of the other security interest. But if the other security interest was perfected before the registration occurred, then the other security interest will have priority over the registered security interest. Thus, priority goes to the first to register or perfect, whichever is earlier. The third case involves a competition between two security interests, neither of which is perfected by registration. In this case, priority is given to the first to perfect its security interest. The fourth case involves a competition between two unperfected security interests. Here, priority is given to the first to attach.

The residual priority rules in the other Acts use a different formulation. The provision sets out three different sub-rules organized according to the perfected or unperfected status of the competing security interests.[3] The first sub-rule covers disputes between two security interests, both of which have been perfected. Priority is determined by the order of occurrence of registration, possession of the collateral if the security interest is perfected by possession, or temporary perfection, whichever is earliest. The second sub-rule covers disputes between a perfected security interest and an unperfected security interest. In this case, the perfected security interest has priority over the unperfected security interest. The third sub-rule involves competitions between two unperfected security interests. In this case, priority is determined according to the order of attachment.

The critical point to note with respect to both these formulations is that a security interest can obtain priority even though it was neither the first security interest to have attached, nor the first to have been perfected. Registration is sufficient to confer priority upon the security interest, even though the security interest may not have even been in existence at the time the competing security interest was perfected. The Ontario formulation differs from the formulation in the other Acts

---

2 OPPSA s. 30(1). See chapter 5 for a more detailed discussion of the concept of perfection.

3 PPSA (A, BC, M, NB, NWT, Nu, PEI, S) s. 35(1); (NS, NL) s. 36(1). YPPSA s. 34(1) contains a somewhat different wording, although it operates in much the same manner as the non-Ontario Acts.

in one important respect. In Ontario, a competition between perfected security interests will be governed by the first to register or perfect, whichever is earlier. In the other jurisdictions there is a second method by which a secured party may obtain priority even though its security interest was not the first to attach or be perfected. If the security interest is perfected by possession, the date of the secured party's possession is used to determine priorities. As in the case of registration, the security interest will be given priority even though it was neither the first to attach, nor the first to be perfected. This is illustrated in the following scenario.

SP1 and D are in loan negotiations. D agrees to give SP1 a possessory security interest in its collateral and leaves the collateral in the possession of SP1 pending the successful completion of the loan negotiations. D then grants a security interest in the collateral to SP2, who perfects it by registration. SP1 and D subsequently enter into a loan agreement.

Outside of Ontario, it is likely that the courts will interpret the Act as conferring priority in favour of SP1 over SP2.[4] At the time of SP2's registration, SP1's security interest was not perfected. Attachment of the security interest is a precondition to its perfection. SP1's security interest had not attached at this point because SP1 had not yet been given any value. Despite this, SP1 will likely be given priority. SP1 has completed a perfection step, and this gives it priority even though it does not yet have an attached or perfected security interest. Under the Ontario formulation, SP2 would be given priority. It is not enough that SP1 has completed a perfection step by taking possession of the collateral. SP1 must have perfected its security interest prior to registration of SP2's security interest in order to obtain priority.

Competitions between two unperfected security interests should be a rare occurrence, since it remains possible for a secured party to register a financing statement or financing change statement to register or correct an error as soon as the secured party realizes that its security interest is unperfected. One would therefore expect that these disputes would usually be resolved by a race to the registry. However, it is possible that the registrations of both the competing secured parties are found to contain invalidating errors well after the collateral has been

---

4   It is possible that a court may hold otherwise if it concludes that that there is no transfer of possession of collateral within the language of the provision unless the parties have entered into a security agreement at the time of the transfer of possession. However, the authors are of the opinion that this interpretation would frustrate the intent of the provision. See chapter 5, C "Perfection Steps."

seized and disposed of. In such a case, the priority competition will be determined according to the order of attachment.[5]

There is one instance in which the residual priority rule does not provide an answer. Where the dispute is between two unperfected security interests, priorities are determined according to the order of attachment. It is quite possible that both the competing security interests attach to the collateral at the same time. This will most likely occur where both security interests cover after-acquired property. In order for attachment to occur, the debtor must have rights in the collateral. The moment the debtor acquires a new asset, both security interests will simultaneously attach to the new asset. Time of attachment therefore cannot be used to determine priorities. In the absence of any statutory priority rule that governs the dispute, a court must resort to common law and equitable principles. The PPSA expressly recognizes that, unless inconsistent with the PPSA, these principles continue to apply to supplement the Act.[6] Under the equitable rule *qui est in tempore potior est jure*,[7] when two equitable mortgages covering after-acquired property are in competition, priority is given to the secured party who first entered into a security agreement with the debtor. In the absence of an express legislative priority rule, this principle should be applied.[8]

2) The Relevance of Knowledge

Unlike some of the other priority rules contained in the PPSA, the residual priority rule does not require that the successful claimant lack knowledge of a prior security interest. The policy reason that is offered in support of this rule is that it produces a priority structure that is simple and predictable. A priority rule that is based on knowledge creates evidentiary requirements that are subjective and much more difficult to establish.[9] A rule that looks to an objective criterion, such

---

5   See *Sperry Inc. v. Canadian Imperial Bank of Commerce* (1985), 17 D.L.R. (4th) 236 (Ont. C.A.) for an example of a case where the order of attachment was used to resolve a priority competition between two unperfected security interests.

6   PPSA (M, NWT, Nu, S) s. 65(2); (NB, PEI) s. 65(1); (NL, NS) s. 66(1); A s. 66(3); BC s. 68(1); O s. 72; Y s. 63(1).

7   He who is prior in time is prior in right. The common law rule of *nemo dat* did not apply, since the common law did not recognize mortgages of after-acquired property unless there was some new act of transfer.

8   *National Bank of Canada v. Merit Energy Ltd.* (2001), 27 C.B.R. (4th) 283 (Alta. Q.B).

9   *Shallcross v. Community State Banks Trust Co.*, 434 A.2d 671 (N.J. Sup. Ct. 1981); *In Re Smith*, 326 F. Supp. 1311 (D. Minn. 1971).

as the date of registration or possession permits a secured party to determine its priority status with less cost and greater certainty. Courts in Canada have refused to read into the statute any requirement that a secured party lack knowledge of a prior unperfected security interest.[10] Although mere knowledge is not enough to preclude a secured party from relying on the residual priority rule, the situation is otherwise if the secured party has acted dishonestly or has engaged in misleading conduct. This conduct may give rise to arguments of bad faith or estoppel, which can disentitle the secured party from obtaining the benefits of the PPSA priority rule.[11]

3) Change in the Method of Perfection

It is possible to change the method of perfection. What impact does a change in the method of perfection have on the operation of the residual priority rule? The PPSA provides that a continuously perfected security interest shall be treated as having been perfected in the manner by which it was originally perfected.[12] The operation of this provision is illustrated in the following scenario.

SP1 and SP2 are both granted security interests in the same collateral by the same debtor. SP1 perfects by possession on 1 January 2001. SP2 perfects by registration on 1 February 2001. SP1 perfects by registration on 1 March 2001 and thereafter releases possession of the collateral to the debtor.

SP1's security interest was continuously perfected, since there was no intervening period in which the security interest was unperfected.[13] Since a continuously perfected security interest is regarded as being perfected in the manner by which it was originally perfected, SP1's security interest will continue to be treated as perfected by possession. SP1 is therefore entitled to claim priority over SP2. This means that the order of registration indicated in a registry search will not always reflect the priority ranking of the parties, since it is possible that the

---

10 *Robert Simpson Co. v. Shadlock* (1981), 31 O.R. (2d) 612 (H.C.J.); *Canadian Imperial Bank of Commerce v. A.K. Construction (1988) Ltd.*, [1995] 8 W.W.R. 120 (Alta. Q.B.); *B.M.P. & Daughters Investment Corp. v. 941242 Ontario Ltd.* (1992), 11 O.R. (3d) 81 (Gen. Div.).

11 See the discussions of bad faith and estoppel in section I, "Other Principles Affecting Priorities."

12 PPSA (A, BC, M, NB, NWT, Nu, PEI, S) s. 35(2); (NL, NS) s. 36(2); O s. 30(2); Y no equivalent provision.

13 PPSA (A, BC, M, NB, NWT, Nu, PEI, S) s. 23(1); (NL, NS) s. 24(1); (O, Y) s. 21(1).

later registration is merely the second part of a continuous period of perfection that predates the earlier registration.

The same analysis holds true where SP1's security interest is originally perfected by registration, but is later perfected by possession. This is illustrated in the following scenario.

SP1 and SP2 are both granted security interests in the same collateral by the same debtor. SP1 perfects by registration on 1 January 2001. SP2 perfects by registration on 1 February 2001. SP1 perfects by possession on 1 March 2001. SP1's registration thereafter lapses or is discharged.

Again, SP1 is entitled to priority over SP2. Despite the lapse or discharge of its registration, SP1's security interest is deemed to be perfected by registration from the time when it was originally perfected. In this case, a current registry search will not disclose SP1's lapsed or discharged registration. It will be necessary for SP1 to adduce other evidence to demonstrate that its registration was in effect during the initial period of perfection.

The foregoing applies only if there is no gap in the continuity of perfection. The situation is otherwise if there is a period of time, no matter how short, during which the security interest was unperfected. In such a case, the priority will date from the time of the new perfection step. This is particularly important in respect of the temporary perfection periods. The PPSA occasionally gives a secured party a short period of temporary perfection within which the secured party may perfect its security interest by one of the other two methods of perfection. If the secured party fails to perfects its security interest by some other means before the expiration of this time period, the benefits of the temporary perfection will be lost.

4) Priorities and Multiple Security Agreements

A secured party will often enter into more than one security agreement with the debtor. Prior to the PPSA, it was necessary that each of these security agreements be separately registered. This was only natural under a document registration system that required registration of the security agreement. But with the introduction of a notice registration system, there was no longer any need to retain a one-to-one correspondence between the security agreement and its registration. So long as the information contained in the registration is sufficient to cover the other security agreements, there is no reason to demand that the secured party conduct multiple registrations. This principle is embodied in the PPSA. Most jurisdictions provide that a financing statement may cover more than one security agreement.[14] The Ontario PPSA takes a more limited approach. It permits a blanket registration for commercial transactions,[15] but makes an exception for security interests in consumer goods.[16] Where consumer goods are involved, the secured party must effect a new registration for each security agreement that is executed.[17]

Unfortunately, old attitudes often linger on. In Ontario, secured parties were more inclined to make multiple registrations as a precaution following a judicial decision which held that a single registration can only cover separate security agreements if they are sufficiently linked.[18] This practice should no longer be required following an amendment in 2000 that made it clear that a financing statement may cover more than one security agreement whether or not the security interests are part of the same or related transactions.[19] Even outside of Ontario where courts[20] have made it clear that no similar limitation exists, many secured parties have not taken advantage of this blanket registration capability. They continue to clutter the registry with multiple registrations that add to their costs but which provide no useful new information to searching parties.

The blanket registration principle when combined with the first to register principle of the residual priority rule may produce unpleasant surprises for parties who cannot break free from the notion that there must be a one to one correspondence between a security agreement and a registration. This is illustrated in the following scenario.

On May 1, SP1 is given a security interest in D's excavator. The security agreement secures a loan for $10,000 and does not contain a future advances clause. SP1 registers on May 10. The debtor then approaches SP2 for further financing and offers the excavator as collateral. Since the excavator is valued at $100,000, SP2 assumes that there is $90,000 in value against which it may lend. SP2 therefore makes the secured loan to the debtor and registers on June 1.

---

14   PPSA (A, BC, M, NWT, NU, S) s. 43(5); (NB, PEI) s. 43(6); (NL, NS) s. 44(6); Y
     no equivalent provision.
15   OPPSA s. 45(3).
16   OPPSA s. 45(2).
17   See chapter 6, B.2 "Advance Registration" and B.3 "One Registration for Multiple Security Agreements."
18   *Adelaide Capital Corp. v. Integrated Transportation Finance Inc.* (1994), 111 D.L.R.
     (4th) 493 (Ont. Ct. Gen. Div.).
19   OPPSA s. 45(4), added by S.O. 2000, c. 26, Sched. B, s. 16.
20   *Royal Bank of Canada v. Agricultural Credit Corp. of Saskatchewan* (1994), 115
     D.L.R. (4th) 569.

SP2 has proceeded upon a flawed understanding of the operation of the priority system that has left it vulnerable to the risk of loss. It is true that if nothing else happens, SP1's security interest will only cover the $10,000 loan obligation. If SP1 makes a further advance, SP1 will not be able to tack it to the security interest claim secured party status in respect of it, since the security agreement does not contain a future advances clause. However, the risk is that SP1 will later execute a new security agreement with the debtor in which a security interest is granted in the same collateral to secure the further advances. Because a financing statement can cover more than one security agreement, SP1's registration will cover the new security agreement as well as the old. SP1 will enjoy first priority in respect of both of its security interests, since both will rank from SP1's registration on 1 May. This is not a question of the priority of future advances at all. Rather, it is a case of two separate security interests, each of which is subject to the first in time principle contained in the residual priority rule.

The outcome in this scenario is not altered by the fact that SP1 may have separately registered in respect of its new security agreement. A secured party may register as many financing statements as it wishes, but it is the earliest one that matters for priority purposes. In order to protect itself, SP2 could take the precaution of obtaining a subordination agreement from SP1 before entering into the transaction.

5) Future Advances and All Obligations Clauses

A security interest is defined as an interest in personal property that secures payment or performance of an obligation.[21] It is left, as a matter of contract, for the secured party and the debtor to decide precisely which obligations are to be secured. The security agreement may cover a single, fixed obligation, or the parties may agree that it covers advances that might later be made in the future. Many security agreements are worded very broadly so as to cover all present or future obligations, indebtedness and liability of the debtor to the secured party.

The PPSA provides that the priority a security interest has under the residual priority rule extends to future advances as well.[22] This has the effect of reversing the common law rule in *Hopkinson v. Rolt*[23] that gives the secured party priority in respect of the future advance only

---

21   PPSA (A, BC, NWT, Nu, O, Y) s. 1(1); (M, NB, PEI) s. 1; (NL, NS) s. 2; S s. 2(1).
22   PPSA (A, BC, M, NB, NWT, Nu, PEI, S) s. 35(5); (NL, NS) s. 36(5); O s. 30(3); Y s. 35(4).
23   (1861), 9 H.L.C. 514.

if the secured party did not have knowledge of an intervening security interest. Under the PPSA, a secured party may make future advances pursuant to a future advances clause in its security agreement. The priority that is given to secured party extends to any further advances, and this is unaffected by knowledge of an intervening security interest.[24] Although the definition of future advance[25] does not contemplate future liabilities that may be secured pursuant to an all obligations clause, its priority should logically be the same as that given to future advances if the parties clearly intended that the security interest secure the future liability.[26]

The analysis becomes considerably more complex where obligations owing to third parties are assigned to the secured party, or where the security agreement is assigned to another. Consider first the case where obligations are originally owed to third parties, but are subsequently assigned by them to the secured party. This is illustrated in the following scenario.

D gives a security interest to SP in its collateral. The security agreement provides that the security interest secures all obligations present or future incurred by the debtor. D owes money to several unsecured creditors. SP obtains an assignment of the claims of some of these unsecured creditors.

The issue is whether the secured party can claim that these assigned debts fall within the "all obligations" provision in its security agreement. Courts are reluctant to interpret "all obligations" clauses in security agreements as covering debts owed to third parties for two reasons. The first involves a concern about unfairness to the debtor. It is unlikely that the debtor contemplates that the security interest will cover obligations assigned by third parties to the secured party. This point was made in the Australian decision *Re Clarke's Refrigerated Transport Pty. Ltd.*:

> It does seem strange that a man can lock up his counting-house and go home for the night, in the comfortable knowledge that his only secured creditor is his banker, to whom he owes a trifling sum secured by the usual boundless bank instrument, and unlock the door in the morning to find that, by virtue of assignments of the large but

---

24 The secured party is, however, affected by knowledge of an intervening enforcement creditor. See the discussion in chapter 10, A.4 "Future Advances and the Position of Unsecured Creditors."

25 PPSA (A, BC, NWT, Nu, O, Y) s. 1(1); (M, NB, PEI) s. 1; (NL, NS) s. 2; S s. 2(1).

26 See chapter 4, J.3 "All Obligations Clauses" regarding the interpretation of "all obligations" clauses.

unsecured debts owed by him to his fellow merchants, and indeed to the butcher, the baker, and the candlestick maker, all his unsecured debts have gone to feed his banker's insatiable security, so that every one of his debts is now secured.[27]

The second concern is that this practice would have the potential to disrupt the equitable distribution of assets on an insolvency of the debtor. This was expressed in the American decision of *In Re E.A. Fretz Company, Inc.*:

> If a senior secured party to a security agreement could, via post-bankruptcy assignment, secure and perfect under the umbrella of prior omnibus arrangements the claims of subsidiaries and strangers (general or unperfected secured creditors), the potential for inequality, and, indeed collusion or fraud, would be enormous. Sanctioning such transactions would truly create "strangers in paradise" violative of a cardinal principle of bankruptcy law.[28]

On bankruptcy, the claims of unsecured creditors are usually worth significantly less than their face value. If, through the alchemy of assignment, the secured party were able to transform some of these unsecured claims into secured claims, these claims would become significantly more valuable. These gains would be shared among the secured party and the assigning creditors at the expense of the remainder of the non-assigning general creditors. This would obviously undermine the principle of pro rata sharing among unsecured creditors in bankruptcy.

This is not to say that courts will always refuse to permit a security interest to cover debts assigned to the secured party. But in order to succeed, the language of the provision must clearly and unequivocally provide that the security agreement covers such claims,[29] and the court must be convinced that the transaction has a legitimate commercial purpose and is not merely a device to subvert the claims of third parties. For example, a security agreement might provide that the obligation secured covers obligations that are assigned to the secured party from specifically identified third parties, and these assignments may have been effected prior to the debtor's insolvency. There seems to be no good reason why this security agreement should not be effective

---

27   [1982] V.R. 989 at 995–96. See also *Re Quest Cae Ltd.*, [1985] B.C.L.C. 266 (Ch. D.); *Kova Establishment v. Sasco Investments Ltd.*, [1998] 2 B.C.L.C. 83 (Ch. D.).
28   565 F.2d 366 (C.A. Tex. 1978).
29   *Thorp Sales Corp. v. Dolese Bros. Co.*, 453 F. Supp. 196 (D.C.W.D. 1978).

according to its terms. If it can be established that the security agreement covers claims assigned to the secured party, the priority afforded the security interest in respect of advances should be applied to the assigned claims as well.

The second scenario concerns the assignment of a security agreement that contains an all obligations clause. Does this permit the assignee to claim the benefit of the future advances clause in respect of obligations incurred by the assignee either before or after the assignment? This problem is illustrated in the following scenario.

D gives a security interest to SP1 in its collateral. The security agreement provides that the security interest secures all obligations present or future incurred by the debtor. SP1 perfects its security interest by registration. D then gives a security interest in the same collateral to SP2, who perfects it by registration. Later, D gives a security interest to SP3 to secure a loan of $50,000. SP1 then assigns the security agreement to SP3.

Clearly, SP3 will have priority over SP2 in relation to the $100,000 obligation owed to SP1 and assigned to SP3. But can SP3 claim priority as well to the $50,000 obligation that D owes to SP3? Furthermore, if SP3 makes a further advance to D, can SP3 claim priority over SP2 in respect of this advance on the basis that this advance was covered by the future advances provision that was contained in D's security agreement with SP1 that was assigned to it?

Courts have been willing to permit an assignee of a security agreement that contains a future advance clause to make advances under the agreement and retain the original secured party's priority status.[30] The courts have pointed out that the intervening secured party (SP2) is in no way prejudiced by the assignment from SP1 to SP3. SP2 took the risk that its subordinate security interest would be subordinate to future advances made by SP1. By virtue of the assignment, SP3 simply stepped into the shoes of SP1 and assumed its role in making the advance. In one such case, the court commented: "[c]reditors who choose to extend credit to a debtor in the face of this knowledge can hardly be heard to complain when the risk they assume materializes."[31]

However, courts have been unwilling to permit an assignee to claim the benefit of an all obligations clause in respect of obligations incurred by the assignee before the assignment. It is not entirely clear whether these courts have decided that this outcome is impossible as a matter of

---

30   *In Re Cycle Products Distributing Co.*, 12 U.C.C. Rep. Serv. 2d 889 (Bankr. SD Ill. 1990); *In Re Robert B. Lee Enterprises, Inc.*, 980 F.2d 606 (9th Cir. 1978).
31   *In Re Robert B. Lee Enterprises, Inc.*, ibid. at 609.

law, or if they have simply determined that the clause used in the agreement was not sufficient to produce this result. In England,[32] Australia,[33] and New Zealand,[34] the courts have embraced the former argument and have held that only the clearest of language in the security agreement would permit an unsecured creditor to obtain secured creditor status by taking an assignment of a security agreement that contains an all obligations clause.

In Canada, some courts take the view that the result is impossible as a matter of law. In *Canamsucco Road House Co. v. Lngas Ltd.*,[35] Justice Mercier rejected the argument that the assignee can add previously unsecured debt to the amount secured since "[t]hat would mean a person with a third charge could gain priority over one with a second charge simply by paying off the first charge and obtaining an assignment of same."[36] The question also arose in *Near Horbay Inc. v. Great West Golf & Industrial Inc.*[37] Justice Watson held that "the priority, in my view, should be for what was given priority in the first place, and not for an amalgam of the original secured claim and any number of unsecured and subsequent claims that an assignee might seek to annex to it under a blanket or dragnet clause."[38] He was particularly concerned that this would weaken the predictability of the priority system by making it more difficult for third parties to determine priorities.

The authors are of the view that the idea that there is a substantive rule of law that prevents the parties from extending all obligations clauses to cover obligations that were originally owed to another person is an overreaction to the problem. In many instances, the same result can be achieved without the use of a broadly drafted all obligations clause simply by obtaining the consent of the debtor.[39] The first-ranking secured party (SP1) may make a further advance to the debtor for the purpose of paying out the third-ranking secured party (SP3). This will give the first-ranking secured party priority over a second-ranking

---

32   *OGB Ltd. v. Allan*, [2001] B.P.I.R. 1111 (Ch.D.).

33   *Katsikalis v. Deutsch Bank (Asia) AG*, [1988] 2 Qd. R. 641; *Re Modular Design Group Pty. Ltd.*, (1994), 35 N.S.W.L.R. 96; *Thomas v. Silvia* (1994), 14 A.C.S.R. 446.

34   *Kerr v. Ducey*, [1993] 1 N.Z.L.R. 577.

35   (1991), 2 P.P.S.A.C. (2d) 203 (Ont. Ct. Gen. Div.), rev'd on other grounds (1997), 12 P.P.S.A.C. (2d) 227 (Ont. C.A.).

36   *Ibid.* at 205 (Ont. Ct. Gen. Div.).

37   [2001] 3 W.W.R. 734 (Alta. Q.B.).

38   *Ibid.* at 755.

39   See R. Wood, "Turning Lead into Gold: the Uncertain Alchemy of 'All Obligations' Clauses" (2004), 41 Alta. L. Rev. 801.

secured party (SP2) for the entire amount. This security interest can then be assigned to SP3 or to any other party. Furthermore, there may be sensible commercial reasons for including an all obligations clause that covers such obligations. For example, a security agreement may provide that the security interest covers any obligation owed to the debtor as well as any obligation owed by the debtor to a subsidiary of the secured party that is assigned to the secured party. The authors are of the opinion that a more selective approach is required that would restrict the effectiveness of broadly drafted all obligations clauses only when they are used to undermine the pro rata sharing principle in bankruptcy or when the assignment takes place after the debtor is no longer a viable economic entity simply as a device to attempt to gain an advantage over another claimant. Outside of Ontario, this outcome could be justified on the basis of the overarching obligation imposed by the PPSA on all parties to act in good faith and in a commercially reasonable manner.[40]

6) "Assignment" of the Financing Statement

A claimant to whom a security agreement has been assigned may attempt to argue that it has obtained not only the benefit of the assignor's security agreement, but also the benefit of the assignor's financing statement. In doing so, the claimant does not assert a claim on the security interest that was assigned to it. Instead, the claimant argues that it has obtained the transfer of a financing statement of another person, and that this gives it the right to treat the registration as its own. The claimant then attempts to use this registration to enhance the priority status of a separate security interest given to the claimant by the debtor.

Although some American commentators have argued that a secured party should be able to assign its financing statement and thereby sell its place in line,[41] the authors are of the view that this argument should be rejected in Canada. It is possible in Canada to register a financing statement against the name of a person without the consent of the per-

---

40   PPSA (M, NWT, Nu, S) s. 65(2); (NB, PEI) s. 65(1); (NL, NS) s. 66(1); A s. 66(3); BC s. 68(1); O s. 72; Y s. 63(1); O no equivalent provision. See also section I.1 "Bad Faith."

41   S. Neth, "The First to File Priority in Article 9: Can You Sell Your Place in Line?" (1998) 31 U.C.C.L.J. 64; S. Walt, "Revisiting Neth's *The First to File Priority in Article 9: Can You Sell Your Place in Line? And Shanker's Response*" (1998) 31 U.C.C.L.J. 217. For an opposing view, see M. Shanker, "A Response to *The First to File Priority in Article 9: Can You Sell Your Place in Line?*" (1998) 31 U.C.C.L.J. 82.

son named as a debtor in the registration.[42] The ability to sell a priority position based upon such a registration would be a startling proposition. Although Canadian authorities[43] have dealt with the effect of an assignment of the security agreement rather than an assignment of the financing statement, there would have been no need to consider the operation of the all obligation clause in the assigned security agreement if the assignee were permitted to claim priority on the basis of the assignor's financing statement.

Quite apart from the case law, there is no mechanism contained in the PPSA for an assignment of a financing statement. The statute provides for the assignment of a security interest, not an assignment of a financing statement. Indeed, a financing statement is not an agreement at all, and to speak of an assignment of it makes little sense. Upon an assignment of a security interest, the assignee may register a financing change statement that discloses the name of the assignee.[44] This simply adds the name of the assignee as a secured party as of the time when the financing change statement is registered.[45] It does not operate as a transfer of the registration from one party to the other.

This analysis also applies where an assignee of a security agreement contractually renegotiates its terms by entering into a new agreement with the debtor that brings in additional collateral or additional obligations that are not covered by the original security agreement. Because the assignment does not involve a transfer of the assignor's financing statement, the assignee cannot use the assignor's financing statement to give it priority in respect of the new security agreement. The assignee must base its priority on its own registration. Often this will take the form of a financing change statement that records the assignee as a new secured party, which is registered at the same time or shortly after the assignment. However, for priority purposes, it is the date of the financing change statement and not of the original financing statement that is used for the determination of priorities in respect of the new security agreement.

---

42   The person named as debtor can require the registering party to discharge the registration if the registration in unwarranted. See PPSA (A, BC, M, NB, NWT, Nu, PEI, Y) s. 50; (NL, NS) s. 51; O s. 56.

43   *Canamsucco Road House Co. v. Lngas Ltd*, above note 35; *Near Horbay Inc. v. Great West Golf & Industrial Inc.*, above note 37.

44   PPSA (A, BC, M, NB, NWT, Nu, PEI) s. 45(1); (NL, NS) s. 46(1); O s. 47(1).

45   PPSA (A, BC, M, NWT, Nu) s. 44(5); (NB, PEI) s. 45(4); (NL, NS) s. 46(4); O s. 47(3); Y s. 44(5).

7) Motor Vehicles and Serial Numbered Goods

There is a fundamental difference of approach between the Ontario and Yukon Acts and the Acts of the other jurisdictions in respect of motor vehicles and other serial numbered goods. In Ontario, a secured party is not required to describe motor vehicles by their serial number on a financing statement unless the motor vehicle is classified as consumer goods.[46] In the Yukon, the situation is the same except that the serial number registration requirement is not limited to motor vehicles but extends to a somewhat wider range of goods.[47] A description of motor vehicles by serial number is optional in the case of goods classified as inventory or equipment. Although optional, description by serial number is recommended where the goods are held as equipment. A secured party who does not register by serial number takes the risk of subordination to a person who buys the equipment without knowledge of the security interest.[48] However, a secured party who fails to describe the motor vehicle by serial number is not exposed to a similar risk of subordination as against competing secured parties. There is no requirement that a secured party describe a motor vehicle held as equipment by serial number in order to obtain priority over another secured party.

If the secured party fails to provide the serial number of a motor vehicle held as consumer goods, its security interest will be unperfected. The secured party will lose priority to a competing secured party who describes the collateral by serial number, since an unperfected security interest is subordinate to a perfected security interest. Where the collateral is classified as equipment or inventory, the priority of the security interest will rank from the time of registration whether or not the collateral is described by serial number. The competition is between two perfected security interests, and priority is given to the first to register.

The approach taken in the other jurisdictions is broader than that of Ontario in two respects. First, they take a more expansive approach to the kinds of goods that can be described by serial number. The regulations bring tractors, combines, aircraft, boats, and outboard boat engines within the definition of serial numbered goods. However, it does not by any means extend to all types of goods containing serial num-

---

46   O Reg., s. 3(7).
47   Y Reg., s. 5(k). The provision extends to motor vehicles, trailers, mobile homes, and aircraft.
48   OPPSA s. 28(5).

bers. Items such as computers, televisions, cameras, and oil rigs all fall outside the definition of serial numbered goods.

As with the Ontario PPSA, description of the collateral by serial number is mandatory in the case of consumer goods classified as serial numbered goods. Unlike the Ontario and Yukon Acts, the other Acts provide that serial numbered goods held as equipment must be described by serial number in order to be considered perfected for the purposes of applying the residual priority rule.[49] If the secured party fails to describe the equipment by serial number, it will be considered perfected in respect of a competition with a trustee in bankruptcy or an enforcement creditor. However, it will be considered unperfected in competitions with other secured parties, and will risk subordination if the competing secured party has described the equipment by serial number. For this reason, a registering party will typically attempt to describe such collateral by serial number whenever possible.

Although it is possible in all the jurisdictions to describe inventory by serial number, there is no particular advantage gained by doing so. It places greater demands upon the secured party who must continually amend the registration by adding new serial numbers when inventory is acquired and deleting serial numbers when items are sold. It also adds considerably to the risk of loss caused by human error since mistakes in transcribing serial numbers will often lead to loss of perfection and priority.

8) The Double-debtor Problem

In most cases, a priority dispute between competing secured parties involves a dispute between two secured parties, both of whom have been granted security interests in the same collateral by a common debtor. The priority rules of the PPSA set out the scheme for determining priorities in such cases. The analysis becomes more complex when the original debtor transfers its interest to another party who subsequently sells, leases, or encumbers it. In such cases, the priority rules of the PPSA will often not apply to resolve the competition. This can be easily illustrated in respect of a transaction involving a flawed title.

SP1 is given a security interest in a piece of heavy equipment. The equipment is stolen and sold to an innocent buyer. The buyer then grants a security interest in the equipment to another secured party (SP2).

---

49   PPSA (A, BC, M, NB, NWT, NU, PEI, S) s. 35(4); (NL, NS) s. 36(4).

A priority competition between SP1 and SP2 cannot be resolved by recourse to the residual priority rule of the PPSA. It therefore would not matter that SP2 may have registered a financing statement before SP1 or that SP1 may have failed to register at all. The buyer obtained a flawed title to the equipment. By virtue of the *nemo dat* rule, the operation of which is preserved by the PPSA, SP2's security interest takes subject to SP1's security interest.

The controversy is more likely to arise when the debtor transfers the collateral to another without the consent of the secured party.

Suppose again that SP1 takes a security interest in the debtor's heavy equipment, but that now the debtor transfers the equipment to a buyer.[50] Assume also that none of the buyer-protection rules of the PPSA, such as the ordinary course buyer rule, apply so as to cut off SP1's security interest. The buyer later grants a security interest in the equipment to SP2.

There are two competing theories concerning the proper resolution of this controversy.[51] One approach is to interpret the residual priority rule of the PPSA as restricted to those cases where a common debtor grants competing interests in the same collateral. In the absence of an applicable statutory priority rule, the rule of *nemo dat* would apply, and SP2's security interest would remain subject to SP1's security interest despite the fact that SP2 may have been the first to register a financing statement. This approach would give SP1 priority over SP2 even if SP1's security interest were unperfected.

The second approach invokes the residual priority rule of the PPSA to give SP2 priority over SP1 in cases where SP1 has failed to perfect its security interest. This will give SP2 the ability to discover the existence of the security interest by searching the registry by serial number where serial number registration is required, or by conducting a search using the names of the former owners of the collateral. However, this approach creates a potential problem. If the residual priority rule is used to give SP2 priority when SP1 fails to perfect its security interest, this suggests that it should also be applied when both security interests

---

50   The same flawed title argument cannot be used. The PPSA contains an express provision to the effect that the rights of a debtor can be transferred consensually by the debtor notwithstanding a provision in the security agreement prohibiting transfer. See PPSA (A, BC, M, NB, PEI, NWT, Nu) s. 33(2); (NL, NS) s. 34(2), O s. 39; Y s. 32.

51   For a detailed discussion of this problem, see R.C.C. Cuming, "Double-Debtor ABCD Problems in Personal Property Security Law" (1992) 7 B.F.L.R. 359.

are perfected but SP2 has registered first. This is illustrated by the following scenario.

D1 gives a security interest in a crane to SP1 which SP1 registers on 1 July 2001. Prior to this, D2 had given SP2 a security interest covering all present and after-acquired personal property which SP2 registered on 1 June 1999. On 1 October 2001, D1 sells the crane to D2. The sale does not occur in D1's ordinary course of business with the result that D2 takes the crane subject to SP1's security interest.

In the absence of any other rule, the application of the second approach would result in SP2 obtaining priority over SP1 on the basis of its earlier registration.

With the exception of the Ontario Act, the PPSA addresses this problem through a specific priority rule.[52] It provides that where a debtor transfers an interest in collateral that is subject to a perfected security interest, that security interest has priority over any other security interest granted by the transferee before the transfer. By virtue of this provision, SP1 is given priority over SP2 notwithstanding that SP2 was the first to register. There are two exceptions to this rule. First, the provision does not operate when the transferee acquires the debtor's interest free from SP1's security interest.[53] Second, this priority cannot be claimed by SP1 in respect of any future advances that are made fifteen days after SP1 learns of the transfer but before SP1 amends the registration to disclose the transferee as a new debtor.

This provision does not cover the entire field. A double debtor problem will also arise in the following scenario.

D1 gives a security interest in a computer to SP1. SP1 fails to register or otherwise perfect its security. D2 gives SP2 a security interest in all present and after-acquired personal property that SP2 perfects by registration. D1 then sells the computer to D2. D2 knows of SP1's unperfected security interest, and therefore is subject to SP1's unperfected security interest.

In the absence of a statutory provision, it is necessary to decide if the matter will be resolved by applying the *nemo dat* approach (which gives priority to SP1), or by applying the residual priority rule (which gives priority to SP2).

---

52   PPSA (BC, M, NB, NWT, Nu, S) s. 35(8); (NL, NS) s. 36(8); A s. 35(9); PEI s. 35(7); Y s. 34(6).

53   PPSA (BC, M, NB, NWT, NU, S) s. 35(9); (NL, NS) s. 36(9); A s. 35(10); PEI s. 35(8); Y s. 34(7).

The inclusion of this additional priority provision in jurisdictions other than Ontario provides convincing evidence that it was intended that the residual priority rule should govern those cases where SP1 did not perfect its security interest. Article 9 of the *Uniform Commercial Code*[54] contains a provision specifically limiting the application of the residual priority rules in cases where SP1 has maintained the perfection of its interest. The provision has substantially the same effect as the PPSA provision, and the Official Comment confirms that it is contemplated that the Article 9 priority rules will normally apply to the double debtor problem.[55] As a result, SP1's perfected security interest should be given priority over SP1's unperfected security interest.[56]

The situation is less clear under the Ontario Act. In the absence of a special priority provision, an Ontario court might apply the *nemo dat* approach where SP1's security interest is properly perfected. Although an Ontario court might be inclined to apply the residual priority rule in cases where SP1 has failed to perfect its security interest, the problem is that this appears to create an inconsistency. If the *nemo dat* approach is used to resolve a dispute when a perfected security interest is involved, this suggests that it should also be used when the dispute is with an unperfected security interest. Nonetheless, some commentators assert that there is no inconsistency with applying the *nemo dat* approach in the former case, and the residual priority rule in the latter.[57]

The foregoing analysis will only apply if the secured party is able to maintain its claim to the collateral against the buyer. If the sale from the debtor to the buyer is one that attracts one of the buyer protection rules, the secured party loses its security interest in the collateral. The secured party will therefore be unable to assert a claim against the buyer or anyone who has obtained an interest in the property from the buyer, including a secured party. This is sometimes referred to as the doctrine of sheltering. The application of this doctrine is illustrated in the following scenario.

---

54   Article 9-325.
55   *Ibid.*, Official Comment 4.
56   The double-debtor problem only arises if D2 gives a security interest in the collateral to another secured party. It does not arise when D2 creates or reserves a security interest in the collateral in its own favour. In such a case, the residual priority rule is not applied, and D2 remains subject to SP1's unperfected security interest. See *Daewoo Heavy Industries America Corporation v. Northwest Equipment Inc.*, [2002] 6 W.W.R. 444 (Alta. C.A.).
57   L. Lysaght and G. Stewart, "Priority between Competing Secured Creditors: Exploring the Borderland Between Personal Property Security Rules and the Common Law" (1995) 74 Can. Bar Rev. 50 at 64.

SP1 takes and perfects a security interest in D's goods. In violation of the security agreement, D sells some of the goods in the ordinary course of business to B. B then grants a security interest in the goods to SP2, who fails to register its security interest.

SP2 has priority over SP1 despite its failure to register its security interest. SP1's security interest in the goods was cut off upon the sale of the goods to B. The competition is resolved by the application of the doctrine of sheltering which gives SP2 the right to shelter its claim under B's indefeasible title.[58]

9) Amalgamations

None of Acts provide any guidance on the resolution of a priority competition that arises when two or more corporations which have given security interests in their existing and after-acquired property amalgamate. This problem is illustrated in the following scenario.

SP1 is given a security interest in all present and after-acquired property of A Inc., which it registers on 1 September 1999. SP2 is given a security interest in all present and after-acquired property of B Inc., which it registers on 1 October 2001. On 1 July 2002, A Inc. amalgamates with B Inc. to form AB Ltd. At the time of the amalgamation, A Inc. owes SP1 $300,000 and B Inc. owes SP2 $100,000. After 1 July, AB Ltd. acquires new property worth $200,000. Following the amalgamation, SP1 advances no additional credit, but SP2 advances a further $200,000.

Under business corporations' statutes, the amalgamated corporation has all the property and rights and is subject to all liabilities and debts of each of the amalgamating corporations. Upon the amalgamation, the security interests of both SP1 and SP2 attach to all present and after-acquired property of AB Ltd.[59] The first issue concerns the resolution of a priority competition between SP1 and SP2 in respect of the assets that were in existence at the time of the amalgamation. Should the residual priority rule be applied so as to give priority to SP1 on the basis of its earlier registration? Application of the residual priority rule would

---

58   An exception to this doctrine is recognized where the collateral is transferred back to the original wrongdoer. See R.M. Goode, *Commercial Law*, 2d ed. (London: Penguin, 1995) at 60–61.

59   *Heidelberg Canada Graphic Equipment Ltd. v. Arthur Anderson Inc.* (1992), 4 P.P.S.A.C. (2d) 116 (Ont. Ct. Gen. Div.); *Pudwill v. Royal Bank of Canada*, [2001] O.J. 2141 (S.C.J.), aff'd [2002] O.J. 1547 (C.A.)

undermine the priority system insofar as it would expose secured parties to the risk that their priority would be lost upon an amalgamation despite the fact that they had the first recorded registration at the time they obtained their security interests. The authors are of the view that the amalgamation should not cause a secured party to lose priority in respect of its security interest in the pre-amalgamation assets. SP1 should have priority over the assets of A Inc. and SP2 should have priority over the assets of B Inc.[60]

Assuming that the residual priority rule will not be applied so as to give priority to the secured party with the earlier registration, the next issue concerns the relative priority of SP1's and SP2's claim to the property acquired by AB Ltd. after the amalgamation. There are two possible approaches. One approach is to share the after-acquired property rateably based on the obligations outstanding at the date of amalgamation. The second approach is to share the assets rateably based on the obligations outstanding at the time of enforcement. Applying the first approach to the above scenario would result in a distribution of $150,000 to SP1 and $50,000 to SP2. Under the second approach, SP1 and SP2 would each receive $100,000 out of the proceeds of the after-acquired property. No guidance on how this issue is to be resolved is to be found in either the PPSA or in common law principles. The first approach has the advantage of producing a precise point in time (the date of the amalgamation) for the calculation of the respective entitlements, and provides an incentive for a secured party to monitor the activities of the debtor. Under the second approach, there is nothing that SP1 can do to prevent an increasing reduction in its proportionate share in after-acquired property due to the lending choices of SP2. For this reason, the authors favour the first approach.

C. PURCHASE MONEY SECURITY INTERESTS

The residual priority rule of the PPSA creates a basic first-in-time rule that governs competitions between secured parties unless a special priority rule governs the dispute. The Act provides a special priority rule

---

60   This is analogous to the approach taken where from the sale of collateral of SP1 are mixed with proceeds from the sale of collateral of SP2, or where goods subject to a security interest of SP1 are mixed or processed with goods subject to a security interest of SP2. See chapter 12, F "Manufactured and Commingled Goods." In both cases, a *pro rata* approach is adopted instead of applying the first in time approach.

in respect of purchase money security interests. So long as certain procedural requirements are satisfied, it substitutes a "second in time, first in right" priority rule. For this reason, it is sometimes said to create a "superpriority." The definition of purchase money security interest is used in several other contexts within the scheme of the PPSA, and the term is also used in other commercial law statutes. However, because of the particular significance of the concept in disputes between secured parties with competing security interests in the same collateral, the definition will be discussed in this chapter.

1) Justification for Superpriority

The rationale for the purchase money security interest superpriority is very much bound up with the approach to security interests in after-acquired property adopted by the PPSA.[61] The PPSA greatly facilitated the ability of parties to take security interests in after-acquired property. The security interest attaches to the new property without the requirement of any new act of transfer. The parties may execute a single security agreement that will automatically attach to new inventory that is acquired or new accounts that are generated without the need to execute new security agreements. Although this was also the rule in equity under pre-PPSA law, unlike the rule under the prior law, a security interest in after-acquired property is not afforded an inferior priority status by the PPSA.

   The effectiveness of an after-acquired property clause when combined with a first-in-time priority rule gives the first secured party a competitive advantage over later secured parties. The first secured party enjoys a situational monopoly over later entrants. The purchase money security interest priority is introduced into the PPSA in order to blunt this situational monopoly and permit the debtor to obtain future loans from secured parties on competitive terms. This is not seen as unfair to the first secured party, since the new asset would not have been obtained by the debtor but for the new credit provided by the purchase money security interest financer. It is, however, necessary to limit the scope of purchase money superpriority. A general second in time, first in right rule of priority would completely undermine the institution of secured credit. For this reason, the purchase money security interest priority is restricted in two respects. First, it only applies if the purpose of the extension of secured credit is to enable the debtor to acquire the

---

61   See T. Jackson and A Kronman, "Secured Financing and Priorities Among Creditors" (1979) 88 Yale L.J. 1143 at 1164–71.

asset in respect of which the secured credit is granted. Second, it only applies to the extent that the funds are actually used by the debtor to acquire the new asset.

Recognition of the purchase money security interest priority means that a debtor who has given a broadly based security interest on present and after-acquired property to one creditor will be able to raise additional secured financing from a different creditor on the basis of new assets so long as the additional financing is used to acquire the new assets. This is subject to one important qualification. Purchase money security interest priority does not give the debtor the right as against an earlier secured party to obtain purchase money financing from another creditor if the security agreement with the earlier secured party prohibits the debtor from entering into such transactions. Although the debtor may have the power to create a purchase money security interest that outranks the earlier security interest, the debtor will nonetheless be in breach of the earlier security agreement in doing so. Most security agreements provide that a breach of covenant contained in a security agreement amounts to an event of default, with the result that the breach will give the secured party the right to exercise its enforcement remedies against the collateral albeit subject to the superpriority enjoyed by the purchase money secured party over those items of collateral that are subject to its security interest.

2) Definition of Purchase Money Security Interests

The definition of "purchase money security interest"[62] contained in the PPSA covers two kinds of financing transactions: (1) security interests taken by sellers in the property sold in order to secure its unpaid purchase price; and (2) security interests taken by lenders for the purpose of permitting the debtor to acquire new assets. The Acts in jurisdictions outside of Ontario also deem certain leases and consignments to be security interests within the scope of the definition.[63]

The definition of purchase money security interest in the PPSA, not including the Ontario Act, makes it clear that the obligation secured by a purchase money security interest is not limited to the purchase price of the property, but extends as well to any credit charges or interest payable in connection with the transaction. Although this language is absent from the Ontario Act, it is likely that the definition would also be interpreted to include these amounts.

---

62 PPSA (A, BC, NWT, Nu, O, Y) s. 1(1); (M, NB, PEI) s. 1; (NL, NS) s. 2; S s. 2(1).
63 See chapter 2, E "The Deemed Security Agreements."

a)   Security Interests Taken by Sellers

The definition of purchase money security interest includes a security interest that secures all or part of its purchase price. This covers the situation where a security interest is taken by the seller in the property sold on credit to a buyer in order to secure the unpaid purchase price. The definition expressly excludes a sale-and-lease-back transaction under which the owner sells an asset to a buyer and then immediately leases it back from the buyer. This type of transaction is excluded since it does not result in any addition to the debtor's pool of assets. Sale and repurchase agreements similarly fall outside the definition of a purchase money security interest. Under this transaction, the owner sells an asset to a buyer and then immediately repurchases it under a secured instalment purchase agreement. Although this does not fall within the sale-and-lease-back exception mentioned in the provision, courts have held that the transaction did not create a purchase money security interest because the transaction did not enhance the debtor's asset pool.[64]

A seller who sells the property to the buyer on unsecured credit terms cannot thereafter execute a security agreement and obtain a purchase money security interest in the property. Upon the sale of the collateral, the buyer becomes the owner of it. The subsequent execution of a security agreement merely gives the seller a security interest in an asset that is now owned by the debtor.

All the Acts apply to security interests that take the form of a consignment or lease, but which secure payment or performance of an obligation. These "security leases" or "security consignments" are essentially disguised sales, and therefore fall within the definition of a purchase money security interest.

b)   Enabling Loans

Two conditions must be satisfied in order for a lender to obtain a purchase money security in collateral. First, the purpose of the loan must have been to enable the debtor to acquire the new assets. Second, the value must have been applied by the debtor to acquire those rights. In order to establish the first requirement, it is not necessary that the security agreement evidence the fact that the purpose of the loan was

---

64   *Wheatland Industries (1990) Ltd. v. Baschuk* (1994), 8 P.P.S.A.C. (2d) 247 (Sask. Q.B.); *Re 1151162 Ontario Ltd.* (1997), 13 P.P.S A C (2d) 16 (Ont. Ct. Gen. Div.).

to enable the debtor to acquire the new asset so long as this can be established by some other means.[65]

In order to satisfy the second requirement, it must be established that the funds advanced by the lender were actually used by the debtor to acquire the new property. This is easy to do if the lender has advanced the funds directly to the seller or has drawn an instrument payable to the debtor and the seller jointly. It is more difficult to establish if the money is paid to the debtor and mixed with other funds. A court would most likely resort to tracing principles to determine if the funds advanced were used to acquire the new asset. This is illustrated in the following scenario.

SP makes a loan to D for the purpose of enabling D to acquire a new rock crusher. A cheque for $20,000 is made payable to D, who deposits the funds in D's bank account. At the time of the deposit, D has $30,000 of D's own funds in the account. D withdraws $40,000 and pays it to a creditor. D later deposits a cheque for $10,000 from another source into the bank account. D then withdraws $20,000 from the account and uses it to purchase a rock crusher.

Under the tracing approach, the intermediate balance rule would be applied. The debtor is presumed to spend the debtor's own funds first.[66] Once this amount is notionally exhausted, further withdrawals erode the purchase money funds in the account. New deposits from other sources do not thereafter revive the purchase money funds once they are adjusted downwards. Under this approach, SP would obtain a security interest in the rock-crusher to secure $20,000. However, its purchase money security interest would only secure $10,000, since it could only establish that $10,000 of the funds advanced was actually used to acquire the rock crusher.

A frequently litigated issue arises where the debtor acquires the property before the lender makes any loan advances to the debtor. Suppose that a debtor acquires the property from a seller on an unsecured basis. The debtor then borrows money from a lender and gives the lender a security interest in the goods that were acquired. The funds are then used by the debtor to pay the account owing to the seller. Some

---

65   *Royal Bank of Canada v. Pioneer Property Management Ltd.*, [1987] 2 W.W.R. 445 (Sask. Q.B.); *Canadian Imperial Bank of Commerce v. Marathon Realty Co.*, [1987] 5 W.W.R. 236 (C.A.); *Royal Bank of Canada v. Gatekeeper Leasing Ltd.* (1993), 91 B.C.L.R. (2d) 357 (S.C.).

66   *Re Hallet's Estate* (1880), 13 Ch. D. 696 (C.A.). See also the discussion in chapter 12, B.3.b "The Lowest Intermediate Balance Rule."

courts in the United States have held that the loan cannot be an enabling loan because the debtor already owned the property at the time the funds were advanced.[67]

Other courts have held that it is sufficient if there was a close nexus between the purchase and the loan.[68] It is enough that the loan transaction is closely allied with the purchase transaction, and "rigid adherence to particular formalities and sequences should not be required."[69] Under this approach, the crucial factor is whether the parties regarded the sale transaction and the loan transaction as two steps in a single transaction.[70] If the debtor obtains a commitment from the lender, then acquires the property, and finally uses the funds advanced by the lender to pay the seller, the loan will be regarded as enabling the acquisition of the asset. But if the debtor acquired the property first without a firm commitment but merely a hope that financing could be arranged, the loan will not be regarded as an enabling loan.[71]

In *Agricultural Credit Corp. of Saskatchewan v. Pettyjohn*,[72] the debtor had acquired the collateral with money that had been advanced by an interim financer. The lender then advanced funds to the debtor, which was used to pay out the interim financier. At the time of acquisition of the collateral, the lender had given the debtor a binding commitment to extend credit. The Saskatchewan Court of Appeal held that the interim financing should be viewed in the first step in a two-step transaction that enabled the debtor to acquire rights in the collateral. The security interest taken by the lender in the collateral was therefore held to be a purchase money security interest even though the loan money had not been used to pay the seller.

The outcome in *Pettyjohn* might also have been reached through the application of tracing principles. There is increasing academic support for the view that it is possible to trace money that was used to pay a debt into property that had been previously acquired by the debtor in

---

67   *North Platte State Bank v. Production Credit Association of North Platte*, 200 N.W.2d 1 (S. Ct. Neb. 1972).

68   *General Electric Capital Commercial Automotive Finance, Inc. v. Spartan Motors, Ltd.*, 675 N.Y.S.2d 626 (N.Y.A.D. 1998).

69   G. Gilmore, *Security Interests in Personal Property*, vol. 2 (Boston: Little, Brown, 1965) at 782.

70   *Thet Mah and Associates, Inc. v. First Bank of North Dakota (NA), Minot*, 336 N.W.2d 134 (N.D. 1983).

71   *In Re Hansen*, 85 B.R. 821 (B. Ct. N.D. Iowa 1988).

72   (1991), 79 D.L.R. (4th) 22 (Sask. C.A.) [*Pettyjohn*].

exchange for the assumption of the debt.[73] This is sometimes referred to as tracing by subrogation or backwards tracing. Although the case law has not given general recognition to tracing under these circumstances, there are a number of cases that provide support for backwards tracing.[74] If this principle were applied, the lender would be required to demonstrate that the money advanced was used to pay out the unsecured obligation owing to the seller or to pay out interim financing, and that it was not used for any other purpose. This will be sufficient to satisfy the requirement that the value was used to acquire the asset. However, the lender will still be required to show that the purpose of the loan was to permit the acquisition of the new asset. For this reason, it will still be necessary for the lender to establish that, at the time of the acquisition of the collateral, it had given a commitment to make an enabling loan.

c) Deemed Security Interests

Outside of Ontario, a "lease for a term of more than one year" and a "commercial consignment" are brought within the scope of the PPSA even though they do not in substance create security interests.[75] These deemed security interests are governed by the same priority rules that govern true security interests. By satisfying the procedural requirements, the lessor or consignor can ensure that it will enjoy priority over an earlier secured party. But if the lessor or consignor fails to satisfy these procedural requirements, it will not be able to assert the purchase money security interest superpriority, and its priority status will be governed by the residual priority rule.[76]

Under the Ontario Act, such transactions are not deemed to be security interests that fall within the scope of the Act. The PPSA priority rules that govern disputes between secured parties therefore will not apply to resolve a competition between a security interest and a lease or consignment that is not in substance a security interest. In such a case, the lease or consignment will be entitled to priority over the security interest without any need for registration or perfection.

---

73   See L. Smith, *The Law of Tracing* (Oxford: Clarendon Press, 1997) at 146–52; J. Penner, *The Law of Trusts*, 2d ed. (London: Butterworths, 2000) at 375–79.

74   *Bishopsgate Investment Management Ltd. v. Homan*, [1995] Ch. 211 at 221–22 (C.A.), Dillon J.; *Foskett v. McKeown*, [1998] Ch. 265 at 283–84 (C.A.), Sir Richard Scott V-C.

75   See chapter 2, E.4 "A Commercial Consignment" and E.5 "A Lease for a Term or More Than One Year."

76   See, for example, *Canadian Imperial Bank of Commerce v. Westfield Industries Ltd.* (1990), 1 P.P.S.A.C. (2d) 142 (Sask. Q.B.).

3) Procedural Requirements

In order to obtain the purchase money security interest priority, a secured party must do two things. First, it must establish that its security interest falls within the definition of a purchase money security interest. Second, it must establish that it satisfied certain procedural requirements. The procedural requirements are separate from the definition. A secured party who fails to satisfy the procedural requirements will not be able to assert a superpriority over an earlier secured party. Instead, it will be subject to the normal first-in-time priority rule. However, the security interest will continue to be classified as a purchase money security interest, and other provisions of the PPSA that provide other special rules for purchase money security interests will continue to apply to it.

The PPSA sets out a simple procedural requirement that is easily satisfied where the collateral is non-inventory. Where inventory is involved, the procedural requirements are more complex.

a) Purchase Money Security Interests in Non-Inventory

A secured party who holds a purchase money security interest in non-inventory is given priority over any other security interest in the same collateral given by the same debtor if the security interest is perfected within a specified time period. The Ontario PPSA provides that it must be perfected before or not later than ten days after the debtor obtains possession of the collateral.[77] The other Acts provide that perfection must occur not later than fifteen days after the debtor obtains possession of the collateral.[78] Where the collateral is an intangible, the time period runs from the date of attachment of the security interest.

In order to claim the benefit of this priority rule, it is necessary to perfect the security interest before the expiration of the specified time period. If the secured party attempts to perfect by registration but there is an invalidating error in a registration, the requirements for the priority rule will not have been satisfied unless a financing change statement is registered before the expiration of the time period.

In order to perfect a security interest in motor vehicles held as consumer goods under the Ontario and Yukon Acts, a secured party must record the serial number on the financing statement. If the motor vehicles are held as equipment or inventory, registration of the serial

---

77   OPPSA s. 33(2).
78   PPSA (A, M, NWT, NU, S) s. 34(2); (BC, NB, PEI) s. 34(1); (NL, NS) s. 35(1); Y s. 33(1).

number is not required. Under the other Acts, a secured party is required to describe serial numbered goods by serial number if they are held as consumer goods. Although registration of a serial number is not required in order to perfect a security interest in equipment as against a trustee in bankruptcy or a judgment enforcement creditor, a failure to do so will render the security interest unperfected in a competition with another secured party who has perfected its security interest.[79]

The Acts in Saskatchewan, Manitoba, Northwest Territories, Nunavut, and the Atlantic provinces extend this rule so that it covers purchase money security interests as well. In order to claim purchase money security interest priority in respect of serial numbered goods held as equipment, the secured party must describe the collateral by serial number. A failure to do so will mean that the security interest is unperfected with the result that the procedural requirements for obtaining the purchase money security interest priority will not have been satisfied. The outcome of the priority competition will therefore fall to be determined by the residual priority rule.

The comparable provisions of the PPSA in British Columbia and Alberta are worded differently and produce a different outcome. The rule that requires registration of serial numbers to perfect a security interest in serial numbered goods held as equipment applies only to the residual priority rule and not to the purchase money security interest priority rule. In Alberta and British Columbia, a secured party who obtains a purchase money security interest in equipment and perfects it by registration will obtain priority over earlier security interests even though the secured party fails to describe the collateral by serial number. Unfortunately, this approach tends to undermine a basic philosophy of the Act in respect of serial numbers. The legislation was designed so that potential secured parties could search the registry by serial number of equipment with a high degree of confidence that the search would disclose any security interests taken in the equipment. This expectation is greatly undermined if a serial number search fails to disclose purchase money security interests.

b)   Purchase Money Security Interests in Inventory

Where the secured party takes a purchase money security interest, stricter procedural requirements must be observed.[80] There are two requirements. First, the secured party must perfect the security inter-

---

79   PPSA (A, BC, M, NB, NWT, NU, PEI, S) s. 35(4); (NL, NS) s. 36(4).
80   PPSA (A, M, NWT, NU, S) s. 34(3); (BC, NB, PEI) s. 34(2); (NL, NS) s. 35(2); O s. 33(1); Y s. 33(2).

est before the debtor obtains possession of the collateral. Second, the secured party must notify prior secured parties who have registered a financing statement that covers the inventory. These requirements may be satisfied in any order; what is critical to superpriority is that both have been satisfied before delivery of possession of the inventory to the debtor. These more stringent requirements are imposed on the theory that a prior secured party with a security interest in the debtor's after-acquired goods is likely to rely upon the debtor's acquisition of new inventory in making new advances to the debtor. The prior secured party should be given notice of an intervening purchase money security interest financer who will have priority over the new inventory. In the absence of this requirement, the secured party would need to continually search the registry to ensure that no purchase money security interest has been registered before making fresh advances against incoming inventory.

The notice must be given before the debtor obtains possession of the collateral. There is no legal requirement that registration of the purchase money security interest occur before the notice is sent. However, by registering first and then obtaining a search result, the inventory financer will be able to identify which parties will need to be given the notice. The notice must be given to any secured party who has registered in respect of the collateral before the purchase money security interest is registered. A party who searches the registry, notifies other secured parties and then registers the purchase money security interest takes the risk that other competing security interests may be registered after it has conducted its search but before its registration is effected.

Some of the earlier versions of the PPSA provided that the notice was only effective for a two-year period. This created a trap for the unwary purchase money security interest financer without providing much in the way of new information to the earlier secured party, and therefore it has been abolished in every jurisdiction except the Yukon.[81]

The notice only needs to be given to a secured party who has an earlier registration covering the inventory. The notice need not be given if the earlier security interest was perfected otherwise than by registration or if it is unperfected. The fact that the secured party who holds the purchase money security interest has actual knowledge of such an interest is irrelevant.[82] The notice is sufficient not only for the purchase money security agreement that is being immediately contemplated, but

---

81   YPPSA s. 34(3)(c).
82   Under the former Ontario PPSA, the notice had to be given to earlier registrations as well as to any other secured party in respect of whose interest the

also any other purchase money security agreement that may be subsequently entered into between the parties.[83] The notice is not invalidated by the fact that it is overbroad and identifies more items or kinds of collateral than are actually granted to the holder of the purchase money security interest.[84]

Although a secured party who holds a purchase money security interest will usually perfect its security interest in inventory by registration, it is conceivable that the secured party might perfect it by possession. For example, this would occur where a feedlot operator sells cattle to a debtor on secured credit terms and relies upon its possession of the animals to perfect its security interest.[85] The PPSA provides that the notice requirement must be satisfied before the debtor, or a third party with the consent of the debtor, obtains possession of the collateral. Here, the debtor never obtains possession of the collateral. The notice requirement therefore does not need to be satisfied unless the cattle are delivered to the debtor.[86] Although the PPSA provides that the notice must be given to any secured party who has registered before the registration of the purchase money security interest, this can have no application where the purchase money security interest is perfected by possession. If the secured party plans to release the cattle to the debtor, it should ensure that it first registers its interest and gives the notice.

The notice must be in writing and indicate that the secured party expects to acquire a purchase money security interest in inventory of the debtor. It must also include a description of the inventory in which it expects to acquire a purchase money security interest that identifies the inventory by item or kind.[87] A reference to the collateral as "inventory" is not a sufficient description for the purposes of this provision.[88]

---

holder of the purchase money security interest had actual knowledge. This latter class of persons has been deleted from the current Act.

83 *Fedders Financial Corp. v. Chiarelli Bros., Inc.*, 289 A.2d 169 (Pa. Super. 1972).

84 *Ibid.* The notice described a wide range of inventory when in fact the purchase money security interest was taken only in air conditioners. This is not objectionable because the notice is not tied to the immediate security agreement, but may cover subsequently created purchase money security interests in the other classes of inventory.

85 See *Kundel v. Sprague National Bank*, 128 F.3d 636 (8th Cir. 1997).

86 *Ibid.*

87 See *Clark Equipment of Canada Ltd. v. Bank of Montreal*, [1984] 4 W.W.R. 519 (Man. C.A.). The court held that the notice may provide a generic description such as "front-end loaders" and "dozers."

88 *Toronto Dominion Bank v. Lanzarotta Wholesale Grocers Ltd.* (1996), 12 P.P.S.A.C. (2d) 30 (Ont. C.A.).

c)   Determining the Date of Possession

The procedural requirements in respect of collateral other than intangibles are triggered when the debtor obtains possession of the collateral. Sometimes the property is delivered to the debtor before a security agreement is signed by the debtor. This is illustrated in the following scenario.

On February 1, SP1 registers a financing statement to perfect a security interest it has been given in all of D's present and after-acquired personal property. On May 1, SP2 delivers possession of goods to D on a trial basis. D is under no obligation to purchase the goods. On June 1, D agrees to purchase the goods from SP2 under a secured instalment credit agreement. On June 5, SP2 registers a financing statement.

If time begins to run from the date of D's actual possession, SP2 will have failed to register within the requisite time period. But if time begins to run from the time that D becomes obligated to SP2 under the terms of their security agreement, SP2 will have registered in time and will take priority over SP1. Courts have adopted the latter approach and have held that time will not begin to run until the debtor has possession of the collateral as a debtor and not in some other capacity.[89] The wording of the Ontario Act confirms that this was the intended result. The legislation was amended to provide that the debtor must "obtain possession of the collateral *as a debtor*" (emphasis added). It is therefore necessary to determine the date that the debtor becomes obligated to the secured party. This is not necessarily the date that the security agreement was signed. If the debtor signs a security agreement which is subject to the secured party approving the transaction, the relevant date is the date of the approval and not the date of the security agreement.[90]

---

89   *Guaranty Trust Co. of Canada v. Canadian Imperial Bank of Commerce* (1989), 2 P.P.S.A.C. (2d) 88 (Ont. H.C.J.), aff'd (1993), 6 P.P.S.A.C. (2d) 51 (Ont. C.A.); *Associates Leasing (Canada) Ltd. v. Humboldt Flour Mills Inc.* (1998), 14 P.P.S.A.C. (2d) 174 (Sask. Q.B.); *Air Products Canada Ltd. v. Farini Corp.* (2000), 16 C.B.R. (4th)18 (Ont. S.C.J.); *Greyvest Leasing Inc. v. Canadian Imperial Bank of Commerce* (1991), 1 P.P.S.A.C. (2d) 264 (Ont. Ct. Gen. Div.), rev'd on other grounds (1993), 5 P.P.S.A.C. (2d) 187 (Ont. C.A.).

90   *McLeod & Co. v. Price Waterhouse Ltd.* (1992), 3 P.P.S.A.C. (2d) 171 (Sask. Q.B.). The debtor was previously in possession of the collateral in a different capacity, and later agreed to purchase it. A security agreement was executed on 16 October 1989, but the secured party did not agree to provide financing until 2 November 1989. The court held that the debtor did not become a debtor until the secured party agreed to accept the debt on November 2

4) The Double-debtor Scenario

A purchase money security interest that meets the procedural requirements discussed above has priority over any other security interest in
the same collateral given by the same debtor. The priority rule does
not apply if the competing security interest and the purchase money
security interest were given by different debtors. This is illustrated in
the following scenario.

**SP1 is given a security interest in D1's goods, which it registers on August
1. On September 1, D1 sells the goods to D2. The sale is not authorized by
SP1 and does not occur in D1's ordinary course of business. SP2 finances the
acquisition of the goods by D2 and takes a purchase money security interest
in them, which it registers on September 5.**

SP2 cannot invoke the purchase money security interest priority against
SP1, since the competing security interests were not given by the same
debtor. The rule only gives SP2 priority over competing security interests that were granted by D2, and not those granted by D1.

5) Maintaining Purchase Money Security Interest Status

Some of the more contentious issues relating to purchase money security interests arise when a purchase money security interest is combined
with another security interest. This might occur where the security
agreement provides that the collateral also secures non-purchase
money obligations. It may also occur where a purchase money obligation is consolidated with other obligations upon a refinancing or where
a secured party pays out a purchase money security interest held by a
third party.

a) The Effect of Cross-collateralization
Most security agreements that create purchase money security interests
involve a direct one-to-one relationship between the collateral acquired
and the purchase money obligation. In other words, the security interest is taken in the new property that is acquired and secures the loan
or credit that permitted the acquisition of that asset. However, some
security agreements provide for a cross-collateralization or add-on feature. The issue is whether the presence of this feature results in the loss
of the purchase money security interest status that would otherwise be
available.

The cross-collateralization or add-on feature may take a number of
different forms. This is illustrated in the following scenarios.

Scenario 1: A secured party makes a loan which enables the debtor to acquire a new fork lift. The security agreement provides that in order to secure this purchase money loan, the debtor grants the secured party a security interest in all present and after-acquired personal property.

The loan in this case is a purchase money loan. The security agreement provides that a security interest is taken in the fork lift. But as well, a security interest is taken in the debtor's other present and after-acquired personal property to secure this obligation. Clearly, the security interest in the debtor's other present and after-acquired personal property cannot qualify as a purchase money security interest since the funds advanced were not used to acquire those assets. The issue is whether the presence of the cross-collateralization or add on feature destroys the purchase money status of the security interest in the fork lift.

Scenario 2: A lender makes a loan that enables the debtor to acquire a truck. The security agreement gives the secured party a security interest in the truck. The security agreement also contains an all obligations clause which provides that the security interest also secures any other obligation that might be owed by the debtor to the secured party.

If the secured party later makes a further loan to the debtor, it will be secured by the security interest in the truck. The later loan will not qualify the security interest as a purchase money security interest since it did not enable the debtor to acquire the truck. The issue is whether the presence of an all obligations or future advances clause in the security agreement will prevent the secured party from claiming a purchase money security interest in the truck.

Scenario 3: A seller sells fifty head of cattle to the debtor for $25,000 under a secured instalment purchase agreement. Later the same seller sells a further 100 head of cattle to the debtor for $50,000 under a similar security agreement. Both security agreements contain a clause that provides that the security interest secures not only the goods sold pursuant to the agreement, but also any other goods that are sold by the seller to the buyer.

Under these clauses, the fifty head of cattle sold under the first agreement secures not only the $25,000 purchase money obligation that permitted their acquisition. It also secures the $50,000 obligation incurred in respect of the acquisition of the 100 head of cattle that were subsequently acquired under a different agreement. Similarly, the 100 head of cattle secures the $50,000 purchase money obligation as well as the $25,000 obligation under the earlier agreement.

Prior to the amendments incorporated in the most recent version of Article 9, the effect of a cross-collateralization or add-on feature was frequently litigated in the United States.[91] Some courts invoked the "transformation" rule and held that a purchase money security interest was transformed into a non-purchase–money security interest through the operation of a cross-collateralization clause.[92] Under this approach, in order to maintain the status of a purchase money security interest, the security agreement must have secured only the purchase money obligation. Any attempt to secure some other obligation would result in a transformation of the obligation so that it would no longer be regarded as a purchase money obligation. Other courts invoked the "dual-status" approach. Under this approach, the security interest was divided into purchase money and non-purchase money components.[93] The current version of Article 9 has now expressly adopted the dual-status approach.[94]

In Canada, the courts that have considered the matter have embraced the dual-status approach.[95] They point out that there is nothing in the PPSA to prevent a purchase money security interest from co-existing with other kinds of security interests. A further argument in support of this view is based on the wording of the PPSA definition of a "purchase money security interest." The definition provides that a security interest is a purchase money security interest "to the extent that" the loan enables the debtor to purchase new property. It is argued that this language recognizes the possibility of a secured obligation that is only partly a purchase money obligation.[96]

In each of the three scenarios set out above, the application of the dual-status approach results in the retention of a purchase money security interest in the property that was financed by the secured party. To the extent that the security agreement provides for the creation of

---

91   See B. Burk, "Preserving the Purchase Money Status of Refinanced or Commingled Purchase Money Debt" (1983) 35 Stan. L. Rev. 1133. Article 9-103 (e) and (f) of the most recent Revision have eliminated much of the controversy in the United States in non-consumer goods transactions.

92   See, for example, *In Re Manuel*, 507 F.2d 990 (5th Cir. 1975); *Southtrust Bank of Alabama, NA v. Borg-Warner Acceptance Corp.*, 760 F.2d 1240 (11th Cir. 1985).

93   See, for example, *John Deere Co. v. Production Credit Association*, 686 S.W.2d 904 (Tenn. App. 1984); *In Re Billings*, 838 F.2d 405 (10th Cir. 1988).

94   Art. 9-103(f).

95   *Clark Equipment of Canada Ltd. v. Bank of Montreal,* above note 87; *Re Paradise Valley Marine Ltd. (c.o.b. Ridge Marine)* (1997), 7 C.B.R. (4th) 252 (B.C.S.C.).

96   See *In Re Billings*, above note 93.

any other type of security interest, it will create only a non-purchase money security interest. This is illustrated in the following scenario.

Scenario 4: SP1 takes a security interest on all present and after-acquired property of the debtor and properly registers it. Thereafter, SP2 sells fifty head of cattle to the debtor for $25,000 under a secured instalment credit agreement. Later SP2 sells a further 100 head of cattle to the debtor for $50,000 under a similar security agreement. Both security agreements contain a clause that provides that the security interest secures not only the goods sold pursuant to the agreement, but also any other goods that are sold by the seller to the buyer. SP2 registers its security interest and completes the procedural steps that are needed in order to obtain the purchase money security interest priority. Following a default by the debtor, all the cattle are sold. There is $15,000 owing to SP2 in respect of the first lot of cattle and $45,000 owing in respect of the second lot. The first lot are sold for $20,000, while the second lot are sold for $40,000.

SP2 cannot simply take the $60,000 in proceeds and apply it against the $60,000 that is owed to it in priority to SP1. SP2 has a purchase money security interest in the first lot of fifty cattle only to the extent that it secures its unpaid purchase price of $15,000. The cross-collateralization clause gives SP2 a security interest in the first lot of cattle in order to secure the obligation owing under the second agreement, but this does not give it the status of a purchase money security interest. In respect of the sale proceeds of the first lot, SP2 will have priority to the extent of $15,000 by virtue of its purchase money security interest. In respect of the remaining $5,000, SP1 will have priority by virtue of its earlier registration. As the proceeds from the sale of the second lot are not sufficient to retire the purchase money obligation, SP2 will be able to claim priority over SP1 for all the proceeds arising from the sale of the second lot.

Unfortunately, courts have sometimes lost sight of this point. In *Chrysler Credit Canada Ltd. v. Royal Bank of Canada*,[97] a priority competition arose between a bank that had taken a security interest in all of the debtor's present and after-acquired personal property and an inventory financer who claimed a purchase money security interest in trade-ins resulting from the sale of new vehicles. The Saskatchewan Court of Appeal held that the inventory financer could claim a purchase money security interest in the trade-ins even though the purchase price of

97   [1986] 6 WWR. 338 (Sask. C.A.).

the new vehicles to which they related were fully paid. This result is difficult to support. In principle, a purchase money security interest should not persist after the purchase money obligation that it secures has been satisfied. Although the cross-collateralization clause in the security agreement was sufficient to give the inventory financer a security interest in these trade-ins, it should not have been given the status of a purchase money security interest. Courts in Ontario have rejected this argument.[98] The Saskatchewan PPSA was subsequently amended to reverse the outcome in this case, and a similar provision has been included in the PPSA in many of the other jurisdictions.[99]

b) Consolidation of Debts and Refinancing

The issue of loss of purchase money security interest status may also arise in the context of a consolidation of debts or refinancing. The simplest case involves the refinancing of a single purchase money security interest. A secured party may agree to refinance the loan by increasing the term of the loan and decreasing the size of the periodic payments. Often this is accomplished by cancellation of the original promissory note and execution of a new note that evidences the new terms of repayment. Under this arrangement, the new loan funds that are advanced are used to pay out the old loan. Although some courts in the United States have held that this extinguishes the first debt and therefore results in a loss of purchase money security interest status,[100] this approach is overly formalistic and it has been rejected by at least one Canadian court.[101]

The issue becomes more complex when a purchase money security obligation is combined with another obligation. This is illustrated in the following scenarios.

---

98 *Unisource Canada Inc. v. Hongkong Bank of Canada* (1998), 14 P.P.S.A.C. (2d) 112 (Ont. Ct. Gen. Div.), aff'd (2000), 15 P.P.S.A.C. (2d) 95 (Ont. C.A.).

99 PPSA (M, NWT, Nu) s. 34(9); (NB, PEI) s. 34(7); (NL, NS) s. 35(7); S s. 34(10) provides that a "purchase money security interest in an item of collateral does not extend or continue in the proceeds of the item after the obligation to pay the purchase price of the item or to repay the value given for the purpose of enabling the debtor to acquire rights in it has been discharged"; (A, BC, O, Y) no equivalent provision.

100 *In Re Matthews*, 724 F.2d 798 (9th Cir. 1984).

101 See *Werner v. Royal Bank of Canada* (2000), 2 P.P.S.A.C. (3d) 119 (Sask. Q.B.).

Scenario 1: SP1 is given a security interest in all of D's present and after-acquired personal property to secure an operating loan, and registers a financing statement on 1 February 2000. SP2 makes a loan to D to enable D to acquire a new truck to be used as equipment. SP2 registers on 1 May 2001 and delivers the truck to D on the same day. As a result, SP2 obtains a purchase money security interest priority over SP1. On 1 March 2002, SP2 agrees to loan an additional $20,000 to D. New documentation is executed which consolidates the two loans into a single obligation, and a security interest in the truck is given to SP2 to secure this consolidated loan obligation.

In this scenario, the purchase money obligation is combined with a non-purchase money obligation to create a single obligation with a single re-payment schedule. In order to maintain its priority SP2 must establish that its purchase money security interest has not been lost by virtue of the refinancing. The application of the transformation approach would result in the complete loss of priority for SP2. The application of the dual-status approach would result in a notional division of the single obligation into two components: the purchase money component and the non-purchase money component. Under this approach, SP2's priority over SP1 would only pertain to the purchase money component.

Scenario 2: SP1 is given a security interest in all of D's present and after-acquired personal property to secure an operating loan, and registers a financing statement on 1 February 2000. On 1 March 2001, SP2 makes a loan to D that enables D to acquire a truck and takes a purchase money security interest in the truck. On 1 May 2001, SP2 makes a loan to D that enables D to acquire a tractor and takes a purchase money security interest in the tractor. SP2 registers a financing statement within the requisite time period and obtains purchase money security interest priority over SP1. On 1 June 2002, SP2 agrees to refinance its loans. The two loans are combined into a single obligation and a security interest is executed which gives SP2 a security interest in both the truck and the tractor to secure the consolidated obligation.

In this scenario, a purchase money obligation is combined with another purchase money obligation to form a single consolidated obligation. In both scenarios, SP2 must establish that its purchase money security interests have not been lost by virtue of the refinancing in order to maintain its purchase money security interest priority over SP1. The application of the transformation approach would result in the complete loss of priority for SP2. The application of the dual-status approach would result in a notional division of the single obligation into two components both of which retain their status as purchase money obligations. Under this approach, SP2 would maintain its priority over SP1 in respect of the truck and the tractor.

The Saskatchewan Court of Appeal has held that the consolidation of debts does not destroy a purchase money security interest.[102] By rejecting the transformation approach in favour of the dual-status approach, the court has made it necessary to come to grips with a second issue. Where money is paid towards the consolidated obligation, how does one determine the amount that is to be attributed to the purchase money component and what portion is to be attributed to the other component? This is illustrated in the following scenario.

Scenario 3: SP is given a purchase money security interest in D's computer. SP is later given a non-purchase money security interest in D's automobile to secure a loan. SP subsequently agrees to refinance the loans, and the two obligations are combined into a single obligation. D executes a new security agreement that gives SP a security interest in the computer and the automobile. At the time of the loan consolidation, $2,500 is left owing on the purchase money loan and $5,000 is left owing on the non-purchase money loan. D later pays a total of $3,000 towards the consolidated loan obligation before defaulting.

What portion of the $3,000 paid towards the combined obligation should be attributed to the purchase money component, and what portion should be attributed to the non-purchase money component? If the new loan documents provide a contractual formula for the allocation of payments, this should govern.[103] But in the absence of a contractual formula, the issue is whether the courts will be willing to provide a method for the allocation of payments. In the United States, some courts applied the first-in, first-out rule and allocated the payment towards the first obligation that was incurred.[104] This was the

---

102 *Bank of Montreal v. Tomyn* (1989), 84 Sask. R. 253 (Q.B.); *Battlefords Credit Union Ltd. v. Ilnicki* (1991), 82 D.L.R. (4th) 69, [1991] 5 W.W.R. 673 (Sask. C.A.).

103 This is the approach adopted by art. 9-103(e)(1)–(2).

104 *In Re Conn*, 33 U.C.C. Rep. 701 (W.D. Ky. 1982). Art. 9-103(e) of the most recent revision now provides an allocation of payment formula for non-consumer transactions. If the parties have agreed to a reasonable allocation formula, it will be applied. In the absence of one, the person owing the obligation can specify at the time of payment how it is to be applied. In the absence of an agreed method or a timely manifestation of intention, it is allocated first against unsecured obligations and then against obligations secured by purchase money security interests in the order that they were incurred.

approach later adopted in current Article 9.[105] In scenario 3, application of this approach would mean that $2,500 would be paid against the purchase money obligation, with the remaining $500 paid against the non-purchase money obligation. As a result, SP could no longer claim a purchase money security interest in the computer. Alternatively, a court may decide to apply a pro rata apportionment formula that would allocate the payment in proportion to the obligation secured. If this approach were applied in scenario 3, one-third of the payments would be allocated against the purchase money component and two-thirds would be allocated against the non-purchase money component. SP could therefore claim a purchase money security interest in the computer to the extent of $1,500.

In choosing between the first-in, first-out rule and the *pro rata* rule, a court might have regard to the type of financing arrangement. The *pro rata* rule may be more appropriate in the case of a consolidation of two separate obligations. In the absence of the consolidation of the two debts, the debtor would have been paying down both of the obligations. On the other hand, a first-in, first-out rule may be more appropriate in respect of a secured instalment purchase arrangement, as there is a stronger expectation that the debtor will pay the price of the first purchase before any of the money is applied against the price of the next purchase.

It is by no means clear that courts will be willing to supply an appropriation of payment formula in the absence of a contractual formula. In *Re Gerrard*,[106] an obligation pertaining to a purchase money security interest was consolidated with a non-purchase money obligation. The court held that it was incumbent on the secured party not only to prove the existence of the purchase money security interest, but also to prove the debt due.[107]

Other cases suggest that a court will not look too closely and indeed may permit some degree of cross-collateralization to occur. This is most likely to occur where the secured party combines several purchase money security interests into a single obligation. In *Battlefords*

---

105   Art. 9-103(e)(3).

106   (2000), 20 C.B.R. (4th) 90 (N.S.S.C.).

107   A purchase money obligation of $2,757.77 was combined with a non-purchase money obligation of $5,000. Apparently, the secured party failed to establish the amount due in respect of the purchase money security interest or even the amount owing in respect of the consolidated loan. The court might have been more willing to provide an allocation formula if the secured party had established the total amount that was due and payable on the consolidated obligation.

Credit Union Ltd. v. Ilnicki,[108] a secured party made a loan that consolidated various purchase money security interests in the farm equipment. The Saskatchewan Court of Appeal held that the secured party held a purchase money security interest in all of the items that had been subject to a purchase money security interest. In doing so, the court did not inquire as to how much of the purchase money obligation in respect of each item was owing or how subsequent payments on the consolidated obligation had been allocated towards these purchase money obligations.

The problem with this approach is illustrated in the following scenario.

Scenario 4: SP1 is given a security interest in all of D's present and after-acquired personal property to secure an operating loan, and registers a financing statement on 1 February 1998. On 1 March 1999, SP2 is given a purchase money security interest in D's truck. On 1 June 2001, SP2 is given a purchase money security interest in D's automobile. On 1 September 2002, the two purchase money loans are consolidated into a single obligation secured by a security interest in the truck and automobile. At the time of the consolidation, the amount owing on the automobile loan is $1,000, and the amount owing on the truck loan is $30,000. D defaults and the collateral is seized. The automobile is valued at $10,000 and the truck is valued at $20,000.

SP2 may argue that it has a purchase money security interest in both the automobile and the truck that secures the consolidated obligation of $31,000. If this argument is accepted, SP2 would be entitled to all the proceeds of realization. The authors are of the view that a consolidation of purchase money security interests should not produce this result. If the loans had not been consolidated, SP2 would have been entitled to recover $1,000 in respect of the automobile, and $20,000 in connection with the truck. A loan consolidation should preserve existing priorities; it should not permit one party to leap frog over others in priority. In respect of the automobile, SP2 should be entitled to priority over SP1 only to the extent of the purchase money obligation associated with this transaction.

108 Above note 102.

c) Paying Out Purchase Money Security Interests Held by Third Parties

A lender may wish to assume a purchase money security interest that was granted to another party. The safest method of accomplishing this is to obtain an assignment of the security interest. However, sometimes this is not done. Instead, the lender advances funds that are used to pay out the secured party, and the debtor executes a security agreement that gives the lender a security interest in the collateral. The issue is whether the lender can successfully claim that it has a purchase money security interest in the collateral. This is illustrated in the following scenario.

Scenario 1: SP1 is given a security interest in all of D's present and after-acquired personal property and registers it on 1 June 2000. On 1 May 2001, SP2 obtains a purchase money security interest in D's tractor and completes the procedural steps necessary for it to obtain priority over SP1. On 1 July 2002, SP3 advances money to D for the purpose of enabling D to pay out SP2's obligation, and D gives SP3 a security interest in D's tractor to secure this loan. SP3 registers a financing statement on 3 July 2002.

The Saskatchewan Court of Appeal in *Battlefords Credit Union Ltd. v. Ilnicki*[109] held on these facts that SP3 obtains a purchase money security interest in the collateral. Observing that a transaction falls within the definition of a purchase money security interest if the secured party gives value "for the purpose of enabling the debtor to acquire rights" in the collateral, the Court held that the loan enabled the debtor to acquire rights in the collateral since it permitted the debtor "to rid the items of the purchase money security interests of others" thereby adding to the debtor's bundle of rights.[110] The case has been followed in a number of other jurisdictions.[111]

Similar reasoning was employed by the Ontario Court of Appeal in *Unisource Canada Inc. v. Laurentian Bank of Canada*.[112] Weiler J. held that the paying out of a purchase money security interest permitted the debtor to acquire additional rights in the collateral.[113] He commented that this interpretation was consonant with sound commercial policy,

---

109 *Ibid.*
110 *Ibid.* at 74 (D.L.R.).
111 *Re Gerrard*, above note 106; *Trans Canada Credit Corp. v. Wonnacott* (2000), 188 Nfld & P.E.I.R. 198 (P.E.I.S.C.T.D.).
112 (2000), 47 O.R. (3d) 616 (C.A.).
113 For a serious critical comment on this reasoning, see Anthony J. Duggan, "Hard Cases, Equity and the PPSA" (2000), 34 Can. Bus. L.J. 129.

since it makes it easier for the debtor to enter into a new financing arrangement without the co-operation of the original lender being required. In order to claim the purchase money security interest priority, the secured party must comply with the necessary procedural steps. As explained earlier, where the collateral is inventory, the secured party must perfect the security interest before the debtor acquires possession of the collateral and must notify secured parties who have earlier registrations covering the collateral. Where the collateral is non-inventory, the secured party need only perfect the security interest before the expiration of the ten-day (Ontario) or fifteen-day (other jurisdictions) time period, which starts to run from the time that the debtor obtains possession of the collateral. The date of the debtor's original possession of the collateral under the purchase money security interest that is paid out is not used. Rather, the debtor is considered to have possession of the collateral as a debtor at the time that the new funds were used to pay out the earlier security interest.[114]

These cases show that the courts are willing to give the refinancing lender the same priority status that was enjoyed by the holder of the purchase money security interest whose interest was paid out. However, the authors are of the opinion — an opinion shared by other commentators[115] — that the theory upon which they have sought to achieve this result is conceptually flawed. By paying out the earlier security interest, the refinancing lender is viewed as having obtained a purchase money security interest in its own right. The lender's priority is therefore not dependent on the priority of the earlier purchase money security interest that is paid out. The problems with this approach are illustrated in the following scenario.

Scenario 2: SP1 is given a security interest in all of D's present and after-acquired personal property and registers it on 1 June 2000. On 1 May 2001, SP2 obtains a purchase money security interest in D's tractor. The tractor is delivered to the debtor on May 5, but SP2 does not register until 30 May 2001. On 1 July 2002, SP3 advances money to D for the purpose of enabling D to pay out SP2's obligation, and D gives SP3 a security interest in D's tractor to secure this loan. SP3 registers a financing statement on 3 July 2002.

SP3's loan enabled D to rid itself of SP2's security interest. In the preceding cases, the courts have held that this satisfies the purchase money security interest definition that value be given that enables the debtor

114 *Farm Credit Corp. v. Gannon*, [1993] 6 W.W.R. 736 (Sask. Q.B.).
115 Duggan, above note 113.

to acquire rights in the collateral. On this theory, SP3 has a purchase money security interest in the tractor. As SP3 registered within the proper time periods, it would be entitled to priority over SP1 despite the fact that SP2 did not have priority over SP1.

Furthermore, the courts' reasoning would appear to apply even where the security interest that is paid out is not a purchase money security interest. This is illustrated in the following scenario.

Scenario 3: SP1 is given a security interest in all of D's present and after-acquired personal property and registers it on 1 June 2000. On 1 May 2001, SP2 takes and perfects a non-purchase money security interest in D's tractor. On 1 July 2002, SP3 advances money to D for the purpose of enabling D to pay out SP2's obligation, and D gives SP3 a security interest in D's tractor to secure this loan. SP3 registers a financing statement on 3 July 2002.

SP3's loan was used to get rid of SP2's security interest and thereby added to D's bundle of rights. Therefore, applying the reasoning of the courts in the above cases, SP3's security interest qualifies as a purchase money security interest and is entitled to priority over SP1 since SP3 met the requisite procedural requirements. Needless to say, this conclusion would completely undermine the entire structure of the PPSA priority system.

The theory that a secured party may obtain a purchase money security interest by paying off an existing encumbrance is wholly inadequate. Courts in the United States have come to the same result by finding that the secured party is entitled to be subrogated to rights of the secured party whose security interest has been paid out.[116] Subrogation is the substitution of one person in the place of another in respect of a claim or right. This permits the secured party to step into the shoes of the prior secured party and obtain the benefit of its security interest. But if SP2 did not take the steps needed to obtain priority over SP1, then SP3 should not obtain any greater priority. Because SP3's priority is derived from SP2's security interest, it is necessary to show that SP2 has not lost its priority due to lapse or discharge of its registration.[117]

---

116 See, for example, *French Lumber Co. v. Commercial Realty & Finance Co.*, 195 N.E.2d 507 (Mass. 1964). See also the discussion later in this chapter in I.3 "Subrogation."

117 *Rinn v. First Union National Bank of Maryland*, 176 B.R. 401 (D. Md. 1995).

6) Purchase Money Security Interests in Accounts or Chattel Paper as Proceeds of Inventory

The PPSA makes it clear that the priority of a purchase money security interest extends to any proceeds as well.[118] Although this represents the general rule, PPSA jurisdictions take divergent approaches in the following scenario.

An accounts financer is given a security interest on all the debtor's accounts that it registers first-in-time. Later, an inventory financer is given a purchase money security interest on all inventory that it supplies to D. The inventory financer takes the necessary procedural steps to ensure that it obtains the purchase money security interest superpriority. Some of the inventory is then sold to customers giving rise to proceeds in the form of accounts owing to the debtor.

There are three distinct approaches that have been adopted in the various PPSA jurisdictions. The Ontario PPSA does not provide any special exception for this situation. As a result, the secured party who has a purchase money security interest will obtain priority over the prior accounts financer in respect of any accounts generated from the sale of the inventory. The Atlantic provinces adopt the same general rule subject to an important qualification.[119] The inventory financer is given priority only if it gives advance notice to the accounts financer of its intention to take a purchase money security interest in the inventory.[120] In the Western provinces and the Territories, the accounts financer is given priority over the inventory financer provided that the accounts financer claims the accounts as original collateral rather than as proceeds and has given new value for it.[121]

The Western and Territorial rule does not apply where the account is not one that is owed to the debtor by a third party but is one which

---

118 PPSA (A, M, NWT, Nu, S) s. 34(2)–(3); (BC, NB, PEI) s. 34(1)–(2); (NL, NS) s. 35(1)–(2); O s. 33(1)–(2); Y s. 33(1)–(2). These provisions state that a purchase money security interest in collateral *or its proceeds* has priority over any other security interest in the same collateral given by the same debtor.

119 PPSA (NL, NS) s. 35(2); NB s. 34(2).

120 The difference between this and the Ontario rule is that under the Ontario rule the inventory financer would obtain priority in respect the accounts even though it did not notify the accounts financer of its intention to take a purchase money security interest. Under the Ontario rule, this notice need only be given to a party who has registered a financing statement covering inventory. In the Atlantic Provinces it must be given also to a party who has a financing statement that covers accounts.

121 PPSA (A, M, NWT, Nu, S) s. 34(6); BC s. 34(5); Y s. 33(7).

is owed to the debtor by the account financer. In *Transamerica Commercial Finance Corp. Canada v. Royal Bank*,[122] the Saskatchewan Court of Appeal held that the rationale for protecting the prior accounts financer was that accounts financing ought not to be jeopardized by subsequent purchase money financing. The Court therefore held that the special protection for accounts financers does not apply where the account arises out of the deposit of cash proceeds from the sale of inventory with an account financer in its capacity of a deposit-taking institution. This limitation has been codified in Saskatchewan, the Northwest Territories, and Nunavut.[123]

Under all the Acts, an inventory financer who claims a purchase money security interest in chattel paper as proceeds of inventory will not be entitled to claim priority over a chattel paper financer who takes possession of the chattel paper in the ordinary course of its business and for new value.[124] This is so regardless of whether the chattel paper financer knew of the inventory financer's claim. This rule permits the debtor to raise additional funds by discounting its chattel paper. If the inventory financer wishes to avoid subordination, it must take possession of the chattel paper.

7) Competing Purchase Money Security Interests

A competition can arise between two purchase money security interests. This may occur where a lender advances money that is used by the debtor as a down payment, and the seller finances the balance of the purchase price through a secured instalment-credit agreement. It may also occur where two lenders have both financed a portion of the total purchase price of the property. The general purchase money security interest priority rule does not provide an answer where both secured parties have a purchase money security interest in the property acquired and have satisfied the procedural requirements.

All the Acts give priority to a purchase money security interest granted in favour of a seller over the purchase money security interest of a lender.[125] Outside of Ontario, leases for a term of more than one year and commercial consignments are deemed to be security interests

---

122 [1990] 4 W.W.R. 673 (Sask. C.A.).

123 See SPPSA s. 34(7); (NWT, Nu) s. 34(6.1).

124 PPSA (A, BC, NB, NWT, Nu, PEI) s. 31(6); (M, S) s. 31(7); (NL, NS) s. 32(6); O s. 28(3); Y s. 30(5).

125 PPSA (A, M, NWT, Nu, S) s. 34(5); (BC, NB, PEI) s. 34(4); (NL, NS) s. 35(4); O s. 33(3); Y s. 33(7). And see *Royal Bank of Canada v. Russell Food Equipment Ltd.* (2001), 28 C.B.R. (4th) 111 (Sask. Q.B.).

within the definition of a purchase money security interest and are afforded a similar priority over purchase money security interests given to lenders assuming the usual procedural requirements are satisfied.

The PPSA is silent on the resolution of a priority competition when both purchase money security interests are given to lenders. In the absence of any special priority rule, the residual priority rule will apply and priority will be given to the first security interest that is registered or perfected.[126]

A competition between two purchase money security interests may also arise where one of the purchase money security interests is taken in the original collateral and the other purchase money security interest attaches to the collateral as proceeds. This type of competition is illustrated in the following scenario.

SP1 finances the acquisition of a purchase money security interest in an automobile which SP1 registers on May 1. D later buys a truck from SP2 under a secured instalment-credit agreement and gives SP2 the automobile by way of a trade-in. SP2 registers in respect of the truck on August 5.

Both SP1 and SP2 have purchase money security interests in the truck. SP2's purchase money security interest is taken in the truck as original collateral. SP1's security interest in the truck arises by operation of law by virtue of the proceeds provisions of the PPSA. The sale of the automobile by D to SP2 involved a dealing with collateral. This gave SP1 a security interest in any proceeds received by the debtor (the truck) as a result of the dealing with the automobile. The purchase money security interest priority of a secured party extends to any proceeds. Therefore, SP1 is able to claim a purchase money security interest in the truck as proceeds.

The Acts in Western Canada and the Territories contain an express priority rule to deal with this situation.[127] Priority is given to the purchase money security interest in the original collateral, over the purchase money security interest in the collateral as proceeds. In order to obtain this priority the non-proceeds purchase money security interest must be perfected not later than fifteen days after the debtor obtains possession of the collateral. In the case of inventory, the secured party must perfect the security interest before the debtor obtains possession of the collateral. This rule gives SP2 priority over SP1 in respect of the truck. This does not mean that SP1 is without a remedy. So long as the

---

126 *National Trailer Convoy of Canada v. Bank of Montreal* (1980), 10 B.L.R. 196 (Ont. H.C.J.); *Polano v. Bank of Nova Scotia* (1979), 95 D.L.R. (3d) 510 (Ont. Dist. Ct.).
127 PPSA (A, M, NWT, Nu) s. 34(7); BC s. 34(6); S s. 34(8); Y s. 33(6).

sale of the automobile to SP2 did not cut off SP1's security interest, SP1 will be able to recover the automobile from SP2 or sue for conversion if SP2 has disposed of it.

The Acts in Ontario, the Yukon, and the Atlantic Provinces contain no comparable provision. Here, SP1 will argue that the residual priority rule applies and that it should be given priority over SP2 since it was the first to register its interest (assuming that it has properly perfected its interest in the proceeds).

D. PRODUCTION MONEY SECURITY INTERESTS IN CROPS AND ANIMALS

The PPSA provides a special priority rule in respect of certain production money security interests. All the Acts provide that a perfected security interest that is given in crops or its proceeds to enable the debtor to produce the crop (the "production money" security interest) has priority over another security interest in the same collateral.[128] The production money security interest is entitled to this priority only if it is created not more than six months before the crops become growing crops.

The Ontario PPSA contains an additional more restrictive limitation. The production money secured party only obtains priority in respect of obligations owing to the earlier secured party that were due more than six months before the crops became growing crops. In other words, the amount owing under the earlier security interest must be overdue by at least six months before the crops became growing crops. Grant Gilmore, in referring to a similar limitation found in an earlier version of Article 9 of the *Uniform Commercial Code*, indicated that this limitation effectively renders it a dead-letter.[129] In respect of current obligations (that is, those less than six months overdue), the usual first in time priority rule will apply.

In order to obtain the production money priority, the purpose of the loan must have been to enable the debtor to produce or harvest the crop. This has been held to cover inputs such as chemicals or fertiliz-

---

128 PPSA (BC, NB, PEI) s. 34(8); (M, NWT, Nu) s. 34(10); (NL, NS) s. 35(8); A s. 34(9); O s. 32(1); S s. 34(11); Y s. 33(6).

129 Gilmore, above note 69 at 870. Appendix II to revised art. 9 creates a production money security interest that is similar that in the non-Ontario Acts. However, since there was a lack of consensus among states, these are presented merely as optional provisions.

ers as well as seed.[130] The section is not restricted to the acquisition of agricultural inputs, but may apply as well when the funds are used to acquire services that enable the crop to be produced. One Alberta decision has interpreted this provision very broadly. The Court held that a security interest in crops given pursuant to a forbearance agreement under which a creditor agreed to hold off from seizing and selling the debtor's equipment allowed the debtor to produce a crop in that growing season.[131] The authors are of the opinion that this case goes too far, and that the section should be restricted to the provision of inputs or services that are directly related to the production of the crop.

The statutory provisions do not require that the funds provided by the production money actually be used to acquire the agricultural inputs. The absence of this requirement makes it unlikely that the courts will apply a strict tracing requirement that the funds can be traced into the acquisition of the inputs. However, it is possible that the courts will require a close nexus between the funds advanced and the purchase of the inputs.[132]

The definition of goods in the PPSA encompasses growing crops.[133] The Ontario and Yukon Acts do not contain a definition of crops. The other Acts provide a definition of crops that covers all types of crops that are grown on land, as well as fruit and other crops grown on trees.[134] The definition also covers trees, but only to the extent that they are grown for uses other than the production of lumber or wood products. The definition therefore covers trees that are grown for nursery stock or trees that will be harvested and sold as Christmas trees. The same idea is captured by the Ontario and Yukon Acts in a different fashion. While the basic definition of goods includes growing crops, the definition then goes on to explicitly exclude "timber to be cut."

In order to obtain the production money security interest priority, the secured party must perfect the security interest. However, the Act does not clearly specify when perfection must be effected. Although it might seem sensible to require the security interest to be perfected at the time the secured party gives new value to enable the production of the crops, this involves reading into the provision a requirement

---

130 *Leu v. N.M. Patterson & Sons Ltd.* (1997), 13 P.P.S.A.C. (2d) 27 (Sask. Q.B.).
131 *Agriculture Financial Services Corp. v. John Hofer Farms Ltd.* (2001), 2 P.P.S.A.C. (3d) 314 (Alta. Q.B.).
132 See section C.2.b "Enabling Loans."
133 PPSA (A, BC, NWT, Nu, O, Y) s. 1(1); (M, NB, PEI) s. 1; (NL, NS) s. 2; S s. 2(1).
134 PPSA (A, BC, NWT, Nu, O, Y) s. 1(1); (M, NB, PEI) s. 1; (NL, NS) s. 2; S s. 2(1).

that does not appear on its face.[135] Issues of cross-collateralization and consolidation or refinancing of a production money security interest may arise in connection with a production money security interest. In principle, these issues should be resolved in accordance with the same policies that apply to purchase money security interests.

A competition may arise between two or more production money security interests that have been granted in the same collateral. The Ontario PPSA contains an express priority rule that provides that the security interests rank equally according to the ratio that the amount advanced by that particular secured party bears to the total amount advanced.[136] The other Acts do not contain an express priority rule to cover such competitions. In the absence of an express priority rule, it is likely that the competition would be resolved through the application of the first in time principle of the residual priority rule.

All the Acts except those of Ontario and the Yukon provide for a production money security interest in animals.[137] A perfected security interest that is taken in animals to enable the debtor to acquire food, drugs, or hormones to be fed to or placed in the animals is given priority over any other security interest created in the animals by the same debtor other than a perfected purchase money security interest. Like the provision dealing with production money security interests in crops, this provision does not resolve uncertainties concerning the timing of perfection and the resolution of disputes between competing production money security interests. Further uncertainty is created by the lack of a requirement that the funds actually be used to acquire the agricultural or accquacultural inputs.

The Ontario and Yukon Acts do not contain a similar production money priority provision in relation to animals. An input supplier that is given a purchase money security interest in the feed or other inputs may attempt to argue that its priority extends to the animals as proceeds of the original collateral. Alternatively, it may argue that its security interest extends to the animals pursuant to the PPSA provisions

---

135   Compare s. 9-324A of Appendix II of revised art. 9 (optional), which provides that a production money security interest obtains priority over an earlier security interest only if the security interest is perfected by filing before the production money secured party gives value and delivers a notice of intention to the earlier secured party.

136   OPPSA s. 32(2).

137   PPSA (BC, NB, PEI) s. 34(9); (M, NWT, Nu) s. 34(11); (NL, NS) s. 35(9); A s. 34(10); S s. 34(12).

covering processed or commingled goods. However, it is highly unlikely that these provisions apply to such biological transformations.[138]

E. PRIORITIES UNDER THE PROPOSED CHANGES ASSOCIATED WITH THE *UNIFORM SECURITIES TRANSFERS ACT*

Upon the enactment of the *Uniform Securities Transfers Act*, the PPSA will be amended to conform to the new concepts and terminology of that Act.[139] Where the collateral is investment property, a priority competition between two or more secured parties will not be governed by the residual priority rule. Instead, it will be governed by a new priority rule that applies exclusively to priority competitions in respect of investment property.[140]

The special priority rules governing investment property completely displace the purchase money security interest priority rules. Prior to the amendments it was possible to create a purchase money security interest in a security or other forms of investment property. Following the amendments, the purchase money security interest priority rules will no longer have any application to competitions between secured parties in respect of investment property. In order to claim purchase money security interest priority, it is necessary to identify the collateral that was acquired with the funds advanced. This exercise becomes highly uncertain under modern securities settlement systems. The control priority rule is better suited to modern settlement systems as it gives a lender the ability to "put into place systems under which it monitors the aggregate levels of credit it is extending, and matches

---

138 Cases in the United States have rejected the argument that a security interest in cattle feed extends to the animals as proceeds or as commingled goods. See *Farmers Co-operative Elevator Co. v. Union State Bank*, 409 N.W.2d 178 (Iowa 1987); *First National Bank of Brush v. Bostron*, 564 P.2d 964 (Colo. App. 1977).

139 See generally *Proposals for a Uniform Securities Transfer Act*, Canadian Securities Administrators' Uniform Securities Act Task Force (consultative draft, 1 August 2003). The reference to the proposed amendments to the APPSA and OPPSA that follow are found in the Task Force's *Proposed Conforming Amendments to Alberta Personal Property Security Act* (1 August 2003) and *Proposed Conforming Amendments to Ontario Personal Property Security Act* (1 August 2003).

140 APPSA, s. 35.1(1); OPPSA, s. 30.1(1) (proposed).

those credit levels against the aggregate value of the collateral to which it is looking for assurance of payment."[141]

The consequential amendments to the PPSA will provide for a new method of perfection in respect of investment property, namely perfection by control.[142] Control is not the only means by which a security interest can be perfected in investment property. It will remain possible to perfect a security interest in investment property through other means. For example, a secured party may choose to perfect a security interest in investment property by registration rather than by control. However, the new priority provision gives priority to a secured party who has control over a secured party who does not have control.[143] Thus, a secured party who perfects by control takes priority over an earlier secured party who has perfected by registration. Knowledge is irrelevant to the operation of the proposed priority rule. A secured party who has perfected by control will have priority even if it knew about the existence of a security interest in favour of a secured party who had perfected by registration.

The rule that a secured party who takes control prevails will also apply where the competing secured party relies upon automatic perfection of its security interest. Automatic perfection will occur where a security interest is given by a broker or securities intermediary to a lender. The new perfection provisions governing perfection of investment property provide that a security interest in investment property created by a broker or securities intermediary is automatically perfected when it attaches.[144] A competition may arise between two lenders, both of whom have been given a security interest by a broker. If one of the secured parties relies on automatic perfection while the other takes the precaution of taking control of the investment property given as collateral, priority will be given to the secured party who takes control.

Under the proposed provisions, a secured party who takes delivery of a certificated security in bearer form thereby obtains control of the certificate.[145] If the security certificate is in registered form, delivery alone will not be enough to give the secured party control of the certificate; the secured party will also need to obtain an effective

---

141   J. Rogers, "Policy Perspectives on Revised U.C.C. Article 8" (1996) 43 U.C.L.A. L. Rev. 1431 at 1486.

142   See chapter 5, H "Perfection by Control."

143   APPSA s. 35.1(2); OPPSA s. 30.1(2) (proposed).

144   APPSA s. 19.2(2); OPPSA s. 19.2(2) (proposed). A similar provision governs a security interest in a commodities contract or commodities account that is created by a commodities intermediary.

145   USTA s. 30(1).

endorsement of the certificate.[146] If this is not done, the certificate will be considered to be perfected by delivery rather than by control.[147] The new priority rules for investment property provide that a security interest that is perfected by delivery has priority over a conflicting security interest that is perfected by a method other than control.[148] Thus, a secured party who takes delivery of the security certificate may claim priority over the holder of a prior registered security interest in it. Here also, knowledge of the prior registration is not a factor in the determination of priorities.

It is possible that more than one secured party will have perfected their security interests by control. The new priority provisions provide a set of rules that will govern such cases. If the collateral is a security entitlement or commodities contract and the competition is between the securities or commodities intermediary and a secured party, the intermediary who obtains control will be entitled to priority.[149] Where a broker or intermediary is not involved, a temporal rule is applied and priority is given to the secured party who was the first to take control.[150]

The new priority provisions also govern the situation where a security intermediary grants competing security interests, none of which are perfected by control. In such a case, the competing security interests rank equally.[151] This would cover the unlikely situation where a broker has given competing security interests to two different secured parties, both or whom rely upon the automatic perfection of their security interests and neither of whom take control of the investment property.

---

146 USTA s. 30(2).
147 APPSA s. 24(3); OPPSA s. 22(2) (proposed). See also USTA s. 79.
148 APPSA s. 35.1(3); OPPSA s. 30.1(3) (proposed).
149 APPSA s. 35.1(5)–(6); OPPSA s. 30.1(5), (6) (proposed). This rule will apply only in narrowly defined situations, since the ordinary control priority rule will usually confer priority upon the intermediary. If the entitlement-holder grants a security interest in the security entitlement to her own securities intermediary, the intermediary has control of the security entitlement. See USTA s. 33. A similar control rule is provided in respect of a commodity contract held by a commodity intermediary. See APPSA, OPPSA s. 1(1.1)(d) (proposed). The special priority rule will only apply where: (1) the debtor has granted security interests to both the intermediary and another lender; (2) the lender has entered into a control agreement with the intermediary; and (3) the parties to the control agreement neglected to specify the priority position of the intermediary and the lender.
150 APPSA s. 35.1(4); OPPSA s.30.1(4) (proposed).
151 APPSA s.35.1(7); OPPSA s. 30.1(7) (proposed).

The new priority provisions state that any other priority competition will be governed by the residual priority rule.[152] This will cover situations where both secured parties have perfected by registration. In such cases, the residual priority rule will apply and priority will be given to the first secured party to register a financing statement that covers the investment property.

F. DATE OF RESOLUTION OF PRIORITY COMPETITIONS

A perfected security interest that is entitled to priority over another security interest may thereafter become unperfected. This will ordinarily result in a loss of priority. But what is the outcome if the security interest becomes unperfected after the secured party enforces its security interest against the collateral? Is it necessary to maintain perfection of the security interest even after the collateral is seized or other enforcement steps are completed? Seizure of the collateral does not constitute perfection in jurisdictions other than Ontario and Manitoba.[153] Therefore, it cannot be argued that the security interest remains perfected by possession following the seizure. Although seizure of the collateral is effective to perfect a security interest in Ontario and Manitoba, this does not provide a complete answer. Some enforcement measures do not involve a seizure of collateral. Nor does the appointment of a privately appointed receiver involve a seizure, since the security agreement will usually contain a provision to the effect that the receiver acts as agent for the debtor.[154]

In order to resolve priority competitions in these types of situations, it is necessary to determine when the PPSA priority rule is to be applied. In *Sperry Inc. v. Canadian Imperial Bank of Commerce*,[155] a competition arose between an unperfected security interest held by a bank and an unperfected security interest held by a manufacturer of farm equipment. The bank enforced its security interest through the appoint-

---

152 APPSA s. 35.1(8); OPPSA s. 30.1(8) (proposed).
153 See chapter 5, section E.3, "Perfection by Seizure or Repossession."
154 *Sperry Inc. v. Canadian Imperial Bank of Commerce*, above note 5; *Bank of Nova Scotia v. Royal Bank* (1987), 8 P.P.S.A.C. 17 (Sask. C.A.).
155 *Sperry Inc. v. Canadian Imperial Bank of Commerce, ibid.* See also *Asklepeion Restaurant Ltd. v. 791259 Ontario Ltd.* (1996), 11 P.P.S.A.C. (2d) 320 (Ont. Ct. Gen. Div.), aff'd (1998) 13 P.P.S.A.C. (2d) 295 (Ont. C.A.). See also *Loeb Canada Inc. v. Caisse Populaire Alexandria Ltée.*, 2004 CarswellOnt 4973 (Ont. S.C.J.).

ment of a receiver. Eleven days later, the bank registered a financing statement and claimed priority over the farm equipment manufacturer on the basis that its perfected security interest was entitled to priority over an unperfected security interest. The Ontario Court of Appeal rejected this argument. It held that the priority issue between the parties should be resolved as of the time when their respective security interests came into conflict. This occurred when the bank enforced its security interest through the appointment of a receiver. An Alberta decision also adopted the time of enforcement as the proper date for the determination of priorities.[156]

The alternative view is that the initiation of enforcement proceedings should have no effect on the determination of priorities. It is not until enforcement proceedings are fully executed that priorities become fixed and crystallized. After all, until this occurs, the debtor retains rights in the collateral and the PPSA priorities rules should therefore be applied to determine the ranking of the competing claims. On this view, a secured party may lose priority if the security interest lapses or otherwise becomes unperfected after the secured party has commenced enforcement measures against the collateral, but before the collateral is sold by the secured party or retained in satisfaction of the obligation.[157] In a competition between two security interests that were unperfected at the time of the enforcement, a secured party, on this theory, would be able to gain priority by perfecting its security interest at any time before final sale of the collateral pursuant to enforcement proceedings (or retention of the collateral in satisfaction of the secured obligation). The authors are of the opinion that this approach is more consonant with the principles, structure, and operation of the PPSA.

G. REPERFECTION OF A SECURITY INTEREST

The Ontario PPSA takes a very different approach from that employed in the other Acts to the priority consequences of reperfection of a security interest following a loss of perfection. The Ontario PPSA covers the situation where a security interest that was originally perfected by registration becomes unperfected and then is later again perfected by

---

156 *John Deere Credit Inc. v. Standard Oilfield Services Inc.* (2000), 16 C.B.R. (4th) 227 (Alta. Q.B.).
157 In the case of an intangible, the priorities would be fixed upon the payment of the money owed by the third party to the secured party.

registration.[158] The security interest is to be considered continuously perfected from the time of its original registration. However, if a person has acquired rights in the collateral during the period in which the security interest is unperfected, the security interest is ineffective against that person.

The operation of this provision is illustrated in the following scenario.

SP1 and SP2 are both given security interests in the debtor's collateral. SP1 registers a financing statement on 1 September 2000. SP2 registers on 30 September 2000. SP1's security interest becomes unperfected on 1 June 2001. On December 2001 SP1 again perfects its security interest by registration.

SP1 obtains priority over SP2, since SP2 did not acquire rights in the collateral during the period that SP1's security interest was unperfected.[159] The provision only operates where both the original perfection and the reperfection is by registration. It would therefore not apply where SP1 subsequently reperfected its security interest by taking possession of the collateral.

Section 30(6) of the Ontario Act applies whenever a security interest is perfected by registration and later becomes unperfected. This may occur where the registration lapses or is discharged, or it may occur where the secured party fails to amend the registration after learning of a change in the debtor's name or a transfer of the collateral to another party. It also applies where a financing statement is amended by deleting an item or class of collateral.[160] The provision does not apply when the original registration contains an invalidating error.

A secured party will not be able to regain a lost priority through reperfection that occurs after the collateral has been seized or enforcement proceedings commenced, unless the courts determine that the date of sale or foreclosure represents a better cut-off date for the determination of priorities.[161] Nor can a secured party take advantage of

---

158 OPPSA s. 30(6).
159 In *Heidelberg Canada Graphic Equipment Ltd. v. Arthur Anderson Inc.*, above note 59, the court held that the intervening secured party must acquire some new right in the collateral. It is not enough that the loss of perfection of the other secured party would have caused it to have been promoted in ranking.
160 *Ibid.* In such a case, a new registration is not required. It is sufficient if a financing change statement is used to amend the registration by adding the collateral description back into the registration.
161 *Asklepeion Restaurant Ltd. v. 791259 Ontario Ltd.*, above note 155. And see the discussion above under the heading: F, "Date of Resolution of Priority Competitions."

section 30(6) if a third party has acquired rights in the collateral during the period in which it is unperfected. There is considerable uncertainty as to which parties will be covered by this exception. Suppose that the security agreement entered into with SP2 contained an after-acquired property clause. SP2's security interest in the after-acquired property attaches when the debtor acquires rights in the collateral. SP2 may argue that its security interest attached and its rights arose during the period when the security interest was unperfected, and therefore it is entitled to priority in respect of these assets. Although consistent with the language of the provision, this interpretation seems contrary to the policy behind the section.

A secured party who makes future advances during the period when the security interest is unperfected should be considered to have acquired rights during the gap in perfection. In *Re Triad Financial Services and Thaler Metal Industries Ltd.*,[162] the court held that a secured party who makes advances during the gap in perfection acquires new rights in the collateral and therefore is entitled to priority over the re-perfecting secured party to the extent of those advances. Although this decision has been criticized,[163] it seems correct in principle. A security interest that secures $10,000 is significantly different from a security interest that secures only $5,000. Although the collateral may be the same, the extent of the interest has been enlarged. This interpretation also accords with the policy behind the provision, since the secured party who makes the advance will often conduct a search of the registry before making the advance.

It is not certain whether the mere act of registration is sufficient to give a secured party new rights in the collateral. Suppose that SP2 is granted a security interest when SP1's security interest is perfected, but registers during the period of unperfection. It might be argued that the elevation of its security interest from an unperfected to a perfected status gives SP2 new rights in the collateral since it has altered the quality of rights that the secured party possesses against third parties. The authors are of the opinion that this interpretation goes too far. Although registration may affect the priority and ranking of a security interest, it does not confer upon a secured party any new rights in the collateral.

---

162 (1979), 1 P.P.S.A.C. 44 (Ont. H.C.J.), aff'd (1979) 27 O.R. (2d) 506 (C.A.).
163 See J.S. Ziegel, "The Quickening Pace of Jurisprudence under the Ontario Personal Property Security Act" (1979–80), 4 Can. Bus. L.J. 54 at 86–88.

The re-registration provision of the Act in jurisdictions outside of Ontario takes an entirely different approach to the problem.[164] The provision is far more limited in its scope. It only applies to a lapse or discharge of a registration. It does not apply where the secured party fails to amend its registration after learning of a transfer or a change of name.[165] Nor does it apply where the secured party mistakenly amends its registration by deleting a category of collateral. Its only function is to provide a mechanism that permits a lapsed or discharged registration to be reactivated. The provision is further limited in that it must be initiated no later than thirty days after the lapse or discharge. Unlike the Ontario provision, re-registration is not effected merely by registration of a new financing statement. A special re-registration procedure must be used. If the secured party fails to invoke the special re-registration procedure within the thirty-day period, the registration cannot be revived.[166] The secured party may register a fresh financing statement to perfect its security interest. The priority of its security interest will not be determined by the re-registration provision. It will be resolved by application of the residual priority rule, which will rank the security interest according to the time of the fresh financing statement.

The registry sends out a verification statement to the registrant as well as the secured party whenever a registration is totally discharged (in the case of the registries in the Atlantic provinces, a verification statement is sent when any change of any kind is made to a registration). This is designed to give a secured party notice in the event that the registration is fraudulently discharged. This gives the secured party an opportunity to re-register pursuant to the special procedure. A verification statement is not sent in the case of lapse.

If the special re-registration procedure is invoked, the secured party retains its original priority against a competing secured party who held a subordinate, perfected security interest immediately before the lapse or discharge, except to the extent that the security interest secures advances made or contracted for before during the gap (that is,

---

164 PPSA (BC, M, NB, NWT, Nu, S) s. 35(7); (NL, NS) s. 36(7); A s. 35(7)–(8); PEI s. 35(7); Y s. 34(5).

165 These events do not result in a general loss of perfection. Instead, PPSA (A, BC, N, NB, NWT, Nu, PEI, S) s. 51; (NL, NS) s. 52; Y s. 45 provides a priority rules that give priority to parties who acquire their interests after the secured party learns of these events but before the secured party amends its financing statement.

166 The financing statement must indicate that the registration is being effected pursuant to the re-registration provision and it must provide the registration number of the lapsed or discharged registration.

after lapse or discharge and before re-registration). The secured party will not obtain priority against a secured party who takes and perfects its security interest during this gap. Nor will it have priority over a competing secured party who had registered before the lapse or discharge, but whose security interest attaches during this gap. Less certain is the outcome where SP2's security interest has attached and is not perfected immediately before the discharge but is perfected before SP1's re-registration. The re-registration provision may be read as applying only where SP2 had a *perfected* security interest before the lapse or discharge. The alternative reading is that the section does not require that the competing security interest of SP2 be perfected immediately before the lapse or discharge, but merely signals that if SP2's security interest is not perfected at the time of the competition, the matter will be resolved by giving priority to the perfected security interest over the unperfected security interest rather than by the application of the re-registration provision. The authors are of the opinion that this latter interpretation is the correct one.

Both the Ontario reperfection provision and the re-registration provisions of the other jurisdictions may produce circular priority problems. This is illustrated in the following scenario.

SP1 is given a security interest in D's collateral which it registers on February 1. SP2 is given a security interest in the same collateral which it perfects by registration on March 1. On April 1, SP1's security interest is discharged. SP3 is given a security interest in the same collateral which it perfects by registration on April 5. On April 20, SP1 reperfects its security interest.

SP1 has priority over SP2, SP2 has priority over SP3, but SP3 has priority over SP1. A similar priority competition may arise if instead of giving a security interest to SP3 the debtor went bankrupt on April 5.[167] Circular priority competitions may arise in a number of different situations within the PPSA as well as in other contexts. There is no easy solution to their resolution. Legislation should generally seek to minimize the potential for such disputes since they must be resolved by costly litigation and introduce uncertainty into the resolution of priority competitions.

---

167 This situation arose in *Frankel v. Canadian Imperial Bank of Commerce* (1997), 12 P.P.S.A.C. (2d) 306 (Ont. Ct. Gen. Div.). The court held that the time for determination of priorities was the time of bankruptcy, so that it was no longer open for SP1 to reperfect its security interest. As a result, the circularity was broken by giving first priority to SP2, and subordinating SP1's security interest to the trustee in bankruptcy. But in *Olympus Plastics Ltd. (Receiver of) v. Olympus Plastics Ltd.* (2000), 1 P.P.S.A.C. (3d) 45 (Ont. Ct. Gen. Div.) the court gave priority to SP1 despite SP1's reperfection after the bankruptcy.

The non-Ontario Acts seek to minimize the risk by placing a thirty-day limit on the time for re-registration. The Ontario PPSA places no limit on the time for reperfection, with the result that there is a much greater potential for these types of competitions to arise.

The reperfection provision under the Ontario PPSA and the re-registration provisions of the other jurisdictions apply equally to purchase money security interests. Although the re-registration provisions are located in the section that establishes the residual priority rule, there is nothing in its wording or in the underlying policy of the section that would operate to prevent it from applying to purchase money security interests.

H. SUBORDINATION AGREEMENTS

1) The Nature and Varieties of Subordination Agreements

The PPSA provides that a secured party, in a security agreement or otherwise, may subordinate its security interest to any other interest, and the subordination is effective according to its terms.[168] Although subordination agreements were common under prior law, they take on an even greater significance under the PPSA. The first to register priority rule in combination with the blanket registration capability that permits a financing statement to cover more than one security agreement, as well as the ability to tack future advances, makes it more risky for a subsequent secured party to advance additional funds unless it is secured by a purchase money security interest. Even if the security agreement of the prior secured party does not purport to cover all obligations or future advances, the parties may enter into a new security agreement at some later time. This new security interest will be entitled to priority over an intervening security interest on the basis of the secured party's earlier registration. In such cases, the subsequent secured party may seek to obtain a subordination agreement from the first secured party before making the loan to the debtor.

The subordination is effective according to its terms. The subordination agreement may provide for a subordination of the entire claim, or it may be limited in nature. For example, the subordination may provide that it is effective only upon the occurrence of a particular set of

---

168 PPSA (A, BC, M, NB, NWT, Nu, PEI, S) s. 40; (NL, NS) s. 41; (O, Y) s. 38. On the question as to whether a subordination agreement creates a security interest, see chapter 2, D.3.

events. The subordination may be limited to certain types of collateral or it may provide that the postponement is effective only in relation to certain types of debts or obligations. The subordination agreement might also provide that the subordination agreement is effective only up to a specified amount.[169]

The PPSA covers essentially two different types of subordination agreements. The first kind is a contractual agreement that is executed directly between the secured party who is subordinating its security interest and the other party who is the beneficiary of that subordination. The terminology used in such agreements often denotes the subordinating party as the junior creditor and the recipient of the subordination as the senior creditor. Sometimes a multilateral agreement, often referred to as an intercreditor agreement, is executed by several different creditors.

The second type of subordination provision is one that is contained in the security agreement between the secured party and the debtor. In such a case, the benefiting creditor is not a party to the contract. At common law, this type of subordination agreement had the potential to run afoul of the principle of privity of contract, since the benefiting creditor was not a party to the agreement and contract law did not generally permit third-party beneficiaries to enforce a contract.[170] The Ontario and Yukon Acts provide that a secured party may in the security agreement or otherwise subordinate its security interest.[171] The Ontario Court of Appeal in *Euroclean Canada Inc. v. Forest Glade Investments Ltd.*[172] held that this language has altered the common law by expressly permitting the subordination agreement to be enforced by the benefiting creditor. This decision has since been followed by

---

169 See generally P. Wood, *The Law of Subordinated Debt* (London: Sweet & Maxwell, 1990) at 6–8.

170 The Supreme Court of Canada in *Fraser River Pile & Dredge Ltd. v. Can-Dive Services Ltd.*, [1999] 3 S.C.R. 108 has displayed a willingness to relax the privity of contract rule in cases where the parties to the contract intended to extend the benefit in question to the third party, at least in those cases where the inchoate contractual right has crystallized prior to any purported amendment by the contracting parties. As a result of this decision, it may well be that subordination provisions contained in a security agreement may be enforced by the beneficiary. The privity doctrine as it relates to third-party beneficiaries has been abolished by statute in New Brunswick. See *Law Reform Act*, S.N.B. c. L-1. 2 s. 4 (1) ("A person who is not a party to a contract but who is identified by or under the contract as being intended to receive some performance or forbearance under it may, unless the contract provides otherwise, enforce that performance or forbearance by a claim for damages or otherwise").

171 PPSA (O, Y) s. 38.

172 (1985), 16 D.L.R. (4th) 289 (Ont. C.A.).

the Alberta Court of Appeal.[173] The subordination provisions in the other jurisdictions are even more explicit on this point. They go on to provide that the subordination "may be enforced by a third party if the third party is the person or one of the class of persons for whose benefit the subordination was intended."

None of the Acts address the issue of variation of the subordination agreement by the contracting parties. Suppose that a security agreement contains a subordination provision that subordinates the security interest to a third party who supplies inventory to the debtor. Later, the secured party and the debtor enter into a refinancing arrangement under which the original security agreement is replaced by a new security agreement which does not contain a subordination provision. What effect does this have on the rights of the benefiting creditor? Very likely, the benefiting creditor will be permitted to rely upon the subordination provision in respect of deliveries of inventory that were contracted while the original security agreement was in force. But it is far less clear whether the benefiting creditor obtains a vested right that permits it to claim priority in respect of deliveries that are contracted for after the replacement of the original security agreement.

Although a subordination provision usually takes the form of a written agreement, it is possible that it may be found in an oral agreement.[174] In practice, it may be difficult to distinguish between an oral statement that is found to create an oral subordination agreement, and a statement that gives rise to an estoppel that prevents the secured party from relying upon the priority status to which it would otherwise be entitled.[175] Although it is also theoretically possible that a subordination agreement may take the form of an implied agreement that is inferred through a course of conduct, such agreements are difficult to prove since courts will generally require that there be evidence of an unequivocal intention to relinquish rights.[176]

A subordination agreement differs from a waiver or release of a security interest. A subordination involves an agreement under which the subordinating creditor agrees to postpone its security interest to the claim of

173 *Chiips Inc. v. Skyview Hotels Ltd.* (1994), 116 D.L.R. (4th) 385 (Alta. C.A.), Foisy J.A.
174 *Royal Bank v. Tenneco Canada Inc.* (1990), 9 P.P.S.A.C. 254 (Ont. H.C.J.).
175 *Furmanek v. Community Futures Development Corp. of Howe Sound* (1998), 162 D.L.R. (4th) 501 (B.C.C.A.).
176 *Sun Life Assurance Co. of Canada v. Royal Bank of Canada* (1995), 129 D.L.R. (4th) 305 (Ont. Ct. Gen. Div.). See also the comments of Jackson J.A. in *Flexi-Coil Ltd. v. Kindersley District Credit Union Ltd.* (1993), 107 D.L.R. (4th) 129 at 134 (Sask. C.A.) that "[w]hether it is even possible for a secured party to subordinate its security interest by a course of conduct is doubtful."

the benefiting creditor. A release or waiver involves an extinguishment of the security interest such that the secured party is precluded from thereafter claiming the benefit of its security interest. A release or waiver is more commonly used when the secured party permits the debtor to sell the collateral to a third party free of the security interest. It is advisable to use terminology that refers to postponement or subordination rather than waiver, release or surrender if the secured party wishes merely to subordinate its security interest to the claim of another.[177]

2) Subordination and Priorities

A creditor who has obtained the benefit of a subordination agreement (the "benefiting creditor") may rely upon a subordination agreement even though it has failed to perfect its security interest.[178] It is not necessary for the benefiting creditor to show that it relied upon the subordination provision or that the benefiting creditor even knew of its existence. Of course, since the subordination depends upon the terms of the contractual provision, it always remains possible to contractually limit its scope. For example, the benefit of a subordination provision may be limited to holders of purchase money security interests who have perfected their security interests.

Although a subordination agreement is effective according to its terms as between the parties affected by it, the situation is less clear where the benefiting party assigns its security agreement to a third party. It is possible that the subordination provision might be interpreted widely so as to extend also to an assignee. To fully protect itself, the assignee should take an assignment of the subordination agreement or include a reassignment provision that compels the assignor to accept a reassignment of the security agreement in the event of a default.[179]

An issue that sometimes arises concerns the effect of a subordination provision on an intervening secured party who is not a party to the subordination agreement. This is illustrated in the following scenario.

---

177 See *In Re Bar C Cross Farms & Ranches*, 1 U.C.C. Rep. Serv. 2d 256 (D. Colo. [Bankr.] 1985).

178 See *Euroclean Canada Inc. v. Forest Glade Investments Ltd.*, above note 172. This case involved a secured party who failed to take the steps needed to obtain a purchase money security interest priority. Luckily for the purchase money financer, a review of the earlier secured party's security agreement revealed that it contained a subordination provision in favour of the inventory financer. See also *Chiips v. Skyview Hotels Ltd.*, above note 173.

179 See *YMCF Inc. v. 406248 B.C. Ltd.* (1998), 13 P.P.S.A.C. (2d) 282 (B.C.S.C.).

SP1, SP2, and SP3 are all given a security interest in the same collateral. SP1 registers first, followed by SP2, then SP3. As a consequence, SP1 has priority over the other two secured parties, while SP2 has priority over SP3. SP1 later enters into a subordination agreement with SP3, under which SP1 agrees to postpone its claim to that of SP3. The debtor defaults, and the collateral is realized, but the proceeds are not sufficient to satisfy the claims of all of the secured parties.

The priority competition is resolved by setting aside the amount of SP1's claim. From this fund, SP3's claim is satisfied. If a surplus remains after SP3's claim is satisfied, it is paid over to SP1. SP2's claim would next be satisfied from the remaining funds. If there is anything left, it is then distributed to SP3, then to SP1. In other words, the subordination agreement between SP1 and SP3 is effective only as between those parties, and has no effect on the relative priority of SP2.[180]

Most subordination agreements provide for a postponement of the subordinating creditor's claim. Under a "step-aside" agreement, a secured party may instead agree that it will not make a claim in respect of a subordinated debt until the benefiting creditor is paid in full. If this form of agreement is used, there is a greater likelihood that it will have the effect of elevating the priority of an intervening party. In the above scenario, SP1 would renounce its claim until SP3 is paid in full. This would seem to have the effect of placing SP1 at the end of the queue, with the result that SP2 would obtain first priority followed by SP3.

A priority competition may also arise where the debtor has gone bankrupt and the benefiting creditor has failed to perfect its security interest. This is illustrated in the following scenario.

SP1 and SP2 are granted security interests in the same collateral. SP1 registers a financing statement, but SP2 fails to do so. Therefore SP1's security interest has priority over that of SP2. SP1 and SP2 subsequently enter into a subordination agreement under which SP1 agrees to postpone its security interest to SP2. The debtor then makes an assignment in bankruptcy.

SP2's unperfected security interest is subordinate to the trustee in bankruptcy. Again the solution is to segregate the amount of SP1's claim against the proceeds of sale of the collateral. SP2's claim is then satisfied from this amount. If there is a surplus, the remainder is paid

---

180 See *Grise v. White*, 247 N.E.2d 385 (Mass. 1969); *ITT Diversified Credit Corp. v. First City Capital Corp.*, 737 S.W.2d 803 (Tex. 1987). See also Gilmore, above note 69 at 1021. But see also *AmSouth Bank, N.A. v. J.&D. Financial Corp.*, 679 So.2d 695 (Ala. 1996), in which the Court elevated SP2 to the top-ranking priority.

over to SP1. Once the share associated with SP1's claim is exhausted, the balance of the fund is paid to the trustee in bankruptcy.[181]

3) Subordination Clauses Distinguished from Other Contractual Provisions

In some cases, the subordination provision is clear and unambiguous on its face. The subordination provision in *Euroclean Canada Inc. v. Forest Glade Investments Ltd.*[182] provided that the debtor was permitted to create security interests in connection with the acquisition of new assets and that such security interests were to rank in priority. In other cases, it is equally clear that the contractual provision performs some other function and is not intended to operate as a subordination provision. Courts in Ontario and Alberta have held that a warranty in a security agreement that states that the collateral is free of encumbrances other than purchase money security interests does not constitute a subordination agreement.[183] The provision simply acknowledges that the collateral may be subject to purchase money security interests without making any statement as to the priority status of such interests.

The controversial case concerns a security agreement that contains a permissive provision. In *Chiips v. Skyview Hotels Ltd.*,[184] the security agreement contained a provision that permitted the debtor to give purchase money security interests. The majority decided that this manifested an intention on the part of the secured party to subordinate its security interest to such interests. The dissenting opinion of Hetherington J.A., pointed out that the purpose of the permissive provision was not to subordinate the security interest to such interests. Rather, it was designed to ensure that the creation of purchase money security interests would not result in a breach of covenant, thereby placing the debtor in default. The security agreement contained a negative coven-

---

181 *Bank of Montreal v. Dynex Petroleum Ltd.* (1997), 12 P.P.S.A.C. (2d) 183 (Alta. Q.B.); *Re Woodroffes (Musical Instruments) Ltd.*, [1985] 2 All E.R. 908 (Ch. Div.). The outcome is the same when the benefiting creditor goes bankrupt. The subordinating creditor must account to the benefiting creditor. This fund is then available to the creditors of the benefiting creditor who prove their claims in bankruptcy. See *Grove Packaging Inc. (Re)* (2001), 31 C.B.R. (4th) 37 (Ont. S.C.J.).

182 Above note 172.

183 *Sperry Inc. v. Canadian Imperial Bank of Commerce*, above note 5; *Asklepeion Restaurants Ltd. v. 791259 Ontario Ltd.*, above note 155; *Kubota Canada Ltd. v. Case Credit Ltd.*, [2005] A.J. 329 (C.A.).

184 Above note 173.

ant that prevented the debtor from creating a competing security interest in the collateral. The permissive provision merely operated to make it clear that the creation of a purchase money security interest would not constitute a breach of the security agreement.[185] The decision of the majority has since been followed in Ontario.[186]

I. OTHER PRINCIPLES AFFECTING PRIORITIES

There are a number of other common law or equitable principles that may operate to modify the outcome that would otherwise be obtained through the strict application of the statutory priority rules contained in the PPSA. The PPSA provides that principles of the common law and equity, including the law merchant, supplement and continue to apply except to the extent that they are inconsistent with the Act.[187] These supplementary principles should be distinguished from the common law and equitable priority rules. Prior to the PPSA, property law principles provided the primary source of rules and principles for the resolution of priority competitions. These priority rules have been largely displaced by the statutory priority rules of the PPSA. These should be distinguished from other supplementary principles of the common law and equity, such as bad faith, estoppel, and subrogation, which may be of continuing relevance.

1) Bad Faith

Although it is well established that mere knowledge of a prior security interest will not prevent a secured party from invoking the priority rules of the PPSA, the situation is otherwise if the secured party has acted dishonestly or in bad faith. This is clearly specified in the non-

---

185 See also K. Morlock, "Floating Charges, Negative Pledges, the PPSA and Subordination: *Chiips v. Skyview Hotels Limited*" (1995), 10 B.F.L.R. 405. Note, however, that a covenant under which the debtor agrees to maintain the collateral free from all liens or security interests other than purchase money security interests does not create an implied subordination. The courts will only imply a subordination where the words are found in the charging provision. See *Kubota Canada Ltd. v. Case Credit Ltd.*, above note 183.

186 *Engel Canada Inc. v. TCE Capital Corp.*, (2003), 4 P.P.S.A.C. (3d) 124 (Ont. S.C.J.).

187 PPSA (M, NWT, Nu, S) s. 65(2); (NB, PEI) s. 65(1); (NL, NS) s. 66(1); A s. 66(3); BC s. 68(1); O s. 72; Y s. 63(1).

Ontario Acts. These provide that all rights duties and obligations "are to be exercised and discharged in good faith and in a commercially reasonable manner."[188] They go on to provide that a person does not act in bad faith merely because the person acts with knowledge of the interests of some other person.[189] Although the Ontario PPSA does not contain similar provisions, it seems likely that the courts will also impose a requirement that the secured party act in good faith. Courts have refused to permit a party to invoke a statute in order to perpetuate a fraud on another,[190] and this attitude will likely be applied to the PPSA as well.

Bad faith involves a subjective test of honesty.[191] Clearly, knowledge alone does not amount to bad faith. There must be some other element involving bad faith. But what additional factors will cause a court to conclude that a secured party is acting in bad faith?

There is little case law in Canada interpreting the good faith requirements of the Acts. The leading case is *Carson Restaurants International Ltd. v. A-1 United Restaurant Supply Ltd.*[192] The sole director and shareholder of the debtor corporation had previously taken a security interest in the corporation's assets, but had never registered his security interest. The debtor corporation subsequently granted a security interest to a restaurant equipment supplier. The supplier registered a financing statement, but an error in the debtor name led to its invalidation. In response to the supplier's demand for payment, the director gave assurances that the debt would be paid. The director later searched the registry and, discovering that the supplier's security interest was unperfected, registered a financing statement and claimed priority in respect of the previously unregistered security interest. The Court held that the director acted in bad faith and therefore was unable to claim the benefit of the residual priority rule.

In order to demonstrate bad faith it is usually necessary to show that the claimant had a duty of disclosure to the secured party or that

---

188 PPSA (M, NWT, Nu, S) s. 65(3); (NB, PEI) s. 65(3); (NL, NS) s. 66(2); A s. 66(1); BC s. 68(3); Y s. 62(1).

189 PPSA (M, NWT, Nu, S) s. 65(4); (NB, PEI) s. 65(2); (NL, NS) s. 66(2); A s. 66(2); BC s. 68(2); Y s. 62(1); Y no equivalent provision.

190 *McCormick v. Grogan* (1869), L.R. 4 H.L. 82.

191 In *Canadian Bank of Commerce v. Munro*, [1925] S.C.R. 302 the court indicated that good faith means "honesty in fact." In *Strach v. Toronto Dominion Bank* (1997), 56 Alta. L.R. (3d) 412 (C.A.) The court indicated that this meaning of good faith has been codified in the APPSA.

192 [1989] 1 W.W.R. 266 (Sask. Q.B.). See also *Bank of Nova Scotia v. Royal Bank of Canada* (1998), 14 P.P.S.A.C. (2d) 10 (B.C.S.C.).

it misled the secured party.[193] A controversial issue is whether bad faith is established when the claimant does not simply have knowledge of the secured party's unperfected security interest, but also knows that the debtor's granting of a security interest to it constitutes a breach of the other secured party's security agreement. Many security agreements contain a "negative pledge" covenant or "restrictive provision" that prohibits the debtor from granting a security interest in the collateral to another secured party. If the security interest is not properly perfected, a subsequent secured party who perfects its security interest may seek to claim priority on the basis of the residual priority rule. Does knowledge of the existence of the negative covenant amount to bad faith?

The PPSA expressly permits the debtor to grant interests in the collateral to third parties, notwithstanding that the security agreement may prohibit such transactions.[194] But this merely gives the debtor the power to transfer an interest in the collateral to a third party. It neither gives the debtor the right to do so, nor immunizes the transferee from liability in connection with the transfer. In *Thompson v. United States*,[195] the debtor granted a security interest to a closely related party despite the fact that the closely related party knew that this transaction was in breach of the terms of a security agreement that had been entered into with a prior unperfected secured party. This was held to amount to bad faith conduct. However, in *Bank of Nova Scotia v. Gaudreau*,[196] the court permitted the claimant to claim the benefits of the residual priority rule. The court rejected the secured party's claim to damages for the tort of inducing breach of contract on the ground that the PPSA provided a defence of justification. The court stated:

> Can it be seriously suggested that institutional lenders and financial intermediaries do not routinely include in their security documents provisions purporting to prohibit the borrower or conditional purchaser from selling or encumbering their collateral? Are we then to have, after all the effort expended upon the P.P.S.A., and after the Legislature has adopted such a clear and strong policy position, a regime in which notice of the fact of an earlier and inconsistent security interest does not prevent a person who perfects first from gaining priority over that earlier interest, but if there were knowledge on the part of the later secured party that the earlier security interest arose under an agreement prohibiting further encumbering of the collat-

---

193 *State of Alaska v. Fowler*, 611 P2d 58 (Alaska 1980).
194 PPSA (A, BC, M, NB, NWT, Nu, PEI, S) s. 33; (NL, NS) s. 34; O s. 39; Y s. 32.
195 408 F.2d 1075 (8th Cir. 1969).
196 (1984), 48 O.R. (2d) 478 at 518–19 (H.C.J.).

eral there would be liability in tort that would virtually reverse the result under the P.P.S.A. itself?

This passage indicates that the court had little doubt that knowledge of a restrictive provision did not preclude a secured party from claiming priority under the PPSA.[197] The authors are of the opinion that knowledge of the existence of a covenant not to encumber the collateral should not constitute bad faith. Bad faith denotes fraudulent or dishonest conduct on the part of the party claiming priority. Knowledge that the debtor is in breach of some other agreement should not amount to bad faith conduct. Further evidence for this view can be found in the wording of the PPSA. Some of the priority rules of the PPSA provide that the priority is not available if the purchaser knows that the transaction constitutes a breach of the security agreement. These provisions would not be necessary if such knowledge amounted to bad faith.

2) Estoppel

Instead of arguing bad faith, a secured party may claim that the other secured party is estopped from claiming the benefit of the PPSA. The advantage of the estoppel argument is that it is not necessary to show that the party who seeks to assert the PPSA priority rule has acted dishonestly. The party relying upon an estoppel argument must establish that the other party has, through words or conduct, made a statement that has been acted upon to the detriment of the other party.[198] An estoppel argument is most likely to arise where the secured party has made a representation concerning the existence or extent of its security interest. In such a case, the secured party will be estopped from denying the accuracy of its statements.

In all jurisdictions except for Ontario and the Yukon, the Acts set out a statutory estoppel principle in connection with the secured party's obligation to disclose information concerning its security interest. A secured party who discloses inaccurate information is estopped from denying the accuracy of the information as against the person making the demand and any other person who can reasonably be expected to rely upon the information.[199] This statutory estoppel does not require

---

197 PPSA (A, BC, M, NB, NWT, N, PEI, S) s. 30(2); (NL, NS) s. 31(2); O s. 28(1); Y s. 29(1); PPSA (A, BC, NB, NWT, N, PEI) s. 31(5); (M, S) s. 31(6); (NL, NS) s. 32(5).
198 See *Furmanek v. Community Futures Development Corp. of Howe Sound* (1998), above note 175.
199 PPSA (M, NB, NWT, Nu, PEI, S) s. 18(14); (NL, NS) s. 19(14); A s. 18(10); BC s. 18(15).

proof that the recipient of the information actually relied upon the information to its detriment.

3) Subrogation

Subrogation involves the substitution of one party for another so that the party who is substituted may exercise the rights of the other party in respect of a claim.[200] The right to subrogation arises in a number of established categories. One such category is where a third party at the request of a debtor pays off a security interest with a view to obtaining a first-ranking security interest on the collateral. In the absence of evidence of an intention to the contrary, the third party is entitled in equity to assert the security interest of the first secured party.[201] This is useful where an intervening party obtains an interest in the collateral before the later secured party obtains its interest. Subrogation permits the later secured party to step into the shoes of the earlier secured party and thereby obtain priority over the intervening interest. This is permitted whether or not the later secured party knew of the intervening interest.

The issue is whether equitable subrogation can be imported into the PPSA. In *N'Amerix Logistix Inc. (Re)*,[202] a secured party made a loan to a debtor which was used to repay the operating loan of an earlier secured party. The secured party registered a financing statement, but recorded the incorrect debtor name, which resulted in the invalidation of its registration. The debtor subsequently went bankrupt, and the trustee in bankruptcy argued that the secured party's unperfected security interest was subordinate. The Ontario Supreme Court held that the secured party was entitled to be subrogated to the security interest of the earlier secured party. As a result, the later secured party was able to assert priority over the trustee in bankruptcy, not on the basis of its unperfected security interest, but pursuant to the earlier secured party's perfected security interest that it was permitted to assert by virtue of equitable subrogation. Courts in the United States have permitted equitable subrogation in similar circumstances.[203]

---

200 See generally C. Mitchell, *The Law of Subrogation* (Oxford: Clarendon Press, 1994).

201 *Coupland Acceptance Ltd. v. Walsh*, [1954] S.C.R. 90; *Gordon v. Snelgrove*, [1932] 2 D.L.R. 300 (Ont. S.C.); *Hayward Lumber Co. v. McEachern*, [1931] 3 W.W.R. 658 (Alta. S.C.T.D.); *Crosbie-Hill v. Sayer*, [1908] 1 Ch. 866.

202 (2001), 57 O.R. (3d) 248 (S.C.J.).

203 See, for example, *French Lumber Co. v. Commercial Realty & Finance Co.*, 195 N.E.2d 507 (Mass. 1964); *Kaplan v. Walher*, 395 A.2d 897 (N.J. Super. A.D.

Because the subrogated party's rights are derived from the creditor who is paid out, the subrogated party is subject to any defects or limitations in relation to that creditor's security interest. This is illustrated in the following scenario.

SP1 registers a financing statement in respect of a security interest that secures a loan of $50,000. Later, SP2 is given a security interest in the same collateral, which SP2 perfects by registration. SP3 then makes a loan of $100,000. Half of these funds are used to pay out SP1's loan, while the other half is used as a general operating loan.

SP3 is subrogated to SP1's security interest. This permits SP3 to claim priority over SP2 to the extent of $50,000. Subrogation only permits SP3 to claim priority over SP2 to the same extent that SP1 had priority over SP2. Therefore, SP3 is limited to the value of the obligation secured by SP1's security interest at the time that it was paid out with SP3's funds. Similarly, if SP1's security interest became unperfected due to lapse or other reason such that SP2 would be entitled to priority over SP1, then the right of subrogation will not help SP3 in a competition with SP2.

FURTHER READINGS

CUMING, R.C.C., "Double-Debtor ABCD Problems in Personal Property Security Law" (1992) 7 B.F.L.R. 359

DUGGAN, A.J., "Hard Cases, Equity and the PPSA" (2000) 34 Can. Bus. L.J. 129

LYSAGHT, L. & G. STEWART, "Priority between Competing Secured Creditors: Exploring the Borderland Between Personal Property Security Rules and the Common Law" (1995) 74 Can. Bar Rev. 50

MITCHELL, C., *The Law of Subrogation* (Oxford: Clarendon, 1994)

MORLOCK, K., "Floating Charges, Negative Pledges, the PPSA and Subordination: *Chiips v. Skyview Hotels Limited*" (1995) 10 B.F.L.R. 405

WOOD, R.J., "Turning Lead into Gold: the Uncertain Alchemy of 'All Obligations' Clauses" (2004) 41 Alta. L. Rev. 801

1978); *Rinn v. First Union National Bank of Maryland*, 25 U.C.C. Rep. Serv. 2d 1057 (D. Md. 1995).

CHAPTER 9

SECURITY INTERESTS IN NEGOTIABLE AND QUASI-NEGOTIABLE COLLATERAL

A. INTRODUCTION

All types of personal property (other than the few expressly excluded by the Act[1]) can be given as collateral under a security agreement. This includes highly negotiable property, such as negotiable instruments and money. Conceptually and functionally, this creates few problems and is an important feature of modern business financing. In addition, it is possible to perfect a security interest in negotiable property, such as money, negotiable instruments and securities, and quasi-negotiable property, such as documents of title and chattel paper, in any one of the three ways available for security interests in other types of collateral. However, it is not feasible to apply the same priority rules to security interests in these types of property that are applicable to most other types. It is unacceptable to require a transferee of negotiable property to obtain a search result from the registry or assume the risk of being subject to a temporarily perfected security interest when acquiring an interest in the property through negotiation. The PPSA recognizes this through a special set of priority rules designed to avoid disruption in traditional patterns of dealing with these types of property.

---

1   PPSA (A, BC, M, NB, O, PEI, S) s. 4; (NWT, Nu, Y) s. 3; (NL, NS) s. 5.

The PPSA not only accommodates transactions in traditional types of negotiable property, but, in addition, it recognizes a new type of property called chattel paper and confers upon it certain characteristics of negotiability.

B. TRADITIONAL NEGOTIABLE PROPERTY

1) Money

A security interest can be taken and perfected in money, the most negotiable of all personal property.[2] As is the case with all other forms of tangible property, perfection can be by possession of the secured party or its agent,[3] by registration,[4] or can be automatic.[5] Where perfection by possession is involved, special measures to protect third-party transferees are unnecessary since negotiation of money requires transfer of physical possession. However, where the security interest is perfected by registration or automatically perfected as proceeds, these measures are required.

The PPSA[6] contains special priority rules designed to protect holders of money. The rules apply to "money"[7] and not to other forms of payment or value such as negotiable instruments.[8] However, not all holders of money receive the same level of protection. A mere holder of money has priority over a security interest in it perfected by registration or automatically as proceeds only if she acquired the money without knowledge that it is subject to a security interest. A holder for value is given this superior priority status whether or not he was aware of a security interest in it when he acquired his interest. The absence of knowledge of a perfected security interest in the money is relevant only in the case of a gift of it to the holder.

---

2   Money is included in the definition of "personal property." PPSA (A, BC, NWT, Nu, O, Y) s. 1(1); (M, NB, PEI) s. 1; (NL, NS) s. 2; S s. 2(1).

3   PPSA (A, BC, M, NB, NWT, Nu, PEI, S) s. 24; (NL, NS) s. 25; O s. 22; Y s. 22.

4   PPSA (A, BC, M, NB, NWT, N, PEI, S) s. 25; (NL, NS) s. 26; (O, Y) s. 23.

5   PPSA (A, BC, NWT, Nu, S) s. 28(3); (NB, PEI) s. 28 (4); (NL, NS) s. 29(1); M s. 28(2); O s. 25(4); Y s. 26(2).

6   PPSA (A, BC, M, NB, NWT, Nu, PEI, S) s. 31(1); (NL, NS) s. 32(1); Y s. 30(1); O no equivalent provision. It takes a "hands-off" position by providing in s. 29(b) that the rights of a transferee from the debtor of money are determined without regard to the Act.

7   Above note 2. It includes Canadian and foreign currency.

8   *Indian Head Credit Union v. Andrew*, [1993] 1 W.W.R. 673 (Sask. C.A.).

This feature of the PPSA is compatible with federal law relating to currency.[9] While, as a result of recent amendments to the *Bank of Canada Act*,[10] it is no longer possible to draw direct analogies between bank notes and bills of exchange governed by the *Bills of Exchange Act*,[11] the rights of a holder of a Bank of Canada note to take free from prior interests in the note are very similar to those of the holder of a negotiable instrument. Indeed, a Bank of Canada note can be viewed as a common law promissory note payable to bearer on demand. Mere physical transfer of a promissory note does not necessarily result in transfer of ownership of it. The gift of a stolen promissory note that has been issued and is payable to bearer on demand does not give the donee a legal right to retain it against its owner, although a transfer of it for value to someone unaware of the thief's defect in title would.

2) Instruments and Negotiable Documents of Title

The PPSA[12] essentially replicates the law applicable to the transfer of negotiable instruments.[13] A purchaser for value of an instrument[14] who takes possession of it has priority over a security interest in the instrument[15] perfected by registration or temporarily perfected if the

---

9   See *Currency Act*, R.S.C. 1985, c. C-52, s. 8 (am. R.S.C. 1985, c. 35 (3d Supp.) s. 181); and *Bank of Canada Act*, R.S.C. 1985, c. B-2, s. 25 (am. S.C. 2001, c. 9, s. 198).
10 *Bank of Canada Act*, R.S.C. 1985, c. B-2, s. 25 (am. S.C. 2001, c. 9, s. 198).
11 R.S.C. 1985, c. B-4.
12 PPSA (A, BC, NB, NWT, Nu, PEI) s. 31(3); (M, S) s. 31(4); (NL, NS) s. 32(3); O s. 28(4); Y s. 30(3).
13 See generally *Flexi-Coil Ltd. v. Kindersley District Credit Union Ltd.*, [1994] 1 W.W.R. 1 (Sask. C.A.).
14 The term "instrument" is defined in PPSA (A, BC, NWT, Nu, O, Y) s. 1(1); (M, NB, PEI) s. 1; (NL, NS) s. 2; S s. 2(1) to include bills of exchange, notes and cheques governed by the *Bills of Exchange Act*, common law instruments in the nature of bills of exchange, and letters of credit or advices of credit that are drawn in such a way as to require surrender on claiming payment (a transferable or assignable credit). However, in addition, the definition appears to include a documentary intangible in the form that provides for transfer of a right to payment through endorsement and delivery even though the transferee is not protected from defects in title of the transferor or an earlier transferor (i.e., a truly negotiable instrument).
    BCPPSA s. 2(i)(v) provides that the term instrument does not include a "negotiable" mortgage or charge on land that is specifically identified in the instrument. Whether a "negotiable mortgage" is an instrument under the OPPSA depends upon the scope given to OPPSA s. 4(1)(e)(ii).
15 A non-negotiable term deposit agreement is not an instrument. *Indian Head Credit Union v. Andrew*, above note 8.

purchaser acquired the instrument without knowledge of a security interest in it.[16] These rights are in addition to those of a holder in due course of a negotiable instrument governed by the *Bills of Exchange Act*[17] or corporations law. The same approach is applied to the transfer of negotiable documents of title,[18] even though the law otherwise applicable to this type of property may not recognize that its transfer through endorsement and delivery cuts off prior interests in it.

The special priority rules applicable to instruments and negotiable documents of title extend to a "purchaser" of an instrument or a negotiable document of title. This term includes a person who acquires an interest in the instrument or document of title through any type of consensual transaction.[19] Consequently, it includes a secured party who takes a security interest in the instrument or document of title and perfects by taking possession. In these circumstances, the secured party would be a purchaser of the instrument or document and, if it acquired its interest without knowledge of the prior security interest, would be able to rely on the priority rules to give it priority over a prior security interest in the instrument or document of title perfected by registration or automatically perfected.

The Saskatchewan Court of Appeal concluded in *Flexi-Coil Ltd. v. Kindersley District Credit Union Ltd.*[20] that when the value of cheques "deposited" in a credit union account reduced a debit balance in the account and entitled the depositor to draw on a line of credit operated through the account, the credit union was a purchaser of the cheques and therefore protected by the PPSA special priority rule. However, to qualify for priority under this provision, it is not necessary that the value of the instrument be applied to a pre-existing debt owing to the deposit-taking

---

16 Several Acts provides a parallel priority rule applicable where the purchaser is in competition with a prior unperfected security interest in the instrument. PPSA (NB, S) s. 20(4); (NWT, Nu) s. 20(2); NL s. 21(3); NS s. 21(4); (A, BC, M, O, Y) no equivalent provision.

17 OPPSA s. 29(a). There is no equivalent in other Acts. However, because of the exclusive jurisdiction of the Federal Parliament over bills of exchange, it is clear that the right of a holder in due course of a bill of exchange cannot be affected by provincial law.

18 A distinction must be drawn between competing security interests in a negotiable document of title and between a security interest in a negotiable document of title and a security interest in the goods covered by the negotiable document of title. PPSA (A, BC, M, NB, NWT, Nu, PEI, S, Y) s. 27(1); (NL, NS) s. 28(1); O s. 26(1).

19 PPSA (A, BC, NWT, Nu, Ont., Y) s. 1(1); (M, NB, PEI) s. 1; (NL, NS) s. 2; S s. 2(1).

20 Above note 13.

institution. Whether the institution is acting as a discounter or collector of the instrument, it will have given value so long as the account of the depositor is credited with the value of the instrument.[21]

The PPSA[22] provides a general test as to what constitutes knowledge for the purposes of the PPSA priority rules.[23] Under this test, a person knows or has knowledge when information comes to the attention of that person under circumstances in which a reasonable person would take cognizance of it. However, this test is qualified where an interest is acquired in an instrument pursuant to a transaction entered into in the ordinary course of the transferor's business.[24] In this context, a purchaser has knowledge only if she acquired the instrument with knowledge that the transaction violated the terms of the security agreement under which the security interest arose.

Several Acts[25] provide that a creditor who receives an instrument drawn or made by a debtor and delivered in payment of a debt owing to that creditor has priority over any security interest in the instrument whether or not the creditor has knowledge of the security interest at the time of the delivery. This provision has the effect of empowering a debtor to use a negotiable instrument to pay debts, even though, as property of the debtor, the instrument is subject to a security interest. The provision appears to have very limited scope. It does not apply to an instrument drawn or made by someone else and endorsed to the debtor. Nor does it appear to apply to the account on which the instrument is drawn. A secured party who enforces the security interest against the account before the instrument is paid would have priority over the creditor to whom the instrument was delivered. However, the Saskatchewan Court of Appeal in *Flexi-Coil Ltd. v. Kindersley Credit*

---

21 It is a separate issue, however, as to whether or not the debtor-creditor relationship that arises between the institution and the depositor creates an account that is proceeds of a security interest in the instrument. See *Belarus Equipment of Canada v. C & M Equipment (Brooks) Ltd.*, [1995] 1 W.W.R. 429 (Alta. Q.B.); *Flexi-Coil Ltd. v. Kindersley District Credit Union Ltd.*, above note 13; *Indian Head Credit Union v. Andrew*, above note 8.

22 PPSA (A, BC, NWT, Nu) s. 1(2); (M, NB, PEI) s. 2(1); (NL, NS) s. 3(1)(c); O s. 69; S s. 2(2); Y no equivalent provision. See also PPSA (A, BC, M, NB, NWT, Nu, PEI, S) s. 47; (NL, NS) s. 48; O s. 47(5); Y s. 52(3).

23 The Act specifically precludes registration being treated as constructive knowledge of an interest to which the registration relates. PPSA (A, BC, M, NB, NWT, Nu, PEI, S) s. 47; (NL, NS) s. 48; O s. 47(5); Y s. 52(3).

24 PPSA (A, BC, NB, NWT, Nu, PEI) s. 31(5); (M, S) s. 31(6); (NL, NS) s. 32(5); (O, Y) no equivalent provision.

25 PPSA (A, BC, NB, NWT, Nu, PEI, S) s. 31(2); (NS, NL) s. 32(2); Y s. 30(2); O no equivalent provision.

Union Ltd.[26] suggested that, as a matter of public policy, the section should be read as applying to payment by an electronic funds transfer. The same court concluded in *Transamerica Commercial Finance Corporation v. Royal Bank*[27] that the provision implicitly encompasses payment with cash.

The Saskatchewan and Manitoba Acts[28] contain provisions that supplement the PPSA policy of ensuring that security interests in currency do not interfere with commercial activity. The effect of these provisions is to give power to a debtor to use various payment mechanisms to pay a debt owing to a creditor. So long as the payment is a "debtor-initiated payment," the creditor takes free from any security interest in the cash and in an instrument used to effect the payment or the account on which the instrument is drawn or against which the debit is made whether or not he has knowledge of the security interest at the time of payment. This includes payment using an instrument or an electronic funds transfer. It also includes a debit, transfer order, or authorization given to a deposit-taking institution by the debtor when the payment is made. However, it does not include a preauthorized debit or transfer order. Consequently, a deposit-taking institution cannot rely on this provision when, with knowledge of a security interest in an account it owes to a debtor, it discharges an obligation owing to it by the debtor by debiting the account unless this occurs pursuant to an authorization made at the time the debit occurs.

---

26   Above note 13.

27   (1990), 79 C.B.R. (N.S.) 127 (Sask. C.A.).

28   PPSA M s. 31(2.1); S s. 31(2)–(3). MPPSA s. 31(3) contains a broader definition of "debtor-initiated payment." The term includes payment under a written authorization executed by the debtor as part of a loan or other credit transaction, under which the debtor became indebted to the deposit-taking institution, which sets out specified amounts to be debited to the deposit account at specified times or intervals, or authorizes debits to the deposit account when the credit in the deposit account exceeds an amount specified in the written authorization, but does not include payment authorized by the deposit-taking institution as agent of the debtor.

3) Securities

The PPSA[29] recognizes the "negotiable" character of publicly traded securities[30] under Canadian business corporations law[31] and provides that purchasers[32] who acquire possession of certificated or uncertificated securities[33] take free from registered or automatically perfected securities interests in the securities.

The PPSA[34] requires that the purchaser give value and acquire his interest in the security without knowledge that it is subject to a security interest. The Act[35] specifies the general test as to what constitutes knowledge for the purposes of the PPSA priority rules. Under this test, a person knows or has knowledge when information comes to the attention of that person under circumstances in which a reasonable person would take cognizance of it. However, this test is qualified[36] where an interest is acquired in a security pursuant to a transaction entered into in the ordinary course of the transferor's business. In this context, a purchaser has knowledge only if she acquired the instrument with knowledge that the transaction violated the terms of the security agreement under which the security interest arose. The transferee of the security must have specific

---

29 PPSA (A, BC, NB, NWT, Nu, PEI) s. 31(3); (M, S) s. 31(4); (NL, NS) s. 32(3); O s. 28(6)–(8); Y s. 30(3).

30 PPSA (A, BC, NWT, Nu, O, Y) s. 1(1); (M, NB, PEI) s. 1; (NL, NS) s. 2; S s. 2(1). While OPPSA s. 1(1) contains a definition of security, as a result of OPPSA s. 28(8), the definition of the term, and the terms "security certificate" and uncertificated security" as they are used in OPPSA ss. 28(6)–(7) are to be found in s. 53 of the *Business Corporations Act*, R.S.O. 1990, c. B.16.

31 See, for example, *Business Corporations Act*, R.S.A. 2000, c. B-9, s. 47(3); Ontario *Business Corporations Act*, *ibid.*, s. 53(3).

32 PPSA (A, BC, NWT, Nu, O, Y) s. 1(1); (M, NB, PEI) s. 1; (NL, NS) s. 2; S s. 2(1). While OPPSA s. 1(1) contains a definition of "purchase," as a result of OPPSA s. 28(8), the definition of the term "purchaser" in OPPSA ss. 28(6)–(7) is to be found in s. 53(3) of the Ontario *Business Corporations Act*, *ibid.*

33 These provisions apply to the transfer of securities held with a clearing agency. However, the protection is not available when the records of the clearing agency indicate the existence of a prior security interest since the recording is treated as perfection of the security interest by possession on the part of the secured party See PPSA (MB, NB, PEI) s. 2(4); (NL, NS) s. 3(4); (NWT, Nu) s. 1(6); BC s. 24(3); S s. 2(5); (A, O, Y) no equivalent provision. But see Ontario *Business Corporations Act*, *ibid.*, ss. 85(1), (3)–(5).

34 Above note 29.

35 As to what constitutes "knowledge," PPSA (A, BC, NWT, Nu) s. 1(2); (M, NB, PEI) s. 2(1); (NL, NS) s. 3(1)(c); O s. 69; S s. 2(2); Y no equivalent provision. PPSA (A, BC, M, NB, NWT, Nu, PEI, S) s. 47; (NL, NS) s. 48; O s. 47(5); Y s. 52(3).

36 PPSA (A, BC, NB, NWT, Nu, PEI) s. 31(5); (M, S) s. 31(6); (NL, NS) s. 32(5); (O, Y) no equivalent provision. However, see OPPSA s. 28(7).

knowledge that the instrument is subject to a security interest and that its transfer is in violation of a security agreement.[37]

Section 28(6) and (7) of the Ontario Act draw a distinction between a "good faith purchaser"[38] of a security and a "purchaser of a security who purchases the security in the ordinary course of (the purchaser's) business." In the latter case, the purchaser takes free from a registered or automatically perfected security interest in the security even though he knows that the security interest exists, so long as he does not know that the purchase constitutes a breach of the security agreement.

The enactment of the *Uniform Securities Transfer Act* (USTA) and complementary amendments to the PPSA[39] will result in a new set of priority rules applicable to competing interests in securities and cut-off rules protecting purchasers and buyers of certificated and uncertificated securities. Set out in the following discussion is a very brief overview of the changes in the PPSA that would result should the USTA and the proposed changes to the PPSA be implemented.

The USTA and complementary amendments to the PPSA would result in a new form of collateral ("security entitlement")[40] and new con-

---

37 See text accompanying notes 22 to 24.

38 As a result of OPPSA s. 28(8), the definition of this term is in s. 53 of the Ontario *Business Corporations Act,* above note 30. The definition imports other defined concepts such as "good faith" and "adverse claim." It also brings indirectly held securities into the operation of s. 28(8).

39 For the full text of these provisions, see the webpage of the Uniform Law Conference of Canada (www.ulcc.ca), Proceedings of the 2003 meeting, Commercial Law Documents, *Report of the Working Group on Reform of Canadian Secured Transactions Law, 2003.* The proposed amendments to the PPSA use the Alberta and Ontario versions and the references that follow therefore refer only to these Acts.

40 USTA s. 106(1) provides as follows:

(1) Except as otherwise provided for in subsections (3) and (4), a person acquires a security entitlement if a securities intermediary

(a) indicates by book entry that a financial asset has been credited to the person's securities account,

(b) receives a financial asset from the person or acquires a financial asset for the person and, in either case, accepts it for credit to the person's securities account, or

(c) becomes obligated under another statute, law, regulation or rule to credit a financial asset to the person's securities account.

(2) If a person acquires a security entitlement under subsection (1), that person has the security entitlement even though the securities intermediary does not itself hold the financial asset.

A feature of the new system that is not obvious from the legislation is that a security "entitlement" is not the equivalent of tangible personal property that is transferred or dealt with in conventional ways. It is not a claim to a specific

figurations of collateral ("investment property," "financial assets,"[41] and "securities account"[42]) in which security interests can be taken. Special rules will deal with attachment and perfection of a security interest in a securities account where the securities intermediary is the secured party. The proposed legislation would grant automatic attachment and perfection to security interests in a security or financial asset arising in the context of transactions between persons in the business of dealing with securities or financial assets that provide for delivery against payment.[43] This special form of attachment and perfection also applies to a security interest in investment property, a commodity account or a commodity contract created by a broker, securities intermediary or commodity intermediary, respectively.[44]

Under the proposed amendments, it would be possible to perfect a security interest in certificated and uncertificated securities through methods permitted under existing law. However, the system would also introduce a new method of perfection, "control,"[45] that can be used with respect to certificated and uncertificated securities and that must be used with respect to a security entitlement.[46]

Revised priority rules protect "buyers" of certificated or uncertificated securities.[47] Parallel rules are provided for purchasers, including "protected purchasers"[48] of "financial assets" (including security en-

---

identifiable thing. It is essentially just a bundle of rights held by an entitlement holder that can be asserted directly only against the entitlement holder's intermediary.

41   Proposed APPSA s. 1(1)(x.1); OPPSA s. (1) "investment property" means a security, whether certificated or uncertificated, security entitlement, securities account, commodity contract, or commodity account. USTA s. 1(1)(m) "financial asset" includes a security, a credit balance in a securities account and any property that is held by a securities intermediary for another person in a securities account if the securities intermediary has expressly agreed with the other person that the property is to be treated as a financial asset under this Act.
42   USTA s. 1(1)(cc) "securities account" means an account to which a financial asset is or may be credited in accordance with an agreement under which the person maintaining the account undertakes to treat the person for whom the account is maintained as entitled to exercise the rights that constitute the financial asset.
43   Proposed APPSA ss. 12.1(3) and 19.2(1); OPPSA ss. 11.1(3) and 19.2(1).
44   Proposed APPSA ss. 19.2(2)–(3); OPPSA ss. 19.2(2)–(3).
45   See a brief discussion of this feature in chapter 5, H "Perfection by Control."
46   Proposed APPSA s. 24.1; OPPSA s. 22(2)–(3). Perfection of a security interest in a securities account also perfects a security interest in the security entitlements carried in the securities account. Proposed APPSA s. 19.1; OPPSA s. 19.1.
47   Proposed APPSA s. 30(9); OPPSA s. 28(6)–(7).
48   As defined in the USTA s. 1(1)(x).

titlements).[49] These rules reflect the unique nature of the rights associated with securities held with an intermediary. Where the competition is between security interests, a special set of priority rules apply. A security interest of a secured party having control of investment property has priority over a security interest of a secured party who does not have control of the investment property. A security interest in a certificated security in registered form that is perfected by taking delivery has priority over a conflicting security interest perfected by a method other than control. Conflicting security interests of secured parties each of which has control rank according to the time of obtaining control. A security interest held by a securities intermediary in a security entitlement or a securities account maintained with the securities intermediary has priority over a conflicting security interest held by another secured party.[50]

C. CHATTEL PAPER

1) Chattel Paper: A *Sui Generis* Type of Collateral

Chattel paper is the only category of collateral "created" by the PPSA. It is a composite of two types of property (a chose in action and tangible personal property) that, under prior law, were governed by different and largely unrelated principles. Chattel paper is composed of one or more writings that evidences both a monetary obligation and a security interest in or lease of specific goods or specific goods and accessions to those goods.[51] Because of the *sui generis* nature of chattel paper, important aspects of security interests in it are governed by special PPSA rules. These rules were designed to reflect established practices associated with a particular segment of the secured financing market. However, it is not possible to treat chattel paper as a single type of property for all purposes.[52] There are circumstances in which this characterization breaks down and the two kinds of property interests involved require separate recognition.

49   Proposed APPSA s. 30(10–11) and 31; OPPSA s. 28(7–8) and 28.1.
50   Proposed APPSA s. 35.1(5); OPPSA s. 30.1(5).
51   PPSA (A, BC, NWT, Nu, O, Y) s. 1(1); (M, NB, PEI) s. 1; (NL, NS) s. 2; S s. 2(1). The OPPSA definition makes no reference to accessions.
52   PPSA (A, BC, M, NB, NWT, Nu, PEI, S) s. 29; (NL, NS) s. 30; O s. 27(1); Y s. 28.

A security interest (or deemed security interest)[53] in chattel paper arises when a secured seller, lender or a lessor[54] gives a security interest in or sells the chattel paper (i.e., his security interest or ownership interest in specific goods[55] and the obligations of the debtor or lessee)[56] to a "purchaser."[57] The chattel paper may be held by the initial purchaser or "securitized" through additional sales. The rules applicable to interests in the chattel paper are not concerned with the perfection and priority status of the transferred security interest or lease and the associated obligation. These issues are addressed in provisions of the Act that are of more general application. However, the commercial value of the chattel paper to a purchaser may well be affected by the priority status of the security interest or lease that comprises the chattel paper. If the security interest is not perfected or otherwise can be defeated under a special priority rule of the PPSA, the purchaser of the chattel paper may not be able to rely on enforcing the security interest should the debtor who has granted it not discharge the obligation it secures.

The picture is somewhat more complicated where the chattel paper is a true lease of goods between the chattel paper debtor and a lessee. The PPSA is ambiguous as to the nature and extent of the interest acquired by the chattel paper purchaser. One view is that its position is equivalent to that of an assignee of the lessor's entire interest. The other view (and, in the opinion of the authors, the better view) is that the chattel paper purchaser acquires the chattel paper only and not the reversionary interest of the lessor in the goods. If he is to have a security interest in the reversionary interest, he must acquire this under a security agreement specifically providing for this. If that interest is already subject to a prior perfected security interest in favour of another financer, the chattel paper purchaser will be subject to it. However, should

---

53   The PPSA applies to sales of chattel paper as well as to security interest in chattel paper. PPSA (A, M, NB, PEI, S) s. 3(2); (NL, NS) s. 4(2); (NWT, N) s. 2(2); (O, Y) s. 2(b); BC s. 3.

54   The lease need not be a security lease or one that otherwise falls within the scope of the PPSA.

55   A security agreement that provides for a security interest in after-acquired property does not qualify as chattel paper.

56   Depending upon the context and the market involved, the transfer contract may provide for either recourse (in whole or in part) or non-recourse back to the seller should the borrower, buyer or lessee default under the loan, sales contract or lease. Where consumer transactions are involved, the chattel paper purchaser is likely to notify the borrower, buyer or lessee and instruct that payments owing their agreements be made directly to the purchaser.

57   This includes a person who takes a security interest in the chattel paper or someone who buys it.

the lease be prematurely terminated and the equipment returned to or repossessed by the lessor, the chattel paper purchaser will have priority to the goods to the extent of the value of the unexpired term of the lease, but not the entire value of the leased goods.

The PPSA treats the seller, lender, or lessor as the "debtor" and the purchaser of the chattel paper as the "secured party" in the context of security interests in chattel paper. Perfection and priority rules relating to chattel paper address priority conflicts involving successive claims to the chattel paper.

2) Competing Security Interests in Chattel Paper

A feature of the priority rules of the PPSA applicable to competing interests in chattel paper[58] is that they give to chattel paper an element of negotiability. As is the case with negotiable instruments, priority is affected by the state of knowledge of the purchaser as to the existence of a prior interest in the chattel paper. A purchaser (secured party or buyer) of chattel paper who takes possession of it in the ordinary course of the purchaser's business and for new value[59] is given priority over a security interest in the chattel paper perfected by registration if she does not have knowledge at the time she took possession that the chattel paper was subject to a security interest. While the matter is not free from doubt, it is the view of the authors that all of the value given for the chattel paper must be new value. If any portion is the cancellation of an antecedent debt, the requirements of the section have not been met. If only some of the value needs to be new, the following situation could result.

SP1 provides an inventory loan for $100,000 and takes a security interest in the inventory purchased by D. SP2 makes a secured loan of $50,010 to D. At this stage, SP1 has priority over SP2. D then sells inventory and generates chattel paper. D sells the chattel paper to SP2 for $50,000 which is then set-off against SP2's loan to D. If the $10 meets the new value requirement, the priority rules of the PPSA would give priority with respect to the chattel paper to SP2 over SP1 who has a first priority, purchase money security interest in the inventory.

---

58   PPSA (A, BC, NB, NWT, Nu, PEI) s. 31(6); (M, S) s. 31(7); (NL, NS) s. 32(6); O s. 28(3); Y s. 30(5).
59   This term is defined in PPSA (A, BC, NWT, N) s. 1(1); (M, NB, PEI) s. 1; (NL, NS) s. 2; S s. 2(1); (O, Y) no equivalent provision.

If the chattel paper is proceeds of inventory, the purchaser who takes possession of the chattel paper in the ordinary course of his business has priority over the perfected security interest in the chattel paper, whether or not the purchaser is aware of the security interest.

The PPSA[60] contemplates two standard situations in which competing interests in chattel paper are likely to arise. The first is where the debtor sells or gives a security interest in chattel paper generated in his business to two or more successive commercial purchasers of chattel paper. The purchaser for new value who takes possession of the chattel paper without knowledge of the other interest is given priority over a secured party who has perfected its interest by registration.[61] The secured party can protect its interest from defeat in this context by indicating clearly on the chattel paper that it is subject to its security interest. This would give notice to any subsequent purchaser who took possession of the chattel paper that the prior interest exists under circumstances in which he would have knowledge of the security interest.[62]

The second situation contemplated by the PPSA[63] is one in which the prior security interest in the chattel paper is one granted by the PPSA or arising under the security agreement as proceeds of inventory. This situation will arise where a supplier who has a perfected security interest in inventory supplied to the debtor acquires a security interest in chattel paper generated by the debtor through the sale of that inventory under a secured instalment sales contract. Assume that after the chattel paper comes into existence, it is transferred to a purchaser who takes possession of it in the ordinary course of his business and for new value. The chattel paper purchaser is given priority[64] even though he may be aware that the chattel paper is subject to a perfected security interest in the chattel paper as proceeds. In this context, the chattel paper has a negotiability that is superior to that of a bill of exchange or other negotiable instrument. Unlike a holder in due course of a negotiable instrument, a purchaser of chattel paper in this context need not be without knowledge of a prior interest in it.

The distinction between the two situations is a product of a policy decision designed to facilitate the use of chattel paper as a financing device. It is based on the assumption that it is commercially more bene-

---

60   Above note 58.
61   *Ibid.*
62   As to what constitutes "knowledge," PPSA (A, BC, NWT, N) s. 1(2); (M, NB, PEI) s. 2(1); (NL, NS) s. 3(1)(c); O s. 69; S s. 2(2); Y no equivalent provision; PPSA (A, BC, M, NB, NWT, Nu, PEI, S) s. 47; (NL, NS) s. 48; O s. 47(5); Y s. 52(3).
63   Above note 58.
64   *Ibid.*

ficial to permit business enterprises to sell their chattel paper than it is to protect the interests of inventory financers in chattel paper generated through the sale of the inventory in which they hold security interests. This priority rule places an inventory financer who wants to protect his proceeds security interest in chattel paper in the position of having to "police" the sales of the inventory so as to ensure that the chattel paper generated in those sales is physically handed over to him.

An interpretive issue arises in the context of the priority rule that give priority to a transferee of chattel paper over a secured party with a security interest in the chattel paper as proceeds.[65] Does the rule apply where the security agreement between the inventory financer and the debtor and the registration relating to the security interest describe the chattel paper as original collateral (and not as proceeds) and where the amount of credit granted to the debtor by the inventory financer is greater because the debtor has granted a security interest in the chattel paper? For example, where both the agreement and the registration provide for a security interest in "all present and after-acquired personal property" of the debtor, one may well conclude that there can be no security interest in proceeds. All property acquired by the debtor, including chattel paper from the sale of the inventory, is original collateral and not proceeds and that the total credit granted was based on the secured party having a security interest is both the inventory and the chattel paper. If this is accepted, the case comes within the alternative priority rule and the knowledge of the purchaser of the chattel paper would then be relevant. The inventory supplier could protect its interest by notifying financial organizations that might be expected to purchase chattel paper generated by the debtor that it has a security interest in chattel paper generated from the sale of the inventory.

It is the view of the authors that the wording of a security agreement and the registration relating to a security interest cannot affect the operation of the priority provisions. The test is objective. If, in fact, the chattel paper is proceeds of inventory, the provisions apply even though the chattel paper may be viewed as original collateral under the wording of the security agreement and the understanding of the parties. Any other approach would result in easy circumvention of the policy that the priority provisions of the PPSA embody.

---

65   *Ibid.*

3) Breakdown of the Chattel Paper Concept

The priority rules of the PPSA relating to chattel paper are based on the assumption that the relationships that underlie chattel paper transactions (for example, the secured loan, instalment sales contract or lease) remain intact and enforceable. However, this will not always be the case. For example, in the context of an instalment sale, the relationship between the seller and the buyer may change as a result of the collateral (for example, an automobile) being returned or repossessed by the seller or by the chattel paper purchaser under circumstances in which the right of the chattel paper purchaser to enforce the payment obligation contained in the instalment sales contract is extinguished or jeopardized. In these circumstances, it will be commercially necessary for the chattel paper purchaser to look to the tangible personal property aspect of the chattel paper. In other words, the purchaser will want to assert priority to an interest in the returned or repossessed automobile. The conceptual difficulty is that the purchaser does not have a security interest in an automobile; it has a security interest in chattel paper, a different form of collateral. An additional problem is that another secured party, for example an inventory supplier, may have a security interest in the automobile as a result of an after-acquired property clause in its security agreement with the seller.

The PPSA addresses these and other issues that arise in this context in a separate set of rules.[66] These rules are examined in detail in chapter 12.

---

66   PPSA (A, BC, M, NB, NWT, Nu, PEI, S) s. 29; (NL, NS) s. 30; O s. 27(1); Y s. 28.

CHAPTER 10

COMPETITIONS WITH OTHER CLAIMANTS

A. COMPETING INTERESTS UNDER MONEY JUDGMENT ENFORCEMENT LAW

1) Introduction

Canadian secured financing law has always recognized that unsecured creditors are one of the categories of persons protected under perfection and priority rules. However, the theoretical basis for this protection and the operation of these rules has not always been consistent. Indeed, there are currently very considerable differences between the approaches taken in the various jurisdictions to the respective priority positions of the secured and unsecured creditors of a debtor. Some of these differences result from recent fundamental changes in the judgment enforcement systems of some jurisdictions. The effect of the new systems is to give to an unsecured judgment creditor the ability to acquire a priority status in relation to other interests, including PPSA security interests, very similar to that of a secured creditor. Because of the very different conceptual and operational differences among judgment enforcement systems, the authors have grouped the systems and treated each group separately.

The PPSAs of British Columbia, Manitoba, Ontario, Saskatchewan, the Northwest Territories, Nunavut, and the Yukon Territory[1] employ a

---

1   PPSA (NB, NWT, Nu, O, S) s. 20(1); (BC, M) s. 20(a); PEI s. 20(2); Y s. 19(1).

more traditional approach to the priority status of an unsecured credit-
or in relation to the secured creditors of a debtor. Saskatchewan and
the Northwest Territories form a sub-group as a result of additional
features contained in their judgment enforcement laws. The newer approach is reflected in the Acts in effect in the Atlantic provinces and
Alberta.

2) The Traditional Approach

a) Binding Effect of a Writ of Execution

The position of a secured party who acquires a security interest in property of a debtor after it is bound by the issue and delivery of a writ of *fieri
facias* to the sheriff is determined by execution law. The common law
early recognized that, while the issue and delivery of a writ of execution against chattels to the sheriff did not give to the judgment creditor
any claim to or interest in goods of the debtor, it did "bind" the goods.[2]
However, this binding effect was never extended to other forms of personal property. Goods "bound" by a writ of execution could be legally
seized by the sheriff from any person who acquired a property interest,
including full ownership, after the delivery of the writ.[3] Consequently,
goods subject to the binding effect of a writ have been treated as being
"encumbered" with the power of the sheriff to seize them.[4] The harsh
consequences that resulted from this conclusion were ameliorated in
many jurisdictions by legislation patterned on section 1 of the English
Mercantile Law Amendment Act, 1856, which provided that no writ of
execution can prejudice the right of any person to goods acquired from
an execution debtor in good faith, for valuable consideration and without notice.[5] The effect of this legislation is to insulate from the binding
effect of writs of execution subsequent interests, including security interests, acquired under the circumstances described in the provision.
In practical terms, this strips the binding effect of a writ of execution
of much of its value in giving priority with respect to goods over subsequent interests in debtors' property. However, the legislation does not
protect a person who acquires an interest from a debtor in possession

---

2   See, for example, *Ross v. Dunn* (1889), 16 O.A.R. 552.
3   See *Young v. Short* (1885), 3 Man. R. 302 (C.A.).
4   See *Lloyds and Scottish Finance Ltd. v. Modern Cars and Caravans (Kingston) Ltd.*,
    [1966] 1 Q.B. 764.
5   See, for example, *Law and Equity Act*, R S B C 1996, c. 253, s. 35(1).

under an undertaking to hold seized goods for the sheriff (a so-called walking possession agreement or sheriff's bond).[6]

The situation under current Ontario law is unclear because of obscure legislative drafting. Section 10(1) of the *Executions Act*[7] provides that a writ of execution binds the goods against which it is issued from the time it has been received for execution and recorded by the sheriff. However, section 10(2) provides:

> despite subsection (1), no writ of execution against *goods other than bills of sale and instruments in the nature of chattel mortgages prejudices the title to such goods* acquired by a person in good faith and for valuable consideration unless such person at the time of acquiring title had notice that such writ or any other writ by virtue of which the goods of the execution debtor might be seized or attached has been delivered to the sheriff and remains in the sheriff's hands unexecuted [emphasis added].

If the section is given its plain meaning, the reference to "instruments in the nature of a chattel mortgage" is a carve out of the category of "goods," even though a bill of sale or chattel mortgage is not "goods." The effect of this interpretation would be that buyers of bills of sale or chattel mortgages would be subject to the binding effect of a writ. Another interpretation — albeit one that strains the wording of the section — is that the reference to bills of sale and instruments in the nature of chattel mortgages was included to ensure that a good faith purchaser does not acquire his interest free from a bill of sale or chattel mortgage.

A security interest that attaches to money in the hands of a sheriff as a result of a levy takes subject to the interest of the execution creditor under whose writ the goods were sold. This is not a product of the binding effect of the writ of execution; it results from the "interest" that an execution creditor is given at common law in the proceeds of sale under an execution.[8] It is not clear whether this same principle applies to money received by a sheriff through seizure of an account. It apparently does not apply to money paid into court pursuant to a garnishee summons.[9]

---

6   See *Lloyds and Scottish Finance Ltd. v. Modern Cars and Caravans (Kingston) Ltd.*, above note 4.
7   R.S.O. 1990, c. E.24.
8   See *British Columbia (Deputy Sheriff) v. Canada* (1992), 90 D.L.R. (4th) 680 (B.C.C.A.); *Giles v. Grover* (1832), 6 E.R. 843 (H.L.).
9   See *Polyco Window Manufacturing Ltd. v. Prudential Assurance Co.* (1994), 119 Sask. R. 131 (Q.B.).

b) Prior Security Interests and Subsequent Writs of Execution

Under the traditional approach employed in the six jurisdictions identi-fied above,[10] the *nemo dat* rule is implicitly employed to give priority to a perfected security interest over the interest of an unsecured creditor who has invoked judgment enforcement measures after the security in-terest has been taken and perfected. A judgment enforcement measure can affect only the unencumbered interest of the judgment debtor.

However, an unperfected security interest (other than a purchase money security interest that is later perfected within a specified period of time after it attaches)[11] is vulnerable under the PPSA to subordina-tion to the interests of judgment creditors. The Ontario Act[12] provides that an unperfected security interest is subordinate to the interest of a person who assumes control of the collateral through execution, at-tachment, garnishment, charging order, equitable execution,[13] or other legal process.[14] The formulation in the other PPSAs in this group is somewhat different.[15] It refers to a person who "causes the collateral to be seized pursuant to legal proceedings to enforce a judgment." This formulation eliminates an ambiguity in the assumption of control test adopted by the OPPSA.[16] Under judgment enforcement law, a judgment creditor does not "assume control" of the property of the debtor. Goods seized under execution are under the control of the sheriff. The execu-tion creditor who has issued the writ under which the seizure occurs has no right to possession of the goods or to instruct the sheriff in the disposition of them.[17] Payment of money into court pursuant to gar-

---

10 Above note 1.
11 PPSA (A, BC, M, NB, NWT, Nu, PEI, S) s. 22(1); (NL, NS) s. 23(1); O s. 20(3); Y s. 20.
12 Above note 1.
13 However, the appointment of a receiver under a power of appointment con-tained in a security agreement does not give the appointing creditor status to attack an unperfected security interest. *Bank of Nova Scotia v. Royal Bank of Canada* (1987), 68 C.B.R. (N.S.) 235 (Sask. C.A.); *Rogerson Lumber Co. v. Four Seasons Chalet Ltd.* (1980), 113 D.L.R. (3d) 671 (Ont. C.A.).
14 Persons entitled to share in a levy under creditors' relief legislation, for example, *Creditors' Relief Act,* R.S.O. 1990, c. C-45, are included in the list of creditors benefiting from the PPSA priority rule applicable to judgment enforce-ment creditors. Above note 1.
15 See above note 1.
16 An additional uncertainty endemic to OPPSA s. 20(1) is whether the concept of assumed control includes delivery of a writ of execution and recording of it by the sheriff. When this occurs, the goods of the debtor are "bound" by the writ. *Execution Act,* above note 7, s. 10(1).
17 See *Corsbie v. J.I. Case Threshing Machine Co.* (1913), 25 W.L.R. 466 (Sask. S.C.).

nishment proceedings does not result in the funds coming under the control of the garnisheeing creditor.[18] Neither a charging order nor an equitable execution results in a judgment creditor obtaining control of the property of the debtor. The formulation adopted by the other Acts in this category addresses another ambiguity in the OPPSA. While it is clear that the priority rules of the other PPSAs apply only to judgment creditors, the reference to "control" in the OPPSA provision can be interpreted as including a creditor who has invoked pre-judgment garnishment or who has obtained a Mareva injunction.

The usual priority conflict to which the PPSA rule applies is one in which a security interest has been taken in property of the debtor but has not been perfected by registration or automatically perfected at the time a judgment enforcement measure,[19] such as seizure under execution or garnishment proceedings,[20] occurs.[21] However, the section applies in another, more controversial, context. This is where a lender effects a registration relating to property owned by a prospective debtor. At the time of registration, no security agreement exists between the lender and the prospective debtor. Thereafter, and before such an agreement is executed, a judgment creditor causes the property of the debtor to be seized to enforce the judgment. Without knowledge of the seizure, the lender enters into a security agreement with the debtor and advances funds under it. Since the security interest arising under the agreement will not attach until the agreement is executed, the security interest would not be perfected at the time of seizure of the collateral

---

18   However, in *Canada Mortgage and Housing Corporation v. Apostolou* (1995), 22 O.R. (3d) 190, an Ontario Court General Division ruled that the service of a garnishee summons gave "control" to a judgment creditor sufficient to give it priority over an unperfected security interest in the account attached. The court focused on the function of OPPSA s. 20(1) rather than the ordinary meaning of its words. See also *Access Advertising Management Inc. v. Servex Computers Inc.* (1993), 21 C.B.R. (3d) 304 (Ont. Ct. Gen. Div.); *Rogerson Lumber Co. v. Four Seasons Chalet Ltd.*, above note 13.

19   Or such further time as is permitted for perfection of purchase money security interests. See above note 11.

20   As to the effect of garnishment proceedings on the property rights of the judgment debtor, see *Polyco Window Manufacturing Ltd. v. Prudential Assurance Co.*, above note 9.

21   In *Denolf v. Brown* (1994), 17 Alta. L.R. (3d) 374, the Alberta Queen's Bench concluded that the provision of the PPSA which subordinates an unperfected security interest to a seizing creditor applies when the execution debtor is a buyer from the debtor under the security agreement. Although this provision has since been repealed in the Alberta Act, and the matter is now governed by s. 35 of the *Civil Enforcement Act*, there is no reason in principle why this interpretation should not extend to the new legislation as well.

under the judgment enforcement proceedings with the result that it would be subject to the judgment.

The above-noted scenario must be distinguished from one that is very similar. This is where a lender effects a registration relating to property of a prospective debtor. At the time of registration, or shortly thereafter, a security agreement is executed between the lender and the prospective debtor. However, at that time the debtor does not have rights in the property described in the agreement as collateral. Thereafter, the debtor acquires such property which, however, is immediately seized under execution to enforce the judgment. Without knowledge of the seizure, the lender advances funds to the debtor. Since the security interest arising under the agreement attached as soon as the debtor acquired the property, the security interest would be perfected at the time of seizure of the collateral and, consequently would have priority.

There is another context within which a priority competition between a security interest and the interest of an unsecured creditor can arise. This is where a perfected security interest becomes unperfected and is then reperfected. If, during the period the security interest was unperfected, the collateral is seized under judgment enforcement proceedings, the PPSA[22] will apply, with the result that the security interest will be defeated. However, if the seizure occurred prior to the termination of perfection, the result may be quite different.

OPPSA section 30(6) treats a security interest reperfected by registration as having been "continuously perfected from the time of first perfection,"[23] except as against a person who acquired rights in all or part of the collateral when the security interest was unperfected. A bankruptcy trustee of the debtor is such a person since the effect of bankruptcy law is to vest in the trustee the debtor's property as of the date of the receiving order or assignment.[24] An unsecured creditor who has caused the collateral to be seized prior to the termination of the initial perfection does not "acquire rights" during the period of non-perfection.[25] The question arises as to whether an unsecured creditor who

---

22 Above note 1, but not including Ontario.
23 The section applies only where there has been reperfection by registration. It is not clear whether it applies where the initial perfection was by registration or by some other method.
24 *Frankel v. Canadian Imperial Bank of Commerce* (1997), 12 P.P.S.A.C. (2d) 306 (Ont. Ct. Gen. Div.).
25 *Re PSINet Realty Canada Limited* (2002), 30 C.B.R. (4th) 226 (Ont. S.C.J.) and *Heidelberg Canada Graphic Equipment Ltd. v. Arthur Andersen Inc.* (1992), 7 B.L.R. (2d) 236 (Ont. Ct. Gen. Div.). Theses cases deals with prior secured creditors, but the reasoning applies as well to unsecured creditors.

"assumes control" of the collateral within the meaning of that term in OPPSA section 20(1) during the period when the security interest is not registered thereby "acquires rights" in the collateral.

Technically, seizure of property under a judgment enforcement proceeding, such as a writ of *fieri facias* or garnishment proceedings, does not give to the judgment creditors who issued the process under which the seizure occurred any property right or right to possession or control of the property seized.[26] The seizing sheriff acquires a "special property" that allows him to maintain an action for trespass or conversion.[27] Consequently, no direct analogy can be made to the position of a trustee in bankruptcy. However, if goods subject to a security interest are sold under execution, the "interest" in the proceeds that the execution creditor acquires at that stage of the process would qualify as rights acquired in the collateral.[28]

There is no equivalent to OPPSA section 30(6) in the other PPSAs in this group.[29] Under the other Acts, the only issue is whether or not the security interest is perfected at the time the unsecured creditor causes the collateral to be seized to enforce a judgment. If the seizure occurs during the period when the security interest is unperfected, the judgment has priority. If the seizure occurs before expiry of the initial perfection or after the subsequent perfection, the security interest will have priority. This priority rule expressly applies only when the security interest is unperfected at the time of seizure.

---

26 See, for example, *Ross v. Dunn* (1889), 16 O.A.R. 552; *Corsbie v. J.I. Case Threshing Machine Co.*, above note 17; *Polyco Window Manufacturing Ltd. v. Prudential Assurance Co.*, above note 9.

27 *Beatty v. Rumble* (1891), 21 O.R. 184 (H.C.J.). The PPSA makes specific reference to the power of the sheriff to defeat an unperfected security interest. See, for example, SPPSA, s. 20(1). There is no such reference in the OPPSA.

28 Above note 8.

29 PPSA (BC, M, NB, NWT, Nu, S) s. 35(7); (NL, NS) s. 36(7); A s. 35(8); PEI s. 35(6); Y s. 34(5), which provides for preservation of priority upon lapse or discharge of a registration and renewal of a registration, applies only to priority competitions between security interests. It does not apply to the interests of judgment creditors or trustees in bankruptcy.

3) The Judgment Creditor as Chargeholder

a) The New Judgment Enforcement Systems

As a result of changes made during the last decade to the judgment enforcement laws of several provinces,[30] priority regimes regulating the respective rights of money judgment creditors and secured parties have been dramatically changed. Under the approach contained in these systems, a judgment creditor can acquire through registration a priority status equivalent under provincial law[31] to that of a secured party with a security interest in the personal property of the debtor. The priority regime applicable to competing claims of judgment creditors and secured creditors parallels that adopted by the PPSA for competitions among secured parties.[32]

These systems follow one or other of two quite similar patterns: that contained in the legislation of the Atlantic provinces and that contained in the legislation of Alberta and Newfoundland. The pattern found in the legislation of the Atlantic provinces is hereafter examined in the context of the New Brunswick *Creditors Relief Act*[33] (the New Brunswick Act), while the pattern used in the Alberta *Civil Enforcement Act*[34] (the Alberta Act) is treated as representative of the Newfoundland legislation that was closely patterned on it.

The concept of the binding effect of a judgment enforcement measure is at the core of the priority rules contained in both the New Brunswick[35] and Alberta[36] regimes. The New Brunswick Act provides that registration of a notice of judgment[37] in the Personal Property Registry

---

30 *Civil Enforcement Act,* R.S.A. 2000, c. C-15, s. 33(2)–(3); *Judgment Enforcement Act,* S.N.L. 1996, c. J-11, ss. 41–58; *Creditors Relief Act,* R.S.N.B. 1973, c. C-33, ss. 2.1–2.6; *Creditors' Relief Act,* R.S.N.S. 1989, c. 112, ss. 2(a)–(e); *Judgments and Executions Act,* R.S.P.E.I. 1988, c. J-2.

31 It is clear from the overwhelming weight of judicial authority that a judgment charge arising under provincial legislation does not give to the judgment creditor the status of secured creditor in the context of section 70(1) of the *Bankruptcy and Insolvency Act. Canadian Credit Men's Trust Assn. v. Beaver Trucking Ltd.* (1959), 38 C.B.R. 1 (S.C.C.); *Re Sklar and Sklar* (1958), 26 W.W.R. 529 (Sask. C.A.).

32 See generally R. Cuming, "When an Unsecured Creditor is a Secured Creditor" (2003) 66 Sask. L. Rev. 255.

33 Above note 30.

34 *Ibid.*

35 NB s. 2.3(2).

36 A s. 33(2).

37 This is an electronic form of notice prescribed by regulations under the *Personal Property Security Act.*

"binds" all of the judgment debtor's present non-exempt, exigible, personal property on registration and all non-exempt, personal property acquired by the judgment debtor after registration from the time of its acquisition. Under the Alberta Act, the registration of a writ of enforcement[38] in the Alberta Personal Property Registry binds all the enforcement debtor's exigible present and after-acquired personal property. The priority status of a money judgment under these systems is based exclusively on registration of the notice of judgment or writ of enforcement.[39]

Each Act contains an extensive set of priority rules. The base rule gives priority to rights resulting from the registration of a notice of judgment or writ of enforcement over any interest acquired in personal property that is "bound" as a result of the registration. This general rule is refined in the Acts and in the related PPSAs. Under section 20(1) of the NBPPSA, a registered judgment is given priority over a security interest that is not perfected at the date of registration of the notice of judgment. Section 35(1)(a) of the Alberta Act gives priority to a registered writ of enforcement over a prior unperfected security interest, unless a registration relating to the security interest was effected before the writ was registered.

The Alberta Act[40] gives priority to a perfected security interest over a registered writ, except with respect to future advances made under the circumstances prescribed in APPSA section 35(5). Both Acts give priority to a purchase money security interest over a registered notice of judgment or writ of enforcement under the same conditions as are applicable to a priority competition between a purchase money security interest and a non-purchase money security interest in non-inventory collateral.[41] Both Acts[42] require registration of the serial number of the same specified types of goods that constitute serial numbered goods in the PPSA context as a condition of priority of the writ or notice of judgment over the interests of secured parties.

The Acts apply to registered judgments or writs the same priority rules that are applicable to registered security interests that are in com-

---

38 This is the writ issued out of the court that provides the authority to seize judgment debtors' property.
39 Section 2.3(1) of the New Brunswick Act and s. 34(1) of the Alberta Act provide that the only way personal property can be bound is by registration in the Personal Property Registry as provided in these Acts.
40 APPSA s. 35(2).
41 NB s. 22(1); A s. 35(3).
42 A 36(3); NB s. 2.3(6).

petition with purchasers (including secured parties) of money, negotiable instruments, securities, documents of title, and chattel paper.[43]

b)   The Saskatchewan and Northwest Territories Approaches

Saskatchewan law contains a hybrid approach: the traditional priority structure contained in the PPSA examined above and priority rules based on registration of writs of execution in the Personal Property Registry. SPPSA section 20(1) subordinates an unperfected security interest to the interest of a person who causes the collateral to be seized to enforce a money judgment. The issue and delivery of a writ of execution against chattels binds all the chattels of the debtor in the province.[44] However, section 2.2 of *The Executions Act*[45] provides that, if the writ is registered, it takes priority over a security interest that has not been registered or that is registered after the writ is registered.[46]

While the two approaches overlap to some extent, they supplement each other. For example, SPPSA section 20(1) does not address the situation where the security interest arises after a seizure of the collateral pursuant to an enforcement measure referred to in the section. It applies only to prior unperfected security interests.[47] Section 2.2 of *The Executions Act* gives priority to a prior registered writ of execution over prior and subsequent unperfected security interests and over subsequent unperfected security interests.

A variant of the Saskatchewan approach is contained in the Northwest Territories *Seizures Act*. Unlike the Saskatchewan legislation, the Northwest Territories legislation does not subordinate a prior unperfected security interest to a registered writ of execution. PPSA section 20(1) applies.[48]

---

43   A s. 38; NB s. 2.3(6).
44   *The Executions Act*, R.S.S. 1978, c. E-12, s. 2.2.
45   *Ibid*.
46   See *Colliar v. Robinson Diesel Injection Ltd.* (1990), 81 Sask. R. 144 (Q.B.), aff'd (1990), 86 Sask. R. 198 (C.A.).
47   However, the Saskatchewan Court of Appeal concluded in *Erjo Investments Ltd. v. Michener Allen Auctioneering Ltd.* (2004), 241 Sask. R. 228, that a writ delivered to the sheriff (but not registered) did not have priority over a subsequent perfected security interest in the judgment debtor's property. It concluded that s. 2.2 of *The Executions Act* does not apply to determine priorities where the writ of execution is not registered.
48   R.S.N.W.T. 1988, c. s-5, s. 3.

4) Future Advances and the Position of Unsecured Creditors

The PPSA provides for "tacking" of advances made by a secured party to a debtor or third party.[49] The effects of these provisions is to give the same priority status to all advances[50] made pursuant to a security agreement even though they may be made after an intervening perfected security interest has been acquired in the collateral.[51]

However, the Acts do not treat the intervening interests of unsecured creditors in the same way. The PPSAs, other than the OPPSA, provide that advances made by a secured party after it acquires knowledge[52] that the collateral has been seized to enforce a judgment cannot be tacked.[53] The effect of this is to preclude a secured party from knowingly reducing or eliminating the priority effect of judgment enforcement measures on the residual value of the collateral. A secured party can tack future advances made pursuant to a statutory requirement or a legally binding obligation owing to a person other than the debtor entered into by the secured party before it acquired knowledge that the collateral was seized.[54] It may also tack reasonable costs and expenses incurred by the secured party for the protection, preservation, maintenance, or repair of the collateral.[55]

Under the Ontario Act,[56] a secured party can knowingly tack against an intervening judgment creditor advances that the secured party is

---

49   PPSA (A, BC, M, NB, NWT, Nu, S) s. 35(6); (NL, NS) s. 36(6); O s. 30(3)–(4); PEI s. 35(5); Y s. 34(4).
50   The wording of OPPSA s. 30(3) is somewhat obscure. It provides that where future advances are made under a perfected security interest, "the security interest has the same priority with respect to each future advance as it has with respect to the first advance." There is nothing in the Act that states specifically what priority is given to the first advance. Priority dates from the date a perfection step has been taken or deemed perfection begins, not from the date an advance has been made.
51   PPSA (A, BC, M, NB, PEI, NWT, Nu, S) s. 35(5); (NL, NS) s. 36(5); O s. 30(3); Y s. 34(4).
52   As to what constitutes "knowledge," see PPSA (A, BC, NWT, Nu) s. 1(2); (M, NB, PEI) s. 2(1); (NL, NS) s. 3(1) (c); S s. 2(2); O s. 69; Y no equivalent provision.
53   PPSA (A, BC, M, NB, NWT, Nu, S) s. 35(6); (NL, NS) s. 36(6); PEI s. 35(9); Y no equivalent provision.
54   In such cases, the secured party is released from any obligation it may have undertaken to the debtor to make the future advances. PPSA (A, BC, MB, NB, NWT, Nu, PEI) s. 13(2); (NL, NS) s. 15(2); S s. 14(2); Y 13(2); O no equivalent provision.
55   Above note 53 and OPPSA s. 30(4).
56   OPPSA s. 30(4)(b).

"bound" to make even though, upon default by the debtor (including, presumably, seizure of the collateral under judgment enforcement process) the secured party is released from the obligation.

The Alberta Act[57] provides that the tacking priority given to secured parties applies to advances made before the secured party acquires knowledge of a writ of enforcement[58] within the meaning of section 32 of the *Civil Enforcement Act,*[59] advances made pursuant to a statutory requirement or a legally binding obligation owing to a person other than the debtor entered into by the secured party before it acquired knowledge that the collateral was seized, and reasonable costs and expenses incurred by the secured party for the protection, preservation, maintenance, or repair of the collateral. A very similar approach is contained in the PPSAs of the Atlantic provinces. Tacking gives priority to secured parties over judgment enforcement creditors to the extent that the advances are made prior to the time the secured party acquires knowledge that a judgment has been registered in the Personal Property Registry.[60] The same exceptions with respect to binding obligations and collateral preservation costs are recognized.

B. PRIORITY COMPETITIONS WITH NON-CONSENSUAL SECURITY INTERESTS

A property interest most often arises out of an agreement under which one party agrees to transfer an interest in the property to another. This transfer may be absolute, as in the case of a sale, or it may involve a transfer of a more limited right, as in the case of a security interest. However, there are other events that can create property rights. These are commonly grouped under the category of property rights arising by operation of law. Property interests that are created by statute or recognized by the common law or equity and that secure payment or performance of an obligation are referred to in this book as non-consensual security interests.

A security interest that is governed by the PPSA will often come into competition with a non-consensual security interest. Non-con-

---

57   A s. 35(5).
58   This requires actual knowledge. The registration of the writ of enforcement in the Personal Property Registry is not sufficient.
59   Above note 30, s. 33(2).
60   PPSA (NL, NS) s. 36(6); NB s. 35(6); PEI s. 35(9)

sensual security interests do not fall within the scope of the PPSA.[61] The priority rules of the PPSA that govern disputes between competing security interests therefore do not apply, as these rules only apply where both of the security interests are governed by the Act. The only exception is the priority rule provided by the PPSA to resolve a priority competition between a security interest and commercial liens. This does not provide a comprehensive priority rule, because liens are only one of a number of different non-consensual security devices, and in any event the provision does not even apply to all categories of liens. It is therefore necessary to look to non-PPSA priority rules and principles to resolve such disputes.

One of the difficulties with this area is that non-consensual security interests originate from several different sources of law. Some are created by statute, others by the common law or equity. There are liens, rights of distress, statutory security interests, deemed statutory trusts, and statutory rights of attachment. There are literally hundreds of non-consensual security interests that have been created by statute in Canada, and there is a wide variation in drafting in the provisions that create them. The area is further complicated by the fact that federal bankruptcy legislation has a profound effect on the resolution of priority competitions involving non-consensual security interests, and the outcome is therefore frequently different depending upon whether or not the debtor is bankrupt. It is accordingly not possible to describe the priority status of every non-consensual security interest. Instead, in the discussion that follows, the authors have provided a brief description of the different types of non-consensual security interests and an examination of the rules and principles that should be applied in resolving a priority competition between a PPSA security interest and a non-consensual security interest. The effect of the bankruptcy of the debtor on the outcome of priority competitions is also examined.[62]

---

61 PPSA (A, BC, M, NB, O, S) s. 4; (NWT, Nu, Y) s. 3; (NL, NS) s. 5. The Ontario formulation is narrower in that it only refers to a lien whereas the other Acts exclude a lien, charge, or other interest given by statute or rule of law. However, there is an even more basic reason why non-consensual security interests fall outside the scope of the Acts. The Acts clearly contemplate that the security interest is created by a security agreement, and this condition is not satisfied in the case of non-consensual security interests. See the definitions of "security agreement" and "security interest" in PPSA (A, BC, NWT, Nu, O, Y) s. 1(1); (M, NB, PEI) s. 1; (NL, NS) s. 2; S s. 2(1).

62 For a more in-depth examination of this topic, see R. Wood and M. Wylie, "Non-consensual Security Interests in Personal Property" (1992) 30 Alta. L. Rev. 1055.

1) Taxonomy of Non-consensual Security Interests

a) Liens
At common law, certain claimants were recognized as having a right to retain goods until a debt or other claim was paid. There are three major classes of common law liens. First, there are liens that were conferred upon persons carrying on a common calling who were required by law to provide goods or services to those willing to pay for them. The lien of the common carrier and the innkeeper's lien fell within this class. Second, there were liens in favour of those who improved goods. The artificer's lien fell within this class. Finally, there were liens of arising by general usage of trade. The solicitor's lien and the stockbroker's lien fell within this class.[63] The common law liens were passive in nature. They permitted the lien-holder to withhold delivery until payment, but did not give the lien-holder the right to sell the property to recover the debt.[64] A right to resell the goods was subsequently created by legislation in respect of most categories of liens. Equitable liens were also available under certain circumstances. For example, a trustee was entitled to a lien on the trust property to secure reimbursement of money expended in carrying out the trust.

Many other kinds of liens have been created by statute. Persons who stored goods of others were not entitled to claim a lien at common law. Statutory liens were created in favour of warehouse keepers and other bailees.[65] Like the common law liens, these liens were possessory and the right to claim the lien was lost if the lien-holder surrendered possession of the property. Jurisdictions also began to create non-possessory liens that could be claimed even though the lien claimant did not have possession of the property. Several provinces have enacted garage keeper's lien statutes that create a non-possessory lien in favour of motor vehicle repairers. Ontario has enacted legislation that covers repairers and storers and that permits the creation of non-possessory liens in respect of these claims.[66] Two jurisdictions have enacted the *Uniform Commercial Liens Act* that rationalizes many of the rules that

---

63 *Re London and Globe Finance Corp.*, [1902] 2 Ch. 416; *Ex parte Sterling* (1809), 16 Ves. 258, 33 E.R. 982.

64 By way of exception, liens that arose out of general trade usage could give the lien-holder a right of resale if the usage of trade accepted this practice. See *Jones v. Davidson Partners Ltd.* (1981), 1 P.P.S.A.C. 242 (Ont. H.C.J.) (right of resale available in respect of stockbroker's lien).

65 Most jurisdictions have enacted the *Uniform Warehousemen's Lien Act* of the Uniform Law Conference of Canada.

66 *Repair and Storage Liens Act*, R.S.O. 1990, c. R.25.

apply to many different types of liens and also broadens the availability of non-possessory liens.[67] Registration is required in order to protect the non-possessory lien.

b) Rights of Distress

At common law, a landlord was given a right to take possession of goods located on the leased premises in order to secure payment of unpaid rent. A right to resell the goods was conferred upon the landlord by statute.[68] There are several limitations on the exercise of the right of distress. The right is an alternative remedy to that of forfeiture of the lease. As well, there are certain restrictions on the kinds of goods covered by the right of distress. Goods that are *in cusodia legis* (in the custody of the law) cannot be distrained.[69]

c) Statutory Security Interests and Charges

Several statutes create a statutory security interest or charge in favour of a claimant. The statutory security interest is typically non-possessory in nature and secures claims that are owing to governmental or quasi-governmental bodies. In some jurisdictions it is used to secure claims owing to unpaid workers or assessments that are owing to workers' compensation boards. The statutes typically do not require that the statutory security interest be registered in the personal property registry.

d) Statutory Deemed Trusts

Several statutes also use the concept of a trust in order to secure an obligation owing to certain claimants. This device is frequently used in connection with taxation statutes where the recipient has collected provincial sales tax and in respect of source deductions, such as income tax and employment insurance and Canada Pension Plan contributions, withheld from an employee by the employer. If the statute simply provides that the recipient is deemed to hold the funds in trust, the provision will not be effective if the funds are not kept separate

---

67   *The Commercial Liens Act*, S.S. 2001, c. C-15.1; *Liens Act*, S.N.S. 2001, c. 33 (not yet proclaimed) and see R. Cuming, "The Spreading Influence of PPSA Concepts: the *Uniform Liens Act*" (1999) 15 B.F.L.R. 1.

68   *Distress for Rent Act, 1689*, 2 W & M, c. 14.

69   *Melton Real Estate Ltd.* v. *National Arts Services Corp. Ltd.* (1977), 2 Alta. L.R. (2d) 180 (Dist. Ct.). Many jurisdictions provide a set of exemptions in relation to the right of distress. See, for example, *Civil Enforcement Act*, above note 30, s. 104(d).

and cannot be traced.[70] For this reason, many deemed statutory trust provisions now provide that the recipient is deemed to keep the money separate and apart, whether or not it has actually been kept separate and apart. Despite this language, the juridical nature of the interest is that of a charge rather than a trust. The recipient does not hold all of the assets on behalf of the claimant, and therefore it is misleading to refer to the claimant's interest as that of a trust beneficiary. In reality, the recipient's assets are subject to a charge that secures the unremitted amounts that were collected or withheld.

e)   Statutory Rights of Attachment of Debts

Some statutes provide a statutory attachment remedy. This permits the claimant to notify third persons who owe money to the debtor and demand that the money be paid to the claimant rather than to the debtor. The device creates a form of statutory garnishment. Without more, the legislation will not be interpreted as creating a proprietary right in the accounts owing to the debtor.[71] The situation is different if the device has been enhanced through the inclusion of a provision to the effect that the claimant obtains a property right to the debt upon notice being given to the third party. This type of provision is effective to create a non-consensual security interest in the debt owed by the third party.[72]

f)   Procedural Devices

Some statutes provide procedural devices in favour of specified claimants. The claimant may be given a statutory preference over other creditors. Without more, this does not operate as a non-consensual security interest and will only give the claimant preference over unsecured creditors.[73] Some statutes provide that upon filing a certificate with the clerk of the court, a claimant is deemed to have a judgment. This does not create a non-consensual security interest, but merely gives the claimant the procedural advantage of being able to commence judgment enforcement proceedings without having commenced an action or obtained a judgment.

---

70   *Dauphin Plains Credit Union Ltd.* v. *Xyloid Industries Ltd.*, [1980] 1 S.C.R. 1182.
71   *Royal Bank of Canada v. Canada (Attorney General)* (1978), 105 D.L.R. (3d) 648 (Alta. S.C.A.D.); *Re Zurich Insurance Co. & Troy Woodworking Ltd.* (1984), 6 D.L.R. (4th) 552 (Ont. C.A.).
72   *Canada Trustco Mortgage Corp.* v. *Port O'Call Hotel Inc.*, [1996] 1 S.C.R. 963.
73   *Alberta (Attorney General)* v. *Alberta (Board of Industrial Relations)*, [1976] 1 W.W.R. 756 (Alta. S.C.T.D.).

2) The Resolution of Priority Competitions

a) Determining the Legal Parameters of the Non-consensual Security Interest

Before resolving a priority competition between a PPSA security interest and a non-consensual security interest, it is necessary to consider the legal parameters of the non-consensual security interest. In particular, it is important to determine the rules that define the nature and extent of the interest. Since there is not a single source of law that governs non-consensual security interests, these rules will differ depending upon the type of interest involved.

It is first necessary to identify the property that is subject to the non-consensual security interest. If the non-consensual security interest is created by statute, the property will be identified in the statute. If the non-consensual security interest is not statutory in origin, one must look to the common law rule. For example, a landlord's right of distress can be exercised only in relation to goods located on the leased premises unless the goods have been fraudulently removed. Second, it is necessary to determine the obligation that is secured by the non-consensual security interest. For example, the common law possessory lien of a repairer only secures claims for labour or services connected with the goods. If the goods are returned to the customer and later brought back to the repairer for further repairs, the lien can only be claimed in respect of the second obligation.[74] Third, one must determine if there are any formal requirements that must be satisfied. For example, the Ontario *Repair and Storage Liens Act*[75] provides that the non-possesory lien recognized by that Act is not enforceable unless the debtor has signed a written acknowledgment of indebtedness. Fourth, it must be determined if there are any perfection requirements, such as possession or registration, that must be satisfied. Finally, because the resolution of the priority competition may depend on the order of creation, it may be necessary to determine the precise point in time when the non-consensual security interest attaches to the property.

b) Priority Rules Contained in the PPSA

The PPSA does not adopt a comprehensive approach to the resolution of a priority competition between a non-consensual security interest and a PPSA security interest. The Act provides a priority rule — examined

---

74 *Senft v. Bank of Montreal* (1986), 69 A.R. 35 (Q.B.).
75 Above note 66, s. 7(5). A similar requirement is found in provinces that have enacted garage keeper's lien legislation.

immediately in the section that follows — that covers competitions with certain kinds of liens, but does not purport to resolve priority competitions with other kinds of interests. There is also a significant difference between the Ontario Act and the other Acts with respect to the effect of non-perfection of a PPSA security interest in a priority competition with a non-consensual lien.

i) Commercial Liens on Goods

The PPSA provides that where a person in the ordinary course of business furnishes materials or services with respect to goods, any lien conferred upon that person will have priority over a competing security interest.[76] There are a number of limitations contained in this provision. It only applies to goods, and not to liens on other forms of property such as securities. It only applies to commercial liens where the lien-holder is in the business of supplying materials or services.[77] And it only applies to liens that secure charges relating to the materials or services as opposed to some other obligation. Unlike the common law, the Act does not draw a distinction between work that maintains the goods and work that enhances its value. Therefore, the PPSA priority rule extends beyond repair liens to storage liens and stable keepers' liens. The provision does not apply to the lien of an innkeeper, because the services that are provided are not connected to the goods against which the lien is claimed.[78]

The PPSA priority rule contains a further limitation. If the lien is created by statute, which provides that the lien does not have priority, the priority provision contained in that statute will govern. The Ontario *Repair and Storage Liens Act*,[79] as well as the garage keeper's legislation in effect in certain other provinces, provide an example of such a provision. These statutes provide that a security interest that

---

76   PPSA (A, BC, M, NB, NWT, Nu, PEI) s. 32; (NL, NS) s. 33; (O, Y) s. 31.
77   The fact that the services that give rise to the lien are only a small percentage of the overall volume is not determinative. The test is whether the provision of such services was an ordinary aspect of the lien claimants business. See *Craddock Trucking Ltd. v. Leclair* (1995), 28 Alta. L.R. (3d) 145 (Q.B.).
78   Despite the non-application of this priority rule, the innkeeper's lien would nevertheless be entitled to priority over a prior security interest. At common law, the innkeeper's lien could be exercised against all property brought into the inn by the guest, even if it is not owned by the guest. See *Bank of Montreal v. 414031 Ontario Ltd.* (1983), 2 P.P.S.A.C. 248 (Ont. Dist. Ct.).
79   Above note 66, s. 10(1).

arises after the lien is created but before it is registered has priority over the lien.[80]

ii) Effect of Non-perfection of the Security Interest

The Ontario PPSA provides that an unperfected security interest is subordinate to a person who has a lien given under any other Act or by a rule of law.[81] The provision does not apply to other forms of non-consensual security interests. The Ontario Court of Appeal has concluded that although a right of distress is not a lien, it becomes a lien when the landlord takes possession of the goods.[82] This ruling gives an Ontario landlord priority over an unperfected security interest in the form of a conditional sales agreement.[83] The Ontario Act contains a further provision that identifies the time when the rights of a lien-holder arise.[84] If the debtor is bankrupt, they arise at the effective date of the bankruptcy. In non-bankruptcy cases, they arise when the lien-holder has taken possession or has otherwise done everything needed to make the lien enforceable.

The Acts of the other jurisdictions provide that an unperfected security interest is subordinate to the interest of a transferee for value without knowledge. The language of the relevant provisions indicates that this priority rule is restricted to consensual transfers and therefore does not extend to non-consensual security interests. In many cases, the priority competition is instead governed by legislative provision outside of the PPSA. For example, in some jurisdictions a purchase money security interest is given priority over a landlord's right of distress provided that the security interest is perfected.[85] In other jurisdictions, the legislation does not require that the purchase money security interest be perfected in order to enjoy such priority.[86] The difference may perhaps be attrib-

---

80 *Repairer's Lien Act*, R.S.B.C. 1996, c. 404, s. 10(b); *Garage Keeper's Lien Act*, R.S.A. 2000, c. G-2, s. 4.

81 OPPSA, s. 20(1)(a)(i).

82 *Commercial Credit Corp. Ltd. v. Harry D. Shields Ltd.* (1980), 29 O.R. (2d) 106 (H.C.J.), aff'd 32 O.R. (2d) 703 (C.A.).

83 Under the *Commercial Tenancies Act*, R.S.O. 1990, s. L-7, s. 31(2) the right of distress has priority over security interests other than conditional sales agreements. Section 20(1)(a)(i) qualifies this by requiring that the conditional sales agreement be perfected.

84 OPPSA, s. 20(2)(a).

85 See, for example, *Rent Distress Act*, R.S.B.C. 1996, c. 403, s. 3(4); *Landlord and Tenant Act*, C.C.S.M., c. L70, s. 37(b).

86 See, for example, *Civil Enforcement Act*, above note 30, s. 104; *Landlord and Tenant Act*, R.S.S. 1978, c.L-6, s. 25, am. S.S. 1979-80, c. 28, ss. 3–4; 1982–83, c. 16, s. 31; 2001, c. 50, s. 9. Courts have indicated that they are unwilling to read

uted to differing views on whether or not a landlord will generally search the registry before exercising the right of distress.

c)   Other Legislative and Common Law Priority Rules

Often a statute that creates a non-consensual security interest will provide a priority rule to govern a competition between a security interest and a non-consensual security interest. When the non-consensual security interest is in favour of the Crown or a quasi-governmental body, it is common to find provisions that purport to give the interest priority over competing security interests. Courts have often adopted a strict interpretation of these provisions. The Supreme Court of Canada decision in *Homeplan Realty Ltd. v. Avco Financial Realty Services Ltd.*[87] is the most frequently cited case on this point. The Court stated that the legislation "should not be construed in a manner that could deprive third parties of their pre-existing property rights." The legislation at issue in that case provided that a non-consensual security interest in favour of employees for unpaid wages was payable "in priority over any other claim or right" and that "such priority shall extend over every assignment, including an assignment of book debts, whether absolute or otherwise, every mortgage of real or personal property, and every debenture."[88]

The Court held that the provision was ambiguous in that there was uncertainty about the identity of the property that was subject to the lien. The statute did not make it clear whether the lien and charge was upon the property of the employer only or if it was upon all property in which the employer held an interest. If the lien only attached to the property of the employer, it would only cover the employer's interest in the property after the prior security interest had been satisfied. If it covered any property in which the employer had an interest, the lien would attach not only to the employer's interest, but also to a pre-existing property interest held by a prior third party. The Court resolved the ambiguity in favour of the pre-existing property interest and therefore gave priority to the prior security interest. The result of this approach is a presumption that, unless the legislation is very clear on the point, the statutory charge was intended by the legislature to affect only the property of the person against whom the Crown claim is made and not the property of others.

---

into a statute a perfection requirement that the security interest be perfected. See *British Columbia v. PT Car and Yacht Rental Inc.* (2003), 5 P.P.S.A.C. (3d) 332 (B.C.S.C.).

87   [1979] 2 S.C.R. 699.

88   *Payment of Wages Act*, S.B.C. 1962, c. 45, as am. by S.B.C. 1973, c. 68.

The deemed statutory trust in respect of federal source deductions required to be made under the *Income Tax Act* gives the Crown's claim priority over prior competing interests. The statute provides that the deemed trust is imposed on the debtor's property as well as the property of any secured creditor.[89] This gives the deemed trust priority over a security interest. The Act defines security interest as "any interest in property that secures payment or performance of an obligation and includes an interest created by or arising out of a debenture, mortgage, lien, pledge, charge, deemed or actual trust, assignment or encumbrance."[90] Courts have held that this definition does not include leases or conditional sales agreements.[91] As a result, these transactions would take priority over the statutory deemed trust.

d) Order of Attachment

If a statute that creates a non-consensual security interest provides a priority rule, that provision will govern. In the absence of such a provision, a priority competition will be governed by the order of creation of the interests. Although this might appear to be a simple application of traditional property law concepts, it is not so. A simple deemed statutory trust would ordinarily create only an equitable interest in the property and would therefore be liable to be defeated by a person who acquires a legal interest for value and without knowledge. The courts have not purported to draw a distinction between legal and equitable interests, but have simply resolved priorities on the basis of a first-in-time rule.[92]

In the past, the first-in-time rule had to deal with the effect of the floating charge. For the purpose of determining the time of creation of the security interest, the courts looked to the time of crystallization of the charge. The concept of the floating charge has no counterpart under the PPSA.[93] A security interest in all present and after-acquired personal property attaches to the collateral when the ordinary requirements for attachment have been satisfied. This will generally mean that the security interest attaches to the collateral at a much earlier point than was the case under the prior law.

---

89 *Income Tax Act*, R.S.C. 1985, c. 1. (5th Supp.), s. 227(4.1).

90 Ibid., s. 224(1.3).

91 See *DaimlerChrysler Financial Services (Debis) Canada Inc. v. Mega Pets Ltd.* (2002), 212 D.L.R. (4th) 41 (B.C.C.A.); *Canada (Deputy Attorney General) v. Schwab Construction Ltd.*, [2002] 4 W.W.R. 628 (Sask. C.A.).

92 *Dauphin Plains Credit Union Ltd. v. Xyloid Industries Ltd.*, above note 70; *Royal Bank of Canada v. Sparrow Electric Corp.*, [1997] 1 S.C.R. 411.

93 See *Royal Bank of Canada v. Sparrow Electric Corp., ibid.*

3) The Effect of Bankruptcy on Priorities

Upon the occurrence of a bankruptcy, unsecured creditors lose their ability to recover their claims through the provincial judgment enforcement system, and must instead prove their claims through the federal bankruptcy process. Secured creditors are not so restricted. Subject to a few minor limitations, they can exercise their remedies against their collateral.[94] The definition of a secured creditor in the *Bankruptcy and Insolvency Act*[95] is not limited to consensual security interests, but extends to liens as well.[96] These parties will be largely unaffected by the bankruptcy. They are entitled to enforce their claims against the property subject to the non-consensual security interest outside of the bankruptcy system, and their priority status *vis-à-vis* competing parties who hold PPSA security interests will be unaffected by the bankruptcy. Thus, in a competition between a repairer who claims a possessory lien on goods and a secured party who has a PPSA security interest in the goods, the priority will be the same whether or not the debtor has gone into bankruptcy.[97]

There are, however, three situations where the resolution of priorities between a non-consensual security interest and a PPSA security interest will be different upon the occurrence of bankruptcy. In each of these situations, the bankruptcy triggers an inversion of priorities. Although the non-consensual security interest has priority outside of bankruptcy, it is subordinated to the PPSA security interest once the bankruptcy takes effect.

a) Crown Claims

Section 86(1) of the *Bankruptcy and Insolvency Act* establishes the general rule that in relation to a bankruptcy or a proposal, all Crown claims[98] and claims of workers' compensation bodies rank as unsecured claims. For convenience of discussion, reference will be made only to Crown claims, but the same analysis applies to claims of workers' compen-

---

94   *Bankruptcy and Insolvency Act,* R.S.C. 1985, c. B-3, s. 69.3(2) [BIA].

95   *Ibid.,* s. 2.

96   *Re Victoria Bed and Mattress Co.* (1960), 24 D.L.R. (2d) 414 (B.C.S.C.).

97   The claimant must be careful not to file a proof of claim in bankruptcy for the full amount, as this may be taken to be a waiver of the non-consensual security interest. See *Re Canadian Exotic Cattle Breeders' Co-Operative* (1979), 14 B.C.L.R. 183 (S.C.).

98   See *Re Richmac Interiors Ltd.* (1994), 25 C.B.R. (3d) 31 (Alta. Q.B.) for a discussion of the test for determining which agencies will be considered to be agents of the Crown.

sation bodies. Any non-consensual security interest that is created in favour of the Crown is rendered inoperative in bankruptcy. The statute recognizes three exceptions to this rule. First, the provision does not apply if the security interest is one that is generally available to other persons besides the Crown.[99] For example, if the debtor gives the crown agency an ordinary PPSA security interest, the security interest will remain effective in bankruptcy. Second, the provision does not apply to the statutory attachment remedy created in favour of the federal Crown in respect of income tax or contributions in respect of employment insurance or the Canada Pension Plan or any provincial income tax or comprehensive provincial pension plan.[100] Third, the non-consensual security interest will escape relegation to the status of a mere unsecured claim if it is registered.[101]

Section 87 of the *Bankruptcy and Insolvency Act* sets out the conditions that must be satisfied before the interest will be considered registered for the purposes of this provision. The interest must be registered before the date of the assignment in the case of a voluntary bankruptcy or the date of the petition for a receiving order in the case of an involuntary bankruptcy.[102] In the case of a commercial proposal, the interest must be registered at the date of filing of the proposal or the date of the filing of a notice of intention to file a proposal.[103]

Section 87(2)(a) of the *Bankruptcy and Insolvency Act* provides a priority rule in respect of a competition between a registered Crown interest and a consensual security interest. It provides that the Crown claim is subordinate to "securities in respect of which all steps necessary to make them effective against other creditors were taken before that registration." Presumably this refers to perfection of a security interest under the PPSA, since this represents the point when a security interest will become effective against judgment enforcement creditors and the trustee in bankruptcy of the debtor. The operation of the provision is illustrated in the following scenario.

---

99 BIA, s. 86(2)(a).

100 BIA, s. 86(3).

101 The *Bankruptcy and Insolvency General Rules*, C.R.C. 368, s. 111 provides that a "prescribed system of registration" referred to in section 86(2) "is a system of registration of securities that is available to Her Majesty in right of Canada or a province and to any other creditor holding a security, and is open to the public for inspection or for the making of searches." This clearly encompasses the Personal Property Security Registry.

102 BIA, s. 87(1)(a), (b).

103 BIA, s. 87(1)(c), (d).

SP registers a financing statement covering all of D's present and after-acquired personal property on March 1. SP and D do not at this time enter into a written security agreement. The Crown registers a claim on March 10. On March 15, D signs a written security agreement that gives SP a security interest in D's assets and SP advances funds to D.

The priority provision in section 87(2)(a) would not operate to give SP priority over the Crown claimant since SP had not perfected its security interest at the time of registration of the Crown claim. Section 87(2)(a) would not appear to give a secured party priority in respect of property acquired by the debtor after registration of the Crown claim.[104] At the time of registration of the Crown claim, the secured party would not have an attached or perfected security interest in such property. All steps necessary to make the security interest effective (that is, perfection of the security interest) would not have been completed until the security agreement was signed. Even if a written security agreement had been obtained in advance of the Crown's registration, the priority provision would not operate in respect of collateral that was acquired by the debtor after registration of the Crown's claim. Because the security interest in the asset would have neither attached nor have been perfected at the time of registration of the Crown's claim, the secured party would be unable to obtain the benefit of section 87(2)(a).

Section 87(2)(b) provides that registration of a Crown claim is valid only in respect of amounts that are owing to the Crown at the date of registration. This effectively prevents the Crown from pre-registering its non-consensual security interest in order to obtain priority. Moreover, successive registrations will be necessary as new arrears arise. Since the assets of the debtor will usually be already subject to registered security interests in favour of consensual secured creditors at the time the Crown debt arises, this provision typically confers priority to the secured party over the Crown claim.

b) Deemed Statutory Trusts

Section 67(1)(a) of the *Bankruptcy and Insolvency Act* provides that "property held by the bankrupt in trust for any other person" is not divisible among the bankrupt's creditors.

---

104 The Personal Property Security Regulations in Alberta, Manitoba and British Columbia all provide for registration of Crown claims in the Personal Property Registry.

The Supreme Court of Canada in *British Columbia v. Henfrey Samson Belair Ltd.*[105] held that section 67(1)(a) did not apply to statutory deemed trusts that lack the common law attributes of a trust. The statutory deemed trust failed to meet the requirement of a valid trust that the property be kept separate and apart and not commingled with the bankrupt's own property. McLachlin J., for the majority, thought that to allow the operation of provincially created trusts that deviated from these requirements would enable provinces "to create their own priorities under the *Bankruptcy Act* and to invite a differential scheme of distribution on bankruptcy from province to province."[106] In the vast majority of cases, it will be impossible to trace the deemed trust into specific property of the debtor, and the deemed trust will therefore not be effective in the bankruptcy of the debtor.

The *Bankruptcy and Insolvency Act* was amended in 1997 by the addition of section 67(2), which provides that a deemed statutory trust in favour of the Crown shall not be considered to be held in trust for the purpose of paragraph 67(1)(a) unless it would be so regarded in the absence of that statutory provision. Section 67(2) only applies to property that is deemed to be held in trust for the Crown. This does not completely displace the judicially created rule. A statutory deemed trust created by employment standards legislation deems the property to be held in trust for unpaid employees rather than the Crown. Its validity will therefore continue to be governed by the principles set out in *British Columbia v. Henfrey Samson Belair Ltd.* rather than by section 67(2).

Section 67(3) provides a significant exception to the rule that renders ineffective deemed statutory trusts in bankruptcy. Amounts that are deemed to be held in trust under the *Income Tax Act*, the *Employment Insurance Act*, and the Canada Pension Plan, as well as any equivalent provision covering provincial income tax or comprehensive pension legislation, are excepted from the application of section 67(2). Thus, the deemed statutory trusts that protect the major source deductions that are required to be deducted from the salary and wages of employees are effective in bankruptcy.

c) Preferred Claims

The third situation where the priority status of a non-consensual security interest is not recognized in a bankruptcy concerns claims that are designated as preferred claims under section 136 of the *Bankruptcy*

---

105 [1989] 2 S.C.R. 24.
106 *Ibid.* at 33.

and Insolvency Act. Certain classes of claims are given the status of preferred claims. These are entitled to be paid in full before any funds are distributed to the unsecured creditors on a *pro rata* basis. Section 136(1)(d) provides that a claim for unpaid compensation for work rendered in the six months immediately preceding the bankruptcy are preferred to the extent of $2,000. Section 136(1)(e) covers municipal taxes that do not constitute a preferential lien or charge against the real property in respect of which the taxes are assessed. Section 136(1)(f) covers a landlord's right of distress for unpaid rent. In each of these instances, these claims are also typically secured by non-consensual security interests governed by provincial law. In many cases, the provincial law also gives the non-consensual security interest priority over a competing security interest.

The Supreme Court of Canada in a series of decisions held that the designation of a claim as a preferred claim in federal bankruptcy legislation precludes the claimant from taking advantage of any provincial law that attempts to give it a higher priority status. The Supreme Court of Canada in *Workers' Compensation Board v. Husky Oil Operators Ltd.*[107] stated that although bankruptcy law necessarily calls upon provincial law for its operation, "provincial law simply cannot apply when to do so would entail subverting the federal order of priorities in the *Bankruptcy Act.*"[108] Upon bankruptcy, these claimants lose the priority they would otherwise enjoy over a competing secured creditor. Instead, they can only claim as a preferred creditor in the bankruptcy.

d) The Use of Bankruptcy to Invert Priorities

It is not uncommon for a secured party to induce a bankruptcy for the sole purpose of enhancing its priority position. This raises two questions. The first has to do with the legal effect of the bankruptcy on the non-consensual security interest. Does the bankruptcy destroy the interest, or does it merely prevent the claimant from asserting it against the trustee in bankruptcy? If the interest is destroyed, the competing secured creditor will be able to assert its claim against the property free of the claim. Bankruptcy will therefore result in an enhancement of the secured creditor's priority. If the interest is merely rendered ineffective against the trustee in bankruptcy rather than destroyed, the outcome is quite different. The trustee in bankruptcy has a representative capacity that permits the trustee to acquire the rights held by the creditors who participate in the bankruptcy. On this view, the benefit of the

107 [1995] 3 S.C.R. 453.
108 *Ibid.* at 506.

non-consensual security interest accrues to the trustee in bankruptcy. The priority that would have been enjoyed by the claimant who holds the non-consensual security interest is turned over to the trustee in bankruptcy. This would not result in an enhancement of the secured creditor's priority. The funds would be turned over to the trustee on bankruptcy, who would then distribute them in accordance with the scheme of distribution set out in the bankruptcy legislation.

The cases that have considered the matter have all dealt with non-consensual security interests that fall within the class of preferred claims set out in the bankruptcy legislation. The leading case is that of the British Columbia Court of Appeal in *Bank of Montreal v. Titan Landco Inc.*[109] The court considered these two alternative views and held that the weight of the authorities favour the proposition that the non-consensual security interest ceases to have any force and effect upon bankruptcy. The wording of the new legislative provisions dealing with deemed statutory trusts[110] and Crown claims also suggests that the intention was that the non-consensual security interest is destroyed upon the occurrence of the bankruptcy.

The second issue concerns the question whether it is legitimate for a secured creditor to petition a debtor into bankruptcy for the sole purpose of destroying the superior priority status of a claimant who has a non-consensual security interest that would otherwise have priority over the secured creditor. Although expressing misgivings about this practice, the British Columbia Court of Appeal in *Bank of Montreal v. Scott Road Enterprises Ltd.* held that this does not amount to an improper purpose that would permit the court to exercise its discretion to refuse the granting of a receiving order.[111]

C. PRIORITY COMPETITIONS OVER TRUST PROPERTY

A competition may arise between a secured party and a beneficiary under an express, resulting or constructive trust. The PPSA does not contain any priority rules that govern this kind of competition unless the trust is in substance a security interest, in which case the competi-

---

109 (1990), 70 D.L.R. (4th) 1 (B.C.C.A.).
110 BIA, s. 67(2) and 86(1).
111 (1989), 73 C.B.R. (N.S.) 273 (B.C.C.A).

tion will be resolved through application of the PPSA priority rules that govern competitions between secured parties.[112]

1) Trust Property Acquired before the Creation of a Security Interest

A person who holds property in trust may subsequently grant a security interest in it to secure an obligation. If the transaction is unauthorized, the trustee will have acted in breach of the trust and the beneficiary will have a variety of potential remedies against the trustee.[113] However, the beneficiary may also assert a claim to the trust property in respect of which a security interest was granted to the secured party. The trustee holds legal title to the trust property, and thus has sufficient rights in the property to permit attachment of the security interest.[114] Both the beneficiary and the secured party claim competing interests in the same property, and it is therefore necessary to apply the appropriate priority rule to resolve this competition. The PPSA does not contain any express priority rules that govern the competition. In such a case, the PPSA directs that principles of the common law and equity continue to apply.[115] The competition will therefore be resolved through application of common law and equitable rules that generally govern competing claims to property.

It is the view of the authors that the competition should be resolved through use of the principle that a *bona fide* purchaser for value of a legal interest in the trust property acquires the property free of any trust obligations. Equity is willing to extend personal trust obligations to third parties who obtain legal title to the property, but will not do so if the person acquired the interest for value and without notice of the trust obligation.[116] A secured party therefore cannot escape the imposition of equitable obligations in respect of the trust property unless the secured party can bring itself within the *bona fide* purchase principle. In applying this rule, the old categories of security devices, such as the legal mortgage and equitable charge, should not be resurrected. Instead, a PPSA security interest should be characterized as a legal in-

---

112 See chapter 2, B.4 "Security Trusts."
113 See P. Birks and A. Pretto, eds., *Breach of Trust* (Oxford: Hart, 2002).
114 See chapter 4, C.2 "Exceptions to *Nemo Dat*."
115 PPSA (M, NWT, Nu, S) s. 65(2); A s. 66(3); BC s. 68(1); (NB, PEI) s. 65(1); (NL, NS) s. 66(1); O s. 72; Y s. 63(1).
116 See J. Penner, *The Law of Trusts*, 2d ed. (London: Butterworths, 2000) at 34.

terest, since the attributes of this form of proprietary interest are now defined by legislation.[117]

2) Trust Property Acquired after the Creation of a Security Interest

A priority competition may arise between a prior secured party and a subsequent trust beneficiary. The resolution of the priority competition is straightforward where the debtor creates an express trust in relation to property that is already subject to a PPSA security interest. The security interest is a legal interest, and by virtue of the *nemo dat* principle of the common law, it is entitled to priority over any subsequent interest.

The issue is more complex where the debtor agrees to give a secured party a security interest in after-acquired property and thereafter acquires property, falling within the description of the property in the security agreement, as trustee from another person. This may occur where a third party transfers property to the debtor in trust for a beneficiary. It may also occur where the debtor acquires property from a third party under circumstances in which a court would impose a resulting or constructive trust. One approach is to resolve the issue through the application of traditional property law principles. However, the characterization of a PPSA security interest as a legal interest now creates a potential difficulty. The secured party may attempt to claim the benefit of the *bona fide* purchaser rule on the basis that the after-acquired property provision has given it a legal interest in the subsequently acquired trust property. Under prior law, this type of priority competition could not arise. A promise to mortgage after-acquired property did not convey legal title to the property upon its acquisition by the debtor.[118] However, under the PPSA there is no longer any differ-

---

117 A similar transformation has occurred in other contexts. The common law did not give legal recognition to an assignment of an intangible, although it was recognized by equity. Legislation was passed which provided for the assignment of intangibles, and thereafter an assignment that conformed to the statute was considered to be a legal assignment. The equitable priority rules were still used for the resolution of priority competitions where a legal assignment was involved, but the reason for this was that the legislation expressly preserved these rules. See *E. Pfeiffer Weinkellerei-Weineinkauf G.m.b.H. v. Arbuthnot Factors Ltd.*, [1988] 1 W.L.R. 150 (Q.B.D.).

118 It would, however, be effective to convey the equitable interest in the property. See *Holroyd v. Marshall* (1862), 10 H.L.C. 191.

ence in characterization between a security interest in existing property and a security interest in after-acquired property.[119]

If the non-PPSA rule were to prevail, it would subordinate a trust beneficiary in circumstances where there has been no prejudice to the secured party. As the situation did not arise under prior law, it involves a novel point that requires judicial determination. Although the *bona fide* purchaser principle was originally conceived as "an inherent jurisdictional limitation upon a court of equity to entertain claims against those whose consciences were clean," the modern tendency is to explain the defence on the basis that it protects innocent parties from prejudice.[120] On this basis, the *bona fide* purchaser defence should be limited to cases where the legal interest in the trust property is subsequently created. If, however, the secured party makes a further advance without notice of the intervening equitable interest, a much stronger case can be made in favour of the secured party.[121]

FURTHER READINGS

BUCKWOLD, T.M., "From Sherwood Forest to Saskatchewan: The Role of the Sheriff in a Redesigned Judgment Enforcement System" (2003) 66 Sask. L.Rev. 219

CUMING, R.C.C., "The Spreading Influences of PPSA Concepts: The Uniform Liens Act" (1999) 15 B.F.L.R. 1

CUMING, R.C.C., "When an Unsecured Creditor is a Secured Creditor" (2003) 66 Sask. L. Rev. 255

WILLIAMSON, J.R. & C.P CURRAN, "Judgment Enforcement and the *Personal Property Security Act*: The Newfoundland Experience" (1999) U.N.B.L.J. 351.

WOOD, R.J. & M. WYLIE, "Non-Consensual Security Interests in Personal Property" (1992) 30 Alta. L.Rev. 1055

WOOD, R.J., "Enforcement Remedies of Creditors" (1996) 34 Alta. L. Rev. 783

---

119 See chapter 4, C.6 "After-acquired Collateral."
120 K. Barker, "Bona Fide Purchase as a Defence to Unjust Enrichment Claims: A Concise Restatement" [1997] R.L.R. 75 at 76.
121 See *Hopkinson v. Rolt* (1861), 9 H.L. Cas. 514.

THE EFFECTS OF BANKRUPTCY AND INSOLVENCY PROCEEDINGS ON SECURITY INTERESTS

A. INTRODUCTION

When a debtor defaults on his credit obligations, it is very common that a range of creditors' claims are affected. If bankruptcy or insolvency proceedings have been invoked either by the debtor or by one or more creditors, a regime different from that otherwise applicable to the regulation of the various claims comes into play. This regime draws on both federal bankruptcy and insolvency law and rules contained in the PPSA that expressly apply to insolvent or bankrupt debtors who have given security interests in their property. The most significant features of this regime are examined in this chapter.

However, the chapter has not been designed to be a comprehensive exposition of all features of bankruptcy and insolvency law that affect the position of secured creditors. Its intended role is to highlight issues that directly affect rights that arise in the context of the PPSA.

B. THE EFFECT OF BANKRUPTCY LAW ON THE RIGHTS OF SECURED CREDITORS

1) The Definition of Secured Creditor under the BIA

Prior to enactment of the PPSA, the appropriate characterization of interests created by the transfer or retention of title to secure loan or sale credit was conceptually problematic under the *Bankruptcy and Insolvency Act* (BIA).[1] At common law, the creditor is the owner of the goods until the contractual conditions are fulfilled. The adoption of a functional concept of security by the PPSA has resolved the characterization problem and the Supreme Court of Canada has now confirmed that the PPSA approach is to be used when interface issues between the PPSA and BIA are involved.[2] The very broad definition of secured creditor in the BIA[3] is subject to one significant exception. Sections 86

---

1   R.S.C. 1985, c. B-3 [BIA].
2   *Re Giffen* (1998), 155 D.L.R. (4th) 332 (S.C.C.), rev'g (1996), 16 B.C.L.R. (3d) 29 (C.A.). Until recently, the characterization problem remained alive in Quebec since the *Civil Code* treats retention or transfer of title as conceptually distinct from hypothecary security in the strict sense: compare *Re Giffen, ibid.*, with *Ouellet (Trustee of)*, [2004] 3 S.C.R. 348 and *Lefebvre (Trustee of); Tremblay (Trustee of)*, [2004] 3 S.C.R. 326. To resolve this uncertainty, the definition of "secured creditor" in section 2 of the BIA was amended to explicitly include title-based security arrangements arising under Quebec law. See below note 3 for the text of the expanded definition.
3   Secured creditor is defined in s. 2 of the BIA to mean

> a person holding a mortgage, hypothec, pledge, charge, or lien on or against the property of the debtor or any part of that property as security for a debt due or accruing due to the person from the debtor, or a person whose claim is based on, or secured by, a negotiable instrument held as collateral security and on which the debtor is only indirectly or secondarily liable, and includes: (*a*) a person who has a right of retention or a prior claim constituting a real right, within the meaning of the *Civil Code of Québec* or any other statute of the Province of Quebec, on or against the property of the debtor or any part of that property, or (*b*) any of
>
> (i)   the vendor of any property sold to the debtor under a conditional or instalment sale,
> (ii) the purchaser of any property from the debtor subject to a right of redemption, or
> (iii) the trustee of a trust constituted by the debtor to secure the performance of an obligation,
>
> if the exercise of the person's rights is subject to the provisions of Book Six of the *Civil Code of Québec* entitled *Prior Claims and Hypothecs* that deal with the exercise of hypothecary rights.

to 87 of the Act deny legal effect to provincial legislatures attempts and, to a much more limited extent, federal statutory provisions designed to give to Crown claims a first-ranking priority in bankruptcy, whether through the statutory creation of superpriority, non-consensual security or through a prior-ranking claim against the proceeds of disposition of a debtor's assets. Governmental claims, including the claims of publicly funded workers' compensation boards for unpaid assessments, are reduced to unsecured status unless secured by a conventional security interest of a type available to private creditors or unless they are registered in provincial registry. In the latter case, the claim is secured only to the amount owing at the date of registration.[4]

2) The Traditional Approach

From its inception, bankruptcy law has been viewed as a regime that does not directly affect the position of secured creditors of the bankrupt. The hands-off approach to security interests in bankrupts' property is highlighted in section 136 of the BIA. This section sets out the priority structure that must be applied by a trustee in bankruptcy when distributing the property of the bankrupt among the various claimants to it. All the priority rules set out in the section are made "subject to the rights of secured creditors." This approach is also evident in section 70(1) that states the effect of an assignment or receiving order in bankruptcy on the rights of creditors of the bankrupt. The "rights of secured creditors" are excepted from the precedence that bankruptcy has over the creditors' rights arising outside of bankruptcy. Section 71(2) vests the bankrupt's property in the trustee "subject to … the rights of secured creditors." Section 69.3, which stays enforcement of creditors' rights against a bankrupt, affects secured creditors, but only in very limited circumstances and for only a short period of time.

The Ontario Supreme Court has concluded that a secured creditor is not subject to section 81 of the BIA that requires a person who claims any interest in property in the possession of the bankrupt at the date of bankruptcy to file a proof of claim.[5] The result is that a secured creditor can seize collateral from a defaulting bankrupt debtor over the objections of the debtor's trustee. If this approach accurately reflects current

---

4   For a detailed discussion of the priority status of non-consensual security interests in bankruptcy proceedings (and the impact of this on the priority of consensual security interests), see chapter 10, B "Priority Competitions with Non-consensual Security Interests."

5   See *R. v. Ford Motor Credit Canada Ltd.* (1990), 78 C.B.R. (N.S.) 266 (Ont. H.C.J.).

law,[6] section 124 that provides that "a secured creditor shall prove his claim" is not binding on a secured creditor unless it intends to claim as an unsecured creditor for the unsecured portion of its claim.[7]

The BIA makes available to trustees a procedure through which the value of collateral in excess of the obligation owing to a secured creditor can be realized for the bankruptcy estate.[8] A secured creditor can force the trustee to elect between redeeming the collateral and accepting the secured creditor's valuation of it.[9]

However, the priority secured creditors have in bankruptcy may ultimately be subject to the doctrine of equitable subordination. The doctrine, which is a feature of United States bankruptcy law, can result in a secured party being treated as having an unsecured or subordinated claim in bankruptcy when it has engaged in some type of inequitable conduct that resulted in injury to creditors of the bankrupt or conferred an unfair advantage on the claimant. The doctrine enables a bankruptcy court, in exercise of its equitable powers, to subordinate the claims of one creditor to those of other creditors. Canadian courts have yet to recognize the doctrine as part of Canadian law.[10]

3) The Effect of Bankruptcy Law on the Priority Rights of Secured Creditors

The traditional hands-off approach of bankruptcy law is subject to qualifications. Security interests that are fraudulent preferences can be set aside under section 95 of the BIA. Section 81.1 provides that unpaid suppliers have the right to demand the return of goods delivered to buyers who become bankrupt or insolvent or are placed in receivership

---

6 However, this approach must be questioned in the light of the decision of the Supreme Court of Canada in *Re Giffen* above note 2 at 352 in which the Court accepted without question that a deemed secured creditor (lessor) holding an unperfected security interest is subject to BIA s. 81(2). This case is examined later in this chapter.

7 *Re Menard (sub nom. Shink v. Gingras)* (1962), 3 C.B.R. (N.S.) 309 (Que. C.S.).

8 BIA, ss. 128–29.

9 BIA, s. 130.

10 See *Canada Deposit Insurance Corp. v. Canadian Commercial Bank* (1992), 97 D.L.R. (4th) 385 (S.C.C.); *C.C. Petroleum Ltd. v. Allen* (2003), 46 C.B.R. (4th) 221 (Ont. C.A.), calling into question the lower court application of the doctrine in (2002), 35 C.B.R. (4th) 22 (Ont. S.C.J.); *Unisource Canada v. Laurentian Bank* (2000), 15 C.B.R. (4th) 315 (Ont. C.A.); *Olympia & York Developments Ltd. v. Royal Trust Co.* (1993), 103 D.L.R. (4th) 129 (Ont. C.A.). See also T.G.W. Telfer, "Transplanting Equitable Subordination: The New Free-Wheeling Equitable Discretion in Canadian Insolvency Law?" (2001) 36 Can. Bus. L.J. 36.

within thirty days after delivery. This right of recapture "ranks above every other claim or right against the purchaser in respect to those goods, other than a right of a bona fides subsequent purchaser of the goods for value without notice that the supplier had demanded repossession of the goods." In practice, the provision has limited effect on security interests in the goods supplied because the supplier's repossession rights are subject to procedural measures that few suppliers are aware of or are capable of timely performing. A companion provision, section 81.2, was designed to give protection to unpaid farmers, fishers, or aquaculturalists who supply perishable products to buyers who become bankrupt or are placed in receivership. The suppliers' claims are deemed to be secured by a charge on the purchaser's general inventory as of the date of bankruptcy or receivership in priority to all other claims except for the repossession claims of unpaid suppliers. However, as is the case with section 81.1, compliance requirements are such that the remedy is largely ineffective.

4) The Effect of Bankruptcy and Insolvency Law on Enforcement Rights of Secured Creditors

Sections 243 to 244 of the BIA require a secured party who intends to enforce a security interest against the inventory, accounts receivable, or other business assets of an insolvent person to give notice of this intention. Enforcement is stayed for a ten-day period following the sending of the notice. In addition, sections 246 to 252 impose additional notice requirements on the secured party and give jurisdiction to the court to order compliance and to require the secured creditor to act honestly and deal with the collateral in a commercially reasonable manner.

The enforcement rights of secured creditors are dramatically delayed or abridged when a non-consumer debtor[11] invokes insolvency proceedings designed to permit reorganization. The filing of a notice of intention to present a proposal under section 50.4 of the BIA, subject to minor exceptions, results in a stay of enforcement rights of secured creditors of the debtor.[12] The stay is extended until the proposal is dealt with or the debtor becomes a bankrupt.[13] While the filing of a reor-

---

11   There is no stay when a consumer proposal is involved since secured creditors are not affected by the proposals unless they file claims. See BIA, ss. 66.11–66.12 and 66.28(1).

12   BIA, s. 69(1).

13   *Ibid.*

ganization proposal under the *Companies' Creditors Arrangement Act*[14] does not trigger an automatic stay, the court almost invariably grants a comprehensive stay on enforcement by all creditors, including secured creditors. As is the case with a proposal under the BIA, this stay is in effect until the proposal is dealt with or bankruptcy occurs. In the latter event, secured creditors are generally free to pursue their enforcement rights against the collateral unimpeded by the bankruptcy process.

C. THE EFFICACY OF AFTER-ACQUIRED PROPERTY CLAUSES IN BANKRUPTCY

An important practical issue is the efficacy in bankruptcy of a clause in a security agreement providing for a security interest in all present and after-acquired property of the debtor or property to come into existence at a future time. In *Holy Rosary Parish (Thorold) Credit Union Limited v. Premier Trust Company*,[15] the Supreme Court held that a security assignment covering the debtor's present and future wages made prior to bankruptcy was effective to capture wages earned by the assignor while a bankrupt. The assignment was effective in equity to transfer property in the wages to the assignee as soon as they were earned. Consequently, the assignment was not affected by BIA sections 67(1)(c) or 70(2). The precise ruling in *Holy Rosary* has since been reversed by amendments to the BIA. Section 68.1 (1) provides that an assignment of existing or future wages made by a debtor before the debtor became bankrupt is of no effect in respect of wages earned after the bankruptcy. Section 68.1(2) goes on to provide that an assignment of amounts receivable as payment for or commission or professional fees in respect of services rendered made by a debtor who is a natural person before the debtor became bankrupt is likewise of no effect in respect of such amounts earned or generated after the bankruptcy. This reverses cases extending the reasoning in *Holy Rosary* to post-bankruptcy income in the form of professional fees and commissions.[16]

---

14   R.S.C. 1985, c. C-36, s. 11.
15   [1965] S.C.R. 503 [*Holy Rosary*].
16   See, for example, *Re Kryspin* (1983), 44 C.B.R. (N.S.) 232, 40 O.R. (2d) 424, 142 D.L.R. (3d) 638 (Ont. H.C.J.): Note, however, that in his decision in *Re Lloyd* (1995), 30 C.B.R. (3d) 113, 9 P.P.S.A.C. (2d) 107, 164 A.R. 59 (Q.B.), Registrar Funduk took the view that section 68.1 cannot be used to avoid a pre-bankruptcy absolute assignment and that the application of section 68.1(2) is directed at grant of security under a general assignment of book debts (as the title of the

In respect of post-bankruptcy accounts that fall outside the scope of these amendments, it is the view of the authors that the reasoning in *Holy Rosary* is open to serious question as a result of the intervening enactment of the PPSA. The *Holy Rosary* case did not involve application of the PPSA. The decision is based on the equitable doctrine that when the debtor, who has given an assignment or mortgage of property he does not own, acquires the property after becoming a bankrupt, the assignment or mortgage is effective against the trustee in bankruptcy since the bankrupt receives the property as trustee for the assignee or mortgagee[17] with the result that it does not vest in the trustee by virtue of the exclusion of trust property from the definition of the property of a bankrupt divisible among his creditors in section 67(1) of the BIA.

It is uncertain that the trust approach applies in the context of the PPSA. The PPSA adopts the principles of equity to the extent they are not inconsistent with the provisions of the Act.[18] However, it is not clear that the doctrine of equity that treats a debtor as a trustee of after-acquired property for the benefit of a secured party to which the debtor has agreed to give a security interest is consistent with the conceptual structure and priority rules of the PPSA. The issue involved is not one that is governed by bankruptcy law; consequently, it must be addressed in the context of non-bankruptcy law. The problem with applying the *Holy Rosary* approach where the debtor is not a bankrupt is demonstrated in the following scenario.

D gives SP a security interest in all of D's present and after-acquired property. However, SP fails to register a financing statement. D then acquires property and SP's security interest attaches. An unsecured creditor of D obtains judgment and a writ of execution under which the property is seized by the sheriff. Is it open to SP to argue that under the doctrine of equity applied in *Holy Rosary* case, the execution was ineffective to give priority to the sheriff pursuant to provision of the PPSA that subordinates an unperfected security interest to an execution creditor who caused the collateral to be seizure under execution because D never acquired ownership of the collateral other than as trustee?

---

provision reads) and therefore does not affect the grant of security in a specific assignment of a specific debt.

17   See *In Re Lind*, [1915] 2 Ch. 345 at 360 (C.A.).

18   PPSA (M, NWT, Nu, S) s. 65(2); (NB, PEI) s. 65(1); (NL, NS) s. 66(1); A s. 66(3); BC s. 68(1); O s. 72; Y s. 63(1).

The answer must surely be "no" because the argument requires the application of a principle of equity that conflicts with the priority regime of the PPSA.[19] It is difficult to accept that the *Holy Rosary* principle applies to preclude property acquired by a bankrupt debtor after bankruptcy from vesting in the trustee but does not have the same effect as against a judgment creditor in the context of the non-bankruptcy scenario set out above. The result reached in the *Holy Rosary* case can only be justified on an analysis that is consistent with PPSA and BIA principles without bringing trust doctrine into the picture.

Under the PPSA, a security interest automatically attaches when the debtor acquires rights in the collateral. Prior to attachment, the secured party cannot have a security interest. It follows that, if a security interest in property acquired after the invocation of bankruptcy is to attach, the debtor-bankrupt must acquire rights in the collateral. As a result of the displacement of trust law by the PPSA in this context, the secured party cannot rely on the exclusion of "property held in trust for another person" from the definition of the "property of the bankrupt" in section 67(1) of the BIA. Consequently, there appears to be little basis for the conclusion that a security interest can attach to property acquired by a bankrupt debtor after bankruptcy.

There is no doubt that a debtor loses the power to create security interests in his property once it has vested in the trustee. Section 71(2) of the BIA provides that the vesting of the present and after acquired property of the debtor in the trustee as a result of an assignment or receiving order is "subject to ... the rights of secured creditors."[20] However, these words have not been interpreted as giving to secured creditors rights to enlarge the scope of the collateral covered by their security interests after the debtor's property vests in the trustee. Consequently, once a receiving order or assignment has been made, a mortgagee cannot invoke the equitable principle of consolidation of mortgages[21] or

---

19   Note, however, that if the security agreement provided for an assignment of present and future accounts of D's business and D were petitioned into bankruptcy, SP1's failure to register in this scenario would avoid its security interest against the PPSA by virtue not of the PPSA but s. 94 of the BIA which provides that a general assignment of book debts (defined to include an assignment by way of security) is void as against the trustee with respect to any book debts that have not been paid at the date of bankruptcy unless the assignment is registered pursuant to a provincial statute providing for the registration thereof.

20   This qualification did not appear in the counterpart section of the BIA at the time of the *Holy Rosary* decision.

21   *Eastern Canada Savings & Loan Co. v. Campbell (No. 2)* (1971), 16 C.B.R. (N.S.) 75 (P.E.I. Ch.).

the right of tacking advances[22] if the effect is to reduce the value of the bankruptcy estate. An assignment of future receivables made before bankruptcy does not affect receivables generated from the post-bankruptcy sale by the trustee of the tangible assets of the estate.[23] Clearly the basis for these decisions is that property that vests in the trustee pursuant to section 71(2) after bankruptcy cannot be collateral under a security interest granted under a pre-bankruptcy security agreement merely because that property falls within the collateral description contained in an after-acquired property clause in the security agreement.

Conversely, if the debtor acquires rights in after acquired property prior to it vesting in the trustee, the security interest attaches pursuant to the PPSA and the trustee acquires the property "subject to the rights of secured creditors" within the meaning of that qualification in section 71(2). It thus becomes critical to determine when a debtor acquires rights in collateral sufficient for the purposes of attachment under the PPSA. The analysis is usually straightforward for tangible assets but poses greater problems where the after-acquired collateral takes the form of accounts and other intangibles owing to the debtor by an account debtor.

In the decided cases, the courts have concluded that it is not necessary for the account debtor's obligation to be due or payable at the point of bankruptcy for the secured party to take precedence over the trustee. It is sufficient if the contract or other event upon which the account debtor's obligation to pay has been completed or occurs prior to bankruptcy. Thus, it has been held that a secured party has priority over a trustee to the proceeds of an insurance settlement reached between the trustee and the bankrupt's insurer after bankruptcy, where the contract of insurance had been concluded and the loss or damage giving rise to the indemnity obligation of the insurer occurred prior to bankruptcy.[24]

---

22   *Camrati Investments Inc. v. Manulife Bank of Canada* (1993), 21 C.B.R. (3d) 118, (Ont. Ct. Gen. Div.).

23   *Re Anderson & Hiltz Limited* (1985), 57 C.B.R. (N.S.) 222 (Ont. H.C.J.).

24   *Re Dominion Used Store Fixtures Ltd.* (1939), 20 C.B.R. 325, [1939] 4 D.L.R. 735 (Ont. S.C. In Bankruptcy). See also *Kent Steel Products Ltd. v. Arlington Management Consultants Ltd.* (1966), 9 C.B.R. (N.S.) 298, 58 W.W.R. 1, 59 D.L.R. (2d) 374 (Man. Q.B.), aff'd (1967), 59 W.W.R. 382, 62 D.L.R. (2d) 502 (Man. C.A.), further appeal quashed as being defective 10 C.B.R. (N.S.) 92, [1967] S.C.R. 497, 61 W.W.R. 119, 62 D.L.R. (2d) 638 holding that the secured party was entitled as against the trustee to the proceeds of a right of compensation for land of the bankrupt which had been expropriated prior to bankruptcy. The Court noted that if the land had been expropriated after bankruptcy, the trustee would have been entitled to the proceeds as the land would have vested in the trustee as of the date of bankruptcy.

The courts have also given priority to a secured creditor over accounts generated by the trustee's post-bankruptcy completion of an agreement of sale covering the debtor's tangible assets that had been entered into by the debtor before bankruptcy.[25] Similarly, a secured party with a security interest in the debtor's future accounts was held to be entitled, in precedence to the trustee, to the proceeds of the account generated by an auction sale of the debtor's tangible assets that took place after bankruptcy where the debtor had entered into the auction agreement before making the assignment in bankruptcy.[26]

The results in these cases can be justified on the basis that the debtor had acquired rights in the property interest that is subject to the security interest — the right to receive payment — sufficient to support attachment of the security interest under the PPSA before the invocation of bankruptcy.[27] The secured party may claim the proceeds of rights to payment in existence at the point of bankruptcy even where collected by the trustee.[28] This conclusion is consistent with the scheme of distribution contemplated by the BIA. As noted earlier, the trustee is empowered to distribute the property of the bankrupt to the debtor's unsecured creditors "subject to the rights of secured creditors." This qualification does not by its own terms depend on whether it is the secured party or the trustee who realizes the collateral.

More problematic are cases in which preference has been given to the secured party over the trustee where the pre-bankruptcy contract that generated the post-bankruptcy account remains executory in nature, with the account debtor's continuing obligations to pay being dependent on continued counterperformance by the debtor. For example, relying on the *Holy Rosary* decision, it has been held that rental payments falling due after bankruptcy under a pre-bankruptcy lease of the bankrupt's personal property accrue to the secured party in preference to the trustee.[29] Also problematic are cases giving precedence to the secured party even where the event triggering the account

---

25 *Irving A. Burton Ltd. v. Canadian Imperial Bank of Commerce* (1982), 41 C.B.R. (N.S.) 217 (Ont. C.A.).

26 *Re Cedarbrooke Sawmills Inc.* (1990), 80 C.B.R. (N.S.) 31 (B.C.S.C.).

27 *Western Surety Co. v. National Bank of Canada* (2001), 22 C.B.R. (4th) 283, 237 N.B.R. (2d) 346, 612 A.P.R. 346 (C.A.).

28 See, for example, *Agricultural Credit Corp. of Saskatchewan v. Featherstone (Trustee of)*, [1996] 8 W.W.R. 281 (Sask. Q.B.); *Re Brookfield Construction Co.* (1963), 5 C.B.R. (N.S.) 283, 42 D.L.R. (2d) 240, 50 M.P.R. 211 (N.S.S.C.).

29 *Re Otea Inc.*, [1976] C.A. 539. Compare with *Re Jason Construction Ltd.*, 16 C.B.R. (N.S.) 297, [1972] 3 W.W.R. 504, 25 D.L.R. (3d) 340 (Alta S.C.T.D.), aff'd 17 C.B.R. (N.S.) 158, [1972] 6 W.W.R. 203, 29 D.L.R. (3d) 623 (Alta. S.C.A.D.).

debtor's obligation to pay does not take place until after bankruptcy, for example, a right to payment of insurance indemnities for loss or damage to the debtor's assets that occurs only after bankruptcy proceedings have been initiated.[30]

In the view of the authors, the results in these cases are open to serious question once it is accepted that the trust theory advanced in *Holy Rosary* is not sustainable with the advent of the PPSA. The results can be sustained only if it can be said that the debtor had acquired sufficient rights in the account prior to bankruptcy to support attachment of the security interest. However, it has been held that where a right to successive payments under a contract is dependent on the continuing satisfaction of certain preconditions by the debtor, a security interest in the payments does not attach until those preconditions are satisfied.[31]

It might be argued that the secured party is entitled to an account falling due under contracts entered into prior to bankruptcy even though the conditions for payment are not satisfied until after bankruptcy on the theory that the account is the proceeds of collateral in existence at the point of bankruptcy, that is, the contractual obligation of the account debtor to pay once the conditions are satisfied.[32] The success of this argument depends on whether the proceeds are treated under

---

30   *In Re Dickie Estate* (1925), 5 C.B.R. 864 (N.S.S.C.).
31   *Western Surety Co. v. National Bank of Canada*, above note 27.
32   In the United States, s. 552(a) of the *Bankruptcy Code* provides the general rule that property acquired after the commencement of bankruptcy is not subject to pre-petition security agreements even if there is an "after-acquired" clause in the security agreement. Section 552(b)(1) states an exception to this general rule. It provides that a pre-petition security interest *does* attach to post-petition proceeds derived from pre-petition collateral if that pre-petition security interest would have attached to those proceeds pursuant to applicable non-bankruptcy law. In interpreting the scope of the proceeds exception, the U.S. courts have held that Congress intended to defer to state law, i.e. the courts interpret the term "proceeds" in the *Bankruptcy Code* by reference to the UCC definition. Until recently, the art. 9 definition of proceeds included whatever was received "upon the sale, exchange, collection or other disposition of collateral or proceeds." The definition of proceeds in 9-102(a)(64) has been expanded to include "whatever is collected on, or distributed on account of, collateral" and "rights arising out of collateral." The expanded definition is expected to significantly increase the range of post-bankruptcy collateral that will be caught by a pre-bankruptcy security interest: see, for example, Warner, "The Anti-Bankruptcy Act: Revised Article 9 and Bankruptcy" (2001) 9 Am. Bankr. Inst. L. Rev. 3; Harris and Mooney, "Revised Article 9 Meets the Bankruptcy Code: Policy and Impact" (2001) 9 Am. Bankr. Inst. L. Rev. 85; Pryor, "How Revised Article 9 Will Turn the Trustee's Strong-Arm into a Weak Finger: A Potpourri of Cases" (2001) 9 Am. Bankr. Inst. L. Rev. 229.

the PPSA as a continuation of the original collateral and, consequently, not new property or as new property subject to the statutorily deemed security interest that is treated as having the same effect and priority as the security interest in the original collateral. If the proceeds are new property, they vest in the trustee pursuant to section 67(1)(c), with the result that the deemed PPSA security interest cannot attach.

The PPSA does not state in explicit term that proceeds are, in property term, an extension of the original collateral. The reality is that proceeds are in fact new and different property. Furthermore, the Acts appear to leave to the common law the question as to whether or not and when the debtor acquires an interest in the property. All the Acts, except that of Ontario, provide that in order for the property to be proceeds, the debtor must acquire an interest in it.[33] This suggests that the PPSA does not treat proceeds as simply an extension of the original collateral. If the debtor does not acquire an interest in property resulting from a disposition of the original collateral, the property is not proceeds. In other words, it is not possible to argue that since the property is proceeds, the debtor is deemed to have an interest in it. The reasoning must go the other way: if the debtor acquired rights in the property it can be proceeds.

The complexity deepens in cases where the post-bankruptcy property that is in dispute is merely an increase in the value of existing property. This issue arises when a security interest attaches to collateral prior to bankruptcy. After bankruptcy and before discharge of the bankrupt, the property increases in value. Is the increased value of the property "new property" that vests exclusively in the trustee or merely the original collateral that is now more valuable than it was prior to bankruptcy?[34]

Where there is no connection of this kind between property acquired by the debtor before bankruptcy and property acquired by the debtor while a bankrupt, the only basis on which to conclude that a security interest in the post-bankruptcy property attaches to the property and gives priority to the secured creditor over the trustee is to conclude that the property momentarily vests in the bankrupt before it vests in the trustee.

---

33   PPSA (A, BC, M, NB,NWT, Nu, PEI, Y) s. 1; (NL, NS, S) s. 2.

34   This issue is closely related doctrinally to the issue addressed later in this chapter that arises when collateral appreciates in value after the discharge of the debtor. See D "The Effect of Discharge of the Bankrupt Debtor on a Security Interest."

The BIA does not expressly provide that property acquired by the bankrupt before discharge vests directly in the trustee. Section 67(1)(c) of the BIA provides that property acquired by a bankrupt before discharge is divisible among his creditors.[35] BIA section 71(2) is the section of the Act that deals with the effect of bankruptcy on the property rights of a bankrupt. However, the section appears not to address the situation contemplated by section 67(1)(c). It appears to refer only to property owned by the debtor at the date of bankruptcy. Consequently, the BIA does not expressly preclude the conclusion that property acquired by the bankrupt vests momentarily in the bankrupt before it vests in the trustee. A court could then conclude that there was a moment in time (a *scintilla temporis*) prior to the revesting of the property in the trustee in which the secured party's security interest might attach to the asset. There is an obvious artificiality to this approach in that it does not adequately explain why the two events are not simply viewed as arising simultaneously. The revesting of the property in the trustee as well as attachment of the security interest both occur immediately upon the bankrupt acquiring an interest in the post-bankruptcy assets. The decision to treat the security interest as arising immediately before the revesting merely masks a judicial choice to prefer the secured party over the trustee for reasons that are not articulated.

In *Wallace v. United Grain Growers Ltd.*,[36] the Court explicitly rejected the conclusion of the Manitoba Court of Appeal that that property owned by the debtor at the date of bankruptcy is treated differently from property acquired during bankruptcy and that the bankrupt is free to deal with that property until intervention by the trustee. The Court concluded that the plain meaning of the BIA indicates that, outside of the circumstances set out in sections 68(1) and 99(1), the bankrupt loses the ability to deal with her property regardless of whether it was acquired before or after the assignment in bankruptcy.[37] Although this ruling is not conclusive, it calls into question the analysis that property acquired by the bankrupt momentarily vests in the bankrupt before vesting in the trustee.

---

35 In *Royal Bank of Canada v. North American Life Assurance Co.*, [1996] 1 S.C.R. 325, [1996] 3 W.W.R. 457, Gonthier J. (speaking for the Court) stated at para. 48: "Unlike provisions of the Act such as ss. 71(2), 91 or 68, s. 67(1) tells us nothing about the property-passing stage of bankruptcy. Instead, it relates to the estate-administration stage by defining which property in the estate is available to satisfy the claims of creditors."

36 [1997] 3 S.C.R. 701.

37 *Ibid.* at 728–29.

D. THE EFFECT OF DISCHARGE OF THE BANKRUPT DEBTOR ON A SECURITY INTEREST

Under BIA section 178(2), an order of discharge releases a bankrupt from all claims provable in bankruptcy other than those specified in section 178(1). However, the discharge does not release or nullify a security interest.[38] The debt that is secured remains in place to the extent of supporting the security interest.

A controversial, and as yet unsettled, issue arises in the context of the following scenarios.

Scenario 1: Prior to bankruptcy, D gives a security interest to SP in all present and after acquired personal property. Once D becomes a bankrupt, SP seizes property of D, but the proceeds of disposition of the collateral are not sufficient to discharge fully the obligation owned by D to SP. In the result, SP is an unsecured creditor in D's bankruptcy.[39] After D's discharge, D acquires new property that falls within the collateral description of the security agreement with SP. SP seizes the property, claiming that it has a security interest in it to secure the portion of the D's debt that was not discharged from the first seizure of the collateral (and any dividend received from D's trustee).

Scenario 2: Prior to bankruptcy, D gives a security interest to SP in all present and after-acquired personal property. Notwithstanding the bankruptcy, SP leaves property that is collateral under the security agreement in possession of D. The value of the collateral at the date of D's discharge is less than the obligation owed by D to SP. In the result, SP is an unsecured creditor to this amount. After D's discharge, the property increases in value. SP seizes the property, claiming that it has a security interest in the total value of the property to secure the entire obligation of D to SP.

Scenario 3: Prior to bankruptcy, D gives a security interest to SP in all present and after-acquired personal property. Notwithstanding the bankruptcy, SP leaves property that is collateral under the security agreement in possession of D. During the time D is a bankrupt, she maintains her payment obligations to SP. The value of the collateral at the date of D's discharge is

---

38   *Toronto-Dominion Bank v. Mulatz* (1994), 111 D.L.R. (4th) 601 (Sask. C.A.).

39   The outcome may, but need not, be affected by the decision of SP to file a claim as an unsecured creditor in the bankruptcy proceedings. See *Andrew v. Farmstart* (1988), 71 C.B.R. (N.S.) 124 (Sask. C.A.), leave to appeal to S.C.C. refused [1989] 4 W.W.R. lxx (S.C.C.).

less than the obligation owed by D to SP. In the result, SP is an unsecured creditor to this amount. After D's discharge, SP seizes and disposes of the collateral and brings action against D for the balance owing under the security agreement.

In all three scenarios, at the date of D's discharge, SP is an unsecured creditor to the extent of the difference between the amount owing by D and the value of the collateral at that date.

The effect of a discharge under BIA section 178(2) is to "release" the bankrupt from unsecured debt owing to the secured party. The release of the debt precluded attachment of the security interest in property acquired thereafter. It would follow from this that SP in scenario 1 could not have a security interest in the new collateral acquired by the debtor after discharge since there would be no debt in existence to support that security interest.[40] For the same reason, SP in scenario 2 could not assert a security interest in the increased value of the collateral that accrued after D's discharge. In scenario 3, SP would be able to enforce its security interest in the collateral, but would not be able to obtain judgment against D for any deficiency.[41]

The logic and symmetry of this was recognized by the Supreme Court of Canada in *Holy Rosary Parish (Thorold) Credit Union Ltd. v. Bye.*[42] In this case the court concluded that a creditor could not rely on an assignment of wages after discharge of the assignor to enforce payment of an obligation that had been discharged. The Court concluded that "[t]he debt has now gone by operation of law. The assignment was given as a means of collection of the debt. The statutory release of the debtor under the *Bankruptcy Act* renders the assignment ineffective as a means of collection."[43] This ruling directly addresses scenario 1.[44] However, it is not apparent to some lower courts that it also addresses scenarios 2 and 3.

---

40   See also *Re Pelyea,* [1970] 2 O.R. 384 (Ont. C.A.); *Patrie v. Royal Bank* (1994), 27 C.B.R. (3d) 89 (Ont. Ct. Gen. Div.).

41   For a complete analysis of the issues involved, see T. M. Buckwold, "Post-Bankruptcy Remedies of Secured Creditors: As Good as it Gets" (1999) 31 Can. Bus. L.J. 436 and "Post-Bankruptcy Remedies of Secured Creditors: A Reply to Professor Ziegel" (2000) 33 Can. Bus. L.J. 128; J.S. Ziegel, "Post-Bankruptcy Remedies of Secured Creditors: Comments on Professor Buckwold's Article" (1999) 32 Can. Bus. L.J. 142 and "Post-Bankruptcy Remedies of Secured Creditors: A Brief Rejoinder" (2000) 33 Can. Bus. L.J. 144.

42   [1967] S.C.R. 271.

43   *Ibid.* at p. 274.

44   Although its authority appears not to be accepted by at least one Canadian expert in secured financing law. See Ziegel, above note 41.

In *Andrew v. FarmStart*[45] the Saskatchewan Court of Appeal found that, because there were prior mortgages for amounts in excess of the value of the mortgaged land, a mortgage held by FarmStart was valueless at the date of discharge of the bankrupt. Nevertheless, it concluded that the mortgage could be enforced against the bankrupt's land when, as a result of the withdrawal of the prior mortgages after the discharge, the debtor regained an equity in the land. This was so even though, at the date of the discharge, the FarmStart debt was completely unsecured. It is the view of the authors that the decision failed to apply the principle set out in the *Holy Rosary* case.[46] The outcome should be the same whether the debtor acquires new equity after the discharge through the satisfaction of prior secured claims, through appreciation in the value of the collateral[47] or through the acquisition of a new item of collateral. [48]

In *Seaboard Acceptance Corporation Ltd. v. Moen*[49] a lessee retained a leased vehicle and paid the lease payments during the period she was in bankruptcy and shortly thereafter. She then defaulted and the lessor brought action against her for the full amount payable under the lease contract. This was more than the unpaid lease payments; it was an amount that, in effect, was equivalent to the purchase price of the vehicle and an applicable credit charge.[50] The British Columbia Court of Appeal rejected the argument of the lessee that she had been released from her obligation to pay amounts owing under the contract when she obtained her discharge in bankruptcy. The Court concluded that the contract continued after the discharge. The fact that there may have been a claim provable in bankruptcy did not affect the "continuing effect" of the contract into the post-discharge period. The actions of the lessee in retaining the vehicle and maintaining the payments throughout the period she was a bankrupt amounted to an endorsement of the contract following the discharge.

If a former bankrupt affirms an obligation discharged in bankruptcy in a new contract entered into after discharge, the obligation is

---

45 Above note 39.
46 Somewhat anomalously, however, leave to appeal to the Supreme Court was denied, *ibid*.
47 *Patrie v. Royal Bank*, above note 40. It is the view of the authors that this decision accurately reflects the operation of BIA, s. 178(2).
48 *Pisiak v. Dyck* (1986), 63 C.B.R. (N.S.) 151, 32 D.L.R. (4th) 287 (Sask. Q.B.).
49 (1986), 62 C.B.R. (N.S.) 143 (B.C.C.A.) [*Seaboard*]; *Burton v. Toronto Dominion Bank* (1976), 22 C.B.R. (N.S.) 207 (Ont. H.C.J.).
50 The so-called lease was an "open-end" lease that, under the PPSA, would be treated as a security agreement. Consequently, any amount owing to the lessor by the lessee would be a debt.

enforceable. However, the Court in *Seaboard* concluded that this had not occurred and that its conclusion was not based on novation. In any event, the facts did not support a finding of novation. This would have required a conscious decision on the part of the debtor to affirm the debt in return for the creditor's agreement to waive its right of repossession of the leased vehicle.[51] This did not occur. Unfortunately, the Court provided no explanation for its ruling that demonstrates conceptual symmetry with bankruptcy law.

The apparently new doctrine of "continuing effect of a contractual obligation" after discharge has been uncritically applied by several trial level courts in cases involving mortgages of land.[52]

E. THE STATUS OF A TRUSTEE UNDER THE PPSA

1) The Interface between the PPSA and the BIA

The PPSA[53] provides that a security interest is not effective against a trustee in bankruptcy if the security interest is unperfected at the date

---

51 *Cleve's Sporting Goods Ltd. v. J.G. Touchie and Associates* (1986), 58 C.B.R. (N.S.) 304 (N.S.C.A.). However, see *Trans Canada Credit Corp. v. Martin*, [2000] 9 W.W.R. 226 (Man. Q.B.).

52 *Manulife Bank of Canada v. Planting* (1996), 43 C.B.R. (3d) 305 (Ont. Ct. Gen. Div.), aff'd [1998] O.J. No. 73 (C.A.); *Scotia Mortgage Corp. v. Winchester* (1997), 205 A.R. 147 (Q.B.) and *CIBC Mortgage Corp. v. Stenerson* (1998), 220 A.R. 248 (Alta. Q.B.); *Tildesley v. Weaver* (1998), 7 C.B.R. (4th) 313 (B.C.S.C.); *CIBC Mortgage Corp. v. Coleski* (1999), 13 C.B.R. (4th) 17 (N.S.S.C.).

53 PPSA (NWT, Nu, O, PEI) s. 20(1); (BC, M) s. 20(b); (NB, S) s. 20(2); A s. 20(a); NL s. 21(1); NS s. 21(2); Y s. 19(1). There is an important difference between the OPPSA and the other Acts with respect to who else has a special status with respect to an unperfected security interest. All PPSAs other than OPPSA give the same status as is given to a trustee to a liquidator appointed pursuant to the *Winding-up and Restructuring Act,* R.S.C. 1985, c. W-11, where the security interest is unperfected at the date the winding-up order is made context. However, they give only a derivative status to a representative of creditors. The representative can assert only the priority status of actual creditors of the debtor. Under OPPSA s. 20(1)(b) an unperfected security interest is not effective against a person who represents the creditors of the debtor, including an assignee for the benefit of creditors. All representatives of creditors, including the trustee in bankruptcy, are given the same status. However, a monitor appointed under the *Companies' Creditors Arrangement Act* and a trustee in a proposal under the *Bankruptcy and Insolvency Act* are is not a representative of creditors for this purpose. *Re PSINet Ltd.* (2002), 30 C.B.R. (4th) 226 (Ont. S.C.J.); *Re Hupfer*, 2003

of bankruptcy. The effect of this is to give to the debtor's trustee in bankruptcy an independent status to defeat unperfected security interests in personal property that vests in the trustee as provided by BIA section 71(2).

As a result of the definitions of bankrupt, bankruptcy, and date of initial bankruptcy event in BIA section 2(1), the date of bankruptcy for the purposes of the PPSA is the date when an assignment by the debtor is made or a receiving order is made against the debtor. The date of bankruptcy is no longer treated as being the date the petition for the receiving order was filed.

In *Re Giffen*,[54] one of the very few judgments of the Supreme Court of Canada involving interpretation of the PPSA, the Court addressed the interface between this feature of the PPSA and the BIA. It rejected the position taken by the British Columbia Court of Appeal[55] and adopted that of the Saskatchewan Court of Appeal,[56] recognizing that provincial law can give to a trustee in bankruptcy the power to prevent a secured party from asserting against the trustee its proprietary rights to the property in which the bankrupt had a possessory interest.

The Court also recognized the underlying rationale of this aspect of the PPSA. The justification for subordinating an unpefected security interest to a trustee in bankruptcy is not based on the conclusion that failure to give public disclosure of the existence of a security interest results in unsecured creditors being induced to give credit to debtors. There is no requirement that the trustee demonstrate that he or she represents an unsecured creditor who gave credit without knowledge of the unperfected security interest. The knowledge of the creditor and the date the credit was given are irrelevant considerations. Further, there is no requirement that the trustee be without knowledge of the unperfected security interest or be misled in any way by the failure of the secured party to provide public disclosure of the security interest. All that is required is that the security interest be unperfected at the date of bankruptcy. The policy basis of the provision can be found in the representative capacity of the trustee and the effect of bankruptcy on the enforcement rights of unsecured creditors.[57]

ABQB 267. A privately appointed receiver is not a representative of creditors for this purpose. *Xerox Canada Inc. v. Bank of Montreal* (1989), 76 C.B.R. (N.S.) 99 (Ont. H.C.J.).

54   Above note 2.

55   *Ibid.*

56   *International Harvester Credit Corp. of Canada Ltd. v. Touche Ross Ltd.* (1986), 61 C.B.R. (N.S.) 193.

57   Above note 2 at 347–48.

A security interest is subordinate to a judgment creditor of a non-bankrupt debtor if the unsecured creditor has caused the collateral to be seized under legal process to enforce a judgment or the judgment[58] or a writ of enforcement is registered before the security interest is perfected.[59] The PPSA in effect treats a judgment enforcement measure or its registration, as the case may be, as a method through which an unsecured creditor can raise his or her claim to a status equivalent for priority purposes to that of a secured creditor.[60] If the unsecured creditor "perfects" his or her claim through seizure or registration before the secured party perfects his or her claim by registration or possession, the unsecured creditor has priority.

However, bankruptcy has a dramatic effect on the rights of unsecured creditors under provincial law. Under BIA section 69.3, the invocation of bankruptcy bars any remedy an unsecured creditor has against the debtor. Section 70(1) completes the picture by giving to bankruptcy law precedence over any provincial judgment enforcement measure not completed by the time the assignment is made or the receiving order is issued. The result is that, as soon a debtor becomes a bankrupt, further possibility of an unsecured creditor pursuing a claim through a provincial judgment enforcement measure terminates. In effect, the judgment enforcement rights of unsecured creditors are merged in the bankruptcy proceedings and the trustee is now the representative of creditors who can no longer bring their claims to a "perfected" status under provincial law. As such repository of enforcement rights, the trustee has status under the PPSA to attack an unperfected security interest in property in which the bankrupt has an interest.[61]

2) Reperfection and the Status of the Trustee

The following scenario raises an issue of practical importance.

D gives a security interest to SP1, who registers a financing statement. However, due to an error on the part of SP1, or due to fraud on the part of someone else, the registration lapses or is discharged. Shortly thereafter, D becomes a bankrupt. When SP1 discovers that the registration no longer exists, he re-registers a financing statement. The trustee takes the position

---

58 PPSA (NWT, Nu, O, S) s. 20(1); (BC, M) s. 20(a); Y s. 19.
59 PPSA A s. 20(B); NB s. 20(1); NL s. 21(2); NS s. 21(1); PEI s. 20(2).
60 For a detailed discussion of the relevant priority event under the different versions of the PPSA — seizure or registration — see chapter 10.
61 Above note 2 at 349.

that the re-registration does not affect her priority over SP1's security interest.

The PPSA, other than the OPPSA, specifically address situations where a registration is terminated as a result of lapse or inadvertent or fraudulent discharge.[62] It provides that in such a case, if the secured party registers its security interest again not later than thirty days after the lapse or discharge, its priority status existing before the lapse or discharge is, in effect, restored with respect to "a competing perfected security interest that, immediately prior to the lapse or discharge had a subordinate priority position." This provision makes no reference to a trustee in bankruptcy where the bankruptcy occurred during the period between the lapse and re-registration. Consequently, SP's security interest is subordinate to the claim of the trustee since it was not perfected at the date of bankruptcy.[63]

Section 30(6) of the OPPSA provides that, when a security interest that is perfected by registration becomes unperfected and is again perfected by registration, the security interest is treated as having been continuously perfected from the time of first registration, except with respect to the "rights" in the collateral of a person acquired during the period when the security interest was unperfected. There can be little doubt that the trustee in bankruptcy qualifies as a person who acquired rights in D's property. The interest that vests in the trustee as provided in BIA section 71(2)[64] qualifies as "rights" under section 30(6). Consequently, in this respect, the result under the OPPSA does not differ from the result under the other Acts.

3) The Special Status of the Trustee under the PPSA

The Supreme Court of Canada in *Re Giffen*[65] appears to have adopted the conclusion of the Saskatchewan Court of Appeal[66] that the PPSA does not confer any property right on the trustee. The PPSA provides only a priority rule; its effect is to prevent the secured party from exercising

---

62   PPSA (A, BC, M, NB, NWT, Nu, PEI, S) s. 30(6)–(7); (NL, NS) s. 31(6)–(7); Y s. 29(2); O no equivalent provision.

63   PPSA (NWT, Nu, PEI) s. 20(1); (BC, M) s. 20(b); (NB, S) s. 20(2); A s. 20(a); NL s. 21(1); NS s. 21(2); Y s. 19(1).

64   See extensive discussion of the issue in *Re Giffen*, above note 2.

65   *Ibid.* at 349.

66   *Re Perepeluk* (1986), 25 D.L.R. (4th) 73 (Sask.C.A.); *International Harvester Credit Corp. of Canada Ltd. v. Touche Ross Ltd.*, above note 56. See also *Direct Rental Centre (West) Ltd. v. A.C. Waring Associates Inc.* (2001), 205 D.L.R. 4th 651 (Alta. C.A.), aff'g (1997), 50 C.B.R. (3d) 200 (Alta. Q.B.).

rights against the trustee. In order for the trustee to have the power to defeat an unperfected security interest under the PPSA, a property interest of the debtor must vest in her pursuant to BIA section 71(2). Where a true security interest is involved, this requirement creates no difficulty since the debtor owns the collateral. In *Re Giffen*, the possessory right of the debtor under a lease for a term of more than one year was sufficient for this purpose.[67] In any event, the Court recognized the power of provincial law to deem a bankrupt to have a property interest sufficient to meet this requirement.

The requirement that some property interest of the bankrupt vest in the trustee under BIA section 71(2) if the trustee is to be able to defeat an unperfected security interest may be seen as source of difficulty in contexts other than unregistered security interests or deemed security interests arising under leases for a term of more than one year or commercial consignments. The PPSA includes within its registration and priority provisions non-security assignments of accounts and transfers of chattel paper.[68] These transactions involve the sale and transfer of the "debtor's" interest to the buyer with the result that there is no property interest left in the transferor to vest in the trustee of the transferor pursuant to BIA section71(2). This issue was addressed in two Ontario decisions.[69] The courts ruled that an unregistered non-security assignment was not effective against the assignor's trustee in bankruptcy as a result of section 20(1)(b) of the OPPSA. Both of these decisions pre-dated the ruling in *Re Giffen*.[70]

---

67   As to whether the trustee could defeat a security interest in property held "in trust" by the bankrupt, see T.M. Buckwold, "Re Giffen: The Personal Property Security Act and the Bankruptcy and Insolvency Act — Peace at Last" (1998) 14 B.F.L.R.173 at 176–77 and 180.

68   PPSA (A, M, NB, PEI, S) s. 3(2); (NL, NS) s. 4(2); (NWT, Nu) s. 2(2); (O, Y) s. 2(b); BC s. 3.

69   *Agent's Equity Inc. v. Hope (Trustees of)* (1996), 40 C.B.R. (3d) 310 (Ont. Ct. Gen. Div.); *TCE Capital Corp. v. Kolenc* (1999), 8 C.B.R. (4th) 165 (Ont. Div. Ct.).

70   In *Agent's Equity, ibid.*, Feldman J. employed a "bootstrap" analysis to address this issue. He concluded:

   The section no longer subordinates the interest of the unperfected security interest to the interest of the trustee in bankruptcy, but rather it now provides that the unperfected security interest in the collateral is no longer effective against the trustee in bankruptcy. In this case, the security interest is the interest of Agent's Equity in the transferred accounts. If it is not effective that is tantamount to saying that it is void against the trustee at the date of bankruptcy. Therefore, as of that date, the property in the accounts or the right to the commissions is not transferred to Agent's Equity but is property of the bankrupt again and can therefore pass to the trustee.

There is another approach that received implicit recognition in *Re Giffen*. The interest of a non-security transferee of an account or chattel paper is defined in the PPSA as a "security interest."[71] If a security interest is in the nature of a hypothec, conceptually one party is owner of the collateral and another party is the holder of a charge on that collateral. By treating the interest of a non-security transferee of an account or chattel paper to be a security interest, the PPSA is implicitly deeming the transferor to have ownership of the account or chattel paper that is deemed to be charged with the security interest. This deemed ownership qualifies as property vesting in the trustee in bankruptcy under BIA section 71(2). The Supreme Court recognized in *Re Giffen* the legitimacy of provincial legislation that redefines what constitutes "property" in any context. In its subsequent decision in *Lefebvre (Trustee of); Tremblay (Trustee of)*,[72] the Supreme Court reaffirmed the power of the provincial legislature to redefine property in the bankruptcy context in this fashion, observing that "[o]f course the legislature may play a more active role in the legal relationships of the parties or other interested persons by recharacterizing the rights established by contracts or giving a more radical scope to the consequences of the failure to publish."[73] This is the effect of the PPSA in its treatment of non-security transfers of accounts or chattel paper.

Where a true lease (lease for a term of more than one year)[74] is involved, the power of the trustee to defeat the lessor's interest is terminated when the lease is terminated and the leased property has been repossessed by the lessor. At this point, the former lessee has no interest of any kind in the leased property.[75] The same would apply to a commercial consignment when the consigned goods have been returned to the consignor. However, where a security agreement in the form of a lease or a consignment is involved, repossession of the leased property does not terminate the interest of the lessee or consignee. Since the transaction is a security agreement, the lessee's interest is that of a debtor, and not a lessee, with all the rights that are protected by Part 5 of the PPSA.[76] If, however, enforcement of a security interest has been completed pursuant to Part 5 before the debtor becomes a bankrupt, there is nothing for the trustee to attack. The security interest no longer exists.

---

71   PPSA (A, BC, NWT, Nu, O, Y) s. 1(1); (M, NB, PEI) s. 1; (NL, NS) s. 2; S s. 2(1).
72   Above note 2.
73   *Ibid.* at para. 30.
74   This term is defined in PPSA (A, BC, NWT, Nu, Y) s. 1(1); (M, NB, PEI) s. 1; (NL, NS) s. 2; S s. 2(1); O no equivalent provision.
75   *Bodnard v. Capital Office Systems Inc.* (1992), 3 P.P.S.A.C. (2d) 71 (Sask. C.A.).
76   It is the view of the authors that, in this respect, the decision in *Re Glencoe Express Inc.* (1992), 3 P.P.S.A.C. (2d) 239 (B.C.S.C.) is incorrect.

The Court in *Re Giffen*[77] addressed the derivative issue as to how
the trustee can effect the transfer of title to the collateral under bankruptcy proceedings. The priority that the PPSA gives to the trustee does
not vest ownership of the collateral in the trustee. All it does is prevent the secured party from asserting its unperfected security interest
against the trustee. The Court concluded that the trustee has, by virtue
of BIA section 81(2), an implied power to confer title free from the unperfected security interest. This section empowers a trustee to sell or
dispose of property free from a third-party claim that has been aban-
doned by the claimant through failure to appeal the trustee's rejection
of the claims. The effect of the PPSA is to prevent the claimant from
successfully making the claim. The effect is the same as it would be if
the appeal were not pursued.

4) The Exemptions Issue

An issue that has generated a considerable amount of litigation[78] in the
context of the interface between the PPSA and the BIA is whether an
unperfected security interest in property that is exempt from seizure
under provincial judgment enforcement law and, consequently, property that cannot be treated as part of the bankruptcy estate as a result
of BIA section 67(1)(b) can be defeated by the debtor's trustee in bankruptcy. The issue arises in two different contexts, but it is the same.
One context is where the property is exempt from seizure under execution but not from seizure under a security agreement. The other is
where the property is exempt from seizure under execution and under
a non-purchase money security interest, but is not exempt from seizure
under a purchase money security interest.[79] The issue is whether the
secured party's failure to perfect its security interest (or, in the second
context, its purchase money security interest) results in subordination
of the interest to the trustee under the PPSA.

---

77   Above note 2.
78   For a recent examination of the various approaches to this issue, see *VW Credit Canada Inc. v. Roberts* (2001), 197 D.L.R. (4th) 274 (N.S.C.A.). See also *Direct Rental Centre (West) Ltd. v. A.C. Waring Associates Inc.*, above note 66; *Rainbow Soil Services Ltd. v. Kada* (1995), 9 P.P.S.A.C. (2d) 22 (Sask. Q.B.); *Spence (Trustee of) v. Yellowhead Feeders Co-operative Ltd.*, [1994] 5 W.W.R. 129 (Sask. Q.B.); *Royal Bank of Canada v. Demyen (Trustee of)* (1986), 53 Sask. R. 224 (Sask. Q.B.).
79   Saskatchewan, New Brunswick, Prince Edward Island, Nova Scotia, and New-foundland have extended the judgment enforcement exemptions so that they apply to secured parties as well. British Columbia, Alberta, Manitoba, Ontario, and all three of the Territories have not done so with the result that a secured party is permitted to seize exempt assets.

The argument that an unperfected security interest in exempt property is not vulnerable to attack by the debtor's trustee under the PPSA is derived from the conclusion that the PPSA does not confer any property right on the trustee. It provides only a priority rule that prevents the secured party from exercising rights against the trustee. In order for the trustee to have the power to defeat an unperfected security interest under the PPSA, a property interest of the debtor must vest in her pursuant to BIA section 71(2). However, if, as a result of under BIA section 67, exempt property does not vest in the trustee, the trustee has no basis on which to defeat the unperfected security interest under the PPSA.

There are several variables that must be taken into account when addressing this issue. One line of cases addresses the effect of the interface between the PPSA and the BIA on the rights of a bankrupt debtor to claim a statutory exemption in jurisdictions where a debtor is given the right to claim exemptions from enforcement of security agreements but may not with respect to property subject to a purchase money security interest.[80] The analysis under which the conclusion is reached that a bankrupt loses her statutory exemptions when she becomes a bankrupt is as follows. The trustee asserts his rights under the PPSA to defeat an unperfected security interest. The trustee is then in the position to assert the secured creditor's rights as the holder of a purchase money security interest against the debtor. The cases that deal with this issue have concluded that the power of the trustee to defeat an unperfected security interest must not be read as defeating the bankrupt's right to claim exemptions under BIA section 67.[81] The way in which they reach this position is to conclude that the trustee does not acquire an interest in exempt property with the result that he does not have standing to defeat the unperfected security interest.

However, this approach might lead to the anomalous result that, when the issue is only the power of the trustee to defeat an unperfected security interest in a case where the bankrupt's claim to the exemption is not directly involved, the policy of the PPSA of giving priority to trustees over holders of unperfected security interests is defeated.[82] A secured

---

80   See PPSA (N B, PEI) s. 58(7); NS s. 59(7); NL s. 59(5); *The Exemptions Act*, R.S.S. 1978, c. E-14, s. 5(2).

81   See *Spence v. Yellowhead Feeders Co-operative Ltd.*, above note 78; *Rainbow Soil Services Ltd. v. K*, above note 78.

82   This was not accepted in *VW Credit Canada Inc. v. Roberts*, above note 78; *Royal Bank of Canada v. Demyen (Trustee of)*, above note 78 and *Re Fields* (2002), 59 O.R. (3d) 611 (S.C.J.) (on appeal, the Court of Appeal recognized the matter as controversial but was able to avoid ruling on it. See (2004), 240 D L R (4th) 494).

party need not comply with the perfections requirements of the Act in order to successfully defend any attack by the debtor's trustee.

Even if this approach is accepted as the prevailing law, it does not follow in every case that an unperfected security interest in exempt property is invulnerable to attack by a trustee under the PPSA. It is necessary to look at the relevant provincial or territorial law that provides for the exemption and determine whether or not the exemption must be claimed by the debtor in order to be recognized. If, under the applicable law, the exemption applies whether or not it is claimed by the debtor, the trustee would not have the status to defeat the unperfected security interest. However, if the exemption does not exist unless it is specifically claimed by the debtor, whether or not an unperfected security interest is vulnerable to defeat by a trustee under the PPSA will depend upon the election of the debtor.[83] Similarly, in jurisdictions where a claim is not required, the outcome of an attack by the debtor's trustee may depend upon whether or not the debtor has waived the exemption.

There is another possible approach to this issue that is conceptually consistent with the policies of the PPSA, the BIA, and exemptions legislation. This approach was employed in the Queen's Bench Court in *Direct Rental Centre (West) Ltd. v. A.C. Waring & Associates Inc.* but rejected by the Alberta Court of Appeal.[84] The starting point is to give full recognition to the ruling of the Supreme Court of Canada in *Royal Bank of Canada v. North American Life Insurance Co.*[85] that upon bankruptcy all the property of the bankrupt, including exempt property, vests in the trustee under BIA section 71(2).[86] BIA section 16(3) requires the trustee to take possession of "all property" of the bankrupt. It is all the

---

83   See *Spence v. Yellowhead Feeders Co-operative Ltd.*, above note 78. See also *Direct Rental Centre (West) Ltd. v. A.C. Waring Associates Inc.*, above note 66. A very peculiar feature of this decision is that, in addition to concluding that exemption is an automatic right under Alberta law, the majority of the Alberta Court concluded that the secured party (lessor) could claim the exemption. However, given the finding that exemptions in Alberta need not be claimed, the reference to the lessor's right to claim the exemption should be treated as irrelevant. As to some of the difficulties involved in the approach adopted by the Court in cases where the debtor is given an election between two or more items of property of the same kind, see the dissenting judgment of Berger J.A.

84   Affirmed on other grounds, above note 66.

85   Above note 35.

86   Admittedly, the BIA, s. 71(2) provides that this vesting is "subject to the rights of secured creditors." However, the BIA defers to provincial law with respect to those rights. While under the PPSA the secured party retains its rights against the debtor to enforce its security interest, the debtor retains its interest in the property that passes to the trustee.

property of the bankrupt that vests in the trustee under BIA section 71(2). This is what the Court referred to as the "property passing stage of bankruptcy."[87] The second stage, the "administration stage," is when BIA section 67(1)(b) comes into play: "Therefore, while an asset that is exempt under provincial law passes into the possession of the trustee at the time of bankruptcy, the exemption itself bars the trustee from dividing the asset among creditors where section 67(1)(b) is operative."[88]

At the very minimum, the trustee acquires on bankruptcy at least a right to possession of all the property of the bankrupt arising from the trustee's obligation under BIA section 16(3) to take possession of it. This includes property that is exempt from execution. The Supreme Court held in *Re Giffen* that possession of the leased goods was sufficient to give the trustee property that would allow the trustee to invoke the PPSA to defeat the unregistered lessor interest. The right to possession under BIA section 16(3) and the vesting of title under BIA section 71(2) give a statutory property interest in the exempt property to the trustee. This meets the requirement that, in order to assert priority over an unperfected security interest, the trustee must have acquired some property right in the collateral.

Since, under the approach set out in *Royal Bank of Canada v. North American Life Insurance Co.*, property in exempt property vests in the trustee, the requirement that the trustee have sufficient property interest in the property to permit a successful attack under the PPSA on an unperfected security interest has been met.

The result of this approach is that the unperfected security interest is defeated by the trustee, but the trustee is precluded by BIA section 67(1)(b) from treating the collateral as property of the estate divisible among creditors. The trustee must then turn possession of the property over to the bankrupt. However, the uncertainty does not stop there. It is necessary to determine the relationship that exists between the bankrupt and the secured party.

One approach is to conclude that the bankrupt's interest in the property is free from the security interest that has been defeated by the trustee. The secured party is precluded from enforcing its security interest against the bankrupt who is sheltered by having acquired the interest through the trustee. This is so even though, under the applicable exemptions law, the debtor would not otherwise be entitled to claim the exemption against the secured party either because there are no exemptions for property subject to a security interest or because of a pur-

---

87   Above note 35 at 354–55 (S.C.R.).
88   *Ibid.* at 358.

chase money security interest in exempt property held by the secured party. The trustee would be estopped by BIA section 67(1) from asserting a property interest in the exempt property, with the result that the debtor would be treated as unencumbered owner of it. The anomaly associated with this approach is that the unperfected security interest that could be enforced against the debtor outside of bankruptcy is lost when the debtor becomes a bankrupt.

An alternative approach is to conclude that the bankrupt is not "sheltered" under the position of the trustee. While the security interest is subordinate to the trustee, it remains effective against the bankrupt on an *inter partes* basis. This approach draws on the principle that perfection of a security interest is relevant only in the.context of·competing priority claims to the collateral. It is not relevant in the context of the relationship between the secured party and the debtor. The practical result of the second approach is to excuse the secured party from the requirement of the PPSA to perfect its security interest in order to protect it from subordination by the trustee in bankruptcy.

FURTHER READINGS

BUCKWOLD, T.M., "Post-Bankruptcy Remedies of Secured Creditors: As Good As It Gets" (1999) 31 Can. Bus. L.J. 436

BUCKWOLD, T.M., "Re Giffen: The Personal Property Security Act and the Bankruptcy and Insolvency Act — Peace at Last" (1999) 14 B.F.L.R. 173

BUCKWOLD, T.M., "Post-Bankruptcy Remedies of Secured Creditors: A Reply to Professor Ziegel" (2000) 33 Can. Bus. L.J. 128

TELFER, T.G.W., "Transplanting Equitable Subordination: The New Free-Wheeling Equitable Discretion in Canadian Insolvency Law?" (2001) 36 Can. Bus. L.J. 36

ZIEGEL, J.S., "Post-Bankruptcy Remedies of Secured Creditors: Comments on Professor Buckwold's Article" (1999) 32 Can. Bus. L.J. 142

ZIEGEL, J.S., "Post-Bankruptcy Remedies of Secured Creditors: A Brief Rejoinder" (2000) 33 Can. Bus. L.J. 144

CHAPTER 12

FOLLOWING AND TRACING INTO NEW FORMS OF COLLATERAL

A. OVERVIEW

1) Following and Tracing

A secured party may assert a personal or proprietary claim based upon the secured party's security interest in the collateral.[1] Before being in a position to do so, the secured party must demonstrate that the property in question was indeed subject to the security interest. There are two distinct processes that may precede the assertion of a claim by a secured party. The first involves following the collateral. The second involves tracing into the proceeds of the collateral.

The objective of following is to locate and identify the collateral. If the secured party wishes to enforce its security interest against the asset, it must show that it was the same asset that was given to the secured party as collateral. Tracing does not seek to identify the original collateral. Instead it looks to new property that was obtained as a result of a dealing with the original collateral. This new property is viewed as a substitute for the original collateral, and the secured party is thereby permitted to claim a security interest in it.

It may be necessary to conduct an exercise in both tracing and following. This is illustrated in the following scenario.

---

1   See chapter 13, A.1 "Personal Claims and Proprietary Claims."

A secured party (SP) holds a security interest in the debtor's (D's) boat. D sells the boat and takes a motorcycle as part of the price. D then sells the motorcycle to a buyer (B).

SP may claim a security interest in the motorcycle as proceeds arising out of the dealing with the original collateral. This step involves tracing. Having done so, SP may then attempt to demonstrate that the motorcycle in the hands of the B is the same one that earlier had been received by D. This step involves following. If the tracing and following exercises are successful, SP may assert that it has a security interest in the motorcycle in the hands of B. This does not mean that SP will necessarily succeed against B. This will be determined by the priority rules of the PPSA. But if SP cannot show a basis for claiming a security interest in the motorcycle in the possession of B, it will not even get out of the starting gate.

The PPSA expressly recognizes the distinction between following collateral and tracing proceeds. It provides that where collateral is dealt with so as to give rise to proceeds, the security interest continues in the collateral and also extends to the proceeds.[2] In order to assert a security interest in the property that has been transferred to a third party, it is necessary for the secured party to demonstrate that this property was subject to its security interest. This is an exercise in following collateral. If the transaction results in the receipt of assets by way of exchange, the security interest will continue in the proceeds. This is an exercise in tracing proceeds.

2) Following Collateral into New Products

A property right is a right in relation to a thing. If the subject matter of the property right is destroyed, the property right comes to an end. A security interest is a kind of property interest, and therefore physical destruction of the collateral will result in a loss of the security interest. However, matters are not always so clear-cut. The collateral may have been transformed in some fundamental way, and the question will arise whether its identity as a separate thing can still be said to exist. This may occur where goods are processed or manufactured into a new product, or where goods are attached to other goods or to land so as to lose their separate identity.

---

2   PPSA (A, BC, M, NB, NWT, Nu, PEI, S) s. 28(1); (NL, NS) s. 29(1); O s. 25(1); Y s. 26(1).

Under the common law, an interest in property can be lost by specification (that is, the transformation of the goods into a new thing), by accession (that is, becoming attached to other goods) or by becoming a fixture (that is, becoming attached to land). However, a property interest is not lost upon the goods being mixed with other goods of the same description. In this case, the owner obtained an interest in the mixture that is proportionate to the owner's contribution to the mixture.[3]

A security interest under the PPSA provides the secured party with a more robust right than is available under the common law. The security interest is not as easily lost upon a transformation of the goods.[4] If the goods become an accession or a fixture, the secured party will typically have the right to remove it. In the case of a loss of identity due to the goods being manufactured or processed, the security interest is not lost but instead continues in the finished product. However, in each of these cases an exercise in following is necessary in order to demonstrate that it was the original collateral, and not some other property of the debtor, that was transformed. Because the secured party has a greater ability to assert its security interest in the fixture, accession, or new product, it becomes necessary to provide an expanded set of priority rules in the PPSA to determine the outcome of the priority disputes that will inevitably arise.

3) Tracing Value into New Assets

Tracing permits "one asset to stand in place of another for certain legal purposes."[5] In the context of a secured transaction, a secured party may seek to claim that assets that were obtained by a debtor upon the disposition of the secured party's collateral are subject to its security interest. Before the PPSA, there was considerable uncertainty concerning the ability of a secured party to claim a security interest in

---

3   There is uncertainty on whether this interest involves co-ownership of the bulk or if it involves recognition of a continuing ownership in the contribution. See P. Birks, "Mixtures" in N. Palmer and E. McKendrick, eds., *Interests in Goods*, 2d ed. (London: LLP Reference Publishing, 1998) at 461 (advocating co-ownership); L. Smith, *The Law of Tracing* (Oxford: Clarendon Press, 1997) at 75–77 (advocating continuing ownership). The rules differ if one of the contributors is a wrongdoer.

4   The PPSA provisions might equally be conceptualized as involving the creation of a new property right in the transformed asset rather than as a continuation of the original right. However, as the PPSA provides a set of rules that govern priority competitions over the transformed asset, it is unnecessary to determine if the property right is conceptually a new right or a continuation of the original right.

5   Smith, above note 3 at 17.

proceeds.[6] The PPSA eliminates any doubt on this matter by expressly providing that a security interest in original collateral extends to any proceeds of disposition.

In some cases, the process can be quite simple. The debtor sells a truck and receives a cheque and an automobile in exchange. So long as the debtor is still in possession of the cheque and the automobile, tracing is simple and uncontroversial. Matters become more complicated if the cheque is deposited in an active bank account and mixed with other funds. It is no longer factually possible to show how much of the funds in the account are proceeds. Here, the tracing exercise operates through the application of a number of legal presumptions that tell us the extent to which the proceeds of the original collateral remain in the account.

The tracing claim is different from a claim based on following the original asset. Tracing is premised on the idea of an exchange or substitution, whereas following is not. In the case of a manufacturing process, it might be thought that this involves a dealing with the original collateral (the raw product) and that this gives rise to proceeds (the finished product). This fails to properly distinguish between following and tracing, and results in an unjustified overlap between the PPSA provisions that deal with proceeds and those that deal with commingled and processed goods. The secured party must demonstrate that its collateral, rather than some other property, was used to form the mixture or the new product. This requires the secured party to follow the original asset to show that it was so used. This is conceptually different from tracing which involves an exchange of one asset for another.

4) Tracing and Identifying Proceeds

When an asset is dealt with by a debtor, the debtor sometimes obtains a straight substitution or swap of one asset for another. This is sometimes referred to as a clean substitution. In other cases, the asset may be mixed with property or value belonging to another person. The classic example of this concerns money that is deposited into an active bank account into which funds of others have been deposited. This is

---

6   A secured party's claim to proceeds was recognized in respect of a Bank Act security by the Supreme Court of Canada in *Flintoft v. Royal Bank of Canada*, [1964] S.C.R. 631. However, it remains unclear whether the claim depended upon the existence of an express trusts proceeds clause in the security agreement, or if it arose because the Bank Act is said to effectively vest "ownership" of the goods in the bank.

sometimes referred to as a mixed substitution. In such a case, it is often necessary to apply a legal presumption to determine how much of a person's value survives in the mixture, because it is no longer possible to factually identify the substituted asset. Under the common law and equity, a claim to the substituted asset, whether or not there is a mixture involved, is referred to as a tracing claim.

The PPSA adopts a different terminology to distinguish between clean substitutions and mixed substitutions. The Act draws a distinction between identifiable and traceable proceeds. Identifiable proceeds are proceeds in which it is possible to factually identify the proceeds. Traceable proceeds are those involving a mixture where it is necessary to apply one of the presumptive rules to determine how much of the secured party's value remains in the mixture of assets. A claim to the substituted asset (the proceeds), whether or not there is a mixture involved, is referred to as a proceeds claim. This PPSA terminology and usage is employed in the balance of this chapter and the other chapters of this book.

B. PROCEEDS

1) Extension of the Security Interest to Proceeds

a) The Statutory Right to Proceeds
The PPSA provides that where collateral gives rise to proceeds, the security interest extends to the proceeds.[7] The right to a security interest in proceeds therefore arises by operation of law and does not depend upon the presence of a trust proceeds clause in the security agreement. Despite this, the Ontario Court of Appeal in *General Motors Acceptance Corp. of Canada Ltd. v. Bank of Nova Scotia*[8] indicated that a trust proceeds clause is needed in order for a secured party to obtain the strongest claim to proceeds. The Court held that the debtor must owe a fiduciary obligation to the secured party to entitle the secured party to invoke the equitable tracing rules which would permit it to trace into a mixed fund.

There are two serious difficulties with this position. First, the view that a fiduciary obligation is needed in order to invoke the equitable

---

7   PPSA (A, BC, M, NB, NWT, Nu, PEI, S) s. 28(1); (NL, NS) s. 29(1); O s. 25(1); Y s. 26(1).
8   (1986), 55 O.R. (2d) 438 (C.A.).

tracing principles,[9] or indeed that there is any difference between the tracing principles of equity and those of the common law, has been challenged.[10] Second, even if it were accepted that a fiduciary obligation is required in order to invoke the equitable tracing principles, there is no reason to think that this requirement has been incorporated into the PPSA. The Act provides that a secured party's security interest continues in any identifiable or traceable personal property that arises out of a dealing with the original collateral. The reference to traceable personal property was simply intended to bring into operation the rules and principles that permit a claim to be made when property or funds are mixed. The Saskatchewan Court of Appeal has held that this creates a statutory right to claim proceeds and that this right is not subject to any of the limitations or preconditions that might have been imposed by the common law or equity.[11] This position has since been codified. All the Acts, other than the Ontario and Yukon Acts, provide that proceeds are traceable whether or not there is a fiduciary relationship between the secured party and the debtor.[12]

There are signs that the Ontario Court of Appeal may reconsider its position. The Ontario Act was amended after the *General Motors Acceptance Corp.* decision by the removal of the words "identifiable or traceable" from the substantive provisions and their insertion into the definition of proceeds. In *Toronto-Dominion Bank v. Co-Pac Ltd.*,[13] the Court raised the possibility that "this change signals a legislative attempt to ensure that full tracing rights including those based on equitable principles are not preconditioned on the existence of a fiduciary relationship between creditor and debtor."[14] Although it is highly

---

9   See Smith, above note 3 at 120–32. This suggestion is even more surprising given the fact that Canadian courts have rejected the idea that it is necessary to establish a fiduciary obligation as a pre-condition for tracing in equity. See P. Maddaugh and J. McCamus, *The Law of Restitution* (Aurora: Canada Law Book, 1990) at 87–93.

10 *F.C. Jones & Sons v. Jones*, [1996] 4 All ER 721 (C.A.). And see Smith, *ibid.*, at 162–74; P. Birks, "The Necessity of a Unitary Law of Tracing" in R. Cranston, ed., *Making Commercial Law* (Oxford: Clarendon, 1997). See also *Grant v. Ste Marie Estate*, [2005] A.J. No. 48 (Q.B.).

11 *Transamerica Commercial Finance Corp. Canada v. Royal Bank of Canada* (1990), 70 D.L.R. (4th) 627 (Sask. C.A.). See also *Indian Head Credit Union v. Andrew*, [1993] 1 W.W.R. 673 (Sask. C.A.); *Flexi-Coil Ltd. v. Kindersley District Credit Union Ltd.* (1993), 107 D.L.R. (4th) 129 (Sask. C.A.).

12 PPSA A s. 1(6); (BC, NWT, Nu) s. 1(4); (M, NB, PEI) s. 2(3); (NL, NS) s. 3(3); S s. 2(4).

13 (1999), 178 D.L.R. (4th) 149 (Ont. C.A.).

14 *Ibid.* at 154.

doubtful whether the amendment was intended to achieve this result, it gives rise to some hope that the Court will revisit its decision.[15]

The parties to a security agreement may by contract limit or eliminate the right to proceeds that a secured party would otherwise enjoy. In *Credit Suisse Canada v. 1133 Yonge Street Holdings Ltd.*,[16] a security interest was given in all existing and future leases and rents arising in connection with commercial premises that had been financed by the secured party. The agreement provided that until notified to the contrary, the debtor "shall be entitled to" all rents and other amounts due under the leases. The court interpreted this contractual language as giving the debtor the right to treat the rental payments as the debtor's own property until notified to the contrary. In effect, the secured party had contracted out of its right to the proceeds prior to notice.

A distinction must be drawn between cases where the secured party contracts out of its right to proceeds and instances where a secured party has merely authorized the debtor to deal with the proceeds. In the latter case, the secured party will have a security interest in the proceeds, but will take subject to any transaction that it authorized. Thus, a secured party who has financed the new vehicle inventory of a car dealership will have a security interest in any trade-in vehicles, but will generally authorize the debtor to sell the trade-in vehicles. The secured party will therefore be able to claim a security interest in the trade-in vehicles that are on the lot, but will not have any claim to the vehicles sold by the debtor to its customers. The same analysis should apply in principle where the proceeds take the form of funds in a bank account. If the secured party permits the debtor to deposit proceeds in its operating account and authorizes the debtor to use the funds to pay operating expenses, the secured party has the right to claim the remaining funds as proceeds (to the extent that they can be traced), but has no claim against any party who obtained payment from this fund.[17]

---

15   See also *Credit Suisse Canada v. 1133 Yonge Street Holdings* (1996) 28 O.R. (3d) 670 (Gen. Div.), var'd on other grounds (1998), 41 O.R. (3d) 632 (C.A.) in which Day J. expressed the view that the position of the Saskatchewan Court of Appeal was to be preferred.

16   *Ibid.*, cited to C.A.

17   The parties who acquire an interest in the proceeds may, of course, have an additional basis for claiming priority. The buyers of trade-ins will likely be able to claim the benefit of the ordinary course buyer rule. See chapter 7. Creditors who are paid by cash or cheque will be able to rely on priority rules that protect holders of negotiable property. See chapter 9.

b) Advantages of a Proceeds Claim

There are two primary reasons why a secured party may seek to claim proceeds under the PPSA. The first concerns the extension of the security interest to assets that were not taken as collateral pursuant to the terms of the security agreement. Suppose that a secured party takes a security interest in the debtor's backhoe and in no other collateral. The debtor later exchanges the backhoe for a bulldozer. The secured party may assert a security interest in respect of the bulldozer as proceeds, despite the fact that the security agreement did not give the secured party a security interest in it as original collateral. If the secured party had taken a security interest in all he debtor's present and after-acquired personal property, the secured party would not need to go to the bother of showing that the bulldozer was proceeds that arose from a disposition of the backhoe. The secured party could claim a security interest in the bulldozer as original collateral in the form of after-acquired personal property.

The second reason a secured party may seek to claim proceeds is that the claim may permit the secured party to assert a special status in respect of the proceeds. This is most commonly observed in respect of a secured party who has been given a purchase money security interest in the collateral. The PPSA provides that a holder of a purchase money security interest in collateral or its proceeds has priority over any other security interest given by the same debtor.[18] A secured party may therefore assert a claim to proceeds in order to obtain an enhanced priority status in relation to them. In such a case, the secured party may want to assert a proceeds claim even though its security agreement gives it a security interest in that property as original collateral. Suppose that a secured party enters into a security agreement that gives it a purchase money security interest in a backhoe, and an ordinary security interest in "all present and after-acquired construction equipment." Although its security agreement gives it a security interest in the bulldozer, this does not allow it to claim priority over a competing secured party who registered first. In order to succeed, the secured party must show that its purchase money security interest status extends to the bulldozer. It does so by demonstrating that the bulldozer is proceeds, that is, by showing that the bulldozer was obtained by the debtor as a result of a dealing with the backhoe.

---

18 See, for example, PPSA (A, M, NWT, Nu, S) s. 34(2); (BC, NB, PEI) s. 34(1); (NL, NS) s. 35(1); O s. 33(2); Y s. 33(1).

The PPSA makes it clear that the superpriority of a purchase money security interest in original collateral extends as well to any proceeds.[19] Other statutes that deal with security interests may be less clear on this point. For example, provincial legislation may provide that a landlord's right of distress or an employee's claim for unpaid wages has priority over a security interest other than a purchase money security interest. The statute therefore may not make it clear whether the priority of the purchase money security interest also extends to the proceeds.[20] Although the outcome in each particular case will depend upon the construction of the individual statute, the courts have been inclined to construe the priority status awarded by these statutes as applying to proceeds as well.[21]

c)   Enforcement against Both the Original Collateral and the Proceeds

The PPSA provides that a security interest continues in the original collateral and as well extends to any proceeds that arise as a result of a dealing with the original collateral.[22] This permits a secured party to claim a security interest in both the original collateral and proceeds. This represents a departure from the general approach of the common law, which typically requires a claimant to make an election between a claim to the original property and a claim to the proceeds.[23] In many instances, the secured party will have authorized the debtor to deal with the original collateral. Where this occurs, the buyer will take free of the security interest and the secured party will only be able to claim a security interest in the proceeds. The ability to go against both the

---

19   PPSA (A, M, NWT, Nu, S) s. 34(2)–(3); (BC, NB, PEI) s. 34(1)–(2); (NL, NS) s. 35(1)–(2); (O, Y) s. 33(1)–(2).

20   Compare with *Employment Standards Code*, R.S.A. 2000, c. E-9, s. 109(4) (priority statutory security interest in favour of unpaid employees does not apply to a purchase money security interest, but no mention of the status of proceeds); *Civil Enforcement Act*, R.S.A. 2000, c. C-15, s. 104(c)(iii) (right of distress subordinate to a purchase money security interest in original collateral or its proceeds).

21   See, for example, *Agricultural Credit Corp. of Saskatchewan v. Pettyjohn* (1991), 79 D.L.R. (4th) 22 (Sask. C.A.) [*Pettyjohn*]. Saskatchewan farm protection legislation provides that farm assets are exempt against a security interest other than a purchase money security interest. The Court held that the exception to the exemption extended also to proceeds of a purchase money security interest.

22   This change in the law was clearly intended. The language used is substantially the same as that of the *Uniform Commercial Code*. The Official Comment to 1978 UCC 9-306 (Comment 3) indicates that "the secured party may claim both proceeds and collateral, but may of course have only one satisfaction."

23   See Smith, above note 3 at 380–83.

proceeds and the original collateral is only available where the debtor has acted wrongfully in disposing of the original collateral.

Unlike the Ontario and Yukon Acts, the Acts of the other jurisdictions impose a limitation on the ability of a secured party to claim a security interest in both the original collateral and the proceeds. Where a secured party enforces a security interest against both the original collateral and the proceeds, the amount secured by the security interest is limited to the market value of the collateral at the date of the dealing.[24] The operation of this provision is illustrated in the following scenario.

SP is given a security interest in D's crane to secure a loan. D sells the crane to B for $50,000 under circumstances such that SP's security interest in the crane is not lost. B pays for the crane by giving D a cheque for $20,000 and a bulldozer in trade. Three years later, the debtor defaults. The crane presently has a value of $35,000 while the bulldozer has a value of $25,000.

SP may claim a security interest in both the crane and the bulldozer. However, SP may not recover more than $50,000 (the market value of the crane at the time of the sale by D to B).

The Ontario and Yukon Acts do not contain a similar limitation. The issue that has yet to be decided is whether the secured party will be able to proceed against the full value of both the original collateral and the proceeds, or whether a court will read into the statute a limitation similar to the one contained in the Acts of the other jurisdictions. The authors are of the opinion that such a limitation would be the most appropriate response. The basic premise behind the proceeds provisions is that the proceeds should stand in the place of the original collateral. Although a secured party has the right to claim both the original collateral and the proceeds where there has been a wrongful dealing by the debtor,[25] this was intended to protect the secured party against a post-disposition deterioration in the value of the original collateral or the proceeds and was not intended to give an unexpected windfall to the secured party at the expense of the debtor or the unsecured creditors of the debtor.

---

24   PPSA (A, BC, M, NB, NWT, Nu, PEI, S) s. 28(1); (NL, NS) s. 29(1); O s. 25(1); Y s. 26(1).

25   If the secured party has authorized the dealing, the secured party will no longer be able to assert a security interest in the original collateral.

2) The Definition of Proceeds

Proceeds are defined in the PPSA to mean identifiable or traceable personal property[26] derived directly or indirectly from any dealing with collateral or proceeds of collateral.[27] The Acts of all jurisdictions except Ontario and the Yukon include an additional requirement that the debtor must acquire an interest in the proceeds. All the Acts provide that the definition of proceeds also includes a payment as indemnity or compensation for loss or damage to the collateral or proceeds. All Acts, except the Ontario and Yukon Acts, also provide that proceeds include a payment made in total or partial discharge or redemption of an intangible, chattel paper, an instrument, or a security. Although the definition may appear to be relatively simple and straightforward, it contains within it several important messages that directly affect the nature and scope of a secured party's claim to proceeds.

a) Application to Later Generation Proceeds

Proceeds are defined as personal property derived directly or indirectly from any dealing with collateral or the proceeds of the collateral. The definition therefore covers second-generation and later-generation proceeds.[28] This is illustrated in the following scenario.

SP takes a security interest in D's truck. D sells the truck to B and takes an automobile in trade. D later sells the automobile to C and takes a snowmobile in trade.

The original collateral is the truck. It was sold to B, giving rise to proceeds in the form of an automobile (first-generation proceeds). When these proceeds are sold to C, the transaction gives rise to further proceeds in the form of a snowmobile (second-generation proceeds).

b) The Debtor's Interest Requirement

The definition of proceeds in the PPSA, except for the Ontario and Yukon Acts, contains a further limitation. It provides that property that would otherwise qualify as proceeds does not fall within the definition

---

26   The definition of proceeds therefore does not cover real property — whether a secured party has a right to proceeds that take the form of real property therefore depends on other law. The registration requirements of real estate law would defeat a proceeds right as against third parties, but not necessarily as against the debtor.

27   PPSA (A, BC, NWT, Nu, O, Y) s. 1(1); (M, NB, PEI) s. 1; (NL, NS) s. 2; S s. 2(1).

28   See *Flexi-Coil Ltd. v. Kindersley District Credit Union Ltd.*, above note 11.

of proceeds unless the debtor acquires an interest in the property. The operation of this limitation is illustrated in the following scenario.

SP takes a security interest in a drill press. D sells the drill press to B1. B1 is unable to assert any of the buyer-priority rules, so that SP has the right to enforce the security interest against it. B1 later sells the drill press to B2 and receives a router in trade.

SP does not have a security interest in the router in the hands of B2. Although the router was derived from a dealing with the original collateral, the router does not fall within the definition of proceeds because D never acquired an interest in it.

There are two reasons for this limitation. The first is the risk of the geometric multiplication of proceeds claims that could otherwise arise. Suppose that a debtor sells an asset that is subject to a security interest to B1. B1 sells it to B2, who in turn sells it to B3, who then sells it to B4. In addition to a claim to the original collateral, the secured party, in the absence of this limitation, would be entitled to claim the proceeds in the hands of D, B1, B2, and B3. The picture is complicated further because D, B1, B2, and B3 may have dealt with these proceeds, giving rise to further proceeds. Since the secured party is not required to make an election between the original collateral and the proceeds, its security interest could easily proliferate into an astonishing collection of assets.

The second reason has to do with the relative strength of the secured party's claim to the proceeds.[29] A claimant who is seeking to assert equitable property rights through tracing is subject to a serious limitation. The tracing claim will be defeated by a *bona fide* purchaser who acquires the legal title to the asset without notice. The same does not hold true in respect of a secured party who asserts a security interest in proceeds. The claim to proceeds enjoys much the same priority status as that pertaining to the original collateral. The PPSA identifies certain circumstances under which buyers of goods or purchasers of negotiable assets obtain priority over a secured party. But these rules are vastly more limited than equity's *bona fide* purchaser rule. Moreover, the registry system will generally not provide a means through which the purchaser can discover the existence of the proceeds claim that is asserted against a person other than the debtor. In the scenario above, B2 would conduct a search of the registry using B1's name as the

---

29   See L. Smith, "Tracing the Proceeds of Collateral under the PPSA: *Flexi-Coil Ltd. v. Kindersley District Credit Union Ltd.*" (1995) 25 Can. Bus. L.J. 460 at 469–72.

search criteria. This would not disclose SP's security interest, since this was registered against D's name.

A similar limitation on the definition of proceeds is not found in the Ontario or Yukon Acts. In the past, the other Acts also did not contain this limitation. However, the Saskatchewan Court of Appeal in *Flexi-Coil Ltd. v. Kindersley District Credit Union Ltd.*[30] read it into the definition of proceeds in the former Saskatchewan Act. Although some Ontario commentators have argued that a similar limitation should not be read into the Ontario Act,[31] the authors are of the opinion that the geometric multiplication of proceeds claims and the enhanced priority status of a secured-party's claim to proceeds are convincing reasons for adopting a uniform approach to this problem across all the PPSA jurisdictions.

c) The Requirement of a Dealing

In order to fall within the definition of proceeds, the personal property in which a proceeds security interest is claimed must arise directly or indirectly from a dealing with the collateral. This clearly encompasses property that is obtained as a result of an exchange. If collateral is sold and a trade-in and a cheque are received by way of payment, the trade-in and the cheque fall within the definition. There are other cases where the property does not arise out of an exchange, and it will become necessary to determine if this property also can be considered to result from a dealing. One might begin by filtering out the more extreme examples. Consider the case of a secured party who has been granted a security interest in a truck that the debtor uses to generate revenue through the transportation of goods. It might be argued that the use of the truck to generate income should be considered to be a "dealing," with the result that the income produced will be considered to be proceeds. This argument should be rejected. The Ontario Court of Appeal in *General Motors Acceptance Corp. of Canada Ltd. v. Cardinali*[32] recognized that in order to fall within the definition there must be an exchange, although the exchange does not necessarily have to result from a voluntary or consensual transaction. In that case, a secured party reserved a security interest in a boat that it sold to the debtor, but the debtor refused to accept it because of defects in the boat. The

---

30 Above note 11.
31 J.S. Ziegel and D.L. Denomme, *The Ontario Personal Property Security Act: Commentary and Analysis* (Aurora: Canada Law Book, 1994) at 198.
32 (2000), 185 D.L.R. (4th) 141 (Ont. C.A.), referring to Ziegel and Denomme, *ibid.* at 179.

seller then tendered a different boat in performance of its obligation. The transaction did not involve an exchange, since the buyer never did acquire an interest in the original collateral. The situation would have been different if the buyer had acquired the boat and later exchanged it for another.

The same analysis should hold true for fruits and products generated by the original collateral or its proceeds. This would include such things as the young of animals, wool taken from sheep, or apples harvested from trees. These should not be regarded as proceeds as they do not involve an exchange. Nonetheless, the Saskatchewan Court of Appeal concluded that the offspring of animals could fall within the definition of proceeds.[33] The definition of proceeds in the Saskatchewan legislation was subsequently amended to provide that it "does not include animals merely because they are offspring of animals that are collateral."[34] Notwithstanding this case, the authors are of the view that the fruit and products of the original collateral or its proceeds should not fall within the definition of proceeds.

d) The "Identifiable or Traceable" Requirement

In order to fall within the definition of proceeds, the personal property must be identified or traceable. The Ontario Court of Appeal in *General Motors Acceptance Corp. of Canada Ltd. v. Bank of Nova Scotia*[35] described the difference between these two concepts as follows: "Proceeds are identifiable when they continue to exist in their original form. They are traceable if they are converted into a substituted form which can be located and determined to be the substitution for the original proceeds."

This passage is ambiguous. On one reading it seems to suggest that a distinction is to be drawn between first-generation proceeds (that is, identifiable proceeds in their original form) and subsequent generations of proceeds (traceable proceeds). Alternatively, the Court may have been intending to draw a distinction between a transaction that involves a simple swap of one asset for another and a transaction in which the proceeds have changed form or are mixed with other assets such that the tracing rules must be invoked. The definition of proceeds in the PPSA makes it clear that both first-generation proceeds and second (or later) generation proceeds can be either identifiable or traceable. This interpretation has been embraced by the Saskatchewan Court of Ap-

---

33   *Weiller & Williams Ltd. v. Ager* (1992), 4 P.P.S.A.C. (2d) 19 (Sask. Q.B.).
34   The legislation of the other jurisdictions does not contain a similar provision.
35   Above note 8 at 442.

peal[36] which concluded that "identifiable" refers to the ability to point to the particular property obtained by the debtor as a result of the dealing with the collateral (or proceeds), while "traceable" refers to the situation where the collateral is commingled with other property so that its identity is lost. Identification of proceeds simply involves a factual inquiry. All that is needed is that the secured party can point to particular assets that were obtained as a result of the dealing. An automobile that is subject to a security interest might be sold in exchange for a trade-in and a cheque. Both are first-generation proceeds and both are identifiable. The cheque might then be deposited in a bank account. At this point a further issue of identifiably arises. If there were no other funds in the bank account other than the cheque that was deposited, the bank account would also be considered to be identifiable proceeds. But if the funds from the deposited cheque became mixed with other funds in an active account, it is no longer possible to identify the proceeds. Instead, one must turn to the rules of tracing in order to determine how much of the funds in the account should be considered to be proceeds.

3) The Tracing Rules

a) Are PPSA Tracing Rules Different from Conventional Tracing Rules?

At one time it seems to have been generally accepted that there were two different sets of tracing rules that had been developed by the courts: common law tracing rules and equitable tracing rules. It was also generally accepted that the common law tracing rules were in many respects inferior to the equitable tracing rules.[37] More recently, there has been a growing acceptance of the idea that this view was mistaken and that there exists a unitary set of tracing rules.[38] These judicially created tracing rules will be referred to as the conventional tracing rules. Several courts have commented that although the PPSA tracing rules incorporate many of the key features of the conventional tracing rules, this does not mean that all their features must be incorporated into the context of the PPSA.[39] In *Flexi-Coil Ltd. v. Kindersley District Credit*

---

36 *Transamerica Commercial Finance Corp., Canada v. Royal Bank of Canada*, [1990] 84 Sask. R. 81 (C.A.), Vancise J.A. at 85. (Sask. C.A.).
37 The problem with the common law tracing rules was that it was thought that the common law could not trace through a mixed fund. See, for example, *Banque Belge pour l' Étranger v. Hambrouck*, [1921] 1 K.B. 321 (C.A.).
38 Above note 10.
39 *Pettyjohn*, above note 21.

Union Ltd.,[40] the Saskatchewan Court of Appeal indicated that it would "use the common law and equitable rules as their base, but, as far as possible, seek to found solutions on the statute and its underlying policy." It is therefore necessary to determine how one goes about deciding which aspects of the conventional tracing rules are appropriately included and which are not.

Part of the problem is terminological. Courts often have failed to distinguish the process of tracing from the process of claiming.[41] Tracing is about identifying a new asset that is acquired following a dealing with the original asset. It is neither a right nor a remedy, but rather a process. Claiming is different from tracing. It involves the assertion of some legal right to the substituted asset. Once this difference is appreciated, it becomes possible to quickly dispose of a number of troublesome arguments. For example, it has been argued that the incorporation of the tracing rules into the PPSA brings with it the equitable priority rules that limit the ability of the claimant to assert a right in respect of the traceable assets in the hands of a bona fide purchaser for value without knowledge. This argument fails to understand the difference between tracing and claiming. The tracing rules are used to identify property in which there is so close and substantial a connection that it should be viewed as a substitute for the original asset. Once this is done, it is necessary to determine who has the better claim to the asset. In order to make this determination, one looks to the priority rules of the PPSA and not to the common law and equitable priority rules of property law.

Problems may also be encountered as a result of confusion between the process of tracing and an event that creates a property right. A trustee who withdraws money in breach of trust may later deposit funds with the intention of replacing the trust funds that were wrongfully withdrawn. If this occurs, the funds so deposited will be impressed with a trust.[42] This has nothing at all to do with the law of tracing. The beneficiary's funds are gone, and the substitute asset is in no way connected to it. Rather, the beneficiary acquires an interest in the replacement funds by virtue of a new express trust.[43] As this is not a tracing rule, it is of no relevance to the tracing of proceeds under the PPSA.

---

40   Above note 11.
41   See Smith, above note 3 at 10–14.
42   *James Roscoe (Bolton) Ltd. v. Winder*, [1915] 1 Ch. 62.
43   J. Penner, *The Law of Trusts*, 2d ed. (London: Butterworths, 2000) at 372.

Once one is able to cut through these terminological difficulties, it is apparent that the PPSA tracing rules are much closer to the conventional tracing rules than was previously thought to be the case.

b) The Lowest Intermediate Balance Rule

The identification or tracing of proceeds involves the search for transactional links between the original collateral and the proceeds. Sometimes this process simply involves a substitution. In this case, the inquiry is purely factual. It simply involves the identification of the proceeds that were obtained by the debtor. The process becomes more complex when the transaction does not involve a simple substitution of one asset for another, but instead involves a mixture of an asset with other assets. This often occurs where the proceeds are deposited in an account and mixed with funds that belong to the debtor. If the debtor sells the collateral and deposits the proceeds in a bank account so that it is "mixed" with the debtor's own funds, the secured party will have a security interest in the bank account that secures the value of the proceeds that were deposited in the account. The problem arises when there are subsequent withdrawals from the account. It then becomes necessary to decide whose contribution to the mixture was withdrawn.

The common law provided a rule for the allocation of payments. A debtor who owed more than one debt to a creditor might make a payment to a creditor. There needed to be some rule to determine which debt was being paid. If neither the debtor nor the creditor specifies the debt against which it is to be allocated, a "first-in, first-out" rule is applied. A bank account is regarded as a series of debts that arise each time the customer deposits money into the account. When the customer withdraws money, a first-in, first-out rule is also applied. Each withdrawal of funds is presumed to extinguish the earliest debts. This is known as the rule in *Clayton's Case*.[44]

Although this rule is used to allocate payments as between the bank and its customer, the rule is not applied where the customer's funds are mixed with those belonging to another. Instead, the debtor is presumed to spend the debtor's own funds first.[45] This rule is said to be justified on the theory that the debtor should be subject to a presumption of honesty.[46] This justification does not necessarily apply in

---

44 *Devaynes v. Noble; Clayton's Case* (1816), 1 Mer. 572, 35 E.R. 781.
45 *Re Hallet's Estate* (1880), 13 Ch.D 696 (C.A.).
46 *Ibid.* Jessel M.R. stated at para. 31, "where a man does an act which may be rightfully performed, he cannot say that the act was intentionally and in fact done wrongly."

the case of a secured transaction. The secured party may have author-ized the sale of the original collateral and permitted the debtor to de-posit the proceeds into the debtor's bank account. Unlike a trustee who mixes trust property with her own in breach of trust, the debtor may have been acting lawfully and with the authorization of the secured party. However, the presumption that the person withdraws his or her own share first has been applied in cases where the mixture has been authorized.[47] It is therefore appropriate to apply this presumption to a secured transaction whether or not the secured party has authorized the sale or permitted the mixing of the funds.

If a withdrawal exceeds the value of the debtor's funds in the ac-count, the excess must necessarily come out of the traceable proceeds held in the account. The debtor's funds in the bank account will have been exhausted, and all remaining amounts will be attributable to the proceeds of the security interest. A subsequent deposit of funds belong-ing to the debtor will not have the effect of resurrecting the previous proceeds balance. This is known as the lowest intermediate balance rule. This rule has been applied in a number of cases in the United States where proceeds arising out of a dealing with collateral are mixed in a bank account with funds belonging to the debtor.[48]

The following scenario illustrates the application of the lowest intermediate balance rule.

A debtor sells collateral and deposits the proceeds in the sum of $1,000 into a bank account. The bank account contains $500 belonging to the debtor. The debtor withdraws $750. This leaves $250 in proceeds in the bank ac-count. The debtor next deposits $500 into the account. The balance in the account is $750, of which $250 is proceeds.

If the proceeds that were withdrawn from the account were used to ac-quire an asset, the secured party could trace its proceeds into this new asset, but this does not affect the operation of the lowest intermediate balance rule in respect of the funds remaining in the account.[49]

---

47   Smith, above note 3 at 208–12.
48   See, for example, *Universal C.I.T. Credit Corp. v. Farmers Bank of Portageville*, 358 F. Supp. 317 (D.C. Mo. 1973); *General Motors Acceptance Corp. v. Norstar Bank, N.A.*, 532 N.Y.S.2d 685 (N.Y. Sup, 1988); *Michigan National Bank v. Flowers Mobile Home Sale, Inc.*, 217 S.E.2d 108 (N.C. App. 1975).
49   For example, if the $750 that was withdrawn from the account (made up of $500 of the debtor's money and $250 representing proceeds of the original col-lateral) is used to buy a computer, the secured party would be able to claim a security interest in the computer to the extent of $250.

c)   Tracing and Multiple Claimants

The proceeds from a disposition of collateral might be mixed with other funds in a bank account that do not belong to the debtor.[50] If the debtor later withdraws funds from the account, the presumption that the debtor spends his or her own money first cannot be used since the other funds do not belong to the debtor. Some other principle must be applied in order to decide whose contribution to the fund has been spent. In England, it would appear that the rule in *Clayton's Case* is applied.[51] This approach has been rejected in Canada. In *Ontario (Securities Commission) v. Greymac Credit Corp.*,[52] the loss was allocated *pro rata* among the innocent contributors.

The *pro rata* depletion rule is illustrated in the following scenario.

D gives SP1 a security interest in an automobile, and gives SP2 a security interest in a truck. The automobile is sold and the proceeds are deposited in a bank account on June 10. On June 15, the truck is sold and the proceeds are deposited in the account. D then withdraws money from the account.

If the account contains any funds belonging to D, then these will be presumed to be withdrawn first. But if D does not have any funds in the account or if D's funds are exhausted, it is then necessary to deplete the proceeds funds of secured parties. An application of the rule in *Clayton's Case* would result in the depletion of SP1's proceeds. Once SP1's proceeds are all gone, any further depletion would come out of SP2's proceeds. Under the *pro rata* depletion rule, SP1 and SP2 would share the loss rateably. Suppose SP1's proceeds amounted to $100 and SP2's proceeds amounted to $300. D then withdrew $200 from the account. Of the $200 remaining in the account, SP1 would be able to claim $50 as proceeds and SP2 could claim $150.

The *pro rata* depletion rule does not, in principle, affect the operation of the intermediate balance rule. In applying the *pro rata* depletion rule, the calculation is based upon the amount of proceeds in existence at the time of the mixing, and not upon the original amount contributed to the fund. If the proceeds of one of the contributors have been depleted, the addition of proceeds from another contributor does not

---

50   The scenarios that are used to illustrate the tracing rules consider a case where proceeds claimed by one secured party are mixed in a bank account with proceeds claimed by another secured party. However, the analysis would apply equally if the proceeds were mixed with funds held in trust by the debtor or were otherwise traceable by the other claimant.

51   *Barlow Clowes International Ltd. v. Vaughan*, [1992] 4 All E.R. 22 (C.A.).

52   (1986), 30 D.L.R. (4th) 1 (Ont. C.A.), aff'd [1988] 2 S.C.R. 172 [*Greymac*].

cause the depletion to be reversed. This is illustrated in a continuation of the last scenario.

There is $200 in the bank account. Both the claims of SP1 and SP2 have been depleted on a *pro rata* basis; $200 of proceeds belonging to SP3 are then deposited into the account.

SP1 and SP2 are only allowed to recover the value of their depleted claims ($50 for SP1 and $150 for SP2). If there are no further withdrawals, SP3 will be able to claim all of the $200 contributed into the fund as proceeds. If D makes further withdrawals from the account, the *pro rata* depletion rule will again operate. Thus, if D later withdraws $200 from the account, the *pro rata* depletion rule will operate on SP1's and SP2's depleted proceeds balance. Therefore, the $200 remaining in the account will be attributed in the following manner: $25 to SP1, $75 to SP2, and $100 to SP3.

However, the Ontario Court of Appeal in *Law Society of Upper Canada v. Toronto-Dominion Bank*[53] has cast some doubt on the applicability of the intermediate balance rule in these circumstances. Instead of applying this approach it applied what it called the *pari passu ex post facto* approach. Under this approach, the court determines the original contribution made to the fund as a percentage of the total contributions of all those with claims against the fund. The claimant's *pro rata* share of the assets is determined by multiplying this factor by the total assets available for distribution. If this approach were applied to the last scenario, their respective percentage claims would be: SP1, 16.7 percent; SP2, 50 percent; and SP3, 33.3 percent. As a result, the allocation of proceeds would be as follows: $33 to SP1, $100 to SP2, and $67 to SP3.

In reaching its decision, the Court said that it was open to it to choose between the lowest intermediate balance rule and the *pari passu ex post facto* approach depending upon which was more just, convenient, and equitable under the circumstances. The Court preferred the *pari passu ex post facto* approach in the circumstances of the case before it, because the large number of claimants and transactions would make the calculation difficult or perhaps impossible. It also thought that it made better sense to treat the fund as an indistinguishable blend of debits and credits rather than as an amalgam of the contributions that were placed into it. The case has been sharply criticized on the ground that it overlooks binding Canadian authority and that it rejects the central underlying idea of tracing, which requires the finding of

---

53   (1998), 169 D.L.R. (4th) 353 (Ont. C.A.) [*Law Society of Upper Canada*].

a transactional link between one asset and another.[54] The authors are persuaded that the intermediate balance rule is an integral feature of the law of tracing and that the *Law Society of Upper Canada* decision should be re-examined by the courts.

d) The Relevance of Wrongdoing

The application of conventional tracing rules are affected by wrongdoing on the part of one of the parties. The issue typically arises in connection with a wrongful mixture of funds. Suppose that A wrongfully mixes funds belonging to B with A's own funds. A then makes a withdrawal from the mixed fund. Where a person is responsible for causing an evidential difficulty, all reasonable inferences will be drawn against the person who caused it. Thus, if A withdraws funds from the mixture and spends it, the law will presume that the wrongdoer spent his own money first. The balance in the account that is attributed to B's contribution is diminished only after all of A's money has been exhausted. This outcome is chosen because it is the more favourable to the innocent party.

There are other situations where an assumption that a wrongdoer spends his own money first would not benefit the innocent party. Suppose that A wrongfully mixes $100 of B's money together with $100 belonging to A in a bank account. A withdraws $50 from the account and uses it to buy a clock. Later, A withdraws the remainder of the funds and spends it in a restaurant. In this case, B is permitted to trace her funds into the clock. Again, the outcome is justified because the wrongdoing of A gives B the right to have any evidential uncertainty resolved against A. Following a withdrawal from a mixed fund, the innocent party is therefore given the option to assert that her contribution remains in the account or alternatively that it is traceable into the new asset acquired with the withdrawn funds. The outcome will be different if A can demonstrate that B's funds could not have been used to acquire the asset. Suppose that A can show that the entire bank account was emptied and used to pay taxes and that later A's own funds were deposited into the bank account. In this case, the addition of A's money into the fund will not permit B to trace into the fund. Because the difficulty was caused by A's wrongful mixing of the monies, the onus will

---

54   L. Smith, "Tracing in Bank Accounts: The Lowest Intermediate Balance Rule on Trial" (2000) 33 Can. Bus. L.J. 75 argues that the *pari passu ex post facto* approach was directly rejected in the *Greymac* decision, which upheld the intermediate balance rule and is binding Canadian authority.

be on A to demonstrate that a specific portion of the fund is traceable to A's contribution.[55]

The issue that will need to be decided is whether the same approach to wrongdoing should be adopted in connection with the PPSA tracing rules. This can be illustrated in the following scenario. Suppose that SP is given a security interest in D's bike. Without authorization, D sells the bike for $100 and deposits the money in a bank account that contains $200 belonging to D. D withdraws $100 and uses it to buy a television. D then withdraws the remaining funds and uses it to buy a meal at a restaurant. Can SP resort to the wrongdoing principle and assert a security interest in the television? Or are the PPSA tracing rules more mechanical in nature such that it should be presumed that the debtor withdraws his own money first regardless of the wrongdoing of the debtor?

If the wrongdoer principle can be invoked by a secured party, two consequences will follow. First, the onus will be on the debtor to establish that funds are attributable to the contribution of the debtor rather than the secured party.[56] Second, the secured party will have the option to assert that money withdrawn from the mixture is proceeds if that is more favourable to the secured party than applying the presumption that the debtor spends the debtor's own money first.[57] This will hold true against the debtor's trustee in bankruptcy as well as against the debtor. The mere fact that the transaction involved a security agreement would not, of course, be sufficient to invoke the wrongdoer principle. It would only come into operation where the debtor wrongfully disposed of the collateral and deposited the proceeds into a bank account. If the secured party had authorized the sale and had permitted the debtor to deposit the proceeds into the debtor's bank account, the secured party would have consented to the debtor's conduct and there would be no basis for applying the wrongdoer principle.

There are two potential difficulties in applying the wrongdoing principle in the context of a secured transaction. The first concerns the distributional impact of the rule. In most cases where the issue arises, the competition is not between a secured party and the debtor. Rather, the dispute is between the secured party and the unsecured creditors or trustee in bankruptcy of the debtor. Although the wrongdoing principle purports to achieve a just result between the secured party and the debtor, in most cases the issue is not misconduct on the part

55   *Re Hallet's Estate*, above note 45.
56   *Ibid.; Re Saskatchewan General Trusts Corp.*, [1938] 3 D.L.R. 544 (Sask. C.A.).
57   *Re Oatway*, [1903] 2 Ch. 356.

of the debtor but whether assets of the debtor should be treated as being subject to the security interest of the secured party or available to the unsecured creditors of an insolvent debtor. The principle punishes unsecured creditors who have not engaged in wrongdoing. A counter-argument to this is that this also holds true in the context of the conventional tracing rules. To the extent that there is a concern about the distributional impact on unsecured creditors, the approach should be the same for both the conventional and PPSA tracing rules.

The second problem concerns the contractual language that is found in security agreements. Frequently security agreements contain provisions that obligate the debtor to segregate and account for the proceeds. It is equally common to find that these provisions are routinely ignored by the debtor with the knowledge and acquiescence of the secured party. There are two possible responses to this problem. One response is to reject the wrongdoer principle outright and apply the presumption that the debtor withdraws the debtor's own money first whether or not the debtor was authorized to mix the funds.[58] This is not the only possible response to the problem. Another approach would be for courts to adopt a less formalistic interpretation of contractual language and to show a greater willingness to recognize a variation of the written contractual provisions through implied conduct and acquiescence. A problem with this approach is that it will often entail factual complexity, leading to uncertainty of outcomes and increased costs of litigation.

In *Agricultural Credit Corp. of Saskatchewan v. Pettyjohn*,[59] the Saskatchewan Court of Appeal considered the case of an unauthorized sale of collateral followed by the deposit of the proceeds into the debtor's bank account. It was possible to trace these proceeds of sale into the acquisition of a replacement herd. Approximately half of the original cattle were subject to a purchase money security interest, while the other half was not. Under Saskatchewan farm security law, the debtor was able to claim an exemption in respect of the cattle unless they were subject to a purchase money security interest. The majority opinion took the view that the tracing principles should be the same whether they arise in cases involving disputes between the secured party and the debtor or whether they involve competitions between a secured party and a competing third-party claimant. As a result, the majority

---

58   See R. Cuming, "Protecting Security Interests in Proceeds: Equity and Canadian Personal Property Acts" in J. Waters, ed., *Equity, Fiduciaries and Trusts, 1993* (Toronto: Carswell, 1993) 423 at 433–35.

59   Above note 21.

held that the debtor could claim the exemption in respect of half of the cattle, notwithstanding the wrongful sale of the cattle. The dissenting opinion took the contrary view and was prepared to presume that any diminishment in the value of the herd was to be taken out of the debtor's interest in the cattle.

e) Tracing through Payment of a Debt

There is considerable uncertainty about whether it is possible to trace value into property acquired on credit where traceable proceeds are used to repay this debt. Suppose that the debtor has a bank account into which proceeds from the sale of collateral have been deposited. Suppose also that after applying the intermediate balance rule, it is determined that all the funds in the account are proceeds. The debtor then buys a car for $10,000, but does not immediately pay for it. Finally, the debtor withdraws $10,000 from the account and uses it to pay the debt incurred as a result of the purchase of the automobile.

The issue is whether the security interest in the funds in the bank account can be traced into the automobile. Some argue that it should not be capable of being traced. They point out that the debtor was the owner of the automobile at the time the money was withdrawn from the account, and therefore it is not possible to show that the money was used to acquire the automobile.[60] However, there is growing support for the idea that it is possible to trace through the payment of a debt.[61] This has also been referred to as "backwards tracing."[62] The Saskatchewan Court of Appeal in *Agricultural Credit Corp. of Saskatchewan v. Pettyjohn*[63] alluded to the possbility of tracing through payment of a debt, which it called "tracing by subrogation," but did not need to decide this question.

There is no reason, in principle, why the statutory tracing principles of the PPSA should be any different from conventional tracing principles on this question. However, if tracing value through the payment of a debt is accepted, it is important to understand the limitations of the concept. It does not mean that everything that was acquired in the past and paid for out of the account will be proceeds. It will still be necessary to show that the debt that was extinguished was related to the acquisition of an asset. If the payment was unconnected to the

---

60   *Bishopsgate Investment Management Ltd. (In. Liquidation) v. Homan*, [1995] Ch. 211 (C.A.), Leggatt L.J.

61   Smith, above note 3 at 146–52.

62   Penner, above note 43 at 375–79.

63   Above note 21.

acquisition of an asset by the debtor, then there will be nothing to trace into. It also follows that a reduction in the size of an overdraft does not permit tracing into subsequent purchases that were made possible by this reduction. In cases involving an overdraft facility, it may be very difficult or impossible to show where the value went. If that is the case, the secured party will simply be unable to trace its proceeds. But if it can show that its funds were used to pay a debt that was incurred in connection with the acquisition of an asset by the debtor, it may argue that it can trace its security interest into that property.

f)   The Functional Equivalence Rule

The Saskatchewan Court of Appeal in *Agricultural Credit Corp. of Saskatchewan v. Pettyjohn*[64] adopted a new tracing principle that has no counterpart in the conventional tracing rules. The secured party had a purchase money security interest in a herd of cattle. The herd was sold and the proceeds were deposited into the debtor's account. The account was overdrawn, but it may have been possible to show that the deposit of funds from the sale of the original herd was used to extinguish debts that had been incurred by the debtor in purchasing a replacement herd. However, the Court did not go through this process. Instead, it articulated a new tracing principle which it expressed at follows: "The appropriate principle of tracing in such a case is that where a set of chattels is replaced by another of like function in the affairs of the debtor, it shall be open to the court to find that the proceeds from the first were used to acquire the second, whatever the formalities of the transactions in question."[65]

The Court stated that in order to trace value from one item of property into another, "it is necessary to establish a close and substantial connection between the two pieces of property, so that it is appropriate to allow the rights in the original property to flow through to the new property."[66] The Court commented that the connection established through the application of the conventional tracing rules is an arbitrary one that focuses on form rather than substance. The Court thought that a close and substantial connection could also be established by looking at the substance of the transaction and recognizing that one set of assets had replaced another of the same kind. The Court concluded that the requisite close connection was established by the nature and function of the property, regardless of the sequence of transactions.

---

64   *Ibid.*
65   *Ibid.* at 43.
66   *Ibid.* at 39.

The functional equivalence approach was also applied in *Re River Industries. Ltd.*[67] The court held that a security interest in inventory that was sold could be traced into replacement inventory that had been acquired. There was no evidence as to the sequence of events, but the financial statements indicated that 77 to 79 percent of the debtor's gross revenues had been used to acquire new inventory during the relevant period. The Court held that the secured party could trace its security interest into the replacement inventory in proportion to the ratio that the inventory it supplied bore to the total inventory.

The difficulty with the functional equivalence rule is that it appears to violate a fundamental principle of tracing. Tracing is about finding transactional links between one asset and another. If it was impossible for the value to have been used to acquire the substitute asset, it is not possible to trace into it. In *Pettyjohn*, the replacement cattle were purchased before most of the original cattle were sold. Under conventional tracing principles, the secured party would need to show that the proceeds from the sale of the original collateral were used to pay down the debt that was incurred in connection with the acquisition of the replacement herd.[68] The Court concluded that although some of the proceeds from the sale of the original herd had been used to repay the bank money that had been loaned to permit the acquisition of the replacement herd, a portion of the proceeds had not been used for this purpose. It also would have been necessary for the secured party to demonstrate that the amounts deposited into the account resulted from a sale of the original cattle, a matter that was not conceded by the defendant. By applying the functional equivalence rule, the court circumvented these two problems, which would have greatly limited the secured party's ability to trace into the replacement herd.

The problematic nature of the functional equivalence rule is illustrated by the following variation on the facts of the *Pettyjohn* case. Suppose that $10,000 resulting from the sale of cattle subject to a security interest is deposited in the debtor's bank account and mixed with $10,000 of the debtor's own funds. The entire $20,000 in the account is then used to pay taxes that were owing by the debtor. The debtor then deposits $20,000 of the debtor's own funds, which it obtains from another source. Finally, the debtor withdraws the $20,000 and uses it to buy a replacement herd. Although the replacement herd in this scen-

---

67   [1992] 6 W.W.R. 257 (B.C.S.C.).

68   The court in *Pettyjohn* was apparently willing to permit tracing through a debt. See B.3.e "Tracing through Payment of a Debt."

ario is functionally equivalent to the original collateral, the transaction through which it was acquired cannot be linked to the original herd.

It might be possible to explain the functional equivalence principle adopted in *Pettyjohn* on the basis that it really involves only a shift in the onus of proof. Normally, it is the secured party who must establish the transactional links through which its security interest in the original collateral can be connected with the proceeds collateral. The *Pettyjohn* case might be interpreted to mean simply that in cases where there is evidential uncertainty, the court will be prepared to presume that the proceeds of the original collateral were used to acquire property that is functionally equivalent to it unless the other party can show that the funds were actually used for another purpose. But is there really any compelling reason to do so? No similar rule is available to a beneficiary where there has been a mixing of funds by a trustee acting in breach of a trust. While the courts have indicated that they may depart from the tracing principles of the common law and equity in order to find solutions based on the underlying principles of the PPSA, there are no underlying principles of the PPSA that suggest why a secured party should obtain the advantage of this presumption when it is denied to other claimants who seek to trace their value.[69]

4) Perfection and Priorities

a) The Ontario and Manitoba Perfection Provisions
There is a fundamental division among the Acts on the treatment of perfection of proceeds. Under the Ontario Act, a security interest in proceeds is automatically perfected so long as the security interest in the original collateral is perfected by registration at the time the interest in the proceeds arose.[70] This is so, even though the proceeds do not fall within the description of the original collateral. As a result, searching parties are expected to know that the secured party has a potential claim to any of the debtor's assets that arose as a result of a dealing with the collateral described in the financing statement. This applies only if the registration in relation to the original collateral was in effect at the

---

69   In *C.O. Funk & Son, Inc. v. Sullivan Equipment, Inc.*, 92 Ill.App.3d 659 (Ill. App. 1981), aff'd 431 N.E.2d 370 (Ill. 1982) the court rejected a "large asset picture" theory of tracing that would presume that proceeds of inventory were used to purchase replacement inventory in favour of the intermediate balance rule. The court further held that the burden of proof to establish the claim lay on the secured party.
70   OPPSA s. 25(2).

time the proceeds arose. If this condition is not satisfied, the secured party will need to ensure that the description in the financing statement covers the proceeds collateral when it effects the registration.

Although registration of a security interest in the original collateral perfects a security interest in any proceeds, this form of perfection is an inferior method of perfection where the proceeds take the form of a motor vehicle classed as consumer goods. The Ontario Act provides that a good faith buyer takes free of the security interest in such proceeds unless the secured party has registered a financing change statement that sets out the vehicle identification number.[71] This ensures that consumer buyers of motor vehicles will be able to rely upon a serial number search of the registry system. The provision is anomalous in two respects. First, it only applies to buyers, whereas most of the buyer protection rules apply to lessees as well. Second, the provision does not require that the buyer acquire the goods without knowledge, but only requires that the buyer acts in good faith. This suggests that a buyer can take advantage of this provision so long as the buyer was not acting fraudulently.

Automatic perfection of a proceeds security interest under the Ontario Act does not occur if the security interest in the original collateral is perfected otherwise than by registration.[72] In this case, the secured party is given a ten-day grace period after the proceeds arise within which it must perfect its security interest in the proceeds by some other means. This can be accomplished by registering a financing statement or by the secured party taking possession of the collateral.

The Manitoba Act provides that perfection of a security interest by registration perfects a security interest in the proceeds without any need for a proceeds description in the financing statement. It does not provide a temporary perfection period if the security interest was perfected otherwise than by registration. Nor does it provide any protection for consumer buyers of serial numbered goods.[73]

b)   The Perfection Provisions of the Other Jurisdictions
The Acts of jurisdictions other than Ontario and Manitoba adopt an entirely different approach. For the most part, they require a description

---

71   OPPSA s. 25(5).

72   OPPSA s. 25(4).

73   Sections 30(6) and (7) of the MPPSA would give a buyer without knowledge priority over the secured party if the secured party did not register the proceeds by serial number in respect of serial number goods held as equipment. However, there is no similar rule that would protect consumer buyers.

of the proceeds in the financing statement in order to perfect a security interest in them.[74] The underlying philosophy behind this approach is that parties who search the registry should be able to rely upon the information contained in the search result. It is therefore incumbent on the secured party to describe the proceeds if it wishes to assert its claim to them against competing third parties. The one exception is where the proceeds take the form of money, cheques, or deposit accounts in a financial institution. In this case, the proceeds are automatically and continuously perfected from the time of registration of the financing statement covering the original collateral. The underlying assumption here is that parties who acquire interests in these types of assets ought to realize that they may have arisen as a result of a disposition of the collateral described in the financing statement, and that, in the case of cheques and money, it is safe to relax the perfection rules as its negotiable character ensures that there is little risk of prejudice to third parties.

If the original collateral description covers the proceeds, then nothing further need be done. Suppose that SP takes a security interest in the debtor's bulldozer held as inventory and describes the collateral as "construction equipment" in the financing statement. The bulldozer is sold and the sale proceeds are used by the debtor to purchase an excavator. The security interest in the excavator will be continuously perfected since it falls within the original collateral description.

In many instances, the proceeds collateral will not fall within the same description as the original collateral. In this case, the secured party may include a description of the proceeds in the financing statement. If this is done, the security interest in the proceeds is continuously perfected. Of course, if the proceeds are serial numbered goods that are held as consumer goods or as equipment, it is almost impossible for the secured party to provide a serial number description of the collateral at the time that it registers its financing statement.

The foregoing perfection rules should be read as subject to the continuity of perfection principle which requires that there be no intermediate period during which the security interest is unperfected.[75] This is illustrated in the following scenario.

D gives SP1 a security interest in its computer and registers a financing statement that describes the collateral as a "computer." D then gives SP2 a

---

74   PPSA (A, BC, NWT, Nu, S) s. 28(2); (NB, PEI) s. 28(3); (NL, NS) s. 29(3); Y s. 26(2).
75   PPSA (A, BC, NB, NWT, Nu, PEI, S) s. 23(1); (NL, NS) s. 24(1); Y s. 21(1)

security interest in all present and after-acquired personal property, which SP2 perfects by registration. D sells the computer and receives a photocopier in trade. SP1's financing statement does not cover the photocopier, and SP2 therefore has priority over SP1. Six months later, D sells the photocopier and receives a different computer and a cheque in payment.

The Act provides that the security interest in the computer and the cheque is continuously perfected if the security interest in the original collateral is perfected by registration. Although this condition is satisfied, the rule must be read subject to the continuity of perfection principle. SP1's proceeds security interest in the cheque and the computer therefore should not be considered to be continuously perfected, since its security interest in the photocopier was not perfected.

If a security interest in proceeds has not been perfected by any of these methods, then the secured party may nevertheless take advantage of a temporary perfection period.[76] So long as the security interest in the original collateral is perfected, the security interest in the proceeds will be temporarily perfected for fifteen days after the proceeds arise. If the security interest in the proceeds is perfected during this temporary perfection period, it will be continuously perfected from the date of perfection of the original collateral. The temporary perfection period is absolute and not conditional in that it is conferred on the secured party whether or not the secured party perfects its security interest in the proceeds during the fifteen-day period. For example, if the secured party fails to perfect its security interest in the proceeds through registration or possession and a bankruptcy occurs within fifteen days after the bankruptcy arises, the secured party can take advantage of the temporary perfection period and claim priority over the trustee in bankruptcy in respect of the proceeds.[77] However, if the bankruptcy occurs after the expiration of the temporary perfection period, the secured party will be subordinate to the trustee in bankruptcy. Moreover, as with all other temporary perfection periods, this form of perfection will not be effective in protecting the security interest against a buyer or lessee who acquires the goods without knowledge of the security interest.[78]

---

76   PPSA (A, BC, NB, NWT, Nu, PEI, S) s. 28(3); (NL, NS) s. 29(3); Y s. 26(3).

77   *Central Refrigeration & Restaurant Services Inc. (Trustee of) v. Canadian Imperial Bank of Commerce* (1986), 47 Sask. R. 124 (C.A.).

78   PPSA (A, BC, NB, NWT, Nu, PEI, S) s. 30(5); (NL, NS) s. 31(5); Y s. 29(5).

c) Priority of Security Interests in Proceeds

A security interest in proceeds is generally afforded the same priority as the security interest in the original collateral. For the purposes of the residual priority rules, the time of registration, possession or perfection of the original collateral is also the time of registration, possession, or perfection of the proceeds.[79] The PPSA also makes it clear that the enhanced priority of a purchase money security interest extends to any proceeds,[80] although there are a number of exceptions to this rule. Several jurisdictions provide that a purchase money security interest in proceeds of inventory does not have priority over a prior registered security interest in accounts.[81] Many jurisdictions also provide a priority rule to govern priority competitions between a purchase money security interest taken in an asset as original collateral and a competing proceeds purchase money security interest in it.[82] All the Acts provide that a purchase money security interest in proceeds of inventory does not have priority over a purchaser of chattel paper, even if the purchaser knew of the security interest.[83]

C. RETURNED OR REPOSSESSED GOODS

The PPSA provides a set of rules that govern the situation where the debtor has sold or leased goods that are later returned as a result of a consensual transaction or repossessed as a consequence of a default on the part of the buyer or lessee. This situation will almost always arise in respect of a return or repossession of goods held as inventory by the

79 PPSA (A, BC, M, NB, NWT, Nu, S) s. 35(3); (NL, NS) s. 36(3); O s. 30(5); Y no equivalent provision. Section 30(5) of the OPPSA only refers to registration or perfection, and not to possession. This reflects a difference in policy in that the residual priority rules in the other provinces use the date of possession for the purposes of the rule, even though the security interest has not attached with the result that it is not yet perfected. See chapter 8, B.1 "The First-in-time Rule."
80 PPSA (A, M, NWT, Nu, S) s. 34(2)–(3); (BC, NB, PEI) s. 34(1)–(2); (NL, NS) s. 35(1)–(2); (O, Y) s. 33(1)–(2).
81 PPSA (A, M, NWT, Nu, S) s. 34(6); BC s. 34(5); Y s. 33(7). See the discussion in chapter 8, C.6 "Purchase Money Security Interests in Accounts or Chattel Paper as Proceeds of Inventory."
82 PPSA (A, M, NWT, Nu, S) ss. 34(7), 34(8); BC s. 34(6); Y s. 33(6). See the discussion in chapter 8, C.7 "Competing Purchase Money Security Interests."
83 PPSA (A, BC, NB, NWT, Nu, PEI) s. 31(6); (M, S) s. 31(7); (NL, NS) s. 32(6); O s. 30(3); Y s. 30(5). See the discussion in chapter 9, C.2 "Competing Security Interests in Chattel Paper."

debtor. The provisions attempt to do two different things. First, they provide for the creation of a security interest in circumstances in which a security interest might not otherwise be created. Second, they provide for the resolution of priority competitions where more than one person asserts a claim to the returned or repossessed goods. For convenience, the discussion will consider the case of a sale, but the same analysis applies where the transaction is in the form of a lease.

When a seller sells some of its inventory to a customer, the buyer will usually take free of any security interest in the inventory that had been given by the seller to a secured party. There are two reasons why this is usually the case. The secured party will usually have authorized the sale. As well, the sale will often occur in the ordinary course of business of the seller so as to attract the ordinary course buyer priority rule. If the seller agrees to defer payment, an account will be created. If the seller agrees to defer payment, but also takes a security interest in the goods that it sells, chattel paper will be generated. If only part of the unpaid price is secured by the security interest, both an account and chattel paper will be created. Any account or chattel paper thus created may in turn have been transferred to another party either absolutely or by way of security.

Difficulties arise when the goods are then returned or repossessed. This may occur because the customer is dissatisfied with the goods, or it may be that they were traded back to the seller in payment of the purchase price of other goods. Alternatively, the goods may have been repossessed as a result of a default by the customer. The Act provides for the reattachment of the security interest of the inventory financer that had been lost upon the sale of the goods to the customer. It also provides for the continuation of the security interest of an account financer and of a chattel paper financer. Since it is possible that the inventory financer, the account financer, and the chattel paper financer all will thus end up with a security interest in the returned or repossessed goods, it is necessary to provide a priority rule that resolves the resulting priority competition.

1) Reattachment of the Inventory Financer's Security Interest

An inventory financer will normally expect the debtor to repay its loan or credit from the proceeds of sale that it received from the sale of the goods. This expectation is obviously frustrated when the goods are returned or repossessed. When this occurs, the PPSA provides that the inventory financer's security interest reattaches to the returned or repossessed goods if the obligation secured has not been performed.[84] Although inventory financing agreements typically provide that the security interest covers any returned or repossessed goods, this provision ensures this result where the agreement is silent on the point. It also ensures that the reattached security interest is afforded the same priority status that it had prior to detachment. If the inventory financer had a purchase money security interest in the inventory, the reattached security interest will also be afforded this status.

There is a variation between the language used in the Ontario Act and that contained in the Acts of the other jurisdictions. The Ontario Act provides for reattachment where the goods are returned to the debtor (that is, the seller). The other Acts are wider in that they provide for reattachment even if the goods were seized by a chattel paper financer.

If the inventory financer's registration is still in effect, nothing further needs to be done in order to perfect the reattached security interest. The Act provides that the perfection and the time of registration of the reattached security interest is to be determined as if the goods had not been sold.[85] If the financing statement has lapsed or discharged, new perfecting steps will need to be taken in order to perfect the reattached security interest.

The reattachment of the inventory financer's security interest does not affect a security interest that was created by the buyer after the sale but before it was returned or repossessed. So long as this security interest is properly perfected, it will have priority over the reattached security interest of the inventory financer. The non-Ontario Acts[86] contain an express provision to this effect, and it is likely that courts would arrive at the same conclusion in Ontario.

2) The Chattel Paper Financer's Interest

Often a commercial seller of durable goods will sell the goods pursuant to a secured instalment credit agreement whereby it takes a security interest in the goods to secure the unpaid purchase price. The seller will frequently transfer the rights it enjoys under this agreement to a transferee. Less commonly, the seller may give a security interest in these

---

84   PPSA (A, BC, M, NB, NWT, Nu, PEI, S) s. 29(1); (NL, NS) s. 30(1); O s. 27(1); Y s. 28(1).

85   PPSA (A, BC, M, NB, NWT, Nu, PEI, S) s. 29(2); (NL, NS) s. 30(2); O s. 27(2); Y s. 28(2).

86   PPSA (A, BC, M, NB, NWT, Nu, PEI, S) s. 29(7); (NL, NS) s. 30(7), Y s. 28(3).

rights in order to secure a loan. Both of these transactions are brought within the scope of the PPSA. The Act regards the rights held by the seller as a separate category of collateral called chattel paper. This represents a fundamental departure from prior law which regarded the transaction as involving two separate kinds of property: a chose in action in the form of the buyer's promise to pay, and title to the goods. The chattel paper transferee will usually notify the buyer of the transfer and direct that payments be made to the transferee rather than the seller. If the debtor defaults, the chattel paper transferee will have the right to enforce the security interest against the buyer through seizure of the goods.

In the event that the goods are returned to or repossessed by the seller, the chattel paper financer no longer has an interest in the chattel paper. In its place, the Act gives the chattel paper financer a security interest in the goods.[87] Since the security interest that is created is in a different category of collateral, the chattel paper financer must ensure that it perfects its security interest in the goods. Usually a chattel paper financer will perfect its security interest in the chattel paper by possession. This represents a superior method of perfection since it will prevent subordination of the interest to a purchaser for value without knowledge. But this method of perfection will not be sufficient to perfect a security interest in the returned or repossessed goods. The chattel paper financer may have taken the precaution of registering a financing statement that describes the goods. If this is so, nothing else need be done in order to perfect the security interest in the returned or repossessed goods. But if no registration has been effected, the chattel paper financer will need to perfect its security interest in the goods.

The Act gives the secured party a period of temporary perfection — ten days in Ontario and fifteen days in the other jurisdictions — within which to perfect its security interest in the returned or repossessed goods. This step is not necessary if the chattel paper financer has taken the precaution of registering in advance a financing statement that contains a description of the goods. Nor is it necessary if it is the chattel paper financer rather than the seller who has repossessed the goods.[88] If, however, the goods are repossessed by the seller rather than by the chattel paper financer, then the chattel paper financer must ensure that

---

87   PPSA (A, BC, M, NB, NWT, Nu, PEI, S) s. 29(3); (NL, NS) s. 30(3); O s. 27(3); Y s. 28(4).

88   This represents a departure from the rule in most of the non-Ontario Acts that possession by way of seizure or repossession does not qualify as a perfection step. See chapter 5, E.3 "Perfection by Seizure or Repossession."

it perfects its security interest in the goods by registration. This holds true even if the transfer to the chattel paper financer was by way of a sale and the seller was acting wrongfully in taking possession of the goods without the consent of the chattel paper financer.

The continuation of the security interest in the returned or repossessed goods will not give the chattel paper financer priority over all competing parties. Ordinary course buyers will take free of the security interest.[89]

3) The Account Financer's Interest

The Act also creates a security interest in returned or repossessed goods in favour of a secured party who had been given a security interest in accounts of the seller.[90] One might well question the wisdom of this legislative policy, since most account financers would not really expect to be able to resort to the goods under these circumstances. As with transfers of chattel paper, the accounts financer must ensure that its security interest in the returned or repossessed goods is perfected. The accounts financer is also given a temporary perfection period within which to effect a registration if it has not taken the precaution of registering in advance a financing statement that contains a description of the goods.

4) The Resolution of Priority Competitions

It is possible that an inventory financer, a chattel paper financer, and an accounts financer may each be able to claim a security interest in returned or repossessed goods. The Acts contain a special set of priority rules that govern such competitions. There is, however, a significant difference between the Ontario and Yukon Acts and the Acts in the other jurisdictions as to how such priority competitions are to be resolved.

a)   The Situation outside of Ontario and the Yukon
Except for Ontario and the Yukon, the PPSA jurisdictions have adopted a common solution to the priority problem. The accounts financer is given the lowest priority ranking. It will be defeated by the reattached security interest of an inventory financer and by the security interest

---

89   PPSA (A, BC, M, NB, NWT, Nu, PEI, S) s. 30(2); (NL, NS) s. 31(2); O s. 28(1); Y s. 29(1).
90   PPSA (A, BC, M, NB, NWT, Nu, PEI, S) s. 29(3); (NL, NS) s. 30(3); O s. 27(3); Y s. 28(4).

of a chattel paper financer in the returned or repossessed goods.[91] The chattel paper financer is given the highest priority, and the inventory financer therefore comes second in the ranking of priorities.[92] The inventory financer is not permitted to circumvent its second ranking by asserting a security interest in the goods as new collateral rather than on the basis of its reattached security interest. The chattel paper financer is given priority over the inventory financer's reattached security interest, and also is given priority over any security interest in the goods as after-acquired property.

The Act provides temporary perfection periods in respect of the continued security interests of chattel paper financers and accounts financers. These secured parties must register or otherwise perfect their security interests within this period in order to maintain priority over the trustee in bankruptcy and other competing claimants such as subsequent transferees and secured parties. What is not made clear is whether this requirement for perfection of the continued security interest also applies to the special priority rule that governs competitions between a reattached security interest of an inventory financer and the continued security interests of a chattel paper financer and an accounts financer. In other words, can a chattel paper financer who fails to register within the temporary perfection period nevertheless claim priority over the reattached security interest of an inventory financer? The PPSA priority rule that governs such disputes does not expressly provide that this priority is dependent on continued perfection of the security interest. However, there is good reason to read this provision as subject to a perfection requirement. In the absence of such a requirement, circular priority problems can easily arise. In the event of the debtor's bankruptcy, the chattel paper financer would have priority over an inventory financer, but would be subordinate to the trustee in bankruptcy. The inventory financer would have priority over the trustee in bankruptcy, but would be subordinate to the chattel paper financer. This problem is eliminated if the special priority rule is available only if the continued security interest of the chattel paper financer is continuously perfected.

b) The Ontario Provision

The Ontario Act provides three basic rules for resolving a priority competition in respect of returned or repossessed goods. As between a chattel paper financer and an inventory financer, the party who has priority

---

91   PPSA (A, BC, M, NB, NWT, Nu, PEI, S) s. 29(5); (NL, NS) s. 30(5).
92   PPSA (A, BC, M, NB, NWT, Nu, PEI, S) s. 29(6); (NL, NS) s. 30(6).

with respect to the chattel paper will also have priority with respect to the returned or repossessed goods.[93] So long as the chattel paper financer purchases the chattel paper in the ordinary course of business and for value, the chattel paper financer will be entitled to priority.[94] In respect of other priority competitions, the chattel paper financer's security interest in the goods is deemed to have been perfected at the time the security interest in the chattel paper was perfected.[95] Finally, an account financer's security interest in the returned or repossessed goods is deemed to have been perfected at the time that its security interest in the accounts was perfected.[96] All of these rules are applicable only if the chattel paper financer or account financer has ensured that its security interest in the returned or repossessed goods was continuously perfected.

Under this scheme, the account financer's security interest in the returned or repossessed goods is not necessarily subordinated to the security interest of the chattel paper financer or the inventory financer. The accounts financer will have priority over the inventory financer if the accounts financer perfected its security interest in the accounts before the inventory financer perfected its security in the inventory. If, however, the inventory financer has taken a purchase money security interest, it will be able to claim priority over the accounts financer. The accounts financer will also have priority over the chattel paper financer if the accounts financer perfected its security interest in the accounts before the chattel paper financer perfected its security in the chattel paper. The chattel paper financer is given priority over the inventory financer so long as it had priority with respect to the chattel paper, and this is so even if it was not the first to perfect its security interest.

The Ontario provision can produce odd results. If an accounts financer registers first, it will have priority over a chattel paper financer. The chattel paper financer will have priority over an inventory financer, but will be subordinate to the accounts financer. The accounts financer will, however, be subordinate to the inventory financer who has taken a purchase money security interest in the inventory. This produces a circular priority problem. There is also an interpretive problem. Unlike the Acts in the other jurisdictions, the Ontario Act only subordinates

---

93   OPPSA s. 27(6)(a).
94   OPPSA s. 28(3)(b). The provision does not require the purchaser to be without knowledge against a secured party who claims the chattel paper as proceeds of inventory.
95   OPPSA s. 27(6)(b).
96   OPPSA s. 27(5).

the reattached security interest of the inventory financer. The inventory financer may therefore attempt to assert priority over the chattel paper financer by claiming priority on the basis of its after-acquired property clause rather than on the basis of the reattached security interest that it is given by statute.

c)   The Yukon Provision

The Yukon Act takes a somewhat different approach than the Ontario Act and the other Acts. It contains two priority rules. The chattel paper financer is given priority over the inventory financer if it takes possession of the chattel paper in the ordinary course of business.[97] The inventory financer is given priority over an accounts financer.[98] The provisions do not provide a special priority rule where there is a competition between an accounts financer and a chattel paper financer.

D. FIXTURES AND CROPS

Under the common law, goods lose their separate identity upon being attached to land so as to become fixtures.[99] The common law developed a number of tests to determine what degree of attachment was needed in order for this to happen. This posed a significant risk to a secured party who had financed the acquisition of the goods. Although the secured party could provide a contractual stipulation that permitted the secured party to remove the fixtures from the land, this provision only operated as against the debtor and gave the secured party no right of removal against a buyer or mortgagee of the land.[100]

The PPSA sets out a comprehensive legal regime governing fixtures. The Act gives the secured party a right to remove fixtures and it regulates the manner by which this right of removal may be exercised. The Act also governs priority disputes that may arise between a secured party who exercises its right of removal and a party with an interest in the real property who claims the fixtures as part of the land. The Act adopts a similar set of rules to govern crops growing on land.

---

97   YPPSA s. 28(4).
98   YPPSA s. 28(5).
99   This was expressed in the Latin maxim: *quicquid plantatur solo, solo cedit* (whatever is fixed in the ground, becomes part of the ground). See *Gough v. Wood & Co.*, [1894] 1 Q.B. 713.
100 *Hobson v. Gorringe*, [1897] 1 Ch. 182 (C.A.).

1) The Definition of Fixtures

The PPSA provides a definition of fixtures, but it is not comprehensive. The definition merely provides that the fixtures do not include building materials.[101] The Ontario Act does not define building materials. The other Acts provide an extensive definition of this term. The term fixtures as it is used in the PPSA therefore refers to goods that are considered to be fixtures according to the common law tests for fixtures, other than goods that are classified as building materials.

From these definitions, a threefold scheme of categorization can be derived. The first encompasses goods that have either become permanently incorporated into the land[102] as well as goods categorized as building materials. These goods will not fall within the definition of fixtures and the secured party will not have a right to remove the goods from the land. The second category encompasses goods that are so slightly attached to the land that they do not satisfy the common law test for becoming fixtures. These goods will not have lost their separate identity. The fixtures provisions will not apply and no priority competition will arise in relation to real property claimants since the goods do not form part of the land. The third category encompasses goods that fall within the definition of fixtures. The secured party will enjoy a right of removal in respect of these goods, and priority competitions with real property claimants will be resolved by the priority rules of the PPSA governing fixtures.

The common law tests for fixtures focus on two elements: (1) the extent to which the goods have been physically attached to the land and the permanence of this condition (the degree of annexation); (2) the purpose of the attachment, that is, whether it was intended to enhance the use or value of the land (the object of annexation).[103] Courts have applied these common law tests in determining if the goods have been sufficiently attached to the land so as to become fixtures for the purposes of determining whether the PPSA fixtures rules apply.[104]

---

101 PPSA (A, BC, NWT, Nu, O, Y) s. 1(1); (M, NB, PEI) s. 1; (NL, NS) s. 2; S s. 2(1).

102 Examples would include topsoil that is spread to create a lawn and trees that are planted on the land.

103 *Holland v. Hodgson* (1872), L.R. 7 C.P. 328. The most frequently cited Canadian case is *Stack v. T. Eaton Co.*, [1902] 4 O.L.R. 335 at 338 (Ont. Div. Ct.).

104 See, for example, *Pezzack v. Irving Bank Canada* (1989), 69 O.R. (2d) 536 (H.C.J.) (furnace, ceiling-suspended gas heaters, electric baseboard heaters, air-conditioning and infrared portable ceiling heaters not considered to be building materials). For a more extensive discussion of the case law, see H. Bennett, "Attachment of Chattels to Land" in Palmer and McKendrick, above note 3 at 461.

The PPSA in jurisdictions other than Ontario contains a definition of building materials. The definition provides that it includes goods that are attached to a building[105] such that their removal would necessarily involve the dislocation or destruction of some part of the building or would weaken the structure or expose it to the elements. The definition excludes heating, air conditioning, and conveyancing devices, as well as machinery for carrying out an activity in the building. The definition recognizes technological advances in building construction. Traditional techniques usually involved a high degree of permanence in the incorporation of the goods into the structure (for example, bricks and mortar). Modern building materials and construction techniques are often modularized so that components such as windows and walls can be easily removed. The PPSA definition of building materials therefore does not look at the degree of annexation but adopts instead a pragmatic approach that asks whether the component is essential to the integrity of the building. Although items such as furnaces and elevators would normally qualify as building materials, they are excluded because they are commonly used as independent goods collateral in commercial practice.

In interpreting the Ontario Act, which does not contain a definition of building materials, one Ontario court has held that the term is not restricted to components such as lumber, brick, and mortar that become incorporated into the structure, but includes materials that are "so closely interlinked and identified with other materials generally described as building material, that they must for all practical purposes be considered as building materials ..."[106] Applying this test, the court concluded that an electric weigh scale that was bolted to concrete footings belonged in the category of building materials, where both the concrete deck and the scale would be destroyed by the removal process.[107]

See also M. Burke, "Fixture Financing under the PPSA: the Ongoing Conflict between Realty and Fixture-Secured Interests" (1986) 24 Osgoode Hall L.J. 547.

105 The term "building" is defined as a structure, erection, mine or work in the non-Ontario Acts. See PPSA (A, BC, NWT, Nu, Y) s. 1(1); (M, NB, PEI) s. 1; (NL, NS) s. 2; S s. 2(1).

106 *Charles A. Hare Ltd. v. Payn* (1982), 18 B.L.R. 209 at 214 (Ont. H.C.), quoting from *Alexander v. McGillivray* (1932), 41 O.W.N. 406 (H.C.).

107 The scale would likely not be classified as building materials in the other jurisdictions that define the term. However, courts in those jurisdictions would probably arrive at the same result by concluding that the goods became permanently incorporated into the land and therefore did not qualify as fixtures.

2) The Priority of a Security Interest in Fixtures

The priority provisions of the PPSA governing fixtures cover two different situations. The first is where a security interest is taken in goods before they are affixed to land. The second is where the debtor gives a security interest in an existing fixture.

Where a security interest is taken in goods before they are affixed to land, the secured party will have priority over a person who has an interest in the land.[108] This is illustrated in the following scenario.

D owns the land upon which a factory is located. D mortgages the land to M. A fixtures financer (SP) takes a security interest in manufacturing equipment which is later installed in the factory in such a manner as to be considered fixtures.

SP will have priority over M. SP does not need to file a notice in the land registration system in order to claim this priority.[109] When M advances funds pursuant to its real property mortgage, it does not do so on the expectation that the value of the land will be enhanced by the presence of the fixture and therefore M is not prejudiced by the exercise of SP's right of removal. Nor does it matter if SP's security interest was unperfected. The lack of perfection of SP's security interest will subordinate its security interest as against other claimants who have competing security interest in the goods, but it will be of no significance where the competition is with a person who holds an interest in the land in view of the absence of any reliance on the PPSA registry by the person with the interest in the land.

A secured party may take a security interest in a fixture that has already been affixed to the land when the security agreement is entered into. In this case, the security interest in the fixture will be subordinate to existing real property interests unless the holders of such interests consent to the security interest or disclaim their interest in the fixtures.[110]

Once the goods are affixed to the land, third parties who thereafter acquire interests in the land will operate under the expectation that they are acquiring the land including the fixture. In order to prevent prejudice to these parties, the secured party must file a fixtures

---

108 PPSA (BC, M, NWT, Nu, S) s. 36(3); (A, NB, PEI) s. 36(2); (NL, NS) s. 37(2); O s. 34(1); Y s. 35(1).

109 *Canadian Imperial Bank of Commerce v. Nelson & Nelson Holdings Inc.* (1988), 68 Sask. R. 278 (Q.B.).

110 PPSA (A, BC, NWT, Nu) s. 36(5); (M, S) s. 36(6); (NB, PEI) s. 36(7); (NL, NS) s. 37(7); O s. 34(1); Y s. 35(1)

notice in the land registration system to alert such parties that the secured party had the right to remove the fixture from the land. If the secured party fails to register this notice, it will lose priority against a subsequent real property interest holder who acquires the interest for value.[111] The security interest will also be subordinate to a prior mortgagee who makes a subsequent advance after the goods are affixed unless a fixtures notice is registered. The subordination is not for the entire mortgage debt, but only for the future advance that was made. The Ontario Act requires that the subsequent real property interest holder must have been without knowledge of the security interest in the fixtures.[112] In the other jurisdictions, it is enough that the real property interest holder acted without fraud.[113]

Outside of Ontario, a failure to register a fixtures notice will result in subordination of the fixtures security interest in two other cases. The security interest will be subordinate to a judgment enforcement creditor who causes a writ or judgment to be registered in the land titles system.[114] If the secured party has a purchase money security interest in the goods, the secured party is given a fifteen-day grace period within which to register the fixtures notice.[115] The security interest will also be defeated by a prior mortgagee who obtains an order for sale or foreclosure of the land before the fixture notice is registered.[116]

The common law recognizes a special class of fixtures known as tenant's fixtures. Fixtures that are installed by a tenant can be removed from the land. This distinction is of no relevance under the PPSA. Goods that become affixed to the land are subject to the Act whether or

---

111 PPSA (A, BC, NWT, Nu) s. 36(5); (M, S) s. 36(6); (NB, PEI) s. 36(7); (NL, NS) s. 37(7); O s. 34(1); Y s. 35(1). The Ontario Act refers to a "subsequent purchaser." The definition of purchaser in s. 1 includes a mortgagee. The Yukon Act operates in the same fashion as the Ontario Act. The other Acts make it clear that the protected purchasers include a person who obtains an assignment of a prior real property interest. The Ontario and Yukon Acts do not indicate if the provision covers an assignment from the real property interest holder or if it is restricted to a transfer from the debtor.
112 OPPSA s. 34(2).
113 PPSA (BC, M, NB, NWT, Nu, PEI, S) s. 36(4); A s. 36(3); (NL, NS) s. 37(4); Y s. 35(2).
114 PPSA (A, BC, NWT, Nu) s. 36(6); (M, S) s. 36(7); (NB, PEI) s. 36(9); (NL, NS) s. 37(9); Y s. 35(3).
115 PPSA (A, BC, NWT, Nu) s. 36(7); (M, S) s. 36(8); (NB, PEI) s. 36(10); (NL, NS) s. 37(10); Y s. 35(4).
116 PPSA (BC, M, NB, NWT, Nu, PEI, S) s. 36(4); A s. 36(3); (NL, NS) s. 37(4); Y no equivalent provision.

not they qualify as tenant's fixtures under the common law.[117] However, the concept may still be of some utility in identifying situations where the owner of land should be considered as having impliedly consented to the removal of the goods.[118] In such cases, the secured party's right to remove the goods will take priority over the interest of the real property interest holder.[119] Although the PPSA does not provide a similar priority rule in respect of real property interests that are created after the goods are affixed to the land, the situation will be governed by general principles of the common law pertaining to consent and waiver with the result that a real property interest holder who consents to the removal of the goods or who disclaims an interest in the fixtures will not be able to assert a claim to the fixtures.

3) The Role of Real Property Priority Rules

The PPSA fixtures provisions are designed to reverse the common law rule that what is fixed to the ground becomes part of the ground. This is accomplished by giving the secured party a right to remove the fixtures. In order to assert the right of removal against subsequent real property interest holders, it is necessary to register a fixtures notice. Where a secured party has not registered a fixtures notice, the security interest in the fixtures may come into competition with both a prior real property interest as well as a subsequent real property interest. It is then necessary to understand the interplay between the real property priority rules and the PPSA fixtures priority rules.

This issue was examined by the Ontario Court of Appeal in *G.M.S. Securities & Appraisals Ltd. v. Rich-Wood Kitchens Ltd.*[120] National Trust (NT) had taken and registered a mortgage of land. It then made several advances pursuant to the mortgage. Rich-Wood Kitchens Ltd. (RW) sold a cabinet to the debtor under a secured instalment purchase agreement. The cabinet was then affixed to the land. RW did not register a fixtures notice in the land registry system. G.M.S. Securities & Appraisals Ltd. (GMS) then took a second mortgage. The debtor later de-

---

117 *Cormier v. Federal Business Development Bank* (1984), 3 P.P.S.A.C. 161 (Ont. Co. Ct.); *Pezzack v. Irving Bank Canada*, above note 104; *859587 Ontario Ltd. v. Starmark Property Management Ltd.* (1997), 12 P.P.S.A.C. (2d) 281 (Ont. Ct. Gen. Div.), aff'd (1998), 14 P.P.S.A.C. (2d) 20 (Ont. C.A.).

118 See *Sawridge Manor Ltd. v. Selkirk Springs International Corp.* (1995), 10 P.P.S.A.C. (2d) 124 (B.C.C.A.).

119 PPSA (A, BC, NWT, Nu) s. 36(5); (M, S) s. 36(6); (NB, PEI) s. 36(7); (NL, NS) s. 37(7); O s. 4(1); Y s. 35(1).

120 (1995), 121 D.L.R. (4th) 278 (Ont. C.A.).

faulted on all its obligations. All but one of NT's advances were made before the goods were affixed to the land. The land was sold pursuant to NT's power of sale, but the proceeds were not sufficient to satisfy all of the outstanding claims. NT clearly had priority over both RW and GMS in respect of the one advance that it made after the goods became fixtures. The controversy concerned the other advances that were made before the goods were attached to the land. If the matter involved only NT and RW, it would have been resolved in RW's favour since registration of a fixtures notice is only necessary as against subsequent real property interests. However, RW's failure to register the fixtures notice resulted in the loss of its right of removal as against GMS.

The Court of Appeal viewed the issue as raising a circular priority problem. RW had priority over NT (because the PPSA gives a security interest in fixtures priority over a prior real property interest). GMS had priority over RW (because the PPSA gives a subsequent real property interest priority over a security interest in fixtures where no fixtures notice is registered). But NT had priority over GMS (because of the first to register priority rule of the real property registry system). The court placed the loss on NT. It reasoned that by exercising its right of sale, NT converted RW's security interest in the fixture. NT was therefore required to compensate RW for this loss. NT was entitled to be subrogated to any right that RW had against GMS. However, since RW did not register a fixtures notice, it had no claim against GMS and therefore this right of subrogation was of no value to NT.

The reasoning of the court is inadequate in two respects. First, it assumes that RW had the right to remove the fixtures from the land. This ignores the fact that RW lost its right to remove the fixture as against GMS by virtue of its failure to register the fixtures notice. If the court had taken into account the PPSA fixtures priority rule that applied between RW and GMS, it would have concluded that RW's right to remove the fixture had been terminated under the PPSA. Second, the reasoning used by the court will result in different outcomes depending upon which party realizes on the collateral. If RW had removed the cabinets from the land and sold them, the analysis would be as follows. GMS would claim that RW's removal of the cabinets interfered with its right to retain them as part of the land. RW would therefore be bound to compensate GMS. RW would be subrogated to any right that GMS had against NT. But because NT was the first to register, it had no claim against NT and therefore this right of subrogation was of no value to GMS. The loss would therefore fall on RW.

The circular priority problem would have been avoided if the court had applied the PPSA priority regime and the real property priority regime only to priority contest within their respective purviews. Applying the PPSA priority rule, one would conclude that RW's right to remove the fixture was lost because of its failure to register the fixtures notice. The competition between NT and GMS would then be resolved by applying the usual first to register real property priority rule. This approach has the advantage of placing the loss on the party (RW) who failed to take the steps necessary to protect its claim. The PPSA in effect in Saskatchewan and the Atlantic provinces include a provision designed to produce this result. The Acts of these jurisdictions provide that the priority that is given to a subsequent real property interest-holder is not affected by the priority rules of the real property registration system.[121]

This approach provides a predictable rule that can be used to solve other apparent circular priority problems. Consider the following scenario.

SP1 and SP2 take competing security interests in goods. SP1 has priority over SP2 because of it registered first in the personal property registry. The goods are then affixed to the land. SP2 registers a fixtures notice, but SP1 does not. The land is then sold to a buyer.

SP1's right to remove the goods has been lost because of its failure to register a fixtures notice. SP2 therefore has the right to remove the goods from the land free from SP1's claim. The loss is again placed on the party that failed to take the steps required to protect its interest.

4) Enforcing Security Interests in Fixtures

The PPSA contains a set of rules that set out the procedural steps that must be undertaken by a secured party who wishes to exercise its right to remove fixtures from the land. The rules attempt to achieve a fair balance between the interest of the secured party who has a security interest in the fixture, and the interests of persons who have an interest in the land, other than the debtor, who will be affected by the removal of the fixture. The underlying assumption, of course, is that the secured party has priority over the real property interest holders and therefore has the right to remove the fixtures from the land.[122]

In most cases, the removal of the fixture will result in some incidental damage to the land. A secured party who removes fixtures must exercise its right in a manner that causes no greater damage or injury

---

121 PPSA (NB, PEI) s. 36(6); (NL, NS) s. 37(6); S s. 36(18).
122 This is expressly provided in s. 34(5) of the OPPSA.

to the land or to other property on it and puts the occupier of the land at no greater inconvenience than is necessarily incidental to the removal of the goods.[123] The person with an interest in the land, other than the debtor, has the right to be reimbursed for any damage caused to the land, other than the diminishment of value to the land caused by the absence of the fixture.[124] The person entitled to this reimbursement may refuse permission to remove the goods until the secured party gives adequate security.[125] The secured party must give notice of its intention to remove the goods to parties who have registered their interests in the land under the real property registry system.[126] The notice must describe the collateral and state the value of the obligation secured by the security interest in the fixture. A real property interest-holder may retain the fixtures by paying out the secured party. The Acts outside of Ontario make it clear that the amount that is to be paid is the lesser of the obligation secured or the market value of the fixtures.[127] The Ontario Act provides for payment of the amount required to satisfy the obligation secured by the security interest, which may be greater than the value of the fixtures.[128]

5) Security Interests in Crops

Growing crops have a hybrid nature at common law. They can be sold or mortgaged separately from the land, but they can also pass to a buyer or mortgagee as part of the land. This raises the possibility of a prior-

---

123 PPSA (A, BC, NWT, Nu) s. 36(8); (M, S) s. 36(6); (NB, PEI) s. 36(11); (NL, NS) s. 37(11); Y s. 35(13). The OPPSA does not contain a comparable provision, but it is likely that a court would interpret the Act as mandating a similar obligation.

124 PPSA (A, BC, NWT, Nu) s. 36(9); (M, S) s. 36(10); (NB, PEI) s. 36(12); (NL, NS) s. 37(12); O s. 34(3); Y s. 35(8).

125 PPSA (A, BC, NWT, Nu) s. 36(10); (M, S) s. 36(11); (NB, PEI) s. 36(13); (NL, NS) s. 37(13); O s. 34(4); Y s. 35(9). Outside of Ontario, the Acts also provide that a secured party may apply to court for an order identifying the person entitled to the reimbursement, an order determining the adequacy of the security or an order authorizing the removal without provision for reimbursement. See PPSA (A, BC, NWT, Nu) s. 36(11); (M, S) s. 36(12); (NB, PEI) s. 36(14); (NL, NS) s. 37(14); Y s. 35(10). The real property interest-holder may also apply for an order postponing removal. See PPSA (A, BC, NWT, Nu) s. 36(16); (M, S) s. 36(17); (NB, PEI) s. 36(19); (NL, NS) s. 37(19); Y s. 35(11).

126 The notice period is ten days in Ontario and fifteen days in the other jurisdictions.

127 PPSA (A, BC, NWT, Nu) s. 36(12); (M, S) s. 36(13); (NB, PEI) s. 36(15); (NL, NS) s. 37(15); Y s. 35(12).

128 OPPSA s. 34(7).

ity competition between a person who takes a PPSA security interest in the crops and a person who acquires an interest in the crops as part of the land. Jurisdictions other than Ontario and the Yukon have included provisions in the PPSA to regulate the priority and enforcement of security interests in crops.[129] These provisions contain priority rules that are substantially similar in structure to the PPSA fixtures priority provisions. The rules governing the procedure for enforcement of a security interest against fixtures are incorporated by reference. Thus, the provisions governing reimbursement for loss, security, notice, and redemption apply to growing crops.

A secured party who takes a security interest in growing crops has priority over a person who had an interest in the land before the crops became growing crops. The crop financer must register a notice in the real property registration system in order to claim priority over a subsequent transferee of the land, a prior mortgagee who makes future advances, or a prior mortgagee who obtains title to the land through enforcement of its land mortgage remedies.[130] Registration is also needed to protect the security interest in crops against a writ or judgment that is subsequently registered against the land.[131]

The PPSA crop priority provisions only apply to crops that are growing crops. If the crops have been severed from the land prior to the creation of the subsequent real property interest, the crops will be treated purely as personal property and a competition with a real property interest will not arise. The crop priority rules will also not apply where the contest is between two competing security interests in the growing crops. Priorities will be determined by applying the ordinary priority rules of the PPSA, and registration of the security interest in the real property registry system will be of no relevance.

E. ACCESSIONS

Difficulties can arise when a secured party has taken a security interest in goods and those goods are then attached to or installed in other goods. For example, tires may be installed on a truck or spare parts

---

129 PPSA (A, BC, M, NB, NWT, Nu, PEI, S) s. 37; (NL, NS) s. 38.

130 PPSA (BC, M, NB, NWT, Nu, PEI, S) s. 37(4); A s. 37(3); (NL, NS) s. 38(4).

131 PPSA (BC, M, NB, NWT, Nu, PEI, S) s. 37(5); A s. 37(4); (NL, NS) s. 38(5). As in the case of fixtures, the secured party is given a fifteen-day grace period from the time that the security interest in the crops attaches if a purchase money security interest is involved.

in an engine. The secured party will wish to assert its right to remove the accessory goods and sell them upon a default under the security agreement. Other third parties may resist the removal. The goods that constitute the whole (that is, the combined goods) may have been sold to a third party who did not know of the security interest, or the debtor may have granted a security interest in the whole to another secured party. The PPSA provides a set of rules that governs the priority of security interests in accessions and also provides a procedure for the removal of the accessory goods from the whole. These rules are similar in structure to the rules that govern fixtures.

1) The Definition of Accessions

At common law, accession occurs when one item is joined to another with the result that the separate identity of one of the items is lost in the other. It is necessary to identify one of the items as the dominant or principal goods which maintain its identity, and the other item as the subordinate or accession goods which lose their separate identity. If both items are significantly changed in the process, then specification rather than accession occurs and both items lose their separate identity. The common law doctrine of accession does not apply to all cases where one item is attached to another. A number of different tests have been devised to determine when accession occurs.[132] One of the principal tests is whether the accessory goods can be removed from the whole without destroying or seriously damaging it.[133] A second test is whether the accessory goods have lost their separate identity. A third test asks if the removal would destroy their commercial identity. A fourth looks to the intentions of the parties and the purpose of the attachment.[134] The problem with the common law tests is that the meaning of the term accession tends to shift depending upon the relationship of the parties, a problem exacerbated by the multiplicity and essential vagueness of the tests.[135] Thus, under pre-PPSA law, where the contest was between a conditional seller who sold tires that were installed on a truck, it was

---

132 See A.G. Guest, "Accession and Confusion in the Law of Hire Purchase" (1964) 27 Mod. L. Rev. 505.

133 *Industrial Acceptance Corp. Ltd. v. Firestone Tire & Rubber Co. of Canada Ltd.* (1970), [1971] S.C.R. 357.

134 The various tests are set out in *Industrial Acceptance Corp. v. Firestone Tire & Rubber Co. of Canada Ltd.* (1969), 8 D.L.R. (3d) 770 (Alta. C.A.), rev'd [1971] S.C.R. 357.

135 This was acknowledged by Laskin J. in *Industrial Acceptance Corp. v. Firestone Tire & Rubber Co. of Canada Ltd.*, above note 133.

generally thought that the goods did not lose their separate identity through the law of accession against a prior conditional seller of the truck. But courts were more inclined to find there to be an accession if the truck, together with the tire, were sold to an innocent buyer.

The definition of accessions contained in the PPSA represents a significant break from the common law. Because the PPSA provides a right to remove the accession and contains a set of priority rules that take into account the different position of the competing claimants, it is possible to replace the common law tests for accession with a much simpler test. The PPSA defines accession simply as goods that are installed in or affixed to other goods.[136] This definition encompasses many situations that would not have been regarded as involving an accession under the common law. Tires attached to a truck will now unquestionably be treated as an accession under the PPSA. There no longer is a requirement that the items must be irreversibly united. It will still be necessary to exclude situations where the joining of the items is so slight and temporary that neither item falls within the definition of an accession. For example, a television linked to a DVD player by a cable would not fall within the definition of an accession since it cannot be said that either item is affixed to or installed in the other.

The definition of accession is limited to goods that are capable of being removed from the whole. The provisions governing accessions are premised on the idea that a secured party who has been given a security interest in the accessory goods has a right to remove them. If the goods are not removable at all, then the situation will likely be governed by the PPSA provisions that govern processed or commingled goods. Situations that at common law were regarded as involving accession will often now be governed by these provisions rather than by the PPSA accession rules.

2) The Priority of a Security Interest in Accessions

The accession provisions of the PPSA contain a set of priority rules. These rules are designed to ensure that a person who acquires an interest in goods is forewarned of the existence of a security interest in accessory goods. This is important because the secured party will be entitled to remove the accessory goods from the whole. However, if the secured party fails to take the necessary steps to protect its interest, the secured party's right to remove the accessions will be subordinate to the interest of any person who has acquired an interest in the whole.

---

136 PPSA (A, BC, NWT, Nu, O, Y) s 1(1); (M, NB, PEI) s. 1; (NL, NS) s. 2, S s. 2(1).

The Act draws a distinction between two situations. The first is where a security interest is taken in the goods and the goods are then affixed to the whole. The second is where the debtor gives a security interest in accessory goods after they have been affixed to or installed in the whole.

Where a security interest is taken in the goods before they are attached to the whole, the secured party has priority over a person who has an interest in the whole.[137] Suppose that SP1 takes a security interest in an automobile. SP2 takes a security interest in an air conditioner. The air conditioner is then installed in the automobile. SP2 will have priority over SP1. This priority does not depend upon registration of SP2's security interest. The rationale for this approach is the same as for the equivalent rule in the context of fixtures. SP1 did not operate under an expectation that the automobile had an air conditioner, and therefore SP2 is permitted to exercise its right to remove the air conditioner free from SP1's claim to it.

A secured party may take a security interest in accessory goods after they have already been affixed to the whole.[138] In this case, the security interest in the accessory goods will be subordinate to any person who had an interest in the whole at the time of accession unless that person consents to the security interest or disclaims an interest in the accessory goods.

Once the goods are affixed, the secured party with a security interest in the accessory goods must register in the personal property registry in order to ensure that it has priority over third parties who thereafter acquire interests in the whole for value and without knowledge. The Ontario Act only protects subsequent buyers.[139] The other Acts go further and protect a person who acquires an interest in the whole in satisfaction of the obligation secured.[140] Prior secured parties are also protected to the extent that they make advances after the accession occurs. The non-Ontario Acts also protect a prior secured party who exercises its right to retain the accessory goods in satisfaction of the obligation secured. Registration is also needed to maintain prior-

---

137 PPSA (A, BC, M, NB, NWT, Nu, PEI, S) s. 38(2); (NL, NS) s. 39(2); O s. 35(1); Y s. 36(1).
138 PPSA (A, BC, M, NWT, Nu, S) s. 38(4); (NB, PEI) s. 38(5); (NL, NS) s. 38(5); O s. 35(1); Y s. 36(2).
139 OPPSA s. 35(2).
140 PPSA (A, BC, M, NB, NWT, Nu, PEI, S) s. 38(3); (NL, NS) s. 39(3); Y s. 36(2). In *Pratt & Whitney Leasing Inc. v. Ellis Air Inc.* (2002), 6 P.P.S.A.C. (3d) 84 (B.C.S.C.), the court held that this did not extend to a court order that lifted a stay of proceedings and permitted a lessor to repossess the leased goods.

ity over subsequent judgment enforcement creditors.[141] A short grace period is provided if the security interest in the accessory goods is a purchase money security interest.[142]

3) Enforcing Security Interests in Accessions

The accession provisions contain a set of rules governing the enforcement of a security interest in accessions. They are very similar in structure to the enforcement rules in respect of fixtures. A secured party who has a security interest in the accessory goods must exercise its right of removal in a manner that causes no greater damage or injury to the whole and puts the other person at no greater inconvenience than is necessarily incidental to the removal of the accessory goods.[143] A person with an interest in the whole, other than the debtor, has the right to be reimbursed for any damage caused to the whole, other than the diminishment of value to the whole caused by the absence of the accession.[144] The person entitled to reimbursement may refuse permission to remove the accessory goods until the secured party gives adequate security.[145] The secured party must give notice of its intention to remove the accessory goods to parties who are known to have an interest in the whole or who have registered a financing statement against the whole in the personal property registry.[146] The notice must describe the acces-

---

141 In Atlantic Canada, the enforcement creditor will win if a notice of judgment is registered in the personal property registry before the security interest in the accessory goods is registered. See NBPPSA s. 38(7); NS s. 39(7); PEI s. 38(6.1). In other jurisdictions, the enforcement creditor will have priority if it seizes or otherwise takes control of the property through the exercise of one of the judgment enforcement remedies. See PPSA (BC, M, NWT, Nu, S) s. 38(5); O s. 35(2); Y s. 36(3); A no equivalent provision. However, s. 35(2) of the *Civil Enforcement Act*, R.S.A. 2000, c. C-15, am. S.A. 2002, c. 17, s. 1 gives priority to an enforcement creditor if the security interest is not registered or perfected at the time the writ is registered.
142 PPSA (BC, M, NWT, Nu, S) s. 38(6); NB s. 38(8); NS s. 39(8); PEI s. 38(6.2); Y s. 36(4) (fifteen-day grace period); OPPSA s. 35(3) (ten-day grace period).
143 PPSA (BC, M, NWT, Nu, PEI, S) s. 38(7); A s. 38(5); NB s. 38(9); NL s. 39(7); NS s. 39(9). The Ontario and Yukon Acts do not contain a comparable provision, but it is likely that a court would interpret the Acts as mandating a similar obligation.
144 PPSA (BC, M, NWT, Nu, PEI, S) s. 38(8); A s. 38(6); NB s. 38(10); NL s. 39(8); NS s. 39(10); O s. 35(4); Y s. 36(8).
145 PPSA (BC, M, NWT, Nu, PEI, S) s. 38(9); A s. 38(7); NB s. 38(11); NL s. 39(9); NS s. 39(11); O s. 35(5); Y s. 36(9).
146 PPSA (A, BC, M, NWT, Nu, PEI, S) ss. 38(12)–(14); NB s. 38(14)–(15); NL s. 39(12)–(14); NS s. 39(14)–(16); O s. 35(6)–(7). The notice period is ten days in Ontario and fifteen days in the other jurisdictions.

sory goods and state the value of the obligation secured by the security interest in the accessory goods. A person with an interest in the whole may retain the accessory goods by paying out the secured party. The Acts outside of Ontario make it clear that the amount that is to be paid is the lesser of the obligation secured or the market value of the accessory goods.[147] The Ontario Act provides for payment of the amount required to satisfy the obligation secured by the security interest, which may be greater than the value of the accessory goods.[148]

F. MANUFACTURED AND COMMINGLED GOODS

The PPSA contains a set of rules that govern where the collateral is manufactured into a different product. These rules also govern where a security interest is taken in fungible goods that are then mixed with other fungibles. These rules have two functions. First, they provide that the security interest in the component goods continues in the finished product or the mixture. Second, they provide rules for the resolution of priority competitions. The Ontario Act is much less complete and contains only a single provision. The other Acts have worked out a more detailed set of rules. Courts in Ontario may therefore find it useful to examine the other Acts to fill in the gaps in the Ontario Act.

1) Continuation of the Security Interest in the Product or Mass

At common law, an interest in goods is lost when the goods are manufactured or otherwise transformed into a new thing. This occurs when the nature of the goods is so altered that their original identity is lost. The common law refers to this principle as specification. Thus, prior to PPSA reform, a seller who retained title in resin to secure its unpaid purchase price could not claim any interest in the chipboard into which the resin was manufactured or in the proceeds of sale of the chipboard.[149] The common law takes a different approach in respect of fungible goods that are mixed. The mixing does not result in a loss

---

147 PPSA (BC, M, NWT, Nu, PEI, S) s. 38(11); A s. 38(9); NB s. 38(13); NL s. 39(11); NS s. 39(13); O s. 35(8); Y s. 36(12).

148 OPPSA s. 35(8).

149 *Borden (U.K.) Ltd. v. Scottish Timber Products Ltd.*, [1981] Ch. 25 (C.A.).

of the interest. Rather, the contributor is able to claim a proportionate share of the mixture.[150]

The PPSA provides that a security interest in goods that are manufactured, processed, assembled or commingled continues in the product or mass.[151] The common law rules governing specification and mixtures are thereby displaced. The manufacturing or processing of the goods into a new product will no longer result in the destruction of the security interest. Under the PPSA, the secured party is able to assert a security interest in the new product. The section will therefore apply where blank paper is manufactured into a book or pamphlet[152] (or resin into chipboard to revert to the earlier example). The PPSA provision also applies when the separate identity of goods is lost through commingling. It therefore will cover cases where fungibles, such as two quantities of wheat, are mixed to form a single mass.

The situation that is covered by the PPSA provisions on commingled and processed goods should be distinguished from a number of other situations. The provisions will not apply where the goods are accessions. Accessions are governed by a different set of PPSA provisions. There should be no overlap between the two sets of rules. The rules governing accessions only apply where the accessory goods are attached to the whole, but do not lose their separate identity (for example, tires installed on a truck). If identification of the goods becomes impossible or if the goods are no longer removable (for example, gold plate applied to jewellery), then the provisions governing commingled and processed goods apply.

The provisions only apply if the goods have been manufactured, processed, assembled, or commingled. The goods may have been consumed in ways that do not fall within the ambit of the provisions. For example, a security interest that is taken in food or drugs that are fed to cattle does not result in a continuation of the security interest in the cattle.[153] Nor will the provisions apply to a security interest in fuel that fires a furnace used to manufacture pottery.

The provisions should also be contrasted with situations that involve a disposition of the original collateral in a manner that gives rise to a proceeds security interest under the PPSA. Proceeds arise when

---

150 See Birks, above note 3.
151 PPSA (A, BC, M, NB, NWT, Nu, PEI, S) s. 39(1); (NL, NS) s. 40(1); O s. 37; Y s. 37(1).
152 *Unisource Canada Inc. v. Hongkong Bank of Canada Inc.* (1998), 14 P.P.S.A.C. (2d) 112 (Ont. Ct. Gen. Div.).
153 See *First National Bank of Brush v. Boston*, 564 P.2d 964 (Colo. App. 1977).

there is a dealing with the collateral. This should not be interpreted as covering a transformation in goods that results from the processing or commingling of the goods. Proceeds will arise only where there has been some kind of exchange under which the collateral is disposed of and substitute property is acquired in its place.[154] Accordingly, there should be no overlap between the two sets of provisions.

2) Perfection of the Security Interest in the Product

The PPSA provides that a security interest in goods that are later commingled or processed continues in the finished product. However, it is also necessary to determine if this security interest in the finished product has been perfected. This will not be an issue in Ontario because the secured party will usually describe the collateral by ticking the inventory box, and an inventory description covers raw materials as well as finished products. The issue is of greater concern in the other jurisdictions, since the collateral description may well describe the component but fail to describe the finished product. For example, a financing statement may describe the collateral as resin. If the resin is processed into chipboard, the collateral description will not cover the finished product. The issue here concerns the effect that this will have on the perfected status of the resin financer's security interest in the finished product.

As just noted, the Ontario Act does not provide a rule to cover this situation, as none is needed. The other Acts provide that for the purposes of the residual priority rule that governs competitions between secured parties, perfection of a security interest in the component shall also be treated as perfection of the security interest given by the Act in the finished product or mass.[155] The security interest will therefore be automatically perfected in respect of a competition that is governed by the residual priority rule. Secured parties who wish to take a security interest in the finished product must therefore not limit their examination of search results to collateral descriptions describing the finished product. They must also look for registrations that contain descriptions of the component goods that were used to produce the product. The perfection provision does not provide for automatic perfection where the competition is with someone other than a secured party. A failure by the secured party to describe the finished product in the financing

---

154 See chapter 12, B.2.c "The Requirement of a Dealing."
155 PPSA (BC, M, NB, NWT, Nu, PEI, S) s. 39(3); A s. 39(2); (NL, NS) s. 40(3); Y no equivalent provision.

statement will result in subordination of its security interest to a non-ordinary course buyer who purchases the finished product without knowledge[156] and to a trustee in bankruptcy.

3) Competing Security Interests in the Separate Components

More than one perfected security interest in components may be continued in the product. In such a case, it will be necessary to resolve a priority competition between two or more secured parties who have perfected security interests in separate components, since each will be able to claim a security interest in the product. Grant Gilmore, one of the chief architects of Article 9 of the *Uniform Commercial Code*, uses the now-classic example of candy that is made from sugar and chocolate. Suppose that SP1 has a perfected security interest in the sugar and SP2 has a perfected security interest in the chocolate. The two components are then manufactured into candy. The Ontario Act provides that "the security interests rank equally according to the ratio that the cost of the goods to which each interest originally attached bears to the cost of the total product or mass."[157] Unfortunately, this wording was imported without modification from an older version of the *Uniform Commercial Code*,[158] despite the fact that Gilmore had provided a detailed analysis of its flaws.[159] The problem with the wording is that it refers to the total cost of the candy, and the total cost is not limited to the costs of the two components but may also include labour and overhead costs. Suppose that the cost of the sugar is $3,000, the cost of the chocolate is $5,000, and the cost of labour and overhead is $2,000. The OPPSA formulae would give SP1 a claim to 30 percent of the value of the candy, SP2 a claim to 50 percent of its value, and the trustee in bankruptcy would be entitled to the remaining 20 percent. The result is that the trustee in bankruptcy may be entitled to claim part of the

---

156 An ordinary course buyer will be protected by the ordinary course buyer priority rule whether or not secured party describes the finished product in the financing statement.

157 OPPSA s. 37.

158 U.C.C. 9-315. The problem has been rectified in the most recent revision. See 1999 Rev. U.C.C. 9-336.

159 G. Gilmore, *Security Interests in Personal Property*, vol. 2 (Boston: Little, Brown, 1965) at 851–54.

value of the finished product even though neither of the claims of the secured parties has been fully satisfied.[160]

This problem in wording is rectified in the Acts of the other PPSA jurisdictions. These provide that the holders of the security interests in the components "are entitled to share in the product or mass in the ratio that the obligation secured by each security interest bears to the sum of the obligations secured by all security interests."[161] Under this rule, SP1 would receive 3/8 or 37.5 percent of the value of the candy, while SP2 would receive 5/8 or 62.5 percent. These Acts also provide that, for the purposes of this provision, the obligation secured cannot be greater than the market value of the component at the time the component becomes part of the product or mass.[162] If the market value of the sugar was $1,000 but the obligation secured by SP1's security interest in the sugar was $3,000, the obligation secured would be capped at the market value of the component ($1,000). If the obligation secured was $1,000, but the market value of the component was $3,000, the $1,000 figure representing the obligation secured would be used for the purposes of the calculation.

The Ontario Act does not provide a priority rule to cover the situation where the security interest in one of the components is a purchase money security interest while the security interest in another of the components is not.[163] The other Acts provide that the proportional sharing rule is displaced in this case and priority is given to the purchase money security interest.[164] This priority is limited to the value of the component goods on the day that they became part of the product.[165]

---

160 For example, if the candy is sold for $5,000, SP1 will receive $1,500, SP2 $2,500, and the trustee $1,000.

161 PPSA (BC, M, NB, NWT, Nu, PEI, S) s. 39(2); A s. 39(4); (NL, NS) s. 40(2); Y s. 37(2).

162 PPSA (BC, M, NB, NWT, Nu, PEI, S) s. 39(4); A s. 39(5); (NL, NS) s. 40(4); Y no equivalent provision.

163 *Unisource Canada Inc. v. Hongkong Bank of Canada Inc.*, above note 152, involved a competition between a purchase money security interest in component goods and a general security interest in all of the debtor's present and after-acquired personal property (i.e., all the component goods and the finished product as well). The court held that the proportionate sharing rule could not be applied in this situation.

164 PPSA (BC, M, NB, NWT, Nu, PEI, S) s. 39(6); (NL, NS) s. 40(6); Y no equivalent provision.

165 PPSA (BC, M, NB, NWT, Nu, PEI, S) s. 39(5); A s. 39(3); (NL, NS) s. 40(5); Y no equivalent provision.

4) Competing Security Interests in a Component and a Product

The proportional sharing rule does not apply where the competition is between a secured party who has a security interest in a component that continues in the product and another secured party who has a security interest in the product as original collateral. If the security interest in the component was not a purchase money security interest, the competition will be resolved by applying the residual priority rule that governs competitions between secured parties. If the security interest in the product was registered before the security interest in the component was registered, the security interest in the product or mass will have priority. This is illustrated in the following scenario.

SP1 is given a security interest in boots produced by a manufacturer, and SP1 registers first in time. SP2 is later given a security interest in leather, which it registers second in time. The leather is then processed into boots.

SP2's security interest continues into the boots, but the priority competition will be resolved by applying the first to register rule of priority. SP1 will therefore have priority over SP2 in respect of the boots.

   The Ontario Act does not provide a priority rule where the competition is between a purchase money security interest in a component and a security interest in the product. In *Unisource Canada Inc. v. Hongkong Bank of Canada Inc.*,[166] the court held that a perfected purchase money security interest in component goods has priority over a security interest in the product. The Acts in the other jurisdictions provide an express set of priority rules to govern such competitions. A purchase money security interest in goods other than inventory that continues in the product has priority over a competing security interest in the product.[167] When inventory is involved, the priority rules parallel the priority rules that govern purchase money security interests in inventory. When the component is inventory, the secured party who holds the purchase money security interest in the component must notify a secured party who has a prior registration covering the product of its intention to take a purchase money security interest in the inventory.[168]

---

166 Above note 152.
167 PPSA (BC, M, NB, NWT, Nu, PEI, S) s. 39(6); (NL, NS) s. 40(6); Y no equivalent provision.
168 PPSA (BC, M, NB, NWT, Nu, PEI, S) s. 39(6); (NB, PEI) s. 39(7); (NL, NS) s. 40(7); PEI s. 39(7); Y no equivalent provision.

The notice must be given before the components are incorporated into the product.

5) Valuation Limits on Continued Security Interests

The PPSA permits a security interest in a component to continue into the product. What happens when the obligation that is secured by the component is greater than the value of the component? This is illustrated in the following scenario. Assume that SP1's security interest in component goods (potatoes) has priority over SP's security interest in the product (frozen french fries). This may occur where SP1 registers before SP2. Or it may occur if SP1 has a purchase money security interest in the component goods and takes the required steps needed to obtain priority. The obligation secured by SP1's security interest is $10,000, but the value of the potatoes is only $3,000. The Ontario Act does not place an express limit on the value of SP1's claim to the french fries. The Acts in the other jurisdictions limit SP1's claim to the value of the component goods at the time they became part of the product. Therefore, SP1's priority over SP2 in respect of the frozen french fries is limited to $3,000.[169]

The valuation limits in some of the Acts apply only in respect of a competition with another security interest. This might be taken to suggest that a secured party can assert a security interest in the product to secure the full secured obligation ($10,000 in the preceding example) when the competition is with a buyer or trustee in bankruptcy or when enforcing the claim against the debtor. This argument should be rejected. The purpose behind the processing and commingling provisions is to allow the security interest in the component to continue into the product. It was not intended to give the secured party a windfall. This is most easily demonstrated where a mixture, rather than a processing of the goods, is involved. Suppose that a secured party has a security interest in 100 kilograms of nails. The nails are worth $1,000. The obligation secured by the security interest is $3,000. The nails are then mixed with 100 kilograms of similar nails belonging to the debtor. The mass is now valued at $2,000. The mixing of the nails provides no justification for giving the secured party a security interest in any more than the value of the nails that were added to the mixture. The Ontario Act and the other Acts to the extent that the competition does

---

169 PPSA (BC, M, NB, NWT, Nu, PEI, S) s. 39(5); A s. 39(3); (NL, NS) s. 40(5): Y no equivalent provision.

not involve another secured party should be read as subject to a value limitation.

The Acts in Atlantic Canada are worded more broadly so as to remove the possibility of arguing that the value limitation only applies to a competition with another secured party. Instead, the value limitation applies whenever a security interest in a component continues in a product.[170]

FURTHER READINGS

BURKE, M., "Fixture Financing under the PPSA: The Ongoing Conflict Between Realty and Fixture-Secured Interests" (1986) 24 Osgoode Hall L.J. 547

CUMING, R.C.C., "Protecting Security Interests in Proceeds: Equity and Canadian Personal Property Acts" in D.W.M. Waters, ed., *Equity, Fiduciaries and Trusts, 1993* (Agincourt, ON: Carswell, 1993) at 423

PENNER, J., *The Law of Trusts*, 2d ed. (London: Butterworths, 2000)

SMITH, L., *The Law of Tracing* (Oxford: Clarendon Press, 1997)

SMITH, L., "Tracing the Proceeds of Collateral under the PPSA: *Flexi-Coil Ltd. v. Kindersley District Credit Union Ltd.*" (1995) 25 Can. Bus. L.J. 460

---

170 PPSA (NB, PEI) s. 39(5); (NL, NS) s. 40(5).

CHAPTER 13

REMEDIES

A. INTRODUCTION

1) Personal Claims and Proprietary Claims

A creditor who is given a security interest in the debtor's property obtains a proprietary right to the collateral. The defining characteristic of a proprietary right (which is also referred to as a real right or a right *in rem*) is that it is a right in a thing that is generally enforceable against the world. By way of contrast, a personal right is a right in respect of a particular person or identifiable group of persons. For example, a creditor who lends money to a debtor has a personal right to recover the debt. This right is owed only by the debtor to the creditor.

A proprietary right in the form of a security interest may be directly vindicated by enforcement of the security interest. This will typically involve the seizure and sale of tangible collateral in the hands of the debtor or in the hands of some third party to whom it has been transferred. The law provides another means by which the secured party's proprietary right in the collateral may be protected. A secured party is given a personal right against a person who wrongfully interferes with the secured party's security interest in the collateral. A security interest therefore provides the foundation for two distinct types of claims that can be made by the secured party: (1) the enforcement of the security interest against the collateral; and (2) a personal claim against persons who wrongfully interfere with the collateral.

Part 5 of the PPSA provides a comprehensive remedial system that sets out in considerable detail the rights and obligations of a secured party who seeks to enforce its claim against the collateral. In contrast, the right of a secured party to bring a personal action against those who interfere with the collateral is almost entirely unregulated by the PPSA. Instead, the Act leaves these matters to be determined by the common law.

This chapter will focus primarily on the remedial system found in Part 5 of the Act. However, in order to appreciate the full range of remedies available to a secured party, it is also necessary to understand how the common law protects proprietary interests through the availability of personal actions against persons who unlawfully interfere with the secured party's interest. This chapter will therefore conclude with a discussion of the available personal actions.

2) Secured and Unsecured Creditors' Remedies

One of the major reasons why a creditor may wish to take a security interest in the debtor's property is that it gives the creditor a superior set of enforcement remedies. Without a security interest, the creditor has no proprietary interest in the debtor's assets, and must enforce the claim through the provincial judgment enforcement system. In order to do this, the creditor must bring a civil action and obtain a judgment. This can produce delays, particularly if the debtor defends the action. Once a judgment is obtained, the creditor will usually obtain a writ of execution or writ of enforcement. The creditor will then seek to enforce the judgment through seizure and sale of the debtor's personal property, garnishment of intangible claims, or sale proceeds against the debtor's land. These proceedings tend to be more cumbersome, particularly in jurisdictions that have not reformed their judgment enforcement systems. As well, the judgment enforcement creditor is generally required to share funds produced as a result of enforcement proceedings with other judgment enforcement creditors.

A creditor who takes a security interest in some or all of the debtor's personal property has a more powerful set of default remedies. The secured creditor does not need to obtain a judgment before commencing enforcement proceedings. Upon default, the secured creditor has the right to take possession of the collateral. In most jurisdictions, a seizure and sale of personal property does not need to be undertaken by the sheriff. In seven PPSA jurisdictions, provincial and territorial exemptions law does not apply to secured creditors (the other five have enacted legislation that makes security interests subject to exemptions).

Despite the superiority of its secured party remedies, a creditor may decide to invoke its judgment enforcement remedies. If the secured party is undersecured (that is, if the anticipated proceeds from the collateral are insufficient to cover the obligation secured), the secured party may wish to obtain a judgment to cover the shortfall. This shortfall is popularly referred to as a "deficiency," and the judgment obtained in respect of it is called a "deficiency judgment." The creditor may then use the judgment enforcement system in order to proceed against the debtor's unencumbered property to collect the deficiency. The PPSA provides that a security interest does not merge merely because the claim has been reduced to judgment.[1] The creditor may therefore invoke its secured party remedies against the collateral and concurrently invoke its judgment enforcement remedies against the debtor's other assets. Of course, the creditor cannot receive more than one satisfaction of the judgment debt. Any amount received from the disposition of the collateral must be applied so as to reduce the amount payable on the judgment.

In other instances, a secured party may decide to enforce its claim using its judgment enforcement remedies instead of its secured party remedies. This might occur if the secured party has a security interest in one piece of equipment, but has obtained judgment and is directing seizure of several other pieces of equipment under judgment enforcement proceedings. Under these circumstances, it may be more convenient to have all the property seized under the judgment enforcement proceedings rather than having to effect two different types of enforcement proceedings. The fact that the secured party instructs seizure of the collateral under judgment enforcement proceedings should not prevent the secured party from asserting its secured party's remedies. Therefore, the secured party may choose to sell its collateral under the sale mechanism set out in the PPSA despite the fact that seizure was undertaken under judgment enforcement proceedings.

Although the remedies are cumulative, a secured party will eventually be required to make an election between inconsistent remedies. For example, a secured party who elects to exercise its right under the PPSA to retain the collateral in satisfaction of the obligation secured thereafter loses the right to recover on a judgment, since the underlying obligation is extinguished. However, a claimant will not be re-

---

1   PPSA (A, NB, PEI, NWT, Nu) s. 55(8); BC s. 55(9); M s. 55(4); (NL, NS) s. 56(8); O s. 59(7), S s. 55(7); Y s. 53(9).

garded as having elected between inconsistent remedies until there is an irrevocable choice of one over the other.[2]

It is less certain whether a secured party may continue to rely upon its security interest after it has caused the collateral to be sold pursuant to judgment enforcement proceedings that it has instructed. In *Trans Canada Credit Corporation Ltd. v. Foubert*,[3] the Ontario Court of Appeal indicated that a secured party makes an irrevocable election to waive its enforcement rights under a conditional sales agreement once it has caused the collateral to be sold pursuant to judgment enforcement proceedings. Although this ruling was rendered under pre-PPSA law, it likely represents the current position in all the PPSA jurisdictions other than Ontario. The position in Ontario is less clear because the Ontario PPSA states that a security interest does not merge in a judgment by virtue of the secured party having levied execution.[4] A levy typically refers to both the seizure and sale of the asset pursuant to a writ.[5] This suggests that the sale of an asset under execution proceedings does not amount to an irrevocable election of remedies.

B. THE NATURE AND SCOPE OF PART 5

Part 5 of the PPSA establishes a set of rules to govern the enforcement remedies of secured parties. This represents a major departure from the prior law, which provided different enforcement remedies depending upon the particular type of security device that was utilized (that is, mortgage, conditional sale, equitable charge). Part 5 adopts a unitary approach to enforcement remedies. It creates a single set of enforcement rules that apply to virtually every type of security agreement, regardless of its form. Differences in treatment are not based on the type of security agreement, but on the nature of the collateral or on the circumstances peculiar to particular modes of enforcement. The PPSA enforcement code is comprehensive in scope, and most rules are mandatory in nature. Unlike the case under prior law, there is little scope

---

2   *United Australia Ltd. v. Barclays Bank Ltd.* [1941] A.C. 1 at 37–39 (H.L.), Lord Atkin.
3   (1960), 26 D.L.R. (2d) 73 (Ont. C.A.).
4   OPPSA s. 59(7). This wording is not found in the other jurisdictions.
5   Section 5 of the *Creditors' Relief Act*, R.S.O. 1990, c. C.45 provides for the distribution of funds where the sheriff "levies money under an execution against the property of a debtor."

for the secured party to contractually modify the statutory enforcement remedies.

Part 5 is not the exclusive source of enforcement rules in the PPSA. Other parts of the Act govern enforcement against fixtures,[6] crops,[7] and accessions,[8] and set out the obligations of a secured party who is in possession of the collateral.[9] Other provincial or territorial statutes may provide additional protection to consumers, and the PPSA provides that in the event of a conflict, these provisions prevail.[10] In some cases, there is a suggestion that the secured party may also rely upon common law secured party remedies.[11] This proposition is doubtful, since the common law remedies varied according to the type of security device that was used, and this philosophy is very much opposed to the unitary approach to security interests adopted by the PPSA.

1) Transactions Not Caught by Part 5

Part 5 does not apply to transactions that are brought within the scope of the PPSA as deemed security interests. The non-Ontario Acts contain an express provision that excludes deemed security interests from the scope of Part 5.[12] Under these Acts, leases for a term of more than one year, commercial consignments, sales of accounts and chattel paper, and non-ordinary course sales of goods without a transfer of possession under the Acts of the Atlantic provinces are not governed by Part 5. If there is a breach of the agreement giving rise to the deemed security interest, the parties' remedies are instead determined by the common law. On the other hand, a transaction that takes the form of a lease or consignment or sale, but which in substance creates a security interest, is a true security interest that will be governed by Part 5.[13]

---

6   PPSA (A, BC, M, NB, NWT, Nu, PEI, S) s. 36; (NL, NS) s. 37, O s. 34; Y s. 35.
7   PPSA (A, BC, M, NB, NWT, Nu, PEI, S) s. 37; (NL, NS) s. 38; (O, Y) no equivalent provision.
8   PPSA (A, BC, M, NB, NWT, Nu, PEI, S) s. 38; (NL, NS) s. 39; O s. 35; Y s. 36.
9   PPSA (A, BC, M, NB, NWT, Nu, O, PEI, S) s. 17; (NL, NS) s. 18; Y s. 16.
10 PPSA s. 69 (M, NWT, Nu, S); A s. 72; BC s. 74; (NB, Y) s. 70; (NL, NS) s. 71; O s. 73.
11 *Tureck v. Hanston Investments Ltd.* (1986), 30 D.L.R. (4th) 690 (H.C.J.).
12 PPSA (A, M, NB, NWT, Nu, PEI) s. 55(2); (BC, S) s. 55(2); (NL, NS) s. 56(3); Y s. 53(3); O no equivalent provision.
13 PPSA (A, M, NB, PEI, S) s. 3(2); BC s. 3; (NWT, Nu) s. 2(2); (NL, NS) s. 4(2); Y s. 2(b) provides that the PPSA applies to a transfer of an account or chattel paper, a lease for a term of more than one year, a commercial consignment, and under the Atlantic Acts a non-ordinary course sale of goods without a transfer of possession, only if they do not secure payment or performance of an obliga-

Under the Ontario Act, only absolute transfers of accounts and chattel paper are deemed to be security interests. Although the Ontario PPSA does not expressly exclude these transactions from the application of Part 5, its provisions cannot sensibly be applied to such transactions. Part 5 permits the secured party to sell the collateral and apply the proceeds against the secured obligation. It also gives the debtor the right to redeem the collateral by paying the amount of the secured obligation. A transaction that takes the form of a sale of an account or chattel paper involves an outright transfer of the property. There is no obligation secured and therefore Part 5 can have no application to it.

Pawn transactions are excluded from the scope of the Ontario PPSA[14] and from Part 5 of the PPSA of other jurisdictions.[15] As a result, the remedies of pawnbrokers in all jurisdictions are governed by the common law and applicable statutes. However, with the exception of the Ontario Act, other parts of the Act, such as section 17, which set out the duties of secured parties who are in possession of the collateral, apply to pawn transactions.

2) Contractual Modifications to Part 5

Although most security agreements contain contractual provisions that set out the enforcement remedies of the secured party, it is not strictly necessary for the security agreement to contain any enforcement provisions at all. The enforcement remedies are conferred by Part 5 rather than by the security agreement.[16] In a few instances, Part 5 provides that the right must be stipulated in the security agreement in order to create the enforcement right. The most significant example is the rule that the security agreement must provide for the appointment of a receiver in order for the secured party to privately appoint a receiver.[17] Except for the Ontario Act, the PPSA also provides that the secured party may dispose of the collateral by lease only if the security agree-

---

tion. The exclusion of Part 5 is limited to the deemed security interests listed in this provision. Therefore, leases that fall within the definition of a "lease for a term of more than one year" or a "commercial consignment" or "a transfer of an account or chattel paper" or "a sale without a change of possession" but which in substance create security interests are not excluded from Part 5.

14   OPPSA s. 4(1)(d).
15   PPSA (A, M, NB, NWT, Nu, PEI) s. 55(3); (BC, S) s. 55(2); (NL, NS) s. 56(3); Y s. 53(3).
16   *Andrews v. Mack Financial (Canada) Ltd.* (1987), 46 D.L.R. (4th) 731 (Sask. C.A.).
17   PPSA (BC, M, NB, NWT, Nu, PEI) s. 64(1); (A, NL, NS) s. 65(1); O, s. 60(1)(a); S s. 64(2); Y s. 54(1).

ment so provides.[18] Some of the Acts also permit a disposition by deferred payment if this is provided for in the security agreement.[19]

For the most part, this scheme of enforcement remedies is mandatory and a secured party has only a limited ability to vary it by contract. The PPSA provides that to the extent that the enforcement provisions give rights to the debtor or impose obligations on the secured party, they cannot be waived or varied except as provided by the Act.[20] The PPSA also states that provisions in a security agreement that purport to exclude a duty or to limit damages recoverable are void.[21] Although the PPSA provides that a secured party also has the rights and remedies provided in the security agreement,[22] these cannot detract from the rights conferred upon the debtor by Part 5 and by section 17. The PPSA permits contractual variation of the remedial scheme if the variation expands the rights available to the debtor on default.

A contractual variation of the secured party's rights is also expressly permitted by the PPSA in the following circumstances:

- A secured party in possession of chattel paper, a security or an instrument may contract out of its obligation to preserve rights against other persons.[23]
- After the occurrence of an event of default, a debtor may in writing consent to the immediate disposition of the collateral without notice.[24]
- A secured party in possession of collateral may contract out of the obligation to keep the collateral identifiable.[25]

---

18   PPSA (BC, M, NWT, Nu, S) s. 59(3); A s. 60(2); (NB, PEI) s. 59(5); (NL, NS) s. 60(5); Y s. 57(2). OPPSA s. 63(2) permits the secured party to dispose of the collateral by sale, lease or otherwise. In Ontario, the secured party is therefore able to lease the goods even in the absence of contractual provision authorizing the secured party to do so.

19   PPSA (BC, M, NWT, Nu, S) s. 59(4); A s. 60(2); (NB, PEI) s. 60(6); (NL, NS) s. 60(6); (O, Y) no equivalent provision.

20   PPSA (BC, M, NB, NWT, Nu, S) s. 56(3); A s. 56(2); (NB, PEI) s. 56(4); (NL, NS) s. 57(4); O s. 59(5); Y s. 53(7).

21   PPSA (M, S) s. 65(10); A s. 67(5); BC s. 69(9); (NB, PEI) s. 66(7); (NL, NS) s. 67(6); (NWT, Nu) s. 65(9); O s. 67(3); Y s. 62(3).

22   PPSA (BC, M, NB, NWT, Nu, PEI, S) s. 56(2); A s. 56(1); (NL, NS) s. 57(2); O s. 59(1); Y s. 53(4).

23   PPSA (BC, M, NB, NWT, Nu, PEI, S) s. 57(2); A s. 57(1); (NL, NS) s. 58(2); O s. 61(1); Y s. 55(1).

24   PPSA (BC, M, NWT, Nu) s. 59(17); A s. 60(15); (NB, PEI) s. 59(18); (NL, NS) s. 60(18); O s. 63(7); S s. 59(16).

25   PPSA (BC, M, NB, NWT, Nu, PEI, S) s. 17(2); (A, O) s. 17(1); (NL, NS) s. 18(2); Y s. 16(1).

- After the occurrence of an event of default, a debtor may surrender the right to redeem the collateral[26] or reinstate the security agreement.[27]

The Ontario and Yukon Acts contain a provision not found in the other Acts. It provides that a security agreement may set out the standards by which rights of the debtor and duties of the secured party are to be measured, so long as those standards are not manifestly unreasonable.[28]

3) Disposition of Real and Personal Property

A secured party may have taken a security interest in both real and personal property to secure the same obligation. In enforcing the security interests, the secured party may proceed against the land and the personal property separately. Alternatively, the secured party may proceed against both the land and the personal property in a single action. In the latter case, the procedure governing enforcement against the land, and not Part 5, governs the enforcement proceedings.[29]

Difficulties may arise if the secured party proposes to proceed against the land and the personal property, but proposes to foreclose against the land or the personal property, or both. Foreclosure proceedings will result in the satisfaction of the obligation secured. The secured party cannot thereafter sue the debtor on the underlying debt or proceed against any other property given as collateral.[30] In *Dor-O-matic of Canada Ltd. (Re)*,[31] the secured party sought an order that would permit it to foreclose against both the land and the personal property in separate proceedings, without accepting either in full satisfaction of the debt. Blair J. held that the single-action foreclosure procedure was chosen as the appropriate mechanism to deal with this problem, and that it must therefore be used when the secured party wishes to fore-

---

26 PPSA (BC, M, NWT, Nu, S) s. 62(1); A s. 63(1); (NB, PEI) s. 62(2); (NL, NS) s. 63(2); O s. 66(1); Y s. 60(1).

27 PPSA (BC, M, NWT, Nu, S) s. 62(1); A s. 63(1); (NB, PEI) s. 62(2); (NL, NS) s. 63(4); Y s. 60(1). OPPSA s. 66(2) restricts the reinstatement right to consumer goods and does not provide for a post-default waiver of the notice requirement.

28 OPPSA s. 59(4); Y s. 53(7).

29 PPSA (A, NB, PEI, NWT, Nu, S) s. 55(4); BC s. 55(6); M s. 55(5); (NL, NS) s. 56(4); O s. 59(6); Y s. 53(8).

30 See *Travel West (1987) Inc. v. Langdon Towers Apartment Ltd.* (2001), 2 P.P.S.A.C. (2d) 99 (Sask. Q.B.), rev'd [2002] 9 W.W.R. 449 (C.A.) (foreclosure against land extinguishes the debt with the result that the secured party loses its security interest in the debtor's personal property).

31 (1996), 28 O.R. (3d) 125 (Gen. Div.).

close against both the land and the personal property. The single action procedure is not restricted to foreclosure proceedings. It also permits a secured party to seek a judicial sale of both the land and the personal property.

All the Acts, except those of Ontario and the Yukon, contain two additional rules that apply when the secured party proceeds against both land and personal property in a single action.[32] Both concern the position of a third party who has a security interest in the personal property. The first provides that the single action procedure does not operate to prejudice any of the rights to which that secured party may be entitled. The third party is therefore entitled to the benefit of any notification requirements provided by Part 5, and its priority position cannot be adversely affected by the use of the single action procedure. The second rule provides an allocation formula to determine the proportion of the sale proceeds that is attributable to the sale of the personal property when the land and the personal property are sold for a single price.[33] This formula would be utilized if the sale produces a surplus, and a subordinate secured party had a security interest in the personal property. In such a case, it is necessary to determine the extent to which the surplus was generated by the sale of the personal property as opposed to the sale of the land, since only the former would be distributable to the subordinate secured party.

4) Enforcement against Third Parties

In most cases when the secured party enforces its security interest, the collateral is in the hands of the original debtor. But the debtor may have sold or otherwise transferred the collateral to a third party. If the buyer or other transferee acquired the collateral in circumstances where it took free of the security interest under the priority rules of the Act or otherwise, then the secured party's right to enforce the security interest is lost. But if the security interest continues in the collateral, the secured party may follow the collateral into the hands of the buyer or transferee and enforce its proprietary claim. This type of enforcement is also regulated by Part 5 of the PPSA. The definition of debtor in the PPSA expressly provides that debtor includes a transferee of or a suc-

---

32 PPSA (A, NB, PEI, NWT, Nu, S) s. 55(5); BC s. 55(7); M s. 55(6); (NL, NS) s. 56(5).
33 The portion attributable to the sale of the personal property is calculated by dividing the market value of the personal property by the total market value of the land and personal property and multiplying this by the total proceeds of sale.

cessor to a debtor's interest in the collateral.[34] The secured party may therefore assert the Part 5 enforcement remedies against a transferee in much the same way that they could be asserted against the original debtor. If the secured party chooses to sell the collateral, a pre-disposition notice must be given to the debtor.[35] If the secured party proposes to foreclose, a notice of intention must be given to the debtor.[36] In both cases, the notice must also be given to a transferee if the secured party knows of the transfer.

This inclusion of a transferee within the definition of a debtor does not mean that a transferee is in the same position as the original debtor for all purposes. Unlike the original debtor, a transferee is not liable to the secured party for any deficiency following the sale of the collateral.[37] Although a transferee is given the right to redeem the collateral, a transferee is not given the right to reinstate the security agreement by paying the sums actually in arrears or otherwise curing the default.[38]

5) Who Is the Debtor?

In most cases, the person who owes the obligation to the creditor is also the owner of the collateral in respect of which the security interest is given. This person is referred to as the debtor. But sometimes the person who gives the security interest may not be the same person who owes the obligation to the secured party. The definition of debtor in the

---

34   PPSA (A, BC, NWT, Nu, O, Y) s. 1(1); (M, NB, PEI) s. 1; (NL, NS) s. 2; S s. 2(1). The definition of debtor in the OPPSA simply provides that "debtor" includes a transferee of or successor to a debtor's interest in collateral. In most of the other Acts the definition of debtor is more precise in that it identifies the specific sections where debtor is to be interpreted as including a transferee or successor in interest.

35   PPSA (BC, M, NWT, Nu, S) s. 59(6); A s. 60(4); (NB, PEI) s. 59(8); (NL, NS) s. 60(8); O s. 63(4); Y s. 57(4).

36   PPSA (BC, NB, NWT, Nu, PEI, S) s. 61(1); (A, NL, NS) s. 62(1); M s. 61(2); O s. 65(2); Y s. 59(1).

37   The definition is not so restricted in Ontario, but it is most unlikely that the provision would be interpreted so as to make a transferee liable for a deficiency.

38   The extended definition of debtor in the non-Ontario Acts does not cover the provision dealing with reinstatement. The definition is not so restricted in Ontario, and therefore it is possible to argue that a transferee has a right to reinstate the security agreement. Presumably this would be done only where the transferee intends to take over the responsibility of making future payments. However, most security agreements provide that a transfer of collateral without the consent of the secured party is an event of default, with the result that a transferee will be unable to cure the default.

non-Ontario Acts[39] provides that if the person who owes payment or performance of an obligation (the obligor) is not the same person as the person who has rights in the collateral (the owner), then debtor means the owner in a provision dealing with the collateral and the obligor in a provision dealing with the obligation. Where the context permits, the term may include both the owner and the obligor. Each provision of the statute must be carefully considered to determine which types of debtor are being referred to.[40] For example, the PPSA requires that notice of intention to sell must be given to the debtor.[41] This should be construed to refer to both the owner of the collateral and the obligor. The owner obviously has an interest in learning of the intended sale, as the owner may wish to redeem the collateral. The obligor also has an interest in learning of the sale, since the failure to properly conduct it may increase the size of the deficiency for which the obligor will be liable. Although the definition of debtor in the Ontario PPSA contemplates that the owner of the collateral and the obligor may be different people, it does not contain an interpretive clause similar to the provision described above. Notwithstanding this omission, it is likely that the Ontario Act would be interpreted in a similar manner.

C. DEFAULT

Default represents a turning point in the secured transaction. It constitutes the very risk that motivated the creditor to take the security interest in the first place. It is upon default that issues of priority come into sharper focus, because there is an immediate need for the secured party to consider how its rights stack up against other third parties who have an interest in the collateral. Default also triggers the right of the secured party to exercise its remedies in respect of the collateral. Before proceeding against the collateral, a secured party must ensure that there has been an event of default. A secured party who seizes the collateral before the occurrence of an event of default may face liability for trespass, conversion, and breach of contract. In appropriate cases,

---

39   PPSA (A, BC, NWT, Nu, O, Y) s. 1(1); (M, NB, PEI) s. 1; (NL, NS) s. 2; S s. 2(1).
40   See the discussion in chapter 1, D.2 "Debtor" on the question whether a guarantor falls within the definition of a debtor.
41   PPSA (BC, M, NWT, Nu, S) s. 59(6); A s. 60(4); (NB, PEI) s. 59(8); (NL, NS) s. 60(8); O s. 63(4); Y s. 57(4).

punitive or exemplary damages may be awarded against the secured party as well.[42]

1) Defining the Events of Default

A failure to pay or otherwise perform the obligation secured when due falls under the definition of default under the PPSA.[43] In addition, the definition provides that the parties are free to specify in the security agreement other events or circumstances as events of default that will cause the security interest to become enforceable. In the words of Grant Gilmore, one of the principal architects of Article 9 of the *Uniform Commercial Code*, default "is a matter of contract and can best be defined as being whatever the security agreement says it is."[44] Most security agreements take advantage of this provision and list a number of different events of default. Some of the more commonly specified events of default are summarized as follows:

- a failure by the debtor to perform or comply with any covenant;[45]
- any representation or warranty that proves to be untrue in a material way;
- the institution against the debtor of bankruptcy or insolvency proceedings;
- the debtor's ceasing to carry on business or the making of a bulk sale of its assets;
- the death or declaration of incompetency of an individual debtor, or the dissolution or liquidation of a corporate debtor;
- the institution of execution, garnishment, attachment, or enforcement proceedings against the debtor;
- any encumbrance becoming enforceable against the collateral;
- the secured party's good faith belief that the prospect of payment or performance of the obligation is impaired or that the collateral is likely to be placed in jeopardy.

---

42   *Royal Bank of Canada v. W. Got & Associates Electric Ltd.*, [1999] 3 S.C.R. 408.

43   PPSA (A, BC, NWT, Nu, O, Y) s. 1(1); (M, NB, PEI) s. 1; (NL, NS) s. 2; S s. 2(1).

44   G. Gilmore, *Security Interests in Personal Property*, vol. 2 (Boston: Little Brown, 1965) at 1193.

45   Sometimes the security agreement will provide that the failure will not constitute a default until a specified time period after the debtor knows of the failure or after the secured party notifies the debtor.

2) Acceleration Clauses and Insecurity Provisions

Security agreements typically contain an acceleration clause that provides that upon the occurrence of an event of default, the secured party has the right to declare all indebtedness that is not payable on demand to be immediately due or payable in a lump sum. This gives the secured party the right to accelerate all future repayments so that they become immediately payable. Many security agreements also include a provision to the effect that there is an event of default if the secured party in good faith believes that the prospect of payment or performance of the obligation is impaired or that the collateral is likely to be placed in jeopardy (sometimes referred to as an "insecurity" provision). Taken at face value, the combination of these two provisions would give the secured party an uncontrolled power to declare an event of default and accelerate the obligation at its sole discretion so long as it acted honestly. This power is curtailed by the PPSA. The Act provides that such a clause is to be interpreted to mean that the secured party is permitted to accelerate performance only if the secured party is in good faith and has commercially reasonable grounds to believe that the prospect of payment is impaired or that the collateral is or is about to be placed in jeopardy.[46] An objective test is used.[47] It is not enough that the secured party has the honest belief that the security is impaired. There must exist commercially reasonable grounds that justify that belief.

3) The Reasonable Notice Doctrine

Courts in Canada have constrained the ability of a secured party to immediately enforce a security interest upon default through the application of the reasonable notice doctrine. The Supreme Court of Canada in *Ronald Elwyn Lister Ltd. v. Dunlop Canada Ltd.*[48] described the operation of the doctrine as follows:

> [T]he debtor must be given "some notice on which he might reasonably expect to be able to act." … Failure to give such reasonable notice places the debtor under economic, but nonetheless real duress, often as real as physical duress to the person, and no doubt explains the eagerness of the courts to construe debt-evidencing or creating documents as including in all cases the requirement of reasonable notice for payment.

---

46   PPSA (A, BC, M, NB, NWT, Nu, O, PEI, S) s. 16; (NL, NS) s. 17; Y s. 15.
47   *Loewen v. Superior Acceptance Corp.* (1997), 46 C.B.R. (3d) 239 (B.C.S.C.).
48   [1982] 1 S.C.R. 726 at 746.

There are three notable features of the Canadian formulation of the reasonable notice doctrine that distinguishes it from that adopted in England and other Commonwealth countries. The first concerns the length of time that is afforded to the debtor. Elsewhere, the courts have adopted a mechanics of payment test that gives the debtor no opportunity to obtain refinancing from another lender or to raise the funds through liquidation of assets, but merely gives the debtor sufficient time to withdraw the funds from an existing bank account or other source of payment.[49] In Canada, the time period is more extensive and can extend for a few days. The amount of time that must be given depends upon a wide range of factors, including the amount of the loan, the risk to the creditor of losing his money or security, the length of the relationship between the debtor and the creditor, the character and reputation of the debtor, the potential ability to raise the money required in a short time, the circumstances surrounding the demand for payment, and any other relevant factors.[50] Second, in Canada the reasonable notice doctrine has been extended so as to apply to debts that are repayable in instalments[51] and to all events of default.[52] Third, the reasonable notice doctrine is treated as a rule of law which cannot be waived or varied by the security agreement.[53]

The reasonable notice doctrine does not fit easily within the remedial scheme set out in Part 5 of the PPSA. The PPSA provides that upon default, the secured party has the right to enforce the security interest by any method permitted by law.[54] This would seem to suggest that

---

49 *Bank of Baroda v. Panessar*, [1987] 2 W.L.R. 208; *Bunbury Foods Pty Ltd. v. National Bank of Australasia Ltd.* (1984), 152 C.L.R. 491 (H.C. Aust.); *ANZ Banking Group (N.Z.) Ltd. v. Gibson*, [1986] 1 N.Z.L.R. 556 (C.A.).

50 *Mister Broadloom Corp. (1968) v. Bank of Montreal* (1979), 25 O.R. (2d) 198 (H.C.J.), var'd (1983), 44 O.R. (2d) 368 (C.A.). If the debtor's circumstances are such that it is unlikely that he can raise the amount owing or if the debtor's conduct is dishonest, the secured party will be permitted to demand payment and almost immediately thereafter enforce its security. See *Kavcar Investments Ltd. v. Aetna Financial Services Ltd.* (1989), 70 O.R. (2d) 225 (C.A.).

51 *Roynat Ltd. v. Northern Meat Packers Ltd.* (1986), 29 D.L.R. (4th) 139 (N.B.C.A.), leave to appeal to S.C.C. refused (1987), 78 N.B.R. (2d) 90.

52 *Jim Landry Pontiac Buick Ltd. v. Canadian Imperial Bank of Commerce* (1987), 40 D.L.R. (4th) 343 (N.S.S.C.); *Kavcar Investments Ltd. v. Aetna Financial Services Ltd.*, above note 50; *Waldron v. Royal Bank* (1991), 78 D.L.R. (4th) 1 (B.C.C.A.).

53 *Kavcar Investments Ltd. v. Aetna Financial Services Ltd.*, ibid.; *Waldron v. Royal Bank*, ibid.

54 PPSA (BC, M, NB, NWT, Nu, PEI, S) s. 58(2); A s. 58(1); (NL, NS) s. 59(2); O s. 62; Y s. 56

upon the occurrence of an event of default, the secured party is given the right to immediately seize the collateral. Courts have continued to apply the reasonable notice doctrine without explaining how the doctrine functions within the context of the PPSA. The doctrine might be explained on the basis that an event of default does not in fact arise until after a reasonable period of time has elapsed, and therefore the secured party has no right to enforce the security agreement until that time. The problem with this rationalization is that the reasonable notice doctrine has been applied in cases where there has been a failure to pay an instalment under a term loan and in cases where an event of default other than a failure to pay has been triggered. Another approach is to explain the application of the doctrine on the basis that it is merely an aspect of the overarching obligation of the secured party to act in good faith and a commercially reasonable manner.[55] The problem with this approach is that it cannot explain the operation of the doctrine in Ontario, as the Ontario Act does not contain a similar provision. Nor does it explain why it is commercially reasonable to require a secured party to give a pre-seizure notice when the debtor has failed to pay an instalment when it is due.

Some PPSAs expressly provide that the right to enforce a security interest is subject to any other Act or rule of law that requires a secured party to give prior notice of its intention to enforce its security interest.[56] The authors are concerned that the reasonable notice doctrine, as it is presently formulated, cannot be reconciled with the enforcement regime of the PPSA, at least in those jurisdictions that do not expressly contemplate its application. To the extent that the reasonable notice doctrine is restricted to a demand for payment under a demand loan, there is no inconsistency. There is no default until a reasonable period has elapsed. However, to the extent that the doctrine has been applied to term loans or to cases where other events of default have been triggered, there is a conflict with the legislation. Courts have failed to develop an underlying theory that explains why the reasonable notice doctrine operates as a substantive rule of law and not simply an implied term that can be varied by the terms of the security agreement. Although it has been suggested that the doctrine is based on unconscion-

---

55   PPSA (M, NWT, Nu, S) s. 65(3); A s. 66(1); BC s. 68(3); (NB, PEI) s. 65(3); (NL, NS) s. 66(2); Y s. 62(1).

56   Such a provision is found in the Acts of Saskatchewan and the Atlantic provinces. See PPSA (NB, PEI, S) s. 58(2); (NL, NS) s. 59(2).

ability,[57] this would appear to involve a surprising expansion of the unconscionability concept because the application of the reasonable notice doctrine does not appear to depend upon the actual conduct or vulnerabilities of the parties.

4) The Statutory Notice of Intention to Enforce a Security

To a large extent, the controversy concerning the reasonable notice doctrine has dissipated since the enactment in 1992 of a statutory notice requirement in the *Bankruptcy and Insolvency Act*.[58]

Section 244(1) provides that a secured party who intends to enforce a security covering all or substantially all of the inventory, accounts, or other property of a business debtor must give the debtor advance notice of this intention.[59] The notice is only required where the debtor is insolvent.[60] A secured party who is required to send a notice of intention is not permitted to enforce the security until the expiry of ten days after the notice is sent.[61] A debtor is permitted to consent to an earlier enforcement of the security, but only after the notice of intention is given to the debtor.[62] Therefore, it is not possible to contract out of the statutory notice requirement through the inclusion of a waiver clause in a security agreement.

The statutory notice provision dovetails neatly with the commercial proposal provisions found elsewhere in the *Bankruptcy and Insolvency Act*.[63] Once the debtor receives the requisite notice of intention to enforce the security, the debtor may attempt to reorganize its affairs by making a proposal to its creditors for the settlement or compromise of their claims. The debtor may file a proposal with a licenced trustee. Alternatively, the debtor may file a notice of intention to file a proposal with the official receiver. In either event, the enforcement rem-

---

57 See *Kavcar Investments Ltd. v. Aetna Financial Services Ltd.*, above note 50; *Waldron v. Royal Bank*, above note 52.

58 R.S.C. 1985, am. S.C. 1992, c. 27 [BIA].

59 BIA s. 244(1). In *London Life Insurance Co. v. Air Atlantic Ltd.* (1994), 27 C.B.R. (3d) 66 (N.S.S.C.) the court held that enforcement against a single aircraft did not constitute an enforcement against substantially all of the debtor's assets.

60 Under s. 2 of the BIA, a debtor is insolvent when (1) he is unable to meet his obligations as they generally become due; (2) he has ceased to pay his current obligations in the ordinary course of business generally as they become due; or (3) the fair market value of his property is not sufficient to enable payment of all his obligations due and accruing due.

61 BIA s. 244(2).

62 BIA s. 244(2) and (3).

63 BIA Part 3, ss. 50–66.

edies of secured and unsecured creditors are immediately stayed until the creditors have had an opportunity to vote on the proposal.[64] If the proposal is rejected, the stay of proceedings comes to an end and the debtor is deemed to have made an assignment in bankruptcy.[65] The secured party may apply to a court to have the stay lifted[66] or to terminate the time period for making the proposal.[67]

If a notice of intention to enforce a security is given to a debtor and the debtor does not file a proposal or a notice of intention to file a proposal, the secured party is permitted to enforce its security interest. If the debtor files either of these documents after the expiry of the ten-day notice period, this will not have the effect of staying the secured party's enforcement remedies.[68] The courts have indicated that the ten-day statutory notice period provides a minimum notice period and is not a substitute for the common law notice period.[69] However, it will be rare that the common law notice period will exceed the statutory period.[70]

5) Other Provincial Pre-seizure Notice Requirements

Some provinces have enacted legislation requiring additional pre-seizure notice requirements. Saskatchewan law requires that the secured party must notify the debtor at least thirty days before seizing a house trailer and the seizure and sale must be carried out by the sheriff.[71] Saskatchewan law also provides a special seizure mechanism for specific

---

64 BIA ss. 69 and 69.1.
65 BIA s. 57.
66 BIA s. 69.4.
67 BIA s. 50.4(11). Where a proposal is filed, s. 50(12) provides that the creditor may apply to a court to have a declaration that the proposal is deemed to have been refused by the creditors.
68 BIA ss. 69(2) and 69.1(2).
69 *Prudential Assurance Co. (Trustee of) v. 90 Eglinton Ltd. Partnership* (1994), 18 O.R. (3d) 201; *Delron Computers Inc. v. ITT Industries of Canada Ltd. (Receiver of)* (1995), 31 C.B.R. (3d) 75 (Sask. Q.B.); *Beresford Building Supplies (1984) Ltd. v. Caisse Populaire de Petit-Rocher Ltée* (1996), 38 C.B.R. (3d) 274 (N.B.Q.B.). These cases also decided that the statutory notice can be combined with the common law notice.
70 In *Whonnock Industries Ltd. v. National Bank of Canada* (1987), 42 D.L.R. (4th) 1 (B.C.C.A.), Seaton J.A. stated at 11: "The Canadian law demonstrated in the decisions does not contemplate more than a few days and cannot encompass anything approaching 30 days. In the decisions noted nothing approaching the seven days permitted here has been classed as unreasonable."
71 *Distress Act*, R.S.S. 1978, c. D-31, ss. 6–6.2 (as am. S.S. 1979-80, c. 23, s. 5).

kinds of goods.[72] The secured party must give the debtor a notice of intention to seize. The secured party is prohibited from seizing the collateral within thirty days of this notice. During this period, the debtor may apply to a court for a hearing. A failure to comply results in the termination of the security agreement and the release of liability of the debtor; as well, the debtor is given the right to recover all payments previously made to the secured party. Manitoba law provides that a secured party cannot seize goods sold under an instalment-sale agreement without a court order if the amount owing is less than 25 percent of the cash price of the goods at the time of the sale.[73] In Ontario, a court order is needed if the consumer has paid two-thirds of the price.[74]

Manitoba and Saskatchewan require a pre-seizure notice in respect of certain types of farm property. The Manitoba legislation provides that a seller who has taken a security interest in farm machinery must obtain the leave of the Farm Machinery Board before seizing the collateral.[75] Saskatchewan provides a system for pre-seizure notification before a seller can seize specified personal property from a farmer. No seizure is permitted for thirty days after the notice has been given in order to give the debtor an opportunity to apply to a court for a hearing. A failure to comply results in the termination of the security agreement, the release of liability of the debtor and the debtor is given the right to recover one and a half times the market value of the property at the time of the seizure.[76]

D. SEIZURE

If the debtor is in default under the security agreement and if the required pre-seizure notices have been given, the PPSA gives the secured party the right to take possession of the collateral or otherwise enforce the security agreement by any method permitted by law.[77] The secured party will generally wish to take possession before selling the collateral or retaining it in satisfaction of the obligation secured. However,

---

72 *Limitation of Civil Rights Act*, R.S.S. 1978, c. L-16, ss. 19–33 (as amended). The provision applies to the seizure of a washing machine, stove, heater, sewing machine or refrigerator.

73 *Consumer Protection Act*, C.C.S.M. c. C200, s. 49.

74 *Consumer Protection Act*, R.S.O. 1990, c. C.31, s. 23.

75 *Farm Machinery and Equipment Act*, S.M. 1998, c. C40, s. 38(2).

76 *The Saskatchewan Farm Security Act*, S.S. 1989–90, c. S-17.1, ss. 47–64.

77 PPSA (BC, M, NB, NWT, Nu, PEI, S) s. 58(2); A s. 58(1); (NL, NS) s. 59(2); O s. 62; Y s. 56.

seizure of the collateral is not a precondition for the exercise of these remedies, and in exceptional cases the secured party may choose to sell or foreclose before the collateral is seized. Sometimes the debtor will voluntarily surrender the collateral to the secured party, thereby eliminating any need for the secured party to seize the collateral.

1) The Right to Seize the Collateral

The PPSA provides that a secured party has the right to take possession of the collateral upon default by any method permitted by law. This incorporates the ancient common law rules governing the self-help remedy of recaption of chattels. This permits the secured party to seize the collateral without the assistance of the courts or any legal process. Alberta, the Northwest Territories, and Nunavut take a different approach. They restrict the exercise of self-help remedies by providing that a seizure pursuant to a security agreement must be undertaken by a civil enforcement bailiff or a sheriff.

a) Peaceable Recaption

In jurisdictions that do not restrict the exercise of the self-help remedy, collateral can be seized by the secured party so long as it does not involve a breach of the peace. The use of unlawful force will render the seizure unlawful and expose the secured party to both civil and criminal liability.[78] The unlawful use of force cannot be validated by a term in the security agreement.[79]

There are two situations where the validity of the seizure may be brought into question. The first occurs where the seizure is undertaken in the presence of the debtor and the debtor resists the seizure. In such cases, the secured party is not permitted to use force. The appropriate response is for the secured party to back down and to obtain a court order for the seizure of the collateral. However, the secured party is entitled to use reasonable force to prevent the debtor from retaking possession of the collateral from the secured party after the secured party has obtained possession.[80] Less clear is the situation where the secured party used deception or trickery to obtain possession of the collateral. There is no Canadian authority, but the case law in the United States

---

78 *Devoe v. Long* (1950), [1951] 1 D.L.R. 203 at 217 (N.B.S.C. (A.D.)); *R. v. Shand* (1904), 7 O.L.R. 190 (C.A.); *R. v. Doucette*, [1960] O.R. 407 (C.A.); *Stackaruk v. Woodward*, [1966] 2 O.R. 32 (C.A.).

79 *R. v. Doucette*, ibid.

80 *Casey v. City National Leasing Ltd.* (1987), 51 Alta. L.R. (2d) 85 (Q.B.).

suggests that making false representations does not constitute a breach of the peace so as to invalidate the seizure after the fact.[81]

The second situation occurs where the seizure is undertaken in the absence of the debtor, and the secured party uses force to gain access to the premises. The security agreement will typically give the secured party an express licence to enter the debtor's land. This licence entitles the secured party to seize a car from a driveway or to seize equipment from a field. More questionable is whether it permits the secured party to use force to break into a building. There is older Canadian authority to the effect that a secured party may use reasonable force that does not cause unnecessary damage to break open a door.[82] On the other hand, there are many cases from the United States that have held that breaking into a building, such as a closed garage, or the cutting of a locked chain on a gate amounts to a breach of the peace.[83] In any event, a secured party is well advised not to break into a home or dwelling on the authorization of the licence, as there is some suggestion that Canadian courts treat this kind of entry differently.[84]

b) Restrictions on Self-help Remedies

Alberta, the Northwest Territories, and Nunavut restrict the exercise of self-help remedies by a secured party.[85] In these jurisdictions, the secured party must use a sheriff or civil enforcement bailiff to conduct a seizure. The powers given to the sheriff and to civil enforcement bailiffs are more extensive than those conferred upon a secured party in the exercise of its self-help remedies. The sheriff is permitted to use force to gain access to a building other than a dwelling.[86] The restriction of

---

81 See, for example, *Thompson v. Ford Motor Credit Co.*, 550 F.2d 256 (C.A. Ala. 1977).
82 *Rayson v. Graham* (1864), 15 U.C.C.P. 36; *Graham v. Green* (1862), 10 N.B.R. 330 (S.C.).
83 See, for example, *Davenport v. Chrysler Credit Corp.* 818 S.W.2d 23 (Tenn. App. 1991); *Martin v. Dorn Equipment Co. Inc.*, 821 P.2d 1025 (Mont. 1991).
84 See D. Paciocco, "Personal Property Security Act Repossession: The Risk and the Remedy" in M.A. Springman and E. Gertner, eds., *Debtor-Creditor Law: Practice and Doctrine* (Toronto: Butterworths, 1984) 365 at 396–97, citing *dicta* in *Devoe v. Long*, above note 78, and *Bennett v. Kent Piano Co. Ltd.* (1921), 29 B.C.R. 465 (C.A.).
85 *Civil Enforcement Act*, S.A. 1994, c. C-10.5, s. 9(3), am. 1996, c. 28, s. 9(4); *Seizures Act*, R.S.N.W.T. 1988, c. S-6, s. 16.
86 See Gordon Turiff & Elizabeth Edinger, *The Office of the Sheriff*, Study Paper (Vancouver: Law Reform Commission of British Columbia, 1983) at 141–45; C.R.B. Dunlop, *Creditor-Debtor Law in Canada*, 2d ed. (Toronto: Carswell, 1995)

self-help remedies does not apply to the appointment of a receiver by a secured party.[87]

A sheriff or civil enforcement agency is not permitted to use force in order to gain access into a dwelling. Instead, a court order must be obtained. These jurisdictions also require that the secured party obtain a court order for the delivery of a mobile home, where the debtor is in occupation of it.[88]

c) Constructive Seizure

A secured party may wish to leave goods in the possession of the debtor following a seizure of the collateral. There are a number of reasons why a secured party may wish to do so. The goods may be difficult to remove or storage facilities may unavailable or expensive. As well, the secured party may wish to avoid the obligations and potential liability that are imposed upon a secured party who is in possession of collateral. This is a particular concern if there is not a ready market for the goods or there is expected to be a delay before they can be disposed of. The PPSA provides that the secured party may in certain circumstances seize collateral without removing it from the premises. The Ontario Act provides that the secured party may do so where the collateral is classified as equipment. In order to effect the seizure, the goods must be rendered unusable.[89] The equivalent provision in the other Acts applies to all categories of goods, but its application is limited to cases where the goods cannot readily be removed or where storage facilities are not readily available.[90]

Since seizure is not a precondition for sale or foreclosure, one may well wonder if a constructive seizure pursuant to the statute is of any real significance. There are two reasons why it may be of relevance. Under the non-Ontario Acts, the secured party has a statutory right to dispose of the collateral on the debtor's premises only if the constructive seizure is effected in accordance with the statute. This statutory right to sell on the premises must not cause the debtor any additional inconvenience or cost than is reasonably incidental to the seizure.[91]

---

at 299–305. In Alberta, the powers of a civil enforcement bailiff are set out in s. 13 of the *Civil Enforcement Act, ibid.*

87   *Civil Enforcement Act, ibid.,* s. 9(8).

88   APPSA s. 59; *Seizures Act*, R.S.N.W.T 1986, c. S-6, s. 22.

89   OPPSA s. 62(b).

90   PPSA (BC, M, NB, NWT, Nu, PEI, S) s. 58(2); A s. 59(2); (NL, NS) s. 59(2); Y s. 56.

91   It is unclear whether a secured party may rely upon a contractual power to do so or whether this would be regarded as an impermissible waiver of the debtor's rights.

This is not a factor in Ontario, since the secured party's right to dispose of the collateral on the premises is not limited to cases where a constructive seizure has been effected.

A second reason why constructive seizure may be useful is that a debtor may be found criminally or civilly liable for interfering with the collateral after its seizure. The secured party will be considered to have possession of the collateral following constructive seizure, and any interference with the secured party's possession will be regarded as unlawful. In the absence of this mechanism, the debtor would be liable in this manner only if the debtor signed a bailee's undertaking under which the debtor agreed to hold the goods as bailee of the secured party and to deliver them to the secured party on demand.

The right to effect a constructive seizure cannot be exercised unless the security interest is perfected by registration.[92] The obvious concern is with third parties who might not realize that the goods are under seizure. Although this might be justified in Ontario and Manitoba where it is possible to perfect a security interest by seizure, the provision makes little sense in the other jurisdictions where perfection by seizure or repossession is not permitted.

d) Seizure by Judicial Action

The common law did not provide a general remedy that permitted an owner of goods to recover possession. The owner's claim was limited to an action for damages for trespass or conversion. The common law provided a limited means by which an owner could regain possession though the ancient writ of replevin. This was later replaced by a statutory replevin action, often provided for in the rules of court. Under this procedure, the plaintiff files an affidavit asserting a wrongful taking or detention and posts a bond or otherwise gives security. The court issues a replevin order that directs the sheriff to seize the property. The security is conditioned on the plaintiff returning the property to the defendant without delay if so ordered by the court.

The replevin procedure is cumbersome, and a secured party may choose to resort instead to the power conferred on the court by the PPSA to make orders under Part 5.[93] Several courts appear to have used

---

92   PPSA (BC, M, NB, PEI, S) s. 58(2); A s. 58(1); (NL, NS) s. 59(2); O s. 62; Y s. 56.
93   PPSA (BC, M, NB, NWT, Nu, PEI, S) s. 63(2); A s. 64; (NL, NS) s. 64(2); O s. 67(1); Y s. 61.

this power to make orders requiring the debtor to deliver the collateral to the secured party.[94]

2) Property Exempt from Seizure

Provincial judgment enforcement law exempts certain types of property held by debtors from seizure. In the absence of legislation expressly extending the application of these exemptions to seizures by secured parties, the secured party is not subject to them unless it elects to forego its enforcement rights against the collateral and sue only on the debt.[95] Saskatchewan, New Brunswick, Prince Edward Island, Nova Scotia, and Newfoundland have enacted legislation extending the exemptions to secured parties. British Columbia, Alberta, Manitoba, Ontario, and all three territories have not done so, with the result that a secured party is permitted to seize assets that would be exempt from enforcement by judgment creditors.

Two general approaches are used to create exemptions that pertain to secured parties. In Saskatchewan, the provincial exemptions statutes applicable to judgment enforcement proceedings are simply extended to cover security agreements as well.[96] This means that the same exemptions that may be claimed by judgment debtors may also be claimed by debtors who have given security interests in their personal property. In the Atlantic provinces, a set of exemptions applicable to seizure by secured parties is incorporated directly into Part 5 of the PPSA. These exemptions are somewhat different from those that pertain to judgment enforcement creditors.[97] Under both approaches, collateral subject to a purchase money security interest is not exempt. The exemptions also do not apply to goods subject to a deemed security interest in the form of a lease for a term of more than one year or a commercial consignment (which are excluded from Part 5 in any event).

---

94   *Canadian Imperial Bank of Commerce v. Northland Trucks (1978) Ltd.* (1985), 38 Sask. R. 95 (Q.B.); *Costley v. Pioneer Credit Union Ltd.* (1992), 2 P.P.S.A.C. (2d) 212 (Sask. Q.B.).

95   *Re Vanhove* (1994), 20 O.R. (3d) 653 (Ont. Ct. Gen. Div.).

96   *The Exemptions Act*, R.S.S. 1978, c. E-14, s. 3, 1979–80, c. 25, s. 4, 1988–89, c. 52, s. 8; *The Saskatchewan Farm Security Act*, S.S. 1989–90, c. s-17.1, ss. 65–75.

97   PPSA (NB, PEI) s. 58(3); (NL, NS) s. 59(3).

3) Custodial Duties of the Secured Party

The PPSA imposes custodial duties upon a secured party who is in possession of the collateral.[98] These obligations are not restricted to a secured party who takes a possessory security interest, but apply as well to a secured party who has seized the collateral upon default.[99] For the most part, these duties cannot be waived or varied in the security agreement or otherwise. These duties apply as well to a receiver.[100] The broad power given by the court to enforce compliance with the Act and to give directions extends also to matters concerning a secured party's duty to take care of the collateral.[101]

The primary obligation imposed by the PPSA on a secured party in possession of collateral is the duty to use reasonable care in the custody and preservation of the collateral.[102] The Act provides that, unless otherwise agreed, reasonable care in the case of collateral in the form of an instrument, a security, or chattel paper includes taking necessary steps to preserve rights against other persons. A secured party who has taken a possessory security interest in a promissory note payable will therefore be under a duty to give proper notice of dishonour in order not to discharge an endorser.[103] The secured party may use the collateral only if the use is authorized by the security agreement, is needed for the preservation of the collateral, or is authorized by a court order.[104]

The PPSA also provides a set of implied terms that apply when the secured party is in possession of the collateral.[105] These rules may be varied by contract, but since most favour the secured party this is unlikely to occur. These rules are summarized as follows:

- The reasonable expenses incurred by the secured party in the custody and preservation of the collateral including the cost of insur-

---

98 PPSA (A, BC, M, NB, NWT, Nu, O, PEI, S) s. 17; (NL, NS) s. 18; Y s. 16.

99 PPSA (BC, M, NB, NWT, Nu, PEI, S) s. 56(2); A s. 56(1); (NL, NS) s. 57(2); O s. 59(1); Y s. 53(4).

100 PPSA (BC, M, NB, NWT, Nu, PEI, S) s. 17(1). In Ontario, Alberta, and the Yukon the provision is found in the definition of "secured party."

101 PPSA (BC, M, NB, NWT, Nu, PEI, S) s. 63(2); A s. 64; (NL, NS) s. 64(2); O s. 67(1); Y s. 61.

102 PPSA (BC, M, NB, NWT, Nu, PEI, S) s. 17(2); (A, O) s. 17(1); (NL, NS), s. 18(2); Y s. 16(1).

103 *Bills of Exchange Act*, R.S.C. 1985, c. B-4, s. 95.

104 PPSA (BC, M, NB, NWT, Nu, O, PEI, S) s. 17(4); A s. 17(3); (NL, NS), s. 18(4); Y s. 16(4).

105 PPSA (BC, M, NB, NWT, Nu, PEI, S) s. 17(3); (A, O) s. 17(2); (NL, NS), s. 18(3); Y s. 16(2).

ance and the payment of taxes or other charges are chargeable to the debtor.

- The risk of loss from accidents (not caused by the negligence of the secured party) is borne by the debtor to the extent that it is not covered by insurance.
- The secured party obtains the benefit of any increase in the value of the collateral or profits derived from the collateral subject to an obligation to apply any money received in respect of the collateral in reduction of the obligation secured.
- The secured party must keep the collateral identifiable, except that fungible goods may be commingled.

The Ontario and Yukon Acts contain an additional provision, not found in the other Acts, which gives the secured party the right to create a security interest in the collateral upon terms that do not impair the debtor's right to redeem it.[106]

E. REDEMPTION AND REINSTATEMENT

The PPSA gives a debtor the right to redeem the collateral and, in certain cases, the right to reinstate the security agreement.[107] These rights can be exercised at any time before the secured party disposes of the collateral or contracts for its disposal or before a secured party irrevocably elects to retain the collateral in satisfaction of the obligation secured. The right is lost if the goods are sold to a good faith purchaser for value notwithstanding that the secured party fails to comply with the appropriate procedural requirements.[108] The debtor may waive the right to redeem or to reinstate in a post-default written agreement, but a pre-default term in the security agreement waiving the right will not be effective.[109]

---

106 OPPSA s. 17(2)(e); Y s. 17(2)(d).
107 PPSA (BC, M, NWT, Nu, S) s. 62(1); A s. 63(1); (NB, PEI) s. 62(2); (NL, NS) s. 63(2)–(4); O s. 66(1)–(2); Y s. 60(1).
108 PPSA (BC, M, NWT, Nu, S) s. 59(14); A s. 60(12); (NB, PEI) s. 59(15); (NL, NS) s. 60(15); O s. 63(9); Y s. 57(10); PPSA (NWT, Nu, S) s. 61(7); A s. 62(7); (NB, PEI) s. 62(7); (NL, NS) s. 62(8); O s. 65(7); Y s. 59(6).
109 PPSA (BC, M, NB, NWT, Nu, S) s. 56(3), A s. 56(2); (NB, PEI) s. 56(4); (NL, NS) s. 57(4); O s. 59(5); Y s. 53(7). See also *Gujral v. Miller* (1994), 8 P.P.S.A.C. (2d) 96 (B.C.S.C.). This confirms that pre-default waiver of the right to redeem is not permitted.

1) The Right to Redeem

Redemption of the collateral occurs when the debtor tenders the obligation secured by the collateral or otherwise cures the default. This has the effect of extinguishing the security interest in relation to the collateral that has been redeemed. The debtor is not the only person who is given the right to redeem the collateral. The right to redeem may be exercised by any person who is entitled to receive the notice of disposition. A subordinate secured party may therefore decide to redeem the collateral by paying out the senior creditor.

a)   What Must Be Tendered?

Redemption of a mortgage traditionally involved payment of the interest and principal together with any reasonable costs associated with enforcement of the mortgage debt. Does the PPSA adopt the same approach? It is arguable that the concept of redemption under the PPSA may be different from the historical approach. The PPSA provides that a person who is entitled to redeem may do so by tendering fulfilment of all obligations secured by the collateral[110] together with payment of the reasonable enforcement costs incurred by the secured party to that point. The critical issue is whether the term "obligations secured" refers to the entire obligation owing by the debtor or is limited to the value of the collateral. The issue becomes important when the obligation secured by the collateral exceeds its value. If the debtor wishes to redeem, must the debtor tender the entire outstanding obligation? Or is it sufficient that the debtor tender the value of the collateral?

It can be argued that the PPSA has adopted a new approach. A security interest only exists to the extent that there is collateral to secure it. The value of the obligation secured is therefore defined by the value of the collateral at any given time.[111] If the amount owing to the secured party is $1,000, but the value of the collateral is only $500, then the obligation secured by the collateral is limited to $500 with the remaining $500 existing as an unsecured obligation. On this logic, a debtor may redeem collateral by paying its current value to the secured party for this will satisfy the obligation secured by the collateral measured as of that date.

---

110   PPSA (BC, M, NWT, Nu, S) s. 62(1); A s. 63(1); (NB, PEI) s. 62(2); (NL, NS) s. 63(23); O s. 66(1); Y s. 60(1).

111   For an elaboration of this argument, see T. Buckwold, "Post-Bankruptcy Remedies of Secured Parties: As Good as it Gets" (1999) 31 Can. Bus. L.J. 436 at 452–67.

Courts have embraced the proposition that *in terrorum* enforcement of a security interest by a secured party is not a legitimate goal or tactic. The exercise of the enforcement remedies should not be permitted by a secured party where it is designed to make an example of the debtor or to hold the collateral to ransom. A refusal by a secured party to permit redemption arguably falls into this category, since there is no prospect that the secured party can obtain a higher price through sale of the collateral.

The idea of redemption by repayment of the value of the collateral is not foreign to Canadian law. The *Bankruptcy and Insolvency Act* permits a trustee to redeem the collateral for the benefit of the creditors by paying the secured party the value of the collateral.[112] Although pre-PPSA law required that the debtor pay the full amount owing to the secured party in order to redeem the collateral, it can be argued that the underlying rationale for this position no longer holds true under the PPSA.[113]

On the other hand, there are arguments that can be made in favour of the view that the PPSA retains the traditional approach that requires a debtor exercising a redemption right to tender the entire outstanding indebtedness. Abandonment of the traditional approach would give rise to difficult issues of proof of value that one would have expected the drafters to establish a procedure or guidelines to resolve. In addition, in at least one other context, the Act uses the term "obligation secured" to refer to the entire obligation of the debtor without regard to the value of the collateral. The PPSA provides that, under specified circumstances, the creditor may take the collateral in full satisfaction of the obligation secured.[114] If, in this context, the obligation secured meant the value of the collateral, a secured party who retains the collateral in satisfaction of the obligation secured would retain a right to maintain an action against the debtor for the difference between the value of the collateral and the total debt owing by the debtor. But the general assumption is that once the creditor takes the collateral in satisfaction of the obligation, no further action on the debt is permissible because the absence of a sale makes it impossible to determine the extent of the deficiency.

---

112 R.S.C. 1985, c. B-3, s. 128.

113 In the case of a mortgage, the full amount had to be tendered since the exercise of the right of redemption involved a buying back of the legal estate after it had passed to the mortgagee.

114 PPSA (BC, M, NB, NWT, Nu, PEI, S) s. 61; (A, NL, NS); O s. 65; Y s. 59. And see G.1 "Statutory Foreclosure" in this chapter.

b) Application of Equitable Principles

A secured party may attempt to assert the equitable doctrine of con-solidation. This doctrine applies where two mortgages are granted to a person by the same mortgagor. The mortgagee is entitled to consolidate the mortgages against the mortgagor, and can refuse to allow the mort-gagor to redeem one of the mortgages without redeeming the other.[115] The doctrine of consolidation does not apply to redemption under the PPSA. At common law, equitable consolidation does not apply where the mortgagor has a legal or statutory right to redeem.[116] Furthermore, the statutory right of redemption created by the PPSA provides that the debtor may redeem by tendering fulfilment of the obligations secured by the collateral. This wording precludes the secured party from de-manding payment of other obligations that are not secured by the col-lateral that the debtor seeks to redeem.

The equitable remedy of subrogation likely will apply when a per-son other than the debtor redeems the collateral. A lender who makes an unsecured loan that is used to pay out a secured party may be sub-rogated to the secured party's rights. These conditions are satisfied when a right to redeem is exercised by a subordinate secured party or other person with an interest in the collateral. The right of subrogation may be displaced by the intention of the parties, but there appears to be a presumption in favour of the right.[117]

2) Reinstatement

The debtor is given a right to reinstate a security agreement by paying the arrears and curing any default.[118] This right may only be exercised by the debtor.[119] The effect of an acceleration clause is ignored when calculating the arrears that must be tendered in order to exercise this right. Where the event of default is something other than a failure to pay an instalment, the debtor may reinstate the agreement by curing the default. If the security agreement provides that it is an event of default if the debtor permits any writs or liens against the collateral, the right to

---

115 P.V. Baker and P. St. J. Langam, *Snell's Equity* (London: Sweet & Maxwell, 1980) at 399–400.

116 *Credit foncier franco-canadien v. Walker*, [1938] O.W.N. 339 (H.C.J.).

117 See R. Goff and G. Jones, *The Law of Restitution*, 5th ed. (London: Sweet & Max-well, 1998) at 151–53.

118 PPSA (BC, M, NWT, Nu, S) s. 62(1); A s. 63(1); (NB, PEI) s. 62(2); (NL, NS) s. 63(3); O s. 66(2); Y s. 60(1).

119 The definition of debtor does not include a transferee for the purposes of the right of reinstatement. See above note 38.

reinstate can be exercised by discharging the liens or writs. Sometimes it may impossible to cure a default, in which case the right to reinstate does not arise. If the secured party relies upon an insecurity clause, the debtor will not be able to cure the defect unless it can demonstrate that the facts which gave the secured party reasonable grounds to believe that the collateral was in jeopardy no longer exist.[120]

Outside of Ontario, the right of reinstatement may be exercised in respect of all classes of collateral, but in Ontario it is available only if the collateral is consumer goods. Under the Ontario Act, a right of reinstatement may only be exercised once during the term of the security agreement.[121] Under the non-Ontario Acts, a debtor is not permitted to reinstate more than twice in each year.[122] The British Columbia Act adopts the non-Ontario approach in relation to consumer goods, but in relation to other types of collateral the debtor must obtain a court order relieving the debtor of the consequences of default or staying enforcement of any provision in the security agreement providing for acceleration.[123]

F. SALE OF THE COLLATERAL

Once the secured party has seized the collateral, it is faced with a choice between two remedies. The secured party may sell the collateral to a buyer and apply the proceeds of sale against the obligation secured together with any reasonable costs associated with the seizure, storage, repair, and disposition of the collateral.[124] Alternatively, the secured party may propose to retain the collateral in satisfaction of the obligation secured (strict foreclosure). The advantage of a sale over a strict foreclosure is that the secured party may bring an action against the debtor to recover any deficiency if the proceeds of sale are not sufficient to cover the secured obligation. The disadvantage of the sale remedy is that there is a greater risk of litigation based on the allegation that the secured party conducted a negligent or improvident sale.

---

120 *Glenn v. General Motors Acceptance Corp. of Canada* (1992), 2 P.P.S.A.C. (2d) 203 (Ont. Ct. Gen. Div.).
121 OPPSA s. 66(3).
122 PPSA (BC, M, S) s. 62(2); A s. 63(2); (NB, PEI) s. 62(5); (NWT, Nu) s. 62(3); (NL, NS) s. 63(5); Y s. 60(2).
123 BCPPSA s. 62(3).
124 PPSA (BC, M, NB, NWT, Nu, PEI, S) s. 59(2); A s. 60(1); (NL, NS) s. 60(2); O s. 63(1); Y s. 57(1).

The PPSA provides that the remedies set out in Part 5 are cumulative.[125] A secured party will therefore not be regarded as having made an election until there is an irrevocable choice of one remedy over the other. A secured party may attempt to sell the collateral by private sale, but may abandon this plan if no suitable offers are obtained. Here there has been no irrevocable election, and therefore the secured party may exercise its right to retain the collateral in satisfaction of the obligation. In addition, the secured party may exercise the sale remedy against some of the collateral, and thereafter exercise its strict foreclosure remedy against the remaining collateral in satisfaction of the balance of the secured indebtedness.

1) Method of Sale

The PPSA gives the secured party considerable latitude in choosing an appropriate method of sale. The secured party may sell by public sale (usually a sale by auction or closed tender) or by private sale.[126] Some of the Acts provide that the disposition may be by lease or by deferred payment only if the security agreement so provides.[127] The Ontario Act would seem to permit such dispositions even in the absence of an express contractual provision.[128] The secured party may generally purchase the collateral only by way of public sale.[129] The secured party is

---

125 PPSA (BC, PEI, NB, S) s. 55(3); (A, M, NWT, Nu, PEI) s. 55(2); (NL, NS) s. 56(3); O s. 58; Y s. 53(3).

126 PPSA, s. 59(3) (BC, M, NWT, Nu, S); A s. 60(2); (NB, PEI) s. 59(5); (NL, NS) s. 60(5); O s. 63(2); Y s. 57(2).

127 PPSA (BC, M, NWT, Nu, S) s. 59(4); A s. 60(2); (NB, PEI) s. 60(6); (NL, NS) s. 60(6); (O, Y) no equivalent provision.

128 Although the OPPSA does not specifically authorize a sale on deferred payment terms, the fact that OPPSA s. 63(2) permits a disposition by way of a lease suggests that deferred payment terms are permissible.

129 PPSA (BC, M, NWT, Nu, S) s. 59(13); A s. 60(11); (NB, PEI) s. 59(14); (NL, NS) s. 60(14); O s. 63(2); Y s. 57(9). The OPPSA provides that a secured party is permitted to purchase the goods by way of private sale if authorized by court order. The other Acts provide that the sale must be for a price that bears a reasonable relationship to the market value of the collateral. A private sale to a secured party should be permitted if the debtor agrees to it in a post-default agreement. In this case, the sale is not a forced sale by the secured party, but a voluntary sale by the debtor, and there is nothing in the PPSA that prevents the debtor from entering into such a transaction. However, if the debtor on a voluntary sale does not obtain the prior consent of subordinate secured creditors and others with a subordinate interest in the collateral, their interests will not be cut off by the sale since the PPSA extinguishes subordinate interests only on a forced sale or a taking in satisfaction of the secured obligation.

permitted to delay disposition for such periods of time as may be commercially reasonable.[130] In Ontario and Manitoba, this must be read subject to the obligation that is imposed on a secured party to dispose of consumer goods if at least 60 percent of the indebtedness has been paid. In such a case, the secured party is given ninety days after seizing the collateral to dispose of it.[131] This requirement can be waived by the debtor in a post-default agreement.

The secured party is not required to sell all the collateral in one lot, but may sell different portions by different means.[132] In appropriate cases, a secured party may decide to sell part of the collateral by public sale and part by private sale. If more than one public sale is conducted, the secured party must send out notices of disposition in respect of each sale.[133]

The PPSA provides that a secured party may dispose of the collateral in its existing condition or may sell it after it is repaired.[134] If it is repaired, the reasonable costs of repair may be added to the obligation secured. Although this provision may seem to suggest that the secured party is under no obligation to repair the goods, the case law in the United States suggests that it will be read subject to the overarching obligation on the secured party to act in a commercially reasonable manner. If a significantly higher return would be obtained by making minor repairs or improvements, then the secured party should take the appropriate steps to prepare the collateral for sale.[135]

---

130 PPSA (BC, M, NWT, Nu, S) s. 59(5); A s. 60(3); (NB, PEI) s. 59(7); (NL, NS) s. 60(7); O s. 63(3); Y s. 57(3). Although the non-Ontario Acts do not specifically provide that the delay must be commercially reasonable, the obligation to act in a commercially reasonable manner pervades all of Part 5.

131 OPPSA s. 65(1); MPPSA s. 61(1).

132 PPSA (BC, M, NWT, Nu, S) s. 59(3); A s. 60(2); (NB, PEI) s. 59(5); (NL, NS) s. 60(5); O s. 63(2); Y s. 57(2).

133 It is probably unnecessary to give multiple notices where the collateral is to be sold by private sale since the notice need only inform the debtor that on the day after which any private disposition of the collateral is to be made.

134 PPSA (BC, M, NB, NWT, Nu, PEI, S) s. 59(2); A s. 60(1); (NL, NS) s. 60(2); O s. 63(1); Y s. 57(1).

135 See, for example, *Franklin State Bank v. Parker*, 346 A.2d 632 (N.J. Dist. Ct. 1975); *Liberty National Bank & Trust Company of Oklahoma City v. Acme Tool Division of the Rucker Company*, 540 F.2d 1375 (C.A. Okl. 1976). Some commentators argue that these cases involve an incorrect reading of the statute and that the secured party should be under no obligation at all to repair. See White and Summers, *Uniform Commercial Code*, vol. 4, (St. Paul: West Publishing, 1995) at 451–52.

2) Notice of Disposition

The secured party must give a written notice to the debtor and to certain other interested parties before disposing of the collateral. The purpose of the notice is to give the recipient an opportunity to redeem the collateral or to reinstate the security agreement. It also permits the recipient to monitor the conduct of the sale to ensure that it is conducted in a commercially reasonable manner or to attempt to find a purchaser for the collateral. The Ontario PPSA provides a fifteen-day notice period,[136] whereas the other Acts provide a twenty-day notice period.[137] The notice must provide a brief description of the collateral, state the amount required to satisfy the obligation secured, and indicate the amount of the expenses of disposition or a reasonable estimate of such expenses.[138] It must also contain a statement that the recipient is entitled to redeem the collateral and a statement that failure to do so means that the debtor may be liable for any deficiency. Under the Ontario Act, the notice must also contain a statement that upon receipt of payment, the payor is entitled to any rebates or allowances to which the debtor is entitled by law.[139] Under the non-Ontario Acts, the notice must also inform the debtor of the right to reinstate the security agreement. The notice also gives information as to the date and place of a public sale or the date after which any private disposition of the collateral is to be made. The non-Ontario Acts provide a different form of notice in respect of a disposition by a receiver.[140] This notice need only contain a description of the collateral, a statement that unless it is redeemed it will be disposed of, and information pertaining to the method of sale.

The notice of disposition must be given to the debtor. Where the owner of the collateral and the obligor are not the same person, both must be notified.[141] There is some debate on whether a guarantor must also be notified,[142] and given this uncertainty the safest course is to

---

136 OPPSA s. 63(4)
137 PPSA (BC, M, NWT, Nu, S) s. 59(6); A s. 60(4); (NB, PEI) s. 59(8); (NL, NS) s. 60(8); Y s. 57(4).
138 PPSA (BC, M, NWT, Nu, S) s. 59(7); A s. 60(5); (NB, PEI) s. 59(9); (NL, NS) s. 60(9); O s. 63(5); Y s. 57(5).
139 OPPSA s. 63(5).
140 PPSA (BC, M, NWT, Nu, S) s. 59(10)–(11); A s. 60(8)–(9); (NB, PEI) s. 60(11); (NL, NS) s. 60(12); Y s. 57(6).
141 This is made clear by the definition of debtor. As well, OPPSA s. 63(4)(b) makes it clear that both must be notified.
142 See the discussion in chapter 1, D.2 "Debtor" on the question whether a guarantor falls within the definition of a debtor.

give the guarantor notice. The notice must also be given to any other person who is known by the secured party to be an owner of the collateral.[143] This ensures that if the debtor has transferred the collateral to a third party, the transferee must be given the notice if the secured party knows of the transfer. Although the wording might also be wide enough to encompass the interest of a co-owner who was not a party to the security agreement, it may be argued that it should not be interpreted so expansively. The interest of the co-owner is not affected by a disposition of the collateral. The sale merely transfers the debtor's co-ownership interest in the collateral, and the buyer obtains this interest subject to the interest of the other co-owner. On the other hand, a co-owner may care very much, depending upon the nature and potential uses of the property and may therefore wish to purchase the debtor's interest on the forced sale. It therefore may make sense to require notice to be given to a co-owner as well.

The PPSA provides that certain other third parties must be given the notice. Secured parties who have a subordinate security interest in the collateral that is registered or perfected by possession prior to the date that the notice of disposition is given to the debtor are entitled to the notice.

Some provinces provide for registration of judgment enforcement writs or notices of judgment in the personal property registry.[144] In these provinces, the notice must be given to the holder of the subordinate writs or judgments.[145] The notice must also be given to other parties who have an interest in the collateral who have delivered a written notice to the secured party before the notice of disposition is given to the debtor.[146]

The PPSA also sets out a list of occasions when the notice of disposition is not required.[147] The notice does not need to be given if the collateral is perishable, or if the secured party believes that the collateral will decline substantially in value. Nor is it needed if the collateral

---

143 PPSA (BC, M, NWT, Nu, S) s. 59(6); A s. 60(4); (NB, PEI) s. 59(8); (NL, NS) s. 60(8); O s. 63(4); Y s. 57(4).

144 See chapter 10, A.3 "The Judgment Creditor as Chargeholder."

145 SPPSA s. 59(6); APPSA s. 60(4) refers to creditors and secured parties who have registered in the personal property registry. In Atlantic Canada, PPSA (NB, PEI) s. 59(8); (NL, NS) s. 60(8) makes specific reference to subordinate judgment enforcement creditors who have registered in the personal property registry.

146 PPSA (BC, M, NWT, Nu, S) s. 59(6); A s. 60(4); (NB, PEI) s. 59(8); (NL, NS) s. 60(8); O s. 63(4); Y s. 57(4).

147 PPSA (BC, M, NWT, Nu, S) s. 59(17); A s. 60(14); (NB, PEI) s. 59(18); (NL, NS) s. 60(18); O s. 63(7); S s. 59(16); Y s. 57(12).

is customarily sold on an organized market. Where a receivership is involved, the notice need not be given in respect of sales conducted in the ordinary course of the debtor's business.[148] A debtor may waive the entitlement to notice in a post-default agreement, but a waiver provision in the security agreement will not be effective.[149] A court may also make an *ex parte* order that notice need not be given.

3) The Standard of Commercial Reasonableness

For the most part, the PPSA does not burden the secured party with rules that dictate how and when the sale must be conducted. Instead, the secured party may choose the method and timing of the sale. The secured party generally has a strong incentive to obtain the highest possible price, since there may be little real prospect of recovering much on an action for the deficiency.[150] There are, however, two iron-clad rules that must be respected by the secured party. The first is that a notice of disposition must be sent prior to the sale, and the second is that the secured party is not permitted to purchase the goods by way of a private sale. But other than these, the PPSA gives the secured party considerable flexibility in choosing the time, place, and terms of the sale of the collateral.

The key element that must constantly be borne in mind by the secured party is that every aspect of the sale must be carried out in a commercially reasonable manner.[151] This obligation has been described as a duty to use every effort to sell the collateral "under every possible advantage of time, place, and publicity,"[152] and to use "best efforts to see that the highest possible price is obtained for the collateral."[153]

Two American commentators have observed:[154]

> The cases sometimes distinguish between two tests for commercial reasonableness: one is optimization of the price; the other is follow-

---

148 PPSA (M, NB, NWT, Nu, PEI) s. 64(9); (A, NL, NS) s. 65(9); BC s. 68(1); O s. 63(7); S s. 64(10); Y s. 54(4).
149 See above note 24.
150 This does not hold true where the value of the collateral exceeds the obligation secured.
151 PPSA (M, NWT, Nu, S) s. 65(3); A s. 66(1); BC s. 68(2); (NB, PEI) s. 65(2); (NL, NS) s. 66(2); O s. 63(2); Y s. 62(1).
152 Gilmore, above note 44 at 1233.
153 *Ibid.* at 1234.
154 P. Coogan and J. McDonnell, "The Secured Party and Default Proceedings" in *Bender's Uniform Commercial Code Service, Secured Transactions Under the U.C.C.*, looseleaf (New York: Matthew Bender, 1963) vol. 1A, chapter 8 at 8-77–8-78.

ing correct procedures. Not surprisingly, the courts do not rule out either test entirely. However, one can generally detect more emphasis on the price obtained in consumer sales and in those involving equipment financed by small businesses. But even in these areas a gross disparity between price and value may be required to invalidate a disposition. On the other hand, more concern for the procedures employed is expressed in commercial situations.

A low price alone will not establish that the secured party has failed to meet the standard of commercial reasonableness in carrying out the sale. But it will cause the courts to look closely at the facts of the case to determine if appropriate measures were taken by the secured party in disposing of the collateral. The fact of a low price will be of little relevance where it has been produced by a downturn in the economy since it represents current market values.[155]

Another relevant consideration is whether the sale was to a related party. Although the PPSA prohibits a secured party from purchasing the collateral at a private sale, the Act does not attempt to regulate sales to related parties. The danger is that the secured party may seek to confer a benefit on the related party by selling the collateral at a price that is less than the fair value of the collateral.

The standard of commercial reasonableness imposes a heavier burden on the secured party than that which was historically imposed upon a mortgagee. Earlier authority suggested that it was enough that the secured party act in good faith and did not conduct the sale in a recklessly improvident manner.[156] However, this "pure heart, empty head" standard has since been replaced with the modern requirement that the secured party make reasonable efforts to obtain a proper price.[157] This is also the approach that is to be adopted under the PPSA. The non-Ontario Acts provide that the secured party must act in good faith and in a commercially reasonable manner.[158] This clearly indicates that commercial reasonableness involves something more than good faith. Ontario case law has also confirmed that the higher standard of commercial reasonableness is to be applied.[159]

---

155 *Doran v. Hare* (1994), 6 P.P.S.A.C. (2d) 295 (Ont. Ct. Gen. Div.).

156 *Kennedy v. De Trafford*, [1897] A.C. 180 (H.L.); *J. & W. Investments Ltd. v. Black* (1963), 41 W.W.R. 577 (B.C.C.A.); *British Columbia Land & Investment Agency v. Ishitaka* (1911), 45 S.C.R. 302.

157 *Cuckmere Brick Co. Ltd. v. Mutual Finance Ltd.*, [1971] Ch. 949 (C.A.).

158 PPSA (M, NWT, Nu, S) s. 65(3); A s. 66(1); BC s. 68(2); (NB, PEI) s. 65(2); (NL, NS) s. 66(2); Y s. 62(1).

159 *Copp v. Medi-Dent Service* (1991), 3 O.R. (3d) 570 (Ont. Ct. Gen. Div.).

All aspects of the sale are governed by the standard of commercial reasonableness. The manner of advertising, the method of sale, and the timeliness of the sale may all come under scrutiny. The question in each case is whether the secured party took all reasonable steps to obtain the best price for it. The PPSA does not set out statutory requirements in relation to the advertising of the sale. It is left to the secured party to decide how best to publicize the sale. With respect to highly specialized equipment, the secured party may be expected to advertise in specialized trade publications.[160] Depending upon the nature of the collateral, the secured party may be required to provide prospective buyers with the opportunity to inspect the goods.[161]

The secured party may also fall short of meeting the standard of commercial reasonableness in choosing the method of sale. A choice of a public sale rather than a private sale may be held to be commercially unreasonable where it is clear that a private sale will fetch a substantially higher price.[162] The decision to sell the collateral as a single parcel may also be commercially unreasonable if it is later shown that a much higher price could have been obtained by selling it by individual item or in smaller lots.

The timing of the sale may also come into question. A delay in selling the goods may be commercially unreasonable, particularly if the collateral is depreciable. On the other hand, the secured party may be accused of selling the collateral too quickly and thereby not obtaining an adequate price. Even though a higher price might be obtained, the secured party is not generally required to seek it out "with protracted waiting for just the right buyer and price."[163]

4) Assessment of the Price: Wholesale or Retail?

In assessing whether the secured party has obtained the best possible price in selling the collateral, should the court have regard to the wholesale or the retail value of the collateral? This question has been frequently litigated in the United States[164] and typically arises in con-

---

160 See, for example, *Contrail Leasing Partners, Ltd. v. Consolidated Airways, Inc.,* 742 F.2d 1095 (C.A. Ind. 1984).

161 *Connex Press, Inc. v. International Airmotive, Inc.* 436 F. Supp. 51 (D.C.D.C. 1977).

162 *U.S. v. Willis,* 593 F.2d 247 (C.A. Ohio 1979).

163 *Canstar Trucking Ltd. v. Bank of Nova Scotia* (1984), 48 Sask. R. 136 at 138 (Q.B.)

164 See, for example, *Piper Acceptance Corp. v. Yarborough,* 702 F.2d 733 (C.A. Ark. 1983); *Cessna Finance Corp. v. Bielenberg Masonary Contracting Inc.,* 35 U.C.C. Rep. Serv. 315 (D. Kan. 1982); *Spillers v. First National Bank of Arenzville,* 441 N.E.2d 872 (Ill. App. 4 Dist. 1982); *Transport Equipment Co. v. Guaranty State*

nection with private sales. In theory, there should be no controversy over this question. If the secured party sells by way of retail sale, the secured party should be entitled to charge as a cost of the sale an amount that compensates the secured party for the time and effort expended in carrying out the sale. Less time and expense should be needed if the secured party sells the collateral in a wholesale transaction, and the costs should be correspondingly less. The difference between the amount recovered in a retail sale and the amount recovered in a wholesale sale should correspond to the extra costs in selling the collateral in the retail market.[165]

Some U.S. courts have held that a retail sale is required if the collateral is financed at the retail level, but only a wholesale disposition is needed if the goods were acquired by the debtor in a wholesale transaction.[166] However, the prevailing view is that expressed in *Spillers v. First National Bank of Arenzville*:[167]

> We believe that the inquiry should not be whether the collateral was financed at retail or wholesale, but rather the inquiry is what price should the secured creditor have obtained under all of the circumstances in view of the available markets open to him. In *Hemken*, the evidence indicated that a wholesale market was a commercially reasonable disposition in view of the small disparity between the retail and wholesale market values which was offset by the expenses required to sell retail. In *Cities Services* and *Vic Hansen & Sons, Inc.*, the secured party was required to sell at retail in view of the retail markets available to the secured creditor. In *Transport Equipment Co.*, in view of the fact that a sale on the retail market was not possible because of the assembly necessary to sell on that market, the wholesale measure was appropriate.

5) Recourse and Repurchase Agreements

In many cases, the original secured party on chattel paper will transfer its rights to a finance company or bank. If this transfer is made with

Bank, 518 F.2d 377 (10th Cir. 1975); *Cities Service Oil Co. v. Ferris*, 9 U.C.C. Rep. Serv. 899 (Mich. Dist.1971); *Hemken v. First National Bank of Litchfield*, 394 N.E.2d 868 (Ill. App. 4 Dist. 1979); *California Airmotive Corp. v. Jones*, 415 F.2d 554 (C.A. Ohio 1969); *Vic Hansen & Sons, Inc. v. Crowley*, 203 N.W.2d 728 (Wis 1973).

165 *Hemken v. First National Bank of Litchfield*, ibid.
166 *California Airmotive Corp. v. Jones*, above note 164.
167 Above note 164 at 877–78.

recourse, the realization process will likely involve two steps. First, the finance company will seize the collateral from the debtor and sell it to the dealer pursuant to the recourse or repurchase agreement for the unpaid balance of the debt owing to the finance company. Second, the dealer will sell the collateral using its retail facilities at a substantially higher value. Under the PPSA, a person who is liable to a secured party under a recourse or repurchase agreement and who receives a transfer of the collateral is subrogated to the rights of the secured party and the transfer of collateral is not considered to be a disposition of the collateral.[168] For the purposes of Part 5, the first sale is not considered to be an enforcement sale. Instead, it is the second sale that triggers the notice of disposition requirement and which is used to determine the extent of any surplus or deficiency.

The situation is different if the dealer transferred the chattel paper to the finance company without recourse. The finance company obtains the rights and obligations of a secured party. If the finance company decides to sell the seized goods to the dealer, this sale is considered to be the enforcement sale, and a notice of disposition must be sent to the debtor before it is concluded.

A further complication may arise where a lender finances the acquisition of inventory by a dealer from a manufacturer. The manufacturer of the inventory may enter into a repurchase agreement under which it undertakes to buy the collateral from the lender in the event that the dealer defaults.[169] The sale price is set at the wholesale price of the goods together with the costs of repossession. In this case, the sale to the manufacturer should be considered to be an enforcement sale. The PPSA repurchase agreement provision should only apply where it is the secured party's interest and not simply the collateral that is being purchased.[170] Therefore, the notice of disposition should be given to the debtor before the sale is concluded, and it is this sale and not the resale by manufacturer that should be tested against the standard of commercial reasonableness.

168 PPSA (NB, NWT, Nu, PEI) s. 59(17); A s. 60(14); (BC, M) s. 59(16); (NL, NS) s. 60(17); O s. 63(11); S s. 59(15); Y s. 57(11).
169 See D. Rapson, "Repurchase (of Collateral) Agreements and the Larger Issue of Deficiency Actions: What Does Section 9-504(3) Mean?" (1993) 29 Idaho L. Rev. 649.
170 The Canadian provisions are based upon § 9-504(5) of the 1972 version of the *Uniform Commercial Code*. § 9-618 of current Article 9 reworks this provision to make it clear that it only applies where the transferee does not merely obtain a transfer of the collateral, but also assumes the position of the secured party.

6) The Purchaser's Title

A buyer who purchases the collateral from a secured party at an enforcement sale takes free of the interest of the debtor and of subordinate interests if the buyer was in good faith and gave value.[171] Where the sale is conducted by a junior secured party, the buyer does not take free of a security interest held by the senior secured party unless the senior secured party consents to the sale. In the same vein, the sale will not cut off the claim of an owner or other person with a superior title than that possessed by the debtor. Unless excluded by contract, the buyer will have an action against the secured party for breach of the implied condition of the right to sell or the warranty of freedom from encumbrances established by sale of goods legislation or other law.

A failure by the secured party to comply with the requirements of Part 5 will not invalidate the enforcement sale. A good faith buyer takes free of the debtor's interest and the interests of subordinate parties.[172] The non-Ontario Acts contain an additional requirement that the buyer must have taken possession of the collateral in order to take advantage of the provision. Under the Ontario Act, two different standards are provided depending upon the type of sale.[173] In the case of a public sale, the buyer takes free if the buyer does not know of any defect in the sale and does not act in collusion with the secured party. In any other type of sale, the buyer takes free if the buyer acts in good faith.

7) Surplus and Deficiency

If the proceeds of sale of the collateral at the enforcement sale are sufficient to satisfy the claim of the enforcing creditor, the excess funds are called a surplus. If the sale proceeds are not enough, the shortfall is referred to as a deficiency. In the words of one commentator, "[t]he surplus to be returned to the debtor after sale is the glittering mirage; the deficiency judgment is the grim reality."[174] In those cases where a surplus does arise, often the real controversy concerns the entitlement of subordinate secured parties and third parties holding other interests in the collateral. The PPSA gives directions to an enforcing secured party on the payment of a surplus. It also confirms that a secured party

---

171 PPSA (BC, M, NWT, Nu, S) s. 59(14); A s. 60(12); (NB, PEI) s. 59(15); (NL, NS) s. 60(15); O s. 63(9); Y s. 57(10).

172 PPSA (BC, M, NWT, Nu, S) s. 59(14); A s. 60(12); (NB, PEI) s. 59(15); (NL, NS) s. 60(15); O s. 63(10); Y s. 57(10).

173 OPPSA s. 63(10)(a).

174 Gilmore, above note 44 at 1188.

will be entitled to sue for a deficiency unless the security agreement or some other statute deprives the secured party of this right.[175] Although there was originally considerable uncertainty in Ontario on whether a deficiency clause in the security agreement is needed in order to sue for a deficiency,[176] the Act has since been amended to make it clear that the secured party has a statutory right to sue for a deficiency.

a) Disposition of a Surplus

After receiving the proceeds of an enforcement sale, the secured party is permitted to deduct any reasonable expenses of seizing or dispos-ing of the collateral including any reasonable costs of repair as well as the obligation secured by the collateral.[177] If a surplus remains, it must be paid according to scheme of distribution set out in the PPSA.[178] It is crucial to recognize that this scheme of distribution is a proced-ural rule and not a priority rule. It merely directs the secured party as to its distribution obligation; it does not alter the substantive prior-ity rights among competing claimants. The reason for its inclusion is that a secured party who holds a surplus often is not in a position to determine who among a number of competing claimants has the next highest ranking claim. The distribution rule permits the secured party to pay the surplus according to the scheme of distribution. The recipi-ent of this fund must then fight it out with other competing claimants. A secured party may pay the money into court instead of paying it ac-cording to the scheme of distribution where there is a question as to entitlement to the surplus.[179]

The surplus must first be accounted and then paid over to any per-son who has a subordinate security interest in the collateral who has

---

175 PPSA (BC, M, NWT, Nu, S) s. 60(5); A s. 61(4); (NB, PEI) s. 60(6); (NL, NS) s. 61(6); O s. 64(3); Y s. 58(4). The former Ontario PPSA did not contain a provi-sion giving a secured party a right to sue for a deficiency.
176 The Ontario Court of Appeal in *Royal Bank of Canada v. J. Segreto Construction Ltd.* (1988), 47 D.L.R. (4th) 761 held that a secured party could not sue for a deficiency unless a clause giving this right was included in the security agree-ment. See also *Bank of Montreal v. Featherstone* (1989), 58 D.L.R. (4th) 567 (Ont. C.A.). The current OPPSA gives the secured party a statutory right to recover a deficiency, and therefore these cases are no longer applicable.
177 PPSA (BC, M, NB, NWT, Nu, PEI, S) s. 59(2); A s. 60(1); (NL, NS) s. 60(2); O s. 63(1); Y s. 57(2).
178 PPSA, (BC, M, NB, NWT, Nu, PEI, S) s. 60(2); A s. 61(1); (NL, NS) s. 61(2); O s. 64(1); Y s. 58(2).
179 PPSA (BC, M, NWT, Nu, S) s. 60(4); A s. 61(2); (NB, PEI) s. 60(5); (NL, NS) s. 61(5); O s. 64(4). There is no comparable provision in the Yukon.

registered or perfected the security interest by possession.[180] The expectation is that a secured party will conduct a search of the registry and pay the surplus to any subordinate secured party that is disclosed by the search. The obligation to search the registry and to pay the surplus to a registered interest-holder only applies if that party is a subordinate security interest. Subject to the qualification noted below for registered judgments in the Atlantic provinces, it does not apply to other parties who may have registered in the personal property registry. In some jurisdictions, judgments and writs can be registered. Certain types of non-consensual security interests may also be registered in the personal property registry. Notwithstanding this registration, these parties must give written notice to the secured party in order to be entitled to receive payment of the surplus. The PPSAs of the Atlantic provinces provide a different scheme of distribution in relation to registered judgments. The judgment creditor is not required to give written notice to the secured party, since the registry search will provide the secured party with the requisite information.[181]

After satisfying the claims of subordinate secured parties, the remainder of the surplus is to be paid next to any other person with an interest in the collateral who has given a written notice to the secured party. If there is anything left over, it is to be paid to the debtor. The Acts, other than the Ontario and the Yukon Acts, impose an additional duty upon the secured party to give a written accounting to the persons mentioned in the scheme of distribution.[182] The accounting must indicate the amount received from the disposition of the collateral, the manner of disposition, the expenses, and the amount and manner of distribution of any surplus.

b) Limitations on Deficiency Actions

Under the common law, a conditional seller was permitted to sue for a deficiency only if the agreement provided for this right.[183] By way of contrast, the right to a deficiency under a mortgage or charge arose by implication from the debtor's covenant to pay. The PPSA, which adopts a unitary concept of a security interest, no longer draws such distinctions. Regardless of the form of the transaction, the Act gives the se-

---

180 PPSA (BC, M, NB, NWT, Nu, PEI, S) s. 60(2); A s. 61(1); (NL, NS) s. 61(2);
     O s. 64(1); Y s. 58(2).
181 PPSA (NB, PEI) s. 60(2); (NL, NS) s. 61(2).
182 PPSA (BC, M, NB, NWT, Nu, S) s. 60(3); A s. 61(3); (NB, PEI) s. 60(4); (NL, NS)
     s. 61(4).
183 *Sawyer v. Pringle* (1891), 18 O.A.R. 218 (C.A.).

cured party a statutory right to sue for a deficiency.[184] This may be excluded by a term in the contract or by legislation which deprives the secured party of this right.

The Western provinces and the territories have enacted various forms of "anti-deficiency legislation." In all of these jurisdictions except Saskatchewan, a "seize-or-sue" system is prescribed.[185] The secured party must elect either to seize the goods pursuant to its security agreement or to bring action as an unsecured creditor (in which case the security interest is extinguished). In Saskatchewan, the secured party is not given the option of recovering the debt as an unsecured creditor. The secured party's only remedy is enforcement against the collateral with no right to claim a deficiency.[186]

The anti-deficiency statutes are generally restricted to consumer goods. The legislation in Saskatchewan is not so limited, but a corporate debtor (other than a farmer) is permitted to contract out of its application. In most jurisdictions, the anti-deficiency legislation covers only security interests that are granted to sellers. The rationale for this limitation is that sellers are better able to structure the repayment schedule to ensure that the instalment payments are sufficient to cover the expected depreciation of the goods. However, in British Columbia the seize-or-sue regime also applies to security interests that have been granted to a lender.[187] Most of these statutes provide that the anti-deficiency provisions do not apply if the debtor has deliberately destroyed the goods or is guilty of some other form of misconduct.

G. RETENTION OF THE COLLATERAL IN SATISFACTION OF THE OBLIGATION

The unifying influence of Part 5 is superbly illustrated in its treatment of the foreclosure remedy. At common law, the ability to retain the collateral in satisfaction of the obligation secured depended upon what type of security device was used. Foreclosure is the classic remedy of the mortgagee, and therefore it was available in its pure form in the case of a chattel mortgage. As with the case of real property, a judicial

---

184 PPSA (BC, M, NB, NWT, Nu, S) s. 60(5); A s. 61(4); (NB, PEI) s. 60(6); (NL, NS) s. 61(6); O s. 64(3); Y s. 58(4).

185 *The Consumer Protection Act*, C.C.S.M. 1987, c. C200, ss. 53–54.

186 *The Limitation of Civil Rights Act*, R.S.S. 1978, c. L-16, s. 18; *The Saskatchewan Farm Security Act*, S.S. 1988-89, c. S-17.1, s. 46.

187 BCPPSA s. 67.

order was needed to foreclose the debtor's equity of redemption. If the secured transaction took the form of a pledge or equitable charge, foreclosure was not available.[188] And if the transaction took the form of a conditional sales agreement, the conditional seller could retain the collateral in satisfaction of the obligation by terminating the contract for default which could be done without the intervention of a court (although the seller's right was somewhat curtailed by the pre-PPSA conditional sales acts and by judicial intervention). The PPSA provides a foreclosure remedy that applies regardless of the form of transaction. Unless an objection is raised, the secured party is permitted to exercise its foreclosure remedy without any need for judicial intervention.

1) Statutory Foreclosure

The PPSA provides a statutory remedy that permits a secured party to retain the collateral in satisfaction of the obligation secured. The remedy is instituted by the secured party giving a notice to the debtor and to other interested third parties. The recipients of this notice are given an opportunity to object to the foreclosure. The usual reason for an objection is the expectation that a properly conducted sale of the collateral would produce a surplus to which the debtor or other subordinate interests would become entitled. If the recipient of the notice objects to the seizure, the secured party must either dispose of the collateral by way of sale, or obtain a court order invalidating the objection.[189] If an objection is made by a person other than the debtor, the secured party may request that the person furnish proof of that interest. If the person does not respond within ten days, the objection may be ignored.[190]

The notice of intention to foreclose must be served on the debtor. There is currently controversy over whether the notice must also be served on a guarantor or indemnitor. Cases from Ontario suggest that the notice need not be served on such parties, but the wording of the

---

188 The reason for this difference in treatment had to do with the form of the transaction. A mortgage was in the form of an absolute sale, and equity intervened in order to preserve the mortgagor's equity of redemption. A pledge and a charge did not involve conveyance of title, and sale was the appropriate method to vindicate the secured party's interest.

189 See *101056998 Saskatchewan Ltd. v. Kipp & Zonen Inc.*, [2004] S.J. 763 (Q.B.) for a discussion of the evidential burden on the secured party and on the opposing party on an application by the secured party for a declaration that the objection is ineffective.

190 PPSA (BC, M, NB, PEI) s. 61(6); A s. 62(5); (NL, NS) s. 62(6); (NWT, Nu, S) s. 61(5); O s. 65(4); Y s. 59(4).

non-Ontario Acts strongly suggests that the term was intended to cover such parties.[191] The same general classes of persons who are entitled to receive a notice of disposition are also given the right to receive a notice of intention to foreclose. The notice period within which the notice of objection may be given is thirty days under the Ontario Act and fifteen days in all other jurisdictions.

2) The Legal Consequences of Foreclosure

If there is no effective objection, the secured party is deemed to have irrevocably elected to accept the collateral in satisfaction of the obligation secured. Upon this event, the obligation secured is extinguished. The exercise of this remedy does not only foreclose the debtor's interest in the collateral. It also extinguishes any claim of subordinate secured parties and other subordinate interests who have been given the notice.[192]

But what is the status of subordinate interest-holders who did not receive the notice? This will include two potential groups of persons. It will cover third parties who were entitled to receive the notice but who were not given it because of some neglect or oversight on the part of the secured party (Class A). It will also include third persons who were not entitled to receive the notice (Class B). For example, a person who has an interest in the collateral other than a security interest (or a registered judgment in the case of the Atlantic provinces' Acts) has a right to be notified only if a written notice of the interest was given to the secured party. In neither case will the foreclosure extinguish that person's interest. The foreclosure operates to extinguish a third party's interest only if that third party has been given a notice of intention to foreclose.

As a consequence, Class A claimants will be entitled to redeem the collateral from the secured party notwithstanding that the notice period has expired. Class A claimants also have the right to object to the foreclosure and demand that the collateral be disposed of by sale until such time as they are properly notified and their interests foreclosed.[193] The position of Class B claimants is more complicated. Class B claimants are not given a statutory right to redeem the collateral, since this right is only conferred on claimants who are entitled to re-

---

191 See above note 24.
192 PPSA (BC, M, NB, PEI) s. 61(8); A s. 62(7); (NL, NS) s. 62(8); (NWT, Nu, S) s. 61(7); O s. 65(7); Y s. 59(6).
193 *Tureck v. Hanston Investments Ltd.* (1985), 30 D.L.R. (4th) 690 (Ont. H.C.J.).

ceive the notice. Class B claimants will therefore have a right to redeem only if they are able to obtain a court order giving the party a right of redemption.[194] Class B claimants do not have the right to object to the foreclosure, since that right is only given to parties that are entitled to the notice.

Non-compliance with the notice requirements will generally give the debtor or third party the right to redeem the collateral and the continuing right to object to the foreclosure and demand that the collateral be sold. However, these rights are lost if the secured party sells and delivers the collateral to a good faith purchaser.[195]

3) Constructive Foreclosure

Sometimes a secured party will seize the collateral, but will not immediately sell it. During this period, the secured party may also use the collateral. There is a line of cases in the United States that treats the secured party as having undertaken a "constructive" or "involuntary" foreclosure through this course of action.[196] A competing line of cases holds that mere delay or use of the collateral by the secured party is not enough, and that the secured party must in some manner manifest an intention to retain the collateral in satisfaction of the obligation secured.[197]

In Canada, the issue was considered in *Angelkovski v. Trans-Canada Foods Ltd.*[198] The secured party repossessed a restaurant and, following a failed attempt to sell it, the secured party operated it as a going concern for more than half a year. The court held that the secured party's right to sue on the debt is not lost until the statutory procedure for foreclosure has been completed. As the secured party had not given notice of its intention to foreclose, the right to sue for a deficiency was not extinguished. The *Angelkovski* case demonstrates a rejection of the

---

194 PPSA (BC, M, NB, NWT, Nu, PEI, S) s. 63(2); A s. 64; (NL, NS) s. 64(2); O s. 67(1); Y s. 61. A court may be reluctant to make such an order where the third party knew that the secured party had seized the collateral, but failed to notify the secured party of its interest. Had the third party done so, the third party would have been entitled to notice and the problem would not have arisen. The power is more likely to be exercised if the third party did not know of the secured party's enforcement of its security interest.

195 PPSA (NWT, Nu, S) s. 61(7); A s. 62(7); (NB, PEI) s. 62(7); (NL, NS) s. 62(8); O s. 65(7); Y s. 59(6). The wording of these provisions is wide enough to cut off claims of Class B claimants as well.

196 See, for example, *National Equipment Rental, Ltd. v. Priority Electronics Corp.*, 435 F. Supp. 236 (DCNY 1977); *Millican v. Turner*, 503 So.2d 289 (Miss. 1987).

197 See, for example, *Nelson v. Armstrong*, 582 P.2d 1100 (Idaho 1978).

198 [1986], 3 W.W.R. 723 (Man. Q.B.) [*Angelkovski*].

notion of "constructive" or "involuntary" foreclosure. To this extent, the decision is persuasive. Instead of applying a fiction that the secured party has by conduct elected to foreclose, a better approach is to apply an estoppel principle or hold that a commercially unreasonable delay or use of the collateral has made the accurate assessment of a deficiency impracticable. However, the *Angelkovski* case should not be applied so as to permit a secured party from taking advantage of its own non-compliance with the foreclosure provisions to preserve its claim to a deficiency. If the secured party has manifested an intention to accept the collateral in satisfaction of the obligation secured, its failure to notify the debtor or other third parties should not allow it to later claim a deficiency. Under such circumstances, the secured party should be precluded from making such a claim.[199]

4) Contractual Foreclosure

It is unclear whether a debtor can agree to a post-default arrangement under which the secured party agrees to retain some or all of the collateral in partial satisfaction of the secured obligation. Almost certainly this cannot be accomplished by including a provision in the security agreement or in some other pre-default agreement. But a post-default arrangement may be beneficial to the debtor as it will limit the debtor's exposure to liability for a deficiency. The PPSA does not contain any provision that covers partial foreclosure and, to the extent that it is permitted at all, partial foreclosure will be contractual in nature.

It may be argued that partial foreclosure is not permitted under the PPSA. Although legal commentators[200] in the United States argued that partial foreclosure was permissible under the 1972 version of Article 9 (the current version provides for it explicitly), the wording of the strict foreclosure provisions provided that the debtor may sign a statement after default renouncing the debtor's rights.[201]

In Canada, the matter is less certain. Partial foreclosure operates in much the same way as a sale of the collateral to the secured party at a price less than the secured obligation. This type of transaction is

---

199 See *Yuan v. Mah Investments Ltd.* (2001), 205 Sask. R. 22 (Q.B.).

200 P. Coogan, "The New Article 9" (1973) 86 Harv. L. Rev. 477 at 521–24; White and Summers, *Uniform Commercial Code*, 4th ed., vol. 4 (St. Paul: West Publishing, 1995) at 428; B. Clark, *The Law of Secured Transactions Under the Uniform Commercial Code*, rev. ed. (Arlington: A.S. Pratt & Sons, 2001) at ¶4.10[3].

201 § 9-505(2). The 1998 Revised Article 9 expressly permits partial foreclosure in a non-consumer transaction if the debtor has agreed to it in a post-default agreement. See § 9-620.

not permitted under the PPSA. A secured party can only purchase the collateral from the debtor at a public sale. Therefore, it might be argued that partial foreclosure violates the rule that the debtor cannot contract out of rights provided to debtors under the PPSA. If a debtor cannot agree to a sale to a secured party by way of a private sale, it would follow that the debtor should not be able to agree to a partial foreclosure.

In support of partial foreclosure, it might be argued that partial foreclosure should not be viewed as a forced sale by the secured party so as to attract the prohibition against a private sale to the secured party. Rather the transaction involves a sale by the debtor to the secured party. Although the PPSA does not generally permit a secured party to contact out of the duties that it owes to the debtor when it exercises its enforcement remedies, the PPSA does not prohibit the debtor from selling the collateral. By the same token a quitclaim on the debtor's interest in return for cancellation of part of the debt is merely a sale by the debtor to the secured party. The limitation on the right of the secured party to purchase the collateral applies only where the sale is being carried out by the secured party. In the view of the authors, courts should therefore strive to give effect to partial foreclosure agreements since these arrangements are most often value-enhancing transactions for both of the parties. The same should hold true for a contractual foreclosure arrangement in which the parties agree that the secured party shall accept the collateral in full satisfaction of the obligation secured. Such agreements should be fully effective between the parties, and should not be regarded as an impermissible contracting out of the requirements of Part 5.

There is an important difference between the legal effect of a statutory foreclosure and a contractual or partial foreclosure. A statutory foreclosure has the effect of foreclosing not only the interest of a debtor, but also the interest of subordinate third parties who were given the notice of intention to foreclose.[202] A partial or contractual foreclosure will not have this effect; it involves merely a contract between the secured party and debtor under which the debtor conveys the debtor's interest in the collateral to the secured party in consideration of the extinguishment of all or part of the debt. The secured party simply obtains the debtor's interest in the property. The transaction does not have the effect of foreclosing the interests of subordinate interest-holders. Unless such parties also agree to surrender their rights to the collateral, the secured party will remain subject to their right to redeem

---

202 PPSA (BC, M, NB, PEI) s. 61(8); A s. 62(7); (NL, NS) s. 62(8); (NWT, Nu, S) s. 61(7); O s. 65(7); Y s. 59(6).

the collateral or to their right to force a sale of it, and a later sale of the collateral by the secured party will not extinguish their rights.

H. ENFORCEMENT AGAINST INTANGIBLES AND CHATTEL PAPER

Often one of the most valuable assets owned by the debtor is its intangible rights such as the accounts that are owed by the debtor's customers. The PPSA provides a direct collection remedy through which a secured party notifies the third party that payment is to be made to the secured party rather than to the debtor. Customers who owe obligations to the debtor may respond that the goods or services that were provided were defective and that therefore the customer is not liable for the full amount. Alternatively, the customer may raise claims that it has against the debtor arising out of separate transactions. This involves the question of defences and set-off. The rules governing defences and set-off are not contained in Part 5 of the Act and therefore they apply to deemed security interests in the form of absolute transfers of accounts and chattel paper as well as to transfers that in substance create a security interest.

1) Direct Collection Rights of Secured Parties

Collateral in the form of an intangible, chattel paper, instrument, or a security often involves an obligation by third parties to pay money to the debtor. Instead of enforcing the security interest by sale of the collateral or by foreclosure of the debtor's interest, the secured party may instead enforce the security interest by collecting the obligation directly from the third party.[203] Any money that is collected is applied against the obligation secured. The secured party is permitted to deduct the reasonable expenses of collection from the amount collected.[204] Since

---

203 PPSA (BC, M, NB, NWT, Nu, PEI, S) s. 57(2); A s. 57(1); (NL, NS) s. 58(2); O, s. 61(1); Y s. 55(1). The OPPSA is drawn more narrowly. It is restricted to accounts, whereas the other Acts cover intangibles. As well, the Acts in Ontario, Alberta, and the Yukon only cover instruments, whereas the other Acts cover securities as well.

204 PPSA (BC, M, NWT, Nu) s. 57(3); A s. 57(2); (NB, PEI, S) s. 57(4); (NL, NS) s. 58(4); O s. 61(1); Y s. 55(2).

the remedies in the PPSA are cumulative,[205] a secured party is permitted to proceed against some of these assets by direct collection, and may enforce its security interest against other of these assets by sale or foreclosure.

Most true security interests in accounts or chattel paper are taken on a non-notification basis. Under these arrangements, the third-party obligor is not notified until after there has been a default. The direct collection provision of the PPSA will therefore apply to these transactions. Notification financing (where the third-party obligor is notified of the transfer and required to pay the obligation to the transferee immediately following the transfer) typically occurs in respect of transactions that involve an absolute transfer of the property, such as the transfer of accounts to a factor or the discounting and sale of chattel paper from a dealer to a bank or finance company. Except for the Ontario Act, the direct collection provision will not apply to these transactions because Part 5 does not apply to deemed security interests. The Ontario PPSA does not contain such an exclusion, with the result that the direct collection provision governs absolute transfers of accounts and chattel paper as well.

A secured party who engages in direct collection is under an obligation to act in a commercially reasonable manner.[206] A lack of diligence in notifying the obligors and collecting the accounts can render the secured party liable for any loss caused by its negligence.[207] If the direct collection produces enough to satisfy the secured obligation and the reasonable costs of collection, the surplus must be turned over to the debtor or a third party in accordance with the PPSA.[208]

Many of the Acts contain an additional notice provision that requires the secured party to notify the debtor not later than fifteen days after the secured party enforces the security interest through direct collection.[209] The Ontario, Alberta, Manitoba, and Yukon Acts do not provide a similar notice requirement.

---

205 PPSA (A, M, NWT, Nu) s. 55(2); (BC, PEI, NB, S) s. 55(3); (NL, NS) s. 56(3); O s. 58; Y s. 53(3).
206 PPSA (M, NWT, Nu, S) s. 65(3); A s. 66(1); BC s. 68(3); (NB, PEI) s. 65(3); (NL, NS) s. 66(2); O s. 61(2); Y s. 62(1).
207 See, for example, *DeLay First Nat. Bank & Trust Co. v. Jacobson Appliance Co.*, 243 N.W.2d 745 (Neb. 1976).
208 PPSA (BC, M, NB, NWT, Nu, PEI, S) s. 60(2); A s. 61(1); (NL, NS) s. 61(2); O s. 64(1); Y s. 58(2). This will not apply where the transaction involves an absolute transfer of an account or chattel paper.
209 PPSA (BC, NWT, Nu) s. 57(4); (NB, PEI) s. 57(3); (NL, NS) s. 58(3); S s. 57(5).

2) Rights of Third-party Account Debtors

The transfer of chattel paper, accounts, or intangibles by a debtor, whether by outright sale or by way of security, will have a direct effect beyond the parties to the transaction. In particular, it will affect the party who owes the obligation to the debtor. For convenience, this party will be referred to as the account debtor, notwithstanding that the obligation may be connected with chattel paper or a form of intangible other than an account.[210] The PPSA provides a set of rules that govern the rights of account debtors *vis-à-vis* secured parties who have obtained an assignment of chattel paper or accounts or other intangibles from the debtor. To a large degree, these provisions mirror the common law rules that govern the relationship between account debtors and assignees. However, in several important respects the common law position has been modified.

a)   Defences and Set-off

The Acts provide that an assignee (which includes both an outright transferee as well as a secured party) takes subject to the terms of the contract between the assignor and the account debtor and is subject to any defences or claims arising out of it.[211] This essentially incorporates the concept of equitable set-off that permits the account debtor to raise any defence that it could assert against the assignor in relation to the contract or a closely connected contract. This form of set-off is available even though the claim is not liquidated. It can be asserted by the account debtor even if the claim arises after the account debtor receives notification of the assignment. This is illustrated in the following scenario.

Buyer A purchases goods on credit from S. S assigns this claim to SP, and SP notifies A of the assignment. If the goods that are delivered are defective, A is permitted to set off any damages in connection with the defective goods when faced with a demand by SP to pay the obligation to it.

The assignee also takes subject to any defences or claims of the account debtor that arise before the account debtor acquires notice of the assignment. This encapsulates the concept of legal set-off. Legal set-off permits the account debtor to set-off claims that arise out of unconnected transactions. In order to do so, the claim must be liquidated and

---

210 This is the terminology adopted in most of the non-Ontario Acts. See PPSA (A, BC, M, NB, NWT, Nu, PEI, S) s. 41(1); (NL, NS) s. 42(1).
211 PPSA (A, BC, M, NB, NWT, Nu, PEI, S) s. 41(2); (NL, NS) s. 42(2); O s. 40(1); Y s. 39(1).

the debts must be mutual (that is, a debt between the same parties in the same right). Legal set-off is available in respect of an existing debt that is payable in the future if payment is subject to no other condition except the passage of time.[212] It is also available in respect of a debt payable on demand even if the demand has not yet been made.[213] Once the account debtor acquires knowledge of the assignment, the account debtor is no longer permitted to claim legal set-off with respect to any debt thereafter arising between the account debtor and the assignor. Registration of a financing statement by the assignee is not sufficient to qualify as knowledge since the Acts provide that registration is not constructive knowledge.[214]

The underlying contract between the account debtor and the assignor may contain a "cut-off clause" or "waiver of defence" clause. These contractual provisions provide that the account debtor waives the right to assert against the assignee defences that are available as against the assignor. The Acts provide that the account debtor's rights may be modified by an enforceable agreement not to assert defences or claims arising out of the contract. This does not validate the use of such provisions. Such clauses are valid at common law, but legislation in many provinces restricts their use in a consumer context.[215]

b)   The Account Debtor's Obligation to Pay on Notification

The account debtor is entitled to make payments to the assignor until the account debtor is given notice of the assignment.[216] Once the account debtor is notified of the assignment, an account debtor who nevertheless makes further payments to the assignor will remain liable to the assignee and will therefore be in the unhappy position of having to pay the debt twice over. The Acts modify this common law position somewhat by giving the account debtor the right to demand that the assignor furnish proof of the assignment. If such a demand is made, the account debtor is allowed to pay the assignor if the assignee fails to furnish such

---

212 *Coopers & Lybrand Ltd. v. Lumberland Building Materials Ltd.* (1983), 150 D.L.R. (3d) 411 (B.C.S.C.).

213 *Belows v. Dalmyn*, [1978] 4 W.W.R. 630 (Man. Q.B.).

214 PPSA (A, BC, M, NB, NWT, Nu, PEI, S) s. 47; (NL, NS) s. 48; O s. 46(5); Y s. 52(3). The Act contains a provision that describes the state of knowledge that is needed to satisfy the knowledge requirement. See PPSA (A, BC, NWT, Nu) s. 1(2); (M, NB, PEI) s. 2; (NL, NS) s. 3; O s. 69; S s. 2(2); Y no equivalent provision.

215 See, for example, *Law of Property Act*, R.S.A. 2000, c. L-7, s. 52(2).

216 PPSA (BC, M, NB, NWT, Nu, PEI, S) s. 41(7); A s. 41(5); (NL, NS) s. 42(7); O s. 40(2); Y s. 39(4).

proof within fifteen days from the date of the request (or within a reasonable time under the Ontario and Yukon formulation).[217]

c)   Post-assignment Contractual Modifications

The Acts make an important change to the common law and equitable principles governing assignments. At common law, an assignee who had given notice of the assignment was not affected by a subsequent modification in the underlying contract between the account debtor and the assignor. This rule is too inflexible as there are situations where new or changed circumstances may make it necessary for the parties to vary the terms of the contract. For example, it may be necessary to change the specifications of the goods ordered and this might entail a change in price or the terms of payment. The Acts permit post-notification contractual modifications under certain conditions.[218] Modifications must be made in good faith and in accordance with reasonable commercial standards without material adverse effect on the assignee's rights under the contract or the assignor's ability to perform. Where such modifications are made, the assignor acquires the rights under the substituted contract that corresponds to those it enjoyed under the original contract.[219]

The non-Ontario Acts further provide that the modification provisions do not affect the validity of a term in an assignment agreement that provides that a modification to the contract is a breach of the agreement between the assignor and the assignee.[220] This will give the assignee the right to sue the assignor for damages for breach of contract, but will not affect the position of the account debtor on the modified contract.

3) Set-off and the Right to Proceeds

An inventory financer who has taken a security interest in goods may attempt to trace the proceeds from the sale of the goods into an account with a bank or other depository institution. The PPSA provides that the

---

217 *Ibid.*
218 PPSA (BC, M, NB, NWT, Nu, PEI, S) s. 41(3)–(4); A, s. 41(3); (NL, NS) s. 42(3)–(4); O s. 40(3); Y s. 39(2).
219 PPSA (BC, M, NB, NWT, Nu, PEI, S) s. 41(5); A s. 41(3); (NL, NS) s. 42(5); O s. 40(3); Y s. 39(2).
220 PPSA (BC, M, NB, NWT, Nu, PEI, S) s. 41(6); A s. 41(4); (NL, NS) s. 42(6); Y s. 39(2); O no equivalent provision.

security interest of the inventory financer continues in the proceeds.[221] The inventory supplier will therefore have a security interest in the account to the extent that it can trace the sale proceeds into the account. The bank or other depository institution may seek to exercise a right of set-off in relation to other claims that the bank may have against its customer. The PPSA provides a statutory right of set-off in relation to assignments of intangibles and chattel paper. However, this provision only applies where these rights have been transferred through an assignment of the intangible or chattel paper. The inventory financer's right to the account as proceeds does not arise by virtue of an assignment between the debtor and the inventory financer. Rather, the right arises automatically by virtue of its statutory right to the proceeds.

The most logical approach would be to apply the common law and equitable rules of set-off. The rules that govern a secured party who has a security interest in accounts as original collateral should also govern a secured party who claims a security interest in the account as proceeds. The bank should therefore have the right to assert the same rights of legal or equitable set-off against the inventory financer that it has against a secured party who obtains an assignment of the account from the debtor.[222]

Frequently, the bank or other depository institution will also hold security in the deposit account to secure a loan or other obligation owing to it by the debtor. In its status as a secured creditor, the bank will normally be subordinated to the inventory financer assuming the latter had satisfied the requirements for purchase money security interest superpriority status. However, it may assert its right of set-off and not rely on its security interest. This is an example of a situation where a bank may have better rights under the law of set-off than it does as a secured creditor. The authors support that result even in cases where the bank has knowledge of the inventory financer's proceeds claim as a result of a notice required by the PPSA. The bank will normally have such knowledge under the Atlantic Acts because they require an inventory financer to give advance notice to any prior-registered secured creditor claiming a security interest in accounts as original collateral. The authors do not regard this element of knowledge as affecting the bank's rights under set off law. The PPSA priority structure is limited to priority competitions involving secured creditors claiming by virtue of

---

221 PPSA (A, BC, M, NB, NWT, Nu, PEI, S) s. 28(1); (NL, NS) s. 29(1); O s. 25(1); Y s. 26(1).

222 See R.C.C. Cuming, "Security Interests in Accounts and the Right of Set-Off" (1991) 6 B.F.L.R. 299.

that status. Except as otherwise explicitly stated, they are not intended to displace the priority rights of creditors enjoyed under other commercial law doctrines such as set-off or negotiable instruments law. To allow this would produce too great a disruption in well-established banking practices.

I. RECEIVERSHIPS

As an alternative to the simple seizure and sale of the collateral, a security interest may be enforced by the appointment of a receiver or receiver-manager. This form of enforcement is most often associated with a security agreement that gives a secured party a security interest in all present and after-acquired personal property. In the vast majority of cases, the secured party appoints the receiver pursuant to a power contained in the security agreement. This is called a privately appointed receiver (also referred to as an instrument appointed or document appointed receiver). The court also has the power to appoint a receiver. In the secured transactions context, most often this occurs when a secured party applies to the court to have a private appointment converted into a court appointment.

A receiver has merely the power to receive income generated by the property. A receiver-manager has, in addition, the power to operate the business. In the vast majority of receiverships, the secured party appoints a receiver-manager with the intention of operating the business for a time before attempting to sell it as a going concern or conducting a liquidation sale. The PPSA in most jurisdictions defines receiver as including a receiver-manager, and this terminology will also be adopted in this book. However, it must be kept in mind that the security agreement or the court order must confer the power to act as both a receiver and manager if the receiver wishes to carry on the business of the debtor.[223]

1) Regulation of Receiverships

At its core, the law respecting receiverships is a mixture of common law and equitable principles. Increasingly, this body of law has been

---

223 In *Standard Trust Co. v. Turner Crossing Inc.* (1993), 4 P.P.S.A.C. (2d) 238 (Sask. Q.B.) the appointment of a receiver-manager to carry on the business of the debtor was set aside on the basis that the contractual provision in the security agreement did not authorize the appointment.

augmented by statutes that are designed to regulate the use of receiver-ships as a device for enforcing security interests. There is considerable variation in the manner in which this statutory supplementation has been carried out. The business corporations legislation in many prov-inces contain provisions that govern receiverships. These provisions are based on provisions found in the federal business corporations legis-lation. In these jurisdictions, the PPSA contains an overlapping layer of regulation.[224] Since the business corporations legislation only gov-erns corporate entities, the parallel PPSA provisions ensure that simi-lar rules govern receiverships of non-corporate entities. The business corporations statutes in Ontario, British Columbia, and Saskatchewan do not contain receivership provisions; in these provinces, the PPSA is therefore the exclusive provincial statutory source of regulation. The *Bankruptcy and Insolvency Act* adds another layer of regulation. Sec-tions 245 to 252 apply to receiverships where the debtor is insolvent.

The receivership provisions in the Ontario PPSA are not very ex-tensive. They simply validate the continued availability of private and court-appointed receivers and receiver-managers, and give the court certain powers over receiverships, such as the power to remove or re-place a receiver, fix remuneration, or give directions. As a result, the receivership provisions of the BIA play a relatively greater role in sup-plementing the PPSA provisions. In most other PPSA jurisdictions, the BIA receivership provisions to a large degree duplicate the provincial or territorial legislation whether found in the PPSA or business corpora-tions legislation or both. Unfortunately, this mass of overlapping and duplicated measures in many instances simply adds to the cost of re-ceiverships by imposing additional costs and delays without producing any corresponding benefit to the parties.

The BIA imposes the following obligations on a receiver:

- the duty to notify the Superintendent of Bankruptcy, the debtor, and all the creditors of the receivership not later than ten days after the appointment;[225]
- the duty to keep records and prepare financial statements of the re-ceivership, and to disclose such information to the debtor and other interested parties;[226] and
- the duty to act honestly and in good faith and to deal with the prop-erty in a commercially reasonable manner.[227]

---

224 PPSA (BC, M NB, NWT, Nu, PEI, S) s. 64; (A, NL, NS) s. 65; O s. 60; Y s. 54.
225 BIA s. 245(1).
226 BIA s. 246.
227 BIA s. 247.

For the most part, the PPSA enforcement regime in Part 5 applies to a receivership. In some Acts, such as Ontario and Alberta, this is accomplished by defining "secured party" to encompass receivers for the purposes of certain sections of the Act. In most of the other Acts, the individual substantive provisions of the PPSA specifically state if they are applicable to receivers.[228] The statutory foreclosure remedy is not applicable, as it is the secured party and not the receiver who retains the collateral in satisfaction of the obligation.

2) The Status and Legal Effect of a Receivership

The appointment of a receiver does not cause the vesting of the debtor's property in the receiver. Upon the appointment of a receiver, the debtor's power of management of the assets is suspended and the receiver obtains the power of control over the assets. The receiver is not required to comply with the usual PPSA advance notice requirements when selling the debtor's assets in the ordinary course of business.[229] Eventually the receiver will attempt to dispose of the business. At this stage, the receiver must exercise the same degree of care and must follow much the same procedure as a secured party who enforces its security interest by sale.[230]

The courts have historically drawn a sharp distinction between a privately appointed receiver and a court appointed receiver in respect of the obligations owed by the receiver. At common law, in the case of a privately appointed receiver, the receiver was traditionally considered to be an agent of the secured party for the purposes of realizing on the collateral. A privately appointed receiver's primary duty is to protect the interests of the secured party and it is under an obligation to act in good faith and ensure that a fair sale is conducted. In the case of a court-appointed receiver, the receiver is under a fiduciary obligation to be an officer of the court with a fiduciary obligation owed to all the creditors. A court-appointed receiver is required to be fair and impartial and to act in the interests of all the creditors, and is under an obli-

---

228 The Yukon Act is silent as to whether the substantive provisions apply to receivers.

229 PPSA (M, NB, NWT, Nu, PEI) s. 64(9); (A, NL, NS) s. 65(9); O s. 63(7)(g); S s. 64(10); Y s. 54(4).

230 The form of the notice of intention to sell is somewhat different in the case of a receivership in jurisdictions other than Ontario. See PPSA (BC, M, NWT, Nu, S) s. 59(10)–(11); A ss. 60(8) and (12); (NB, PEI) s. 59(11)–(12); (NL, NS) s. 60(11)–(12); Y s. 57(6).

gation to give the same degree of care that a reasonable person would give to his own personal affairs.

The PPSA alters the common law position in several respects. Although the concept of a privately appointed receiver and a court appointed receiver remain distinct under the PPSA, there is a greater convergence in the nature and character of their status and obligations.[231] The PPSA gives to receivers a special status separate and apart from the secured party. A privately appointed receiver is no longer merely an agent of the secured party. The receiver has obligations (and rights) under the PPSA that are independent of the secured party. This is a fundamental change from the position of a privately appointed receiver at common law. At common law, a court appointed receiver has a status independent of the secured party who seeks his appointment. Under the PPSA, both court appointed and privately appointed receivers have an independent status and have obligations that are owed independently from those owed by the secured party.

Historically, the courts of equity had no jurisdiction over privately appointed receivers. This has been altered by legislation and this has been carried over to the PPSA receivership provisions. The court is now empowered to make orders in respect of privately appointed receivers as well.[232] This goes part of the way toward reducing the differences that exist between court appointed and privately appointed receivers. It seems likely that the duty of care owed by the receiver in preserving the assets or realizing on the collateral does not differ depending upon the type of appointment, but is the same standard of good faith and commercial reasonableness that is required of a secured party.

Court appointed receivers are typically more costly, and for this reason the vast majority of receiverships involve privately appointed receivers. In some cases, a secured party will apply to court to have a private appointment converted into a court appointment. This is often done when the secured party believes that the receivership may be challenged by the debtor or by an interested third party. In *Royal Bank of Canada v. White Cross Properties Ltd.*,[233] the Saskatchewan Court of Queen's Bench refused to grant the application. The court was of the

---

231 See generally T. Buckwold, "The Treatment of Receivers in the Personal Property Security Acts: Conceptual and Practical Implications" (1997) 29 Can. Bus. L.J. 277.

232 PPSA (M, NB, NWT, Nu, PEI) s. 64(7); (A, NL, NS) s. 65(7); O s. 60(2); S s. 64(8); Y s. 54(2).

233 (1984), 34 Sask. R. 315 (Q.B.). See also *Bank of Nova Scotia v. Sullivan Investments Ltd.* (1982), 21 Sask. R. 14 (Q.B.) and *Royal Trust v. D.Q. Plaza Holdings Ltd.* (1985), 54 C.B.R. (N.S.) 18 (Sask. Q.B.).

568   PERSONAL PROPERTY SECURITY LAW

opinion that the risk of priority competitions were not a sufficient basis for granting the order since a secured party is able to bring a summary application before the court for the determination of priorities. If a privately appointed receiver is later appointed by the court, the private appointment comes to an end. The receiver is bound by the terms of the court appointment and can no longer invoke any of the powers that were conferred by the security agreement.[234]

3) Deemed Agency Clauses

Most security agreements that provide for the appointment of a receiver also include an agency clause that deems the receiver to be the agent of the debtor. There are two reasons for the inclusion of a deemed agency clause. First, the clause ensures that the receiver will be fully empowered to carry on the business of the debtor. Second, there is some suggestion that it will insulate the secured party from liability for the receiver's debts or for any wrongful act of the receiver.[235]

In reality, a deemed agency clause does not necessarily provide a safe harbour for the secured party. The Ontario Court of Appeal in *Peat Marwick Ltd. v. Consumers' Gas Co.*[236] held that a deemed agency clause is only effective when the receiver is carrying on the business of the debtor and not when the receiver is disposing of the assets. In the latter capacity, the receiver acts as the agent of the secured party.

The question of the secured party's liability for misconduct of a receiver is uncertain under the PPSA. If a privately appointed receiver is regarded as having an independent status, this may lead to the conclusion that a secured party is not liable for the misconduct of the receiver and that a deemed agency clause is no longer of any relevance in this regard. The Acts in jurisdictions other than Ontario and the Yukon and some business corporations statutes[237] provide that a court may order that either the receiver or the secured party make good any default in connection with the receiver's custody, management, or disposition of the assets.[238] This may lend some support to the view that a secured party, in the absence of a court order, will not normally be responsible for the misfeasance of a receiver that it appoints. On the other hand, it

---

234 *Price Waterhouse Ltd. v. Creighton Holdings Ltd.* (1984), 36 Sask. R. 292 (Q.B.).

235 See D. Milman, "Receivers as Agents" (1981) 44 Mod. Law Rev. 658. This explanation now seems doubtful given the widespread practice of receivers demanding an indemnity from the secured party before agreeing to act.

236 (1981), 113 D.L.R. (3d) 754 (Ont. C.A.).

237 See, for example, *Canada Business Corporations Act*, R.S.C. 1985, c. C-44, s. 100(d).

238 PPSA (M, NB, NWT, Nu, PEI) s. 64(7); (A, NL, NS) s. 65(7); BC s. 66(1); S s. 64(8).

can be argued that the Part 5 obligations are imposed on secured parties as well as receivers and that they should be jointly liable. If this is accepted, then a deemed agency clause will not be effective in insulating the secured party from liability since the PPSA does not permit a contracting out of a secured party's obligations to the debtor. Thus, in the view of the authors, on either approach a deemed agency clause has no role to play in the determination of the secured party's liability.

J. ENFORCEMENT BY SUBORDINATE SECURED PARTIES

The enforcement remedies of the PPSA are not limited to secured parties who have the highest-ranking security interest. They may also be exercised by secured parties who hold subordinate security interests. Several different issues can arise when it is a subordinate secured party who is enforcing its security interest.[239]

1) Pre-emption by the Senior Secured Party

Although a junior secured party has a right to seize the collateral, problems may arise when the senior secured party demands that the collateral be surrendered so that the senior secured party may enforce its security interest. Does the senior secured party have a better right to possession of the collateral such that it can compel the junior secured party to turn it over to so that the senior secured party may exercise its enforcement remedies against the collateral? Although a junior secured party clearly is given a right to enforce its security interest by the PPSA, the issue is whether that right can be exercised in face of a demand by the senior secured party for possession. Although both the senior and the junior secured parties have the right to enforce their security interests on default, the senior secured party's right should be given precedence in the event of a competition. This higher right is derived from the priority of its security interest. In other words, a priority right should be seen as giving the senior creditor two distinct rights: (1) a su-

---

239 See generally S. Nickles, "Rights and Remedies between U.C.C. Article 9 Secured Parties with Conflicting Security Interests in Goods" (1983) 68 Iowa L. Rev. 216 at 229; C. Dobbs, "Enforcement of Article 9 Security Interests — Why So Much Deference to the Secured Party" (1994) 28 Loyola L.A. L. Rev. 113; C. Starnes, "U.C.C. Section 9-504 Sales by Junior Secured Parties: Is a Senior Secured Party Entitled to Notice an Proceeds?" (1991) 52 U. Pitt. L. Rev. 563.

perior property right in respect of other competing interests; and (2) a superior enforcement right against other secured parties. Courts in the United States have, for the most part, given recognition to the superior right of the senior secured party by permitting it to take possession from a junior secured party.[240]

In *Holnam West Materials Ltd. v. Canadian Concrete Products Ltd.*,[241] an unconditional stay of enforcement was ordered against a subordinate secured party on application of the secured party. The unusual feature of this decision was that the senior secured party was not asserting its superior right of possession. Rather, it was seeking to prevent the junior secured party from enforcing its security interest in order to allow the debtor to retain possession of the collateral and continue to carry on business. The court noted that it was highly unlikely that a buyer could be found. It granted the stay on the basis that failure to do so would be commercially unreasonable as it would force the debtor into liquidation against the wishes of its senior creditor and yet it would not result in the junior creditor receiving any of the funds generated by the sale.

The case is problematic since the decision is based on the assumption that the proceeds of sale would have to be applied first to the senior secured party's claim.[242] However, even if it were accepted that a secured party does not have a claim to the proceeds of an enforcement sale conducted by a junior secured party, the junior secured party nevertheless faces a number of practical difficulties in attempting to sell the collateral in such a case. The junior secured party would ordinarily need to determine the value of the senior secured party's security interest. The junior secured party could thereby discount the price paid so that the buyer would be in a position to pay off the senior secured party's claim should the secured party come after the buyer. However, this becomes difficult if the senior secured party has a security interest in other collateral as well, since it will be uncertain whether the senior secured party will resort to the particular item of collateral subject to the junior security interest. The buyer's position can be further undercut if the senior secured party's security interest secures future advances made to the debtor. A buyer is unlikely to purchase the goods

---

240 See, for example, *American Heritage Bank & Trust Co. v. O. & E., Inc.*, 576 P.2d 566 (Colo. App. 1978). See also Comment 5 to § 9-609 of current art. 9, which states: "Conflicting rights to possession of collateral among secured parties are resolved by the priority rules of this Article. Thus, a senior secured party is entitled to possession as against a junior claimant."

241 [1995] 1 W.W.R. 155 (Alta. Q.B.).

242 This issue is addressed in J.3 "Obligations of the Junior Secured Party."

from a junior secured party under these circumstances unless the senior secured party consents to the transaction.

2) Marshalling of Securities

The equitable doctrine of marshalling of securities applies when a senior secured party has a security interest in two different funds, and the junior creditor has resort against only one of the funds. In such a case, the courts will marshal the securities to ensure that the maximum recovery is obtained without prejudicing the rights of the senior secured party. Although some courts initially took the view that the doctrine is in conflict with the priority structure of the PPSA,[243] more recently courts have indicated a willingness to apply the doctrine to PPSA security interests.[244]

There is presently some uncertainty concerning how the doctrine of marshalling effects this result. The more conventional view is that marshalling operates by subrogation. On this theory of marshalling, the court does not compel the senior secured party to enforce its claim only against the fund in which it alone has an interest. The senior secured party is free to proceed against the common fund, but if it does so, the junior secured party will be subrogated to the rights of the senior secured party in relation to the fund in which the senior secured party alone holds an interest.[245] The competing view is that a court effects a marshalling of securities by compelling the senior secured party to proceed first against the fund in which it alone holds an interest.[246] Although this approach has been endorsed by courts in the United

---

243 *National Bank of Canada v. Makin Metals Ltd.*, [1993] 3 W.W.R. 318 (Sask. Q.B.), rev'd [1994] 4 W.W.R. 707 (Sask. C.A.); *Royal Trust Co. v. H.A. Roberts Group Ltd.*, [1995] 4 W.W.R. 305 (Sask. Q.B.).

244 *National Bank of Canada v. Makin Metals Ltd.*, [1994] 4 W.W.R. 707 (Sask. C.A.); *Surrey Metro Savings Credit Union v. Chestnut Hill Homes Inc.* (1997), 30 B.C.L.R. (3d) 92 (S.C.); *Steinbach Credit Union Ltd. v. Manitoba Agricultural Credit Corp.*, [1991] 4 W.W.R. 36 (Man. Q.B.). In *Holnam West Materials Ltd. v. Canadian Concrete Products*, above note 241, and *Fiatallis North America, Inc. v. Piggott Construction Ltd.* (1992), 3 P.P.S.A.C. (2d) 30 (Ont. Ct. Gen. Div.), the courts assumed that the doctrine is applicable to PPSA security interests but rejected its application on the particular facts of the cases.

245 *Ernst Bros. Co. v. Canada Permanent Mortgage Corp.* (1920), 57 D.L.R. 500 (Ont. S.C.(A.D.)); *C.I.B.C. Mortgage Corp. v. Branch* (1999), 68 B.C.L.R. (3d) 334 (S.C.).

246 See B. MacDougall, "Marshalling and the Personal Property Security Acts: Doing Unto Others…" (1994) 28 U.B.C.L. Rev. 91.

States,[247] the case law in Canada has generally not recognized marshalling by compulsion.[248] Although courts in the United States have held that a trustee in bankruptcy can resort to the doctrine of marshalling of securities,[249] Canadian courts have decided that the doctrine is not available to unsecured creditors.[250]

A situation may arise where the choice of which asset to proceed against will directly affect one or the other of two subordinate parties. This is illustrated in the following scenario.

SP1 has a security interest in assets A and B. SP2 has a subordinate security interest in asset A. SP3 has a subordinate security interest in asset B. If SP1 proceeds against asset A, SP2 will suffer the loss. If SP1 decides to proceed against asset B, SP3 will suffer the loss.

In this situation, SP1 may choose which asset to proceed against, and the claims of SP2 and SP3 will be satisfied rateably out of the other asset.[251]

3) Obligations of the Junior Secured Party

The PPSA does not impose a general requirement that the junior secured party give a notice of the intended sale to a senior secured party prior to the sale, unless the senior secured party sends a written notice of its interest to the junior secured party. A sale by a junior secured party does not have the effect of extinguishing the senior secured party's security interest in the collateral. The senior secured party may therefore enforce its security interest against the collateral in the hands of the purchaser. Notice must be given to junior secured parties, since their interests are extinguished upon a sale of the collateral. For similar reasons, a notice of an intended foreclosure does not need to be given to a senior secured party. The effect of the foreclosure is that junior interests will be extinguished, but the senior secured party will retain its interest in the collateral.

The junior secured party should not be required to account to the senior secured party or to pay the proceeds of disposition to the senior

247 See, for example, *Community Bank v. Jones*, 566 P.2d 470 (Or. 1977); *Shedoudy v. Beverly Surgical Supply Co.*, 161 Cal. Rptr. 164 (Cal. App. 1980).

248 *Canada Trustco Mortgage Co. v. Wenngatz Construction & Holdings Ltd.* (1986), 60 C.B.R. (NS) 270 (B.C.S.C.).

249 *In Re Jack Green's Fashions for Men Big & Tall Inc.*, 597 F.2d 130 (8th Cir. 1979); *Shedoudy v. Beverly Surgical Supply Co.*, above note 247.

250 *Williamson v. Loonstra* (1973) 34 D.L.R. (3d) 275 (B.C.S.C.); *Re Bread Man Inc.* (1978), 89 D.L.R. (3d) 599 (Ont. H.C.J.).

251 *Victoria & Grey Trust Co. v. Brewer* (1970), 14 D.L.R. (3d) 28 (Ont. H.C.J.).

secured party. The sale does not discharge the senior secured party's security interest. The purchaser obtains the collateral subject to this interest, and presumably this is reflected in the price paid by the purchaser. Thus, there is no reason why the senior secured party should have any claim to the proceeds.[252] Courts have sometimes lost sight of this point, and have required the junior creditor to pay the proceeds of the sale to the senior secured party.[253] Current Article 9 has remedied this misconception by making it clear that a junior secured party is under no obligation to pay the proceeds to the senior secured party.[254] Of course, the secured party is entitled to the proceeds of sale if the secured party has consented to the sale by the junior secured party on the condition that it first be paid out from the sale proceeds. In this case, the junior secured party acts as agent of the senior secured party in conducting the sale, and the purchaser will take free of both security interests.

The junior secured party must also account to the secured party where the junior secured party exercises the direct collection remedy and receives payment of obligations that are owed by third parties to the debtor. In this case, the senior secured party does not have a continuing security interest in the collateral following the enforcement by the junior secured party. Once the money is collected, the obligation owing by the account debtor is discharged and therefore the existence of the collateral comes to an end[255] and the senior secured party's pro-

---

252 See Clark, above note 200 at ¶4.06[4]: "The best approach is for the courts to recognize the right of a junior to hold an Article 9 foreclosure sale without being obliged to turn over the proceeds to the senior." The definition of proceeds in all the PPSAs except for the Ontario Act and the Yukon Act provide that the debtor must acquire an interest in the proceeds collateral. This requirement is not met in the case of an enforcement sale by a subordinate secured party, as it is the secured party and not the debtor that acquires an interest in the funds. Although the matter is not as clear-cut in Ontario and the Yukon, the authors are of the opinion that the same requirement should be read into these Acts as well. See chapter 12, B.2.b "The Debtor's Interest Requirement."

253 See *Consolidated Equipment Sales, Inc. v. First Bank & Trust Co. of Guthrie*, 627 P.2d 432 (Okl. 1981). And see *Holnam West Materials Ltd. v. Canadian Concrete Products*, above note 241, in which the court seems to assume that on a sale by the junior secured party, the senior secured party will have the first claim to the proceeds of sale.

254 See § 9-615(a) and (g) and Official Comment 5 to § 9-610.

255 The foregoing assumes that the junior secured party notified the account debtor and the senior secured party did not. If the senior secured party was the first to notify the account debtor, but the account debtor chose to pay the money to the junior secured party, the senior secured party would have an action against the account debtor. In this case, the senior secured party should not be able to

prietary right in the collateral also comes to an end. Therefore, the monies collected by the junior secured party must be applied first towards the satisfaction of the senior secured party's secured obligation, although presumably the junior secured party will be entitled to first deduct its reasonable costs of collection.

K. SUPERVISORY POWER OF THE COURT

The PPSA provides a summary method by which a secured party, a debtor, or an interested third party may bring a matter before a Court.[256] The advantage of this procedure is that the applicant is not required to commence an action before seeking a court order. This provides a useful mechanism where a dispute arises concerning the enforcement of rights. A similar procedure is also available for the determination of priority competitions where the facts are not in dispute.[257]

The court has the power to make an order, including a binding declaration of rights or an order for injunctive relief, to ensure compliance with Part 5, with the custodial obligations of the secured party or with obligations respecting the removal of a fixture or accession. The court also has the power to give directions concerning the exercise of these rights or the discharge of these obligations. This power may be used to enjoin the debtor or a third party from interfering with the secured party's seizure.[258] It may also be used by a secured party to obtain a court authorized seizure. This is most likely to be used where the debtor has resisted peaceable enforcement of the security interest, with the result that the secured party cannot effect a seizure without breaching the peace.[259]

The PPSA permits a court to stay the enforcement of rights or to relieve a party from compliance with the Act. There is presently some uncertainty concerning the circumstances under which a court will be

---

recover from the junior secured party, since the payment to the junior secured party did not affect its entitlement to recover the money from the account debtor.

256 PPSA (BC, M, NB, NWT, Nu, PEI, S) s. 63(2); A s. 64; (NL, NS) s. 64(2); O s. 67(1); Y s. 61.

257 PPSA (M, NWT, Nu, S) s. 66; A s. 69; BC s. 70; (NB, PEI) s. 67; (NL, NS); O s. 67(1); Y no equivalent provision. Section 64 of the SPPSA is the mechanism used for matters concerning the Part 5 default remedies. Section 66 provides a similar mechanism for the resolution of priority disputes.

258 *Martin v. Toronto Dominion Bank* (1985), 43 Sask. R. 212 (Q.B.).

259 *Costley v. Pioneer Credit Union Ltd.*, above note 94.

prepared to make an order that varies the remedies given to the secured party or the debtor under Part 5. The issue most often arises when a debtor applies to court for an order extending the time for redemption. Normally, a debtor may redeem at any point before the secured party sells the collateral or enters into a binding contract for sale or has irrevocably elected to retain the collateral through its foreclosure remedy. The application for an extension is in fact an application for a stay of proceedings for a period of time in order to permit the debtor to redeem or reinstate. In the absence of such an order, the secured party could proceed with its default remedies, with the result that the debtor's opportunity to redeem or reinstate would be lost.

For the most part, the courts have taken a relatively conservative approach to the exercise of their discretion. In *Andrews v. Mack Financial (Canada) Ltd.*,[260] the Saskatchewan Court of Appeal indicated that the PPSA does not authorize a court to rewrite or change the substance of a contract. In its view, the intervention of a court would be warranted only in order to ensure compliance with the requirements of the Act. This would permit a court to make an order requiring a secured party to comply with the statutory notice requirements or enjoining a secured party from exercising its remedies when the debtor was not in default. In the opinion of the Court, the discretion would be properly exercised in the case of an order relieving a secured party of the requirement to notify the debtor where the debtor had absconded so that notification was not possible. The Court held that the section did not permit a court to set aside a valid seizure of the collateral, but that it could be employed to give a debtor additional time to redeem.

In *Rapid Transit Mix Ltd. v. Commcorp. Financial Services Ltd.*,[261] the Alberta Court of Appeal held that the court should not exercise its discretion so as to take away contractual or statutory rights. Furthermore, it was of the view that the broad discretion to grant relief must be read subject to the more specific provisions of the Act which define a debtor's right to redeem. The Court therefore doubted that it is ever appropriate for a court to extend the time for redemption except perhaps to order a short extension causing no prejudice.

There are two distinct stages to the analysis. The first stage is to determine if a Court has the power to modify or vary the statutory rights set out in Part 5. If the answer is "no," that is an end to the matter. If

---

260 (1988), 46 D.L.R. (4th) 731 (Sask. C.A.). See also *Boychuk v. Hunterline Trucking (B.C.) Ltd.* (1997), 122 Man. R. (2d) 114.
261 (1998), 156 D.L.R. (4th) 366 (Alta. C.A.).

the answer is "yes," the second stage is to determine the circumstances under which this discretion ought to be exercised.

On the first question, the authors are of the view that a court has the power to extend the time for redemption in appropriate cases. A court is expressly empowered to stay enforcement of rights provided by Part 5. This recognizes that the statutory rights of a secured party can be overridden. Similarly, the power to relieve a secured party from compliance with the Act recognizes that statutory requirements can be overridden by a court order.[262]

In the view of the authors, the question should instead centre on whether there is a sound commercial justification for judicial intervention. The court should consider the conduct of the parties, the potential prejudice to the secured party if the relief is granted, and the potential harm to the debtor or third parties, if it is not. The court should refuse relief where it would interfere with the interest of an innocent third-party purchaser or if it would cause unwarranted delay.[263] Nor is an extension of time warranted if the debtor's financial conditions are such that there is no real prospect that the debtor will be able to redeem or reinstate.[264] An extension of time may be warranted where there is a real prospect that the debtor will be able to redeem and there is no substantial prejudice to the secured party (as where the value of the collateral exceeds the obligation secured).[265]

L. REMEDIES AGAINST A SECURED PARTY FOR NON-COMPLIANCE WITH THE PPSA

The PPSA creates a statutory right of action against persons who breach any of the duties or obligations imposed by the PPSA. This gives the aggrieved party a right to sue for damages. In many cases, a common law action will also be available. A secured party who purports to enforce a security interest when the security agreement is not in default can be

---

262 In *General Motors Acceptance Corp. of Canada v. Kennedy* (1993), 5 P.P.S.A.C. (2d) 32 (Sask. Q.B.), the court stripped a debtor of the right to reinstate on the basis of the conduct of the debtor.

263 See *Rapid Transit Mix Ltd. v. Commcorp. Financial Services Ltd.*, above note 261.

264 *Andrews v. Mack Financial (Canada) Ltd.*, above note 16.

265 See, for example, *Morris Industries Ltd. v. Remeshylo Farm Equipment (1988) Ltd.* (1995), 9 P.P.S.A.C. (2d) 93 (Sask. Q.B.); *Krolyk v. Carson*, [1997] 6 W.W.R. 373 (Sask. Q.B.).

sued for conversion and breach of contract. In appropriate cases, the aggrieved party may seek an injunction or other relief.[266]

1) The Statutory Right of Action

The PPSA creates a statutory right of action in favour of a person to whom a duty of obligation is owed for reasonably foreseeable loss or damage that is suffered as a result of its breach.[267] Under the Ontario Act, it is available only in respect of duties or obligations that are imposed by Part 5, the secured party's custodial duties in respect of collateral in its possession, or the duty of care in removing fixtures or accessions. The other Acts are wider in that they apply to all duties and obligations imposed by the Act. An action may be brought by the debtor against a secured party, but may also be brought by a third party who suffers loss. This allows a third party to bring an action against a secured party for loss caused through the failure to properly care for collateral in its possession or by an improvident sale of the collateral. In such a case, the third party seeks to recover the value of the surplus that would otherwise have been available to satisfy its claim.

In certain circumstances, the PPSA also gives the debtor the right to deemed damages. The Ontario Act provides that if the collateral is consumer goods, the debtor has a right to recover the greater of $500 or the amount of the actual loss. The Acts in all the other jurisdictions, except the Yukon, give the debtor the right to claim deemed damages in respect of consumer goods if the secured party fails to take reasonable care of collateral in its custody or if the secured party fails to comply with the obligations imposed on it when seizing and selling the collateral or exercising its foreclosure remedy. Deemed damages are available in consumer and non-consumer transactions where the secured party fails to give the debtor a copy of a financing statement (unless this right is waived) or fails to comply with a demand to amend or discharge a financing statement or a fixtures notice. Deemed damages are also available under the Acts of the Atlantic Provinces where the debtor proceeds to discharge a registered financing statement in circumstances where it is not entitled to do so. This rule reflects a difference in the procedure for compelling discharge in the Atlantic Acts as compared to the other non-Ontario Acts.

---

266 PPSA (BC, M, NB, NWT, Nu, PEI, S) s. 63(2); A s. 64; (NL, NS) s. 64(2); O s. 67(1); Y s. 61.

267 PPSA (M, NWT, Nu, S) s. 65(5); A s. 67(1); BC s. 69(3); (NB, PEI) s. 66(2); (NL, NS) s. 67(2); O s. 67(2); Y s. 62(2).

2) Effect on Deficiency Claims

If a secured party fails to comply with the obligations imposed on it by Part 5, what effect does this have on its ability to sue the debtor for a deficiency? This issue most often arises when a secured party fails to give the debtor advance notice of its intention to sell the collateral. In theory, this has the potential to detrimentally effect a debtor in two ways. The notice of intention notifies the debtor of the right to redeem the collateral. In jurisdictions other than Ontario, the notice of intention also notifies the debtor of the right to reinstate the security agreement. A debtor who does not know of its right to redeem or reinstate might not realize that it had the right to do so. As well, the notice gives the debtor the opportunity to monitor the sale or to attempt to find interested buyers.

A failure to comply with the notice requirements or other obligations does not automatically result in a loss of the right to sue for a deficiency.[268] In Ontario and the Yukon, the secured party is only liable for any loss caused by the failure to comply with the Act. The other Acts address this issue by providing that the onus is on the secured party to show that the failure to comply with the Act did not cause loss to the debtor by rendering the determination of the deficiency impracticable or, in the case of consumer goods, by affecting the debtor's ability to redeem or reinstate.[269] This onus might be discharged by demonstrating that the debtor knew of the right to redeem or reinstate, or by showing that the redemption or reinstatement was not feasible given the financial situation of the debtor.[270]

M. PERSONAL CLAIMS AVAILABLE TO A SECURED PARTY

Instead of pursuing its Part 5 remedies against the collateral, a secured party may choose to bring a personal claim against a third person who deals with the collateral or its proceeds. There are several reasons why a secured party may prefer to assert a personal claim in preference to its proprietary claim in respect of the collateral.

---

268 *Bank of Montreal v. Featherstone* (1989), 58 D.L.R. (4th) 567 (Ont. C.A.); *Canada Permanent Trust Company v. Thomas* (1983), 149 D.L.R. (3d) 338 (Sask. Q.B.).

269 PPSA (M, S) s. 65(8)–(9); A s. 67(3)–(4); BC s. 69(7)–(8); (NB, PEI) s. 66(5)–(6); (NL, NS) s. 67(5)–(6); (NWT, Nu) s. 66(8)–(9).

270 See *Indian Head Credit Union Ltd. v. R. & D. Hardware Ltd.* (1986), 54 Sask. R. 161 (Q.B.), aff'd (1988), 66 Sask. R. 90 (C.A.).

The availability of a personal claim is important when the collateral is lost or destroyed, or its value has depreciated. It is also important when the collateral is intact, but the secured party's security interest in the collateral has been lost through the operation of a priority rule following the disposition of the collateral by the defendant to another party. As well, if the collateral is not readily marketable, a secured party may prefer to bring a personal claim in order to avoid potential liability for negligent realization of the collateral. The major disadvantage of a personal remedy is that it ranks merely as an unsecured claim and is affected by the bankruptcy of the defendant.

In most cases, the personal claim for interference with the collateral will be brought against a third party who obtained possession or control over it. Although a personal claim for wrongful interference may also be available against the debtor, there is little point in bringing such an action because the debtor will typically be liable to the secured party on the underlying debt obligation. These personal claims will only be available if the secured party is entitled to priority over the third party. If a buyer is able to assert priority over the secured party on the basis of one of the buyer protection rules of the PPSA, the secured party will not be able to exercise any proprietary claim to the collateral and will be unable to bring a personal action against the buyer for wrongful interference with the collateral.

1) Conversion and Detinue

A secured party may be able to bring a personal claim against a transferee for conversion. The tort of conversion is committed when a person intentionally interferes with a chattel in a manner that is inconsistent with the right of another to it. It is only necessary to show that the wrongdoer intend to commit the act in question. The tort is one of strict liability in the sense that a wrongdoer will be liable despite the fact that she acted innocently and did not intend to challenge the right of the plaintiff.[271] If successful, the plaintiff will obtain damages that are normally assessed at the market value of the goods at the time of the wrongful conduct. Upon paying the value of the goods to the plaintiff, title to the goods is transferred to the wrongdoer.

In order to bring the action, the plaintiff must be in actual possession of the property or have had an immediate right of possession to it at the time of the conversion. Unless the secured party has perfected its security interest by possession or has seized the collateral, the secured

---

271 *Sun Mortgage Corp. v. Kumar* (2000), 146 Man. R. (2d) 89 (Q.B.).

party will not have possession of it. But a secured party will often be able to bring its claim on the basis of an immediate right of possession. This will typically occur where the debtor is in default under the terms of the security agreement. Most security agreements expressly stipulate that an authorized sale of the collateral constitutes an event of default. This is sufficient to give the secured party an immediate right to possession upon a default.[272]

The secured party may also bring an action in the tort of detinue, where a person wrongfully withholds possession of the collateral. In order to bring the action, the secured party must have an immediate right to possession and the secured party is usually required to have first made a demand for the property. There is considerable overlap between detinue and conversion, since the withholding of possession will often represent a denial of the secured party's interest in the collateral. There are some important differences between the two torts. In a conversion action, damages are normally assessed at the time of the act that denies the plaintiff's title. In detinue, damages are assessed at the time of the wrongful refusal to turn over the property.

There is some uncertainty as to what acts by third parties will entitle a secured party to pursue an action in conversion. The issue most commonly arises where a buyer, a junior secured party, or a judgment enforcement creditor takes possession of the collateral. The central question is whether the mere acquisition of possession by the third party will impose liability on the third party, or whether some other act such as a refusal to surrender the collateral to the secured party is necessary.

In the case of a buyer, the mere receipt of the collateral by the buyer was sufficient to impose liability on the buyer under the common law since the buyer was exercising dominion over the goods inconsistent with the title of the true owner.[273] There is some uncertainty whether this principle continues to apply under the PPSA. The PPSA specifically provides that the rights of a debtor in collateral may be transferred voluntarily or involuntarily, notwithstanding a provision in the security

---

272 There is considerable pre-PPSA authority which recognized a secured party's right to sue in conversion on the basis of an immediate right to possession of property arising upon a default under a security agreement. See, for example, *Toronto-Dominion Bank v. Dearborn Motors Ltd.* (1968), 64 W.W.R. 577 (B.C.S.C.); *General Securities Ltd. v. Parsons* (1955), 14 W.W.R. 424 (B.C.C.A.); *Traders Finance Corp. Ltd. v. Stan Reynolds Auto Sales Ltd.* (1954), 13 W.W.R. (N.S.) 425 (Alta. S.C.(T.D.)); *Battlefords Credit Union Limited v. Korpan Tractor & Parts Ltd.* (1983), 28 Sask. R. 215 (Q.B.).

273 See, for example, *Mackenzie v. Blindman Valley Co-operative Association Ltd.*, [1947] 4 D.L.R. 687 (Alta. S.C.(T.D.)),

agreement that prohibits the transfer.[274] The provision goes on to provide that a transfer of the collateral does not prejudice the rights of the secured party. American commentators have argued that the Article 9 counterpart[275] to this provision will "shield a buyer from liability when a conversion action is predicated solely on his purchase of collateral after a debtor's default."[276] On this view, the buyer only becomes liable if the buyer refuses to deliver the property to the secured party or if the buyer has made it more difficult for the secured party to repossess the goods by transferring them to another party or by removing them to another jurisdiction.[277] The competing view is that the PPSA provision has not altered the substantive law of conversion. On this theory, a sale to a buyer constitutes a conversion because the act of sale itself involves an assertion by the buyer of unencumbered ownership over the property. The buyer will be relieved of liability only if it is clear that the property is being sold to the buyer subject to the secured party's security interest, since the buyer's assertion of dominion will not in this case be inconsistent with the secured party's security interest.

The mere act of seizure by a judgment enforcement creditor or a junior secured party should also not constitute a conversion of the property.[278] The PPSA recognizes that the debtor's interest in the property may be transferred voluntarily or involuntarily. The conduct should only be considered wrongful where the enforcement creditor or junior secured party refuses to surrender the property to the secured party when requested to do so.[279]

2) Restitutionary Claims

As an alternative to an action for conversion, a secured party may bring a restitutionary claim against the wrongdoer for the value of the proceeds obtained by the wrongdoer as a result of the disposition of the collateral.[280]

---

274 PPSA (A, BC, M, NB, NWT, Nu, PEI, S) s. 33; (NL, NS) s. 34; O s. 39; Y s. 32.
275 § 9-311; 1999 Rev. Art. 9, § 9-401.
276 S. Nickles, "Enforcing Article 9 Security Interests Against Subordinate Buyers of Collateral" (1982) 50 Geo. Wash. L. Rev. 511 at 526.
277 *Ibid.* at 529.
278 See *Clow v. Gershman Transport International Ltd.* (2000), 265 A.R. 181 (Q.B.).
279 See D. Frisch, "The Priority Secured Party/Subordinate Lien Creditor Conflict: Is 'Lien-Two' Out in the Cold?" (1984) 33 Buffalo L. Rev. 149; J. Justice, "Secured Parties and Judgment Creditors — The Courts and Section 9-311 of the Uniform Commercial Code" (1975) 30 Bus. Lawyer 433.
280 *Jackson v. Penfold*, [1931] 1 D.L.R. 808 (Ont. S.C.(A.D.)); *Overn v. Strand*, [1931] S.C.R. 720 at 725, Lamont J.; *Canadian Imperial Bank of Commerce v. Royal Bank of Canada* (1982), 19 Man. R. (2d) 67 (Q.B.).

In the past, this was referred to as an action for money had and received upon a waiver of tort, but today it is recognized as a restitutionary claim founded on wrongdoing (restitution for wrongs) as opposed to a restitutionary claim founded on a reversal of the defendant's unjust enrichment. A restitutionary claim is available where the wrongdoing is conversion, and is available to a secured party provided that the secured party has a right to sue for conversion of the property.

A critical difference between a restitutionary claim and a compensatory claim (such as an action for conversion) is that a restitutionary claim measures recovery by the gain received by the defendant rather than by the loss suffered by the plaintiff. The plaintiff may therefore bring a personal action for the value of the sale proceeds received by the defendant without any need to investigate the market value of the goods at the time of the sale. Because the claim is personal and not proprietary, the claim is available even though the proceeds of sale are no longer identifiable or traceable. Of course, the amount recoverable by the secured party may never exceed the amount of the secured obligation. There is one potential limitation to a restitutionary claim. The defendant may attempt to assert the change of position defence. Although it has been held that the defence is not available where the defendant is a wrongdoer,[281] some commentators have argued that a more selective approach should be adopted that would allow a court to consider the nature of the wrongdoing.[282]

The secured party may bring an action for conversion as well as a restitutionary action, but because these are inconsistent remedies, an election between them must ultimately be made. Normally, an election must be made at the time of the judgment.[283]

3) Actions for Recovery of Money

The action for conversion is only available in respect of tangible personal property and is therefore unavailable where the collateral is in the form of intangible personal property such as an account.[284] Where there is

---

281 *Lipkin Gorman (a firm) v. Karpnale* Ltd., [1991] 2 A.C. 548 at 540 (H.L.), Lord Goff.

282 See P. Birks, "Overview: Tracing, Claiming and Defences" in P. Birks, ed., *Laundering and Tracing* (Oxford: Clarendon, 1995) 289 at 324.

283 *United Australia Ltd. v. Barclays Bank Ltd.*, [1941] A.C. 1 (H.L.).

284 *Bank of Montreal v. Tourangeau* (1980), 118 D.L.R. (3d) 293 (Ont. H.C.J.). An action for conversion is available where the collateral is not a pure intangible, but takes the form of a negotiable document such as an instrument or security. See *Arrow Transfer Co. Ltd. v. Royal Bank of Canada* (1971), 19 D.L.R. (3d) 420

a wrongful interference with a secured party's security interest in accounts, the secured party may bring an action to recover the money. As this is a personal remedy, it is not necessary to establish that the property received by the defendant can still be identified or traced. It is sufficient to show that the plaintiff had a proprietary interest in the asset.

The action is most likely to be used by a secured party who has a senior security interest in accounts. The senior creditor may bring a personal action for the recovery of money against a junior secured party who enforces its security interest in the accounts or against a judgment enforcement creditor who garnishes the debts. Although the senior secured party's security interest in accounts or their proceeds will generally be defeated when the debtor uses these funds to pay its creditors, this protection does not apply where payment is coerced through enforcement measures undertaken by the creditor.[285]

FURTHER READINGS

BUCKWOLD, T., "The Treatment of Receivers in the Personal Property Security Acts: Conceptual and Practical Implications" (1997) 29 Can. Bus. L.J. 277

NICKLES, S., "Rights and Remedies between U.C.C. Article 9 Secured Parties with Conflicting Security Interests in Goods" (1983) 68 Iowa L. Rev. 216

ONTARIO LAW REFORM COMMISSION, *Study Paper on Wrongful Interference with Goods* (Toronto: The Commission, 1989)

PACIOCCO, D., "Personal Property Security Act Repossession: The Risk and the Remedy," in M.A. Springman & E. Gertner, eds., *Debtor-Creditor Law: Practice and Doctrine* (Toronto: Butterworths, 1984) at 365

WOOD, R.J., "Enforcement Remedies of Creditors" (1996) 34 Alberta L. Rev. 783

ZIEGEL, J.S., "The Enforcement of Demand Debentures — Continuing Uncertainties" (1990) 69 Can. Bar Rev. 718

(B.C.C.A.), aff'd (1972), 27 D.L.R. (3d) 81 (S.C.C.). The same should also hold true in respect of chattel paper and negotiable documents of title.
285 *Canadian Western Bank v. Gescan Ltd.* (1991), 82 Alta. L.R. (2d) 366 (Q.B.).

CHAPTER 14

NATIONAL AND INTERNATIONAL SECURITY INTERESTS

The impact of federal bankruptcy and insolvency law on PPSA security interests is discussed in chapter 11 of this book. Several additional statutes of the Parliament of Canada regulate security interests in personal property. In some cases, the statute essentially provides for a secured transactions regime that governs certain types of assets or certain types of lenders. The federal *Bank Act*[1] makes it possible for certain kinds of debtors to grant security in certain classes of assets to a bank. The *Canada Shipping Act*[2] provides a regime governing ship mortgages. In such cases, competitions may arise between a provincial PPSA security interest and a federal security interest taken in the same asset. In other cases, the federal statute regulating the security interest is less pervasive in scope. Rather than creating a separate and distinct federal secured-transactions regime, the federal statute provides an additional rule that has the effect of pre-empting the otherwise applicable provincial law. This is the approach taken in several of the intellectual property statutes as well as in the provisions of the *Canada Transportation Act*[3] relating to security interests in railway assets and rolling stock.

Over the last two decades, there has been increased international activity in the field of secured transactions law. Canada is close to ratifying and implementing an international convention that creates

---

1   S.C. 1991, c. 46.
2   R.S.C. 1985, c. S-9 [CSA].
3   S.C. 1996, c. 10.

an international regime within which secured financing and leasing of large aircraft will occur. The major features of this regime will also be examined in this chapter. Chapter 1 gives a brief introduction to several other recent international initiatives, notably the *United Nations Convention on the Assignment of Receivables in International Trade* (2001) and the *Hague Convention on the Law Applicable to Certain Rights in respect of Securities Held with an Intermediary* (2002).

A. *BANK ACT* SECURITY

A separate federal system of secured transactions law is set out in sections 427 to 429 of the *Bank Act* (the provisions are frequently renumbered upon revision of the *Bank Act*, and the security is referred to as section 88 security or section 178 security in the older cases). Although the *Bank Act* security regime was one of the first Canadian chattel security statutes to facilitate inventory financing, it is increasingly showing signs of obsolescence. Banks are not limited to the *Bank Act* security. Banks may choose to take provincial (PPSA) security interests to secure their loans or they may take *Bank Act* security. They may also take both federal and provincial security interests to secure the same obligation. Unfortunately, the co-existence of two separate security systems premised on fundamentally different principles gives rise to difficult issues of scope and priority.

1) Availability of the Security

The availability of the *Bank Act* security is restricted in two ways. First, only banks may take the security. Other lenders such as credit unions and trust companies cannot take *Bank Act* security, and therefore their security interests will be governed solely by the PPSA. The second limitation is that only certain categories of debtors may grant the security, and only certain classes of goods can be taken as collateral. The major categories are summarized as follows:

1. wholesale or retail purchasers, shippers or dealers in products of agriculture, products of aquaculture, products of the forest, products of the quarry and mine, products of the sea, lakes, and river, or goods, wares, and merchandise on the security of such products or goods;[4]

---

4   Above note 1, s. 427(1)(a).

2. manufacturers on the security of the goods produced or goods pro-
    cured for the production or packing of the manufactured goods;[5]
3. farmers on the security of crops, agricultural equipment, agricul-
    tural implements;[6]
4. farmers or other persons engaged in livestock raising on the secur-
    ity of feed or livestock;[7]
5. fishers on the security of fishing vessels, fishing equipmentf or
    products of the sea;[8]
6. forestry producers on the security of fertilizer, pesticide, forestry
    equipment, forestry implements, or products of the forest;[9] and
7. aquaculturists on the security of aquaculture stock, aquacultural
    equipment, or aquacultural implements.[10]

The *Bank Act* provides a definition for most of the classes of debtors
(such as "manufacturer") and the classes of collateral (such as "agricultural equipment").[11] Although these definitions are comprehensive in
scope, there may still be a few cases in which the debtor or the collateral
falls outside the permitted categories. These restrictions prevent *Bank
Act* security from being used in many cases. *Bank Act* security cannot
be used to secure consumer loans (for example, a loan to a consumer
on the security of her automobile). Nor can it be used to take a security interest in many kinds of equipment (for example, the ovens of a
bakery or the computers and cash registers of a retail seller).[12] Furthermore, *Bank Act* security does not cover intangible personal property
(although the question of accounts produced by the sale of collateral
subject to *Bank Act* security requires separate consideration).[13]

2) The Security Agreement

In order to create a valid *Bank Act* security, it is necessary for the debtor
to deliver a security agreement to the bank.[14] As delivery of the security agreement is a precondition to the validity of the security, it is
not possible for a bank to claim rights under the *Bank Act* regime in

---

5   *Ibid.*, s. 427(1)(b).
6   *Ibid.*, s. 427(1)(d),(f),(j),(l), and (n).
7   *Ibid.*, s. 427(1)(h).
8   *Ibid.*, s. 427(1)(o).
9   *Ibid.*, s. 427(1)(p).
10 *Ibid.*, s. 427(1)(c),(e),(g),(i),(k), and (m).
11 *Ibid.*, s. 425.
12 *Waldron v. Royal Bank of Canada* (1991), 78 D.L.R. (4th) 1 (B.C.C.A.).
13 See A.7.d "Bank Act Security and Proceeds."
14 *Bank Act*, above note 1, s. 427(2),

respect of an oral security agreement. The form of security agreement is prescribed by regulation.[15] It provides that the collateral must be described and its location specified. It is not essential that a bank use this prescribed form so long as the document that is used is of like effect.[16]

A bank may take a *Bank Act* security to secure a revolving line of credit. The *Bank Act* provides that if a written promise to give security is executed, the security agreement may secure loans or advances made before, at the time of or after the acquisition of the security.[17] In the absence of a written promise to give security, the *Bank Act* security only secures loans or advances made at the time the security is acquired. However, courts have undercut this requirement by giving effect to a new advance that is used to pay out a previously unsecured loan.[18]

3) The Rights Obtained by the Bank

Section 427(2) of the *Bank Act* has two functions: (1) it identifies the property to which the security interest attaches; and (2) it describes the nature of the bank's security interest in that property. Section 427(2) provides that the security interest does not attach until delivery of the security document to the bank. Section 427(2)(a) provides that the *Bank Act* security attaches to property which is owned by the debtor. The security will therefore not attach if the debtor is merely a bailee or lessee.[19] Section 427(2)(b) provides that the security attaches to after-acquired property once the debtor acquires ownership of it.

Upon acquiring its interest in the collateral, the *Bank Act* provides that the bank obtains the same rights as if it had acquired a bill of lading or warehouse receipt in which such property was described.[20] This obscurely worded provision is sufficient to vest in the bank the right and title that the debtor has in the collateral. Where the collateral is affixed to land or is a growing crop, the bank obtains a "first and preferential lien."[21] This presumably gives the bank priority to the crop or fixtures over a prior real property interest.

---

15 *Registration of Bank Special Security Regulations*, SOR/92-301 as amended SOR/94-367 and SOR/95-171.

16 *Royal Bank of Canada v. Mackenzie*, [1932] S.C.R. 524.

17 *Bank Act*, above note 1, s. 429(1).

18 *Canadian Imperial Bank of Commerce v. Fletcher* (1978), 82 D.L.R. (3d) 257.

19 *Port Royal Pulp & Paper Co. Ltd. v. Royal Bank of Canada*, [1941] 4 D.L.R. 1 (J.C.P.C.); *Barry v. Bank of Ottawa* (1908), 17 O.L.R. 83 (H.C.J.).

20 *Bank Act*, above note 1, s. 427(2)(c).

21 *Ibid.*, s. 427(2)(d).

4) Registration

Bank Act security is subject to a registration requirement. A notice of intention must be registered in the office of the Bank of Canada[22] in the province or territory of the debtor's principal place of business (which may be a different jurisdiction than the one where the goods are located). The notice of intention sets out the name of the debtor and the name of the secured party and must be signed by the debtor. It does not contain a description of the collateral. This information must be obtained from the secured party. The *Bank Act* does not contain a disclosure requirement similar to that contained in the PPSA that requires a secured creditor to disclose this information. The notice of intention is cancelled after five years, but can be renewed on an annual basis.[23] The notice of intention can also be cancelled by registering a certificate of release.[24] Cancellation of the notice of intention does not simply result in subordination of the bank's security. It operates as a full release of the security and therefore results in the termination of the security even as against the debtor.[25]

The rights and powers of a bank are void as against creditors of the debtor and against subsequent purchasers or mortgagees in good faith unless a notice of intention is registered not more than three years immediately before the security was given.[26] A failure to register a notice of intention before the security is given cannot be cured by late registration.[27]

Registration does not confer any positive priority status; it simply protects the bank from subordination to creditors and subsequent purchasers or mortgagees. This point is illustrated in the following scenario.

Bank A registers a notice of intention on May 1. Bank B registers a notice of intention on May 15 and obtains a security agreement from the debtor on May 18. On May 21, Bank A obtains a security agreement from the debtor granting security in the same collateral.

Bank B obtains priority over Bank A. The fact that Bank A was the first to register is irrelevant. Bank B was the first to take security and therefore obtained all the right and title of the debtor on May 18.

---

22   *Ibid.*, s. 427(4) and (5).
23   *Registration of Bank Special Security Regulations*, above note 15, s. 7(1).
24   *Bank Act*, above note 1, s. 427(4)(b); *Registration of Bank Special Security Regulations, ibid.*, ss. 4–5.
25   *Re Weiss Air Sales Ltd.* (1982), 134 D.L.R. (3d) 706 (Ont. H.C.J.).
26   *Bank Act*, above note 1, s. 427(4)(a).
27   *Canadian Imperial Bank of Commerce v. Crockett's Western Wear*, [1984] 5 W.W.R. 282 (Alta. C.A.).

5) Fixtures

The *Bank Act* creates special rules governing fixtures. The bank's rights subsist, notwithstanding that the collateral is affixed to real property,[28] and the bank has the right to remove the fixture.[29] The bank does not obtain priority over a real property interest that is acquired after the goods become fixtures unless a caveat or notice is registered in the land titles or land registry office for the locality in which the land is located.[30] The fixtures provisions are a primitive version of the fixtures provisions contained in the PPSA. They are less comprehensive than the PPSA fixtures provisions in that a number of important issues are not addressed. For example, it is not clear whether a prior real property mortgage-holder who makes an advance after the goods become fixtures is within the class of persons who have priority if a caveat or notice is not registered.

6) Fishing Vessels

A security that has been given to a bank pursuant to section 427 of the *Bank Act* on a fishing vessel that is recorded or registered under the *Canada Shipping Act* does not have priority over rights that are subsequently acquired in the vessel unless a copy of the security document has been previously recorded or registered under the *Canada Shipping Act*.[31] Accordingly, a bank that takes a security interest in a fishing vessel must register in both the *Bank Act* registry and the *Canada Shipping Act* registry to fully protect its interest.

7) Resolution of Priority Competitions with PPSA Security Interests

In most jurisdictions, the PPSA excludes security devices taken under the *Bank Act* from its scope.[32] In these jurisdictions, the priority rules of the PPSA do not apply, and a priority competition between a *Bank Act* security and a PPSA security interest is resolved by applying the provisions of the *Bank Act*. If the *Bank Act* is silent, then the issue will be resolved by applying the property law principles of the common law.

---

28 *Bank Act*, above note 1, s. 427(2)(d).
29 *Ibid.*, s. 427(3).
30 *Ibid.*, s. 428(3).
31 *Ibid.*, s. 428(5).
32 PPSA (A, BC, M, NB) s. 4; (NWT, Nu) s. 3; (NL, NS) s. 5; (O, Y) no equivalent provision.

The PPSA in effect in Ontario and the Yukon does not exclude *Bank Act* security from the scope of the legislation. In these two jurisdictions, the resolution of priority competitions is more complex. In the first instance, it is necessary to resolve a priority competition between a PPSA security interest and a *Bank Act* security through precisely the same analysis that is used in the other jurisdictions. However, a bank that holds a *Bank Act* security may then argue that it may take advantage of the PPSA priority rules to give it a priority it would not otherwise obtain.

The discussion will begin with an examination of the general principles that are used to resolve priority competitions between PPSA security interests and *Bank Act* security. This analysis is applicable to all PPSA jurisdictions. It will then examine attempts by banks to invoke PPSA priority rules to enhance the priority status of their *Bank Act* security. This analysis is applicable only in Ontario and the Yukon, since these jurisdictions do not expressly provide for the non-application of the PPSA to *Bank Act* security.

a)   The *Bank Act* Priority Provisions

The *Bank Act* contains a set of rules that establish a priority system. The Act provides that a bank obtains the same rights as if it had obtained a warehouse receipt or bill of lading that described the property. The effect of this provision is that a bank takes the debtor's property subject to any pre-existing interest held by a third party. This means that a prior PPSA security interest will have priority over a subsequent *Bank Act* security.[33] This holds true even if the prior PPSA security interest was not perfected.[34] There is nothing in the *Bank Act* that subordinates a prior PPSA security interest for lack of perfection.

The *Bank Act* also contains a number of provisions that apply where the competition is between a prior *Bank Act* security and a subsequent PPSA security interest. Section 428(1) provides that the bank obtains priority "over all rights subsequently acquired in, on or in respect of that property." Section 427(4) provides for the invalidation of the bank's security interest in the event that it is not registered in the Bank of Canada registry. Thus, a *Bank Act* security will generally obtain priority over a subsequent PPSA security interest so long as the *Bank Act* security is properly registered in the Bank of Canada registry.

---

33   *Agricultural Credit Corp. of Saskatchewan v. Royal Bank of Canada*, [1994] 7 W.W.R. 305 (Sask. C.A.).

34   *Rogerson Lumber Co. v. Four Seasons Chalet Ltd.* (1980), 113 D.L.R. (3d) 671 (Ont. C.A.).

A competition may arise between a PPSA security interest and a *Bank Act* security, both of which cover after-acquired property. Here it is not possible to apply the first-in-time priority rule of the *Bank Act*, since both security interests will attach to the new asset the moment the debtor acquires rights in it. The Saskatchewan Court of Appeal held that priority should be given to the creditor who first obtained a security agreement[35]

A competition may also arise between a prior *Bank Act* security and a subsequent PPSA security interest in the form of a purchase money security interest. The special priority rules of the PPSA that give an enhanced priority status to purchase money security interests are inapplicable. Instead, the *Bank Act* priority rules and traditional property law concepts are used to resolve the priority competition. If a PPSA security interest is taken by a seller under a contract providing that the seller retains title to the collateral, the *Bank Act* security interest will be subordinate to it. A *Bank Act* security interest gives the bank whatever right and title the debtor has in the property. The debtor obtains the property subject to the seller's title (security interest), and therefore the bank also takes subject to this interest.[36]

A competition may also arise between a *Bank Act* security and a purchase money security interest given to a lender. In *Royal Bank of Canada v. Moosomin Credit Union*,[37] the Saskatchewan Court of Appeal concluded that the bank has priority in this situation. The court held that the bank's *Bank Act* security was first-in-time and therefore it was entitled to priority. The case is not authority for the proposition that a *Bank Act* security will always have priority over a subsequent purchase money security interest taken by a lender. The facts of the case were that the debtor bought a truck on 12 August 1998 and obtained financing from a credit union on 20 August 1998. There can be no doubt that the bank's *Bank Act* security attached to the truck before that of the credit union. This fact pattern should be distinguished from cases where the financer of the asset has entered into a security agreement with the debtor before the debtor acquires the new asset. If there is a pre-existing agreement for the creation of a purchase money charge, the charge binds the property the moment the debtor acquires an interest in it. The purchase money financer therefore has priority over

35 *Bank of Montreal v. Pulsar Ventures Inc.*, [1988] 1 W.W.R. 250 (Sask. C.A.); *Agricultural Credit Corp. of Saskatchewan v. Royal Bank of Canada*, above note 33.
36 *Bank of Montreal v. Pulsar Ventures*, ibid.; *Agricultural Credit Corp. of Saskatchewan v. Royal Bank of Canada*, ibid.
37 [2004] 5 W.W.R. 494 (Sask. C.A.).

the secured party who claims it pursuant to an after-acquired property clause contained in a prior security agreement.[38]

A dispute may also arise between a bank with a *Bank Act* security that covers after-acquired crops or livestock and a subsequent lender who has provided financing to the debtor to permit the debtor to acquire agricultural inputs (such as fertilizer or feed) that permit the debtor to produce the crops or livestock. Although the PPSA contains priority rules that give the agricultural input supplier a superpriority, the PPSA priority rules do not govern a competition with a *Bank Act* security. Again, the matter is to be determined by applying the *Bank Act* and traditional property law principles. It is arguable that an input supplier who supplies credit pursuant to a pre-existing agreement should be afforded the same priority as a charge taken by a purchase money lender on the basis that financing that permits the creation of a thing should be afforded the same position as financing the permits the acquisition of a thing.[39] On the other hand, a Saskatchewan court has held that the bank should be given priority over the agricultural input supplier.[40]

b) Application of the PPSA Priority Rules

A bank that holds *Bank Act* security may attempt to invoke the priority rules of the PPSA in order to give it priority over a PPSA security interest. Banks have sometimes adopted the practice of registering a financing statement in the personal property registry in the hope that they would be able to invoke the PPSA priority rules. In most jurisdictions, an attempt to invoke the PPSA priority rules will be wholly ineffective. The PPSA excludes *Bank Act* security from its scope. Therefore, the general priority rule that ordinarily governs competitions between two competing security interests will not apply.[41] Although the PPSA contains a priority rule

---

38   *Abbey National Building Society v. Cann*, [1991] 1 A.C. 56 (H.L.). There is still some uncertainty under English law on whether it is essential that there be an agreement to grant the charge prior to the execution of the charge in favour of the purchase money lender. See R.M. Goode, *Commercial Law*, 2d ed. (London: Penguin, 1995) at 723–25.

39   *Abbey National Building Society v. Cann*, ibid.

40   *Royal Bank of Canada v. United Grain Growers Ltd.*, [2001] 6 W.W.R. 664 (Sask. Q.B.), aff'd [2001] 6 W.W.R. 677 (Sask. C.A.), leave to appeal to S.C.C. dismissed, [2001] S.C.C.A. No. 271. In this case, a lender who supplied seed potatoes was subordinate to a prior bank that held *Bank Act* security.

41   See *Agricultural Credit Corp. of Saskatchewan v. Royal Bank of Canada*, above note 33.

that subordinates an unperfected security interest to transferees for value and without knowledge, this does not apply where the transaction secures payment or performance of an obligation.[42]

Unlike the PPSA in other jurisdictions, the legislation in Ontario and the Yukon does not expressly exclude *Bank Act* security from its scope. In *Bank of Nova Scotia v. International Harvester Credit Corporation of Canada Ltd.*,[43] the Ontario Court of Appeal held that a *Bank Act* security is a security interest under the Ontario PPSA.[44] The Court indicated that the bank could potentially obtain the benefit of the priority rules of the *Bank Act* as well as the benefit of the priority rules of the PPSA. On this theory, if the bank failed to register its *Bank Act* security in the *Bank Act* registry, it nevertheless could obtain priority over a subsequent PPSA security interest if the security interest was perfected under the PPSA.

Houlden J.A. gave the example of a bank which failed to register the security in the *Bank Act* registry. He indicated that the bank would nevertheless be able to obtain priority under the PPSA if it perfected its security interest by possession. The decision appears to permit the bank to pick the most favourable features of both statutes. The case is therefore problematic in two respects. First, it seems to violate the doctrine of federal paramountcy. The *Bank Act* contains an express priority rule that provides that the security is void if it is not registered. The provincial statute provides a priority rule that would nevertheless give priority to the *Bank Act* security. This would seem to constitute an operational conflict between the legislative provisions.[45] Second, there is nothing in the Ontario PPSA that supports the Court's view that a secured party has the power to opt in or opt out of its provisions. It is

---

42 PPSA (A, BC, S, M, NB, NWT, Nu, O) s. 20; (NL, NS) s. 21; Y s. 19.
43 (1990), 74 O.R. (2d) 738 (Ont. C.A.). In reaching this conclusion the court appears to have given inadequate recognition to its own judgment in *Rogerson Lumber Co. v. Four Seasons Chalet*, above note 34. For a fuller analysis of the case, see R. Cuming, "PPSA — Section 178 *Bank Act* Overlap — No Closer to Solutions" (1991) 18 Can. Bus. L.J. 135 and J.S. Ziegel, "The Interaction of Section 178 Security Interests and Provincial PPSA Security Interests: Once More into the Black Hole" (1991) 6 B.F.L.R. 323; R. Wood, "The Nature and Definition of Federal Security Interests" (2000) 34 Can. Bus. L.J. 65.
44 *Bank of Nova Scotia v. International Harvester Corporation of Canada Ltd*, ibid. at 750. See also *Bank of Montreal v. Pulsar Ventures Inc.*, above note 35, and *Birch Hills Credit Union v. Canadian Imperial Bank of Commerce* (1988), 52 D.L.R. (4th) 113 (Sask. C.A.). The Saskatchewan PPSA was later amended to make it clear that *Bank Act* security is not brought within the scope of the PPSA.
45 See *Bank of Montreal v. Hall*, [1990] 1 S.C.R. 121 at 150–55.

not a question of an election between the two regimes. If the security interest that is created by the security document is governed by the PPSA, then all the priority and enforcement rules of the PPSA should, in principle, apply to it. Their application should be limited only to the extent that they are constitutionally impaired by the application of the federal paramountcy doctrine.

The priority competition in *Bank of Nova Scotia v. International Harvester Corporation of Canada Ltd.* was between an unperfected PPSA security interest and a subsequent *Bank Act* security given to a bank and registered in the Bank of Canada registry. The bank had also registered its security interest in the Personal Property Registry. The bank wished to assert the PPSA priority rule that gives a perfected security interest priority over an unperfected security interest. The availability of the PPSA priority rules did not ultimately benefit the bank on the facts of this case. Normally, a perfected PPSA security interest would take priority over an unperfected security interest. However, this priority rule is subject to the more general principle that a security interest is effective according to its terms. The Court held that the *Bank Act* security document that was used by the bank did not purport to give the bank anything other than the interest that the debtor had in the collateral. Although most PPSA security agreements would not produce this result, the *Bank Act* security document contained this limitation and precluded it from obtaining priority over a prior unperfected security interest under the PPSA. Although *Bank Act* security holders in Ontario may be able to take the benefit of PPSA priority rules, this will not give them any priority over prior unperfected PPSA security interests.

c)   Double Documentation and Election

Sometimes banks will take both a *Bank Act* security and a PPSA security interest on the same collateral to secure the same obligation. The goal of banks that adopt this practice is to be in a position to take advantage of either or both the PPSA (so as to have priority over a prior unperfected PPSA security interest) and section 427 of the *Bank Act*, as the circumstances warrant. The approach allows the bank to avoid some of the limitations of the *Bank Act* and to circumvent public policy choices of Parliament contained in the Act through reliance on its provincial security interest.[46] To date, the courts have failed to address

---

46   See, for example, *Kassian v. National Bank* (1998), 4 C.B.R. (4th) 295 (Alta. Q.B.), aff'd (1999), 10 C.B.R. (4th) 20 (Alta. C.A.) in which the court concluded that the special priority given to unpaid employees of a debtor under section 427(7) of the *Bank Act* does not apply when the bank took both a *Bank Act*

the anomaly of having two systems of law apply to the same transaction and the applicability in this context of the principle of election.[47] Only one provincial legislature has addressed this anomaly. Section 9(2) of the Saskatchewan PPSA provides that a security interest in collateral ceases to be valid with respect to that collateral to the extent that and for so long as the security interest secures payment or performance of an obligation that is also secured by a security in favour of the secured party created under the *Bank Act*. The restriction does not apply to a security interest that secures payment or performance owing to a person who is not a party to the security agreement between the debtor and the bank holding the section 427 security.

d) *Bank Act* Security and Proceeds

Unlike the PPSA, the *Bank Act* does not expressly provide that the security interest in collateral extends to any proceeds obtained by the debtor upon a disposition of the collateral. Banks typically include in their security agreements a trust proceeds clause that requires the debtor to hold the proceeds in trust for the bank. If the claim to proceeds is founded upon the contractual agreement to hold the property in trust, then it can be argued that it falls within the definition of a security interest and is governed by the PPSA. In other words, if the bank's interest in the proceeds arises by virtue of an agreement, it is the agreement and not the *Bank Act* that creates the interest in the proceeds. This would mean that it would be necessary to register under the PPSA in order to obtain priority over the debtor's trustee in bankruptcy in respect of any proceeds. If, however, the interest in the proceeds arises by operation of law, then the PPSA would not govern the interest in the proceeds.

Unfortunately, there is great uncertainty in the law at present concerning the legal basis or the priority of the bank's claims to proceeds. Some of the cases seem to suggest that the bank becomes the legal owner of the proceeds. This theory is premised on the view that the *Bank Act* gives the bank legal ownership of the collateral and that the debtor deals with the property merely as agent for the owner.[48] Even where this view is accepted, there appears to be a difference in opinion

---

security and a provincial security interest but relied on the provincial security interest when the debtor failed to repay the bank.

47   See R. Cuming and R. Wood, "Compatibility of Federal and Provincial Personal Property Security Law" (1986) 65 Can. Bar Rev. 267 at 287–92.

48   See *Goodfallow, Traders' Bank v. Goodfallow (Re)* (1890), 19 O.R. 299 (H.C.J. (Ch. D)).

concerning the nature and status of the bank's claim to the proceeds. In one decision, the court concluded that "the proceeds are subject to the same statutory interest and priority under the *Bank Act* as is the original collateral itself."[49] In another, the court concluded that the debtor held the proceeds in trust for the bank.[50] There is a significant difference between these two views. In the former case, the bank could assert its legal title to the proceeds as against competing third parties who subsequently obtained an interest in the proceeds. In the latter case, the bank would have merely an equitable interest that would be defeated by a *bona fide* purchaser for value and without notice who acquired a legal interest in the proceeds. Other cases seem to base the claim on the agreement between the bank and its customer under which the customer agrees to hold the proceeds in trust for the bank.[51] On this view, it can be argued that the parties have created a security interest in the proceeds by virtue of an agreement and that it therefore falls within the scope of the PPSA. Because of this uncertainty, the authors are unable to make any prediction as to outcome where there is a priority competition that involves proceeds.

8) Other Priority Competitions

A holder of a *Bank Act* security will generally have priority over a subsequent buyer, since section 428(1) gives the bank priority over any subsequently created interest.[52] This general principle is modified where the bank has expressly or impliedly authorized the debtor to sell the goods.[53]

The *Bank Act* also contains an obscure provision that subordinates an unpaid vendor who has a lien on the goods to the bank if the bank acquired its interest without knowledge of the lien.[54] The provision does not apply to consensually created security interests, but only applies to the lien of a seller in possession and the seller's right of stoppage in

---

49   *Royal Bank of Canada v. United Grain Growers Ltd.* above note 40 at para. 33 (Sask. Q.B.).

50   *Re Richmac Interiors Ltd.* (1996), 38 Alta. L.R. (3d) 38 (Q.B.) at 50.

51   *Flintoft v. Royal Bank of Canada,* [1964] S.C.R. 631 at 634–35. And see Cuming and Wood, above note 47 at 292–301.

52   *Toronto-Dominion Bank v. Dearborn Motors Ltd.* (1968), 64 W.W.R. 577 (B.C.S.C.).

53   *Hurly v. Bank of Nova Scotia,* [1966] S.C.R. 83; *Indian Head Trading Co. v. Royal Bank of Canada,* [1976] 5 W.W.R. 583 (B.C.C.A.).

54   *Bank Act,* above note 1, s. 428(2).

transit conferred by provincial sales of goods legislation.[55] Finally, the *Bank Act* contains a unique priority provision that subordinates the bank to certain kinds of unsecured creditors. Unpaid wage claimants as well as growers or producers of agricultural products that are owed money by manufacturers are given priority over the bank.[56]

9) Enforcement

The *Bank Act* contains the following set of enforcement provisions:

1. The bank has a statutory right to seize the collateral, to care for it and to enter and remove it from any land to which it has become affixed.[57] These statutory rights only arise in connection with loans referred to in section 427(1)(c) to (p) (that is, they do not cover inventory held by a wholesaler, retailer or manufacturer under section 427(1)(a) or (b)). The statutory right of seizure is available only upon the occurrence of one of six events of default. It is expressed to be in addition to any other rights or powers given to the bank.

2. The bank has a statutory power of sale in the event of non-payment of a debt, liability, loan, or advance. This power of sale must be by public auction, unless the debtor "has agreed to the sale of the property otherwise than as herein provided" or if the collateral is perishable.[58]

3. A buyer of the goods who acquires them pursuant to the exercise by the bank of the statutory power of sale acquires all right and title enjoyed by the bank.[59]

4. In exercising the statutory power of sale, the bank is required to act honestly and in good faith and must give the debtor reasonable notice unless the goods are perishable and to do so would result in a substantial reduction in the value of the property.[60]

5. Where a statutory power of sale is exercised, the bank must as soon as reasonably practical sell the property.[61]

---

55 See B. Crawford and J.D. Falconbridge, *Banking and Bills of Exchange*, 8th ed., vol. 1, (Toronto: Canada Law Book, 1986) at 446–48; J.S. Ziegel, "Interaction of Provincial Personal Property Security Legislation and Security Interests under the *Bank Act*" (1986–87) 12 Can. Bus. L.J. 73 at 84–8; Cuming and Wood, above note 47 at 273–74.

56 *Bank Act*, above note 1, s. 427(7)–(8).

57 *Ibid.*, s. 428(3).

58 *Ibid.*, s. 428(8).

59 *Ibid.*, s. 428(9).

60 *Ibid.*, s. 428(10).

61 *Ibid.*, s. 428(11).

This enforcement scheme contains some gaps. For example, it does not provide a statutory right of seizure where the goods are inventory of a wholesaler, retailer, or manufacturer. The PPSA in jurisdictions other than Ontario and the Yukon excludes *Bank Act* security from its scope. In these jurisdictions, a bank cannot resort to Part 5 of the PPSA as a source of additional rights or remedies. Instead, the right to take possession of the goods on default must be derived from a contractual right contained in the security document. The loan documents used by banks typically give the bank the right to take possession of the goods and the right to appoint a receiver or an agent for the purpose of disposing of the property. The Supreme Court of Canada in *National Bank of Canada v. Atomic Slipper Co. Ltd*[62] held that section 178(3) (the former numbering for what is now section 428) merely confers additional rights on a bank and that a bank is entitled to rely on a contractual right to take possession of the collateral in cases where the statutory right does not operate. The common law permitted the exercise of a contractual right of seizure so long as it did not involve a breach of the peace. Accordingly, a contractual right of seizure contained in the security document would give a bank the right to take possession of the collateral in those cases where the statutory power to seize is not available.

Alone among the common law provinces, Alberta restricts the exercise of the self-help remedy of recaption and requires that the seizure be undertaken by a civil enforcement agency. The Alberta legislation does not contain a limitation that would prevent it from applying to a *Bank Act* security interest. Where the collateral is goods covered by section 427(1)(a) or (b), the bank does not have a statutory right to seize the collateral and must rely on its contractual right to seize. In such cases, there is nothing that would prevent the provincial legislation from applying. However, a bank that is exercising a statutory right of seizure under section 427(3) in respect of any of the other classes of goods would probably not need to comply with the Alberta statute because the paramountcy doctrine likely renders the provincial statute inoperative.[63]

The position in Ontario and the Yukon differs because the PPSA in those jurisdictions does not contain a provision that excludes *Bank Act* security from the application of the Act. As a result, the provisions of Part 5 of the PPSA will govern in the event that the *Bank Act* does not provide an enforcement rule. The PPSA would provide the applicable enforcement rules governing a seizure of inventory covered by section

---

62   (1991), 80 D.L.R. (4th) 134.
63   *Bank of Montreal v. Hall*, above note 45.

427(1)(a) or (b). In many other instances, the *Bank Act* and the PPSA both provide enforcement rules that could apply. For example, both the PPSA and the *Bank Act* give the secured party a statutory right to sell the collateral. Here, the issue is whether a bank is required to comply with the PPSA provisions in the conduct of the sale when conducting a sale pursuant to enforcement rules contained in the *Bank Act*. Both the PPSA and the *Bank Act* provide for pre-sale notification, but the PPSA notice is more extensive in terms of the information that is required and it must be given to parties in addition to the debtor. The application of the provincial statute would likely not be constitutionally limited by the doctrine of paramountcy. There appears to be no operational conflict, since it is possible for the bank to comply with both notice requirements.

A bank holding *Bank Act* security might also attempt to use the PPSA as a source of additional enforcement remedies. For example, the PPSA gives a secured party a right to retain the collateral in satisfaction of the obligation secured. Although there is no *Bank Act* counterpart to this remedy, section 428(11) provides that a bank that exercises its statutory right of seizure under section 427(3) must sell the collateral as soon as reasonably practical. This would preclude the exercise of the retention of collateral option whenever the bank exercised its statutory right of seizure under section 427(3).

10) Reform of the *Bank Act* Security Provisions?

There are a number of different problems associated with the current *Bank Act* security provisions.[64] The first arises because of the obsolete concepts and archaic terms that are used in the legislation. This has produced many interpretive difficulties for lawyers and courts. The second problem is the legal uncertainty that exists when attempting to resolve priority competitions between a provincial security interest and *Bank Act* security. The third problem concerns the co-existence of two registry systems and the added costs that are generated because searching parties are required to conduct searches in more than one registry. The fourth problem is that banks that hold *Bank Act* security are insulated from provincial legislation, such as farm protection legislation, that would otherwise be of general application within the

---

64   For a more detailed discussion of this topic, see Law Commission of Canada, *Modernizing Canada's Secured Transactions Law: The* Bank Act *Security Provisions* (Ottawa: Law Commission of Canada, 2004).

province.[65] This also produces a non-level playing field by giving an economic advantage to banks that is not conferred on non-bank financial institutions. This has led the Uniform Law Conference of Canada as well as the Law Commission of Canada to recommend the abolition of the *Bank Act* security provisions.[66]

B. SECURITY INTERESTS IN SHIPS

1) *Canada Shipping Act* Ship Mortgages

The *Canada Shipping Act*[67] provides a system for the registration of the ownership of ships. Transfers of ownership are recorded in this registry. Smaller vessels are not required to be registered, although registration is permitted.[68] Ship mortgages are also registerable, although it is not possible to register a ship mortgage unless the ship is registered. The registry also permits the recording of mortgages against ships that are under construction.[69]

The CSA adopts a hybrid that is somewhere between a notice registration system and a document-filing system. The mortgage must be prepared in the proper prescribed statutory form. This single-page document contains only the barest of details concerning the contractual terms of the mortgage. It sets out the following:

1. the official number and name of the ship, its number, time, and date of registration, its place of registration, and a few details concerning its dimensions and tonnage;
2. the name and address of the debtor;
3. the name and address of the secured party;
4. the amount secured by the mortgage; and
5. the signature or other form of execution of the debtor.

The details concerning the terms of the mortgage (the representations, warranties, covenants, events of default, acceleration clauses, and remedy provisions standard in personal property security agreements) are typically included in a collateral loan agreement that is not

---

65   *Bank of Montreal v. Hall*, above note 45.
66   Law Commission of Canada, above note 64. And see the 2003 Civil Section Resolutions of the Uniform Law Conference of Canada: www.ulcc.ca.
67   Above note 2.
68   CSA s. 17 provides for optional registration if the vessel does not exceed 15 tons.
69   CSA s. 37(1).

registered.[70] It is the usual practice for the statutory mortgage to make reference to the collateral loan agreement, but likely a failure to do so is not of any legal significance.

The CSA provides a single, centralized registry system.[71] The unique name and number of registered ships eliminates the similar name problem that arises under other personal property security registration systems. The registrar records the mortgages in the order in which they are produced and assigns a number, time, and date to the registration.[72] Priority between registered ship mortgages is determined on the basis of the order of registration.[73] Although the CSA only purports to deal with priority competitions between registered statutory mortgages, it seems to be accepted that the registered statutory mortgage will also have priority over a prior or subsequent unregistered security interest in the ship.[74] An alteration to the priority ranking is permitted if all mortgagees file their written consent.[75]

The CSA contains further provisions for a discharge of a mortgage[76] and a transfer of a mortgage.[77] The mortgagee is not considered to be the owner by virtue of the mortgage except to the extent necessary to make the ship available as security under the mortgage.[78] Registration of a security agreement not in the form of a statutory mortgage is not permitted. The one exception to this rule is created by section 428(5) of the *Bank Act* which provides for the registration of a section 427 *Bank Act* security covering a fishing vessel in the CSA ship registry.

2) The Relevance of Canadian Maritime Law

The CSA provides only a skeletal framework for the regulation of statutory ship mortgages. Principles of Canadian maritime law are used to

---

70 See J.D. Buchan, *Mortgages of Ships, Marine Security in Canada* (Toronto: Butterworths, 1985) at 33–40 and 209–24. The document is also referred to as a "collateral deed."

71 CSA s. 13(1).

72 CSA s. 37(3).

73 CSA s. 39(1).

74 *Royal Bank of Canada v. 273050 B.C. Ltd.* (1996), 86 D.L.R. (4th) 551 (B.C.S.C.). A competition between a statutory ship mortgage and an invalid *Bank Act* security that might nevertheless be treated as an unregistered equitable mortgage was resolved by the application of the first to register principle contained in the statute.

75 CSA s. 39(2).

76 CSA s. 38.

77 CSA ss. 43–44.

78 CSA s. 40.

602 PERSONAL PROPERTY SECURITY LAW

fill in the gaps in the federal statute. Canadian maritime law is a comprehensive body of federal law dealing with all claims in respect of maritime and admiralty matters. It is uniform throughout Canada and it is not the law of any province.[79]

The CSA ship mortgage provisions create a registry and provide a priority rule for competitions between registered mortgages. The statutory regime is silent on many issues concerning the validity and enforcement of statutory ship mortgages. For example, the legislation does not indicate if the priority obtained by virtue of a prior registration extends to further advances made after the mortgagee knows of an intervening mortgage. Under mortgage law, a legal mortgagee making a further advance without notice that the mortgagor had granted a second mortgage was entitled to tack the advance, thereby giving it the same priority as the original loan. However, if the mortgagee had notice of the intervening mortgagee, the first mortgagee did not obtain priority in respect of the further advance.[80] The fact that the first mortgagee may have been contractually obliged to make the advance did not alter the outcome, but only had the effect of releasing the mortgagee from the obligation to make the further advance.[81] Although the PPSA has altered this rule and has provided that the first to register rule of priority extends to future advances, the CSA draws upon traditional English mortgage law referentially incorporated into Canadian law as Canadian maritime law and not PPSA principles to fill in the gaps in the legislation. Because these traditional property law concepts are a component of Canadian maritime law principles, they will apply equally to a statutory ship mortgage executed in Quebec.

3) Priority Competitions with Provincial Security Interests

If a secured party takes a ship mortgage on a vessel, the PPSA will not apply to the transaction. The PPSA in all jurisdictions except Ontario

---

79 *Ordon Estate v. Grail*, [1998] 3 S.C.R. 437 at 488–91. The judgment is a synthesis of the Court's previous decisions beginning with *ITO International Terminal Operators Ltd. v. Miida Electronics Inc.*, [1986] 1 S.C.R. 752 and followed by *Q.N.S. Paper Co. v. Chartwell Shipping Ltd.*, [1989] 2 S.C.R. 683; *Whitbread v. Walley*, [1990] 3 S.C.R. 1273; *Monk Corp. v. Island Fertilizers Ltd.*, [1991] 1 S.C.R. 779; *Bow Valley Husky (Bermuda) Ltd. v. Saint John Shipbuilding Ltd.*, [1997] 3 S.C.R. 1210; and *Porto Seguro Companhia DeSeguros Gerais v. Belcan S.A.*, [1997] 3 S.C.R. 1278.

80 *Hopkinson v. Rolt* (1861), 9 H.L.C. 514.

81 *West v. Williams*, [1899] 1 Ch. 132 (C.A.).

and the Yukon contains an express provision that excludes ship mortgages from the scope of the Act.[82] Even in the absence of this provision, the PPSA cannot apply to ship mortgages on constitutional grounds.[83] A ship mortgage that is registered under the CSA is governed by the federal law. As a result, registration of the ship mortgage under the PPSA is not necessary to protect it as against a trustee in bankruptcy of the debtor or other competing parties. In the event of default, it is federal law and not the PPSA that will govern the enforcement remedies of the parties. Section 42 of the CSA provides expressly that the mortgage of a ship or a share in a ship is not affected by the bankruptcy of the mortgagor after the date of the registration of the mortgage, and the mortgagee has priority over the other creditors of the bankrupt or any trustee or assignee on their behalf.

Instead of taking a ship mortgage under the federal statute, a secured party may take a PPSA security interest in a ship.[84] This is a somewhat risky practice, since a PPSA security interest will be defeated by a competing creditor who subsequently takes a ship mortgage and registers it in the federal registry. However, the security interest will be effective against other parties, such as judgment enforcement creditors, and the trustee in bankruptcy of the debtor if it is properly perfected under the PPSA. Competitions with other provincial PPSA security interests in the ship will also be governed by the PPSA.

4) Enforcement of the Ship Mortgage

The CSA ship mortgage provisions have very little to say about the enforcement of the statutory ship mortgage. The CSA gives the holder of a registered ship mortgage a statutory power of sale and provides that the power of sale cannot be exercised if there are prior registered mortgagees, unless their consent to the sale is obtained.[85] The principles governing enforcement of a ship mortgage are the traditional common law principles governing mortgages imported into Canadian maritime law.[86]

---

82   In many jurisdictions, the legislation expressly excludes ship mortgages. See PPSA (BC, M, NB, PEI) s. 4; (NWT, Nu) s. 3; (NL, NS) s. 5. In others, the statute provides that the PPSA does not apply to a security agreement that is governed by an Act of Parliament that deals with the rights of the parties to the security agreement or rights of third parties affected by it. See PPSA (A, S) s. 4.

83   *Re Doucet* (1983), 42 O.R. (2d) 638 at 644 (H.C.J.).

84   *Ford v. Petford* (1996), 11 P.P.S.A.C. (2d) 227 (B.C.S.C.).

85   CSA s. 41.

86   See W. Tetley, *Maritime Liens and Claims*, 2d ed. (Montreal: Yvon Blais, 1998) at 483–87 for a discussion of the common law rights of a ship mortgagee.

In addition to the mortgage enforcement remedies, Canadian maritime law gives a mortgagee of a ship the right to enforce its security through an action *in rem* against the ship. The arrest of the ship is an essential component of the *in rem* action. The Federal Court rules set out the framework for the exercise of the right of arrest.[87] The mortgagee may seek an order for sale of the ship. This sale will have the effect of providing the purchaser with title free of maritime liens and other claims in respect of the ship. The proceeds of sale are then distributed in accordance with a priority system that ranks the maritime liens and other *in rem* claims.[88]

As a general rule, ship mortgagees prefer to exercise their enforcement rights through an *in rem* proceeding in the Federal Court. Under Canadian maritime law, a ship mortgage is subordinate to any maritime liens that attach to the vessel whether before or after the mortgage is registered. The risk that such liens have attached means that selling the ship pursuant to the power of sale procedure renders the property less marketable compared to a sale pursuant to the *in rem* procedure available in the Federal Court under which the purchaser acquires clean title to the ship.

C. SECURITY INTERESTS IN INTELLECTUAL PROPERTY

There are six different federal statutes that provide for the creation or regulation of intellectual property rights in Canada. These statutes cover patents, copyrights, trademarks, plant breeder's rights, industrial designs, and integrated circuit topographies. Unlike the *Bank Act* security provisions or the ship mortgage provisions of the *Canada Shipping Act*, these statutes do not create a legal regime governing security interests in such property. The statutes provide a system for registration of assignments of these federal intellectual property rights. Three of the statutes — the *Trade-marks Act*, the *Industrial Design Act*, and the *Integrated Circuit Topography Act* — are merely permissive. Registration is not a required in order to render the assignment effective against third parties. A failure to register an assignment will therefore be of no significance in the resolution of priorities, which will be governed by the ordinary priority rules of the PPSA.

---

87   SOR/98-106, Rules 475–95.
88   See *Scott Steel Ltd. v. The Alarissa*, [1996] 2 F.C. 883 at 893, aff'd (1997), 125 F.T.R. 284. And see W. Tetley, above note 86 at 890–91.

The other three statutes — the *Patent Act*, the *Copyright Act*, and the *Plant Breeders' Rights Act* — not only create a registry system, but also specify the consequences of non-compliance with the registration requirements. These statutes provide that an assignment of an intellectual property right is void against any subsequent assignee for value and without knowledge. There is fundamental uncertainty over the operation of these avoidance provisions in respect of security interests in intellectual property. First, it is not clear whether these provisions apply at all to secured transactions. Under the common law, an assignment could include a transfer by way of security as well as an absolute transfer of an asset. This suggests that the term is wide enough to include a security assignment.[89] On the other hand, it can be argued that a PPSA security interest is best characterized as a legal charge, which does not involve the conveyance of title to the secured party.[90] If this argument is accepted, then a security interest would not fall within the definition of an assignment and the PPSA would govern all aspects of the security interest in the intellectual property right.[91] Alternatively, a court might conclude that the application of the federal avoidance provisions applies only to security documents that purport to transfer legal title to the secured party by way of security. If the security document merely purports to grant to the secured party a security interest or charge, the transaction would not be governed by the federal avoidance provisions.

If one concludes that the voidable assignment provisions of the intellectual property statutes apply to security interests in intellectual property, then it is likely that priority competitions involving patents, copyrights, and plant breeders' rights will be governed by the concur-

---

89   See *Colpitts v. Sherwood*, [1927] 3 D.L.R. 7 (Alta. C.A.). This pre-PPSA decision appears to assume that an assignment by way of security would fall within the federal avoidance provision.

90   Courts have recognized that the PPSA has redefined traditional property law concepts. The PPSA adopts a unitary concept of a security interest which no longer depends upon the form of the transaction or the locus of title. See *Re Giffen*, [1998] 1 S.C.R. 91.

91   The PPSA in jurisdictions other than Ontario and the Yukon exclude from its scope a security agreement governed by an Act of the Parliament of Canada that deals with the rights of third parties affected by a security interest. This analysis proceeds on the assumption that this provision was designed to exclude federal statutes that create a comprehensive legal regime such as the *Bank Act* security provisions or the *Canada Shipping Act, 2001* ship mortgage provisions, and that the PPSA is not rendered inapplicable by the inclusion of an isolated priority rule (the voidable grant provision) in the federal intellectual property statutes. See also chapter 2, F.2 "Security Interests Arising under Federal Law."

rent operation of both the provincial and federal provisions. Perfection of a security interest in such assets under the PPSA will be necessary to protect the security interest as against the trustee in bankruptcy and judgment enforcement creditors. This will be the case whether or not the secured party has registered the security interest in the federal intellectual property registry. However, registration under the PPSA alone carries a risk. A failure to register the security interest in the federal intellectual property registry will result in subordination of the security interest as against a competing transferee who registers in the federal registry. For this reason, many secured parties will elect to register in both the provincial and federal registries.

In the event that there is an operational conflict between the federal and provincial priority rules, the doctrine of federal paramountcy will be invoked. This might occur in the following situation.

SP1 and SP2 are both given a security interest in a patent. SP1 registers the security interest under the PPSA, but does not register it the federal registry. SP2 fails to register under the PPSA (or registers second in time), but does register in the federal registry not knowing of SP1's prior interest.

The PPSA gives priority to SP1 on the basis of SP1's earlier registration. However, the *Patent Act* gives priority to SP2. There is an operational conflict which is resolved by giving effect to the federal provision by virtue of the paramountcy doctrine. As a result, SP2 would prevail over SP1.

There is little doubt that the law governing security interests in intellectual property is in need of reform. In order to reduce this uncertainty, the Law Commission of Canada has made recommendations for reform of the law that would create a federal registry system in respect of security interests in intellectual property while still preserving a broad scope for the supplementary application of the PPSA.[92]

---

92 *Leveraging Knowledge Assets: Reducing Uncertainty for Security Interests in Intellectual Property* (Ottawa: Law Commission of Canada, 2004). See also H. Knopf, ed., *Security Interests in Intellectual Property* (Toronto: Carswell, 2002) for a collection of essays discussing the problems with the law and the possible reform solutions.

D. SECURITY INTERESTS IN RAILWAY ASSETS AND ROLLING STOCK

The *Canada Transportation Act*[93] contains three provisions that govern security interests in railway assets and rolling stock. Section 104 provides that a mortgage or hypothec issued by a railway company may be deposited with the Registrar General of Canada. When this is done, it is treated as if it had been filed under any other law respecting real or personal property. Section 105 provides that a lease, sale, conditional sale, mortgage, hypothec, bailment, or security agreement relating to rolling stock may also be filed with the Registrar General of Canada. When this is done, it does not need to be registered under any other law or statute respecting real or personal property, and the document is valid against all persons. These provisions only partially pre-empt the operation of the PPSA in respect of security interests in railway assets or in rolling stock. The PPSA will continue to govern issues of enforcement and priorities. The federal provisions merely provide an alternative place for registration. Where a secured party has filed federally, registration under the PPSA will therefore not be required in order to perfect the security interest.

The *Canada Transportation Act* contains its own procedure for reorganization of insolvent railway companies, and section 106(5) provides that the enforcement remedies of secured creditors are not affected by a court ordered stay unless the railway company agrees to perform all its obligations under the security agreement and cures any default.

E. THE *CONVENTION ON INTERNATIONAL INTERESTS IN MOBILE EQUIPMENT*, 2001

1) Introduction

The *Convention on International Interests in Mobile Equipment,* 2001 and an associated *Protocol on Matters Specific to Aircraft Equipment* (unless otherwise moderated, hereafter cumulatively referred to as "the Convention")[94] were adopted at a diplomatic conference in November 2001.

---

93 S.C. 1996, c. 10.
94 The Convention was designed to apply to a range of different types of mobile equipment each addressed in a separate protocol. However, to date, the Aircraft Protocol is the only one that has been adopted at a diplomatic conference and

When the Convention comes into force in a Canadian jurisdiction, it will provide an international regime within which secured financing and leasing of large aircraft will occur. While at the date this book was being written Canada had not ratified the Convention, the authors assumed that this would occur in the foreseeable future since Canada was an active participant in the development of the Convention and since the pre-implementation preparatory work has been completed. Full implementation of the Convention in a province will require enactment of these instruments as provincial legislation. Implementing legislation has been passed by the Ontario and Nova Scotia Legislatures.[95] Other provincial legislatures are expected to follow shortly. The Uniform Law Conference of Canada (ULCC) has prepared draft legislation, the *Uniform International Interests in Mobile Equipment Act* (Aircraft Equipment),[96] designed to facilitate a uniform or substantially uniform approach to the implementation of the Convention.

The Convention addresses a wide range of issues that arise in the context of the types of transactions falling within the scope of the Convention including, the creation of international interests, enforcement of creditors', lessors', and sellers' rights in the event of non-performance by debtors, lessees or buyers, public disclosure of international interests (registration), priority status of holders of international interests, assignment of rights associated with international interests, and jurisdictional matters. However, while its comprehensiveness is unprecedented, it is not a complete code of law addressing all aspects of aircraft financing, leasing, and sales. Several important issues relating to the types of transactions within its scope are expressly referred to the otherwise applicable law. In addition, there are issues that are not addressed at all or are only partially addressed and others with respect to which contracting states can make elections that will affect the operation of the Convention. As a result, the *Personal Property Security Act* and rules of the common law, including conflict of laws rules, will continue to play an important role, notwithstanding the implementation of the Convention in a PPSA jurisdiction.

As a result of Article 3, the Convention applies when, at the time of the agreement creating or providing for the international interest, the

---

the only one that is likely to have significance to Canadian jurisdictions for the foreseeable future.

95   *International Interests in Mobile Equipment Act (Aircraft Equipment)*, 2002 S.O. 2002, c. 18, Sched. B, s. 10(1); *International Interests in Mobile Aircraft Equipment Act*, S.N.S. 2004, c. 5.

96   See www.ulcc.ca and follow the link to "Proceedings of Annual Meeting, Toronto, 2001."

debtor is situated in a Contracting State. However, this does not dictate what law applies to the matters associated with the agreement that are not addressed in the Convention. Article 5(2) provides a method to determine the applicable law with respect to "matters governed by the Convention" but "not expressly settled in it." These matters are to be settled "in conformity with the general principles on which [the Convention] is based or, in the absence of such principles, the applicable law." Article 5(3) provides that the matters referred to in Article 5(2) "are to be settled under the law designated by private international law of the forum State." Most matters falling within the test of Article 5 will be governed by the law of the location of the debtor, buyer or lessee of an aircraft object. The PPSA provides that issues of validity of security interests or interests arising in the context of title reservation sales agreements (conditional sales contracts) and leases for a term of more than one year when the collateral is mobile equipment[97] are governed by the law of the location of the debtor at the time the interest "attaches." Consequently, whether the matter is one that is implicitly governed by the Convention or not governed by the Convention at all, the law applicable to it is likely to be the law of the location of the debtor when the international interest comes into existence.[98]

2) Types of Transactions to Which the Convention Applies

a) Approach to Characterization of Transactions: Security Agreements, Leases, and Conditional Sales Contracts

The Convention employs both a functional and a formal approach to the identification of transactions falling within its scope. Article 2(2)(a) provides that the Convention applies to a "security agreement" defined in Article 1(ii) in generic terms. However, this approach is not applied universally. Article 2(2) of the Convention includes two additional types of agreements solely by reference to their form: a title reservation

---

97 See PPSA (A, BC, M, NB, NWT, Nu, PEI, S) s. 7(2); Y s. 6 (1); O s. 7(1); (NL, NS) s. 8(2). The section refers to "goods of a type that are normally used in more than one jurisdiction if the goods are equipment or inventory leased or held for lease by a debtor to others."

98 For an examination of the issues involved in determining the applicable law for the purposes of Article 2(4) and the characterization of interests as property or otherwise in the context of the types of interest to which the Convention applies, see R. Cuming, "The Characterization of Interests and Transactions Under The Convention on International Interests in Mobile Equipment, 2001" in I. Davies, ed., *Security Interests in Mobile Equipment* (Aldershot: Dartmouth, 2002) at 377–95.

agreement (defined in Article 1(ll)) and a leasing agreement (defined in Article 1(q)).

As noted above, Article 2(4) refers the characterization of transactions falling within the scope of the Convention to the "applicable law" which, under Article 5(3) is the domestic law applicable by virtue of the rules of private international law of the forum. It is the view of the authors that the applicable law in this respect is the PPSA of the jurisdiction in which the debtor, buyer, or lessee is located when the international interest comes into existence. As noted elsewhere in this book, conditional sales contracts and "security leases" are security agreements under the Act and, consequently, would be viewed as such by a court of a common law province.

While the characterization of a particular transaction as a security agreement rather than a lease or title reservation agreement does not affect the application of the priority rules of the Convention or its registration requirements, it does affect the remedies of a defaulting chargor, lessee or buyer. Under Article 10 the remedies of a lessor or conditional seller are those of an owner: simple recovery of the leased or sold object is permitted. Under Articles 8 and 9, the remedies of a chargee are those of a secured party. These remedies are designed to provide protection to the chargor's interest in the object.

b)   Non-consensual Rights or Interests

The Convention provides for the extension of the registration and priority rules to a "non-consensual right or interest," such as repairers' or suppliers' liens, tax liens, and wage liens, that a contracting state in its declaration elects to treat in the same way as consensual international interests. The term "non-consensual right or interest" is defined in Article 1(s) as a right or interest conferred by law to secure the performance of an obligation, including an obligation to a state or state entity. Under Article 40, a state may declare that specified non-consensual rights or interests are to be treated as interests to which the Convention applies with the result that they will be subject to the registration requirements and priority rules of the Convention and Protocol. An alternative approach is offered by Article 39. It provides that a state may make a declaration setting out a list of non-consensual rights or interests having priority under the national law of that state and that will have priority under the Convention. These rights or interests are not subject to the registration requirement or priority regime of the Convention. Article 23 provides that the list of such interests will be kept on record at the international registry. It is expected that all Canadian jurisdictions will adopt the approach permitted by Article 39 with the result that the *status quo* relating to non-consensual rights or interests will be maintained once the Convention comes into force in a jurisdiction.

c) Assignments

The effect of Chapter IX (Articles 31–38) is to bring assignments of "associated rights" within the scope of the Convention. However, in order for the Convention to apply, the international interest and at least some of the payment rights associated with it must be transferred together. Article 32(3) provides that the Convention does not apply to an assignment of associated rights that is not accompanied by the transfer of the related international interest. The term "associated rights" is defined in Article 1(c) as "all rights to payment or other performance by a debtor under an agreement which are secured by or associated with" equipment to which the Convention applies. This definition is in effect limited by Article 36(2) that restricts application of the priority rules of the Convention to situations in which the competing assignments involve specified kinds of payment rights.

d) Sales of Aircraft Objects

The effect of Article III of the Aircraft Protocol and Article 41 of the Convention is to bring within the priority and registration provisions of the Convention sales of aircraft and aircraft engines. While this feature will not provide a title registration system for these items, it will have this effect with respect to aircraft and engines purchased from manufacturers after the Convention and Protocol come into effect. A potential buyer will be able to search the "chain of ownership" from the manufacturer to the seller. A person who buys on the strength of this information will take free from an intervening transfer of ownership that has not been registered.

3) The International Element

The location of the chargor, lessee or buyer in a contracting state at the time of execution of the security agreement, lease, or conditional sale is the factor that invokes application of the Convention.[99] The location of the secured party, lessor, or seller is not relevant. Article IV of the Aircraft Protocol provides, however, that the Convention will apply to a transaction involving an airframe (but not to an aircraft engine)[100]

---

99 See arts. 3 and 4 of the Convention and art. III, Aircraft Protocol.

100 The Aircraft Protocol distinguishes between an aircraft airframe and the aircraft engines. This feature reflects the fact that only airframes (and helicopters)

or helicopter if the airframe or helicopter is registered in a contracting state or an agreement exists that the aircraft will be registered in a contracting state.

The Convention applies to what in other contexts would be a transaction governed by national law because all or most of the factors relating to the agreement and the equipment are located in a single state. However, a limited exception is allowed. Under Article 50, a contracting state is entitled to declare that the Convention will not apply to "an internal transaction."[101] However, the effect of such a declaration will be limited because it will not exempt the transaction from the registration and priority rules of the Convention.[102] It is not likely that any Canadian jurisdiction will make this declaration.

4) The Priority Structure

The priority structure of the Convention is dependent upon an international registry for international interests and registerable non-consensual interests.[103] The priority rules of the Convention are very simple. Competing registered interests will rank in order of their registration,[104] and a registered interest will have priority over an unregistered interest.[105] Knowledge of a prior unregistered interest will not affect the priority status of a holder of a registered interest.[106] Similarly, an unregistered international interest will be subordinate to the interest of a person who buys the property subject to an international interest from the chargor, lessee, or conditional buyer. This is so whether or not the buyer's interest was acquired with or without actual knowledge of the unregistered international interest.[107] A registered international

---

are registered under the *Chicago Convention on International Civil Aviation,* 1944, online: International Civil Aviation Organization, Document 7300: www.icao.int/icaonet/dcs/7300.html .

101 Defined in art. 1(n).

102 See art. 50(2)–(3).

103 The international registry will be operated by an Irish company named Aviareto.

104 As to priority in the case of competing buyers, see Protocol, art. XIV (1)–(2). The Convention does not affect the rights of a person in an item held prior to its installation on property to which the Convention applies if under the applicable law those rights continue after installation. Nor does it prevent the creation of rights recognized under the applicable law in such an item when it is installed. See Convention, art. 29(7).

105 Art. 29(1).

106 Art. 29(2).

107 Art. 29(3)–(4).

interest will have priority over a trustee in bankruptcy and execution or attaching creditors. Otherwise, an international interest will have the same priority in insolvency proceedings that it has under the law applicable to the proceedings.[108] If, under that law, the interest is valid against the trustee or administrator without registration, the lack of registration in the international registry will not be relevant. For example, since under Ontario law, other than the Convention, an unregistered true lease can be asserted against a trustee in bankruptcy, there is no requirement that the interest of a lessor under a true lease of an aircraft object be registered in the international registry in order to have priority over the lessee's trustee in bankruptcy.

5) Post-default Rights and Remedies

Articles 8 to 15 of the Convention provide a regime of post-default rights and remedies of secured parties that bears close resemblance to the secured transactions laws of most Canadian jurisdictions. However, the Articles contain qualifications designed to accommodate approaches to enforcement employed elsewhere in the world and to address what are perceived to be special needs. Article 15 provides that the parties may agree in writing to derogate from or vary most of the rights and obligations specified by the Convention. Article 12 provides that the parties may agree to additional remedies not inconsistent with its mandatory provisions.

The remedies given to secured parties, lessors, and title-retention sellers under the Convention must be read in light of Article 14, which makes it clear that the procedural laws of the place of exercise of the remedy must be followed.[109] In addition, Article 54(2) empowers a contracting state to declare that enforcement rights may be exercised only with leave of a court.

6) Insolvency

An issue that caused great difficulty for the drafters of the Convention was the interface between national insolvency law (reorganization law) and the rights of secured parties in the event of default by debtors. One group of states wanted to have the Aircraft Protocol specify the right of a secured party, lessor, or seller to have an aircraft object surren-

---

108 Art. 30.

109 The Aircraft Protocol also modifies and supplements the remedial structure of the Convention. See, for example, arts. IX and X.

dered by the debtor or insolvency administrator in possession within a very short period of time after default unless, within that time, the default has been remedied. This concept, while a feature of Canadian[110] and United States law[111] is not a feature of the insolvency law of many states. Another group of states wanted a "softer" rule that would give the insolvency administrator greater flexibility. The compromise that was finally accepted is set out in Article XI of the Protocol. A contracting state that is a "primary insolvency jurisdiction" (defined in Article I(2)(n)) may make a declaration as to which of two alternative approaches set out in the Protocol will be applied. Under Article XI, Alternative A, the aircraft object must be surrendered to the creditor as provided in the security agreement following the occurrence of an insolvency related event (defined in Article I(m)), unless the default that gave rise to the event is remedied within a specified period of time. Under Article XI, Alternative B, the insolvency administrator can be given a longer period of time (specified in the declaration of the contracting state) to cure the default that resulted in the opening of the bankruptcy proceedings.

Recent amendments to the *Bankruptcy and Insolvency Act*[112] and the *Companies' Creditors Arrangement Act* suggest that Canada will not formally adopt either approach, but will exempt secured creditors from the stays of section 69 of the *Bankruptcy and Insolvency Act* and section 11 of the *Companies' Creditors Arrangement Act*.

7) Features of the International Registry

a) A Single International Registry
The Convention provides for a single registry based in Ireland for the registration of all international interests and registerable non-consensual interests in aircraft objects. There will be no direct reliance on or coordination with existing national registries.[113] All registration information will be communicated directly to the Convention registry.

---

110 *Canada Transportation Act*, S.C. 1996, c. 10, s. 106(5) (applicable to railway rolling stock only).
111 11 U.S.C. § 1110 (applicable to aircraft and vessels).
112 See Bill C-4, 1st Sess., 38th Parl., 53 Elizabeth II, 2004.
113 Some states have central national or regional registries for interests in aircraft and aircraft engines created under domestic law. These existing facilities could be designated under the Aircraft Protocol as exclusive or non-exclusive transmitters of registration data. However, the designation can apply only with respect to international interests in, or sales of, helicopters or airframes and

b)   Guarantee of Reliability

Article 28 of the Convention provides that the registrar will "be liable for compensatory damages for loss suffered by a person directly resulting from an error or omission of the Registrar and its officers and employees or from a malfunction of the international registry system." However, exceptions are recognized. There is no liability where the malfunction of the registry is "caused by an event of an inevitable and irresistible nature which could not be prevented by using the best practices in current use in the field of electronic registry design and operation." Nor is the registrar liable for factual inaccuracy of registration information or acts or circumstances for which the registrar is not responsible and arising prior to receipt of registration information at the international registry.

c)   Notice Registration

The international registry will provide for notice, not document registration. What will be entered into the database of the system will be minimal information relating to an existing or potential interest. Apart from the description of the property that is subject to the international interest,[114] the Convention and Aircraft Protocol leave to the regulations the types of data that will constitute a registration.

d)   Pre-agreement Registration

Articles 16(1)(a) and 19(4) of the Convention provide for registration of a "prospective international interest"[115] and a "prospective assignment"[116] (as is the case under the PPSA, it will be possible to effect a registration relating to an aircraft object before the transaction creating an interest in that object has been executed). The priority of this interest dates from the date of the registration of it as a prospective interest and not from the date the interest arises.

---

registerable non-consensual interests. It cannot include international interest in or sales of aircraft engines. Similarly, the national agency will not be the conduit for discharges, amendments or subordinations of registrations. It is the understanding of the authors that no designation will be made by Canada under art. 18(5) of the Convention and art. XIX of the Protocol.

114 A description that allows the equipment to be specifically identified is necessary since this will be the registration-search criterion used to store registration data in and retrieve them from the registry database. See Aircraft Protocol, art. XX (1).

115 Defined in art. 1(y).

116 Defined in art. 1(x).

e) Compulsory Discharge

Article 25 of the Convention requires discharge of a registration relating to an international interest arising under a security agreement or title retention sale, or a registration relating to a prospective interest or an assignment of a prospective interest when the obligations protected by the interest have been performed or where no such obligations were created.[117] As a result of Article 44, when the person who effected the registration fails to discharge the registration, the aggrieved party must seek a remedy in a court having the power to enforce compliance against that person. This order can be enforced by the court of the place in which the registrar has its centre of administration. However, where the person who effected the registration cannot be found or has ceased to exist, this court has original jurisdiction to order discharge of the registration.

8) Interface between the Convention and the PPSA

a) Side-by-side Secured Financing Systems

The implementation of the Convention in PPSA jurisdictions will result in the introduction of very little that is novel to or asymmetrical with personal property security law. The underlying concepts of the Convention and the central role of a registry in its priority structure are very familiar to Canadian legal practitioners. Indeed, the structure and many of the provisions of the Convention were patterned on Canadian and similar North American secured financing regimes. However, it does not follow from this that the Convention can be treated as a simple one-for-one replacement of domestic law, or that its implementation will be completely free from legal uncertainty.

b) Matters Implicitly Left to Domestic Law

i)   Limited Application of the Convention: Size and Use of Aircraft
The scope of the Convention as it applies to aircraft financing is determined by the Protocol. Article II of the Aircraft Protocol makes the Convention applicable to "aircraft objects." This term includes airframes, aircraft engines and helicopters. These are defined in Article I(2). The term "airframe" is defined as an airframe that, when appropriate engines are installed thereon, is certified by the competent aviation authority to transport at least eight persons or goods in excess of 2,750

---

117 Under art. 21 of the Convention, a registration is effective until discharged or until expiry of the period specified in the registration.

kilograms. The term "aircraft engine" is defined as an engine powered by jet propulsion technology having at least 1,750 pounds of thrust or powered by turbine or piston technology having at least 550 rated take-off shaft horsepower. A "helicopter" is defined as a helicopter that is supported in flight chiefly by reaction of the air on power-driven rotors certified by the competent aviation authority to transport at least five persons or goods in excess of 450 kilograms. An additional factor is determining the scope of the Convention is the use of the aircraft. The Convention does not apply to transactions involving aircraft used for military, customs, or police services.[118] These tests focus on the size and use of the aircraft object and not on the parties involved. It is irrelevant that the debtor, buyer, or lessee is or is not engaged in business activity or is a government. The PPSA will continue to govern all aspects of secured financing and leasing transactions involving aircraft having a capacity below that specified in the Protocol and those being used in the three specified governmental functions.

ii) Proceeds

Article 2(5) of the Convention provides that an international interest in an object "extends to proceeds of that object." The term "proceeds" is defined in Article 1(w) to mean "money or non-money proceeds arising from the total or partial loss or physical destruction of the object or its total or partial confiscation, condemnation or requisition." As a result, an international interest does not extend to property received from a voluntary disposition or other dealing with an aircraft object.[119] The Convention provides no answer to the question as to whether or not the international interest in proceeds is lost once the insurance or expropriation payments have lost their original form where, for example, the money is deposited in an active bank account.

An aircraft object financer[120] can invoke the much broader and more refined concept of proceeds in the PPSA to protect its interest in proceeds other than money or non-money proceeds property received

---

118 Aircraft Protocol, art. II(2)(e).
119 Art. 2(5) leads to the conclusion that, when either money or non-money proceeds are involved, the priority status the international interest has under art. 29 carries over to the proceeds, even though this would not be the case under the otherwise applicable law. Whether this would result in the defeat of the transferee of a negotiable instrument is open to question. This may be a matter falling within art. 5(2) that is to be settled in conformity with the applicable law.
120 Hereinafter, the term "aircraft object financer" should be read to include a chargee, a lessor, or a conditional seller as those terms are defined in art. 1 of the Convention.

as insurance or expropriation payments. Under the Act a security interest in collateral "extends to proceeds." The term "proceeds" includes any kind of "identifiable or traceable personal property derived directly or indirectly from any dealing with the collateral or proceeds of the collateral and in which the debtor acquires and interest."[121]

The concepts of identification and tracing proceeds contained in the PPSA can be employed to extend the meaning of proceeds beyond a change in the original form in which they were initially received by the debtor. If the agreement that creates the international interest is a security agreement falling within the PPSA,[122] by complying with the registration requirements of both the Convention and the PPSA, an aircraft object financer can obtain the maximum available protection of its interest in the original collateral and all forms of Convention proceeds and identifiable or traceable proceeds recognized by the PPSA.

iii) Accessions

There are many very costly items, such as avionics, food preparation equipment, and entertainment systems installed in "airframes" that, under the definition of this term in the Protocol, are treated as parts of airframe.[123] A part installed in an engine is treated as a feature of the engine.[124] As a result, an agreement that creates an international interest in an airframe or engine encompasses these items. However, there is no provision in the Convention dealing with interests in these items apart from the interests of debtors in the airframe or engine to which the items are attached.

Article 29(7) provides that the Convention does not affect the rights of a person in an item, other than an airframe or engine, held prior to its installation on the airframe or engine if, under the applicable law, those rights continue to exist after the installation; and does not prevent the creation of rights in such an item after it has been installed where those rights are created under the applicable law. The effect of this provision is to leave to the applicable law resolution of issues associated with creation and priority of separately created interests in these items.

---

121 PPSA (A, BC, MB, NB, NWT, O, PEI, Y) s. 1; (NS, NL, S) s. 2.
122 Leases of aircraft objects that are not "security leases" do not fall within the scope of the Ontario Act. Consequently, it is not possible to look to that Act as method of extending the Convention right in proceeds beyond the narrow forms of property set out in the definition of proceeds in the Convention.
123 The term "airframe" is defined in art. I(e) of the Aircraft Protocol as including "all installed, incorporated or attached accessories, parts and equipment..."
124 The term "aircraft engine" is defined in art. I(b) as including "all modules and other installed, incorporated or attached accessories, parts and equipment."

It is unlikely that these items are accessions under the common law test[125] with the result that their attachment to the airframe or engine does not result in transfer of ownership in them to the owner of the airframe or engine. However, they are "accessions" under the PPSA.[126] As a result, they could be collateral under a security agreement[127] between the owner of the airframe or engine and a financer, other than the holder of an international interest in the airframe or engine, or between someone other than the owner of the airframe or engine and a financer. Under the PPSA, the owner of the accession can grant an effective security interest in the accession goods, either before or after they are attached to the other goods, that can be separately protected by registration from the effects of any disposition of or grant of an interest in the property to which they are attached.[128]

A secured creditor that takes a security interest in an airframe or engine under the Convention cannot rely on the international registry to disclose security interests taken under a PPSA in items that have been attached before the international interest arises. As a result of Article 29(7), the holders of such interests are not required to register their interest under the Convention and its priority regime does not apply to them. Furthermore, a prior security interest in an accession taken under the PPSA can prevail over a later international interest taken in the airframe or engine and accession whether or not the security interest is perfected (registered) in a personal property registry.[129] Consequently, there is no registry that the secured party can rely upon to disclose the existence of a prior security interest in the accession. The position of the aircraft object financer is much stronger in the unlikely event that the debtor gives a security interest in an accession after it has been attached and after the international interest has been created. A security interest granted by the owner of the accession goods after it has been attached to the airframe or engine is valid only if the holder of an interest in the airframe or engine consents to the interest being created. In this case, the

---

125 The general view under Canadian case law is that a minor item becomes an accession to a major item only when removal of the minor item would involve serious injury to the major item. *Industrial Acceptance Corp. v. Firestone Tire & Rubber Co. of Canada Ltd.*, [1971] S.C.R. 357; *Ilford-Riverton Airways Ltd. v. Aero Trades (Western) Ltd.*, [1977] 5 W.W.R. 193 (Man. C.A.).
126 The term "accession" is defined as "goods that are installed in or affixed to other goods." PPSA (BC, NWT, Nu, O, Y) s. 1(1); (M, NB) s. 1; (NFLD, NS) s. 2(a); A s. 2(a); PEI s. 1(a); S. s. 2(1)(a).
127 Including a title reservation agreement or long-term lease.
128 PPSA (A, BC, M, NB, PEI, NWT, N, S) s. 38 (NFLD, NS) s. 39; O s. 35(1); Y s. 36.
129 *Ibid.*

aircraft object financer can preserve its priority by refusing to consent to the security interest in the accession or waive its rights in it.[130]

iv) Transition

A very important matter that must be addressed any time a new regime regulating contractual and property rights is implemented is the extent to which that regime applies to transactions entered into, but not completely executed, before it came into effect. A related matter is the determination as to the rules applicable where there is a conflict between an interest arising before and one arising after the regime comes into effect.

Article 60 provides that the Convention does not apply to a pre-existing right or interest. It expressly preserves the priority such right or interest enjoyed under prior applicable law. However, this is subject to a qualification. A contacting state may by declaration specify a date, not earlier than three years after the date the declaration becomes effective, when the Convention will become applicable, for the purposes of determining priority, including any existing priority, to pre-existing rights or interests arising under an agreement made at a time when the debtor was situated in a contracting state.

When a state does not make a declaration, pre-Convention law continues to govern rights arising under a contract existing at the date of the Convention comes into effect. These rights remain intact for the duration of the contract without regard to the date the Convention comes into effect in the state where the debtor is located. This should not be problem when all competing interests in the aircraft object arose under pre-Convention law or when a pre-Convention interest is in conflict with an international interest. The PPSA of the jurisdiction where the debtor is located when the interests came into existence will provide appropriate priority rules.[131]

The issue can best be addressed in the context of a specific scenario.

Assume that, prior to the Convention becoming effective in a province where the debtor is located, an Airline Company obtained financing from a Canadian bank under a security agreement providing for a security interests in all of the present and future assets of the company as permitted by the *Personal Property Security Act*. The bank registered its interest as required by the Act.

---

130 *Ibid.*
131 Of course, whether or not rights determined under a Canadian PPSA will be recognized by a foreign court cannot be predicted.

After the Convention came into effect, Airline Company contracted with the owner of an aircraft (as defined the Aircraft Protocol) to lease the aircraft for a period of five years. This lease would create an international interest falling within the Convention. Assume that Aircraft Company defaults on its obligations under both the security agreement and the lease and both the bank and the owner of the aircraft claimed priority to it.

Both the bank's security interest and the lessor's international interest fall within the priority regime of the PPSA. If the lease was a "security lease" and was timely registered in the personal property registry, the lessor will have priority. The bank would have priority if no registration was effected or the period for registration of purchase money security interests elapsed before registration.[132] If the transaction was a true lease (that is, not a security agreement) the result would be the same if the debtor were located in any PPSA jurisdiction other than Ontario when the lease was executed. If the debtor were located in Ontario, the lessor would have priority since the applicable priority rule would be the common law principle of *nemo dat quod non habet*.

Should Canada make a declaration permitted by Article 60, the priority regime of the relevant PPSA would apply during the three-year period following the declaration. Thereafter, the relevant features of the priority regime of the Convention set out in the declaration will govern priority competitions, including those involving pre-Convention interests and international interests.

v) Sales of Aircraft Objects
Article III of the Protocol provides that the registration and priority provisions[133] of the Convention apply to contracts of sale aircraft objects. However, this will not create a title or ownership register for these objects. It will provide a record of their transfers occurring after the Convention comes into force. When such transfers are from the original owners, for example, the manufacturers, the practical effect is that a potential buyer or secured creditor can determine through a search of the international registry the "chain of title."

---

132 The international interest would be a purchase money security interest in the aircraft object.

133 Also art. 1, art. 5, cc. X and XII, and most provisions of cc. XII and XIV.

FURTHER READINGS

CUMING, R.C.C. & WOOD, R.J., "Compatibility of Federal and Provincial Personal Property Security Law" (1986) 65 Can. Bar Rev. 267

CUMING, R.C.C., "The Characterization of Interests and Transactions under the Draft Convention on International Interests in Mobile Equipment" (2001) Journal of International Commercial Law 1

GOLD, E., H. KINDRED & A. CHIRCOP, *Maritime Law* (Toronto: Irwin Law, 2003) c. 6

GOODE, R.M., *Official Commentary on the Convention on International Interests in Mobile Equipment and the Protocol thereto on Matters Specific to Aircraft Equipment* (as approved for distribution by the UNIDROIT Governing Council pursuant to Resolution No. 5 of the Cape Town Diplomatic Conference, 2001)

KNOPF, H., ED., *Security Interests in Intellectual Property* (Toronto: Carswell, 2002)

LAW COMMISSION OF CANADA, *Leveraging Knowledge Assets — Reducing Uncertainty for Security Interests in Intellectual Property* (Ottawa, 2004)

LAW COMMISSION OF CANADA, *Modernizing Canada's Secured Transactions Law: The* Bank Act *Security Provisions* (Ottawa, 2004)

WOOD, R.J., "The Nature and Definition of Federal Security Interests" (2000) 34 Can. Bus. L.J. 65

TABLE OF CASES

101056998 Saskatchewan Ltd. v. Kipp & Zonen Inc., [2004] S.J. No. 763,
    7 C.B.R. (5th) 148 (Q.B.), aff'd 2005 SKCA 66, [2005] S.J. No. 335............ 553
1151162 Ontario Ltd. (Re) (1997), 13 P.P.S.A.C. (2d) 16 (Ont. Ct. Gen. Div.) .. 332
243930 Alberta Ltd. v. Wickham (1990), 75 O.R. (2d) 289, 73 D.L.R. (4th)
    474 (C.A.)... 153
356447 British Columbia Ltd. v. Canadian Imperial Bank of Commerce (1998),
    157 D.L.R. (4th) 682, 13 P.P.S.A.C. (2d) 155, [1998] 9 W.W.R. 59,
    [1998] B.C.J. No. 417 (C.A.).. 60, 92, 183
547592 Alberta Ltd. (Re), [1995] A.J. No. 408, 10 P.P.S.A.C. (2d) 62 (Q.B.)...... 292
674921 B.C. Ltd. v. Advanced Wing Technologies Corp., [2005] B.C.J.
    No. 1704, 2005 Carswell BC 1837 (S.C.).. 181
859587 Ontario Ltd. v. Starmark Property Management Ltd. (1997), 34 O.R.
    (3d) 43, 12 P.P.S.A.C. (2d) 281, [1997] O.J. No. 2474 (Gen. Div.), aff'd (1998),
    40 O.R. (3d) 481, 14 P.P.S.A.C. (2d) 20, [1998] O.J. No. 3022
    (C.A.) 494
977380 Ontario Inc. v. Roy's Towing Co. (1997), 13 P.P.S.A.C. (2d) 201
    (Ont. Ct. Gen. Div.) 178

Abbey National Building Society v. Cann, [1991] 1 A.C. 56 (H.L.) 592
Access Advertising Management Inc. v. Servex Computers Inc., [1993]
    O.J. No. 2439, (1993), 15 O.R. (3d) 635, 21 C.B.R. (3d) 304,
    6 P.P.S.A.C. (2d) 113 (Ont. Ct. Gen. Div.)..175, 399
Access Cash International, Inc. v. Elliot Lake and North Shore Corporation for
    Business Development, [2000] O.J. No. 3012, [2000] O.T.C. 617,
    1 P.P.S.A.C. (3d) 209 (S.C.J.) 76
Acmetrack Ltd. v. Bank Canadian National (1984), 12 D.L.R. (4th) 428,
    4 P.P.S.A.C. 199 (Ont. C.A.) 169–70
Adair (Re) (sub. nom. Ward Mallette Inc. v. General Motors Acceptance Corp.)
    (1985), 49 O.R. (2d) 583, 15 D.L.R. (4th) 596, 54 C.B.R. (N.S.) 281,
    4 P.P.S.A.C. 262, 7 O.A.C. 262 (C.A.) 131, 135

Adelaide Corp. v. Integrated Transportation Finance Inc. (1994), 16 O.R.
    (3d) 414, 111 D.L.R. (4th) 493, 6 P.P.S.A.C. (2d) 267, [1994]
    O.J. No. 103 (Gen. Div.) 69–70, 74, 230, 315
Advance Diamond Drilling Ltd. (Receiver of) v. National Bank Leasing Inc.
    (1992), 67 B.C.L.R. (2d) 173, 3 P.P.S.A.C. (2d) 154 (S.C.) 135
Affinity International Inc. v. Alliance International Inc., [1994] M.J. No. 471,
    8 P.P.S.A.C. (2d) 73 (Q.B.), additional reasons at [1994] M.J. No. 608,
    8 P.P.S.A.C. (2d) 73 at 82 (Q.B.), aff'd [1995] M.J. No. 507, 9 P.P.S.A.C.
    (2d) 174 (C.A.) 174
Afton Band of Indians v. Attorney General of Nova Scotia (1978), 29 N.S.R.
    (2d) 226, [1978] N.S.J. No. 615, 3 R.P.R. 298 (N.S.T.D.) 114
Agar v. 762250 Ontario Ltd., [1994] O.J. No. 128, 6 P.P.S.A.C. (2d) 292
    (Ont. Ct. Gen. Div.) 165
Agent's Equity Inc. v. Hope (Trustees of) (1996), 40 C.B.R. (3d) 310,
    12 P.P.S.A.C. (2d) 48, 30 O.R. (3d) 557, [1996] O.J. No. 2895
    (Gen. Div.) 91, 445
Agricultural Commodity Corp. v. Schaus Feedlots Inc., [2001] O.J. No. 2908,
    2 P.P.S.A.C. (3d) 270 (S.C.J.), aff'd [2003] O.J. No. 744, 4 P.P.S.A.C.
    (3d) 266 (C.A.) 292
Agricultural Credit Corp. of Saskatchewan v. Featherstone (Trustee of),
    [1996] 8 W.W.R. 281, [1996] S.J. No. 319, 11 P.P.S.A.C. (2d) 194
    (Sask. Q.B.) 110, 434
Agricultural Credit Corp. of Saskatchewan v. Pettyjohn (1991), 79 D.L.R.
    (4th) 22, [1991] 3 W.W.R. 689, [1991] S.J. No. 129, 1 P.P.S.A.C.
    (2d) 273 (Sask. C.A.) 163, 281, 334, 460, 466, 474–78
Agricultural Credit Corp. of Saskatchewan v. Royal Bank of Canada
    (1994), 115 D.L.R. (4th) 569, [1994] 7 W.W.R. 305, 7 P.P.S.A.C.
    (2d) 1 (Sask. C.A.) 27, 590, 591, 592
Agriculture Financial Services Corp. v. John Hofer Farms Ltd.,
    2001 ABQB 692, 2 P.P.S.A.C. (3d) 314 357
Air Canada v. M. & L. Travel Ltd., [1993] 3 S.C.R. 787, 108 D.L.R.
    (4th) 592, [1993] S.C.J. No. 118... 81
Air Products Canada Ltd. v. Farini Corp., [2000] O.J. No. 1396,
    16 C.B.R. (4th) 18 (Ont. S.C.J.)..340
Alberta (Attorney General) v. Alberta (Board of Industrial Relations) (1975),
    64 D.L.R. (3d) 293, [1976] 1 W.W.R. 756 (Alta. S.C.T.D.)............................410
Alberta (Attorney General) v. Findlay, [1996] 3 W.W.R. 514, 10 P.P.S.A.C.
    (2d) 321 (Alta. Prov. Ct.)... 281, 283
Alberta Opportunity Co. v. Dobko, 167 A.R. 205, [1995] A.J. No. 184,
    9 P.P.S.A.C. (2d) 72 (Q.B.) 107
Alberta Pacific Leasing Inc. v. Petro Equipment Sales Ltd., [1995]
    A.J. No. 877, 10 P.P.S.A.C. (2d) 69 (Q.B.) 293
Alberta Treasury Branches v. Faja Bison Ranch Inc. (1994), 152 A.R. 112,
    6 P.P.S.A.C.(2d) 205 (Q.B.) 183

Alberta Treasury Branches v. Triathlon Vehicle Leasing, [1992] A.J. No. 1258,
    4 P.P.S.A.C. (2d) 163 (Q.B.), aff'g (1992), 134 A.R. 100, 4 P.P.S.A.C.
    (2d) 147 (Q.B.) 272
Alcock, Ingram & Co. (Re) (1923), 53 O.L.R. 422, [1924] 1 D.L.R. 388,
    [1923] O.J. No. 148 (S.C.A.D.) 80
Alda Wholesale Ltd. (Re), 2001 BCSC 921, 3 P.P.S.A.C. (3d) 52,
    26 C.B.R. (4th) 1 .... 273, 274
Alduco Mechanical Contractors (Re) (1979), 27 O.R. (2d) 323,
    1 P.P.S.A.C. 142 (H.C.J.) 263, 265
Alexander v. McGillivray (1932), 41 O.W.N. 406 (H.C.) 491
Alves Worms Ltd. v. Ford Credit Canada Ltd. (1995),10 P.P.S.A.C. (2d) 25,
    [1995] O.J. No. 1950 (Gen. Div.) 152
Amchem Products Inc. v. British Columbia Worker's Compensation Board,
    [1993] 1 S.C.R. 897, 102 D.L.R. (4th) 96 123
American Heritage Bank & Trust Co. v. O. & E. Inc., 576 P.2d 566
    (Colo. App. 1978) 570
Amherst Boot & Shoe Co. v. Carter (1922), 70 D.L.R. 110, 50 N.B.R. 315
    (S.C.A.D.) 197
AmSouth Bank, N.A. v. J & D Financial Corp., 679 So.2d 695 (Ala. 1996) 372
Anderson & Hiltz Limited (Re), [1985] O.J. No. 1758, 57 C.B.R. (N.S.)
    222 (Ont. H.C.J.) 433
Anderson's Engineering Ltd. (Re) (2002), 33 C.B.R. (4th) 1, 3 P.P.S.A.C.
    (3d) 129 (B.C.S.C.) 289, 291
Andrew v. Farmstart, [1988] S.J. No. 687, 71 C.B.R. (N.S.) 124 (C.A.),
    leave to appeal to S.C.C. refused 57 D.L.R. (4th) viii, [1989]
    4 W.W.R. lxx (S.C.C.) 438, 440
Andrews v. Mack Financial (Canada) Ltd. (1987), 46 D.L.R. (4th) 731,
    8 P.P.S.A.C. 110 (Sask. C.A.) 516, 575, 576
Angelkovski v. Trans-Canada Foods Ltd., [1986] 3 W.W.R. 723,
    6 P.P.S.A.C. 1 (Man. Q.B.) 555–56
ANZ Banking Group (N.Z.) Ltd. v. Gibson, [1986] 1 N.Z.L.R. 556 (C.A.) 524
Armory v. Delamirie (1722), 1 Str. 505, 93 E.R. 664 (K.B.) 165
Armour v. Thyssen Edelstahlwerk AG, [1991] 2 A.C. 339 (H.L.) 66
Armstrong, Thomson & Tubman Leasing Ltd. v. McGill Agency Inc. (Trustee of)
    (1993), 15 O.R. (3d) 292, 5 P.P.S.A.C. (2d) 231 (Gen. Div.) 252
Arrow Transfer Co. v. Royal Bank of Canada (1971), 19 D.L.R. (3d) 420,
    [1971] 3 W.W.R. 241 (B.C.C.A.), aff'd [1972] S.C.R. 845,
    27 D.L.R. (3d) 81 582–83
Arseneau (Re) (2005), 7 P.P.S.A.C. (3d) 165, 230 N.S.R. (2d) 33 (S.C.) 132
Askin (Re), [1960] O.J. No. 423, 1 C.B.R. (N.S.) 153 (H.C.J.) 76
Asklepeion Restaurant Ltd. v. 791259 Ontario Ltd., [1996] O.J. No. 1456,
    11 P.P.S.A.C. (2d) 320, 6 O.T.C. 326 (Gen. Div.), aff'd [1998] O.J.
    No. 2273, 13 P.P.S.A.C. (2d) 295 (C.A.) 164, 268, 362, 364, 373
Associates Commercial Corp. v. Scotia Leasing Ltd. (1995), 10 P.P.S.A.C.
    (2d) 195, 24 B.L.R. (2d) 310 (Ont. Ct. Gen. Div.) 31, 129, 131

Associates Leasing (Canada) Ltd. v. Humboldt Flour Mills Inc., [1998]
    S.J. No. 841, 14 P.P.S.A.C. (2d) 174 (Q.B.) 340
Astral Communications Inc. v. 825536 Ontario Inc. (Trustee of) (2000),
    46 O.R. (3d) 477, 128 O.A.C. 362, 183 D.L.R. (4th) 455,
    15 C.B.R. (4th) 1, 15 P.P.S.A.C. (2d) 256 (C.A.)..................... 182–83, 184, 189
Atlas Industries Ltd. v. Federal Business Development Bank, Royal Bank,
    [1983] S.J. No. 143, 50 C.B.R. (N.S.) 14, 3 P.P.S.A.C. 39
    (Sask. Q.B.) 87, 180, 184
Axelrod (Re) (1994), 20 O.R. (3d) 133, 119 D.L.R. (4th) 37, [1994] O.J. No. 2277,
    8 P.P.S.A.C. (2d) 1 (C.A.), aff'g (1994), 16 O.R. (3d) 649,
    111 D.L.R. (4th) 540, [1994] O.J. No. 137 (Gen. Div.) 112

B.M.P. & Daughters Investment Corp. v. 941242 Ontario Ltd. (1992),
    11 O.R. (3d) 81, 4 P.P.S.A.C. (2d) 220 (Gen. Div.) 313
Bachand v. Trans Canada Credit Corp. (1980), 12 B.L.R. 247, 30 O.R. (2d) 405,
    1 P.P.S.A.C. 185, 117 D.L.R. (3d) 653 (C.A.), aff'g (1979), 1 P.P.S.A.C. 41
    (Ont. Co. Ct.)... 131
Baitinger (Re), 2002 SKQB 220, [2002] 8 W.W.R. 686, [2002] S.J. No. 304 113
Ball v. Royal Bank (1915), 52 S.C.R. 254, 26 D.L.R. 385 188
Bank of Baroda v. Panessar, [1987] 2 W.L.R. 208 524
Bank of Montreal v. 414031 Ontario Ltd., [1983] O.J. No. 2352,
    2 P.P.S.A.C. 248 (Dist. Ct.) 412
Bank of Montreal v. Bale (1991), 5 O.R. (3d) 155, [1991] O.J. No. 1541,
    2 P.P.S.A.C. (2d) 194 (Gen. Div.), aff'd [1992] O.J. No. 2395, 4 P.P.S.A.C.
    (2d) 114 (C.A.)..110
Bank of Montreal v. Colossal Carpets Ltd. (1977), 2 B.L.R. 196 (B.C.S.C) ... 76, 79
Bank of Montreal v. Dynex Petroleum Ltd. (1999), 1999 ABCA 363,
    255 A.R. 116, [2000] 2 W.W.R. 693, aff'd 2002 SCC 7,
    [2002] 1 S.C.R. 146, [2001] S.C.J. No. 70 104
Bank of Montreal v. Dynex Petroleum Ltd., [1997] A.J. No. 341,
    12 P.P.S.A.C. (2d) 183 (Q.B.) 373
Bank of Montreal v. Featherstone (1989), 58 D.L.R. (4th) 567,
    9 P.P.S.A.C. 139 (Ont. C.A.) 550, 578
Bank of Montreal v. Hall, [1990] 1 S.C.R. 121, 9 P.P.S.A.C. 177 .... 593, 598, 600
Bank of Montreal v. Kalatzis, [1984] S.J. No. 788, 37 Sask. R. 300 (Q.B.)......... 283
Bank of Montreal v. L.S. Walker Machine Tools Inc. and Whitman Engineering
    Ltd., [2000] O.J. No. 943, 15 P.P.S.A.C. (2d) 236 (S.C.J.) 285
Bank of Montreal v. Pulsar Ventures Inc. (1987), [1988] 1 W.W.R. 250,
    7 P.P.S.A.C. 258 (Sask. C.A.) 591, 593
Bank of Montreal v. Scott Road Enterprises Ltd., [1989] B.C.J. No. 485,
    57 D.L.R. (4th) 623, 73 C.B.R. (N.S.) 273 (C.A.)................................291, 421
Bank of Montreal v. Titan Landco Inc. (1990), 70 D.L.R. (4th) 1,
    [1990] B.C.J. No. 1074 (C.A.)... 421
Bank of Montreal v. Tomyn, [1989] S.J. No. 695, 84 Sask. R. 253 (Q.B.)........... 347
Bank of Montreal v. Tourangeau (1980), 31 O.R. (2d) 177, 118 D.L.R.
    (3d) 293 (H.C.J.) ....,,,,,,,,,........... 582

Bank of Nova Scotia v. Gaudreau (1984), 48 O.R. (2d) 478, 27 B.L.R. 101,
    4 P.P.S.A.C. 158 (H.C.J) 156, 376
Bank Of Nova Scotia v. International Harvester Credit Corp of Canada Ltd.
    (1990), 74 O.R. (2d) 738, 1 P.P.S.A.C. (2d) 93 (Ont. C.A.) 593
Bank of Nova Scotia v. Phenix (Trustee of), [1989] S.J. No. 69,
    74 Sask. R. 143, 9 P.P.S.A.C. 95 (C.A.)... 113
Bank of Nova Scotia v. Royal Bank of Canada (1998), 14 P.P.S.A.C. (2d) 10,
    [1998] B.C.J. No. 3220 (B.C.S.C.) 264–65, 273, 375
Bank of Nova Scotia v. Royal Bank of Canada, [1987] S.J. No. 541, 68 C.B.R.
    (N.S.) 235, 8 P.P.S.A.C. 17 (Sask. C.A.) 216, 362, 398
Bank of Nova Scotia v. Steffens, 2002 NSSC 144, 645 A.P.R. 299..................... 302
Bank of Nova Scotia v. Sullivan Investments Ltd. (1982), 21 Sask. R. 14,
    [1982] S.J. No. 706 (Q.B.).. 567
Banque Belge pour l' Étranger v. Hambrouck, [1921] 1 K.B. 321 (C.A.)............. 466
Banque Nationale de Paris (Canada) v. Pine Tree Mercury Sales Ltd. (1983),
    42 O.R. (2d) 303, 47 C.B.R. (N.S.) 300, 3 P.P.S.A.C. 51 (Co. Ct.) 65, 87
Bar C Cross Farms & Ranches (In Re), 48 B.R. 976, 1 U.C.C. Rep. Serv.
    2d 256 (D. Colo. [Bankr.] 1985).. 371
Barclays Bank Ltd. v. Quistclose Investments Ltd., [1970] A.C. 567 (H.L.)........ 83
Barclays Business Credit, Inc. v. Fletcher Challenge Canada Ltd. (1993),
    13 O.R. (3d) 118, [1993] O.J. No. 927, 5 P.P.S.A.C. (2d) 105 (Gen. Div.).... 108
Barlow Clowes International Ltd. v. Vaughan, [1992] 4 All E.R. 22 (C.A.)........470
Barous (Re), [1983] S.J. No. 601, 3 P.P.S.A.C. 61 (Q.B.)..................................... 271
Barry v. Bank of Ottawa (1908), 17 O.L.R. 83, [1908] O.J. No. 34 (H.C.J.) 587
Battlefords Credit Union Ltd. v. Ilnicki (1991), 82 D.L.R. (4th) 69,
    [1991] 5 W.W.R. 673 (Sask. C.A.) 347, 349, 350
Battlefords Credit Union Ltd. v. Korpan Tractor & Parts Ltd. (1983),
    28 Sask. R. 215, [1983] S.J. No. 675 (Q.B.).. 580
Bauer Enterprises Ltd. v. Chrysler Credit Canada Ltd. (1999), 181 Sask. R. 278,
    [1999] S.J. No. 516 (Q.B.)... 31
Beals v. Saldanha, 2003 SCC 72, [2003] 3 S.C.R. 416 122
Beaton (Re) (1979), 25 O.R. (2d) 614, 101 D.L.R. (3d) 338, 30 C.B.R.
    (N.S.) 225 (C.A.) 106
Beatty v. Rumble, [1891] O.J. No. 64, (1891), 21 O.R. 184 (H.C.J.) 401
Bedard (Re) (1983), 46 C.B.R. (N.S.) 172, 3 P.P.S.A.C. 29 (Ont. H.C.J.) 128
Belarus Equipment of Canada v. C & M Equipment (Brooks) Ltd. (1994),
    [1995] 1 W.W.R. 429, [1994] A.J. No. 724 (Q.B.) 384
Bellini Manufacturing & Importing Ltd. (Re) (1981), 32 O.R. (2d) 684,
    1 P.P.S.A.C. 259 (C.A.).. 271
Belows v. Dalmyn, [1978] 4 W.W.R. 630, 4 B.L.R. 205 (Man. Q.B.)................... 561
Bennett v. Kent Piano Co. (1921), 29 B.C.R. 465, [1921] B.C.J. No. 107 (C.A.) 530
Beresford Building Supplies (1984) Ltd. v. Caisse Populaire de Petit-Rocher
    Ltée. (1996), 38 C.B.R. (3d) 274, [1996] N.B.J. No. 84 (Q.B.) 527
Berman (Re) (1979), 26 O.R. (2d) 389, 105 D.L.R. (3d) 380,
    1 P.P.S.A.C. 81 (C.A.) 84–85

Better (Re), [1989] O.J. No. 2625, 9 P.P.S.A.C. 158 (S.C.)................................. 230
Bigstone Band Enterprises Ltd. (Re), 1999 ABQB 868, 15 P.P.S.A.C. (2d) 240 268
Billings (In Re), 838 F.2d 405 (10th Cir. 1988)... 343
Birch Hills Credit Union Ltd. v. Canadian Imperial Bank of Commerce
    (1988), 52 D.L.R. (4th) 113, 8 P.P.S.A.C. 199 (Sask. C.A.)........................... 593
Bird v. Ft. Frances, [1949] 2 D.L.R. 791 (Ont. H.C.) 165
Bishopsgate Investment Management Ltd. (In Liquidation) v. Homan, [1995]
    Ch. 211, [1995] 1 W.L.R. 31, [1995] 1 All E.R. 347 (C.A.).................... 335, 475
Black Hills Credit Union v. C.I.B.C., [1988] S.J. No. 782, 8 P.P.S.A.C. 199
    (C.A.) 267
Blouin (Re) (sub nom. Caisse Populaire Desjardins de Val-Brillant v. Blouin),
    2003 SCC 31, [2003] 1 S.C.R. 666.. 54
Blower v. Hepburn (1980), 112 D.L.R. (3d) 474, 13 Alta. L.R. (2d) 100 (Q.B.)..... 169
Bodnard v. Capital Office Systems Inc. (1992), 3 P.P.S.A.C. (2d) 71
    (Sask. C.A.).. 446
Borden (U.K.) Ltd. v. Scottish Timber Products Ltd., [1981] Ch. 25 (C.A.) 503
Bow Valley Husky (Bermuda) Ltd. v. Saint John Shipbuilding Ltd., [1997]
    3 S.C.R. 1210, 153 D.L.R. (4th) 385 602
Boychuk v. Hunterline Trucking (B.C.) Ltd. (1997), 122 Man. R. (2d) 114,
    [1997] M.J. No. 403 (Q.B.) 575
Bread Man Inc. (Re) (1978), 21 O.R. (2d) 59, 89 D.L.R. (3d) 599 (H.C.J.) 572
Bristol Yacht Sales Inc. (Re), [1984] B.C.J. No. 2703, 52 B.C.L.R. 246,
    51 C.B.R. (N.S.) 279 (S.C.) 79
British Columbia (Deputy Sheriff) v. Canada (1992), 90 D.L.R. (4th) 680,
    [1992] B.C.J. No. 810 (C.A.)..397, 401
British Columbia Land & Invesment Agency Ltd. v. Ishitaka (1911),
    45 S.C.R. 302, 20 W.L.R. 308 545
British Columbia v. Henfrey Samson Belair Ltd., [1989] 2 S.C.R. 24,
    [1989] S.C.J. No. 78 419
British Columbia v. PT Car and Yacht Rental Inc., 2003 BCSC 1073,
    5 P.P.S.A.C. (3d) 332...414
Bronson (Re), [1996] B.C.J. No. 216, 18 B.C.L.R. (3d) 195, 39 C.B.R.
    (3d) 33 (S.C.) 73, 75
Brookfield Construction Co. (Re) (1963), 5 C.B.R. (N.S.) 283, 42 D.L.R.
    (2d) 240, 50 M.P.R. 211 (N.S.S.C.) 434
Buchan v. Saskatchewan Government Insurance, [1997] S.J. No. 726,
    13 P.P.S.A.C. (2d) 61 (Q.B.) 272, 273
Bunbury Foods Pty Ltd. v. National Bank Of Australasia Ltd. (1984),
    152 C.L.R. 491 (H.C. Aust.) 524
Burton v. Toronto Dominion Bank, [1976] O.J. No. 809, 22 C.B.R. (N.S.) 207
    (H.C.J.) 440
Business Development Bank of Canada v. ABN Amro Leasing, 2002 PESCTD
    14, [2002] P.E.I.J. No. 18, aff'd 2003 PESCAD 5, 5 P.P.S.A.C. (3d) 76.........276
Business Development Bank of Canada v. S & S Mobile Refrigeration (1996),
    12 P.P.S.A.C. (2d) 298, 28 O.T.C. 48 (Ont. Ct. Gen. Div.) 163

C.C. Motor Sales Ltd. v. Chan, [1926] S.C.R. 485, [1926] 3 D.L.R. 712 64

C.C. Petroleum Ltd. v. Allen, [2003] O.J. No. 3726, 46 C.B.R. (4th) 221
    (C.A.), var'g [2002] O.J. No. 2203, 35 C.B.R. (4th) 22 (S.C.J.) 428, 466

C.I.B.C. Mortgage Corp. v. Branch (1999), 68 B.C.L.R. (3d) 334, [1999]
    B.C.J. No. 503 (S.C.).. 571

C.I.B.C. v. Melnitzer (Trustee of), [1993] O.J. No. 3021, 6 P.P.S.A.C. (2d) 5,
    23 C.B.R. (3d) 161 (Gen. Div.) 216, 250

C.O. Funk & Son, Inc. v. Sullivan Equipment, Inc., 92 Ill.App3d 659,
    415 N.E.2d 1308 (Ill. App. 1981), aff'd 431 N.E.2d 370, 89 Ill.2d 27
    (Ill. 1982) 478

Caisse Populaire Desjardins de Val-Brilliant v. Blouin, 2003 SCC 31, [2003]
    1 S.C.R. 666, 225 D.L.R. (4th) 577 113

California Airmotive Corp. v. Jones, 415 F.2d 554, 24 Ohio Misc. 255
    (C.A. Ohio 1969) 547

Camco Inc. v. Frances Olson Realty (1979) Ltd., [1986] 6 W.W.R. 258,
    6 P.P.S.A.C. 167 (Sask. C.A.)...287, 290, 292–93

Cammell v. Sewell (1860), 5 H & N 728, 157 E.R. 1371 (Exch. Ct.)................. 134

Camrati Investments Inc. v. Manulife Bank of Canada, [1993] O.J. No. 1332,
    21 C.B.R. (3d) 118 (Gen. Div.)... 433

Canada (Attorney General) v. Brock, [1991] B.C.J. No. 2745, 59 B.C.L.R.
    (2d) 261 (S.C.) 165

Canada (Deputy Attorney General) v. Schwab Construction Ltd., 2002
    SKCA 6, [2002] 4 W.W.R. 628 415

Canada Deposit Insurance Corp. v. Canadian Commercial Bank, [1992]
    3 S.C.R. 558, 97 D.L.R. (4th) 385 .... 428, 466

Canada Mortgage and Housing Corporation v. Apostolou (1995),
    22 O.R. (3d) 190, 9 P.P.S.A.C. (2d) 89 (Gen. Div.)..................................... 399

Canada Permanent Trust Co v. Thomas (1983), 149 D.L.R. (3d) 338,
    3 P.P.S.A.C. 66 (Sask. Q.B.)... 578

Canada Trustco Mortgage Co. v. Wenngatz Const & Holdings Ltd. (1986),
    60 C.B.R. (N.S.) 270, [1986] B.C.J. No. 3115 (S.C.) 572

Canada Trustco Mortgage Corp. v. Port O'Call Hotel Inc., [1996] 1 S.C.R. 963,
    11 P.P.S.A.C. (2d) 1...410

Canadian Acceptance Corporation Limited v. Matte (1957), 9 D.L.R.
    (2d) 304, 22 W.W.R. 97 (Sask. C.A.) 153

Canadian Bank of Commerce v. Munro, [1925] S.C.R. 302, [1925]
    2 D.L.R. 928 375

Canadian Commercial Bank v. Tisdale Farm Equipment Ltd., [1984]
    6 W.W.R. 122, [1984] S.J. No. 590 (Q.B.), aff'd [1987] 1 W.W.R. 574,
    [1985] S.J. No. 684 (C.A.) 285

Canadian Credit Men's Trust Assn. v. Beaver Trucking Ltd., [1959]
    S.C.R. 311, 38 C.B.R. 1.. 402

Canadian Exotic Cattle Breeders' Co-Operative (Re), [1979] B.C.J. No. 1218,
    14 B.C.L.R. 183 (S.C.) 416

Canadian Imperial Bank of Commerce v. 64576 Manitoba Ltd., [1990]
M.J. No. 248, 67 Man.R. (2d) 172, 79 C.B.R. (N.S.) 308 (Q.B.),
aff'd (1991), 77 D.L.R. (4th) 190, [1991] 2 W.W.R. 323, [1991]
M.J. No. 32, 2 C.B.R. (3d) 4 (C.A.) 60, 97
Canadian Imperial Bank of Commerce v. A.K. Construction (1988) Ltd.,
[1995] 8 W.W.R. 120, 9 P.P.S.A.C. (2d) 257, [1995] A.J. No. 412
(Q.B.) 28, 313
Canadian Imperial Bank of Commerce v. A.K. Construction (1988) Ltd.
(1996), 186 A.R. 1, 11 P.P.S.A.C. (2d) 280 (Alta. Q.B.), aff'd [1998]
A.J. No. 997, 223 A.R. 115 (C.A.) 145
Canadian Imperial Bank of Commerce v. Bedard, [1985] N.B.J. No. 209,
63 N.B.R. (2d) 223 (Q.B.T.D.) 199
Canadian Imperial Bank of Commerce v. Crockett's Western Wear, [1984]
5 W.W.R. 282, 9 D.L.R. (4th) 765 (Alta. C.A.) 588
Canadian Imperial Bank of Commerce v. E & S.L. Liquidators (1994), [1994]
B.C.J. No. 2710, [1995] 1 C.N.L.R. 23, 34 C.P.C. (3d) 338 (S.C.) 115
Canadian Imperial Bank of Commerce v. Fletcher (1978), 82 D.L.R. (3d) 257,
18 O.R. (2d) 289 (H.C.J) 587
Canadian Imperial Bank of Commerce v. Hallahan (1990), 69 D.L.R.
(4th) 449, [1990] O.J. No. 861, 1 P.P.S.A.C. (2d) 58 (C.A.), leave to
appeal to S.C.C. refused [1991] 1 S.C.R. vi, 74 D.L.R. (4th) viii,
129 N.R. 238n 110
Canadian Imperial Bank of Commerce v. International Harvester Credit
Corp. of Canada Ltd. (1986), 4 P.P.S.A.C. 329 (Ont. H.C.J.), rev'd on
other grounds [1986] O.J. No. 1315, 6 P.P.S.A.C. 273 (C.A) 168
Canadian Imperial Bank of Commerce v. Klunkovski, [1983] O.J. No. 1058,
3 P.P.S.A.C. 216 (H.C.J.) 267
Canadian Imperial Bank of Commerce v. Lush, [2001] N.B.J. No. 28,
2 P.P.S.A.C. (3d) 61 (Q.B.T.D.) 286
Canadian Imperial Bank of Commerce v. Maidstone Farming Ltd. (1984),
46 O.R. (2d) 699, 52 C.B.R. (N.S.) 174, 4 P.P.S.A.C. 127 (Co. Ct.)............... 97
Canadian Imperial Bank of Commerce v. Marathon Realty Co., [1987]
5 W.W.R. 236, 7 P.P.S.A.C. 230 (C.A.) 333
Canadian Imperial Bank of Commerce v. Moshi (1989), 9 P.P.S.A.C. 275,
[1989] O.J. No. 2491 (H.C.J.), rev'd on other grounds (1992),
3 P.P.S.A.C. (2d) 86, [1992] O.J. No. 593 (C.A.) 15
Canadian Imperial Bank of Commerce v. Nelson & Nelson Holdings Inc.
(1988), 68 Sask. R. 278, [1988] S.J. No. 266 (Q.B.) 492
Canadian Imperial Bank of Commerce v. Northland Trucks (1978) Ltd.
(1985), 38 Sask. R. 95, 4 P.P.S.A.C. 254 (Q.B) 533
Canadian Imperial Bank of Commerce v. Royal Bank of Canada (1982),
19 Man. R. (2d) 67, [1982] M.J. No. 159 (Q.B.) 581
Canadian Imperial Bank of Commerce v. Westfield Industries Ltd., [1990]
S.J. No. 341, 86 Sask. R. 1, 1 P.P.S.A.C. (2d) 142 (Q.B.) 94, 335

Canadian Imperial Bank of Commerce v. Yorkshire & Canadian Trust Ltd.,
[1939] S.C.R. 85, [1939] 1 D.L.R. 401 103

Canadian Pacific Airlines Ltd. v. Canadian Imperial Bank of Commerce
(1987), 61 O.R. (2d) 233, 42 D.L.R. (4th) 375, [1987] O.J. No. 856 (H.C.J.) 81

Canadian Western Bank v. Baker (1999), 1999 SKQB 252, [2000]
4 W.W.R. 105, 15 P.P.S.A.C. (2d) 247, aff'd 2000 SKCA 108,
[2000] S.J. No. 584, 2 P.P.S.A.C. (3d) 33 .... 72, 73

Canadian Western Bank v. Gescan Ltd. (1991), 82 Alta. L.R. (2d) 366,
2 P.P.S.A.C. (2d) 142 (Alta. Q.B.) 583

Canamsucco Road House Co. v. Lngas Ltd., [1991] O.J. No. 1752, 2 P.P.S.A.C.
(2d) 203 (Gen. Div.), rev'd on other grounds [1997] O.J. No. 1689,
12 P.P.S.A.C. (2d) 227 (C.A.) 320, 322

Canron Inc. v. Ferrofab Ltée. (1986), 7 B.C.L.R. (2d) 291, [1986]
B.C.J. No. 889 (Co. Ct.) 156

Canstar Trucking Ltd. v. Bank Of Nova Scotia (1986), 48 Sask. R. 136,
7 P.P.S.A.C. 105 (Q.B.) 546

Capital City Savings & Credit Union Ltd. v. Alberta Motor Products Ltd.,
2003 ABQB 129, 5 P.P.S.A.C. (3d) 171 183

Capital Plymouth Chrysler Inc. v. Euro Sport Auto Sales Ltd., 1998
ABQB 449, 14 P.P.S.A.C. (2d) 30 183

Cardel Leasing Ltd. v. Maxmenko (1991), 2 P.P.S.A.C. (2d) 302,
[1991] O.J. No. 2163 (Gen. Div.) 151

Carr v. Shamrock Credit Union, [1987] S.J. No. 328, 7 P.P.S.A.C. 66 (Q.B.) 280

Carson Restaurants International Ltd. v. A-1 United Restaurant Supply Ltd.
(1988), [1989] 1 W.W.R. 266, [1988] S.J. No. 660, 8 P.P.S.A.C. 276
(Sask. Q.B.) 28–29, 375

Case Credit Ltd. v. Poirer, 1999 SKQB 151, [1999] S.J. No. 682,
186 Sask. R. 153 72

Case Power & Equipment v. 366551 Alberta Inc. (Receiver of) (1994),
23 Alta. L.R. (3d) 361, 8 P.P.S.A.C. (2d) 267, 118 D.L.R. (4th) 637,
157 A.R. 212, 77 W.A.C. 212 (C.A.) 252, 271, 272, 273

Casey v. City National Leasing Ltd. (1987), 51 Alta. L.R. (2d) 85, [1987]
A.J. No. 238 (Q.B.) 529

Cedarbrooke Sawmills Inc. (Re), [1990] B.C.J. No. 1785, 80 C.B.R.
(N.S.) 31 (S.C.) 434

Centennial Plymouth Chrysler (1973) Ltd. v. Conlin, [2000] O.J. No. 709,
[2000] O.T.C. 138, 15 P.P.S.A.C. (2d) 206 (S.C.J.) 68

Central Guaranty Trust Co. v. Bruncor Leasing Inc. (1992), 97 D.L.R.
(4th) 133, 4 P.P.S.A.C. (2d) 229 (Ont. Ct. Gen. Div.) 164

Central Refrigeration & Restaurant Services Inc. (Trustee of) v. Canadian
Imperial Bank of Commerce (1986), 47 Sask. R. 124, 5 P.P.S.A.C. 262,
[1986] S.J. No. 4 (C.A.) 220, 481

Century Credit Corporation v. Richard (1962), 34 D.L.R. (2d) 291,
[1962] O.R. 815 (C.A.) 134

Cessna Finance Corp. v. Bielenberg Masonary Contracting Inc., 3
    5 U.C.C. Rep. Serv. 315, 1982 W.L. 171037 (D. Kan. 1982) 546
Charles A. Hare Ltd. v. Payn (1982), 18 B.L.R. 209, 2 P.P.S.A.C. 93,
    [1982] O.J. No. 2519 (H.C.) 491
Charter Financial Co. v. Royal Bank (2002), 159 O.A.C. 201, 4 P.P.S.A.C.
    (3d) 4 (C.A.) 266
Chiips Inc. v. Skyview Hotels Ltd. (1994), 116 D.L.R. (4th) 385, 155 A.R. 281,
    [1994] 9 W.W.R. 727, 73 W.A.C. 281, 21 Alta. L.R. (3d) 225,
    27 C.B.R. (3d) 161, 7 P.P.S.A.C. (2d) 23 (C.A.) 87, 370, 371, 373–74
Chrysler Credit Canada Ltd v. Webber, [1993] A.J. No. 720, 6 P.P.S.A.C.
    (2d) 106 (Q.B.), rev'd on reconsideration [1994] A.J. No. 292,
    18 Alta. L.R. (3d) 117 (Q.B.) 272
Chrysler Credit Canada Ltd. v. M.V.L. Leasing Ltd., [1993] O.J. No. 931,
    5 P.P.S.A.C. (2d) 92 (Gen. Div.) 288, 292
Chrysler Credit Canada Ltd. v. Royal Bank of Canada, [1986]
    6 W.W.R. 338, 6 P.P.S.A.C. 153 (Sask. C.A.) 344–45
CIBC Mortgage Corp. v. Coleski, [1999] N.S.J. No. 336, 13 C.B.R. (4th) 17
    (S.C.) 441
CIBC Mortgage Corp. v. Stenerson, 1998 ABQB 482, 220 A.R. 248 441
CIBC v. Otto Timm Enterprises (1996), 26 O.R. (3d) 724, 10 P.P.S.A.C.
    (2d) 228 (C.A.) 168
Cities Service Oil Co. v. Ferris, 9 U.C.C. Rep. Serv. 899, 1971 W.L. 17911
    (Mich. Dist. 1971) 547
Clark Equipment of Canada Ltd. v. Bank of Montreal, [1984] 4 W.W.R. 519,
    (1984) 8 D.L.R. (4th) 424, 4 P.P.S.A.C. 38 (Man. C.A.) 191, 339, 343
Clarke's Refrigerated Transport Pty., Ltd. (Re), [1982] V.R. 989 (S. Ct.) 317–18
Cleve's Sporting Goods Ltd. v. J.G. Touchie and Associates, [1986]
    N.S.J. No. 179, 58 C.B.R. (N.S.) 304 (C.A.) 441
Clow v. Gershman Transport International Ltd. (2000), 265 A.R. 181, 1
    P.P.S.A.C. (3d) 117 (Q.B.) 581
Colliar v. Robinson Diesel Injection Ltd. (1990), 81 Sask. R. 144,
    9 P.P.S.A.C. 266 (Q.B.), aff'd (1990), 86 Sask. R. 198, 1 P.P.S.A.C.
    (2d) 123 (C.A.) 404
Colpitts v. Sherwood, [1927] 3 D.L.R. 7 (Alta. C.A.) 605
Commcorp Financial Services Inc. v. R & R Investments Corp. (1995),
    173 A.R. 1, 10 P.P.S.A.C. (2d) 87 (Q.B.) 276
Commercial Credit Corp. Ltd. v. Harry D. Shields Ltd. (1980), 29 O.R.
    (2d) 106, 112 D.L.R. (3d) 153, 1 P.P.S.A.C. 99 (H.C.J.), aff'd (1981),
    32 O.R. (2d) 703, 122 D.L.R. (3d) 736, 1 P.P.S.A.C. 301 (C.A.) 97, 413
Commercial Credit Corp. v. Niagara Finance Corp., [1940] S.C.R. 420,
    [1940] 3 D.L.R. 1 64
Community Bank v. Jones, 566 P.2d 470, 278 Or. 647 (Or. 1977) 572
Conn (In Re), 16 B.R. 454, 33 U.C.C. Rep. Serv. 701 (W.D. Ky. 1982) 347
Connex Press, Inc. v. International Airmotive, Inc. 436 F. Supp. 51
    (D.C.D.C. 1977) 546

Consolidated Equipment Sales, Inc. v. First Bank & Trust Co. of Guthrie,
627 P.2d 432 (Okl. 1981) 573

Continental Bank v. Sheridan Equipment Ltd., [1986] O.J. No. 489,
60 C.B.R. (N.S.) 14 (Ont. H.C.J.) 72, 73, 75

Contrail Leasing Partners, Ltd. v. Consolidated Airways, Inc.,
742 F.2d 1095 (C.A. Ind. 1984) 546

Convoy Supply Canada Ltd. v. Northern Credit Union Ltd., [2001]
O.J. No. 1483, 2 P.P.S.A.C. (3d) 231 (S.C.J.) 78, 79

Coopers & Lybrand Ltd. v. Lumberland Building Materials Ltd. (1983),
150 D.L.R. (3d) 411, 49 B.C.L.R. 239 (S.C.) 561

Copp v. Medi-Dent Service (1991), 3 O.R. (3d) 570, 2 P.P.S.A.C. (2d) 114
(Gen. Div.) 545

Cormier v. Federal Business Development Bank (1984), 25 B.L.R. 194, 3
P.P.S.A.C. 161, [1983] O.J. No. 924 (Ont. Co. Ct.)............................... 163, 494

Corsbie v. J.I. Case Threshing Machine Co. (1913), 25 W.L.R. 466
(Sask. S.C.).. 398, 401

Corscadden v. Crown Life Insurance Co. (1994), 129 Sask. R. 244,
8 P.P.S.A.C. (2d) 177 (Q.B.) 113

Costley v. Pioneer Credit Union Ltd. (1991), 2 P.P.S.A.C. (2d) 212,
[1991] S.J. No. 503 (Q.B.)..533, 574

Country Kitchen Donuts Ltd. (Re) (1980), 34 C.B.R. (N.S.) 252,
1 P.P.S.A.C. 176 (Ont. H.C.J.).. 31

Coupland Acceptance Ltd. v. Walsh, [1954] S.C.R. 90, [1954] 2 D.L.R. 129..... 378

Craddock Trucking Ltd. v. Leclair, [1995] A.J. No. 250, 28 Alta. L.R.
(3d) 145 (Q.B.) 412

Credit foncier franco-canadien v. Walker, [1938] O.W.N. 339 (H.C.J.)............. 538

Credit Suisse Canada v. 1133 Yonge Street Holdings (1996), 28 O.R. (3d) 670,
11 P.P.S.A.C. (2d) 375, 40 C.B.R. (3d) 214, 26 B.L.R. (2d) 282, [1996]
O.J. No. 1264 (Gen. Div.), var'd on other grounds (1998), 41 O.R.
(3d) 632, 5 C.B.R. (4th) 174, 14 P.P.S.A.C. (2d) 61, 41 B.L.R. (2d) 1,
[1998] O.J. No. 4468 (C.A.) 175, 176, 286, 458

Cronin Fire Equipment Ltd. (Re) (1993), 14 O.R. (3d) 269, [1993]
O.J. No. 1749, 21 C.B.R. (3d) 127 (Gen. Div.) 74

Crop & Soil Service Inc. v. Oxford Leaseway Ltd. (2000), 48 O.R.
(3d) 291, 186 D.L.R. (4th) 85, [2000] O.J. No. 1372 (C.A.) 74

Crosbie-Hill v. Sayer, [1908] 1 Ch. 866.. 378

Cuckmere Brick Co. Ltd. v. Mutual Finance Ltd., [1971] Ch. 949 (C.A.) 545

Cycle Products Distributing Co. (In Re), 118 B.R. 643, 12 U.C.C.
Rep. Serv. 2d 889 (Bankr. S.D. Ill. 1990) 319

Daewoo Heavy Industries America Corporation v. Northwest Equipment Inc.,
2002 ABCA 79, [2002] 6 W.W.R. 444... 327

DaimlerChrysler Financial Services (Debis) Canada Inc. v. Mega Pets Ltd.,
2002 BCCA 242, 212 D.L.R. (4th) 41 415

Dale Tingley Chrysler Plymouth Ltd. v. Chris & Don Enterprises Ltd.,
    [1994] S.J. No. 686, 8 P.P.S.A.C. (2d) 191 (Q.B.), rev'd on other grounds
    [1995] S.J. No. 537, 10 P.P.S.A.C. (2d) 112 (C.A.) 163
Darzinskas (Re) (1981), 34 O.R. (2d) 782, 132 D.L.R. (3d) 77 (H.C.J.)............. 213
Dauphin Plains Credit Union Ltd. v. Xyloid Industries Ltd., [1980]
    1 S.C.R. 1182, 108 D.L.R. (3d) 257..410, 415
Davenport v. Chrysler Credit Corp. 818 S.W.2d 23 (Tenn. App. 1991)............. 530
David Allester Ltd. (Re), [1922] 2 Ch. 211 62
David Morris Fine Cars Ltd. v. North Sky Trading Inc. (1994), 158 A.R. 117,
    [1994] 9 W.W.R. 680, [1994] A.J. No. 558, 27 C.B.R. (3d) 252 (Q.B.),
    aff'd (1996), 38 Alta. L.R. (3d) 428, 11 P.P.S.A.C. (2d) 142,
    184 A.R. 291, [1996] A.J. No. 392 (C.A.) 95, 293
Dearle v. Hall (1823), 3 Russ. 1, [1824–34] All E.R. Rep. 28,
    38 E.R. 475 (Ch.) 100, 226, 227
Dedrick v. Ashdown (1888), 15 S.C.R. 227 285
Delaney v. Downey (1912), 2 W.W.R. 599, 21 W.L.R. 577 (Sask. K.B.).............. 285
DeLay First Nat. Bank & Trust Co. v. Jacobson Appliance Co.,
    243 N.W.2d 745, 196 Neb. 398 (Neb. 1976) 559
Delisle (Re) (1988), 69 C.B.R. (N.S.) 89, 27 B.C.L.R. (2d) 198, 52 D.L.R.
    (4th) 106 (B.C.S.C.) 156
Delron Computers Inc. v. ITT Industries of Canada Ltd. (Receiver of),
    [1995] 5 W.W.R. 174, (1995), 31 C.B.R. (3d) 75 (Sask. Q.B.) 527
Dempster's Custom Sheet Metal Ltd. (Re) (1983), 41 O.R. (2d) 424,
    2 P.P.S.A.C. 308 (C.A.)... 183
Denolf v. Brown (1994), 17 Alta. L.R. (3d) 374, 6 P.P.S.A.C. (2d) 181
    (Q.B.)...283, 399
Devaynes v. Noble; Clayton's Case (1816), 1 Mer. 572, 35 E.R. 781,
    [1814-23] All E.R. Rep. 1 ....468–69, 470
Devoe v. Long (1950), [1951] 1 D.L.R. 203, 26 M.P.R. 357
    (N.B.S.C.(A.D.)) 183, 529, 530
Dickie Estate (In Re), [1925] 4 D.L.R. 527, 5 C.B.R. 864 (N.S.S.C.) 435
Direct Rental Centre (West) Ltd. V. A.C. Waring Associates Inc.,
    2001 ABCA 233, 205 D.L.R. 4th 651, aff'g (1997), 50 C.B.R.
    (3d) 200, 13 P.P.S.A.C. (2d) 299 (Alta. Q.B.) 444, 447, 449
Dominion Used Store Fixtures Ltd. (Re), [1939] 4 D.L.R. 735,
    20 C.B.R. 325 (Ont. S.C. In Bankruptcy) 433
Donnelly v. International Harvester Credit Corp. of Canada Ltd. (1983),
    2 P.P.S.A.C. 290, [1983] O.J. No. 2426 (Co. Ct.).. 15
Doran v. Hare (1994), 6 P.P.S.A.C. (2d) 295, [1994] O.J. No. 51 (Gen. Div.) 545
Dor-O-Matic of Canada Inc. (Re) (1996), 28 O.R. (3d) 125, 11 P.P.S.A.C.
    (2d) 149 (Gen. Div.)... 518
Doucet (Re) (1983), 42 O.R. (2d) 638, 150 D.L.R. (3d) 53, 3 P.P.S.A.C. 78
    (Ont. H.C.J.).. 99, 603
Dubé v. Bank of Montreal (1986), 27 D.L.R. (4th) 718, [1986] S.J. No. 14,
    5 P.P.S.A.C. 269 (C.A.)... 97

Dupuis Frères Limitée (Re) (1979), 28 C.B.R. (N.S.) 313 (Que. S.C.) 79

E. Pfeiffer Weinkellerei-Weineinkauf G.m.b.H. v. Arbuthnot Factors Ltd.,
    [1988] 1 W.L.R. 150 (Q.B.D.)... 423
E.A. Fretz Company, Inc. (In Re), 565 F.2d 366 (5th Cir. 1978) 318
East Central Development Corp. v. Freightliner Truck Sales (Regina) Ltd.,
    [1997] 5 W.W.R. 231, [1997] S.J. No. 25, 12 P.P.S.A.C. (2d) 328 (Q.B.) 95
Eastern Canada Savings & Loan Co. v. Campbell (No. 2) (1971), 1 Nfld. &
    P.E.I.R. 448, 16 C.B.R. (N.S.) 75 (P.E.I. Ch.) 432
Econo Transport Inc. (Re), [1982] O.J. No. 2438, 43 C.B.R. (N.S.) 230, 2
    P.P.S.A.C. 208 (Ont. S.C. (Mast.)) 72
Elmcrest Furniture Manufacturing Ltd. v. 216200 Alberta Ltd (Receiver
    Manager of) (1985), 41 Sask. R. 125, 5 P.P.S.A.C. 22 (Q.B.) 274
Engel Canada Inc. v. TCE Capital Corp., [2002] O.J. No. 2361, 4 P.P.S.A.C.
    (3d) 124, [2002] O.T.C. 407, 34 C.B.R. (4th) 169 (S.C.J.) 87, 374
Ens Toyota Ltd. v. Megill Stephenson Co. (1989), 81 Sask. R. 22,
    9 P.P.S.A.C. 169 (Q.B.) 138
Ensign Pacific Leasing Ltd. v. Lumar Auto Sales (1998), 52 B.C.L.R.
    (3d) 218, 13 P.P.S.A.C. (2d) 249 (S.C.)... 294
Erjo Investments Ltd. v. Michener Allen Auctioneering Ltd. (2004),
    241 Sask. R. 228, 6 P.P.S.A.C. (3d) 220 (C.A.) 404
Ernst Bros. Co. v. Canada Permanent Mortgage Corp. (1920), 57 D.L.R. 500
    (Ont. S.C.(A.D.)) 571
Estevan Credit Union Limited v. Dyer, [1997] 8 W.W.R. 49, additional
    reasons given [1997] 8 W.W.R. 458 (Sask. Q.B.)...................................287, 292
Euroclean Canada Inc. v. Forest Glade Investments Ltd. (1985), 49 O.R.
    (2d) 769, 4 P.P.S.A.C. 271, 54 C.B.R. (N.S.) 65, 16 D.L.R. (4th) 289,
    8 O.A.C. 1 (Ont. C.A.), leave to appeal to S.C.C. refused (1985), 55 C.B.R.
    (N.S.) xxvii, 16 D.L.R. (4th) 289n (S.C.C.) 87, 166, 369–70, 371, 373
Ex parte Sterling (1809), 16 Ves. 258, 33 E.R. 982 (Ch.) 408

F.C. Jones & Sons v. Jones, [1996] 4 All E.R. 721 (C.A.) 457
F.W.C. Land Co. (Receiver-Manager of) v. Turnbull, [1997] B.C.J. No. 1985,
    49 C.B.R. (3d) 82 (S.C.)... 105
Fairline Boats Ltd. v. Leger, [1980] O.J. No. 216, 1 P.P.S.A.C. 218
    (H.C.J.)...287, 292
Farm Credit Corp. v. Gannon, [1993] 6 W.W.R. 736, 5 P.P.S.A.C. (2d) 52
    (Sask. Q.B.) 351
Farm Credit Corp. v. ValleyBeef Producers Co-operative Ltd., 2002 SKCA 100,
    [2002] S.J. No. 499, 36 C.B.R. (4th) 121 85
Farmers Co-operative Elevator Co. v. Union State Bank, 409 N.W.2d 178
    (Iowa 1987)... 359
Farm-Rite Equipment Ltd. (Receiver of) v. Robinson Alamo Sales Ltd.,
    [1986] S.J. No. 256, 5 P.P.S.A.C. 286 (Q.B.)... 167
Farwest Systems (Receiver of) v. Omron Business Systems Corp., [1988]
    B.C.J. No. 1051, 69 C.B.R. (N.S.) 82 (S.C.) 78

Fedders Financial Corp. v. Chiarelli Bros., Inc., 289 A.2d 169
    (Pa. Super. 1972) 339
Federal Business Development Bank v. Bramalea Ltd. (1983), 144 D.L.R.
    (3d) 410, [1983] O.J. No. 297, 2 P.P.S.A.C. 317 (H.C.J.), aff'd (1983),
    150 D.L.R. (3d) 768 (Ont. C.A.) 71
Federal Business Development Bank v. Ontario (Registrar of Personal Property
    Security) (1984), 7 D.L.R. (4th) 479, 4 P.P.S.A.C. 1 (Ont. Div. Ct.) 244
Feduk v. Bank of Montreal, [1992] S.J. No. 254, 3 P.P.S.A.C. (2d) 310 (Q.B.).... 173
Fiatallis North America Inc v. Pigott Construction Ltd. (1992),
    3 P.P.S.A.C. (2d) 30, [1992] O.J. No. 178 (Gen. Div.) 571
Fields (Re) (2002), 59 O.R. (3d) 611, 32 C.B.R. (4th) 216 (S.C.J.),
    aff'd (2004), 71 O.R. (3d) 11, 240 D.L.R. (4th) 494 (C.A.) 448
Finchside International Ltd. v. Roy Foss Motors Ltd., [1994] O.J. No. 3266,
    29 C.B.R. (3d) 108, 10 P.P.S.A.C. (2d) 33 (Gen. Div.) 73
First City Capital Ltd. v. Arthur Andersen Inc. (1984), 46 O.R. (2d) 168,
    4 P.P.S.A.C. 74 (H.C.J.) 175
First National Bank of Brush v. Bostron, 564 P2d 964, 39 Colo. App. 107
    (Colo. App. 1977) 359, 504
First National Bank v. Cudmore (1917), 34 D.L.R. 201, 2 W.W.R. 479,
    10 Sask. L. R. 201 (C.A.) 86
First Nations Farm Credit (Manitoba) Corp. v. McKay (2001), [2000]
    M.J. No. 392, 149 Man. R. (2d) 311, [2001] 3 C.N.L.R. 114 (Q.B.) 115
Fisher v. Seton Lake Indian Band, [1995] B.C.J. 2512 (S.C.)............................. 115
Fleurke (Re) (1992), 133 A.R. 104, 4 P.P.S.A.C. (2d) 59 (Q.B) 273
Flexi-Coil Ltd. v. Kindersley District Credit Union Ltd. (1993),
    107 D.L.R. (4th) 129, [1994] 1 W.W.R. 1, [1993] S.J. No. 546
    (C.A.) 370, 381, 382, 384–85, 457, 462, 464, 466–67
Flintoft v. Royal Bank of Canada, [1964] S.C.R. 631, 47 D.L.R.
    (2d) 141, 49 W.W.R. 301 ....81, 83, 455, 596
Ford Credit Canada Ltd. v. Percival Mercury Sales Ltd., [1986] S.J. No. 93,
    50 Sask.R. 268, 6 P.P.S.A.C. 288 (C.A.), additional reasons at [1986]
    S.J. No. 515, 50 Sask.R. 270, aff'g on other grounds [1984] S.J. No. 437,
    34 Sask.R. 134, 4 P.P.S.A.C. 92 (Q.B.) 167
Ford Motor Credit Corp. v. Centre Motors of Brampton (1982), 38 O.R.
    (2d) 516, 137 D.L.R. (3d) 634 (H.C.J.) 292
Ford Tractor Equipment Sales Co. of Canada Ltd. v. Otto Grundman
    Implements Ltd. (Trustee of) (1979), 9 D.L.R. (3d) 206, 72 W.W.R. 1,
    13 C.B.R. (N.S.) 322 (Man. C.A.) 81, 83
Ford v. Petford (1996), 11 P.P.S.A.C. (2d) 227, [1996] B.C.J. No. 1074 (S.C.) 603
Foskett v. McKeown, [1998] Ch. 265 (C.A.) 335
Foster (Re) (1992), 8 O.R. (3d) 514, 89 D.L.R. (4th) 555, [1992] O.J. No. 352
    (Gen. Div.) 110, 212
Fotti v. 777 Management Inc. [1981] M.J. No. 317 (1981), 2 P.P.S.A.C. 32,
    [1981] 5 W.W.R. 48 (Man. Q.B.) 29, 267

Frado v. Bank of Montreal (1984), 60 A.R. 102, [1984] A.J. No. 706,
    34 Alta. L.R. (2d) 293 (Q.B.) 86
Frankel v. Canadian Imperial Bank of Commerce, [1997] O.J. No. 2671,
    12 P.P.S.A.C. (2d) 306 (Gen. Div.) 367, 400
Franklin National Bank of Morrill, Nebraska, 20 UCC Rep. Serv. 2d 1409,
    848 P.2d 775 (Wyo. 1993) 288
Franklin State Bank v. Parker, 346 A.2d 632, 136 Super. 476
    (N.J. Dist. Ct. 1975) 541
Fraser (Re), [1994] B.C.J. No. 410, 6 P.P.S.A.C. (2d) 235 (S.C.) 251
Fraser River Pile & Dredge Ltd. v. Can-Dive Services Ltd., [1999]
    3 S.C.R. 108, [1999] S.C.J. No. 48 369
Fraser v. Macpherson (1898), 34 N.B.R. 417 (C.A.) 169
French Lumber Co. v. Commercial Realty & Finance Co., 195 N.E.2d 507
    (Mass. 1964) 352, 378
Furmanek v. Community Futures Development Corp. of Howe Sound
    (1998), 162 D.L.R. (4th) 501, 14 P.P.S.A.C. (2d) 1 (B.C.C.A.) 370, 377

G.M.S. Securities & Appraisals Ltd. v. Rich-Wood Kitchens Ltd. (1995), 1
    21 D.L.R. (4th) 278 , 21 O.R. (3d) 761, [1995] O.J. No. 44 (C.A.) 494
Garry v. Sternbauer Estate, [2000] O.J. No. 2704, 1 P.P.S.A.C. (3d) 51 (S.C.J.) 184
Gates Fertilizers Ltd. v. Waddell, [1985] S.J. No. 523, 5 P.P.S.A.C. 79 (Q.B.) 274
Gatx Corporate Leasing Ltd. v. William Day Construction Ltd., [1986]
    O.J. No. 806, 6 P.P.S.A.C. 188, 60 C.B.R. (N.S.) 319 (H.C.J.) 70
Gauntlet Energy Corp. (Re), 2003 ABQB 718, 336 A.R. 302, 36 B.L.R.
    (3d) 250 112
Gauthier Estate v. Capital City Savings & Credit Union Ltd. (1992),
    129 A.R. 12, [1992] A.J. No. 250, 3 P.P.S.A.C. (2d) 176 (Q.B.) 107
GE Capital Canada Acquisitions Inc. v. Dix Performance (Trustee of)
    (1994), [1995] 2 W.W.R. 738, 99 B.C.L.R. (2d) 241, 8 P.P.S.A.C.
    (2d) 197 (B.C.S.C.) 26, 191, 192
Gelowitz v. Garcon Enterprises Ltd., [1995] S.J. No. 351, 132 Sask. R. 273,
    9 P.P.S.A.C. (2d) 212 (Q.B.) 94, 167
Gencare Services Ltd. v. Tolpuddle Housing Cooperative Inc., [1993]
    O.J. No. 2263, 6 P.P.S.A.C. (2d) 340 (Gen. Div.) 285
General Electric Capital Commercial Automotive Finance, Inc. v. Spartan
    Motors, Ltd., 675 N.Y.S.2d 626 (N.Y.A.D. 1998) 334
General Electric Capital Equipment Finance Inc. v. Inland Kenworth Inc. (1993),
    81 B.C.L.R. (2d) 384, 5 P.P.S.A.C. (2d) 272 (S.C.) 270
General Electric Credit Corp. v. R.A. Heintz Construction Co.,
    302 F. Supp. 958 (D. Or. 1969) 288
General Motors Acceptance Corp. of Canada Ltd. v. Bank of Nova Scotia
    (1986), 55 O.R. (2d) 438, 6 P.P.S.A.C. 53 (C.A.) 456–47
General Motors Acceptance Corp. of Canada Ltd. v. Cardinali (2000), 185
    D.L.R. (4th) 141, 15 P.P.S.A.C. (2d) 168, [2000] O.J. No. 864 (C.A.) ...464–65
General Motors Acceptance Corp. of Canada Ltd. v. Furjanic, [1994]
    F.C.J. No. 728, 79 F.T.R. 172, 7 P.P.S.A.C. (2d) 52 (T.D.) 99

General Motors Acceptance Corp. of Canada Ltd. v. Kennedy (1993),
    5 P.P.S.A.C. (2d) 32, 111 Sask. R. 318 (Q.B.) 576
General Motors Acceptance Corp. of Canada Ltd. v. Midway Chrysler
    Plymouth Ltd. (1987), 7 P.P.S.A.C. 156, 50 Man.R. (2d) 185 (Q.B.),
    aff'd (1987), 8 P.P.S.A.C. 13 (Man. C.A.)... 31
General Motors Acceptance Corp. of Canada Ltd. v. Owens (1993),
    11 Alta. L.R. (3d) 269, 5 P.P.S.A.C. (2d) 242 (Q.B.) 294
General Motors Acceptance Corp. of Canada Ltd. v. Stetsko (1992),
    8 O.R. (3d) 537, 3 P.P.S.A.C. (2d) 79 (Gen. Div.) 270
General Motors Acceptance Corp. of Canada Ltd. v. Town & County
    Chrysler Ltd., 2005 CarswellOnt 1393, 2005 CanLII 23110
    (Ont. S.C.J.)... 133, 135
General Motors Acceptance Corp. of Canada Ltd. v. Trans Canada Credit
    Corp. (1994), 147 A.R. 333, 6 P.P.S.A.C. (2d) 216 (Q.B.) 270, 272
General Motors Acceptance Corp. v. Norstar Bank, N.A., 532 N.Y.S.2d 685,
    141 Misc.2d 349 (N.Y. Sup. 1988) 469
General Securities Ltd. v. Parsons (1955), 14 W.W.R. 424 (B.C.C.A.) 580
Gerrard (Re) (2000), 188 N.S.R. (2d) 224, 20 C.B.R. (4th) 90 (S.C.) 348, 350
Gervais (Guardian ad litem of) v. Yewdale, [1993] B.C.J. No. 2504,
    86 B.C.L.R. (2d) 374, 6 P.P.S.A.C. (2d) 62 (S.C.).. 81
Gibbons (Re) (1984), 45 O.R. (2d) 664, 4 P.P.S.A.C. 53 (C.A.) 271
Giffen (Re), [1998] 1 S.C.R. 91, 155 D.L.R. (4th) 332, (1998) 13 P.P.S.A.C.
    (2d) 255, rev'g (1996), 16 B.C.L.R. (3d) 29, 10 P.P.S.A.C. (2d) 277
    (C.A.) 12, 426, 428, 442, 443, 444–47, 450, 605
Gignac, Sutts v. National Bank of Canada, [1987] O.J. No. 298,
    5 C.B.R. (4th) 44 (H.C.J.) 83
Giles v. Grover (1832), 9 Bing. 128, 6 E.R. 843 (H.L.) 397, 401
Gimli Auto Ltd. v. BDO Dunwoody Ltd. (sub. nom Gimli Auto Ltd. v.
    Canada Campers Inc. (Trustee of)), 1998 ABCA 154, 219 A.R. 166,
    160 D.L.R. (4th) 373, [1999] 1 W.W.R. 459, 62 Alta. L.R. (3d) 40,
    13 P.P.S.A.C. (2d) 378 (Alta. C.A.) 25, 67, 123, 124, 138
Glencoe Express Inc. (Re) (1992), 14 C.B.R. (3d) 68, 3 P.P.S.A.C.
    (2d) 239 (B.C.S.C.) 446
Glengarry A.E.T. Inc. (Trustee of) v. Manhattan Electric Cable Corp.,
    [1986] O.J. No. 533, 6 P.P.S.A.C. 112 (H.C.J.) 78–79
Glenn v. General Motors Acceptance Corp. of Canada (1992),
    3 P.P.S.A.C. (2d) 203, [1992] O.J. No. 1959 (Gen. Div.)............................. 539
GMAC Commercial Credit Corp. Canada v. TCT Logistics Inc. (2004),
    70 O.R. (3d) 321, 238 D.L.R. (4th) 487, 6 P.P.S.A.C. (3d) 163,
    45 B.L.R. (3d) 68, 2004 CarswellOnt 1283 (C.A.), aff'g (2002),
    36 C.B.R. (4th) 37, 4 P.P.S.A.C. (3d) 107 (Ont. S.C.J.) 25, 67, 70, 124, 156
GMAC Leaseco Ltd. v. Royal Bank, [1992] B.C.J. No. 1969, 4 P.P.S.A.C.
    (2d) 4 (S.C.) 252

Gold Key Pontiac Buick (1984) Ltd. v. 464750 B.C. Ltd. (Trustee of),
    2000 BCCA 435, 2 P.P.S.A.C. (3d) 206, rev'g [1999] B.C.J. No. 1837,
    15 P.P.S.A.C. (2d) 46 (S.C.)...273, 274
Goodfallow, Traders' Bank v. Goodfallow (Re) (1890), 19 O.R. 299,
    [1890] O.J. No. 149 (H.C.J.(Ch.D.)) 595
Gordon v. Snelgrove, [1932] 2 D.L.R. 300 (Ont. S.C.)..378
Gough v. Wood & Co., [1894] 1 Q.B. 713, 63 L.J.Q.B. 564, 70 L.T. 297 (C.A.) 489
Graff v. Bitz (Trustee of), [1991] S.J. No. 605, 10 C.B.R. (3d) 126,
    2 P.P.S.A.C. (2d) 262 (Q.B.) 81
Graham v. Green (1862), 10 N.B.R. 330 (S.C.) 530
Granite Jewellery Ltd. (Re), [1964] O.J. No. 463, 7 C.B.R. (N.S.) 215 (H.C.J.).... 76
Grant v. Ste Marie Estate, 2005 ABQB. 35, 8 C.B.R. (5th) 81, [2005]
    A.J. No. 48...457
Gray v. Royal Bank (1997), 143 D.L.R. (4th) 179, 12 P.P.S.A.C. (2d) 126
    (B.C.S.C.) 165
Greenshields Inc. v. Johnston (1981), 119 D.L.R. (3d) 714, [1981]
    3 W.W.R. 313 (Alta. Q.B.), aff'd (1981), 131 D.L.R. (3d) 234,
    [1981] A.J. No. 695 (C.A.)..152
Greyvest Leasing Inc. v. Canadian Imperial Bank of Commerce (1991),
    1 P.P.S.A.C. (2d) 264 (Ont. Ct. Gen. Div.), rev'd on other grounds
    [1993] O.J. No. 2525, 5 P.P.S.A.C. (2d) 187 (C.A.) 340
Grise v. White, 247 N.E.2d 385 (Mass. 1969) 372
Grisenthwaite (Re), [1987] O.J. No. 2389, 7 P.P.S.A.C. 71 (S.C. (Mast.)) 250
Grove Packaging Inc. (Re), [2001] O.J. No. 5502, 31 C.B.R. (4th) 37 (S.C.J.).... 373
Guaranty Trust Co. of Canada v. Canadian Imperial Bank of Commerce,
    [1989] O.J. No. 1081, 2 P.P.S.A.C. (2d) 88 (H.C.J.), aff'd [1993]
    O.J. No. 2152, 6 P.P.S.A.C. (2d) 51 (C.A.) 167, 340
Gujral v. Miller (1994), 8 P.P.S.A.C. (2d) 96, [1994] B.C.J. No. 2179 (S.C.) 535
Guntel v. Kocian, [1985] 6 W.W.R. 458, 5 P.P.S.A.C. 109 (Man. Q.B.) 183

Haasen (Re) (1992), 8 O.R. (3d) 489, 3 P.P.S.A.C. (2d) 250 (Gen. Div.) 250
Haibeck v. No. 40 Taurus Ventures Ltd. (1991), 59 B.C.L.R. (2d) 229,
    2 P.P.S.A.C. (2d) 171 (S.C.) 65, 166
Hallet's Estate (Re) (1880), 13 Ch.D. 696, [1874–80] All E.R. Rep. 793,
    49 L.J. Ch. 415 (C.A.) 333, 468, 473
Hansen (In Re), 85 B.R. 821 (B. Ct. N.D. Iowa 1988).......................................334
Harder v. Alberta Treasury Branches (2004), A.R. 320, 6 P.P.S.A.C
    (3d) 346 (Atla. Q.B.)..270, 273
Harrison v. Sterry (1809), 5 Cranch 289..124
Harry D. Shields Ltd. v. Bank of Montreal (1992), 7 O.R. (3d) 57,
    3 P.P.S.A.C. (2d) 115 (Gen. Div.) 168
Hayward Lumber Co. v. McEachern, [1931] 3 W.W.R. 658 (Alta. S.C.T.D.) 378
Heidelberg Canada Graphic Equipment Ltd. v. Arthur Andersen Inc. (1992),
    7 B.L.R. (2d) 236, 4 P.P.S.A.C. (2d) 116, [1992] O.J. No. 2530
    (Gen. Div.) 164, 265, 281, 328, 364, 400
Helby v. Mathews, [1895] A.C. 471 (H.L.)...71

Hemken v. First National Bank of Litchfield, 394 N.E.2d 868,
76 Ill. App.3d 23 (Ill. App. 4 Dist. 1979).. 547
Henry Weiner Ltd. v. Royal Bank, [1986] O.J. No. 1111, 61 C.B.R.
(N.S.) 317 (H.C.J.) 207
Hewstan (Re) (1996), 42 C.B.R. (3d) 186, 12 P.P.S.A.C. (2d) 36 (B.C.S.C.) 263
Hickman Equipment (1985) Ltd. (Re) (2003), 224 Nfld. & P.E.I.R. 73,
5 P.P.S.A.C. (3d) 93 (Nfld. S.C.T.D.) 191, 192
Hickman Equipment (1985) Ltd. (Re) (2003), 40 C.B.R. (4th) 69,
223 Nfld. & P.E.I.R. 21 (Nfld. S.C.T.D.) 263
Hickman Equipment (1985) Ltd. (Re) (2004), 7 P.P.S.A.C. (3d) 56
(Nfld. C.A.) 230
Hickson (Re), [1984] M.J. No. 136, 3 P.P.S.A.C. 263 (C.A.) 271
Hobson v. Gorringe, [1897] 1 Ch. 182, [1895–99] All E.R. Rep. 1231,
75 L.T. 610 (C.A.)... 489
HOJ Franchise Systems Inc. v. Municipal Savings & Loan Corp. (1994), 110
D.L.R. (4th) 645, [1994] O.J. No. 24, 6 P.P.S.A.C. (2d) 302 (Gen. Div.)........ 74
Holland v. Chrysler Credit Canada Ltd. (1992), 5 Alta. L.R. (3d) 258,
134 A.R. 130, 4 P.P.S.A.C. (2d) 250 (Q.B.) 121, 138
Holland v. Hodgson (1872), L.R. 7 C.P. 328, [1861–73] All E.R. Rep. 237,
26 L.T. 709 490
Holnam West Materials Ltd. v. Canadian Concrete Products Ltd. (1994),
[1995] 1 W.W.R. 155, 159 A.R. 296 (Q.B.)...................................570, 571, 573
Holroyd v. Marshall (1862), 10 H.L.C. 191, 11 E.R. 999, [1861–73]
All E.R. Rep. 414 (H.L.) 169, 423
Holy Rosary Parish (Thorold) Credit Union Limited v. Premier Trust
Company, [1965] S.C.R. 503, 51 D.L.R. (2d) 591, 7 C.B.R.
(N.S.) 169..110, 430–32
Holy Rosary Parish (Thorold) Credit Union Ltd. v. Bye, [1967] S.C.R. 271, 61
D.L.R. (2d) 88... 439
Holy Spirit Credit Union v. McMullan (Trustee of), [1994] M.J. No. 105
(Q.B.)... 135
Homeplan Realty Ltd. v. Avco Financial Realty Services Ltd., [1979]
2 S.C.R. 699, 98 D.L.R. (3d) 695 414
Hopkinson v. Rolt (1861), 9 H.L.C. 514.................................... 197, 316, 424, 602
Hovey v. Whiting (1887), 14 S.C.R. 515 .... 186, 188
HSBC Bank Canada v. Expressway Concrete Supply Ltd. (1999), 1 B.L.R.
(3d) 147, 14 C.B.R. (4th) 1 (Ont. S.C.J.) 31
Humboldt Credit Union Ltd. v. Empire Shoe Store Ltd., [1986] S.J. No. 743,
7 P.P.S.A.C. 63 (C.A.).. 196
Hunt v. Long (1916), 27 D.L.R. 337 (Ont. S.C.A.D.)... 275
Hunt v. T & N plc, [1993] 4 S.C.R. 289,109 D.L.R. (4th) 16............................. 122
Hupfer (Re), 2003 ABQB 267, [2003] A.J. No. 369 (Q.B.) 441–42
Hurly v. Bank Of Nova Scotia (1965), [1966] S.C.R. 83, 53 W.W.R. 627........... 596
Huxley Catering Ltd. (Re) (1982), 36 O.R. (2d) 703, 2 P.P.S.A.C. 22 (C.A.) 175

Ilford-Riverton Airways Ltd. v. Aero Trades (Western) Ltd., [1977]
    5 W.W.R. 193, 76 D.L.R. (3d) 742 (Man. C.A.) 619
Imperial Life Assurance Co. of Canada v. Colmenares, [1967] S.C.R. 443,
    62 D.L.R. (2d) 138 151
Indian Head Credit Union Ltd. v. R & D Hardware Ltd. (1986),
    54 Sask. R. 161, [1986] S.J. No. 598 (Q.B.), aff'd (1988),
    66 Sask. R. 90, [1988] S.J. No. 203 (C.A.) 578
Indian Head Credit Union v. Andrew (1992), 97 D.L.R. (4th) 462,
    [1993] 1 W.W.R. 673, [1992] S.J. No. 554, 4 P.P.S.A.C. (2d) 95
    (C.A.) 381, 382, 384, 457
Indian Head Trading Co. v. Royal Bank of Canada, [1976] 5 W.W.R. 583
    (B.C.C.A.) 596
Industrial Acceptance Corp. Ltd. v. Firestone Tire & Rubber Co. of Canada
    Ltd. (1969), 8 D.L.R. (3d) 770, 70 W.W.R. 547 (Alta. C.A.), rev'd (1970),
    [1971] S.C.R. 357, 17 D.L.R. (3d) 229, 75 W.W.R. 621 .... 499, 619
International Harvester Credit Corp. of Canada Ltd. v. Bell's Dairy Ltd.,
    [1986] S.J. No. 520, 6 P.P.S.A.C. 138 (C.A.), rev'g [1984] S.J. No. 574,
    4 P.P.S.A.C. 149 (Q.B.) 167
International Harvester Credit Corp. of Canada Ltd. v. Frontier Peterbilt
    Sales Ltd. (1983), 149 D.L.R. (3d) 572, [1983] 6 W.W.R. 328, [1983]
    S.J. No. 644 (Q.B.) 97
International Harvester Credit Corp. of Canada Ltd. v. Touche Ross Ltd.
    (1986), 61 C.B.R. (N.S.) 193, 6 P.P.S.A.C. 138 (Sask. C.A.) 442, 444
International Terminal Operators Ltd. v. Miida Electronics Inc., [1986]
    1 S.C.R. 752, 28 D.L.R. (4th) 641 34
Intex Moulding Ltd. (Re) (1987), 59 O.R. (2d) 454, 38 D.L.R. (4th) 111,
    7 P.P.S.A.C. 91, [1987] O.J. No. 346 (H.C.J.) 67, 156
Irving A. Burton Ltd. v. Canadian Imperial Bank of Commerce (1982),
    36 O.R. (2d) 703, 134 D.L.R. (3d) 369, 2 P.P.S.A.C. 22, 41 C.B.R. (N.S.),
    17 B.L.R. 170 (C.A.) 103, 110, 175, 434
ITO International Terminal Operators Ltd. v. Miida Electronics Inc., [1986]
    1 S.C.R. 752, 28 D.L.R. (4th) 641 602
ITT Diversified Credit Corp. v. First City Capital Corp., 737 S.W.2d 803
    (Tex. 1987) 372
Iverson Heating Ltd. v. Canadian Imperial Bank of Commerce (1983),
    43 A.R. 142, [1983] A.J. No. 905 (Q.B.) 103

J & W Investments Ltd. v. Black (1963), 38 D.L.R. (2d) 251, 41 W.W.R. 577
    (B.C.C.A) 545
J.I. Case Credit Corp. v. Canadian Imperial Bank of Commerce, [1985]
    S.J. No. 78, 5 P.P.S.A.C. 181 (Q.B.) 184
J.J. Riverside Manufacturing Ltd. v. E.J.W. Development Co., [1981]
    M.J. No. 319, 1 P.P.S.A.C. 330 (Co. Ct.) 183
Jack Green's Fashions for Men Big & Tall Inc. (In Re), 597 F.2d 130
    (8th Cir. 1979) 572
Jackson v. Penfold, [1931] 1 D.L.R. 808 (Ont. S.C.(A.D.)) 581

James Roscoe (Bolton) Ltd. v. Winder, [1915] 1 Ch. 62....................................... 467

Jason Construction Ltd. (Re) (1972), 16 C.B.R. (N.S.) 297, [1972]
  3 W.W.R. 504, 25 D.L.R. (3d) 340 (Alta. S.C.A.D.), aff'd 17 C.B.R.
  (N.S.) 158, [1972] 6 W.W.R. 203, 29 D.L.R. (3d) 623 (Alta. S.C.A.D.) 434

Jim Landry Pontiac Buick Ltd. v. Canadian Imperial Bank of Commerce
  (1987), 40 D.L.R. (4th) 343, [1987] N.S.J. No. 273 (T.D.) 524

John Deere Co. v. Production Credit Association, 686 S.W.2d 904
  (Tenn. App. 1984)... 343

John Deere Credit Inc. v. Standard Oilfield Services Inc. (2000),
  258 A.R. 266, 79 Alta. L.R. (3d) 166, [2000] A.J. No. 84,
  16 C.B.R. (4th) 227 (Q.B.).. 254, 363

Jones v. Davidson Partners Ltd. (1981), 31 O.R. (2d) 494, 1 P.P.S.A.C. 242
  (H.C.J.) 408

Joseph Group of Companies Inc. v. Pickles Tents and Awnings Ltd. (1981),
  127 D.L.R. (3d) 176, [1981] M.J. No. 48, 2 P.P.S.A.C. 1 (C.A.).........65, 87, 184

Joseph v. Lyons (1884), 15 Q.B. 280 (C.A.) 169

Josephine V. Wilson Family Trust v. Swartz (1993), 16 O.R. (3d) 268,
  [1993] O.J. No. 2735, 6 P.P.S.A.C. (2d) 76 (Gen. Div.) 112

Juckes (Trustee of) v. Holiday Chevrolet Oldsmobile (1983) Ltd. (sub nom.
  Juckes, Re) (1990), 79 C.B.R. (N.S.) 143, 68 D.L.R. (4th) 142,
  1 P.P.S.A.C. (2d) 24, 82 Sask. R. 303, [1990] S.J. No. 103 (Q.B.) ...67, 128, 156

K.J.M. Leasing Ltd. v. Grandstrand Bros. Inc. (Receiver Manager of) (1994),
  158 A.R. 78, 7 P.P.S.A.C. (2d) 197 (Q.B.) 252, 271, 272

Kampman (Re), [2000] A.J. 1211, 20 C.B.R. (4th) 243 (Q.B.) 131

Kaplan v. Walker, 395 A.2d 897 (N.J. Super. A.D. 1978) 378–79

Kassian v. National Bank of Canada, [1998] 10 W.W.R. 63, 4 C.B.R. (4th)
  295 (Q.B.), aff'd [1999] 11 W.W.R. 500, 10 C.B.R. (4th) 20 (C.A.)............. 594

Katsikalis v. Deutsch Bank (Asia) AG, [1988] 2 Qd. R. 641 (S. Ct.).................. 320

Kavcar Investments Ltd. v. Aetna Financial Services Ltd. (1989), 70 O.R.
  (2d) 225, 62 D.L.R. (4th) 277 (C.A.) 524, 526

Kawartha Consumers Co-Operative Inc. v. Debenture Holders of Kawartha
  Consumers Co-Operative Inc., [1999] O.J. No. 4367, 14 C.B.R. (4th) 210
  (S.C.J.) 180

Kelln (Trustee of) v. Strasbourg Credit Union Ltd., [1992] 3 W.W.R. 310,
  3 P.P.S.A.C. (2d) 44 (Sask. C.A.) 270, 273

Kennedy v. De Trafford, [1897] A.C. 180 (H.L.) 545

Kent Steel Products Ltd. v. Arlington Management Consultants Ltd. (1966),
  9 C.B.R. (N.S.) 298, 58 W.W.R. 1, 59 D.L.R. (2d) 374 (Man. Q.B.), aff'd
  (1967), 59 W.W.R. 382, 62 D.L.R. (2d) 502 (Man. C.A.), further appeal
  quashed as being defective, [1967] S.C.R. 497, 61 W.W.R. 119,
  62 D.L.R. (2d) 638, 10 C.B.R. (N.S.) 92...110, 433

Kerr v. Ducey, [1993] 1 N.Z.L.R. 577 320

Kevill v. Trans-Canada Credit Corp. (1979), 23 O.R. (2d) 432 (Co. Ct.) 261

Key State Bank v. Voz, [1989] O.J. No. 213, 9 P.P.S.A.C. 47 (Dist. Ct.).............. 216

Key West Ford Sales Ltd. v. Rounis, [1998] B.C.J. No. 54, 13 P.P.S.A.C.
(2d) 102 (S.C.) 214
Kingsclear Indian Band v. J.E. Brooks & Associates (1991), 118 N.B.R.
(2d) 290, [1991] N.B.J. No. 816, 2 P.P.S.A.C. (2d) 151 (C.A.) 114
Kniaziew (Re), [1994] O.J. No. 4182, 8 P.P.S.A.C. (2d) 13 (Gen. Div.) 250
Kodak Canada Ltd. v. Jesi Estates Inc. (1990), 1 P.P.S.A.C. (2d) 154
(Ont. Ct. Gen. Div.) 69
Kostyshyn (Johnson) v. West Region Tribal Council Inc. (1992), [1992]
F.C.J. No. 730, 55 F.T.R. 48 [1994] 1 C.N.L.R. 94 (T.D.)............................114
Kova Establishment v. Sasco Investments Ltd., [1998] 2 B.C.L.C. 83 (Ch. D.) 318
Kozak v. Gruza, [1989] S.J. No. 529, 9 P.P.S.A.C. 221 (C.A.) 173
Krolyk v. Carson, [1997] 6 W.W.R. 373, 154 Sask. R. 85 (Q.B.)........................576
Kryspin (Re) (1983), 44 C.B.R. (N.S.) 232, 40 O.R. (2d) 424, 142 D.L.R.
(3d) 638 (Ont. H.C.J.) 430
Kubota Canada Ltd. v. Case Credit Ltd., 2005 ABCA 139, [2005] A.J. 329 373,
374
Kundel v. Sprague National Bank, 128 F.3d 636 (8th Cir. 1997) 339

Lambert (Re), [1991] O.J. No. 3469, 2 P.P.S.A.C. (2d) 160 (Gen. Div.), rev'd
(1994), 20 O.R. (3d) 108, 7 P.P.S.A.C. (2d) 240 (C.A.), leave to appeal
to S.C.C. refused (1995), [1994] S.C.C.A. No. 555, 33 C.B.R.
(3d) 291n 270, 271, 273, 274
Langley v. Kahnert (1905), 36 S.C.R. 397 (S.C.C.)..78, 80
Lanson v. Saskatchewan Valley Credit Union Ltd. (1998), 172 Sask. R. 106,
14 P.P.S.A.C. (2d) 71 (C.A.) 284
Law Society of Upper Canada v. Toronto-Dominion Bank (1998),
169 D.L.R. (4th) 353, 116 O.A.C. 24, [1998] O.J. No. 5115 (C.A.) 471–72
Lazarchuk (Re), [1994] B.C.J. No. 1047, 7 P.P.S.A.C. (2d) 155 (S.C.) 251
Leaseway Autos Ltd. v. Sinco Sportswear Ltd. (1986), 25 D.L.R. (4th) 294,
45 Sask. R. 254, [1986] S.J. No. 178 (Q.B) 72
Leavere v. Corporation of The City of Port Colborne (1995), 22 O.R. (3d) 44,
122 D.L.R. (4th) 200, [1995] O.J. No. 217 (C.A.) 97
Leavitt (Re) (1997), [1998] 3 W.W.R. 140, [1997] B.C.J. No. 666,
89 B.C.A.C. 132 (C.A.)..113
Lee v. Butler (1893), 2 Q.B. 318 (C.A.)..71
Lefebvre (Trustee of); Tremblay (Trustee of), 2004 SCC 63, [2004]
3 S.C.R. 326 .... 49–50, 426, 446
Legaarden v. Abernethy Credit Union Ltd. (1991), 3 P.P.S.A.C. (2d) 292
(Sask. Q.B.) 173
Leu v. N.M. Patterson & Sons Ltd., [1997] S.J. No. 324, 13 P.P.S.A.C. (2d) 27
(Q.B.)..357
Lewinsky v. Toronto-Dominion Bank (1995), 9 P.P.S.A.C. (2d) 169, [1995]
O.J. No. 579 (Gen. Div.)..15
Liberty National Bank & Trust Company of Oklahoma City v. Acme Tool
Division of the Rucker Company, 540 F.2d 1375 (C.A. Okl. 1976) 541
Lind (In Re), [1915] 2 Ch. 345 (C.A.)..431

Lipkin Gorman (a firm) v. Karpnale Ltd., [1991] 2 A.C. 548 (H.L.) 582

Livesley v. E. Clemens Horst Co. (1924), [1924] S.C.R. 605, [1925]
   1 D.L.R. 159 153

Lloyd (Re) (1995), 30 C.B.R. (3d) 113, 9 P.P.S.A.C. (2d) 107, 164 A.R. 59, [1995]
   A.J. No. 69 (Q.B.) 105, 430

Lloyd v. European and North American Railway (1878), 18 N.B.R. 194
   (C.A.) 169

Lloyds and Scottish Finance Ltd. v. Modern Cars and Caravans (Kingston)
   Ltd., [1966] 1 Q.B. 764 (C.A.) 396, 397

Loeb Canada Inc. v. Caisse Populaire Alexandria Ltée. (2004), 7 P.P.S.A.C.
   (3d) 194, 2004 CarswellOnt 4973 (S.C.J.) 362

Loewen v. Superior Acceptance Corp. (1997), 46 C.B.R. (3d) 239,
   12 P.P.S.A.C. (2d) 230 (B.C.S.C.) 523

Logan (Re) (1992), 73 B.C.L.R. (2d) 377, 4 P.P.S.A.C. (2d) 200 (S.C.) 251

London and Globe Finance Corp. (Re), [1902] 2 Ch. 416 408

London Life Insurance Co v. Air Atlantic Ltd. (1994), 133 N.S.R. (2d) 185,
   27 C.B.R. (3d) 66 (S.C.T.D.) 526

M.C. United Masonry Limited (Re) (1983), 40 O.R. (2d) 330, 142 D.L.R.
   (3d) 470, 2 P.P.S.A.C. 237 (C.A.) 63

MacEwen Agricentre Inc. v. Bériault, [2002] O.J. No. 3314, 61 O.R. (3d) 63
   (S.C.J.) 184

Mackenzie v. Blindman Valley Co-operative Association Ltd., [1947]
   4 D.L.R. 687, [1947] 2 W.W.R. 443 (Alta. S.C.(T.D.)) 580

Maden v. Long, [1983] 1 W.W.R. 649, 41 B.C.L.R. 6 (B.C.S.C.) 134

Magellan Aerospace Ltd. v. First Energy Capital Corp. (2000),
   274 A.R. 195, [2000] A.J. No. 1176, 1 P.P.S.A.C. (3d) 297 (Q.B.),
   aff'd 2001 ABCA 138, 281 A.R. 389, [2001] 8 W.W.R. 448 86

Manuel (In Re), 507 F.2d 990 (5th Cir. 1975) 343

Manulife Bank of Canada v. Planting, [1996] O.J. No. 4594, 43 C.B.R.
   (3d) 305 (Gen. Div.), aff'd. [1998] O.J. No. 73 (C.A.) 441

Maracle v. Ontario (Minister of National Revenue), [1993] O.J. 1173
   (Gen. Div.) 115

Marlex Petroleum Inc. v. The "Har Rai," [1987] 1 S.C.R. 57, 72 N.R. 75,
   aff'g [1984] 2 F.C. 345, 4 D.L.R. (4th) 739 (C.A.) 126

Martin v. Dorn Equipment Co. Inc., 821 P.2d 1025, 250 Mont. 422
   (Mont. 1991) 530

Martin v. Toronto Dominion Bank (1985), 43 Sask. R. 212,
   5 P.P.S.A.C. 144 (Sask. Q.B.) 574

Marzetti v. Marzetti, [1994] 2 S.C.R. 765, 116 D.L.R. (4th) 577, [1994]
   S.C.J. No. 64 112

Matthews (In Re), 724 F.2d 798 (9th Cir. 1984) 345

McArthur (Trustee of) v. Canadian Imperial Bank of Commerce, [1986]
   O.J. No. 2634, 58 C.B.R. (N.S.) 230 5 P.P.S.A.C. 187 (Ont. H.C.J.) 84

McCall v. Wolff (1885), 13 S.C.R. 130 186

McCormick v. Grogan (1869), L.R. 4 H I 82 375

McDiarmid Lumber Ltd. v. God's Lake First Nation, 2005 CarswellMan 33
(C.A.) 115
McLean (Trustee of) v. General Motors Acceptance Corp. (sub. nom Peat
Marwick Thorne Inc v. GMAC), [1992] 3 W.W.R. 524, 101 Sask R. 178
(Q.B.).. 156
McLeod & Co. v. Price Waterhouse Ltd., [1992] S.J. No. 104, 3 P.P.S.A.C.
(2d) 171 (Q.B.) 340
McMahon v. Canada Permanent Trust Co. (1979), 108 D.L.R. (3d) 71, [1980]
2 W.W.R. 438, [1979] B.C.J. No. 1951 (C.A.)...................................... 85
Mearford Energy Services Inc. v. Class M Planet Corporation, 2002 ABQB 107,
3 P.P.S.A.C. (3d) 289.. 236
Media Corporation (In Re), [1984] O.J. No. 2557, 3 P.P.S.A.C. 253
(H.C.J.) 263, 265
Melton Real Estate Ltd. v. National Arts Services Corp. Ltd., [1977]
A.J. No. 537, 2 Alta. L.R. (2d) 180 (Dist. Ct.)................................... 409
Menard (sub. nom Shink v. Gingras) (Re), [1962] C.S. 297, 3 C.B.R.
(N.S.) 309 (Que. C.S.)... 428
Michigan National Bank v. Flowers Mobile Home Sale, Inc., 217 S.E.2d 108,
26 N.C. App. 690 (N.C. App. 1975) 469
Miller, McClelland Ltd. v. Barrhead Savings & Credit Union Ltd. (1995),
165 A.R. 106, 9 P.P.S.A.C. (2d) 102 (C.A.), rev'g (1993), 142 A.R. 155,
5 P.P.S.A.C. (2d) 163 (Q.B.) 251
Millican v. Turner, 503 So.2d 289 (Miss. 1987)..................................... 555
Mister Broadloom Corp (1968) Ltd. v. Bank of Montreal (1979), 25 O.R.
(2d) 198, 101 D.L.R. (3d) 713 (H.C.J.), var'd (1983), 44 O.R. (2d) 368,
4 D.L.R. (4th) 74 (C.A.) 524
Mithras Management Ltd. v. New Visions Entertainment Corp. (1992),
90 D.L.R. (4th) 726, [1992] O.J. No. 842 (Gen. Div.) 123
Modular Design Group Pty. Ltd. (Re) (1994), 35 N.S.W.L.R. 96 (Eq.) 320
Moncton Motor Homes & Sales Inc. (Re), 2003 NBCA 26, 4 P.P.S.A.C.
(3d) 211.. 273
Monk Corp. v. Island Fertilizers Ltd., [1991] 1 S.C.R. 779, 80 D.L.R. (4th) 58.... 602
Moose Jaw v. Pulsar Ventures, [1985] S.J. No. 85, 5 P.P.S.A.C. 133 (Q.B.)......... 267
Morguard Investments Ltd. v. De Savoye, [1990] 3 S.C.R. 1077, 76 D.L.R.
(4th) 256 122
Morris Industries Ltd. v. Remeshylo Farm Equipment (1988) Ltd. (1995),
129 Sask. R. 86, 9 P.P.S.A.C. (2d) 93 (Q.B.) 576
Moskun v. Toronto-Dominion Bank (1985), 5 P.P.S.A.C. 221, [1985]
O.J. No. 2040 (H.C.J.) 15
MTC Leasing Inc. v. National Bank, [1997] 9 W.W.R. 228, [1997]
M.J. No. 384, 12 P.P.S.A.C. (2d) 319 (Q.B.), aff'd (1998), [1999]
6 W.W.R. 587, [1998] M.J. No. 453, 14 P.P.S.A.C. (2d) 303 (C.A.).............. 74
Munr (Re) (1992), 77 B.C.L.R. (2d) 98, 4 P.P.S.A.C. (2d) 245 (S.C.) 270
Mutual Life Assurance Co. v. Toronto Dominion Bank, [1995] M.J. No. 310, 10
P.P.S.A.C. (2d) 182 (Q.B.) 274

N'Amerix Logistix Inc. (Re), [2001] O.J. No. 4875, 57 O.R. (3d) 248 (S.C.J.) ... 378

Nathanson, Schachter & Thompson v. Sarcee Indian Band, [1994]
6 W.W.R. 203, [1994] B.C.J. No. 690, 90 B.C.L.R. (2d) 13 (C.A.) 115

National Bank of Canada v. Atomic Slipper Co. Ltd., [1991] 1 S.C.R. 1059,
80 D.L.R. (4th) 134 598

National Bank of Canada v. Grinnell Corp. of Canada (1993), 5 P.P.S.A.C.
(2d) 266 (Ont. Div. Ct.) 175

National Bank of Canada v. Makin Metals Ltd. (1992), [1993] 3 W.W.R. 318,
4 P.P.S.A.C. (2d) 167 (Sask. Q.B.), rev'd [1994] 4 W.W.R. 707, 6 P.P.S.A.C.
(2d) 164, [1994] S.J. No. 75, 116 Sask. R. 237 (Sask. C.A.) 93, 571

National Bank of Canada v. Merit Energy Ltd., [2001] A.J. No. 776,
27 C.B.R. (4th) 283, 294 A.R. 1 (Q.B) 171, 312

National Equipment Rental, Ltd. v. Priority Electronics Corp.,
435 F. Supp. 236 (DCNY 1977) 555

National Trailer Convoy of Canada Ltd. v. Bank of Montreal, [1980]
O.J. No. 3031, 10 B.L.R. 196, 1 P.P.S.A.C. 87 (Ont. H.C.J.) 65, 355

National Trust Co. v. Bouckhuyt (1987), 59 O.R. (2d) 556, 39 D.L.R.
(4th) 60, [1987] O.J. No. 323 (H.C.J.), rev'd. 61 O.R. (2d) 640,
43 D.L.R. (4th) 543, [1987] O.J. No. 930 (C.A.) 110, 111

National Trust Co. v. Kirch, [1993] O.J. No. 765, 12 O.R. (3d) 781
(Gen. Div.) 294, 303

Near Horbay Inc. v. Great West Golf & Industrial Inc. (2000),
2000 ABQB 861, [2001] 3 W.W.R. 734 .... 320, 322

Nelson v. Armstrong, 582 P.2d 1100 (Idaho 1978) 555

New World Screen Printing Ltd. (c.o.b.) New World Print) v. Xerox Canada
Ltd., 2003 BCSC 1685, [2003] B.C.J. No. 2559 191

Noriega (Re), [2003] 7 W.W.R. 566, 42 C.B.R. (4th) 274, 15 Alta. L.R. (4th) 79
(Q.B.) 274

North Platte State Bank v. Production Credit Association of North Platte,
200 N.W.2d 1 (S. Ct. Neb. 1972) 334

North Western Bank Ltd. v. Poynter, [1895] A.C. 56 (H.L.) 213

Northwest Equipment Inc. v. Daewoo Heavy Industries America Corp.,
2002 ABCA 79, [2002] 6 W.W.R. 444, 299 A.R. 250, 266 W.A.C. 250,
3 P.P.S.A.C. (3d) 101, 1 Alta. L.R. (4th) 14 (C.A.) 129, 138, 145, 284, 287, 292

Nourse v. Canadian Canners Ltd., [1935] O.R. 361 (C.A.) 285

O'Brien v. Stebbins, [1927] 3 D.L.R. 274 (Sask. C.A.) 164

Oatway (Re), [1903] 2 Ch. 356 473

OGB Ltd. v. Allan, [2001] B.P.I.R. 1111 (Ch.D.) 320

Ogden v. Award Realty Inc., [1999] B.C.J. No. 422, 46 C.C.E.L. (2d) 121,
14 P.P.S.A.C. (2d) 99 (S.C.) 83, 105

Olympia & York Developments Ltd. v. Royal Trust Co. (1993), 14 O.R.
(3d) 1, 103 D.L.R. (4th) 129 (C.A.) 428, 466

Olympus Plastics Ltd. (Receiver of) v. Olympus Plastics Ltd., [2000]
O.J. No. 2093, 1 P.P.S.A.C. (3d) 45 (Gen. Div.) 367

Ontario (Securities Commission) v. Greymac Credit Corp. (1986),
    55 O.R. (2d) 673, 30 D.L.R. (4th) 1, [1986] O.J. No. 830 (C.A.),
    aff'd [1988] 2 S.C.R. 172, 52 D.L.R. (4th) 767, 65 O.R (2d) 479 ....470, 472
Ontario Dairy Cow Leasing Ltd. v. Ontario Milk Marketing Board, [1990]
    O.J. No. 1864, 1 P.P.S.A.C. (2d) 149 (Gen. Div.), rev'd on other grounds
    [1993] O.J. No. 464, 4 P.P.S.A.C. (2d) 269, 38 A.C.W.S. (3d) 807 (C.A.).....110
Ontario Equipment (1976) Ltd. (Re) (1981), 33 O.R. (2d) 648, 125 D.L.R.
    (3d) 321, 1 P.P.S.A.C. 303 (H.C.J.), aff'd (1982), 35 O.R. (2d) 194,
    141 D.L.R. (3d) 766n, 6 P.P.S.A.C. 229 (C.A.) 73
Ordon Estate v. Grail, [1998] 3 S.C.R. 437, 166 D.L.R. (4th) 193 602
Orion Truck Centre Ltd. (Re), 2003 BCSC 1167, 17 B.C.L.R. (4th) 337
    (S.C.) 261, 263, 266
Orr & Co. v. Saskatchewan Economic Development Corp. (1994),
    119 Sask. R. 121, 24 C.B.R. (3d) 196, 6 P.P.S.A.C. (2d) 350 (Q.B.),
    aff'd [1994] S.J. No. 504, 125 Sask. R. 80, 8 P.P.S.A.C. (2d) 83
    (C.A.) 112, 174, 188
Osman Auction Inc. v. Murray (1991), 123 A.R. 22, 2 P.P.S.A.C. (2d) 236
    (Q.B.).. 183
Osman Auction v. Murray (1994), 6 P.P.S.A.C. (2d) 211, 16 Alta. L.R.
    (3d) 292 (Alta. Q.B.) 26
Otea Inc.(Re), [1976] C.A. 539.. 434
Ouellet (Trustee of), 2004 SCC 64, [2004] 3 SCR 348 .... 49, 426
Ovens (Re) (1979), 26 O.R. (2d) 468, 1 P.P.S.A.C. 131 (C.A.)........................... 271
Overn v. Strand, [1931] S.C.R. 720, [1932] 1 D.L.R. 490 581

P.E.I. Lending Agency v. Island Petroleum Products Ltd. (1999),
    185 Nfld. & P.E.I.R. 78, 562 A.P.R. 78, 15 P.P.S.A.C. (2d) 111,
    1999 CarswellPEI 111 (P.E.I.S.C.T.D) 271, 272
Paccar Financial Services v. Chubey, [1992] 2 W.W.R. 751, [1992]
    M.J. No. 107 (Q.B.).. 285
Paccar Financial Services v. Sinco Trucking Ltd., [1987] 5 W.W.R. 492, [1987]
    S.J. No. 454, 7 P.P.S.A.C. 176 (Q.B.), rev'd on other grounds (1989),
    57 D.L.R. (4th) 438, [1989] 3 W.W.R. 481, [1989] S.J. No. 86 (C.A.)........... 95
Paquette (Re) (1993), 142 A.R. 305, 5 P.P.S.A.C. (2d) 136 (Q.B.), aff'd
    (1994), 152 A.R. 286, 6 P.P.S.A.C. (2d) 190 (Q.B.), application for
    reconsideration refused (1994), 154 A.R. 79, 6 P.P.S.A.C. (2d) 401
    (Q.B.)..251, 273
Paradise Valley Marine Ltd. (c.o.b. Ridge Marine)(Re), [1997] B.C.J.
    No. 2126, 7 C.B.R. (4th) 252 (S.C.) 343
Paterson (Re) (1994), 29 C.B.R. (3d) 133, 8 P.P.S.A.C. (2d) 126 (Ont. Ct.
    Gen. Div.)... 273
Patrie v. Royal Bank, [1994] O.J. No. 1546, 27 C.B.R. (3d) 89
    (Gen. Div.) 439, 440
Paul (Re) (1986), 53 O.R. (2d) 225, [1986] O.J. No. 2328, 5 P.P.S.A.C. 86
    (H.C.J.) 100

Peat Marwick Ltd. v. Consumers Gas Co. (1980), 113 D.L.R. (3d) 754,
1 P.P.S.A.C. 149 (Ont. C.A.) 568

Pelyea (Re) (1969), [1970] 2 O.R. 384, 11 D.L.R. (3d) 35 (C.A.)........................ 439

Perepeluk (Re) (1986), 25 D.L.R. (4th) 73, 5 P.P.S.A.C. 317 (Sask. C.A.) 444

Pezzack v. Irving Bank Canada (1989), 69 O.R. (2d) 536, [1989]
O.J. No. 1321 (H.C.J.) 490, 494

Philip Services Corp. (Re), [1999] O.J. No. 5117, [1999] O.T.C. 136,
15 C.B.R. (4th) 107 (S.C.J.) 68, 70, 72, 75

Phillips v. Hunter (1795), 2 H. Bl. 409 120

Pierce v. Canada Permanent Loan and Savings Co. (1894), 25 O.R. 671,
[1894] O.J. No. 195 (H.C.J. Ch. D.) 197

Piper Acceptance Corp. v. Yarborough, 702 F.2d 733 (C.A. Ark. 1983)............ 546

Pisiak v. Dyck (1986), 63 C.B.R. (N.S.) 151, 32 D.L.R. (4th) 287 (Sask. Q.B.) 440

Planwest Consultants Ltd. v. Milltimber Holdings Ltd. (1995),
172 A.R. 237, [1995] A.J. No. 720, 32 Alta. L.R. (3d) 397 (Q.B.) 95

Polano v. Bank of Nova Scotia (1979), 95 D.L.R. (3d) 510, 1 P.P.S.A.C. 36
(Ont. Dist. Ct.).. 355

Polyco Window Manufacturing Ltd. v. Prudential Assurance Co., [1994]
S.J. No. 137, 119 Sask. R. 131 (Q.B.) 397, 399, 401

Port Royal Pulp & Paper Co v. Royal Bank of Canada, [1941] 4 D.L.R. 1
(J.C.P.C) 587

Porto Seguro Companhia De Seguros Gerais v. Belcan S.A., [1997]
3 S.C.R. 1278, 153 D.L.R. (4th) 577 602

Pratt & Whitney Leasing Inc. v. Ellis Air Inc. (2002), 3 C.B.R. (5th) 81,
6 P.P.S.A.C. (3d) 84 (B.C.S.C.)... 501

Price Waterhouse Ltd. v. Creighton Holdings Ltd. (1984), 36 Sask. R. 292,
[1984] S.J. No. 34 (Q.B.) 568

Primus Automotive Financial Services Canada Ltd. v. Kirkby (Trustee of),
1998 ABQB 347, 14 P.P.S.A.C. (2d) 273.. 273

Prudential Assurance Co (Trustee of) v. 90 Eglinton Ltd. Partnership (1994),
18 O.R. (3d) 201, [1994] O.J. No. 868 (Gen. Div.) 527

PSINet Ltd. (Re), [2002] O.J. No. 633, 32 C.B.R. (4th) 102 (C.A.), aff'g
(2002), 30 C.B.R. (4th) 226, 3 P.P.S.A.C. (3d) 208
(Ont. S.C.J.)... 265, 268–69, 400, 441

Pudwill v. Royal Bank of Canada, [2001] O.J. 2141, [2001] O.T.C. 404
(S.C.J.), aff'd [2002] O.J. 1547 (C.A.) 266, 328

Q.N.S. Paper Co. v. Chartwell Shipping Ltd., [1989] 2 S.C.R. 683,
62 D.L.R. (4th) 36 602

Quest Cae Ltd. (Re), [1985] B.C.L.C. 266 (Ch. D.)..318

R v. Doucette, [1960] O.R. 407, 25 D.L.R. (2d) 380 (C.A.) 529

R v. Shand (1904), 7 O.L.R. 190 (C.A.).. 529

R. Clancy Heavy Equipment Sales Ltd. v. Joe Gourley Construction Ltd.
(2000), 2000 ABQB 589, [2001] 1 W.W.R. 681, [2000] A.J. No. 947 ....67, 73

R. v. Ford Motor Credit Canada Ltd. (1990), 78 C.B.R. (N.S.) 266,
     1 P.P.S.A.C. (2d) 13 (Ont. H.C.J.) 427
Rainbow Soil Services Ltd. v. Kada (1995), 32 C.B.R. (3d) 47, 9 P.P.S.A.C.
     (2d) 22 (Sask. Q.B.) 447, 448
Rapid Auto Collision Ltd. (Re), [1983] O.J. No. 2332, 49 C.B.R. (N.S.) 142,
     3 P.P.S.A.C. 187 (Ont. S.C.) 101
Rapid Transit Mix Ltd. v. Commcorp Financial Services Inc. (1998),
     156 D.L.R. (4th) 366, 212 A.R. 199 (C.A.) 575, 576
Rayson v. Graham (1864), 15 U.C.C.P. 36, [1864] O.J. No. 229 530
Redi-Mix Ltd. v. Hub Dairy & Barn Systems Ltd., [1987] S.J. No. 505,
     7 P.P.S.A.C. 165 (Q.B.) 175
Rehm v. DSG Communications Inc., [1995] 4 W.W.R. 750, 9 P.P.S.A.C.
     (2d) 114, 33 C.B.R. (3d) 65, 129 Sask. R. 297 (Q.B.) 174–75
Rektor (Re), [1983] O.J. No. 957, 47 C.B.R. (N.S.) 267, 3 P.P.S.A.C. 32
     (H.C.J.) 100
Richardson (Re) (1931), 13 C.B.R. 38 (Ont. S.C.) 79, 80
Richmac Interiors Ltd. (Re) (1996), 38 Alta. L.R. (3d) 38, [1996]
     6 W.W.R. 216 (Q.B.) 596
Richmac Interiors Ltd. (Re), [1994] A.J. No. 12, 25 C.B.R. (3d) 31 (Q.B.) 416
Rinn v. First Union National Bank of Maryland, 176 B.R. 401,
     25 U.C.C. Rep. Serv. 2d 1057 (D. Md. 1995) 353, 379
Rivabo Truck Bodies Ltd. (Re), [1975] O.J. No. 1632, 20 C.B.R. (N.S.) 252
     (Ont. S.C. Reg.) 79
River Industries (Re), [1992] 6 W.W.R. 257, 70 B.C.L.R. (2d) 19, [1992]
     B.C.J. No. 1346 (S.C.) 477
Robert B. Lee Enterprises, Inc. (In Re), 980 F.2d 606 (9th Cir. 1978) 319
Robert Simpson Co. v. Shadlock, [1981] O.J. No. 2448, 31 O.R. (2d) 612
     (H.C.J.) 313
Rodaro v. Royal Bank of Canada, [2000] O.J. 272, [2000] O.T.C. 85 (S.C.J.) 114
Rogerson Lumber Co v. Four Seasons Chalet Ltd. (1980), 29 O.R. (2d) 193,
     113 D.L.R. (3d) 671, 1 P.P.S.A.C. 160 (Ont. C.A.) 181, 398, 399, 590, 593
Ronald Elwyn Lister Ltd. v. Dunlop Canada Ltd., [1982] 1 S.C.R. 726,
     135 D.L.R. (3d) 1 523
Rose (Re) (1993), 16 O.R. (3d) 360, 6 P.P.S.A.C. (2d) 53 (Gen. Div.) 270
Ross v. Dunn, [1889] O.J. No. 42, 16 O.A.R. 552 (C.A.) 396
Royal Bank of Canada v. 216200 Alberta Ltd. (1986), [1987] 1 W.W.R. 545,
     6 P.P.S.A.C. 277 (Sask. C.A.) 288, 292
Royal Bank of Canada v. 273050 British Columbia Ltd. (1991), 86 D.L.R.
     (4th) 551, [1991] B.C.J. No. 3683 (S.C.) 601
Royal Bank of Canada v. Agricultural Credit Corp. of Saskatchewan,
     [1994] S.J. No. 313, (1994), 115 D.L.R. (4th) 569, 7 P.P.S.A.C. (2d) 1
     (C.A.), rev'g [1991] S.J. No. 437, 2 P.P.S.A.C. (2d) 338 (Q.B.) 230, 315
Royal Bank of Canada v. Anderson (Trustee of) (1986), 62 C.B.R. (N.S.) 1,
     6 P.P.S.A.C. 252, 50 Sask. R. 297, [1987] 1 W.W.R. 140 (Q.B.) 131

Royal Bank of Canada v. Autotran Manufacturing Ltd., [1991]
    6 W.W.R. 238, [1991] S.J. No. 388, 95 Sask. R. 250 (Q.B.), aff'd
    [1992] 3 W.W.R. 455, [1992] S.J. No. 152, 97 Sask. R. 232 (C.A.) 94
Royal Bank of Canada v. Canada (Attorney General), [1978] A.J. No. 934,
    105 D.L.R. (3d) 648 (S.C.A.D.) 410
Royal Bank of Canada v. Dawson Motors (Guelph) Ltd. (1981), 39 C.B.R.
    (N.S.) 304, 1 P.P.S.A.C. 359 (Ont. Co. Ct.) 280
Royal Bank of Canada v. Demyen (Trustee of), [1986] S.J. No. 775,
    53 Sask. R. 224, 6 P.P.S.A.C. 240 (Q.B.)...267, 447
Royal Bank of Canada v. G.M. Homes Inc., [1984] S.J. No. 443,
    4 P.P.S.A.C. 116 (C.A.) 174, 175
Royal Bank of Canada v. Gatekeeper Leasing Ltd., [1993] B.C.J. No. 2199,
    (1993), 91 B.C.L.R. (2d) 357, 6 P.P.S.A.C. (2d) 92 (S.C.)..................... 285, 333
Royal Bank of Canada v. Inmont Canada Ltd. (1980), 1 P.P.S.A.C. 197
    (Ont. Co. Ct.)...175
Royal Bank Of Canada v. J. Segreto Construction Ltd. (1988), 47 D.L.R.
    (4th) 761, 8 P.P.S.A.C. 43 (C.A.) 550
Royal Bank of Canada v. Kiska, [1967] 2 O.R. 379, 63 D.L.R. (2d) 582 (C.A.) 164
Royal Bank of Canada v. Mackenzie, [1932] S.C.R. 524, [1932] 2 D.L.R. 12..... 587
Royal Bank of Canada v. Moosomin Credit Union (2003), [2004]
    5 W.W.R. 494, 241 Sask. R. 1 (Sask. C.A.).. 591
Royal Bank of Canada v. North American Life Assurance Co., [1996]
    1 S.C.R. 325, [1996] 3 W.W.R. 457 .... 437, 449–50
Royal Bank of Canada v. Pioneer Property Management Ltd. (1986),
    [1987] 2 W.W.R. 445, [1986] S.J. No. 735 (Q.B.) 333
Royal Bank of Canada v. Russell Food Equipment Ltd., 2001 SKQB 404,
    28 C.B.R. (4th) 111 354
Royal Bank of Canada v. Sparrow Electric Corp. (sub nom. R. v. Royal
    Bank), [1997] 1 S.C.R. 411, 193 A.R. 321, 135 W.A.C. 321, [1997]
    2 W.W.R. 457, 46 Alta. L.R. (3d) 87, 208 N.R. 161, 143 D.L.R. (4th) 385,
    44 C.B.R. (3d) 1, 97 D.T.C. 5089, 12 P.P.S.A.C. (2d) 68 .... 12, 175, 176, 415
Royal Bank of Canada v. Steinhubl's Masonry Ltd. (2003),
    2003 SKQB 299, [2004] 1 W.W.R. 267, [2003] S.J. No. 520 ..... 238, 257–58, 295
Royal Bank of Canada v. Tenneco Canada Inc. (1990), 72 O.R. (2d) 60,
    9 P.P.S.A.C. 254 (H.C.J.) 370
Royal Bank of Canada v. United Grain Growers Ltd. (2000), 21 C.B.R.
    (4th) 123, 1 P.P.S.A.C. (3d) 283 (Sask. Q.B.), aff'd (2001), 24 C.B.R.
    (4th) 125, 2 P.P.S.A.C. (3d) 143 (Sask. C.A.), leave to appeal to S.C.C.
    dismissed [2001] S.C.C.A. No. 271 .... 592, 596
Royal Bank of Canada v. W. Got & Associates Electric Ltd., [1999]
    3 S.C.R. 408, 15 P.P.S.A.C. (2d) 61 522
Royal Bank of Canada v. Wheaton Pontiac Buick Cadillac GMAC Ltd.
    (1990), 88 Sask. R. 151, 1 P.P.S.A.C. (2d) 131 (Q.B.) 295
Royal Bank of Canada v. White Cross Properties Ltd. (1984),
    34 Sask. R. 315, [1984] S.J. No. 30 (Q.B.) 567

Royal Trust Co. v. H.A. Roberts Group Ltd., [1995] 4 W.W.R. 305,
129 Sask. R. 161 (Q.B.) 571

Royal Trust Co. v. Kritzwiser, [1924] 3 D.L.R. 596 (Sask. C.A.) 150

Royal Trust Corp. of Canada v. D.Q. Plaza Holdings Ltd. (1984), 54 C.B.R.
(N.S.) 18, 36 Sask. R. 84 (Q.B.) 567

Roynat Inc. v. United Rescue Services Ltd., [1982] M.J. No. 91,
2 P.P.S.A.C. 49 (C.A.)...175

Roynat Ltd. v. Northern Meat Packers Ltd. (1986), 71 N.B.R. (2d) 212,
29 D.L.R. (4th) 139 (C.A.), leave to appeal to S.C.C. refused
78 N.B.R. (2d) 90 524

Russelsteel Inc. v. Lux Services Ltd., [1986] S.J. No. 222,
6 P.P.S.A.C. 107 (Q.B.) 175

Sanders v. British Columbia (Milk Board) (1991), 77 D.L.R. (4th) 603,
[1991] B.C.J. No. 236, 53 B.C.L.R. (2d) 167 (C.A.) 110

Saskatchewan Credit Union v. Bank of Nova Scotia, [1985] S.J. No. 618,
5 P.P.S.A.C. 123 (Q.B.) 267

Saskatchewan Economic Development Corporation v. Pryor, [1992]
S.J. No. 285, 3 P.P.S.A.C. (2d) 235 (Q.B.)... 275

Saskatchewan General Trusts Corp. (Re), [1938] 3 D.L.R. 544, [1938]
2 W.W.R. 375 (Sask. C.A.) 473

Saskatchewan Wheat Pool v. Smith (1996), 142 Sask. R. 285, 11 P.P.S.A.C.
(2d) 212 (Q.B.), aff'd [1997] S.J. No. 76, 152 Sask.R. 79 (C.A.)................... 292

Saskatoon Auction Mart Ltd. v. Finesse Holsteins, [1993] 1 W.W.R. 265,
[1992] S.J. No. 518, 104 Sask. R. 154 (Q.B.) 111

Sawridge Manor Ltd. v. Selkirk Springs International Corp., [1995]
9 W.W.R. 651, 10 P.P.S.A.C. (2d) 124, [1995] B.C.J. No. 1735 (C.A.) 494

Sawyer v. Pringle (1891), 18 O.A.R. 218, [1891] O.J. No. 9 (C.A.) 551

Scotia Mortgage Corp. v. Winchester (1997), 205 A.R. 147, [1997]
A.J. No. 509 (Q.B.) 441

Scott Steel Ltd. v. The Alarissa (1996), 111 F.T.R. 81, [1996] 2 F.C. 883
(T.D.), aff'd (1997), 125 F.T.R. 284, [1997] F.C.J. No. 139 (T.D.) 604

Seaboard Acceptance Corporation Ltd. v. Moen (1986), 62 C.B.R.
(N.S.) 143 (B.C.C.A.) 440

Searcy (Re) (1991), 2 P.P.S.A.C. (2d) 219, 8 C.B.R. (3d) 11 (B.C.S.C) 31

Senft v. Bank of Montreal, [1986] A.J. No. 1692, 69 A.R. 35 (Q.B.) 411

Seven Limers Coal & Fertilizer Co. Ltd. v. Hewitt (1986), 52 O.R. (2d) 1,
10 O.A.C. 132, 56 C.B.R. (N.S.) 319 (C.A.)...76

Shallcross v. Community State Banks Trust Co., 434 A.2d 671 (N.J. Sup. Ct.
1981) 312

Shedoudy v. Beverly Surgical Supply Co., 161 Cal. Rptr. 164, 100 Cal.
App.3d 730 (Cal. App. 1980)... 572

Simi Ltd. (Re) (1987), 59 O.R. (2d) 139, 7 P.P.S.A.C. 100 (H.C.J.), aff'd
(1988), 66 O.R. (2d) 640, 9 P.P.S.A.C. 46 (C.A.) 31

Simonot v. Burlingham Associates Inc. (sub nom. Collins (Bankrupt), Re)
(1998), 165 Sask. R. 209, [1998] 8 W.W.R. 365, 4 C.B.R. (4th) 115 (Q.B.) 180

Sims Battle Brewster & Associates Inc. (Re), 1999 ABQB 830, 253 A.R. 313,
    13 C.B.R. (4th) 269 82
Sinco Trucking Ltd. (Re), [1987] S.J. No. 454, 7 P.P.S.A.C. 176 (Q.B.) 293
Sklar and Sklar (Re) (1958), 15 D.L.R. (2d) 750, 26 W.W.R. 529 (Sask. C.A.) .. 402
Skybridge Holidays Inc. (Re), [1998] B.C.J. No. 1296, 54 B.C.L.R. (3d) 222,
    13 P.P.S.A.C. (2d) 387 (S.C.), aff'd 1999 BCCA 185, [1999] B.C.J. No. 672,
    11 C.B.R. (4th) 130 .... 81, 83
Smith (In Re), 326 F. Supp. 1311 (D. Minn. 1971) 312
Smith Brothers Contracting Ltd. (Re), [1998] B.C.J. No. 728, 53 B.C.L.R.
    (3d) 264, 13 P.P.S.A.C. (2d) 316 (S.C.) 70, 73
Sokoloski (Re), 2002 ABQB 1022, 4 P.P.S.A.C. (3d) 178 230
Southtrust Bank of Alabama, NA v. Borg-Warner Acceptance Corp.,
    760 F.2d 1240 (11th Cir. 1985) 343
Spar Aerospace Ltd. v. American Mobile Satellite Corp., [2002] 4 S.C.R. 205,
    220 D.L.R. (4th) 54 123
Spence (Trustee of) v. Yellowhead Feeders Co-operative Ltd., [1994]
    5 W.W.R. 129, 6 P.P.S.A.C. (2d) 359 (Sask. Q.B.) 447, 448, 449
Sperry Inc. v. Canadian Imperial Bank of Commerce (1985), 50 O.R.
    (2d) 267, 17 D.L.R. (4th) 236, 4 P.P.S.A.C. 314 (C.A.) 216, 312, 362, 373
Spillers v. First National Bank of Arenzville, 441 N.E.2d 872,
    109 Ill. App.3d 1100 (Ill. App. 4 Dist. 1982) 546, 547
Spir-l-ok Industries v. Bank of Montreal, [1985] S.J. No. 405,
    41 Sask. R. 128 (Q.B.) 207
Spittlehouse v. Northshore Marine Inc (1994), 18 O.R. (3d) 60,
    7 P.P.S.A.C. (2d) 67 (C.A.) 289–91
Stack v. T. Eaton Co., [1902] 4 O.L.R. 335, 1 O.W.R. 511 (Div. Ct.) 490
Stackaruk v. Woodward, [1966] 2 O.R. 32, 55 D.L.R. (2d) 577 (C.A.) 529
Stafford v. Sumbler, [1989] O.J. No. 213, 9 P.P.S.A.C. 47 (Dist. Ct.) 183
Standard Finance Corp. v. Coopers & Lybrand Ltd., [1984] 4 W.W.R. 543,
    [1984] M.J. No. 115, 28 Man. R. (2d) 99 (Q.B.) 72, 74, 75
Standard Trust Co v. Turner Crossing Inc., [1993] 2 W.W.R. 382,
    4 P.P.S.A.C. (2d) 238 (Sask. Q.B.) 564
State Bank of India (Canada) v. Trutzschler GmbH & Co. KG., [1997]
    O.J. No. 254, 44 C.B.R. (3d) 299 (C.A.) 184
State of Alaska v. Fowler, 611 P.2d 58 (Alaska 1980) 376
Steed (Re), [2001] A.J. No. 262, 2 P.P.S.A.C. (3d) 92 (Q.B.) 131, 132
Steinbach Credit Union Ltd. v. Manitoba Agricultural Credit Corp.,
    [1991] 4 W.W.R. 36, 2 P.P.S.A.C. (2d) 81 (Q.B.) 571
Stelco Inc. (Re) (2004), 6 P.P.S.A.C. (3d) 268 (Ont. S.C.J.), rev'd 2005
    CarswellOnt 1537, [2005] O.J. No. 1575 (C.A.) 25, 100–101
Stephanian's Persian Carpets Ltd. (Re), [1980] O.J. No. 156, 34 C.B.R.
    (N.S.) 35, 1 P.P.S.A.C. 119 (H.C.J.) 78, 79, 80
Stevens (Re) (1993), 17 Alta. L.R. (3d) 99, 23 C.B.R. (3d) 46, 6 P.P.S.A.C.
    (2d) 231, (Q.B.) 263

Strach v. Toronto Dominion Bank, [1997] A.J. No. 986, 56 Alta. L.R. (3d) 412
(C.A.) 375

Stusick v. C & M Holdings Inc., [1995] S.J. No. 661, 10 P.P.S.A.C. (2d) 213 (Q.B.)
173

Sugarman v. Duca Community Credit Union Ltd. (1998), 38 O.R. (3d) 429,
[1998] O.J. No. 837, 13 P.P.S.A.C. (2d) 117 (Gen. Div.), aff'd (1999), 44 O.R.
(3d) 257, [1999] O.J. No. 1830, 14 P.P.S.A.C. (2d) 264 (C.A.) 110

Sun Life Assurance Co. of Canada v. Royal Bank of Canada (1995), 129 D.L.R.
(4th) 305, 10 P.P.S.A.C. (2d) 246 (Ont. Ct. Gen. Div.)................................ 370

Sun Mortgage Corp. v. Kumar, [2000] 4 W.W.R. 700, 146 Man. R.(2d) 89 (Q.B.)...
579

Surrey Metro Savings Credit Union v. Chestnut Hill Homes Inc. (1997), 30
B.C.L.R. (3d) 92, [1997] B.C.J. No. 241 (S.C.) 571

Swiss Bank Corp. v. Lloyds Bank Ltd. (1981), [1982] A.C. 584, [1981] 2 W.L.R.
893;[1981] 2 All. E.R. 449 (H.L.).. 86

T. Eaton Co. (Re), [1999] O.J. No. 4216, 14 C.B.R. (4th) 288 (S.C.J.) 110

Tailby v. Official Receiver (1888), 13 App. Cas. 523 (H.L.)........................169, 188

Takhatalian (Re), [1982] O.J. No. 2509, 2 P.P.S.A.C. 90 (H.C.J.) 250

TCE Capital Corp. v. Kolenc (1999), 44 O.R. (3d) 148, 172 D.L.R. (4th) 186,
[1999] O.J. No. 1226, 8 C.B.R. (4th) 165, 14 P.P.S.A.C. (2d) 257
(Ont. Div. Ct.), aff'g [1998] O.J. No. 129, 51 O.T.C. 124, 3 C.B.R.
(4th) 98 (Gen. Div.) 91, 92, 445

Thet Mah and Associates, Inc. v. First Bank of North Dakota (NA),
Minot, 336 N.W.2d 134 (N.D. 1983) 334

Thomas v. Silvia (1994), 14 A.C.S.R. 446 320

Thompson v. Ford Motor Credit Co., 550 F.2d 256 (C.A. Ala. 1977)................ 530

Thompson v. United States, 408 F.2d 1075 (8th Cir. 1969)..........................29, 376

Thorp Sales Corp. v. Dolese Bros. Co., 453 F. Supp. 196 (D.C.W.D. 1978)........318

Tildesley v. Weaver, [1998] B.C.J. No. 1838, 7 C.B.R. (4th) 313 (S.C.) 441

Tisdale Credit Union Ltd v. Fritshaw Farms Meat Processing Ltd., [1989]
S.J. No. 403, 79 Sask. R. 162 (Q.B.).. 262

Todd Shipyards Corp. v. Altema Compania Maritima S.A. (1972), [1974]
S.C.R. 1248, 32 D.L.R. (3d) 571, [1974] 1 Lloyd's Rep. 174 126

Tolofson v. Jensen, [1994] 3 S.C.R. 1022, 120 D.L.R. (4th) 289 149

Toronto-Dominion Bank v. Co-Pac Ltd. (1999), 178 D.L.R. (4th) 149,
123 O.A.C. 325, [1999] O.J. No. 2986 (C.A.) 457–58

Toronto-Dominion Bank v. Dearborn Motors Ltd. (1968), 64 W.W.R. 577,
69 D.L.R. (2d) 123 (B.C.S.C.) 580, 596

Toronto-Dominion Bank v. East Central Feeder Co-operative Ltd., [2001]
O.J. No. 2159, [2001] O.T.C. 419, 2 P.P.S.A.C. (3d) 283 (S.C.J.)................... 85

Toronto-Dominion Bank v. Flexi-Coil Ltd., [1993] S.J. No. 23, 4 P.P.S.A.C.
(2d) 288 (Q.B.).. 180, 273

Toronto-Dominion Bank v. Gottdank, [2000] O.J. No. 2274, 1 P.P.S.A.C.
(3d) 67 (S.C.J.) 86

Toronto-Dominion Bank v. Howitt Enterprises Ltd., [1998] O.J. No. 1112,
13 P.P.S.A.C. (2d) 368 (Gen. Div.) 285
Toronto-Dominion Bank v. Hudye Soil Services Inc., [2000] 9 W.W.R. 272,
149 Man. R. (2d) 56 (Q.B.) 123
Toronto-Dominion Bank v. Lanzarotta Wholesale Grocers Ltd., [1996]
O.J. No. 4395, 12 P.P.S.A.C. (2d) 30 (C.A.) 339
Toronto-Dominion Bank v. McCowan, [1995] O.J. No. 1102, 81 O.A.C. 151,
20 B.L.R. (2d) 138 (C.A.) 86
Toronto-Dominion Bank v. Mulatz, [1994] S.J. No. 77, 111 D.L.R.
(4th) 601 (C.A.) 438
Toronto-Dominion Bank v. Nova Entertainment Inc. (1992), 7 Alta. L.R.
(3d) 132, 4 P.P.S.A.C. (2d) 323 (Q.B.) 281
Toronto-Dominion Bank v. RNG Group Inc. (2002), 61 O.R. (3d) 567,
38 C.B.R. (4th) 110, 4 P.P.S.A.C. (3d) 182 (S.C.J.) 25, 123, 138
Toyerama (Re), [1980] O.J. No. 157, 1 P.P.S.A.C. 126, 34 C.B.R.
(N.S.) 153 (H.C.J.) 77, 79
Traders Finance Corp. v. Casselman, [1960] S.C.R. 242, 22 D.L.R. (2d) 177 ... 153
Traders Finance Corp. v. Stan Reynolds Auto Sales Ltd. (1954), 13 W.W.R.
(N.S.) 425, [1955] 1 D.L.R. 670 (Alta. S.C.(T.D.)) 580
Trailmobile Canada Ltd. v. Kindersley Transport Ltd. (1986), 7 P.P.S.A.C. 75,
54 Sask. R. 1 (Q.B.) 137, 138
Trans Canada Credit Corp v. Foubert, [1961] O.R. 57. 26 D.L.R. (2d) 73
(C.A.) 514
Trans Canada Credit Corp. v. Martin, 2000 MBQB 109, [2000]
9 W.W.R. 226 441
Trans Canada Credit Corp. v. Walko, [1991] S.J. No. 666, 2 P.P.S.A.C.
(2d) 334 (Q.B.) 273
Trans Canada Credit Corp. v. Wonnacott, 2000 PESCTD 11,
188 Nfld & P.E.I.R. 198 350
Transamerica Commercial Finance Corp. Canada v. Karpes, [1994]
B.C.J. No. 1907, 8 P.P.S.A.C. (2d) 86 (.C.) 174
Transamerica Commercial Finance Corp. Canada v. Royal Bank of Canada
(1990), 70 D.L.R. (4th) 627, 79 C.B.R. (N.S.) 127, [1990] 4 W.W.R. 673,
1 P.P.S.A.C. (2d) 61, [1990] 84 Sask. R. 81, [1990] S.J. No. 177
(C.A.) 354, 385, 457, 466
Transport Equipment Co. v. Guaranty State Bank, 518 F.2d 377
(10th Cir. 1975) 546–47
Transport North American Express Inc. v. New Solutions Financial Corp.,
2004 SCC 7, [2004] 1 S.C.R. 249 197
Travel 'N' Save Inc. v. Roynat Inc. (1992), 13 C.B.R. (3d) 21, [1992]
O.J. No. 1356 (Gen. Div.) 15
Travel West (1987) Inc. v. Langdon Towers Apartment Ltd. (2001),
204 Sask. R. 184, 2 P.P.S.A.C. (3d) 99 (Q.B.), rev'd [2002]
9 W.W.R. 449, 217 Sask. R. 233 (C.A.) 518

Triad Financial Services and Thaler Metal Industries Ltd. (Re) (1979),
    24 O.R. (2d) 423, 1 P.P.S.A.C. 44 (H.C.J.), aff'd (1979), 27 O.R.
    (2d) 506, 106 D.L.R. (3d) 706 (C.A.) 365
Tunney (Re), 2000 BCSC 1144, 18 C.B.R. (4th) 311, 1 P.P.S.A.C. (3d) 277 156
Tureck v. Hanston Investments Ltd. (1986), 30 D.L.R. (4th) 690,
    5 P.P.S.A.C. 210 (Ont. H.C.J.) 515, 554
Tureck v. Hanston Investments Ltd. (1987), 56 O.R. (2d) 393, 30 D.L.R.
    (4th) 690, [1986] O.J. No. 18 (H.C.J.) 63
Twinsectra Ltd. v. Yardley, [2002] UKHL 12, [2002] 2 A.C.164, [2002]
    H.L.J. No. 12 83

U.S. v. Willis, 593 F.2d 247 (C.A. Ohio 1979) 546
UF Media Inc. (Re) (2003), 6 P.P.S.A.C. (3d) 16, 2003 CarswellBC 1760
    (C.A.) 268, 274
Unisource Canada Inc. v. Hongkong Bank of Canada Inc. (1998),
    43 B.L.R. (2d) 226, 14 P.P.S.A.C. (2d) 112, [1998] O.J. No. 5586
    (Gen. Div.), aff'd (2000), 131 O.A.C. 24, 15 P.P.S.A.C. (2d) 95,
    [2000] O.J. No. 947 (C.A.) 345, 504, 507, 508
Unisource Canada Inc. v. Laurentian Bank of Canada (2000), 47 O.R.
    (3d) 616, 15 C.B.R. (4th) 315, 15 P.P.S.A.C. (2d) 105 (C.A.) 350, 428, 466
United Australia Ltd. v. Barclays Bank Ltd., [1941] A.C. 1,
    1940 W.L.3 2899, [1940] 4 All E.R. 20 (H.L.) 514, 582
Universal C.I.T. Credit Corp. v. Farmers Bank of Portageville,
    358 F. Supp. 317 (D.C. Mo. 1973) 469
Universal Handling Equipment v. Redipac Recycling, [1992] O.J. No. 1763,
    4 P.P.S.A.C. (2d) 15 (Ont. Ct. Gen. Div.) 183, 184, 252
Urman (Re) (1983), 44 O.R. (2d) 248, 3 P.P.S.A.C. 191 (C.A.), rev'g (1981),
    1 P.P.S.A.C. 340, 128 D.L.R. (3d) 33 (Ont. H.C.J.) 23

Valley Vista Golf Course Ltd. (Receiver of) v. Maximum Financial Services
    Inc., 2003 NSSC 97, 214 N.S.R. (2d) 91 276
Vanhove (Re) (1994), 20 O.R. (3d) 653, 8 P.P.S.A.C. (2d) 240 (Gen. Div.) 533
Vassie v. Vassie (1882), 22 N.B.R. 76 (C.A.) 169
Vic Hansen & Sons, Inc. v. Crowley, 203 N.W.2d 728, 57 Wis.2d. 106
    (Wis. 1973) 547
Victoria & Grey Trust Co v. Brewer, [1970] 3 O.R. 704, 14 D.L.R. (3d) 28
    (H.C.J.) 572
Victoria Bed and Mattress Co. (Re) (1960), 24 D.L.R. (2d) 414,
    35 W.W.R. 259 (B.C.S.C.) 416
Vincent c. Quebec (sous-ministre du Revenu) (1994), [1994] A.Q. no 553,
    64 Q.A.C. 255 [1995] 3 C.N.L.R. 204 (C.A) 116
Vita Food Products Inc. v. Unus Shipping Co., [1939] A.C. 277, [1939]
    1 All E R 513 (P.C.) 150
VW Credit Canada Inc. v. Roberts (2001), 197 D.L.R. (4th) 274,
    2 P.P.S.A.C. (3d) 124 (N.S.C.A.) 447, 448

W.H. Fraser v. Imperial Bank of Canada (1912), 47 S.C.R. 313 197
Wahpeton Dakota First Nation v. Lajeunesse, 2002 SKCA 27, [2002]
    S.J. No. 114, 223 Sask. R. 77, leave to appeal to S.C.C. refused
    (2002), 232 Sask. R. 160n, [2002] S.C.C.A. No. 131 115
Waldron v. Royal Bank of Canada (1991), 78 D.L.R. (4th) 1, [1991]
    4 W.W.R. 289 (B.C.C.A.).. 524, 526, 586
Wallace v. United Grain Growers Ltd., [1997] 3 S.C.R. 701, [1997]
    S.C.J. No. 94... 437
Wal-Mac Amusements Ltd. v. Jimmy's Dining and Sports Lounge (1997),
    200 A.R. 31, [1997] A.J. No. 490, [1997] 7 W.W.R. 358 (C.A.) 109
Walter E. Heller Western Inc. v. Bohemia, Inc., 655 P.2d 1073
    (Or. App. 1982)... 288
Weber (Re) (1990), 73 O.R. (2d) 238, 1 P.P.S.A.C. (2d) 36 (H.C.J.).................. 271
Weiller & Williams Ltd. v. Ager (1992), 104 Sask. R. 260, 4 P.P.S.A.C.
    (2d) 19, [1992] S.J. No. 455 (Q.B.) 465
Weiss Air Sales Ltd. (Re) (1982), 134 D.L.R. (3d) 706, 35 O.R. (2d) 344
    (H.C.J.), aff'd (1982) 140 D.L.R. (3d) 576, 39 O.R. (2d) 800 (C.A.)........... 588
Werner v. Royal Bank of Canada, 2000 SKQB 338, 2 P.P.S.A.C. (3d) 119......... 345
West Bay Sales Ltd. v. Hitachi Sales Corp of Canada Ltd. (Re) (1978),
    20 O.R. (2d) 752, 88 D.L.R. (3d) 743 (H.C.J.)....................................... 26
West v. Williams, [1899] 1 Ch. 132, 79 L.T. 575 (C.A.)..............................197, 602
Western Canada Pulpwood & Lumber Co. Ltd. (Re) (1929), [1930]
    D.L.R. 652, 11 C.B.R. 125 (Man. C.A.).. 291
Western Express Air Lines Inc. (Re), 2005 BCSC 53, 7 P.P.S.A.C. (3d) 229 168
Western Surety Co. v. National Bank of Canada (2001), 22 C.B.R. (4th) 283,
    237 N.B.R. (2d) 346, 612 A.P.R. 346 (C.A.) 434, 435
Westman Equipment Corp. v. Royal Bank, [1982] 5 W.W.R. 475, 24 Man. R.
    (2d) 297, 2 P.P.S.A.C. 171 (Co. Ct.) 138
Whaling (Re), [1998] O.J. No. 5340, 117 O.A.C. 51, 6 C.B.R. (4th) 1
    (C.A.) 85, 113
Wheatland Industries (1990) Ltd. v. Baschuk (Re), [1994] S.J. No. 625,
    8 P.P.S.A.C. (2d) 247 (Q.B.) 332
Whitbread v. Walley, [1990] 3 S.C.R. 1273, 77 D.L.R. (4th) 25 602
Whonnock Industries Ltd. v. National Bank of Canada (1987), 42 D.L.R.
    (4th) 1, [1987] 6 W.W.R. 316 (B.C.C.A.)... 527
Willi v. Don Shearer Ltd., [1992] B.C.J. No. 194, 3 P.P.S.A.C. (2d) 188 (S.C.),
    aff'd (1993), 107 D.L.R. (4th) 121, [1994] 2 W.W.R. 312, 5 P.P.S.A.C.
    (2d) 179 (B.C.C.A.) 25, 280
Williamson v. Loonstra (1973), 34 D.L.R. (3d) 275 (B.C.S.C.) 572
Wilson (Re) (1984), 46 O.R. (2d) 28, 4 P.P.S.A.C. 69 (H.C.J.) 271
Winans v. Attorney-General, [1910] A.C. 27.. 120
Windham Sales Ltd. (Re) (1979), 26 O.R. (2d) 246, 102 D.L.R. (3d) 459,
    31 C.B.R. (N.S.) 130 (Ont. H.C.J.) 87
Winkworth v. Christie Manson and Woods Ltd., [1980] 1 Ch. 496 134
Woodroffes (Musical Instruments) Ltd. (Re), [1985] 2 All E.R. 908
    (Ch. Div.) 373

Woolf (Re), [1992] O.J. No. 2280, 7 P.P.S.A.C. (2d) 268 (Gen. Div.), aff'd on
    other grounds without addressing this point, [1994] O.J. No. 2152,
    7 P.P.S.A.C. (2d) 268 at 276 (C.A.) 271
Workers' Compensation Board v. Husky Oil Operators Ltd., [1995]
    3 S.C.R. 453, [1995] S.C.J. No. 77 420

Xerox Canada Inc. v. Bank of Montreal (1989), 76 C.B.R. (N.S.) 99,
    9 P.P.S.A.C. 215 (Ont. H.C.J.) 442

Yablonski v. Cawood (c.o.b. Cawood Walker) (1997), 143 D.L.R. (4th) 65,
    [1997] S.J. No. 17, 152 Sask. R. 54 (C.A.) 114
YMCF Inc. v. 406248 B.C. Ltd., [1998] B.C.J. No. 316, 13 P.P.S.A.C.
    (2d) 282 (S.C.) 371
Young v. Lambert (1870), L.R. 3 P.C. 142 213
Young v. Short (1885), 3 Man. R. 302 (C.A.) 396
Yuan v. Mah Investments Ltd. (2001), 205 Sask. R. 22, 2 P.P.S.A.C.
    (3d) 159 (Q.B.).. 556
Yustin Construction (Re) (1986), 5 P.P.S.A.C. 154 (Ont. H.C.J.) 266

Zurich Insurance Co. & Troy Woodworking Ltd. (Re) (1984), 6 D.L.R.
    (4th) 552, 3 P.P.S.A.C. 290 (Ont. C.A.) 410

INDEX

Accessions
  after-acquired consumer goods, 172
  aircraft, 618–20
  consumer goods, 172
  definition of, 499–500
  distinguished from processed goods, 504
  enforcement, 502–3
  priorities, 500–2
Accounts
  accounts financer v. inventory financer, 154, 353–54
  anti-assignment clauses, 113–14
  cut-off clauses, 561
  deemed security interests, 92
  enforcement against, 558–59
  exclusion from PPSA, 105–8
  post-bankruptcy accounts, 434–35
  returned or repossessed goods, 486
  set-off, 560–64
After-acquired property
  attachment, 169–74
  purchase money security interests, 330–31
  bankruptcy, 430–37, 438–41
Aircraft, *see Cape Town Convention on International Interests in Mobile Equipment*

Amalgamations
  effect on registration, 265–66
  priorities among secured parties, 328–29
Animals
  attachment, 172–74
  production money security interests, 358
Application of PPSA
  accounts, transfers of, 92–93
  annuities and insurance, 99–101
  borderline transactions, 85–89
  chattel paper, transfers of, 92–93
  commercial consignments, 93–94
  deemed security agreements, 90–96
  federal security interests, 98–99
  First Nation's property, 114–16
  land-related payments, 101–5
  leases for a term of more than one year, 94–95
  licences and quotas, 112–14
  non-consensual security interests, 96–97
  pawnbrokers, 101
  remuneration for personal services, 105–6
  sale of business, 106
  sales of goods, 96

security consignments, 75–80
security leases, 67–75
seller's right of disposal, 107–8
subordination agreements, 87–89
"substance" test, 69–70
tort claims, 107
trusts, 80–85
unassignable property, 112–14
unearned right to payment, 106
Article 9, *Uniform Commercial Code*
2001 revision, 44–47
comparison with PPSA, 43–47
influence of, 42–43
Attachment
after-acquired collateral, 169–72
concept of, 17
conditional sales contracts, 166
conflict of laws, 126–27
consumer goods, 171–72
deemed security interests, 91,
168–69
exceptions to *nemo dat*, 165–66
floating charges, 174–77
future property, 172–74
non-consensual security interests,
415
post-bankruptcy property, 432–33
postponement of, 175–77
priority based on, 311–12, 415
returned and repossessed goods,
483–84
rights in collateral, 164–77
significance of, 161–63
value, meaning of, 163–64

Bad faith, *see* Good faith and commercial reasonableness
Bailment, 69, 217
Bank Act security
application of PPSA, 98, 592–94,
598–99
double documentation, 594–95
enforcement, 597–99
fishing vessels, 589
fixtures, 589
priority rules, 589–92, 596–97
proceeds, 595–96
purchase money security interests,
591–92
reform of, 39, 599–600

restrictions on availability, 585–86
registration, 588
rights obtained by bank, 587
security agreement, 586–87
Bankruptcy and insolvency
affirmation agreements, 440–41
after-acquired property clauses,
430–37
aircraft, 613–14
assignments of claims, 318
choice of law, 157–58
Crown claims, 416–18, 426–27
deemed trusts, 418–19
discharge of bankrupt, 438–41
equitable subordination, 428
exempt property, 447–51
inversion of priorities, 420–21
notice of intention to enforce, 526–27
passage of property to buyer, 290–91
preferred claims, 419–20
reperfection, 443–44
secured creditor, definition of,
426–27
secured party priorities, 428–29,
441–43, 447–51
secured party remedies, 427–30
status of trustee, 444–47
unpaid suppliers, 428–29
Bill of lading
seller's right of disposal, 107–8
Buyers and Lessees
authorized transactions, 284–86
automatic perfection, 298–302
buyer in possession, 302
low-value consumer goods, 297–98
ordinary course sales and leases,
286–95
passage of property to buyer, 289–91
relocation of goods, 132–33, 135
seller in possession, 303–7
serial numbered goods, 295–97
unperfected security interest, 279–83

*Cape Town Convention on International
Interests in Mobile Equipment*
implementation of, 38–40
interface with PPSA, 616–21
priorities, 612–13
proceeds, 617–18
purpose of, 607–9

registration, 257, 614–16
remedies, 613–14
transactions covered, 609–12, 621
transition, 620–21
Chattel Paper
  competing security interests in,
    391–94
  deemed security interests, 92–93
  definition of, 389–91
  enforcement against, 558–59
  proceeds of inventory, 353–54
  returned or repossessed goods, 394,
    484–86
  set-off, 560–64
Cheques, *see also* Instruments
  perfection of proceeds, 480
Civil Code, see Quebec secured transactions law
Collateral
  categories of, 20–21
  custodial duties, 534–35
  definition of, 19
  description in registration, 255–59
  description in security agreement,
    186–93
  following and tracing, 452–56
  registration errors, 274–75
  registration on transfer, 262–66
  rights in, 164–77
Common law and equity, 25–26, 374–79,
  538, 571–72, 578–83
Conditional sales contracts
  attachment, 166
  Bank Act security, 591
  characterization of, 64–67
  Indian Act, 116
Conflict of laws
  attachment and perfection, meaning
    of, 126–29
  automatic perfection of foreign secur-
    ity interests, 218–19, 298–300
  bankruptcy proceedings, 157–58
  characterization of security interests,
    155–56
  documentary collateral, 137, 139–40
  enforcement, 149–53
  goods intended for export, 135–36
  interjurisdictional uniformity,
    122–24

investment property, future reforms,
  158–59
jurisdiction of courts, 122–24
lex rei sitae rule
  relocation of goods, effect of,
    130–35
  scope of rule, 129–30, 136–37
location of debtor rule
  debtor's location, 141–42
  lack of registry system, 145–47
  mobile goods, 137–39
  pure intangibles, 140–41
  relocation of debtor, effect of,
    143–44
  transfer of collateral, 144–45
  mandatory nature of, 124–25
  proceeds, 153–55
  proper law of the contract, 150–51
  purpose of PPSA conflict rules, 8,
    118–21
  renvoi, 147–49
  territorial scope of PPSA, 121–22
Consignments
  agency relationship, 77–78
  bankruptcy, 446
  characterization as security interest
    factors pointing to, 79–80
    relevance of, 75–76
    tests for, 76–78
  commercial consignments, 93–94
Consumer goods
  accessions, 172
  advance registration, 228–29
  after-acquired property, 171–72
  buyers of low-value consumer goods,
    297–98, 479
  definition of, 20
  mandatory discharge of registration,
    234
  multi-agreement registration, 230–31
  use of term as description, 187, 255
Conversion and detinue, 579–81
Crops
  after-acquired property, 172–74
  priorities against real property inter-
    ests, 497–98
  production money security interests,
    356–58
Cut-off clauses, 561

Damages, *see* Remedies
Debt Consolidation and Refinancing, 345–49
Debtor
    application of definition
        to guarantors, 14–15
        to transferees, 15–16, 519–20
    birth date, 251
    change in debtor name or transfer of collateral, 262–66
    definition of, 13–14, 168–69, 520–21
    double debtor problem, 324–25
    enterprise debtor name, 251–54
    errors in registration, 270–72
    individual debtor name, 249–51
    location of, 141–42
    registration, 247–54
    right to copy of security agreement, 199
    signature of, 184–85
Deemed security interests
    application of Part 5, 515–16
    non-perfection and bankruptcy, 445–47
    policy of PPSA towards, 12–13
    time of attachment, 168–69
Default
    acceleration clauses and insecurity provisions, 523
    curing default, 538–39
    definition of, 522
    notice of intention to enforce, 526–27
    provincial pre-seizure notice requirements, 527–28
    reasonable notice doctrine, 523–26
    significance of, 521–22
Distress, *see also* Non-consensual security interests
    common law, 409
    contractual, 86
Documents of title,
    perfection of, 217
    priorities, 382–84

Electronic commerce legislation, 185
Electronic funds transfers, 384–85
Enforcement, *see* Remedies
Equipment
    buyers and lessees, 296–97
    definition of, 20

ordinary course sale, 293–94
    serial number registration, 258
    use of term as description, 187, 255
Equitable subordination, 428
Estoppel, 210, 377–78
Exemptions, 11, 447–51, 533

Federal Security Interests
    Bank Act security, 585–600
    federal jurisdiction over, 33–35
    intellectual property, 604–6
    railway assets, 607
    ship mortgages, 600–6
Fixtures
    Bank Act security, 589
    building materials, 491
    definition of, 490–91
    enforcement, 496–97
    priorities, 492–96
Floating charge
    attachment, 174–77
    under pre-PPSA law, 3
Future Advances
    all obligations clauses, 198–99
    interest and costs, 197
    priority of, 316–21, 405–6
    ship mortgages, 602
    tacking, 197–98

Good faith and commercial reasonableness
    effect on priorities, 374–77
    enforcement against intangibles, 559
    meaning of, 27–28
    sale of collateral, 544–46
Goods
    classification, 20
    conflict of laws, 129–39
    fixtures and crops, 489–98
    land-related goods, 21
Guarantees
    application of PPSA, 86
    definition of debtor, 14–15

Indian Act, 114–16
Instruments, 382–85
Intangibles
    definition of, 20
    enforcement against, 558–59
    land-related intangibles, 22
    set-off, 560–64

Intellectual property
    application of PPSA to, 98–99
    priorities, 605–6
    registration, 604–5
International conventions
    Cape Town Convention on International Interests in Mobile Goods, 39–40, 257, 607–21
    Hague Convention on Investment Securities held with an Intermediary, 41
    Rome Convention on the Law Applicable to Contractual Obligations, 127
    UN Convention on the Assignment of Receivables in International Trade, 41–42
Interpretive Principles
    common law supplementation, 25–26
    conflict with other statutes, 23–24
    good faith and commercial reasonableness, 27–28
    interprovincial harmonization, 24–25
    terminology in other Acts, 24
    underlying policies, 26–27
Inventory
    authorized transactions, 286
    definition of, 20
    proceeds, 353–54, 392–93
    purchase money security interest, 338–39
    returned or repossessed goods, 482–84
    serial number registration, 258–59
    use of term as description, 187, 255

Judgment enforcement creditors
    binding effect of writ, 396–97
    fixtures, 493
    future advances, 197–98, 405–6
    registration of judgments and writs, 11, 402–4
    unperfected security interests, 398–401
    use by secured party, 512–14, 551–52
Junior Secured Parties
    marshalling of securities, 571–72
    obligations of junior, 572–74
    pre-emption by senior, 569–71

Knowledge
    bad faith, 376–77
    constructive knowledge, 205–6, 245
    meaning of, 29–31, 384, 386–87
    relevance of, 312–13

Land, *see* Real property
Leases
    bankruptcy, 446
    characterization as security interest
        factors pointing to, 70–75
        relevance of, 67–68
        role of the lessor, 74–75
        tests for, 68–70
    disguised sales, 71–72
    leases for a term of more than one year, 94–95
    open-end leases, 73–74
    options to purchase, 72–73
Licences and quotas, 109–12
Liens, *see also* Non-consensual security interests
    priorities, 411–15
    types of, 408–9

Manufactured and commingled goods
    continuation of security interest, 503–5
    distinguished from accessions and proceeds, 504–5
    perfection of, 505–6
    priorities, 506–10
    valuation limits, 509–10
Marshalling of Securities, 571–72
Money
    perfection of proceeds, 480
    priorities, 381–82

Negative pledge covenants, 86, 376–77
Negotiable property, 380–94
Nemo Dat, 165–66
Non-consensual security interests
    aircraft, 610–11
    effect of bankruptcy, 416–21, 426–27
    exclusion from PPSA, 96–97
    interpretation of, 414–15
    priorities, 411–15
    sources of law, 406–7

Pawnbrokers, 101, 516
Perfection

attachment, need for, 204
by automatic perfection, 218–23,
    298–302, 360
by control, 223–24, 360
by possession, 211–17
by registration, 205–11
by seizure, 214–17
change in method of, 202–3, 313–14
collateral returned to debtor, 221–23
conflict of laws, 127–29
continuity of, 202–3
effect of non-perfection on,
    Bank Act security, 590
    bankruptcy, 441–44, 447–51
    buyers and lessees, 279–83
    judgment enforcement creditors,
        398–401
    non-consensual security interests,
        413–14
goods held by bailee, 217
manufactured and commingled
    goods, 505–6
meaning of, 200–2
perfection steps, 203–5
proceeds, 220, 478–82
reperfection, 363–68, 443–44
returned or repossessed goods, 394,
    484–86
Personal Actions
conversion and detinue, 579–81
recovery of money, 582–83
restitution, 581–82
Pledge, *see* Possession
Possession
custodial duties, 534–35
evidentiary requirements, 178–80
meaning of, 212–14
perfection by, 211–12
pledge, relevance of concept, 62–63
purchase money security interests,
    340
residual priority rule, 204–5, 311
Postponement agreements, *see* Subordin-
    ation agreements
PPSA
CCPPSL model, 9
comparison with Quebec law, 43–47
comparison with Article 9, *Uniform
    Commercial Code*, 43–47
interpretive principles, 23–29

interprovincial harmonization, 9
key concepts, 12–19
objectives of, 4–7
origins of, 3–4
provincial variations, 8–11
reform initiatives, 38–39
Priorities
accessions, 500–2
aircraft, 612–13
amalgamations, 328–29
assignment of financing statement,
    321–22
bad faith, 374–77
Bank Act security, 589–97
bankruptcy, 426–51
buyers and lessees, 278–307
change in debtor name or transfer of
    collateral, 262–66
change in method of perfection,
    313–14
chattel paper, 389–94
circular priorities, 269, 367–68,
    487–88, 494–96
crops, 356–58, 497–98
date for resolution of, 362–63
double debtor problem, 324–28
electronic funds transfers, 384–85
equitable subordination, 428
estoppel, 377–78
evidentiary requirements, 180–82
fixtures, 492–96
future advances and all obligation
    clauses, 316–21, 405–6
instruments and documents of title,
    382–85
intellectual property, 605–6
judgment enforcement creditors,
    395–406
knowledge, relevance of , 312–13
manufactured and commingled
    goods, 506–10
money, 381–82
multiple security agreements, 314–16
need for certainty, 7–8
non-consensual security interests,
    406–24
perfection by possession, 204–5, 311
pre-PPSA law, 7–8
proceeds, 353–54, 355–56, 482

production money security interests,
356–58
purchase money security interests,
329–56
reperfection of security interest,
363–68, 400–1, 443–44,
residual priority rule, 308–29
returned or repossessed goods,
482–89
securities, 386–89
serial numbered goods, 323–24
shelter principle, 25
subordination agreements, 368–74
subrogation, 351–52, 378–79, 495,
538
trust property, 422–24
Proceeds
accounts financer v. inventory financer, 154, 353–54
advantages of proceeds claim,
459–60
aircraft, 617–18
Bank Act security, 595–96
bankruptcy, 435–36
definition of
dealing requirement, 464–65
debtor's interest requirement,
462–64
identifiable or traceable requirement, 465–66
later generation proceeds, 462
description in security agreement,
193
distinguished from processed goods,
504
enforcement against proceeds and
original collateral, 460–61
chattel paper, 392–93
conflict of laws, 153–55
perfection of, 220, 259, 300–1,
478–82
priority of, 353–54, 355–56, 482
set-off, 562–64
statutory right to, 456–58
tracing and identification, 455–56
tracing rules, 466–78
Production money security interests,
356–58
Purchase money security interests

accounts financer v. inventory financer, 154, 353–54
Bank Act security, 591–92
cross-collateralization, 341–45
date of possession, 340
debt consolidation and refinancing,
345–49
deemed security interests, 335
definition of, 331–35
double-debtor scenario, 341
dual status approach, 343–44
extension to proceeds, 459–60
fixtures, 493
justification for super-priority,
330–31
paying out purchase money security interests held by third party,
350–52
priority between two purchase
money security interests, 354–56
priority over *Bank Act* security,
591–92
priority over writs and judgments,
403
procedural requirements
inventory, 338–39
non-inventory, 336–37
taken by lenders, 332–35
taken by sellers, 332
Purchaser, definition of, 383, 387

Quebec secured transactions law
advance registration, 51
assignment of claims, 50
comparison with PPSA, 47–48
consumer credit, 52–54
enforcement remedies, 55–56
failure to publish, 51
forms of security, 48–50
leases, 50
ordinary course buyers, 54
purchase money super-priority,
51–52
serial number registration, 54

Real property
application of PPSA to, 101–5
enforcement against real and personal property, 518–19
fixtures and crops, 489–98

Receiverships
deemed agency clauses, 568–69
perfection by possession, 216–17
regulation of, 564–66
status and legal effect, 566–68
Redemption, 535–38, 575–76
Registration, *see also* Registration errors;
    Registry
A-B-C-D problem, 255–56
access to information, 207–11, 231–
    33, 377–78
additional collateral, 266–67
advance registration, 228–29
aircraft, 614–16
amalgamations, 265–66
assignment of financing statement,
    321–22
Bank Act security, 588
change in debtor name or transfer of
    collateral, 262–66
collateral description,
    general collateral, 254–55
    proceeds, 259
    serial numbered goods, 255–59
comparison with title registry, 231
constructive knowledge, 205–06, 245
Crown claims, 416–18, 426–27
debtor name, 247–54
duration of, 259–60
electronic registration, 239–42
intellectual property, 604–06
lapse or discharge, 267–69, 363–68,
    443–44
liability for errors, 242–45
mandatory discharge or amendment,
    233–37
multiple security agreements, 229–
    31, 368
non-PPSA registrations, 246–47,
    402–04, 416–18
notice registration, 206, 227–28
perfection by registration, 205–11
pre-PPSA registration systems,
    226–27
renewal, 267
search criteria, 238–39
subordination agreements, 262
time of, 240–42
transfer of security interest, 261–62
verification statements, 269

writs and judgments, 402–4
Registration errors
debtor name, 270–72
dual search criteria, 273–74
general collateral description, 274–75
serial numbers, 273, 275–76
test for invalidity, 269–70
Registry
access to registry, 239–40
efficiency of, 6–7
inexact matches, 271–72
provincial variations, 11
Reinstatement, 538–39
Remedies
accessions, 502–3
aircraft, 613
Bank Act security, 597–99
conflict of laws, 149–53
consolidation of mortgages, 538
contractual modifications, 516–18
deemed damages, 577
default, 521–28
deficiency actions, 551–52, 577–78
demand for information, 209–11
effect of bankruptcy on, 427–30
election of remedies, 513–14, 595
failure to discharge registration,
    236–37
fixtures, 496–97
foreclosure, 552–58
intangibles and chattel paper, 558–64
junior secured parties, 569–74
liability for registry errors, 242–45
marshalling of securities, 571–72
non-compliance with PPSA, 577–78
original collateral and proceeds,
    460–61
personal actions, 579–83
personal and proprietary claims,
    511–12
purpose of, 5
real and personal property, 518–19
receiverships, 564–66
redemption, 536–38
reinstatement, 538–39
sale of collateral, 539–52
scope of Part 5, 515–16
seizure of collateral, 528–35
ship mortgages, 603–04
supervisory power of court, 574–76

third parties, 519–20
unsecured creditors' remedies, use
   of, 512–14, 551–52
Retention of collateral in satisfaction
   constructive foreclosure, 555–56
   effect on third parties, 557–58
   legal consequences, 554–55
   partial foreclosure, 556–58
   statutory foreclosure, 553–54
Returned or repossessed goods
   accounts financer, 486
   chattel paper financer, 484–86
   inventory financer, 483–84
   priorities, 486–89
   purpose of PPSA provisions, 482–83
RRSP, 84–85, 112–14

Sale of goods
   buyer in possession, 302
   COD sales, 86
   deemed security interests, 96
   meaning of, 288
   passage of property, 289–91
   seller in possession, 303–7
   seller's right of disposal, 107–8
   writing requirements, 184–85
Sale or disposition of collateral
   adequacy of price, 546–47
   Bank Act security, 597–98
   commercial reasonableness, 544–46
   deficiency, 551–52
   method of sale, 540–41
   notice of disposition, 542–44
   on debtor's premises, 531–32
   purchaser's title, 549
   recourse and repurchase agreements,
      547–48
   surplus, 549–51
Secured credit
   concept of, 1
   PPSA, origins of, 3–4
   pre-PPSA law, origins of, 2–3
   Quebec law of, 47–56
Secured party
   custodial duties, 534–35
   deemed security interests, 17
   definition of, 16–17
   obligation to amend registration,
      233–37
   obligation to disclose, 207–11

registration of secured party name,
   254
transfer of security interest, 261–62
Security, see also Uniform Securities
   Transfer Act
   perfection by possession, 213–14
   priorities, 386–89
Security agreement
   acceleration clauses, 523
   access to information about, 207–11
   all obligation clauses, 198–99,
      316–21
   authorized transactions, 284–86
   charging clause, 183–84
   collateral description,
      ambiguity and extrinsic evidence,
         192–93
      location and supplier qualifiers,
         190–92
      permissible descriptions, 186–90
      proceeds, 193
   contractual modifications to Part 5,
      516–18
   cross-collateralization, 341–45
   debtor's signature, 184–85
   deemed agency clauses, 568–69
   delivery of copy to debtor, 199
   dragnet clauses, 198–99
   events of default, 522
   evidentiary requirements, 177–182,
      222
   freedom of contract, 194–96
   future advance clauses, 197–99,
      316–21
   insecurity provisions, 523
   multiple documents, 183
   possessory security agreements,
      178–80
   priorities on assignment, 317–21
   proceeds clauses, 193, 456–58,
      474–75
   registering transfer of, 261–62
   reinstatement of, 538–39
   secured obligation, 196–99
   subordination clauses, 369–70
   typical provisions, 182
Security depository, 36–37, 214
Security interest
   characterization and conflict of laws,
      155–58

concept of, 12, 58–63
definition of, 4
hypothecation, 60–61
non-traditional transactions, 64–67
relevance of title, 58–59, 65
Seizure
Bank Act security, 597–99
constructive seizure, 531–32
custodial duties, 534–35
effect on priorities, 362–63
exempt property, 533
judicial action, 532–33
peaceable recaption, 529–30
perfection by possession, 214–17
pre-seizure notice requirements,
523–28
pursuant to judgment enforcement,
398–99, 401
restrictions on, 530–31
seizure by debtor, effect of, 482–89
use of force, 529–30
Serial numbered goods
A-B-C-D problem, 255–56
dual search criteria, 275–76
errors in registration, 273–74
motor vehicle, definition of, 257–58
perfection and proceeds, 479
priority among secured parties,
323–24
priority of buyers, 295–97
purchase money security interests,
337
registration, 238, 255–59
writs and judgments, 403
Service of notices and demands, 31–33
Set-off
application of PPSA to, 87
contractual modifications, 562
cut-off clauses, 561
defences and set-off, 500–1
notification, effect of, 561–62
proceeds, 562–64
Ship mortgages
application of PPSA, 98–99
Canada Shipping Act, 600–1
Canadian maritime law, 601–2
enforcement, 603–4
future advances, 602
priorities, 602–3
registration, 257, 600–1

Signature, 184–85
Subordination agreements
application of PPSA, 87–89
distinguished from other provisions,
373–74
distinguished from waiver or release,
370–71
effect on priorities, 371–73
nature and varieties of, 368–71
oral agreements, 370
registration, 262
Subrogation
application of PPSA, 86–87
effect on priorities, 378–79
fixtures, 495
marshalling securities, 571–72
paying out security interest, 351–52
redemption, 538
repurchase agreements, 548

Tracing
backwards tracing, 334–35, 475–76
Clayton's Case, rule in, 468–69
comparison with conventional
tracing rules, 466–68, 472–75,
476–78
distinguished from claiming, 467–68
distinguished from following, 452–55
distinguished from identification,
455–56
functional equivalence rule, 476–78
lowest intermediate balance rule,
333, 468–69
multiple claimants, 470–72
purchase money security interests,
333–35
wrongdoing, relevance of, 472–75
Trusts
bankruptcy and after-acquired property, 431–32
characterization as security interest,
80–82
co-existence of security interest and
trust, 82–83
deemed trusts, 409–10, 418–19
priority competitions over, 422–24
Quistclose trusts, 83
security interest and trust in related
transaction, 84–85

Uniform Securities Transfers Act
    automatic perfection, 223
    conflict of laws, 158–59
    key concepts and definitions, 36–38
    objectives of, 35–36
    perfection by control, 223–24
    priorities, 359–62, 387–89

Value, 163–64, 280–81

ABOUT THE AUTHORS

Ronald C.C. Cuming has taught and researched domestic and international commercial law for over thirty-five years including secured transactions law, sales law, leasing law, debtor-creditor law, insolvency law, and bankruptcy law. He was the principal draftsperson for Alberta, British Columbia, and Saskatchewan in the preparation of Personal Property Security Acts. This legislation provided models for the secured transactions law for six other jurisdictions in Canada. Professor Cuming is a technical advisor to World Bank and has been a consultant to the Asian Development Bank and other international agencies in the area of commercial law reform of developing countries. He prepared draft secured transactions and leasing legislation for countries in Eastern Europe, Africa, the Middle East, and Asia. He was the originator and principal consultant to the International Institute for the Unification Private Law and the Government of Canada in the development of the *Convention on International Interests in Mobile Equipment*, 2001 which will provide an international regime for secured financing of large aircraft.

Professor Cuming served as chairperson of the Uniform Law Conference Study Committee on Reform of Secured Transactions Actions Law. He received the University of Saskatchewan Distinguished Researcher Award in 1998. Recent publications include Personal Property Security Act handbooks for the western provinces, which he co-authored, a handbook on Albanian secured transactions law and numerous reports, articles and book chapters published in Canada and internationally.

Catherine Walsh joined the McGill University Faculty of Law in 2001. From 1981 to 2001, she was a member of the Law Faculty of the University of New Brunswick. Her principal teaching and research interests are in secured transactions law, comparative commercial law, and private international law. Professor Walsh is a member of the International Academy of Commercial and Consumer Law, a founding member of the Canadian Conference on Personal Property Security Law, and a former counsel to the Atlantic law firm Stewart McKelvey Stirling Scales.

Professor Walsh is the author of numerous reports, articles, and book chapters on secured transactions law. Her handbook on the New

Brunswick *Personal Property Act* grew out of her work as project director for the implementation of the New Brunswick PPSA and its innovative electronic registration system. She is the co-author of a law reform study on security interests in intellectual property and the author or co-author of a variety of reform reports for the Uniform Law Conference of Canada. Currently, Professor Walsh is a member of the Canadian delegation to the United Nations Commission on International Trade Law (UNCITRAL) Working Group charged with the preparation of a Secured Transactions Legislative Guide. Formerly she was a delegate to the UNCITRAL Working Group that produced the *UN Receivables Convention*. She has played an advisory or consultative role on a number of other secured transactions reform initiatives outside Canada and co-authored with Professor Cuming a guide on secured transactions registration systems for the Asian Development Bank.

Roderick J. Wood joined the University of Alberta Law Faculty in 1987 after working for several years as a legal research officer with the Saskatchewan Law Reform Commission. He researches and teaches in the areas of secured transactions law, bankruptcy and insolvency law, and debtor-creditor law. Professor Wood has been a Commissioner on the Law Commission of Canada since 2001, and was a member of the board of the Alberta Law Reform Institute from 1997 to 2001. He is a founding member of the Canadian Conference on Personal Property Security Law, and has served as a delegate on the Uniform Law Conference of Canada for the past five years. In 2005, Professor Wood received the University of Alberta Rutherford Award for Excellence in Undergraduate Teaching.

Professor Wood has written extensively in the area of personal property security law. He is the co-author of a series of handbooks on personal property security legislation in the western provinces and in New Zealand. He is the author of a number of chapters in books, including one of the recovery of pay in a leading textbook on Canadian employment law, and has contributed many articles in academic journals. Professor Wood is presently a member of the Canadian delegation on the International Institute for the Unification Private Law (Unidroit) committee of governmental experts that is preparing a draft protocol for a future international registration system for security interests in space assets.